T0234678

Lecture Notes in Computer Science 12878

More information about this subseries at http://www.springer.com/series/7412

Jianjiang Feng · Junping Zhang ·
Manhua Liu · Yuchun Fang (Eds.)

Biometric Recognition

15th Chinese Conference, CCBR 2021
Shanghai, China, September 10–12, 2021
Proceedings

 Springer

Editors
Jianjiang Feng 🆔
Tsinghua University
Beijing, China

Junping Zhang 🆔
Fudan University
Shanghai, China

Manhua Liu 🆔
Shanghai Jiao Tong University
Shanghai, China

Yuchun Fang 🆔
Shanghai University
Shanghai, China

ISSN 0302-9743   ISSN 1611-3349   (electronic)
Lecture Notes in Computer Science
ISBN 978-3-030-86607-5   ISBN 978-3-030-86608-2   (eBook)
https://doi.org/10.1007/978-3-030-86608-2

LNCS Sublibrary: SL6 – Image Processing, Computer Vision, Pattern Recognition, and Graphics

This Springer imprint is published by the registered company Springer Nature Switzerland AG
The registered company address is: Gewerbestrasse 11, 6330 Cham, Switzerland

Preface

Biometric recognition technology has been widely used in law enforcement, government, and consumer applications around the world. Biometrics offers a number of advantages over traditional password- or token-based solutions. However, current biometric technology is not perfect and still faces problems such as low-quality samples, identification in large populations, and spoofing. Researchers in this field have been actively studying these questions. In China, due to the large number of smartphone users and the government's investment in public safety, the biometrics market is developing rapidly, and the research of biometrics is attracting the attention of many researchers. The Chinese Conference on Biometric Recognition (CCBR), an annual conference held in China, provides an excellent platform for biometric researchers to share their ideas and advances in the development and applications of biometric theory, technology, and systems.

CCBR 2021 was held in Shanghai during September 10–12, 2021, and was the 15th event in the series, which has been successfully held in Beijing, Hangzhou, Xi'an, Guangzhou, Jinan, Shenyang, Tianjin, Chengdu, Shenzhen, Urumqi, and Zhuzhou since 2000. CCBR 2021 received 72 submissions which were subject to a double-blind review process involving 85 experts from the Program Committee. Each submission was reviewed by at least three experts from the Program Committee and received at least two review feedback reports. We are very grateful to all the reviewers for their hard work in reviewing up to five submissions. Based on the rigorous review comments, 20 papers were selected for oral presentation and 33 papers for poster presentation. These papers make up this volume of the CCBR 2021 conference proceedings covering a wide range of topics: multi-modal biometrics, emerging biometrics, hand biometrics, facial biometrics, speech biometrics, etc.

We would like to thank all the authors, reviewers, invited speakers, volunteers, and Organizing Committee members, without whom CCBR 2021 would not have been successful. We also wish to acknowledge the support of the Chinese Association for Artificial Intelligence, the Institute of Automation of Chinese Academy of Sciences, Springer, Shanghai University, ZKTeco, IrisKing, DeepRobotics, and Watrix in sponsoring this conference.

July 2021

Xiaofan Wang
Zhenan Sun
Lin Mei
Jianjiang Feng
Junping Zhang
Manhua Liu
Yuchun Fang

Organization

Advisory Committee

Anil K. Jain	Michigan State University, USA
Tieniu Tan	Institute of Automation, Chinese Academy of Sciences, China
Dapeng Zhang	Hong Kong Polytechnic University, China
Jie Zhou	Tsinghua University, China
Yunhong Wang	Beihang University, China
Xilin Chen	Institute of Computing Technology, Chinese Academy of Sciences, China
Jianhuang Lai	Sun Yat-sen University, China

General Chairs

Xiaofan Wang	Shanghai University, China
Zhenan Sun	Institute of Automation, Chinese Academy of Sciences, China
Lin Mei	The Third Research Institute of Ministry of Public Security, China

Program Committee Chairs

Jianjiang Feng	Tsinghua University, China
Junping Zhang	Fudan University, China
Manhua Liu	Shanghai Jiao Tong University, China
Yuchun Fang	Shanghai University, China

Program Committee Members

Zhicheng Cao	Xidian University, China
Caikou Chen	Information Engineering College of Yangzhou University, China
Cunjian Chen	Canon Information Technology (Beijing) Co., Ltd., China
Fanglin Chen	Harbin Institute of Technology, Shenzhen, China
Ying Chen	Nanchang Hangkong University, China
Beifen Dai	Beihang University, China
Weihong Deng	Beijing University of Posts and Telecommunications, China
Lunke Fei	Guangdong University of Technology, China
Jianjiang Feng	Tsinghua University, China

Keren Fu	Sichuan University, China
Guangwei Gao	Nanjing University of Posts and Telecommunications, China
Quanxue Gao	Xidian University, China
Shenghua Gao	ShanghaiTech University, China
Yongxin Ge	Chongqing University, China
Xun Gong	Southwest Jiaotong University, China
Zhe Guo	Northwestern Polytechnical University, China
Zhenhua Guo	Tsinghua University, China
Hu Han	Institute of Computing Technology, Chinese Academy of Sciences, China
Zhaofeng He	Institute of Automation, Chinese Academy of Sciences, China
Zhenyu He	Harbin Institute of Technology, Shenzhen, China
Qianhua He	South China University of Technology, China
Dewen Hu	National University of Defense Technology, China
Di Huang	Beihang University, China
Kekun Huang	Jiaying University, China
Wei Jia	Hefei University of Technology, China
Xu Jia	Liaoning University of Technology, China
Lianwen Jin	South China University of Technology, China
Yi Jin	Beijing Jiaotong University, China
Xiaoyuan Jing	Wuhan University, China
Wenxiong Kang	South China University of Technology, China
Ubul Kurban	Xinjiang University, China
Zhihui Lai	Shenzhen University, China
Yinjie Lei	Sichuan University, China
Zhen Lei	Institute of Automation, Chinese Academy of Sciences, China
Bo Li	Wuhan University of Science and Technology, China
Dong Li	Guangdong University of Technology, China
Huibin Li	Xi'an Jiaotong University, China
Jinghua Li	Beijing University of Technology, China
Qi Li	Institute of Automation, Chinese Academy of Sciences, China
Weijun Li	Institute of Semiconductors, Chinese Academy of Sciences, China
Wenxin Li	Peking University, China
Yanxiong Li	South China University of Technology, China
Yuenan Li	Tianjin University, China
Zhifeng Li	Institute of Advanced Technology, Chinese Academy of Sciences, China
Dong Liang	Nanjing University of Aeronautics and Astronautics, China
Lingyu Liang	South China University of Technology, China
Shengcai Liao	Inception Institute of Artificial Intelligence, UAE

Eryun Liu   Zhejiang University, China
Fan Liu   Hohai University, China
Feng Liu   Shenzhen University, China
Hao Liu   Ningxia University, China
Heng Liu   Anhui University of Technology, China
Leyuan Liu   Central China Normal University, China
Manhua Liu   Shanghai Jiao Tong University, China
Shu Liu   Central South University, China
Yanli Liu   Sichuan University, China
Yiguang Liu   Sichuan University, China
Zhi Liu   Shandong University, China
Guangming Lu   Harbin Institute of Technology, Shenzhen, China
Jiwen Lu   Tsinghua University, China
Xiao Luan   Chongqing University of Posts and
                        Telecommunications, China
Lizhuang Ma   Shanghai Jiao Tong University, China
Weihua Ou   Guizhou Normal University, China
Bo Peng   Institute of Automation, Chinese Academy of Sciences,
                        China
Fei Peng   Hunan University, China
Huafeng Qin   Chongqing Technology and Business University,
                        China
Haifeng Sang   Shenyang University of Technology, China
Shiguang Shan   Institute of Computing Technology, Chinese Academy
                        of Sciences, China
Chao Shen   Xi'an Jiaotong University, China
Fumin Shen   University of Electronic Science and Technology
                        of China, China
Linlin Shen   Shenzhen University, China
Xiangbo Shu   Nanjing University of Science and Technology, China
Xiaoning Song   Jiangnan University, China
Yunlian Sun   Nanjing University of Science and Technology, China
Zhenan Sun   Institute of Automation, Chinese Academy of Sciences,
                        China
Chaoyin Tang   Nanjing University of Aeronautics and Astronautics,
                        China
Huawei Tian   People's Public Security University of China, China
Qing Tian   Nanjing University of Information Science
                        and Technology, China
Jun Wan   Institute of Automation, Chinese Academy of Sciences,
                        China
Zengfu Wang   Hefei Institutes of Physical Science, Chinese Academy
                        of Sciences, China
Haixia Wang   Zhejiang University of Technology, China
Huiyong Wang   Guilin University of Electronic Technology, China
Kejun Wang   Harbin Engineering University, China

Ruiping Wang	Institute of Computing Technology, Chinese Academy of Sciences, China
Sujing Wang	Institute of Psychology, Chinese Academy of Sciences, China
Wei Wang	Institute of Automation, Chinese Academy of Sciences, China
Yiding Wang	North China University of Technology, China
Yi Wang	Dongguan University of Technology, China
Yunlong Wang	Institute of Automation, Chinese Academy of Sciences, China
Xiangqian Wu	Harbin Institute of Technology, China
Lifang Wu	Beijing University of Technology, China
Shanjuan Xie	Hangzhou Normal University, China
Weicheng Xie	Shenzhen University, China
Xiaohua Xie	Sun Yat-sen University, China
Wanjiang Xu	Yancheng Teachers University, China
Yuli Xue	Beihang University, China
Haibin Yan	Beijing University of Posts and Telecommunications, China
Yan Yan	Xiamen University, China
Gongping Yang	Shandong University, China
Jinfeng Yang	Shenzhen Polytechnic, China
Jucheng Yang	Tianjin University of Science and Technology, China
Lu Yang	Shandong University of Finance and Economics, China
Wankou Yang	Southeast University, China
Yingchun Yang	Zhejiang University, China
Lin You	Hangzhou Dianzi University, China
Shiqi Yu	Southern University of Science and Technology, China
Weiqi Yuan	Shenyang University of Technology, China
Baochang Zhang	Beihang University, China
Kunbo Zhang	Institute of Automation, Chinese Academy of Sciences, China
Lin Zhang	Tongji University, China
Man Zhang	Institute of Automation, Chinese Academy of Sciences, China
Shiliang Zhang	Peking University, China
Shunli Zhang	Beijing Jiaotong University, China
Weiqiang Zhang	Tsinghua University, China
Yongliang Zhang	Zhejiang University of Technology, China
Zhaoxiang Zhang	Institute of Automation, Chinese Academy of Sciences, China
Cairong Zhao	Tongji University, China
Dongdong Zhao	Wuhan University of Technology, China
Qijun Zhao	Sichuan University, China
Fang Zheng	Tsinghua University, China
Kaijun Zhou	Hunan University of Technology and Business, China

Xiancheng Zhou	Hunan University of Technology and Business, China
Xiuzhuang Zhou	Beijing University of Posts and Telecommunications, China
Hui Zhu	Xidian University, China
Xiangyu Zhu	Institute of Automation, Chinese Academy of Sciences, China
En Zhu	National University of Defense Technology, China
Wangmeng Zuo	Harbin Institute of Technology, China

Publicity Chairs

Junping Zhang	Fudan University, China
Wei Jia	Hefei University of Technology, China
Shiliang Sun	East China Normal University, China

Doctoral Consortium Chairs

Shiqi Yu	Southern University of Science and Technology, China
Zhaoxiang Zhang	Institute of Automation, Chinese Academy of Sciences, China

Publication Chairs

Manhua Liu	Shanghai Jiao Tong University, China
Angelo Marcelli	Università degli Studi di Salerno, Italy
Qi Li	Institute of Automation, Chinese Academy of Sciences, China
Jinfeng Yang	Shenzhen Polytechnic, China

Organizing Committee Chair

Yuchun Fang	Shanghai University, China

Organizing Committee Members

Yunlong Wang	Institute of Automation, Chinese Academy of Sciences, China
Qicai Ran	Shanghai University, China
Zhengye Xiao	Shanghai University, China
Liangjun Wang	Shanghai University, China
Yaofang Zhang	Shanghai University, China
Menglu Zhou	Shanghai University, China
Chen Chen	Shanghai University, China
Shiquan Lin	Shanghai University, China

Contents

Facial Biometrics

Speech Biometrics

Multi-modal Biometrics and Emerging Biometrics

A Novel Dual-Modal Biometric Recognition Method Based on Weighted Joint Sparse Representation Classifaction

Chunxin Fang, Hui Ma$^{(\boxtimes)}$, and Zedong Yang

College of Electronic Engineering, Heilongjiang University, Harbin, China
2011043@hlju.edu.cn

Abstract. The dual-modal biometric recognition based on feature-level fusion is an important research direction in identity recognition. To improve the performance of identity recognition, we propose a novel dual-modal biometric recognition method based on weighted joint sparse representation classification (WJSRC). The method introduces joint sparse representation classification (JSRC) to fuse fingerprint and finger-vein features at first. Then, a penalty function is constructed between the test and training samples to optimize the sparse representation. Finally, the image quality scores of samples are utilized to construct a weight function to optimize the decision-making. The experimental results on two bimodal datasets demonstrate that the proposed method has significant improvement for the accuracy and reliability of identity recognition.

Keywords: Joint sparse representation · Weighted joint sparse representation · Dual-modal biometric recognition · Feature-level fusion

1 Introduction

With the continuous development of science and technology, biometric recognition has been widely used in daily life [1]. Compared with traditional identifications, such as passwords, tokens, and so on, biometric traits are difficult to be forgotten or lost. However, unimodal biometric recognition has several drawbacks [2,3]: (1) Sensitivity to spoof attacks. (2) Lack of discriminability. (3) Intra-class variation. The above problems cause an increase in the error rate of the recognition system and a decrease in the system security. To overcome these problems, multimodal biometric recognition techniques that fuse two or more biometric traits (e.g., fingerprint, finger-vein, etc.) are a good option to improve reliability and accuracy [4].

Compared with other biometric traits, such as the face, iris, and so on, fingerprint and finger-vein are easily accepted by the public and have been extensively studied by many scholars [5,6]. Fingerprint, as one of the widely used biometric traits, has a high degree of versatility. However, fingerprints are generally acquired by contact, which can easily leave traces and be copied and stolen.

© Springer Nature Switzerland AG 2021
J. Feng et al. (Eds.): CCBR 2021, LNCS 12878, pp. 3–10, 2021.
https://doi.org/10.1007/978-3-030-86608-2_1

Even with contactless fingerprint recognition [7], it is also difficult to identify the wrinkled fingerprints that have been immersed in liquid for a long time [8]. As an internal trait of the human body, finger-vein is highly resistant to deception and has a high level of security. However, the blood vessels of fingers will be narrow when people with Raynaud's disease feel pressure, making it difficult to identify the finger-veins [9].

Dual-modal biometric recognition based on fingerprint and finger-vein has richer discriminative information, which can alleviate the impact caused by the above mentioned problems to some extent. At the same time, it has congenital fusibility since fingerprint and finger-vein images can be obtained simultaneously on the same finger. However, the dual-modal biometric recognition with fused fingerprint and finger-vein has not been adequately researched yet.

To solve this problem, we propose a dual-modal biometric recognition method based on weighted joint sparse representation classification. The method considers the locality of training samples while using the JSRC to fuse features. Besides, we propose a novel decision function to improve the final recognition performance. Therefore, the main contributions of the paper are as follows:

(1) The JSRC is introduced into dual-modal biometric recognition to avoid the problem of feature space incompatibility. Meanwhile, we propose a penalty function between the test sample and training sample.
(2) A weight function utilizing the quality scores of fingerprint and finger-vein images is constructed to improve the final recognition performance.

The rest of the paper is organized as follows: In Sect. 2, the JSRC is briefly reviewed. Section 3 detailly describes our WJSRC method. Adequate experiments are conducted in Sect. 4. Finally, Sect. 5 concludes the paper.

2   Multimodal Joint Sparse Representation Classification

Joint sparse representation means to consider multiple related sparse representation problems in the same framework. Shekhar et al. [10] proposed a multimodal biometric recognition method utilizing the JSRC, which can be expressed in mathematical as Eq. (1).

$$\hat{\boldsymbol{\beta}} = arg \min_{\boldsymbol{\beta}} \frac{1}{2} \sum_{i=1}^{D} \left\| \boldsymbol{Y}^i - \boldsymbol{X}^i \boldsymbol{\beta}^i \right\|_F^2 + \lambda \left\| \boldsymbol{\beta} \right\|_{1,q} \tag{1}$$

where $\boldsymbol{Y}^i$ denotes the observed value of the ith modal test sample and $\boldsymbol{X}^i$ is the dictionary data of the ith modality. $\boldsymbol{\beta}$ represents sparse coefficient matrix, which is composed of the sparse coefficient matrix of various modalities.

After obtaining $\hat{\boldsymbol{\beta}}$, the test sample is marked as the class with the minimum reconstruction error, as Eq. (2).

$$\hat{j} = arg \min_{j} \sum_{i=1}^{D} \left\| \boldsymbol{Y}^i - \boldsymbol{X}^i \boldsymbol{\delta}_j^i \left(\boldsymbol{\beta}^i \right) \right\|_F^2 \tag{2}$$

where $\boldsymbol{\delta}_j^i$ is the matrix indicator function.

3   Proposed Method

The fusion recognition of fingerprint and finger-vein at feature-level needs to consider the problem of feature space incompatibility [11]. The JSRC fuses features by sharing sparse representation, which can avoid the above problem. However, the JSRC treats all training samples indiscriminately when solving the sparse coefficients. At the same time, it also ignores the quality of different modal images when using reconstruction errors for decision-making.

To address the above problems, we propose a weighted joint sparse representation classification for dual-modal biometric recognition. Specifically, for the first problem, the proposed method constructs a penalty function between the training sample and test sample. The penalty coefficients are used to constrain the sparse coefficients. For the second problem, we utilize the image quality score [12] to construct the weight function for improving the final recognition performance. The overview of the proposed method is shown in Fig. 1.

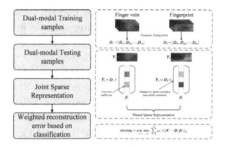

Fig. 1. The overview of the proposed method

The proposed method can be expressed in mathematical as Eq. (3).

$$\hat{\boldsymbol{\beta}} = arg\,\min_{\boldsymbol{\beta}} \frac{1}{2}\sum_{i=1}^{2} \|\boldsymbol{Y}_i - \boldsymbol{D}_i\boldsymbol{\beta}_i\|_2^2 + \lambda\,\|\boldsymbol{\delta}\otimes\boldsymbol{\beta}\|_{1,2} \tag{3}$$

where λ is the balance parameter. And $\boldsymbol{Y}_i \in \boldsymbol{R}^{m\times 1}$ is the test sample of the ith modality, $\boldsymbol{D}_i \in \boldsymbol{R}^{m\times n}$ is the dictionary matrix composed of all training samples of the ith modality. Meanwhile, $\boldsymbol{\beta}_i \in \boldsymbol{R}^{n\times 1}$ means the sparse coefficient vector corresponding to the ith modal test sample. $\boldsymbol{\beta} = [\boldsymbol{\beta}_1, \boldsymbol{\beta}_2] \in \boldsymbol{R}^{n\times 2}$ is the sparse coefficient matrix, which is formed by concatenating the sparse coefficient vectors. Besides, $\otimes$ denotes the multiplication in element-wise, and $\boldsymbol{\delta} = [\boldsymbol{\delta}_1, \boldsymbol{\delta}_2] \in \boldsymbol{R}^{n\times 2}$ means the penalty coefficient matrix whose element $\boldsymbol{\delta}_i$ is $[\delta_{i1}, \delta_{i2}, \cdots, \delta_{ij}, \cdots \delta_{in}]^T$. In particular, δ_{ij} is defined as Eq. (4).

$$\delta_{ij} = \exp\left(\frac{\|\boldsymbol{Y}_i - \boldsymbol{d}_{ij}\|_2}{\sigma_i}\right) \quad i = 1, 2; j = 1, 2, \cdots, n \tag{4}$$

where $\|\boldsymbol{Y}_i - \boldsymbol{d}_{ij}\|_2$ denotes the Euclidean distance between the ith modal test sample and the jth training sample of the ith modality. Meanwhile, σ_i is the bandwidth parameter corresponding to the ith modality.

The result of fusion recognition with fingerprint and finger-vein is not only related to the selection of training samples, but also related to the sum of reconstruction errors among modalities. Therefore, we introduce the quality score of the image to construct the weight function for improving the final recognition performance. The decision function of the proposed method is as follows:

$$identity = \arg \min_{c=1,2,\cdots,C} \sum_{i=1}^{2} \omega_i^c \times \|\boldsymbol{Y}_i - \boldsymbol{D}_i^c \boldsymbol{\beta}_i^c\|_2 \tag{5}$$

where ω_i^c denotes the weight coefficient corresponding to the class c reconstruction error of the ith modality, which is calculated as follows:

$$\omega_i^c = \frac{\exp\left(-\frac{\eta_i^c}{\sigma_i}\right)}{\sum_{i=1}^{2} \exp\left(-\frac{\eta_i^c}{\sigma_i}\right)} \tag{6}$$

where σ_i is the bandwidth parameter corresponding to the ith modality, and η_i^c denotes the ratio of the image quality score of the ith modal test sample to the mean image quality score of the class c training sample in the ith modality.

4   Experiments

We carry out experiments from two different aspects including parameter selection experiments and comparison experiments. Meanwhile, to evaluate the experiments from various perspectives, accuracy (ACC) and kappa coefficient [13] are chosen as the evaluation metrics in this paper. In addition, we use Histogram of Oriented Gradient (HOG) [14] to extract features from fingerprint and finger-vein images. Meanwhile, Principal Component Analysis (PCA) [15] is also utilized to reduce the dimension of the hog feature vector.

It should be noted that the hardware platform used in this paper is 3.00 GHz CPU and 16 GB RAM, and Matlab2018b software is used to run the experiments.

4.1   Datasets

Fingerprint Dataset: The fingerprint database FVC2006 DB2_A [16] is chosen in our testing, which contains 140 fingers. And each finger is collected 12 times. In this paper, the first and last six images of all fingers are formed into DB1 and DB2 fingerprint datasets, respectively.

Finger-vein Dataset: The finger-vein databases FV_USM [17] and PolyU [18] are chosen in our testing. Among them, the FV_USM contains 123 volunteers and the PolyU contains 156 objects. Each finger in both datasets is collected six times. In the paper, all images of the first 140 fingers from the FV_USM and PolyU are selected to compose the FV_USM1 and PolyU1, respectively.

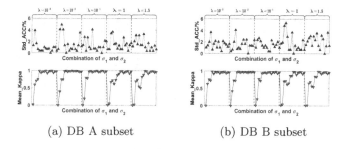

| (a) DB A subset | (b) DB B subset |

Fig. 2. The standard deviation of ACC and average kappa coefficient of three experiments

Dual-modal Dataset: We establish two dual-modal biometric datasets called DB_A and DB_B. In the DB_A, we combine the DB1 with FV_USM1, that is, six fingerprint images and six finger-vein images of each finger are combined as one object. Similarly, the combination of the DB2 and PolyU1 forms the DB_B dataset.

4.2   The Experiments for Selecting Parameter Values

The main purpose of these experiments is to determine the values of the balance parameter λ and four bandwidth parameters (σ_1 for finger-vein and σ_2 for fingerprint in the penalty function, σ_3 for finger-vein and σ_4 for fingerprint in the weight function). There is no direct mathematical relationship between the penalty function and weight function, so the selection of bandwidth parameters is divided into two steps. The first is to change the value of σ_1 and σ_2 to determine the optimal values without introducing the weight function. In the second step, the optimal values of σ_3 and σ_4 are determined by using the optimal parameter values $\lambda, \sigma_1, \sigma_2$ in the first step while introducing the weight function.

The experimental setting is as follows: 50 fingers are randomly chosen from the dual-modal dataset in each experiment to form the subset that contains 300 images. For each finger, the first three images are used for training and the remaining images for testing. Meanwhile, the feature dimension of fingerprint and finger-vein is set to 90 by using PCA. The ACC and kappa coefficient are calculated by varying $\lambda, \sigma_1, \sigma_2$ in their ranges in turn. Each experiment is repeated three times independently.

The standard deviation of ACC and average kappa coefficient are shown in Fig. 2. From the figures, we can see that the standard deviation ACC and average kappa coefficient show different degrees of oscillation with the increase of λ. On the whole, the standard deviation of ACC is relatively small and the average kappa coefficient is close to 1 when λ is 10^{-3}. Therefore, we set λ to 10^{-3}, making WJSRC have better stability and higher accuracy.

When λ is 10^{-3}, the average ACC of DB_A and DB_B subsets are shown in Fig. 3. As we can see from figures that the average ACC on two subsets is relatively higher when $\sigma_1 = \{1, 3, 5\}, \sigma_2 = 0.1$. Comparing the average ACC

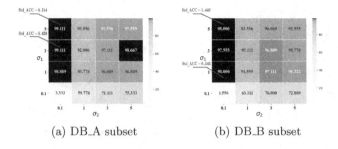

(a) DB_A subset   (b) DB_B subset

Fig. 3. The average ACC on subsets when $\lambda = 10^{-3}$

and standard deviation of ACC, we set the bandwidth parameters in DB_A to $\sigma_1 = 5, \sigma_2 = 0.1$, and the bandwidth parameters in DB_B to $\sigma_1 = 1, \sigma_2 = 0.1$, which can make the proposed method have higher recognition performance and stability.

After selecting the $\lambda, \sigma_1, \sigma_2$, the experiment is conducted again according to the above experimental settings to choose the σ_3, σ_4. The average ACC is shown in Fig. 4.

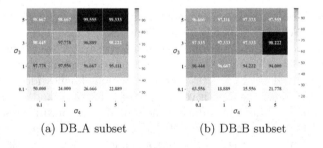

(a) DB_A subset   (b) DB_B subset

Fig. 4. The average ACC on subsets when $\lambda = 10^{-3}$, (a) $\sigma_1 = 5, \sigma_2 = 0.1$ (b) $\sigma_1 = 1, \sigma_2 = 0.1$

It can be seen from the above figures that DB_A and DB_B subsets can obtain higher recognition results when σ_3 takes larger values (e.g., 3 and 5). For the comparison of the follow-up experiments, the values of σ_3 and σ_4 corresponding to the highest average ACC are chosen in this paper. Therefore, we set the bandwidth parameters in DB_A to $\sigma_3 = 5, \sigma_4 = 3$, and the bandwidth parameters in DB_B to $\sigma_3 = 3, \sigma_4 = 5$.

4.3   Comparison Experiments

To verify the effectiveness of the proposed method, we compare it with JSRC [10] and other approaches based on the concatenated feature. Among them, the concatenated feature is classified by sparse representation classification (SRC)

[19] and locality-constrained linear coding (LLC) [20], respectively. For each finger in the dual-modal datasets, the first three images are selected for training and the remaining images are used for testing. The comparison results are shown in Table 1.

Table 1. The results of ACC and kappa coefficient for different fusion methods

Database	DB_A		DB_B	
	ACC (%)	Kappa	ACC (%)	Kappa
SRC	91.191	0.9113	87.619	0.8753
LLC	92.143	0.9209	90.476	0.9041
JSRC	96.429	0.9640	93.333	0.9329
Proposed	**97.619**	**0.9760**	**96.905**	**0.9688**

We can see from the above table that the ACC and kappa coefficient of the proposed method are higher than other fusion methods on different datasets, reflecting that the recognition performance of the proposed method is significantly better than other approaches in the table. Meanwhile, the method based on JSRC can obtain more satisfactory results compared with the approaches based on the concatenated feature. Besides, comparing the experimental results of JSRC with those of the proposed method, it can be found that the addition of penalty and weight coefficients optimizes the JSRC.

5   Conclusion

In this paper, we propose a novel dual-modal biometric recognition method based on weighted joint sparse representation classification. The method fuses fingerprint and finger-vein at the feature-level by sharing sparse representations. Meanwhile, the penalty function constructed between the training sample and test sample optimizes the selection of training samples in the sparse representation. In addition, the weight function constructed in the decision-making process also improves the final recognition results to some extent. The experimental results on two dual-modal datasets show that the proposed method effectively improves the performance of identity recognition. In the future work, we will optimize the dictionary matrix to raise operational efficiency.

References

1. Adiraju, R.V., Masanipalli, K.K., Reddy, T.D., Pedapalli, R., Chundru, S., Panigrahy, A.K.: An extensive survey on finger and palm vein recognition system. Mater. Today Proc. **48**, 1804–1808 (2020)
2. Modak, S.K.S., Jha, V.K.: Multibiometric fusion strategy and its applications: a review. Inf. Fusion. **49**, 174–204 (2019)

3. Vig, R., Iyer, N., Arora, T.: Multi-modal hand-based biometric system using energy compaction of various transforms and wavelets. In: 2017 International Conference on Computing and Communication Technologies for Smart Nation (IC3TSN), pp. 385–390. (2017)
4. Lumini, A., Nanni, L.: Overview of the combination of biometric matchers. Inf. Fusion **33**, 71–85 (2017)
5. Liu, F., Liu, G., Zhao, Q., Shen, L.: Robust and high-security fingerprint recognition system using optical coherence tomography. Neurocomputing **402**, 14–28 (2020)
6. Zhao, D., Ma, H., Yang, Z., Li, J., Tian, W.: Finger vein recognition based on lightweight CNN combining center loss and dynamic regularization. Infrared Phys. Technol. **105**, 103221 (2020)
7. Liu, F., Zhang, D.: 3D fingerprint reconstruction system using feature correspondences and prior estimated finger model. Pattern Recognit. **47**, 178–193 (2014)
8. Khodadoust, J., Khodadoust, A.M., Mirkamali, S.S., Ayat, S.: Fingerprint indexing for wrinkled fingertips immersed in liquids. Exp. Syst. Appl. **146**, 113153 (2020)
9. Khodadoust, J., Medina-Pérez, M.A., Monroy, R., Khodadoust, A.M., Mirkamali, S.S.: A multibiometric system based on the fusion of fingerprint, finger-vein, and finger-knuckle-print. Exp. Syst. Appl. **176**, 114687 (2021)
10. Shekhar, S., Patel, V.M., Nasrabadi, N.M., Chellappa, R.: Joint Sparse Representation for Robust Multimodal Biometrics Recognition. IEEE Transactions on Pattern Analysis and Machine Intelligence. **36**, 113–126 (2014)
11. Yang, W., Wang, S., Hu, J., Zheng, G., Valli, C.: A fingerprint and finger-vein based cancelable multi-biometric system. Patt. Recognit. **78**, 242–251 (2018)
12. Peng, J., Li, Q., Niu, X.: A novel finger vein image quality evaluation method based on triangular norm. In: 2014 Tenth International Conference on Intelligent Information Hiding and Multimedia Signal Processing, pp. 239–242 (2014)
13. Shazeeda, S., Rosdi, B.A.: Finger vein recognition using mutual sparse representation classification. IET Biom. **8**, 49–58 (2019)
14. Xu, J., Fuming, S., Haojie, L., Yudong, C.: Hand vein recognition algorithm based on NMF with sparsity and clustering property constraints in feature mapping space. Chin. J. Electron. **28**, 1184–1190 (2019)
15. Hu, N., Ma, H., Zhan, T.: Finger vein biometric verification using block multi-scale uniform local binary pattern features and block two-directional two-dimension principal component analysis. Optik. **208**, 163664 (2020)
16. Cappelli, R., Ferrara, M., Franco, A., Maltoni, D.: Fingerprint verification competition 2006. Biomet. Technol. Today **15**, 7–9 (2007)
17. Mohd Asaari, M.S., Suandi, S.A., Rosdi, B.A.: Fusion of band limited phase only correlation and width centroid contour distance for finger based biometrics. Exp. Syst. Appl. **41**, 3367–3382 (2014)
18. Kumar, A., Zhou, Y.: Human Identification Using Finger Images. IEEE Trans. Image Process. **21**, 2228–2244 (2012)
19. Chen, L., Wang, J., Yang, S., He, H.: A finger vein image-based personal identification system with self-adaptive illuminance control. IEEE Trans. Instrum. Meas. **66**, 294–304 (2017)
20. Wang, J., Yang, J., Yu, K., Lv, F., Huang, T., Gong, Y.: Locality-constrained linear coding for image classification. In: 2010 IEEE Computer Society Conference on Computer Vision and Pattern Recognition, pp. 3360–3367. IEEE (2010)

Personal Identification with Exploiting Competitive Tasks in EEG Signals

Menglu Zhou, Yuchun Fang$^{(\boxtimes)}$, and Zhengye Xiao

School of Computer Engineering and Science, Shanghai University, Shanghai, China
ycfang@shu.edu.cn

Abstract. Electroencephalography (EEG) is the spontaneous and rhythmic electrical brain cell activity recorded by amplifying the biological potential from the scalp with precise electronic instruments. EEG highly satisfy the requirements of a biometric system such as uniqueness and circumvention, but when recording EEG signals, different events which subject performs, such as opening eyes, closing eyes, clenching fists and so on, will cause signal fluctuation. In this paper, we propose a EEG-based personal identification method. Linear-frequency cepstrum coefficients (LFCC) is used as input feature to get the frequency information from raw EEG signals. A gradient reverse layer (GRL) is added to eliminate the noise caused by different events. Personal identification task and event recognition task are trained together in an adversarial way to extract event-independent feature. Experimental results validate the effectiveness of the proposed method.

Keywords: EEG · Personal identification · Adversarial learning · Competitive task

1 Introduction

Traditional human identification and authentication methods such as passwords, usernames and ID cards could be easily forgotten or stolen. By contrast, biometrics technology utilizes the inherent physiological characteristics that the subject has intrinsically to conduct personal identification, such as fingerprints, iris, face, DNA, etc. As a non-invasive imaging technique, EEG is also simple, portable, and relatively low cost when compared to other brain acquisition techniques.

However, raw EEG signals are often influenced by noise and artifacts. In audio feature processing, the frequency band power feature [1] and mel-frequency cepstral coefficient (MFCC) [2] are two most common frequency feature. But there is no proof that nonlinear scale is also meaningful to EEG signals. Liu et al. [3] therefore proposed the modified-MFCC for EEG signals named LFCC by replacing the mel-scale filters in MFCC with linear-scale filters. We employ LFCC in this paper to extract frequency feature from EEG signals.

Another problem is that when collecting EEG signals, subjects are often performing different events, such as opening eyes, closing eyes, clenching fists and

© Springer Nature Switzerland AG 2021
J. Feng et al. (Eds.): CCBR 2021, LNCS 12878, pp. 11–19, 2021.
https://doi.org/10.1007/978-3-030-86608-2_2

so on. The EEG fluctuation caused by different events is noise to the identification task and may interfere the model to recognize the person. Thus the identification and event recognition of EEG signal is a pair of competitive tasks. In this paper, event recognition is used as the competitive task to identity recognition to improve the performance by learning event recognition adversarially.

The overview of our approach is shown in Fig. 1.

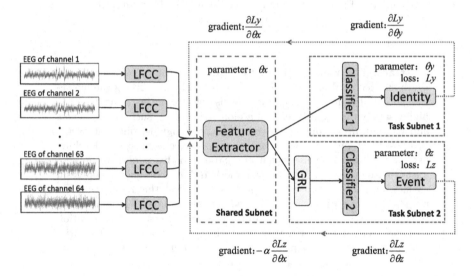

Fig. 1. Overview of the proposed method.

2 Related Work

2.1 EEG Based Personal Identification

Li et al. [4] proposed an EEG based biometrics system which contains automatic channel selection, wavelet feature extraction and Deep Neural Network (DNN) classifier. Thomas et al. [5] proposed a biometric identification system which combines subject-specific alpha peak frequency, peak power and delta band power values to form discriminative feature vectors and templates. Keshishzadeh et al. [6] proposed an EEG based human authentication system on a large dataset by extracting Autoregressive (AR) coefficients as the feature set, selecting the features using a statistical based method. Zhang et al. [7] proposed a identification method named MindID which feeds the decomposed Delta pattern EEG data into an attention-based Encoder-Decoder Recurrent Neural Networks (RNNs) structure which assigns varies attention weights to different EEG channels.

2.2   Multi-task Adversarial Learning

Caruana [8] put forward the concept of multi-task learning as early as 1995. Multi-task learning is a machine learning method to improve generalization performance by training multiple related tasks together.

But not all related tasks will improve each other's performance. For example, competitive task is a kind of task that has a competitive relationship with the main task. Its training goal conflicts with the main task, or even the opposite. Although the competitive task is related to the main task, if they are directly trained together with multi-task learning, the performance of the model on the main task will be damaged. On the contrary, by training the main task and the competitive task in the way of adversarial learning, the competitive relationship between these tasks can be transformed into constraints beneficial to the model. The obtained expression can be beneficial to the main task and adversarial to the competitive task. Shinohara [9] proposed an adversarial multi-task learning of DNNs which constantly uses the opposite information contained in the auxiliary task to eliminate the noise of the speech recognition, so as to enhance invariance of representations. Inspired by the above references, we apply this idea to EEG based personal identification.

3   Method

3.1   LFCC

The MFCC [2] is the most commonly used feature in speech recognition. It uses nonlinear frequency scale since human ears have different auditory sensitivity to different frequencies of sound waves. However, although EEG signals are very similar to audio signals, there is no evidence that nonlinear scale is also meaningful to EEG signals. Liu et al. [3] therefore proposed the modified-MFCC for EEG signals named LFCC by replacing the mel-scale filters in MFCC with linear-scale filters. We employ LFCC in this paper to extract frequency feature from raw EEG signals. The process of feature extraction is shown in Fig. 2.

Fig. 2. The process of LFCC feature extraction.

The preprocessing operations include framing and windowing. The frame length is set to 1s and the 1s Hamming window moves at a 0.5s frame interval for EEG signal analysis. Then we use Fast Fourier Transform (FFT) to obtain the spectrum $X(f)$ of each frame. After that, linear-scale filter banks in Eq. 1 is used to smooth the signals and highlight the main frequency components.

$$Y_n = \sum_{f_n^{(lowest)}}^{f_n^{(highest)}} L_n(f)|X(f)|^2, 1 \leqslant n \leqslant N \tag{1}$$

where $L_n(f)$ represents the frequency response of the n-th linear filter, $f_n^{(lowest)}$ represents the lowest frequency, and $f_n^{(highest)}$ represents the highest frequency for the n-th filter. N is the total number of linear filters and is set to 24 in this paper.

Finally, given the dimension D, the LFCC feature can be calculated by Eq. 2.

$$F_{LFCC}(d) = \sum_{n=1}^{N} \log(Y_n) \cos\left(\frac{(2n-1)d\pi}{2N}\right), 1 \leq d \leq D \tag{2}$$

where $F_{LFCC}(d)$ is the d-th dimension of the extracted LFCC feature. Since D is set to 12, we get a 12-dimension vector for each frame. The same operation is repeated for each frame to get the final LFCC feature of one sample.

3.2   Adversarial Multi-task Learning

We define θ_x as the shared parameters in the feature extractor. Personal identification is employed as the main task and event recognition as the competitive task to form adversarial multi-task learning. θ_y and θ_z represent the parameters specific to the identity recognition task subnet and the event recognition task subnet, respectively. Let X denote the set of the input LFCC vectors. The prediction of the identification and the event task can be calculated in Eq. 3 and Eq. 4.

$$\hat{Y} = F(X; \theta_x, \theta_y) \tag{3}$$

$$\hat{Z} = F(X; \theta_x, \theta_z) \tag{4}$$

where F is the function that maps the input samples to output prediction.

The objective function of the model is defined in Eq. 5.

$$\arg\min_{\theta_x, \theta_y, \theta_z} = L_y\left(\hat{Y}, Y\right) + \lambda L_z\left(\hat{Z}, Z\right) \tag{5}$$

where L_y and L_z denote the cross-entropy loss function of the identity recognition task and the event recognition task, respectively. Y and Z represent the label of the identity recognition task and the event recognition task. λ is a factor to balance the contribution of the losses.

For each training batch, the gradient will be calculated to update the parameters of all subnets by a learning rate η. The gradient back propagation of task subnets can be formulated in Eq. 6.

$$\theta_y \leftarrow \theta_y - \eta\frac{\partial L_y}{\partial \theta_y}, \theta_z \leftarrow \theta_z - \eta\frac{\partial L_z}{\partial \theta_z} \tag{6}$$

The optimization direction of feature extractor's parameters is up to the main task and the competitive task simultaneously. In order to let the model better extract features that are beneficial to the main task, the parameters of feature extractor are updated by Eq. 7.

$$\theta_x \leftarrow \theta_x - \eta \frac{\partial L_y}{\partial \theta_x} \tag{7}$$

However, if we handle the competitive task in the same way, the performance of the model will be impaired. Therefore, it is necessary to optimize the parameters in reverse to eliminate the influence of the competitive task. A gradient reverse layer is added between the feature extractor and the classifier to reverse the gradient. After multiplying α with the gradient of the competitive task subnet, the parameters of feature extractor are updated by Eq. 8.

$$\theta_x \leftarrow \theta_x - \eta \left(-\alpha \frac{\partial L_z}{\partial \theta_x} \right) \tag{8}$$

where α is the hyperparameter to control the degree of adversarial learning.

With Eq. 7 and Eq. 8, the parameter update of the feature extractor can be reformulatd in Eq. 9.

$$\theta_x \leftarrow \theta_x - \eta \left(\frac{\partial L_y}{\partial \theta_x} - \alpha \frac{\partial L_z}{\partial \theta_x} \right) \tag{9}$$

Through reversing the optimization direction of the competitive task, we form an adversarial relationship between the feature extractor and the event recognition task subnet. The GRL helps to converge the model while prevents the noises from the different events. Once the model converges, the event classifier can not recognize which event the subject is performing. The features extracted by the feature extractor is event-independent, which can significantly improve the performance of the personal indentification classifier.

4   Experiment

We have carried out several experiments to prove the effectiveness of our method. The dataset used and some experimental details are first introduced. Then we analyze the results of ablation study and the comparison with other methods.

4.1   Dataset

EEG Motor Movement/Imagery Dataset. This dataset consists of 109 subjects. Each subject performed 14 experimental runs: two one-minute baseline runs (one with eyes open, one with eyes closed), and three two-minute runs of each of the four following events: open and close left or right fist, imagine opening and closing left or right fist, open and close both fists or both feet, and imagine opening and closing both fists or both feet. EEG signals were recorded by a 64-channel system (BCI2000 instrumentation system [10]) and sampled at 160 samples per second. The experiment protocal is decribed in [11].

4.2   Implementation Details

Three two-minute runs of four events performed by 109 subjects are chose to conduct the experiment. For each run, we cut the EEG signals into 10 segments to increase the samples. Thus we obtain $3*4*10 = 120$ samples for one subject. ResNet-18 is employed as the backbone of our model. The value of α increases gradually during the training process to control the influence of the competitve task and stabilizes after reaching a specific value as in Eq. 10.

$$\alpha = \begin{cases} 0.01 * epoch & \text{if } epoch \in [0, 50] \\ 0.5 & \text{if } epoch \in (50, +\infty) \end{cases} \tag{10}$$

4.3   Ablation Study

In this section, we conduct ablation study with different cross validation strategy and different components, respectively. The results in Table 1 show that the model achieves the best performance when 90% samples are used for training and the rest are used for testing, hence we use this cross validation method in subsequent experiments.

Table 1. Recognition accuracy with different cross validation strategy.

Cross validation	Accuracy
50% samples for train, 50% samples for test	87.0
80% samples for train, 20% samples for test	96.3
90% samples for train, 10% samples for test	**99.2**

Table 2. Recognition accuracy with different components.

Method	Accuracy
Raw EEG signals	76.5
LFCC	98.2
LFCC + multi-task learning	97.7
LFCC + adversarial multi-task learning	**99.2**

Next, we verify the effectiveness of the LFCC feature and the adversarial learning. As showed in Table 2, the LFCC feature greatly improves the accuracy by 21.7%. However, if we exploit the event recognition task in common multi-task way, the result is even worse than single task model. The competitve task impacts the main task and reduces the accuracy by 0.5%. In contrast, the proposed approach can further improve the accuracy of identity recognition.

4.4   Comparison with Other Methods

We first compare with other research works in the field of EEG-based personal identification in recent years, the comparative results are reported in Table 3.

Table 3. Comparison with other methods for the recognition problem.

Reference	Method	Subject	Accuracy
Yifan et al. [4]	Channel selection + wavelet feature + DNN	32	88
Thomas et al. [5]	Delta band EEG + cross-correlation values	109	90.21
Keshishzadeh et al. [6]	AR + SVM	104	97.43
Xiang et al. [7]	Delta pattern EEG + attention-based RNNs	8	98.82
Ours	LFCC + adversarial learning	109	**99.2**

Our experimental result is the best of all the methods, which is bold in the Table 3. We mainly compare the recognition accuracy with Thomas et al. [5], since the subject number is the same 109 as ours. The proposed method increases the accuracy by 8.89%. Although it can be noticed that the accuracy of Xiang et al. [7] is very close to our method, they only use 8 subjects while we conduct the experiment on a large dataset with 109 subjects. These comparison results prove that our method is effective for personal identification task.

Then we conduct the experiment for the verification problem. The false acceptance rate (FAR) and the false rejection rate (FRR) are used as the evaluation criterion.

$$FAR = FN/(TN + FN) \tag{11}$$

$$FRR = FP/(TP + FP) \tag{12}$$

where TN is true negative, FN is false negative, TP is true positive, and FP is false positive.

Table 4. Comparison with other methods for the verification problem.

Reference	Method	Subject	FAR	FRR
Shinohara et al. [12]	PSD + cross-correlation values	109	1.96	1.96
John et al. [13]	Customized threshold	15	0	2.2
Ours	LFCC + adversarial learning	109	**0**	**0.76**

As shown in Table 4, the proposed method achieves zero FAR and gives a FRR of 0.76, which is lower than Shinohara et al. [12] and John et al. [13].

5   Conclusion

In this paper, we propose a method that adopting LFCC as input feature and applying adversarial learning to eliminate the inference of different events for EEG-based personal identification. Several experiments are conducted to evaluate the effectiveness of our method. The results show the superiority over other methods, and it is promising in EEG-based personal identification for large number of subjects.

Acknowledgments. The work is supported by the National Natural Science Foundation of China under Grant No.: 61976132, U1811461 and the Natural Science Foundation of Shanghai under Grant No.: 19ZR1419200.

References

1. Robert Jenke, A.P., Buss, M.: Feature extraction and selection for emotion recognition from EEG. IEEE Trans. Affective Comput. **5**(3), 327–339 (2014)
2. Picone, J.W.: Signal modeling techniques in speech recognition. Proc. IEEE **81**(9), 1215–1247 (1993)
3. Ningjie, L., Yuchun, F., Ling, L., Limin, H., Fenglei, Y., Yike, G.: Multiple feature fusion for automatic emotion recognition using EEG signals. In: ICASSP IEEE International Conference on Acoustic Speech Signal Process Proceedings, pp. 896–900 (2018)
4. Li, Y., Zhao, Y., Tan, T., Liu, N., Fang, Y.: Personal identification based on content-independent EEG signal analysis. In: Zhou, J., et al. (eds.) CCBR 2017. LNCS, vol. 10568, pp. 537–544. Springer, Cham (2017). https://doi.org/10.1007/978-3-319-69923-3_58
5. Thomas, K.P., Vinod, A.: Utilizing individual alpha frequency and delta band power in EEG based biometric recognition. In: IEEE International Conference on Systems, Man and Cybernetics, SMC - Conference Proceedings, pp. 4787–4791 (2016)
6. Keshishzadeh, S., Fallah, A., Rashidi, S.: Improved EEG based human authentication system on large dataset. In: Iranian Conference on Electrical Engineering, ICEE, pp. 1165–1169 (2016)
7. Xiang, Z., Lina, Y., Salil S., K., Yunhao, L., Tao, G., Kaixuan, C.: MindiD: person identification from brain waves through attention-based recurrent neural network. Proc. ACM Interact. Mob. Wearable Ubiquitous Technol. **2**(3) (2018)
8. Caruana, R.: Learning many related tasks at the same time with backpropagation. In: Advances in Neural Information Processing Systems, pp. 657–664 (1995)
9. Shinohara, Y.: Adversarial multi-task learning of deep neural networks for robust speech recognition. In: Proceedings of the Annual Conference of the International Speech Communication Association, INTERSPEECH, pp. 2369–2372 (2016)
10. Schalk, G., McFarland, D., Hinterberger, T., Birbaumer, N., Wolpaw, J.: BCI 2000: a general-purpose brain-computer interface (BCI) system. IEEE Trans. Biomed. Eng. **51**(6), 1034–1043 (2004)
11. Goldberger, A., et al.: Physiobank, physiotoolkit, and physionet: components of a new research resource for complex physiologic signals. Circulation **101**(23), e215–e220 (2000)

12. Thomas, K.P., Vinod, A.P.: EEG-based biometric authentication using gamma band power during rest state. Circ. Syst. Signal Process **37**(1), 277–289 (2018)
13. Chuang, J., Nguyen, H., Wang, C., Johnson, B.: I think, therefore i am: usability and security of authentication using brainwaves. In: Adams, A.A., Brenner, M., Smith, M. (eds.) FC 2013. LNCS, vol. 7862, pp. 1–16. Springer, Heidelberg (2013). https://doi.org/10.1007/978-3-642-41320-9_1

A Systematical Solution for Face De-identification

Songlin Yang[1,2], Wei Wang[1(✉)], Yuehua Cheng[2], and Jing Dong[1]

[1] Institute of Automation, Center for Research on Intelligent Perception
and Computing, Chinese Academy of Sciences, Beijing, China
yangsonglin2021@ia.ac.cn, {wwang,jdong}@nlpr.ia.ac.cn
[2] College of Automation, Nanjing University of Aeronautics and Astronautics,
Nanjing, China
chengyuehua@nuaa.edu.cn

Abstract. With the identity information in face data more closely related to personal credit and property security, people pay increasing attention to the protection of face data privacy. In different tasks, people have various requirements for face de-identification (De-ID), so we propose a systematical solution compatible for these De-ID operations. Firstly, an attribute disentanglement and generative network is constructed to encode two parts of the face, which are the identity (facial features like mouth, nose and eyes) and expression (including expression, pose and illumination). Through face swapping, we can remove the original ID completely. Secondly, we add an adversarial vector mapping network to perturb the latent code of the face image, different from previous traditional adversarial methods. Through this, we can construct unrestricted adversarial image to decrease ID similarity recognized by model. Our method can flexibly de-identify the face data in various ways and the processed images have high image quality.

Keywords: Face de-identification · Adversarial attacks · Attribute disentanglement · StyleGAN · Face swapping

1 Introduction

The privacy of biometrics becomes increasingly important, with face recognition widely used. Face data contains important identity information, which is closely related to personal credit and property security. Face data is collected more and more frequently, and people tend to show photos on the Internet, which can be easily obtained by others. As lots of abuse of face data is exposed, people pay increasing attention to the security of face data privacy.

The traditional face anonymization, such as mosaic or blurring of face region, has the disadvantage of degrading the quality of the images significantly. These operations destroy the original data distribution and reduce the detection rate in exchange for the reduction of recognition rate, which makes users or data mining researchers unable to further effectively use anonymous face data.

With the concepts of adversarial attacks [1] and generative adversarial networks [2] proposed, many related works have been published, such as Fawkes [3] and CIA-GAN [4]. However, there are still some unsolved problems in these methods: the perturbations of random noise will lead to the degradation of image quality, and the face swapping will generate some artifacts which are easily perceived by human eyes.

To meet the various needs reflected in the above description, our method of face de-identification is proposed. On the one hand, it can realize the de-identification for human visual perception, i.e., completely changing the identity by face swapping. This can meet the requirements of high-intensity anonymization, for De-ID preprocess of face dataset or removing the identification completely when the information is shown to the public. On the other hand, our method can realize the de-identification for face recognition model, i.e., using the adversarial examples to perturb the identification results of the model. Therefore, for an individual user, face privacy data protection is carried out without the loss of original information, while his sharing needs are satisfied. For example, the De-ID images can be displayed on social platforms, which can be recognized by his friends without being collected identity information maliciously.

The contributions of this paper can be summarized as follows:

a. A systematical solution for face de-identification is constructed, which can De-ID for the human visual perception by face swapping, and De-ID for face recognition model by adversarial attacks.

b. Our method perturbs the latent vector of the image in the latent space and maps this vector to the latent space of StyleGAN [5], to get adversarial images with high quality.

c. Different from traditional adversarial methods which add noise to the original image, our method propagates the gradient back to the mapping network of the adversarial vector. This is to explore a new universal and unrestricted adversarial sample generation [6] way for face images.

2   Background and Related Work

De-identification (De-ID). Considering different needs of privacy protection, de-identification has the following two definitions: one is for human visual perception, with the purpose of completely hiding the identity information of the original image. This is mainly for the applications of public display (complete anonymization) and dataset desensitization (massive data anonymization), represented by mosaic, blurring and face swapping. The other is for face recognition model. In order to prevent the abuse of identity information, it is mainly aimed at the privacy protection of individual users, under the premise of meeting the sharing needs, represented by adversarial examples.

Attribute Disentanglement. Many works such as FaceShifter [7] and Style-GAN, connect the visual facial attributes with high-dimensional vectors, which can enhance the ability of controlling the generative network. For the De-ID problem, we put forward higher requirements for attribute disentanglement. We hope that the information used by the models to recognize human identity can be decoupled from other facial features, such as eyes, nose, jawline, etc., so that the De-ID problem can be solved. These works [8,9] have made some contributions, but they still cannot meet the needs of De-ID tasks.

StyleGAN. Inspired by the paper [10], our method takes the pre-trained synthesis network of StyleGAN as the generator. We train a mapping network to map the latent vector of other latent spaces to the latent space of StyleGAN, which inherits its capacity of generating highly realistic and high quality images. Through this operation, we can split the attribute disentanglement and image generation, to avoid the degradation of image quality.

Adversarial Attacks on Face Recognition Systems. Bose et al. [11] make the faces cannot be detected by detectors, while others use patches [12], glasses [13], hats [14] and other methods to realize physical adversarial attacks. However, these methods are not suitable for the De-ID preprocess of large datasets. Our method will explore the universal adversarial features of the data, and get a network that can describe the common patterns of the adversarial samples corresponding to each class of images.

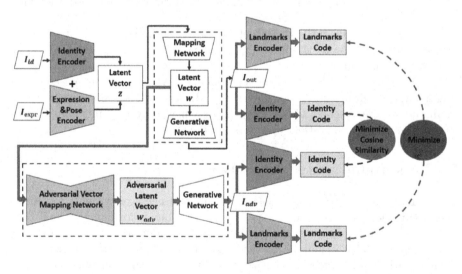

Fig. 1. Framework of our algorithm.

3   Method

3.1   Attribute Disentanglement and Generative Network

As shown in Fig. 1, the identity encoder (En_{id}) extracts the code of facial features from I_{id}. The expression and pose encoder (En_{expr}) extracts the code of expression and pose from I_{expr}. The latent vector z is combined by these two codes, and feed it into the mapping network M to obtain the latent vector w, which will be sent into the generative network to output the I_{out}, thus completing the fusion of identity and expression from different faces. Therefore, the function of **different-input-and-face-swap** and **same-input-and-face-reconstruct** can be realized.

Network Architecture. The ResNet-50 face recognition model, which is pre-trained on VGGFace2 dataset, is used as En_{id} to extract the information of identity, while using the Inception-V3 network as the En_{expr} to extract information of expression and pose. The outputs of both encoders are taken from their last feature vector before the fully-connected classifier and the latent vector z is obtained by combining the outputs of the two encoders:

$$z = [En_{id}(I_{id}), En_{expr}(I_{expr})] \tag{1}$$

The mapping network is a four-layers MLP using LReLU as activation layers, which maps the latent vector z to the latent vector w, thus satisfying the distribution of the generative network. The generator is the synthesis network of StyleGAN. Feed the latent vector w into the generator and get the output image. Landmarks encoder (En_{lnd}) is implemented using a pre-trained landmarks regression network and we only use the 52 inner-face landmarks, removing the jawline landmarks. Discriminator D_W is used to judge whether the latent vector w obtained by mapping network satisfies the distribution of generative network.

Loss Function. The loss functions can be divided into adversarial loss and non-adversarial loss. For adversarial loss, the non-saturating loss with R_1 regularization is selected:

$$
\begin{aligned}
L_{adv}^D =& -E_{w \sim W}[log(D_W(w)] - E_z[log(1 - D_W(M(z)))] \\
& + \frac{\gamma}{2} E_{w \sim W} \|\nabla_w D_W(w)\|_2^2
\end{aligned}
\tag{2}
$$

$$L_{adv}^G = -E_z[log(D_W(M(z)))] \tag{3}$$

For the non-adversarial loss, the overall generator non-adversarial loss $L_{non-adv}^G$ is a weighted sum of L_{id}, $L_{landmark}$ and $L_{reconstruct}$:

$$L_{non-adv}^G = \lambda_1 L_{id} + \lambda_2 L_{landmark} + \lambda_3 L_{reconstruct} \tag{4}$$

As known to all, human perception is highly sensitive to minor artifacts, because not only does every individual frame must look realistic, but the motion across frames must also be realistic.

To enforce visual identity preservation, we use L_1 cycle consistency loss between I_{id} and I_{out}:

$$L_{id} = \|En_{id}(I_{id}) - En_{id}(I_{out})\|_1 \tag{5}$$

To model the possible motion of human face better, we use L_2 cycle consistency landmarks loss between I_{expr} and I_{out}:

$$L_{landmark} = \|En_{lnd}(I_{expr}) - En_{lnd}(I_{out})\|_2 \tag{6}$$

To encourage pixel-level reconstruction of the image when I_{id} and I_{expr} are the same, we use the 'mix' loss suggested by Zhao et al. [15], and use a weighted sum of L_1 loss and MS-SSIM loss. Furthermore, to prevent this reconstruction loss to effect the training of disentanglement, we only employ the reconstruction loss when I_{id} and I_{expr} are the same:

$$L_{reconstruct} = \begin{cases} L_{mix}, & I_{id} = I_{expr} \\ 0, & I_{id} \neq I_{expr} \end{cases} \tag{7}$$

$$L_{mix} = \alpha(1 - (MS - SSIM(I_{id}, I_{out}))) + (1 - \alpha)\|I_{id} - I_{out}\|_1 \tag{8}$$

We sample 70K random Gaussian vectors and feed them through pre-trained StyleGAN, and then we get the latent vector w and its corresponding generative image. The $(image, w)$ data is randomly sampled from the training dataset, and the sampled image data is used as the input of I_{id} and I_{expr}, while the latent vector w will be used as the positive sample for training discriminator. The cross-face training and the same-face training are carried out alternately according to the frequency. The parameters of En_{expr}, discriminator D_W and mapping network M will be updated after each round of training. Note that we separately update the adversarial and non-adversarial parts of parameters, to make the process of training more stable.

3.2   Adversarial Vector Mapping Network

As shown in Fig. 1, take the latent vector w in the pipeline of attribute disentanglement and generative network, and feed it into the adversarial vector mapping network. Then get the adversarial latent vector w_{adv}, and feed it into the generative network. Finally, we can obtain the adversarial image I_{adv} which ID similarity recognized is low against the target ID, but looks very similar to the original image, thus perturbing the identical results of face recognition systems.

Network Architecture. Based on the attribute disentanglement and generative network, our method adds an adversarial vector mapping network M_{adv} into the framework. This is a four-layers MLP using LReLU as activation layers, which maps the latent vector w to the adversarial latent vector w_{adv}.

Loss Function. To better maximize the inner-class distance between the original image and the adversarial image in the latent space, we use the cosine similarity to measure the distance between both images:

$$L_{id}^{model} = \frac{En_{id}(I_{id}) \cdot En_{id}(I_{adv})}{\|En_{id}(I_{id})\| \cdot \|En_{id}(I_{adv})\|} \tag{9}$$

Note that we have to restrict the cosine similarity between the original image and the adversarial image in the latent space, and clip w_{adv} by some selected value δ, after the adversarial vector mapping network outputs the w_{adv}:

$$w_{adv} = Clip_\delta(w_{adv}, w) \tag{10}$$

At the same time, we expect that the human perception similarity between the original image and the adversarial image is high, so we minimize the L_2 cycle consistency distance between landmark codes of these two images:

$$L_{id}^{visual} = \|En_{lnd}(I_{expr}) - En_{lnd}(I_{adv})\|_2 \tag{11}$$

Finally, we adopt a weighted sum of two loss functions as the optimization objective:

$$L_{adv} = \lambda_4 L_{id}^{model} + \lambda_5 L_{id}^{visual} \tag{12}$$

Note that we only use the same-face training in this training stage. Calculate the gradients of the adversarial vector mapping network and update the parameters of it after getting the adversarial latent vector w_{adv}.

4   Experiment

This section will evaluate the performance of the two parts of our method qualitatively and quantitatively, from the ability of disentanglement, the quality of generative images, the adversarial performance of adversarial images and so on. We use FGSM [16], ALAE [17] (generates the whole image) and FSGAN [18] (generates the region of face) as the comparisons. We use the FID [19] (Fréchet Inception Distance) as the objective metric to measure the similarity between the original image and the generative image. We choose MTCNN [20] and Arc-face [21] as face recognition networks, which will respectively measure the face detection rate and identity similarity of the adversarial images in test. We select pre-trained Resnet-50 and Inception-V3 to calculate the loss of facial attributes and expression respectively. Note that the test dataset is FFHQ at 256×256, which all the models used in the following part are not trained on it.

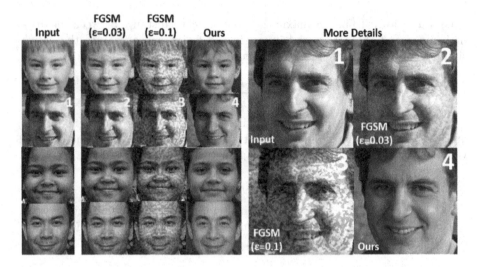

Fig. 2. The result of qualitative comparisons between FGSM and ours.

4.1 De-ID by Adversarial Attacks

In order to evaluate the adversarial performance of our model, we select the FGSM as the comparison. The step sizes of 0.03 and 0.1 are selected respectively, as shown in the Fig. 2. The previous traditional adversarial methods exchange low face detection rate for low identity recognition rate, which have a great impact on the original data distribution. And if you need to keep a low visual artifacts rate, the step size needs to be set very small, but it will degrade its adversarial performance. The image generated by our model has obvious advantages in quality, and can also maintain a high visual ID-similarity and a low model ID-similarity against the original image, which is suitable for De-ID tasks. The quantitative comparative results of the two methods are shown in Table 1. The visual artifacts rate is measured by MOS experiment: We select 100 images randomly with equal probability 12 times (including original images and De-ID images generated by the three methods), and invite 12 people to judge whether there are any artificial De-ID operations. The influence on other applications of De-ID operation is measured by face detection rate. The cosine similarity with the original ID is used to measure the effect of the method on the level of disturbing ID. The FID metric is used as an objective index to determine the visual ID loss between the original images and the adversarial images.

Table 1. Quantitative comparison results of FGSM and our method.

Method	Artifacts rate ↓	Face detect rate ↑	ID similarity ↓	FID ↓
FGSM ($\epsilon = 0.03$)	0.9946 ± 0.014	0.999	0.842 ± 0.005	$\mathbf{33.494 \pm 0.653}$
FGSM ($\epsilon = 0.1$)	1	0.989	0.603 ± 0.008	145.923 ± 2.276
Ours	$\mathbf{0.1442 \pm 0.173}$	1	$\mathbf{0.531 \pm 0.006}$	61.438 ± 0.533

4.2   De-ID by Face Swapping

Disentanglement: Different-Input-and-Face-Swap. Compared with ALAE and FSGAN, the qualitative results of the three methods are shown in Fig. 3. Both ALAE and our method use the whole image generation method, but our method is superior to ALAE in the preservation of identity, expression and pose. At the same time, our method can control the region outside the face and reduce artifacts, better than ALAE. FSGAN focuses on the face region, so it can preserve the features of target identity well. However, the quality of the image generated by FSGAN is obviously poor, and it cannot make the pose and expression provided by target identity, as effectively as our method. This shows that our method can disentangle between visual identity and expressions well. We select FID as a metric to measure the similarity between the original image and the new image. Finally, we evaluated the retention of identity and expression for the model, and the experimental results are summarized in Table 2.

Table 2. Evaluation of ALAE, FSGAN and our method on disentanglement.

Method	FID ↓	Source ID identity loss ↓	Target ID expression loss ↓
ALAE	69.632 ± 1.803	0.033	2.165 ± 0.018
FSGAN	102.324 ± 3.429	0.028	$\mathbf{0.958 \pm 0.038}$
Ours	$\mathbf{37.780 \pm 0.100}$	$\mathbf{0.014}$	1.320 ± 0.012

Reconstruction: Same-Input-and-Face-Reconstruct. When I_{id} and I_{expr} are the same, attribute disentanglement and generative network needs to complete the function of reconstruction, so our model is faced with the problem of GAN inversion [22]. We compare our method with ALAE and FSGAN, to study the quality of reconstruction of our method. Some visual results are shown in Fig. 4. In horizontal contrast, FSGAN, which only focuses on the face, has better performance in the task of reconstruction, but its quality of the generated image is degraded. Both our method and ALAE have undertaken the task of generating the whole image, but our method can better complete GAN inversion, which can preserve most of the features of the original image and reduce the artifacts

Fig. 3. The qualitative results of ALAE, FSGAN, and ours on disentanglement.

at the same time. We verified the reconstruction ability of the model from FID, LPIPS [23] and semantic information such as identity and expression, as shown in Table 3.

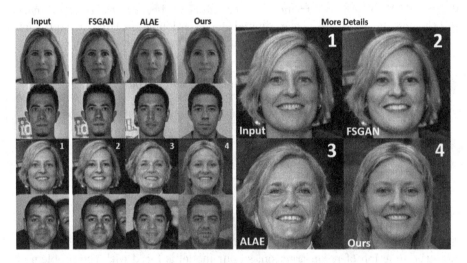

Fig. 4. The qualitative results of ALAE, FSGAN, and ours on reconstruction.

Table 3. Evaluation of ALAE, FSGAN and our method on reconstruction.

Method	FID ↓	LPIPS ↑	Identity loss ↓	Expression loss ↓
ALAE	77.270 ± 1.852	$\mathbf{0.535 \pm 0.003}$	0.032	1.491 ± 0.014
FSGAN	96.010 ± 5.027	0.260 ± 0.003	**0.008**	$\mathbf{0.650 \pm 0.034}$
Ours	$\mathbf{32.889 \pm 0.374}$	0.440 ± 0.004	0.012	0.869 ± 0.008

5   Conclusion

We propose a systematical solution for various levels of de-identification, and the processed images have high image quality. We compare our method with several SOTA methods in specific tasks like adversarial attacks, disentanglement and reconstruction. The experimental results show that our method has achieved good results in these tasks. It is worth mentioning that our method has better generalization than other methods when being tested in non-training dataset. When generating the adversarial sample of the latent vector of the target image, the gradient is back propagated to a mapping network of the adversarial vector, so as to characterize the common features of the adversarial samples. This is to explore a general and unrestricted adversarial sample generation way for face images. However, because the expressive ability of StyleGAN in latent space is limited, we cannot reconstruct the region outside the face. Combined with GAN inversion and unrestricted adversarial attacks, our further research will pay attention to the mechanism of GANs and apply it to De-ID problem of face data.

Acknowledgements. This work was supported by the National Natural Science Foundation of China 61772529, Beijing Natural Science Foundation under Grant 4192058, National Natural Science Foundation of China 61972395 and National Key Research and Development Program of China 2020AAA0140003.

References

1. Szegedy, C., et al.: Intriguing properties of neural networks. arXiv preprint arXiv:1312.6199 (2013)
2. Goodfellow, I.J., et al.: Generative adversarial networks. arXiv preprint arXiv:1406.2661 (2014)
3. Shan, S., et al.: Fawkes: protecting privacy against unauthorized deep learning models. In: 29th USENIX Security Symposium (USENIX Security 2020) (2020)
4. Maximov, M., Elezi, I., Leal-Taixé, L.: CIAGAN: conditional identity anonymization generative adversarial networks. In: Proceedings of the IEEE/CVF Conference on Computer Vision and Pattern Recognition, pp. 5447–5456 (2020)
5. Karras, T., Laine, S., Aila, T.: A style-based generator architecture for generative adversarial networks. In: Proceedings of the IEEE/CVF Conference on Computer Vision and Pattern Recognition, pp. 4401–4410 (2019)
6. Song, Y., Shu, R., Kushman, N., Ermon, S.: Constructing unrestricted adversarial examples with generative models. arXiv preprint arXiv:1805.07894 (2018)
7. Li, L., Bao, J., Yang, H., Chen, D., Wen, F.: FaceShifter: towards high fidelity and occlusion aware face swapping. arXiv preprint arXiv:1912.13457 (2019)
8. Chen, X., et al. InfoGAN: interpretable representation learning by information maximizing generative adversarial nets. arXiv preprint arXiv:1606.03657 (2016)
9. Higgins, I., et al.: beta-VAE: learning basic visual concepts with a constrained variational framework (2016)
10. Nitzan, Y., Bermano, A., Li, Y., Cohen-Or, D.: Face identity disentanglement via latent space mapping. ACM Trans. Graph. (TOG) **39**(6), 1–14 (2020)

11. Bose, A.J., Aarabi, P.: Adversarial attacks on face detectors using neural net based constrained optimization. In: 2018 IEEE 20th International Workshop on Multimedia Signal Processing (MMSP), pp. 1–6. IEEE (2018)
12. Kaziakhmedov, E., Kireev, K., Melnikov, G., Pautov, M., Petiushko, A.: Real-world attack on MTCNN face detection system. In: 2019 International Multi-Conference on Engineering, Computer and Information Sciences (SIBIRCON), pp. 0422–0427. IEEE (2019)
13. Sharif, M., Bhagavatula, S., Bauer, L., Reiter, M.K.: Accessorize to a crime: real and stealthy attacks on state-of-the-art face recognition. In: Proceedings of the 2016 ACM SIGSAC Conference on Computer and Communications Security, pp. 1528–1540 (2016)
14. Komkov, S., Petiushko, A.: AdvHat: real-world adversarial attack on arcface face id system. arXiv preprint arXiv:1908.08705 (2019)
15. Zhao, H., Gallo, O., Frosio, I., Kautz, J.: Loss functions for image restoration with neural networks. IEEE Trans. Comput. Imaging 3(1), 47–57 (2016)
16. Goodfellow, I.J., Shlens, J., Szegedy, C.: Explaining and harnessing adversarial examples. arXiv preprint arXiv:1412.6572 (2014)
17. Pidhorskyi, S., Adjeroh, D.A., Doretto, G.: Adversarial latent autoencoders. In: Proceedings of the IEEE/CVF Conference on Computer Vision and Pattern Recognition, pp. 14104–14113 (2020)
18. Nirkin, Y., Keller, Y., Hassner, T.: FSGAN: subject agnostic face swapping and reenactment. In: Proceedings of the IEEE/CVF International Conference on Computer Vision, pp. 7184–7193 (2019)
19. Heusel, M., Ramsauer, H., Unterthiner, T., Nessler, B., Hochreiter, S.: GANs trained by a two time-scale update rule converge to a local nash equilibrium. arXiv preprint arXiv:1706.08500 (2017)
20. Zhang, K., Zhang, Z., Li, Z., Qiao, Y.: Joint face detection and alignment using multitask cascaded convolutional networks. IEEE Signal Process. Lett. 23(10), 1499–1503 (2016)
21. Deng, J., Guo, J., Xue, N., Zafeiriou, S.: ArcFace: additive angular margin loss for deep face recognition. In: Proceedings of the IEEE/CVF Conference on Computer Vision and Pattern Recognition, pp. 4690–4699 (2019)
22. Xia, W., et al.: GAN inversion: a survey. arXiv preprint arXiv:2101.05278 (2021)
23. Zhang, R., Isola, P., Efros, A.A., Shechtman, E., Wang, O.: The unreasonable effectiveness of deep features as a perceptual metric. In: Proceedings of the IEEE Conference on Computer Vision and Pattern Recognition, pp. 586–595 (2018)

Skeleton-Based Action Recognition with Improved Graph Convolution Network

Xuqi Yang, Jia Zhang, Rong Qin[✉], Yunyu Su, Shuting Qiu, Jintian Yu,
and Yongxin Ge[✉]

School of Big Data and Software Engineering, Chongqing University,
Chongqing, China
{qinrongzxxlxy,yongxinge}@cqu.edu.cn

Abstract. Most previous skeleton-based action recognition methods ignore weight information of joints and data features beyond labels, which is harmful to action recognition. In this paper, we propose a skeleton-based action recognition with improved Graph Convolution Network, which is based on Spatial Temporal Graph Convolutional Network (STGCN). And we add a predictive cluster network, weight generation networks on it. The model uses K-means algorithm to cluster and get the data information beyond the labels. Besides, each cluster traines weight generation networks independently. To find the best clusters, we propose a evaluation criterion with less computational effort. We perform extensive experiments on the Kinetics dataset and the NTU RGB+D dataset to verify the effectiveness of each network of our model. The comparison results show that our approach achieves satisfactory results.

Keywords: Clustering algorithm · Skeleton-based action recognition · Deep learning

1 Introduction

Human action recognition has become an active research area in recent years, as it plays a significant role in computer vision research. In general, existed approaches to recognize human actions can be grossly divided into two categories according to the input data type: RGB videos [1] and 3D skeleton sequences [2]. Compared with RGB video, human 3D skeleton sequences can convey more information about human posture, and our work is based on human 3D skeleton sequences.

Motion recognition based on the human skeleton structure draws much attention in recent years and some accurate motion capture systems can extract skeletal data in real time. In [3], a general network combining human pose estimation is proposed to extract human joint features by using human pose estimation, and then stitching human features into blocks for the first time using an action-based multi-tasking network with LSTM for temporal feature modeling recognition. In [4], a spatio-temporal convolutional graph network is proposed to construct

© Springer Nature Switzerland AG 2021
J. Feng et al. (Eds.): CCBR 2021, LNCS 12878, pp. 31–38, 2021.
https://doi.org/10.1007/978-3-030-86608-2_4

spatio-temporal human skeleton topologies in space and time. Si et al. [5] proposed a GCN-LSTM network, replacing the convolutional operation in LSTM with GCN graph convolutional operation, to make LSTM be able to model data with topological structure.

Above mentioned methods [4–6] are still limited by two urgent problems. First, These methods treat all joint points to the same degree. For some simple body movements such as running, better results can be obtained by setting the body and trunk joints with the same weight. However, for some movements with severe local joint movement, such as boxing or jumping, the movement intensity of different joints varies greatly. If all joints are given the same weight, the result of movement recognition will be affected. Second, these methods only focus on the label information but neglect the information beyond the label.

In this paper, we propose Skeleton-Based Action Recognition with Improved Graph Convolution Network (GCN), which can effectively solve the above challenges. Specifically, we cluster the human skeleton information using the k-means algorithm and find the best clustering method based on our proposed evaluation criteria which is inspired by [6]. Then, the weight generation network is trained independently for each cluster. Noted that STGCN is trained with all the clusters. To maintain the independence of clusters, we propose a cluster-predicted network to distinguish each cluster. The experimental results show that the method does improve the classification accuracy. The main contributions of this paper are summarized as follows:

- K-means algorithm is utilized to mine the data features beyond labels, which is benefit to the skeleton-based action recognition task.
- A cluster-predicted network is proposed to promise the independence between clusters.
- An evaluation criterion is designed for selecting the best clustering results.

2   Method

In this section, we detailedly illustrate the proposed method in three parts. First, we explain the framework of the approach in Sect. 2.1. Second, a improved GCN is proposed in Sect. 2.2. Finally, the process of cluster training is introduced in Sect. 2.3.

2.1   Approach Overview

We detailedly explain the framework of the proposed approach in Fig. 1. First, after the k-means algorithm clustering and selecting the best clustering method X, the human node vector of each cluster of X will be input to the fully connected neural network, and the output will generate its own corresponding learnable weight generation module. Second, we let each cluster share a STGCN for the reason that the method is mainly to improve the accuracy of the weight generation module and reduce the impact of data dispersion due to clustering, we

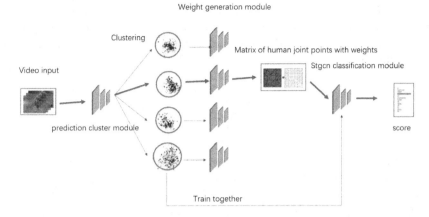

Fig. 1. Overview of our network. The skeleton-based data is classified by cluster-predicted network into corresponding clusters. The data in the cluster is fed into the weight generation network to obtain the weight matrix. Finally, matrixs of human joint points with weight are fed into STGCN to get classification scores.

let each cluster share a STGCN. Since STGCN is a classical action recognition network that uses graph convolution to construct the spatio-temporal human skeleton topology in space and time, respectively, and then classifies the action recognition, the structure of the classification network is the same as the main network structure of the spatio-temporal graph convolution network. In X, for each human node vector data's there is a determined cluster, and a predictive cluster network is generated using supervised learning for predicting which cluster the human nodal vector belongs to.

2.2   Improved GCN

We enhance the graph convolutional network in three ways. First, we construct a weight matrix to represent the importance of the nodes. Second, we have separate weight generation modules for each cluster, which makes the weights more accurate. Third, we use k-means clustering labels as constraints, which can get a lot of off-label information. Finding the best clustering method is indispensable if the above operation is to be performed. In the following, we will describe how to find the best clustering method.

All data in the dataset are clustered using the k-means clustering algorithm, and we divide the dataset into k clusters ($k = 1, 2...50$). First of all, we have to select the best method of clustering, and the violent solution is too computationally intensive to be of practical application, so we propose an evaluation criterion based on the Silhouette Coefficient [6]. We clustered the human posture data according to the k-means clustering number k from 1 to 50, respectively, and calculated the Silhouette Coefficient for each cluster $di(i = 0, 1, 2......k)$ separately. The total Silhouette Coefficient SC of clustering is the mean of all $sc(di)$

when $k = N$:a is Average of the dissimilarity of the vector of human joint coordinates to other points in the same cluster. b is the *minimum* value of the average dissimilarity of the human joint coordinate point vector to other clusters. And the formula are as follows

$$sc = \frac{b - a}{\max(a, b)}$$

$$SC = \frac{1}{N} \sum_{i=1}^{N} sc(d_i)$$

And we find that as the number of clusters increases, The percentage decrease in sample size for the minimum clustering is roughly in the same order of magnitude as the percentage increase in the Silhouette Coefficient. Therefore, we propose a relatively optimal evaluation criterion:

$$Y = SC * \min\{d_i\}$$

Where Y is clustering effect score. Using this evaluation criterion, a higher y cluster represents a better training effect, and we have verified its reliability in experiments.

2.3   Cluster Training

For each cluster of X (the best clustering method), a vector of human joint point samples in each cluster is used as network input, and these samples are first fed to the corresponding weight generation network to obtain a matrix graph with weights (an $n \times n$ matrix, n being the number of sample joints, with a fixed number in the homogeneous dataset). Next, we constructed a custom $n \times n$ initial joint adjacency matrix map of the same size as the weight matrix map, representing whether the joints are adjacent to each other, with 1 for adjacent and 0 for non-adjacent. The weight matrix map was multiplied with our own custom initial joint matrix map to obtain the joint matrix map with weights. The joint matrix with weights and the human joint point vector samples are then fed into the STGCN network to output the classification score. Finally, the classification score p and the label information q do cross entropy substitution into the loss function. At this point, we back-propagate the loss and optimize the weight generation network and STGCN classification network corresponding to this cluster.

$$H(p, q) = \sum_{x} p(x) \cdot \log(\frac{1}{q(x)})$$

3   Experiment

In this part, we evaluate the performance of our method by enhanced graph convolutional network based on k-means clustering and constructing weight matrices. We track the two main data sets processed and used by STGCN and NTU

RGB+D experiments [11], and test the influence of our model on them. Then the experimental results are compared with the effectiveness of other methods in this field.

3.1 Datasets

Kinetics. The Kinetics human action dataset (Kinetics) is the largest unconstrained action recognition dataset in 2017 and includes four hundred human action categories, each with at least 400 video clips, each taken from a different Youtube video and lasting roughly ten seconds. The action categories in the dataset include human-object interactions, such as playing a musical instrument, and human-human interactions, such as shaking hands.

NTU RGB+D. NTU-RGB+D is the largest dataset with 3D joint labeling in the 2016 Human Action Recognition Task, consisting of 56,880 action samples containing RGB video, depth map sequences, 3D skeleton data and infrared video for each sample. There are 25 joints per body in the skeleton sequence and the provided data labels contain the 3D positions of all joint points (X, Y, Z).

3.2 Implementation Details

First, we use the k-means algorithm to classify the sample data in the Kinetics and NTU-RGB+D datasets. We obtain the optimal number of clusters x for the Kinetics human action dataset as 7 and the optimal number of clusters x for NTU-RGB+D as 4. For best sub-clusters on each dataset, we take a uniform batch size of 64 with a learning rate of 0.001, put samples into each of them as network inputs, and train the corresponding adaptive adjacency matrix generation network and perform STGCN network on a Tesla V100 gpu. For the test set, we predict the clusters corresponding to each set of test data with a batch size of 1.

3.3 Ablation Learning

In this section, our main objective is to verify whether the cluster-based multi-weight module approach is valid for STGCN and whether our proposed criteria have applicability. Therefore we change the number of clusters to retrain the test. Considering the computational volume, the experiment is repeated for 5, 10, 15, 20, 25, and 30 clusters, and the weight generation network corresponding to each cluster and the common STGCN are trained on each dataset, and the accuracy of the models corresponding to different number of clusters on the test set is obtained following the above steps. Finally, the test results of x, the test results corresponding to other number of clusters, and the test data corresponding to the original STGCN are compared. We find that the results corresponding to x are the best most of the time. Even though sometimes it is not the best result, the result corresponding to x is similar to the best result and always higher than the result of the original STGCN. The experimental results of ablation learning demonstrate the effectiveness of our proposed cluster-based multi-weight generation module approach and the better applicability of the evaluation criteria based on the minimum number of clusters and Silhouette Coefficient (Fig. 2).

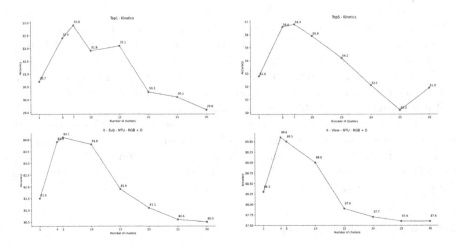

Fig. 2. Comparison of the results corresponding to different number of clusters on the two datasets.

3.4   Compared with the State-of-the-Art

As can be seen from the graphs, our method outperforms the original STGCN on both the NTU-RGB+D dataset and the Kinetics dataset. On the NTU-RGB+D dataset, the model proposed in this paper improves by 2.4% relative to STGCN on x-sub and by 0.7% relative to STGCN on x-view. On the Kinetics dataset, our model outperformed STGCN by 2.2% on TOP-1 and 4.0% on TOP-5. Considering that the structure of our action classification network and the loss function are basically the same as STGCN, the improvement is due to the fact that we train multiple joint adjacency matrix graph weight generation modules based on the k-means clustering results to better generate the joint adjacency matrix graph weights using high-level semantic information other than labels, thus enhancing the graph convolution. This demonstrates the effectiveness of our enhanced graph convolution-based skeleton action recognition method.

Compared with STGCN, the time cost is almost the same, only one percent higher than the original time, but the accuracy is improved considerably. If the cluster-predicted network and weight generation network are not trained by back propagation of all data, then the classification results are not obviously better then STGCN due to data dispersion (Tables 1 and 2).

Table 1. The performance of other methods and ours on the NTU-RGB+D.

Methods	X-Sub (%)	X-View (%)
Lie group [7]	50.1	82.8
HBRNN [2]	59.1	64.0
Deep LSTM [8]	60.7	67.3
ST-LSTM [9]	69.2	77.7
VA-LSTM [10]	79.2	87.7
ARRN-LSTM [11]	80.7	88.8
Ind-RNN [12]	81.1	88.0
Two-Stream 3DCNN [13]	66.8	72.6
Synthesized CNN [14]	80.0	87.2
3scale ResNet152 [15]	85.0	92.3
ST-GCN [4]	81.5	88.3
DPRL+GCNN [16]	83.5	89.8
Ours	83.9	89.6

Table 2. The performance of other methods and ours on Kinetics-Skeleton.

Methods	Top-1 (%)	Top-5 (%)
Feature Enc.	14.9	25.8
Deep LSTM [8]	16.4	35.3
TCN [17]	20.3	40
ST-GCN [4]	30.7	52.8
Ours	32.9	56.8

4   Conclusion

In this paper, we propose an approach to enhance graph convolutional networks. This new action recognition method not only mines off-label information by clustering, but also enhances graph convolution by building a weight generation network to differentiate different human joints. Experimental results on the test set show that this approach is feasible and improves the training results with almost no increase in computational effort. Our proposed evaluation criteria also prove to be effective in comparison experiments, further demonstrating that the method enables the network to obtain information beyond the labels.

Acknowledgments. The work described in this paper was partially supported by the National Natural Science Foundation of China (Grant no. 61772093), Chongqing Research Program of Basic Science and Frontier Technology (Grant no. cstc2018jcyj AX0410), and the Fundamental Research Funds for the Central Universities (Grant no. 2021CDJQY-018).

References

1. Simonyan, K., Zisserman, A.: Two-stream convolutional networks for action recognition in videos. In: Advances in Neural Information Processing Systems 1 (2014)
2. Du, Y., Wang, W., Wang, L.: Hierarchical recurrent neural network for skeleton based action recognition. In: 2015 IEEE Conference on Computer Vision and Pattern Recognition, pp. 1110–1118 (2015)
3. Du, W., Wang, Y., Qiao, Y.: RPAN: an end-to-end recurrent pose-attention network for action recognition in videos. In: 2017 IEEE International Conference on Computer Vision (ICCV) (2017)
4. Yan, S., Xiong, Y., Lin, D.: Spatial temporal graph convolutional networks for skeleton-based action recognition (2018)
5. Si, C., Chen, W., Wang, W., Wang, L., Tan, T.: An attention enhanced graph convolutional LSTM network for skeleton-based action recognition (2019)
6. Silhouettes, R.P.J.: A graphical aid to the interpretation and validation of cluster analysis. J. Comput. Appl. Math. **20**, 53–65 (2021)
7. Vemulapalli, R., Arrate, F., Chellappa, R.: Human action recognition by representing 3d skeletons as points in a lie group. In: 2014 IEEE Conference on Computer Vision and Pattern Recognition, pp. 588–595 (2014)
8. Shahroudy, A., Liu, J., Ng, T., Wang, G.: NTU RGB+D: a large scale dataset for 3d human activity analysis. In: 2016 IEEE Conference on Computer Vision and Pattern Recognition (CVPR), pp. 1010–1019 (2016)
9. Liu, J., Shahroudy, A., Xu, D., Wang, G.: Spatio-temporal LSTM with trust gates for 3D human action recognition. In: Leibe, B., Matas, J., Sebe, N., Welling, M. (eds.) ECCV 2016. LNCS, vol. 9907, pp. 816–833. Springer, Cham (2016). https://doi.org/10.1007/978-3-319-46487-9_50
10. Zhang, P., Lan, C., Xing, J., Zeng, W., Xue, J., Zheng, N.: View adaptive recurrent neural networks for high performance human action recognition from skeleton data (2017)
11. Zheng, W., Li, L., Zhang, Z., Huang, Y., Wang, L.: Relational network for skeleton-based action recognition (2019)
12. Li, S., Li, W., Cook, C., Zhu, C., Gao, Y.: Independently recurrent neural network (INDRNN): building a longer and deeper RNN. In: 2018 IEEE/CVF Conference on Computer Vision and Pattern Recognition, pp. 5457–5466 (2018)
13. Liu, H., Tu, J., Liu, M.: Two-stream 3d convolutional neural network for skeleton-based action recognition, May 2017
14. Liu, M., Liu, H., Chen, C.: Enhanced skeleton visualization for view invariant human action recognition. Pattern Recogn. **68**, 346–362 (2017)
15. Li, B., Dai, Y., Cheng, X., Chen, H., Lin, Y., He, M.: Skeleton based action recognition using translation-scale invariant image mapping and multi-scale deep CNN. In: 2017 IEEE International Conference on Multimedia Expo Workshops (ICMEW), pp. 601–604 (2017)
16. Tang, Y., Tian, Y., Lu, J., Li, P., Zhou, J.: Deep progressive reinforcement learning for skeleton-based action recognition. In: 2018 IEEE/CVF Conference on Computer Vision and Pattern Recognition, pp. 5323–5332 (2018)
17. Kim, T.S., Reiter, A.: Interpretable 3d human action analysis with temporal convolutional networks. In: 2017 IEEE Conference on Computer Vision and Pattern Recognition Workshops (CVPRW), pp. 1623–1631 (2017)

End-To-End Finger Trimodal Features Fusion and Recognition Model Based on CNN

Mengna Wen, Haigang Zhang$^{(\boxtimes)}$, and Jinfeng Yang

Institute of Applied Artificial Intelligence of the Guangdong-HongKong-Macao Greater Bay Area, Shenzhen Polytechnic, Shenzhen 518000, Guangdong, China
zhg2018@sina.com

Abstract. Finger which contains abundant biometric information, has played an important role in the field of identification recognition. Due to the complexity of fingerprint (FP), finger-vein (FV) and finger-knuckle (FKP), traditional feature-level fusion methods perform poorly. This paper proposed an end-to-end finger trimodal features fusion and recognition model based on CNN. For the purpose of constructing an end-to-end model, finger three-modal features extraction module and finger trimodal features fusion module are embedded in CNN. The finger three-modal features extraction module is composed of three parallel and independent CNNs, which are used to extract features from finger trimodal images separately. The finger trimodal features fusion module contains two convolution layers, through which fusion feature can be obtained. The experimental results show that the model proposed in this paper can get high recognition accuracy 99.83%. It shows that the fusion feature obtained by the proposed model possessing good individual characterization ability can effectively improve recognition accuracy.

Keywords: Biometric recognition · FP · FV · FKP · Trimodal fusion · CNN

1 Introduction

At present, biometric identification technology has been widely used in many areas of social life, and market demand keeps growing. Compared with traditional mediums used in identity authentication such as card, password, etc., biometrical characteristics have many advantages such as it is difficult to be forgotten, never to be lost, easy to be carried [1]. Human biometrics can be roughly divided into physiological characteristics (such as face, iris, fingerprint, palm-print, finger-vein) and behavioral characteristics (such as gait, signature, keystroke habits). According to the location of carrier, human biometrics can be classified as head characteristics (such as face, iris, ear shape, voice), hand characteristics (such as fingerprint, palm-print, finger-knuckle, finger-vein, palm-veins) and body characteristics (such as gait). Human biometrics can be contained in a single image or video sequence using special imaging technology. With the gradual diversification of application scenario of identity authentication, single-modal biometric technology will probably fail to meet requirement for security [2]. In order to improve the

© Springer Nature Switzerland AG 2021
J. Feng et al. (Eds.): CCBR 2021, LNCS 12878, pp. 39–48, 2021.
https://doi.org/10.1007/978-3-030-86608-2_5

accuracy, stability and reliability of biometric recognition technology, multi-modal biometric fusion technology which uses fusion information of a variety of biological features to represent individual identity attribute has become a research focus. As finger carries FP, FV and FKP simultaneously, it is prominent among various carriers of hand. Finger naturally integrates physiological characteristics of inner and outer layer of biological tissue, and the features from FP, FV and FKP are sufficiently complementary [3]. For example, fingerprint recognition is not related to whether the object is alive, finger-vein recognition requires that the identified individual must be alive; fingerprint is on the stressed surface, which is easy to wear, while finger-knuckle-print (the dorsal side) is on the non-stressed surface and it is relatively complete; finger-vein image is blurring, finger-knuckle-print image is clear and stable. The complementarity of finger trimodal characteristics demonstrates that fusion feature of FP, FV and FKP is beneficial to get a good performance.

In recent decades, the rapid development of deep learning has brought new opportunities for multi-modal biometric fusion techniques. Researchers have built various artificial neural network models, such as AlexNet, VggNet, GoogleNet, ResNet, DenseNet and SENET [4]. Biometric identification technologies based on deep learning have been tested on several public datasets, and have achieved extraordinary results, which significantly outperform traditional algorithms. It is important to note that convolutional neural network (CNN) models have been widely used in multiple sub-fields of single-modal biometric recognition, such as image enhancement, feature extraction, and improving the robustness of algorithm [5–8]. In 2015, Wang et al. proposed a framework based on CNN to learning multimodal features for identifying RGB-D target [9] and then they designed a deep learning framework to learn specific features of multimodality [10]. Zhang et al. proposed a face recognition method based on RGB-D image in 2018, which can learn a variety of complementary face features through a deep learning network [11]. In the same year, Sobhan et al. proposed a CNN-based multi-level features extraction and fusion method, which was used to extract features of different modalities and realize the fusion expression of multi-level features [12]. In 2019, Zhang et al. proposed a graph-based feature extraction method and designed two features fusion frameworks [13]. However, deep learning has not been well applied in the field of finger multimodal fusion recognition.

Due to the influence of acquisition environment and the properties of FP, FV and FKP, sizes of finger trimodal images are not consistent. Traditional features fusion algorithms adjust size of image by simply cropping or proportion normalization. Overall structure of image will be destroyed and useful information will be lost by the simple and crude methods.

To solve the above problems, this paper proposed a finger trimodal features fusion and recognition model based on CNN, which embedded three feature extraction CNN-based models for extracting fingerprint features, finger-vein features, finger-knuckle-print features separately and a features fusion module. The model can realize features extraction, features fusion and identity recognition through end-to-end working mode. This working mode is superior to the traditional methods which are implemented stage-by-stage. End-to-end working mode is efficient and can save natural resources well.

2   Integrated Acquisition System

The spatial position relationship of fingerprint, finger-vein and finger-knuckle-print located on a same finger is fixed, and the position information can be retained in the finger trimodal images acquired by the integrated finger trimodal images acquisition system. The principle of integrated finger trimodal images acquisition system is shown in Fig. 1.

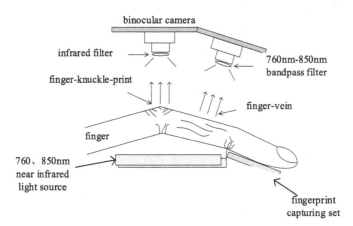

Fig. 1. Integrated finger trimodal images acquisition system

Images of fingerprint, finger-vein and finger-knuckle-print can be captured in a same time using the integrated acquisition device designed above. The sizes of finger-vein, fingerprint and finger-knuckle-print images are 91×200 pixels, 152×152 pixels and 200×90 pixels respectively. Finger trimodal images are shown in Fig. 2. Taking trimodal images of a same finger acquired by integrated images acquisition system as input of three-channel convolutional neural network, fusion features which contain position relationship between FP, FV and FKP will be obtained. Therefore, fusion features from finger trimodal images can commendably describe individual identity information.

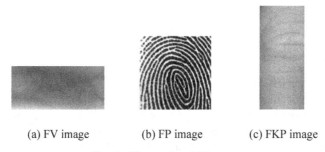

(a) FV image   (b) FP image   (c) FKP image

Fig. 2. Finger trimodal images

3 Preliminaries

3.1 Asymmetric Convolution Kernel

In the respect of function, convolution can be counted as the process of linear transformation at each position of the image and the pixel value is mapped to a new value. Multi-layer convolution can be regarded as mapping layer by layer, and the entire neural network can be treated as a complex function. The weights required for each local mapping can be learned during training.

The weights of convolution kernels are represented by a vector W, the pixels at the corresponding positions of the image are represented by a vector X, and n is the number of pixels in the receptive field, and the convolution result at this position is shown in formula (1).

$$Z(W, X) = f\left(\sum_{i=1}^{n} w_i x_i + b\right) \tag{1}$$

Where, b is bias of the layer, f is the activation function, and X can be transformed into Z by formula (1).

For 2-dimensional data with symmetric information density in x-axis and y-axis, it is reasonable to use symmetric convolution kernels for extracting features. However, for data with asymmetric information density, in which information density is biased toward a certain direction, it is more reasonable to use an asymmetric convolution kernel to extracting features in the direction of greater information density. In addition, asymmetric convolution kernel can be used to adjust the size of feature maps with different pooling method and moving step.

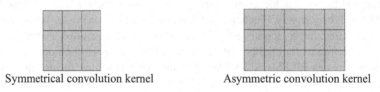

Symmetrical convolution kernel   Asymmetric convolution kernel

Fig. 3. Different types of convolution kernel

3.2 Multi-channel Convolution

The number of channels of input layer in CNN model is determined by the dimension of input data. Color image is formed by superimposing the data from R channel, G channel and B channel, and when the input of CNN is a color image, its input layer needs to be designed with three channels, which are used to deal with data of R, G and B channel respectively. In the convolution process of 3-dimensional data, convolution kernels can be regarded as a cube, and each cube is composed of three 2-dimensional convolution kernels of the same size. The value in cube is convolved with the value at corresponding position of the relevant channel from the 3-dimensional image, and then the values obtained by convolution in three channels are added to produce the first data of the output. Figure 4 depicts three-channel convolution process. 3-dimensional data is scanned from upper left corner to lower right corner using 3-dimensional convolution kernels to complete the convolution of the whole image. In summary, multi-channel convolution can not only extract features from input data of each channel, but also can perform features fusion automatically.

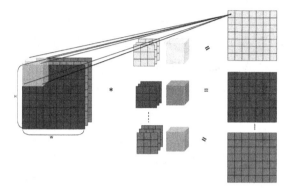

Fig. 4. Three-channel convolution

The three-channel convolution process with multiple convolution kernels described in Fig. 4 can be expressed by Eq. (2).

$$H_1 \times W_1 \times n = \left(\frac{H - k_1}{s_1} + 1 \right) \times \left(\frac{W - k_2}{s_2} + 1 \right) \times n \qquad (2)$$

Where, H and W represent the length and width of input image respectively, n is the number of convolution kernels, size of the convolution kernel is $k_1 \times k_2 \times n$, length and width of the output are H_1 and W_1, s_1 and s_2 are the moving steps in different directions.

4 Model Architecture

In this paper, we construct a finger trimodal features fusion and recognition model, in which the theories of asymmetric convolution kernel and multi-channel convolution are incorporated. The finger three-modal features extraction module embedded at the head of proposed model is used to capture finger trimodal features; The finger trimodal features fusion module existing in the middle part is for fusing features; The last part of the model is to implement recognition. The structure of proposed model is shown in Fig. 5.

The input layer of the model contains three channels, which are original images of finger-vein, fingerprint, and finger-knuckle-print. Aiming at targets of extracting finger trimodal features and carrying out finger trimodal features fusion, we designed two modules named finger trimodal features extraction module and features fusion module,

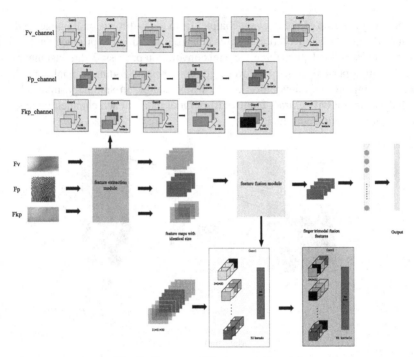

Fig. 5. Structure of the proposed model

and the two modules can be embedded in other networks to achieve an end-to-end working mode. The features fusion module is followed by a fully connected layer (FC) in the proposed model to "flatten" the fusion feature matrices into a 1-dimensional vector. At the end of proposed model, softmax layer is used for classification. In order to solve the problem that convergence speed of neural network is slow which is caused by gradient exploding, rectified linear units (ReLu) is used as the activation function. In addition, batch normalization layer (BN) is designed after the activation layer to accelerate training speed. "Convolution layer" that appears later in this paper including convolution layer, activation function, and batch normalization layer.

Because sizes of finger trimodal images are different, the finger trimodal features extraction module is made up of three CNN models. The network used to extract finger-vein features consists of six convolution layers, and the asymmetric convolution kernel proposed above is selected in each convolution layer. The fingerprint features extraction network is composed of four convolution layers, and symmetrical convolution kernels are used in all convolution layers. The network used to extract finger-knuckle-print features is also composed of six convolution layers, and asymmetrical convolution kernels are designed in each convolution layer. The details of finger trimodal features extraction module are shown in upper half part of Fig. 5. The features fusion module is composed of two convolution layers. Sizes of feature maps obtained from finger trimodal features extraction module are same, so symmetrical convolution kernels are used in features fusion module. The details of features fusion module are shown in the bottom half of Fig. 5. The specific parameters of the proposed model are shown in Table 1.

Table 1. Parameters of proposed model

Input layer	Finger trimodal features extraction module		Features fusion module	FC layer	Output
Fv 91×200	**Conv1**	3×5×32			
	Conv2	3×5×64			
	Conv3	5×7×128			
	Conv4	5×7×10	**Conv1** 3×3×32		
	Conv5	5×7×10			
	Conv6	3×7×10			
Fp 152×152	**Conv1**	3×3×32			
	Conv2	3×3×64			
	Conv3	5×5×128			
	Conv4	5×5×10		4096	585
Fkp 90×200	**Conv1**	5×3×32			
	Conv2	5×3×64			
	Conv3	7×5×128	**Conv2** 3×3×64		
	Conv4	7×5×10			
	Conv5	7×5×10			
	Conv6	7×3×10			

5 Experiments and Analysis

5.1 Experimental Dataset

The dataset used in this paper is consisted of finger-vein images, fingerprint images and finger-knuckle-print images, and the finger trimodal images in this dataset are from 585 fingers. Ten images are obtained for each modality of each finger, and there are 17550 images in the dataset. Pixel depth of the images is 8, and as mentioned above, the images used in experiments are of poor quality. In order to make peculiarity of the experimental data evenly distributed, the dataset was randomized. First, all the data and corresponding label are shuffled out of order. Then, the dataset is randomly divided into training set and test set using "hold-out" method, where the training set accounts for 80% of the entire dataset, and the remaining 20% of the data is test set.

5.2 Experimental Results and Analysis

In order to verify the effectiveness of proposed model in this paper, the network is built using keras-based deep learning framework. In the iterative training process, cross entropy function is used as loss function to calculate the difference between output and label, and weights of all nodes in each layer of the network are updated by back propagation. The difference is gradually reduced by SGD optimizer in the way of gradient

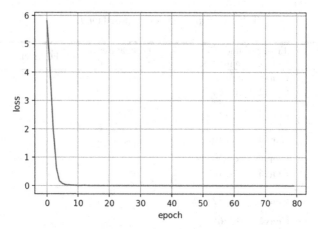

Fig. 6. Changing trend of loss during training

descent under a specific learning rate of 0.01, and the batch size of input data is set to 50. The loss during training process is shown in Fig. 6.

As shown in Fig. 6, during the training process, loss gradually decreases with the increasing of iteration, and it indicates that the proposed model is trainable. Ultimately, the result that loss is near 0 and is in a stable state shows that the model is trained and stable.

In this part, recognition accuracy and calculation efficiency of the proposed model are tested, and the results are compared with the recognition effect of single-mode biometric algorithm based on deep learning. The results of the experiments are shown in Table 2.

Table 2. Recognition performance of different models

Model	Recognition acc (%)	Avg recognition time (s)
Fv_model	97.53	0.0012
Fp_model	92.91	0.00064
Fkp_model	96.97	0.0012
Proposed model	99.83	0.0027

In Table 2, we can see that compared with finger single-mode biometrics, finger tri-modal features fusion and recognition model proposed in this paper can get higher identification accuracy and rational average recognition time, which show that the proposed model can achieve satisfactory result in the field of finger trimodal fusion recognition.

We compared the method proposed in this paper with other fusion algorithms, and the ROC curve (Receiver Operating Characteristic) is shown in Fig. 7. Fusion method based on Graph is described in detail in reference [13]. References [14, 15] introduce pix-based granular fusion method and fusion method based on code in detail respectively.

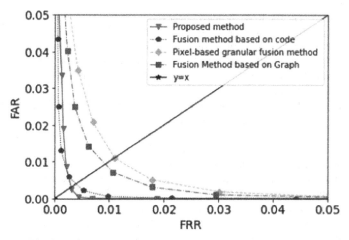

Fig. 7. Comparion results of ROC for different fusion methods

It can be clearly seen from Fig. 7 that the proposed fusion method is outstanding than other fusion algorithms. Fusion features with good identification ability obtained by using the model proposed in this paper is helpful to improve recognition accuracy.

6 Conclusion

In this paper, an end-to-end finger trimodal features fusion and recognition model based on CNN is constructed, which solves the problem of fusion constraint of finger trimodel images with different size. The experimental results show that fusion feature of finger trimodal obtained by the proposed method can effectively improve the accuracy, universality and reliability of biometric recognition technology.

Acknowledgments. This work was supported in part by the National Natural Science Foundation of China under Grant 62076166 and 61806208, in part by the Rural Science and Technology Commissioner Project of Guangdong Provincial Science and Technology Department under Grant KPT20200220.

References

1. Kien, N., Clinton, F., Sridha, S., et al.: Super-Resolution for biometrics: a comprehensive survey. Pattern Recogn. J. Pattern Recogn. Soc. **78**, 23–42 (2018)
2. Shaikh, J., Uttam, D.: Review of hand feature of unimodal and multimodal biometric system. Int. J. Comput. Appl. **133**(5), 19–24 (2016)
3. Asaari, M.S.M., Suandi, S.A., Rosdi, B.A.: Fusion of band limited phase only correlation and width centroid contour distance for finger based biometrics. Expert Syst. Appl. **41**(7), 3367–3382 (2014)
4. Loffe, S., Szegedy, C.: Batch normalization: accelerating deep network training by reducing internal covariate shift. arXiv preprint arXiv:150203167 (2015)

5. Fang Yuxun, W., Qiuxia, K.W.: A novel finger vein verification system based on two-stream convolutional network learning. Neurocomputing **290**, 100–107 (2018)

6. Qin, H.F., El-Yacoubi, M.A.: Deep representation-based feature extraction and recovering for finger-vein verification. IEEE Trans. Inf. Forensics Secur. **12**(8), 1816–1829 (2017)

7. Tang, S., Zhou, S., Kang, W.X., et al.: Finger vein verification using a Siamese CNN. IET Biom. **8**(5), 306–315 (2019)

8. Hou, B.R., Yan, R.Q.: Convolutional auto-encoder model for finger-vein verification. IEEE Trans. Instrum. Meas. **64**(5), 2067–2074 (2020)

9. Wang, A.R., Cai, J.F., Ji, W.L., et al.: MMSS: Multi-modal sharable and specific feature learning for RGB-D object recognition. In: Proceedings of the IEEE International Conference on Computer Vision, Santiago, pp. 125–1133 (2015)

10. Wang, A.R., Lu, J.W., Cai, J.F., et al.: Large-margin multimodal deep learning for RGB-D object recognition. IEEE Trans. Multimedia **17**(11), 1887–1898 (2015)

11. Zhang, H., Han, H., Cui, J.Y., et al.: RGB-D face recognition via deep complementary and common feature learning. In: IEEE International Conference on Automatic Face & Gesture Recognition, pp. 8–15. IEEE Computer Society (2018)

12. Sobhan, S., Ali, D., Hadi, K., et al.: Multi-level feature abstraction from convolutional neural networks for multimodal biometric identification. In: 24th International Conference on Pattern Recognition (2018)

13. Zhang, H.G., Li, S.Y., Shi, Y.H.: Graph fusion for finger multimodal biometrics. IEEE Access, 28607–28615 (2019)

14. Bai, G.Y., Yang, J.F.: A new pixel-based granular fusion method for finger recognition. In: Eighth International Conference on Digital Image Processing. International Society for Optics and Photonics (2016)

15. Li, S.Y., Zhang, H.G., Yang, J.F.: Novel local coding algorithm for finger multimodal feature description and recognition. Sensors **19**, 2213 (2019)

Mouse Dynamics Based Bot Detection Using Sequence Learning

Hongfeng Niu, Jiading Chen, Zhaozhe Zhang, and Zhongmin Cai$^{(\boxtimes)}$

MOE KLINNS Lab, Xi'an Jiaotong University, Xi'an 710049, China
zmcai@sei.xjtu.edu.cn

Abstract. The abuse of web bots poses a great threat to daily life. There are lots of methods proposed to detect web bots. However, these web detection methods focus on specific application tasks such as chat bot, game bot, spam bot, and so on. In this paper, a web bot detection model based on mouse dynamics is proposed. Mouse dynamics, which analyzes user's behavioral patterns, has been proven very effective in distinguishing human users from web bots. We propose a new time series representation method that combines position differences and directional speed values in one time step simultaneously to cover the raw mouse movement sequence into suitable input formats for deep learning models. Experimental results demonstrate that our method outperforms existing machine learning methods with handcrafted features and the deep learning method with visualization representation with a detection accuracy of 99.78% for the bot.

Keywords: Bot detection · Mouse dynamics · Time series representation

1 Introduction

Web bots refer to automated scripts that perform repetitive and complex tasks on behalf of human, which are responsible for a large percentage of web traffic. Web bots are double-edged swords. On one hand, some of are designed for benign purposes, for example, chat bots can assist retailers in serving customers in an effective and convenient way. On the other hand, malicious bots can be exploited to gain illegitimate benefits, such as spamming, fake comments, spreading malware links, et al. According to Bad Bot Report 2021 [1], bad bots take over more than 25.6% of traffic in 2020, which poses a great threat to ecosystem of the Internet. In order to detect bots, various approaches have been proposed. As the representative of human interactive proofs (HIPs), CAPTCHA (Completely Automated Public Turing test to tell Computers and Humans Apart) [2] has been adopted in most websites to detect bots actively. CAPTHCA offers a challenge that human can easily pass but difficult for web bots. However, it can

H. Niu and J. Chen—Contribute equally to this work.

be ineffective with the assistant of human or the image recognition methods. Moreover, with the rapid development of deep learning, it becomes easy and effective to break various types of CAPTCHA [3]. Besides, it can just only offer one-time detection process. Another approach to detecting bots is to resort to human observable proofs (HOP) [4]. Its rational is human's inherent irregularity and complexity [5]. It provides an amazing method to detect web bots. As one of behavioral biometrics, mouse dynamics [6], which analyzes users' mouse operating behaviors, has proved prominent advantages over current state-of-the-art detection methods. Firstly, it can provide a continuous detection through the entire interactive session, representing more stable security. Secondly, it is non-interactive and completely transparent to users and the detection can be accomplished without the user being aware of the detection process.

How to represent the mouse movement sequence is an important issue for mouse dynamics. Previous works relied on handcrafted features extracted from the sequence and fed the features into a shallow machine learning model. However, the detection performance is susceptible to the feature engineering. With the success of deep learning in various fields, researchers attempt to employ deep learning to bot detection via mouse dynamics. In this work, we propose a new time series representation for the mouse movement sequence by which we can employ deep learning to bot detection. Experimental results demonstrate that our method outperforms classical machine learning with handcrafted features and existing deep learning methods. The main contributions of this work are as follows:

1. We propose to employ sequence learning for bot detection based on mouse dynamics.
2. A new time series representation of mouse movement sequence based on time series is proposed, which combines position differences and directional speed values in one time step simultaneously. Comparisons between our method and existing time series representations are conducted using three deep learning models competent at handling sequence data, including 1D-CNN, LSTM, and a hybrid CNN-LSTM.
3. Experimental results prove that our representation method can reach up to 99.78% in the case of web bot detection, which outperforms state-of-the-art baselines. In the meantime, it can also obtain an accuracy of 99.71% when detecting human samples.

The rest of this paper is organized as follows: Sect. 2 introduces the related works and background. Section 3 describes the frameworks of our proposed bot detection. Section 4 provides the data collection. Section 5 conducts the experiments and analysis. In Sect. 6, we conclude our work.

2 Related Works and Background

2.1 Mouse Dynamics

With the success of the mouse dynamics in the field of identity authentication, researchers also attempted to apply it in bot detection area. Lee et al. [7] proposed a method based on machine learning detection game bot by analyzing the self-similarity of the mouse action to effectively measure the frequency of the active activity within a period of time as an important feature. Zi et al. [5] proposed a bot detection system designed based on mouse and keyboard behavioral characteristics. The system could collect user mouse movement and keyboard keystroke behavior data, and send these data to the machine learning model. The experimental results showed that the detection system could effectively distinguish human from bots. In the era of Internet, mouse, as the most important human machine interaction device, is widely used in various scenarios, providing a solid foundation for human machine detection based on mouse dynamics. Most previous research works on mouse dynamics are primarily based on machine learning methods, which first extracts handcrafted features and send them into machine learning models. It is easily influenced by the feature engineering. With the development of deep learning, some researchers attempted to apply deep learning to study mouse dynamics. Chong et al. [8,9] are the first to apply deep learning to mouse dynamics. They proposed to apply 1D-CNN for mouse dynamics via time series representation for mouse movement sequences. Specifically, they utilized position differences, (dx, dy) and directional speed values, $(dx/dt, dy/dt)$ to maintain invariant translation of the movement sequence. Then Antal et al. [10] applied $(dx/dt, dy/dt)$ to user recognition and also validated its effectiveness. Recently, Wei et al. [11] proposed to map raw mouse data into a picture by which employs deep learning to detect web bots via mouse dynamics. Inspired by the success of previous work, in this work, we propose to position differences, (dx, dy), and directional speed values, $(dx/dt, dy/dt)$, to make up a new representation, $(dx, dy, dx/dt, dy/dt)$. And based on this, we can employ deep learning to web bot detection.

2.2 Preliminary Knowledge

Mouse movement is a sequence of data points, each of which has a timestamp and a pair of 2-dimensional coordinates, denoted as: $[(x_1, y_1, t_1), (x_2, y_2, t_2)...(x_n, y_n, t_n)]$. As for machine learning, some statistical characteristics are extracted to represent the mouse movement.

3 Framework of Our Bot Detection

Figure 1 illustrates our bot detection framework, including four parts, data collection, data preprocessing, time series representation, and deep model building. Descriptions are as follows: **Data Collection** When the mouse cursor moving, the built-in JavaScript records the timestamp and Cartesian coordinate points of the mouse movement to generate a set of discrete sequence point coordinates and timestamps in a timely manner. **Data preprocessing** This part is used for cleaning the raw data and segmenting the sequence into appropriate lengths. It may involve insufficient information if the sequence is too short. **Data representation** Position-related (dx, dy) and speed-related $(dx/dt, dy/dt)$ in one time step are combined into a new time series representation format $(dx, dy,$

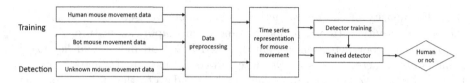

Fig. 1. Framework of bot detection via sequence learning

dx/dt, dy/dt) simultaneously to represent the mouse movement sequence. Based on our statistical analysis, we choose the fixed-size length of 60 to represent the sequence for deep neural networks. The length would be padded with 0 if necessary. **Deep model building** This part is discussed separately in two 2 stages. In the training stage, a detection model would be built using mouse movement sequences based on deep neural networks. In the detection stage, the new mouse movement data would be sent to trained model to output the detection result.

4   Data Collection

This section describes our collection platform, human data collection and bot design and data collection.

4.1   Mouse-Operation Task Design

We design a typical web login scenario as our data collection platform. To be specific, the web page consists of 3 textboxes, including username, password, CAPTCHA and a confirm button. Under normal conditions, 4 pieces of mouse movement sequences at least would be collected during a collection process. We implement the platform in 6 computers with the same configuration. When a user conducts the mouse cursor to complete the login task, the builtin JavaScript in the web page in advance would record each mouse event silently. The whole data collection process is transparent to users.

4.2   Human Data Collection

We recruited 120 students (28 females, 92 males) to participate in our data collection tasks. All of them were right-handed and asked to familiar to the task in advance. Students were asked to complete 5 rounds of data collection each week and the whole task last 6 weeks. Finally, we collected valid 8229 pieces of mouse movement sequences in all.

4.3   Web Bot Data Collection

In order to escape from the detection method that the server only relies presence or absence of mouse operation behavior, bot designers try their best to make web bots imitate the operation behaviors of normal users. Therefore, when designing a web bot, designers need to understand the normal user's operating behavior and make the web bot produce anthropomorphic operating behaviors, such as mouse movement, mouse clicks. To characterize the bot behaviors, we use existing bot tools or libraries to configure the four types of web bots to mimic humans' behaviors, that is, straight-line, regular curve, irregular curve, and semi-straight line. And, we generate 2200 pieces of mouse movement sequences with different parameters for each type of bots and obtain 8800 pieces in total, which is roughly the same as the number of human mouse movement sequences. Figure 2 shows templates for 4 types of bots.

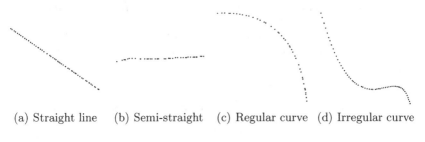

(a) Straight line   (b) Semi-straight   (c) Regular curve   (d) Irregular curve

Fig. 2. Templates for 4 types of bots

5   Experiments and Analysis

5.1   Models Implementation

In this work, we employ 4 classical binary classifiers, SVM, KNN, Adaboost and Logistic Regression as our machine learning baselines. To conduct our performance, LSTM [12], 1D-CNN [13] and a hybrid CNN+LSTM [14] deep learning models are adopted in our time series representation method. These deep neural networks are trained in Keras [15] with Adam optimizer (learning rate: 0.005, decay: 0.0001, loss function: binary cross-entropy). 50 epochs were used for training with a batch size of 16 and employ the dropout layer with 0.3 probability to avoid overfitting.

5.2   Evaluation Metrics

With the goal to distinguish the bots, we define bot samples as positive and human samples as negative. True positive rate (TPR) and true negative rate (TNR) are employed. Here, TPR is defined as the ratio between the number of correctly classified bots samples and the number of bot samples in the testing stage and TNR is defined as the ratio between the number of correctly classified human samples and the number of human samples in the testing stage.

5.3   Training and Testing Procedure

We employ 5-fold cross validation [16] to train the detection model and examine its ability to distinguish human from bots by the following steps. We randomly divide each bot into 5 folds. For each kind of bot, we take 4 folds of data to make up our training set. Half of the remaining data is used to build the validation set and half for the test set. As for human samples, we take the same data partition as bots. Specifically, to remove the interference of the authentication effect, samples from the same human subject are used for one stage, that is, training, validation or testing stage.

5.4   Comparison Among Different Time Series Representations

This experiment conducts the comparison between our representation method and existing time series representations. All of them are conducted in the identical experimental settings.

Table 1. Results of deep neural networks using different time series representations of mouse movement sequences in bot detection

Features	Model	TPR (%)	TNR (%)
(dx, dy)	LSTM	99.28	99.38
	1D-CNN	99.36	99.21
	CNN+LSTM	99.08	98.86
(dx/dt, dy/dt)	LSTM	97.42	96.88
	1D-CNN	96.57	98.24
	CNN+LSTM	98.05	97.88
(dx, dy, dx/dt, dy/dt)	LSTM	**99.78**	99.67
	1D-CNN	99.64	**99.71**
	CNN+LSTM	99.67	99.10

From Table 1, we can see that our method can achieve the best detection accuracy with TPR of 99.78% and TNR of 99.71% obtained by LSTM and 1D-CNN, respectively, which validates the effectiveness of our method. Besides, we also find that models with position differences outperforms models with directional speed values. The reason maybe lie in that the latter would lose some discriminate information after processing.

5.5   Comparison with Baselines in Bot Detection

In this experiment, we select machine learning with handcrafted features and deep learning models with visualization representation [11] as our baselines. Ten handcrafted features are extracted based according to the literature on mouse dynamics, including mean and standard deviation of interval time, step size, movement angle, speed, and acceleration. Here, interval time and step size are the time and Euclidean distance between two adjacent points, respectively, and we define movement angle as the angle between three consecutive points.

Table 2. Results of comparison with baselines in bot detection

Category	Method	TPR (%)	TNR (%)
Machine learning	SVM+ 10 handcrafted features	97.85	97.11
	KNN+ 10 handcrafted features	98.55	97.61
	Logistic Regression + 10 handcrafted features	96.12	95.88
Deep learning	Visualization (Wei's work [11])	99.48	99.55

Table 2 shows the performance of machine learning methods with handcrafted features and deep learning with visualization. Despite that the best result is obtained by Wei's work with TPR of 99.48% and 99.55% of TNR, respectively, it is still weaker than our method (TPR: 99.78%; TNR: 99.71%. See Table 1). Besides, Wei'method takes much more time than ours when building the detection model. The reason is not hard to understand. Our representation for mouse movement is a numeric vector and Wei's method is to map the mouse movement sequence into a picture, which takes more memory space when modeling. The best performance for machine learning is TPR of 98.55% and TNR of 97.61% obtained by KNN. Besides, we speculate handcrafted features cannot characterize the differences fully. Our new representation takes position differences and directional speed values into considerations characterizing more differences in one time step, which makes it possible for deep neural networks to learn more discriminative information. Therefore, our method in combination with deep learning models achieve a best performance.

6   Conclusion

In this work, we propose to employ deep learning with mouse dynamics for web bot detection. Specifically, we propose a new time series representation method by which we can convert the mouse movement sequence into a suitable input format for deep neural networks. Conducted by three different deep neural models, our method outperforms existing time series representation methods. Besides, our method can address the problem that classical machine learning methods are susceptible to feature engineering. Finally, compared with the existing visualization representation method, our method has the advantages of fast modeling speed and small amount of data.

Acknowledgments. This work is supported by National Key R&D Program of China 2018AAA0101501, Science and Technology Project of SGCC (State Grid Corporation of China): Fundamental Theory of Human-in-the-loop Hybrid-Augmented Intelligence for Power Grid Dispatch and Control.

References

1. Imperva: Bad bot report 2021 (2020). https://www.imperva.com/resources/resource-library/reports/bad-bot-report//
2. von Ahn, L., Blum, M., Hopper, N.J., Langford, J.: CAPTCHA: using hard AI problems for security. In: Biham, E. (ed.) EUROCRYPT 2003. LNCS, vol. 2656, pp. 294–311. Springer, Heidelberg (2003). https://doi.org/10.1007/3-540-39200-9_18
3. Stark, F., Hazırbas, C., Triebel, R., Cremers, D.: Captcha recognition with active deep learning. In: Workshop New Challenges in Neural Computation, vol. 2015, p. 94, Citeseer (2015)
4. Gianvecchio, S., Wu, Z., Xie, M., Wang, H.: Battle of botcraft: fighting bots in online games with human observational proofs. In: Proceedings of the 16th ACM Conference on Computer and Communications Security, pp. 256–268 (2009)
5. Chu, Z., Gianvecchio, S., Wang, H.: Bot or human? A behavior-based online bot detection system. In: Samarati, P., Ray, I., Ray, I. (eds.) From Database to Cyber Security. LNCS, vol. 11170, pp. 432–449. Springer, Cham (2018). https://doi.org/10.1007/978-3-030-04834-1_21
6. Shen, C., Cai, Z., Guan, X., Maxion, R.: Performance evaluation of anomaly-detection algorithms for mouse dynamics. Comput. Secur. **45**, 156–171 (2014)
7. Lee, E., Woo, J., Kim, H., Mohaisen, A., Kim, H.K.: You are a game bot!: Uncovering game bots in MMORPGs via self-similarity in the wild. In: Network and Distributed System Security Symposium (2016)
8. Chong, P., Tan, Y.X.M., Guarnizo, J., Elovici, Y., Binder, A.: Mouse authentication without the temporal aspect-what does a 2d-CNN learn? In: IEEE Security and Privacy Workshops (SPW), pp. 15–21. IEEE (2018)
9. Chong, P., Elovici, Y., Binder, A.: User authentication based on mouse dynamics using deep neural networks: a comprehensive study. IEEE Trans. Inf. Forensics Secur. **15**, 1086–1101 (2019)
10. Antal, M., Fejér, N.: Mouse dynamics based user recognition using deep learning. Acta Universitatis Sapientiae Informatica **12**(1), 39–50 (2020)
11. Wei, A., Zhao, Y., Cai, Z.: A deep learning approach to web bot detection using mouse behavioral biometrics. In: Sun, Z., He, R., Feng, J., Shan, S., Guo, Z. (eds.) CCBR 2019. LNCS, vol. 11818, pp. 388–395. Springer, Cham (2019). https://doi.org/10.1007/978-3-030-31456-9_43
12. Greff, K., Srivastava, R.K., Koutník, J., Steunebrink, B.R., Schmidhuber, J.: LSTM: a search space odyssey. IEEE Trans. Neural Netw. Learn. Syst. **28**(10), 2222–2232 (2016)
13. Eren, L., Ince, T., Kiranyaz, S.: A generic intelligent bearing fault diagnosis system using compact adaptive 1d CNN classifier. J. Signal Process. Syst. **91**(2), 179–189 (2019)
14. Wang, J., Yu, L.C., Lai, K.R., Zhang, X.: Dimensional sentiment analysis using a regional CNN-LSTM model. In: Proceedings of the 54th Annual Meeting of the Association for Computational Linguistics (volume 2: Short Papers), pp. 225–230 (2016)
15. KERAS: Keras. https://keras.io
16. Fushiki, T.: Estimation of prediction error by using k-fold cross-validation. Stat. Comput. **21**(2), 137–146 (2011)

A New Age-Groups Classifying Method for Irrawaddy Dolphin

Min Sheng[1,2], Qingxuan He[1,2], Kangwei Wang[3,4], Daoping Yu[3,4(✉)], and Benyue Su[1,5(✉)]

[1] The University Key Laboratory of Intelligent Perception and Computing of Anhui Province, Anqing Normal University, Anqing 246133, China
bysu@aqnu.edu.cn
[2] School of Mathematics and Physics, Anqing Normal University, Anqing 246133, China
[3] Research Center of Aquatic Irganism Conservation and Water Ecosystem Restoration in Anhui Province, Anqing Normal University, Anqing 246133, China
[4] College of Life and Science, Anqing Normal University, Anqing 246133, China
[5] School of Mathematics and Computer Science, Tongling University, Tongling 244061, China

Abstract. Rare species such as Irrawaddy dolphins are in urgent need of conservation, especially for population reproduction status. The study of age structure of them is one of the key issues for the conservation of their populations. Based on this, a new age-groups classifying (AGC) method was constructed in this paper to investigate the age structure of Irrawaddy dolphins. Considering correlations between the dorsal fin characteristics of the Irrawaddy dolphin and the ages of the population, this paper discussed the dorsal fin shape and its internal related features and given a relevant classifying model for the Irrawaddy dolphins age-groups recognition. The experimental demonstrated that the presented algorithm has a high recognition accuracy of up to 82.71% for older dolphins. Differ from the current recognition of individual biological populations, AGC method focused on age-groups, which possesses the important reference significance for the study of the population reproduction status of the Irrawaddy dolphin.

Keywords: Irrawaddy dolphin · AGC · Age structure · Dorsal fin · Shape feature

1 Introduction

Nowadays the study of cetaceans is importance as an attempt to understand marine ecosystem. In a sense, the state of the quality of the ecological environment can be reflected by Cetaceans' abundance, spatio-temporal distribution and migration as well as habitat use. An increase in cetacean populations is important for maintaining a healthy marine environment, and a stable cetacean population helps maintain the robustness of the global marine ecology. As a link at the top

© Springer Nature Switzerland AG 2021
J. Feng et al. (Eds.): CCBR 2021, LNCS 12878, pp. 57–65, 2021.
https://doi.org/10.1007/978-3-030-86608-2_7

of the marine biological chain once cetaceans are extinct, it would cause a rampant reproduction of marine plankton and other marine organisms, resulting in an imbalance in the ratio of marine animals, and the resulting ecological disaster would be incalculable. Cetaceans have great economic value, however, with the development of society and human economy, various human economic activities have caused different degrees of damage to the marine ecosystem. The number of cetaceans, represented by the Irrawaddy dolphins (*Orcaella brevirostris*, Fig. 1 [1]), is rapidly decreasing, and many species are on the verge of extinction. The Irrawaddy dolphin living in the Mekong River basin is categorized as Data Deficient by IUCN Red List due to small subpopulations, declining ranges, and increasing anthropogenic threats [2]. Five recognized subpopulations, only one of which is exclusively marine, are considered Critically Endangered [3]. The protection of cetaceans cannot be delayed, and now human beings have taken action to carry out various research activities for the protection of them, which has far-reaching significance for human beings. There are many existing

Fig. 1. Irrawaddy dolphins (*Orcaella brevirostris*) in the River of Mekong.

conservation methods, mainly divided into two methods: ecological conservation and information technology conservation. The traditional ecological conservation methods including the marker recapture method are more complicated to operate and require a certain amount of time and effort. In recent years, the rapid development of science and technology has led to the application of information technology in the fields of education, industry and biological conservation. The application of information technology methods in the field of biological conservation has achieved considerable results, which can collect information about the characteristics of organisms in an indirect way without affecting the ecosystem and analyze them, providing an important reference basis for the government and experts to implement relevant conservation measures and decisions. The information technology method is mainly based on the video images and collected sound to detect and identify individuals. Stefan et al. [4] trained four multitasking network architectures: DenseNet201, InceptionNetV2, Xception, and MobileNetV2 to predict fish and dolphin populations, reduce ecological conservation costs, and accelerate real-time data analysis of fish and dolphin abundance in the

Amazon and worldwide river systems; Yadira Quiñonez et al. [5] used convolutional neural networks (CNN) to recognize the Dolphin images; Caruso et al. [6] trained a number of supervised machine learning algorithms to automatically classify the echolocation clicks of different types of short broadband pulses from the Indo-Pacific humpback dolphin with the aim of investigating the spatio-temporal patterns of distribution and acoustic behavior of this species; V. Renò et al. [7,8] used the collected photographs to study the individual identification of gray dolphins using a convolutional neural network approach to dichotomize the presence or absence of dorsal fins within the photographs, and then further studied the dorsal fins of the species for individual identification.

On the other hand, the population age structure of an organism reflects the survival ability of the species to a certain extent. If the population of an organism shows a high number of old species, the population structure of the species performs poorly and has a weak reproductive capacity, and the population will be threatened with extinction; If the number of young and middle-aged species of the species is high, the reproductive capacity of the species is strong and has a large reproductive potential. Based on the literature review and consultation with dolphin conservationists, existing biological studies tend to identify individuals and census the amount of species, while less studies have been reported on the maturity of biological populations and the age structure of species populations. The biological study revealed that the dorsal fin characteristics of the Irrawaddy dolphins are more obvious, and there is a correlation between dorsal fin characteristics and age. Starting from these considerations, this paper constructs AGC method study the age structure distribution of Irrawaddy dolphins, and selects and extracts a total of 16 characteristics such as the length of the leading edge of the dorsal fin, the anterior outer curvature and the height of the fin from the expert experience, and classifies Irrawaddy dolphins into three age groups: juvenile, middle-aged and older.

The paper is organized as follows. Section 1 introduces background and significance of this study. In Sect. 2, the details about methodology is provided, and the Sect. 3 is the description discussions of the experiments and results. Lastly, the Sect. 4 concludes this paper.

2   Proposed Method

2.1   Methodology

The methodology proposed in this paper can be summarized as shown in Fig. 2.

Firstly, the training images are input, and then, the biological features of the dorsal fin of the Irrawaddy dolphins are defined using the Feature Engineering module, and then feature selection and extraction are performed to finally obtain the feature vector, and then the acquired feature vector is trained with a support vector machine (SVM) to finally obtain the training model. Whenever a test image is captured, it first goes through a Feature Engineering module in order to extract its biometric information and finally obtain the feature vector. Lastly,

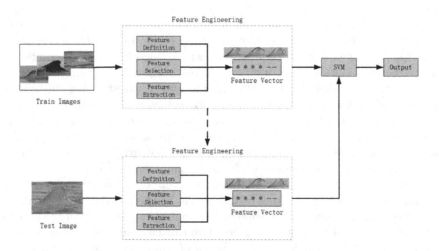

Fig. 2. Overview of the proposed methodology.

SVM method is responsible for classifying its age groups which is trained by a set of previously labeled samples' biometric information.

Feature Extraction and Selection. Note that, according to the growth characteristics of Irrawaddy dolphins, the height of the dorsal fin varies according to age, with juvenile dolphins having immature dorsal fins, older dolphins having degenerative dorsal fins, and middle-aged dolphins having mature dorsal fins at their peak of development. Therefore, the dorsal fins of middle-aged dolphins are relatively stronger and fuller, and the dorsal fin height in middle-aged dolphins is longer than that of juvenile and older dolphins. Based on this biology, review of relevant papers [9,10] and in consultation with dolphin conservationists, this paper defines 16 bio-geometric features of the dorsal fins of the Irrawaddy dolphin, including the length of the anterior edge, the anterior outer curvature and the height of the fin, and performs feature extraction. Finally, the geometric features are transformed into function-type features, and Su *et al.* [11–13] applied this method to the direction of human behavior recognition and achieved better results. Figure 3 shows a schematic diagram of partial feature extraction, and the parts of solid lines portray the corresponding biometric features. By selecting the obtained biometric features, a feature vector about the biometric feature information of the Irrawaddy dolphin is finally obtained.

SVM Classifier. Support vector machine (SVM) is strong classifiers that performs better in dealing with small-sample statistical problems, overlearning and solving dimensional catastrophe problems. It is now widely used in several fields to solve classification problem now widely used in several fields to solve classification problems. Linear SVM (soft-margin) were proposed by Cortes and Vapnik [14]. At the same time, Boser, Guyou and Vapnik [15] introduced and

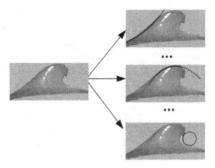

Fig. 3. Partial feature extraction.

proposed the techniques of nonlinear SVM. The original SVM was a two-class classification model, which was then generalized to a multi-class classification. As for the linear indistinguishability problem, the nonlinear support vector machine was constructed by introducing the kernel functions to solve the optimal classification hyperplane. The original linearly indistinguishable case in R^n space is mapped to a higher dimensional *Hilbert* feature space, which is then linearly distinguishable. The commonly used kernel functions are polynomial kernel function, which corresponds to a support vector machine as a sub-polynomial classifier; Gaussian kernel function, which corresponds to a support vector machine as a Gaussian radial basis function classifier; String kernel function, which is more widely used in text classification, information retrieval, bioinformatics, etc.

3   Experiments

3.1   Data Collection and Feature Selection

Images of Irrawaddy dolphin's dorsal fin were taken during a 34-day expedition in the Mekong River Basin in 2019 under different weather conditions and some images shown in Fig. 4. Some of the images were corrupted due to shooting and other reasons, and 208 images were retained in the end. A total of 16 features data such as the height etc. of dorsal fins are extracted from the 208 images in the dataset, and the age labels of dolphins are labeled from the training images.

3.2   Experiments and Results

We use an AMD Ryzen 7 4800H with Radeon Graphics @2.90 GHz, 16 GB RAM, with a Windows 10 64-bit operating system and Python 3.6, and use the dataset introduced in Sect. 3.1.

Due to the high dimension of data features, there may be a certain amount of feature expression repetition. In order to reduce the complexity of the calculation and improve the classification performance of the algorithm, the collected data features were processed by collinearity analysis for dimensionality reduction.

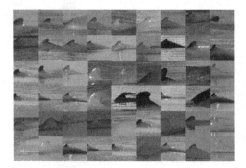

Fig. 4. Some images of Irrawaddy dolphins.

Lastly, after consulting with experts, a total of 9 features such as the height of dorsal fins etc. were obtained by screening.

The basic idea of cross-validation is to group the original data, one part is used as the training set to train the model, and the other part is used as the test set to evaluate the model. K-fold cross-validation [16] is used to evaluate the prediction performance of the model, especially the performance of the trained model on new data, which can reduce the overfitting of the model to a certain extent and check the generalization ability of the model. In this paper, SVM is used as a classifier, and a grid search method is used to find the optimal parameters, and ten times four-fold cross-validation is used to conduct two experiments.

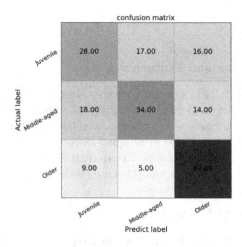

Fig. 5. Single-experiment confusion matrix for classifying Irrawaddy dolphins into juvenile, middle-aged and older dolphins.

Table 1. Recognition results for the juvenile, middle-aged and older Irrawaddy dolphins.

Category	Juvenile	Middle-aged	Older
Mean accuracy	40.61%	54.15%	80.20%

The first experimental results are shown in Fig. 5 and Table 1. The mean recognition rate of juvenile dolphins and middle-aged dolphins were 40.61% and 54.15%, respectively, while the mean recognition rate of old dolphins was 80.20%. In contrast, the dorsal fins of juvenile and middle-aged dolphins were not obvious due to the imperfect development of dorsal fins, and the misclassification was more serious. In order to verify this conclusion, a second experiment was conducted in this paper, in which juvenile and middle-aged dolphins were combined into non-elderly dolphins with the same total sample size, and older and non-elderly dolphins were classified and identified. The results of the experiments are shown in Fig. 6 and Table 2. The number of non-elderly dolphins was significantly higher than that of the elderly dolphins, and the mean recognition rate of the elderly dolphins could still reach 77.79%, while the mean recognition rate of the non-elderly dolphins was 82.95%. From the comparative analysis of the results of the two experiments, the dorsal fin development of the elderly dolphins was more mature and distinguishable, while the juvenile dolphins and middle-aged dolphins had similar characteristics due to the incomplete development of the dorsal fin, resulting in low distinguishability. It also proved that there was a correlation between the dorsal fin characteristics and the age of Irrawaddy dolphins.

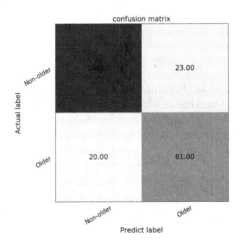

Fig. 6. Single-experiment confusion matrix for classifying Irrawaddy dolphins into non-older and older dolphins.

Table 2. Recognition results for the non-elderly and elderly Irrawaddy dolphins.

Category	Non-older	Older
Mean accuracy	82.95%	77.79%

4   Conclusions and Discussions

In this paper, an age-groups based classifying recognition method for Irrawaddy dolphin was presented, whose dorsal fins show evident and distinctive signs that can be effectively employed to classify their age groups. The main contribution of this work is represented by the innovative application of a feature-based automatic classification method, aiming to effectively classify the age groups of a new dolphin need to be analyzed. In addition, the comparison of the two groups of experiments revealed that the recognition effect of juvenile and middle-aged dolphins was poor, and the recognition effect of older dolphins was better, and their recognition rate was stable above 75%. Therefore, in the future work, we will acquire more photos to expand the data sample size, and continue to explore more biometric features related to the age of Irrawaddy dolphins. Furthermore, we will introduce the deep learning methods to try to automatically select biometric features to improve the performance of dolphin age recognition, especially for juvenile and middle-aged dolphins, when the sample size is sufficient.

Acknowledgements. This work was supported in part by the Study on Habitat Protection and Field Rescue Technology of Irrawaddy Dolphin. This work was supported in part by the Science and Technology Major Project of Anhui Province (No. 18030901021), the Leading Talent Team Project of Anhui Province, and the Anhui Provincial Department of Education outstanding topnotch talent-funded projects (No. gxbjZD26) in China.

References

1. Jackson-Ricketts, J., et al.: Habitat modeling of Irrawaddy dolphins (Orcaella brevirostris) in the Eastern Gulf of Thailand. Ecol. Evol. **10**, 2778–2792 (2020)
2. The IUCN Red List of Threatened Species 2017: e.T15419A123790805. https://www.iucnredlist.org/species/15419/123790805
3. Guidelines for Using the IUCN Red List Categories and Criteria. http://www.iucnredlist.org/documents/RedListGuidelines.pdf
4. Schneider, S., Zhuang, A.: Counting fish and dolphins in sonar images using deep learning. arXiv:2007.12808 (2020)
5. Quiñonez, Y., Zatarain, O., Lizarraga, C., Peraza, J.: Using convolutional neural networks to recognition of dolphin images. In: Mejia, J., Muñoz, M., Rocha, Á., Peña, A., Pérez-Cisneros, M. (eds.) CIMPS 2018. AISC, vol. 865, pp. 236–245. Springer, Cham (2019). https://doi.org/10.1007/978-3-030-01171-0_22
6. Caruso, F., et al.: Monitoring of a nearshore small dolphin species using passive acoustic platforms and supervised machine learning techniques. Front. Mar. Sci. **7**, 267 (2020)

7. Renó, V., et al.: A SIFT-based software system for the photo-identification of the Risso's dolphin. Ecol. Inform. **50**, 95–101 (2019)
8. Renó, V., et al.: Combined color semantics and deep learning for the automatic detection of dolphin dorsal fins. Electronics **9**, 758 (2020)
9. Nasby-Lucas, N., Domeier, M.L.: Impact of satellite linked radio transmitting (SLRT) tags on the dorsal fin of subadult and adult white sharks (Carcharodon carcharias). Bull. Mar. Sci. **96**, 23–30 (2020)
10. Simes-Lopes, P.C., Daura-Jorge, F.G., Lodi, L., Bezamat, C., Wedekin, L.: Bottlenose dolphin ecotypes of the western South Atlantic: the puzzle of dorsal fin shapes, colors and habitats. Aquat. Biol. **28**, 101–111 (2019)
11. Su, B., Jiang, J., Tang, Q., Sheng, M.: Human periodic activity recognition based on functional features. In: SIGGRAPH ASIA 2016 Symposium on Education, pp. 1–9 (2016)
12. Su, B., Jiang, J., Tang, Q., Sheng, M.: Human dynamic behavior recognition based on functional data analysis method. Acta Autom. Sinica. **43**, 866–876 (2017). (In Chinese)
13. Su, B., Zheng, D., Sheng, M.: Single-sensor daily behavior recognition based on time-series modeling of function-based data. Pattern Recogn. Artif. Intell. **31**, 653–661 (2018). (In Chinese)
14. Cortes, C., Vapnik, V.: Support-vector networks. Mach. Learn. **20**, 273–297 (1995). https://doi.org/10.1007/BF00994018
15. Boser, B.E., Guyon, I.M., Vapnik, V.N.: A training algorithm for optimal margin classifiers. In: Proceedings of the Fifth Annual Workshop on Computational Learning Theory, pp. 144–152. Association for Computing Machinery, New York (1992)
16. Rodriguez, J.D., Perez, A., Lozano, J.A.: Sensitivity analysis of k-fold cross validation in prediction error estimation. IEEE Trans. Pattern Anal. Mach. Intell. **32**, 569–575 (2009)

Auricular Point Localization Oriented Region Segmentation for Human Ear

Li Yuan[✉], Xiaoyu Wang, and Zhichun Mu

School of Automation and Electrical Engineering, University of Science and Technology
Beijing, Beijing, China
Lyuan@ustb.edu.cn

Abstract. Auricular acupressure therapy is a simple and effective means of health care and has gradually gained popularity. As an important prerequisite for auricular acupressure therapy, auricular point localization is difficult for general public. Most auricular points are distributed within eight regions, including helix, scapha, fossa triangularis, antihelix, concha, antitragus, tragus, and earlobes, which are divided according to the auricle's anatomical structure. In this paper, an improved YOLACT method is applied to segment the eight regions of the auricle automatically, and the accuracy is up to 93.2% on the ear dataset of 1000 images. Achieving segmentation of the auricular region, which can greatly narrow the localization area of auricular point, will provide an important foundation for the automatic localization of auricular point, favoring nonexperts to increase their understanding of auricular acupressure therapy or the development of an intelligent instrument related to auricular acupressure therapy.

Keywords: Auricular point localization · Ear region segmentation · Improved YOLACT

1 Introduction

Traditional Chinese medicine (TCM) holds that the health of human body can be reflected through the ears, every organ on the human body has corresponding stimulating points on the ears. So auricular acupressure therapy [1] can prevent and treat diseases by stimulating auricular points. Auricular points localization is an important prerequisite for auricular acupressure therapy, but the dense distribution of acupoints and the difference in the shape of the auricle lead to the difference in acupoints location, which is difficult for beginners or non-professionals of TCM. Figure 1 shows a schematic diagram of auricular acupressure localization according to the national standard of auricular acupressure GB/T13734-2008 "Nomenclature and location of auricular points" [2]. In this paper, we conceive that most auricular points are distributed within eight regions, including helix, scapha, fossa triangularis, antihelix, concha, antitragus, tragus, and earlobes, which are divided according to the auricle's anatomical structure. Automatic precise segmentation of the above-mentioned eight regions will simplify the automatic auricular points localization, and favor nonexperts to increase their understanding of auricular acupressure therapy or promote the development of intelligent instrument related to auricular acupressure therapy.

© Springer Nature Switzerland AG 2021
J. Feng et al. (Eds.): CCBR 2021, LNCS 12878, pp. 66–73, 2021.
https://doi.org/10.1007/978-3-030-86608-2_8

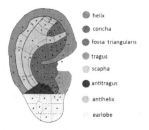

Fig. 1. Schematic representation of auricular points localization.

The research on automatic auricular points localization is relatively less. In [3], Active Shape Model was applied to locate some key points, and then extract the acupoint area by connecting those key points. However, the traditional ASM [4] maybe over relying on the initialization position of the average model [5], and sensitive to lighting variation and noise, which affects the accuracy rate of auricular point localization. With the rapid development of deep learning, many network models with high accuracy have emerged in the field of image segmentation. The semantic segmentation model is able to predict which class of objects each pixel point in the input image belongs to. Instance segmentation model, on the basis of semantic segmentation, is also possible to distinguish different individuals in the same class. Full convolutional instant aware mechanical segmentation [6] is the first algorithm to implement end-to-end instance segmentation using a full convolution scheme. Mask R-CNN [7] adds a branch of semantic segmentation to the target detection pipeline of the Faster R-CNN [8], predicts mask for semantic segmentation, and uses a bilinear interpolation algorithm to better complete pixel level segmentation. YOLACT [9] is a representative instance segmentation method. It adds a mask branch on the basis of the target detection network, which has advantages such as high speed, good mask quality and high applicability. In 2020, Zhang X et al. [10] proposed an improved YOLACT algorithm. In the stage of network prediction, it removes the module in the original network that uses the target prediction box to crop the mask, adds a selecting mask module so as to get new mask with intact edges and errorless detection area, and then improves the accuracy of segmentation. In this paper, the improved YOLACT algorithm is applied to the division of the auricle, completing the segmentation of eight areas, including helix, scapha, fossa triangularis, antihelix, concha, antitragus, tragus, and earlobes, on which important auricular points are located.

2   Improved YOLACT Model with Selecting Mask Module

The network structure of improved YOLACT with selecting mask module is shown in Fig. 2. ResNet101 [11] extracts different sizes of ear image features at different network layers. Then three smaller feature maps are selected as input, Feature Pyramid Networks (FPN) [12] structure is used to fuse feature maps of different sizes to improve the detection accuracy for different size targets. After the above feature extraction is completed, the YOLACT network uses two parallel branches to complete the instance segmentation task. The prediction head branch is the target detection module, which is used to predict the location and category of the target, and also to predict the mask coefficients of each instance. The protonet branch uses the FCN [13] algorithm to generate a set of image-sized prototype masks to separate the background from the foreground, corresponding to the mask coefficients in the other branch. The prediction head branch filters the bounding box using non-maximum suppression to get the prediction box and mask coefficients of the target, then weights the mask coefficients and the mask obtained from protonet branch to sum the predicted n sample masks, which correspond to the mask of the target area of the 8 regions predicted in this paper. Finally, threshold the obtained mask, and a new mask with more complete edges and no error detection area is computed using the selecting mask module to obtain more accurate segmentation results.

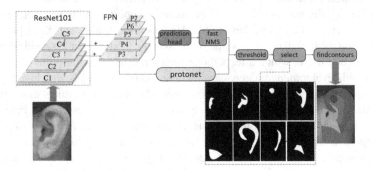

Fig. 2. Network structure of improved YOLACT with selecting mask module.

2.1 Protonet Module and Target Detection Module

The protonet module is a branch of semantic segmentation function of YOLACT, which is used to achieve pixel level classification task. Because the larger size of the feature map contains more detailed information, which is conducive to obtaining pixel level segmentation results, the protonet module selects the feature map with the largest size output of the FPN as input. First, it passes through three convolution layers, and then uses bilinear interpolation for up sampling which reduces the size of the feature map to 1/4 of the original size, improves the resolution of the subsequent generated prototype mask, so as to improve the quality of the overall mask and the segmentation accuracy for small targets. Next, it obtains a K-channel output through two convolution layers. Each channel in the output corresponds to a prototype mask.

Target detection module is the branch of YOLACT that can predict target locations, categories, and prototype mask coefficients. Target detection branch receives five sizes of feature maps generated by the FPN as input. The input feature map first generates anchor, and each pixel generates 3 anchors, with the scale of [0.5, 1, 2] respectively, to increase the adaptability to various targets with different ratios of length and width. According to the feature maps of five sizes, the basic edge length of anchor is 24, 48, 96, 192 and 384 respectively. The basic side length is adjusted according to different proportions to ensure that the area of anchor is equal. Each anchor predicts three kinds of output, which are target location coordinate parameter, target category parameter and prototype mask weighting coefficient.

2.2 Selecting Mask Module

To improve the performance of small target segmentation, YOLACT crops the mask with a true bounding box during training and uses the target prediction box to crop the mask generated by the weighted combination during prediction, preserving only the segmentation results within the target prediction box. Therefore, the segmentation results depend heavily on the accuracy of the target prediction box. When the target prediction box is smaller than the actual boundary box, cropping the composite mask with the target prediction box will destroy the integrity of the original composite mask edge, and the result of the split will appear a straight line edge caused by the cropping. When the target prediction box is too large, the prediction mask will contain a portion of the mask from other instances, which will degrade the quality of the mask.

In order to solve the above problems, the improved YOLACT maintains the operation of cropping the mask with the real bounding box in the training phase and uses the selecting mask module in the testing phase [10]. In the selecting mask module, an outer rectangle is generated for each independent area in the prediction mask, and then the IOU values between the prediction bounding box corresponding to the prediction mask and the outer rectangle of each independent area are calculated in turn. A new mask is generated using the independent area corresponding to the largest IOU value calculated to replace the original mask. The edges of new mask are complete and accurate, and there are no areas of error detection.

2.3 Loss Function

As with the original network, the improved YOLACT network uses four loss functions for training model, namely, classification loss L_{cls}, target prediction box loss L_{box}, mask loss L_{mask} and the last loss of semantic segmentation L_{segm}. The total loss formula is as follows:

$$Loss = \alpha_{cls}L_{cls} + \alpha_{box}L_{box} + \alpha_{mask}L_{mask} + \alpha_{segm}L_{segm}. \tag{1}$$

Where α represents the weight of each loss in accumulation. In this network, the preset values of the weight are $\alpha_{cls} = 1$, $\alpha_{box} = 1.5$, $\alpha_{mask} = 6.125$, $\alpha_{segm} = 1$. The definition of the four types of loss can be referred to "Physiological Curves Extraction of Human Ear Based on Improved YOLACT" [10], which will not be detailed here.

3 Ear Region Segmentation Based on Improved YOLACT

In this paper, the above mentioned improved YOLACT model is applied for ear region segmentation. The ear image dataset used in the experiment is selected from the USTB-Helloear database [10], 200 images of the left ear from 200 individuals are selected as training data. The helix, scapha, fossa triangularis, antihelix, concha, antitragus, tragus, and earlobes of each image were labeled using Labelme as the annotation tool, as shown in Fig. 3. The deep learning framework used is Pytorch 1.2.0. The operating system is ubuntu 16.04. The python version is 3.6.10. The adopted GPU model is Titian RTX and the graphics card memory is 24G.

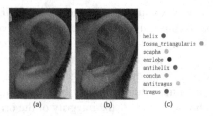

Fig. 3. Dataset example. (a) Original image. (b) Target regions. (c) Labels list.

During the training process, batch size is set to be 16. The learning rate is adjusted every 30000 rounds and the adjustment method is exponential attenuation with the base of 0.1. The maximum number of iterations is 120000 rounds. Under the condition that other parameters being identical, two kinds of learning rates are set for model training, which are 0.001 and 0.0001 respectively. The loss curve is shown in Fig. 4. The horizontal axis is epoch, and the vertical axes are prediction box loss, classification loss and segmentation mask loss respectively. It shows that with higher learning rate, the three kinds of loss values are lower.

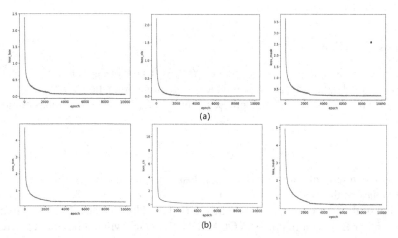

Fig. 4. Loss curve. (a) Learning rate with 0.001. (b) Learning rate with 0.0001.

Mean average precision (mAP) is a common index to evaluate the instance segmentation model. Under different IOU thresholds in the range of 0.5–0.95, the mAP are calculated respectively with the stepsize of 0.05. The results under two kinds of learning rates are shown in Table 1. "lr" represents the learning rate. "box" and "mask" represent the accuracy of target detection and semantic segmentation respectively. "mAP50", "mAP70" and "mAP90" represent the mAP values calculated when the IOU threshold is 0.5, 0.7 and 0.9 respectively. "all" represents the average value of mAP under different IOU thresholds. It can be seen that the average value of mAP under the two learning rates can reach more than 88%, but when the learning rate is set to 0.001, the mAP is significantly higher, which is very close to 100%. Judging from this, the model with higher learning rate has higher mAP value.

Table 1. Model evaluation under different learning rates.

		All	mAP50	mAP70	mAP90
lr = 0.001	Box	97.75	100.00	100.00	98.33
	Mask	98.57	100.00	100.00	99.61
lr = 0.0001	Box	88.85	99.84	99.56	80.74
	Mask	90.65	99.84	99.84	87.32

To test the generalization of the model, the test set contains 1000 ear images taken from 1000 people outside the training set with lighting variation. The results of the models with two different learning rates on the test set are shown in Table 2. Generally, the model can accurately segment 8 regions and is robust to lighting variation, as shown in Fig. 5. However, there are also some problems: the case of missed region is shown in Fig. 6(a); The case of classification error for a certain region is shown in Fig. 6(b); The case of inaccurate boundary segmentation is shown in Fig. 6(c).

It can be seen from the Table 2 that the accuracy of the auricle's 8 regions segmented correctly can reach more than 90% under both learning rates. The model with better performance (learning rate of 0.001) achieves an accuracy of 93.2%. From the perspective of model evaluation indexes, the model with the learning rate of 0.001 has a smaller loss value and a larger mAP value, so its overall accuracy is higher, and the boundary segmentation is more accurate, and the case of misclassification is less. But the model with the learning rate of 0.0001 has the advantage of fewer missed regions.

Table 2. Segmentation performance with different learning rates.

	8 regions segmented accurately	1 region missed	2 regions missed	1 region classification error	Inaccurate boundary segmentation	Total number of images
lr = 0.001	932	40	1	5	22	1000
lr = 0.0001	912	34	0	13	41	1000

In addition, we also use the original YOLACT network to test these 1000 images. With a learning rate of 0.001 and the other parameters being identical, the original YOLACT shows poor results on the ear edge segmentation. Straight edge appears in

382 out of 1000 images as shown in Fig. 7(a). The improved YOLACT network used in this paper overcomes this problem, as shown in Fig. 7(b).

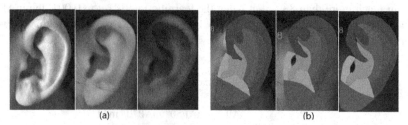

Fig. 5. Segmentation results under different illumination intensities. (a) Original picture. (b) Segmentation results.

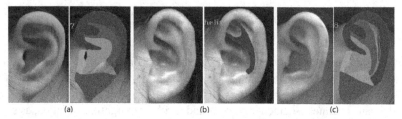

Fig. 6. Examples of wrong segmentation results. (a) Missed detection of the antitragus. (b) Mistaking the antihelix as the helix. (c) Inaccurate segmentation of scapha boundary.

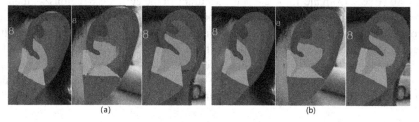

Fig. 7. Segmentation results under different network. (a) The original YOLACT network. (b) The improved YOLACT network.

4   Conclusion

In this paper, an improved YOLACT algorithm is applied for the automatic segmentation of eight areas of human ear, which are helix, scapha, fossa triangularis, antihelix, concha, antitragus, tragus, and earlobes respectively. With only 200 annotated images, the improved YOLACT model can achieve the segmentation accuracy of 93.2% on a 1000-image dataset. This conclusion is of high significance. Our follow-up research will focus on more specific segmentation of the auricle and locate the auricular points on those smaller areas, so as to achieve the effect of automatic location of the auricular points, and lay the foundation for the development of intelligent instruments related to auricular acupressure therapy.

References

1. Hou, P.W., Hsin-Cheng, H., Lin, Y.W., et al.: The history, mechanism, and clinical application of auricular therapy in traditional Chinese medicine. Evid. Based Complement Alternat. Med. **2015**, 1–13 (2105)
2. General Administration of Quality Supervision, Inspection and Quarantine of the People's Republic of China: GB/T 13734-2008 Nomenclature and Location of Auricular Points. Standards Press of China, Beijing (2008)
3. Wang, Y., Jiang, M., Huang, N., et al.: A location method of auricular acupoint divisions based on active shape model algorithm. Beijing Biomed. Eng. **40**, 145–150 (2021)
4. Cootes, T.F., Taylor, C.J., Cooper, D.H., et al.: Active shape models-their training and application. Comput. Vis. Image Underst. **61**, 38–59 (1995)
5. Fan, Y., Ma, J.: ASM and improved algorithm for facial feature location. J. Comput. Aided Des. Comput. Graph. **19**, 1411–1415 (2007)
6. Li, Y., Qi, H., Dai, J., et al.: Fully convolutional instance-aware semantic segmentation. In: Proceedings of the IEEE Conference on Computer Vision and Pattern Recognition, pp. 2359–2367 (2017)
7. He, K., Gkioxari, G., Dollar, P., et al.: Mask R-CNN. In: Proceedings of the IEEE International Conference on Computer Vision, pp. 2961–2969 (2017)
8. Ren, S., Girshick, R., Girshick, R., et al.: Faster R-CNN: towards real-time object detection with region proposal networks. IEEE Trans. Pattern Anal. Mach. Intell. **39**, 1137–1149 (2017)
9. Bolya, D., Zhou, C., Xiao, F., et al.: YOLACT: real-time instance segmentation. In: Proceedings of the IEEE/CVF International Conference on Computer Vision, pp. 9157–9166 (2019)
10. Zhang, X., Yuan, L., Huang, J.: Physiological curves extraction of human ear based on improved YOLACT. In: 2020 IEEE 2nd International Conference on Civil Aviation Safety and Information Technology, pp. 390–394 (2020)
11. He, K., Zhang, X., Ren, S., et al.: Deep residual learning for image recognition. In: Proceedings of the IEEE Conference on Computer Vision and Pattern Recognition, pp. 770–778 (2016)
12. Lin, T.Y., Dollár, P., Girshick, R., et al.: Feature pyramid networks for object detection. In: Proceedings of the IEEE Conference on Computer Vision And Pattern Recognition, pp. 2117–2125 (2017)
13. Long, J., Shelhamer, E., Darrell, T.: Fully convolutional networks for semantic segmentation. In: Proceedings of the IEEE Conference on Computer Vision and Pattern Recognition, pp. 3431–3440 (2015)

Portrait Thangka Image Retrieval via Figure Re-identification

Xire Danzeng[1], Yuchao Yang[2], Yufan Yang[1], Zhao Hou[1], Rui Xi[2],
Xinsheng Li[2], Qijun Zhao[1,2], Pubu Danzeng[1], Gesang Duoji[1(✉)],
and Dingguo Gao[1]

[1] School of Information Science and Technology, Tibet University,
Lhasa, Tibet, People's Republic of China
gsdj@utibet.edu.cn
[2] College of Computer Science, Sichuan University, Chengdu, Sichuan,
People's Republic of China

Abstract. Recognizing figures in portrait Thangka images is fundamental to the appreciation of this unique Tibetan art. In this paper, we focus on the problem of portrait Thangka image retrieval from the perspective of re-identifying the figures in the images. Based on state-of-the-art re-identification methods, we further improve them by exploiting several tricks. We also investigate the impact of different cropping methods to evaluate the contribution of different features. Our evaluation results on an annotated portrait Thangka image dataset collected by ourselves demonstrate the necessity of further study on this challenging problem. We will release the data and code to promote the research on Thangka.

Keywords: Portrait Thangka · Image retrieval · Re-identification

1 Introduction

Thangka, a scroll painting framed by colorful satin interpreted from the book *Tibet Thangka*, is a unique painting art form in Tibetan culture. It is called the "encyclopedia" of Tibetans. Nowadays, the digitalization of Thangka images has notably promoted its protection and dissemination, enabling more people interested in Thangka to access this unique art easily. However, Thangka appreciation is not easy, even for Tibetan people. Taking portrait Thangka for example, there are thousands of different figures, many of which are very difficult to distinguish between each other. Therefore, it is highly demanded to develop tools that can automatically retrieve portrait Thangka images that have same figures in them.

In this paper, we focus on the following portrait Thangka image retrieval task: given a gallery of portrait Thangka images and a probe portrait Thangka image, we generate a candidate list in which the gallery portrait Thangka images are retrieved in descending order according to their similarity to the probe in terms of the figures in them. To demonstrate the difficulty of this task, we feed a query Thangka image that depicts Padmasambhava, a well-known figure in Tibet, into

© Springer Nature Switzerland AG 2021
J. Feng et al. (Eds.): CCBR 2021, LNCS 12878, pp. 74–83, 2021.
https://doi.org/10.1007/978-3-030-86608-2_9

Google and Baidu search engines. The retrieval results are shown in Fig. 1. As can be seen, the retrieved images by both engines mostly resemble the query image in style and color rather than the primary figure. These results reveal that special methods should be designed for portrait Thangka image retrieval to deal with the high similarity between different figures and the large difference between different instances (e.g., multiple incarnations) of a same figure.

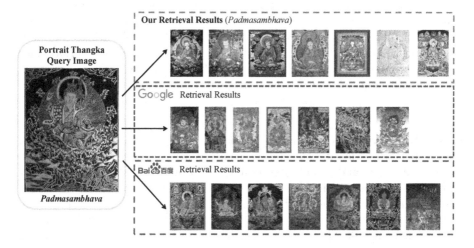

Fig. 1. Portrait Thangka retrieval results by different search engines for a query image of Padmasambhava. The retrieval results of Baidu are mostly black gold Thangkas, but they do not depict the same figure. Most of Google's retrieval results are Thangkas, but their style and figures are not much related to the query image.

We approach the task of portrait Thangka retrieval as a re-identification problem. Specifically, we use two network structures that perform well in the person re-identification task as our baselines which are based on global features and local features, respectively; and we employ some tricks to improve them particularly for the portrait Thangka retrieval task. We finally achieve Rank1 = 76.83% and mAP = 69.42% with the model based on local features, namely MGN-Thangka, which is slightly better than the global feature based model BoT-Thangka. The ablation studies further prove the effectiveness of the employed tricks for portrait Thangka retrieval. The contributions of this paper can be summarized as follows. 1) We discuss the challenges in portrait Thangka image retrieval from the perspective of figure re-identification. 2) We improve the state-of-the-art re-identification methods for portrait Thangka image retrieval by exploiting several tricks. 3) We investigate the contribution of different features to recognizing figures in Thangka, suggesting future research direction for this challenging task. 4) We will release the dataset we collected and the baseline models we developed to promote the research on Thangka as well as on image retrieval and re-identification.

2   Related Work

Thangka Images. As a precious cultural heritage, digitalized Thangka images have been studied for many years. Most of the existing work has focused on the composition elements of Thangka images, such as headdresses [1], religious tools [2], and gestures [3]. Combining image processing and machine learning methods, researchers have studied several tasks such as background-based and content-based Thangka image classification, as well as semantic-based Thangka image retrieval [4]. However, they employ traditional hand-crafted features and shallow-learning-based classifiers, and thus cannot effectively utilize the high-level semantic features in Thangka images. Given the overwhelming performance of deep learning in many computer vision tasks, it is highly necessary to study how the challenging portrait Thangka image retrieval task can benefit from deep learning.

Image Retrieval. Image retrieval technology has applications in many fields, such as person re-identification [5] to ensure security, landmark retrieval [6] to assist positioning, and product retrieval [7,8] to improve user efficiency. Compared with previous methods that aggregate a set of handcrafted local features into a single global vector [9], deep convolutional neural networks trained with ranking-based or classification losses greatly improve the expressive ability of retrieval models [10]. Some researchers optimize the global features by using improved attention mechanism and loss function [11]. In order to get more detailed information, some researchers combine global features with local features, resulting in better retrieval performance [12].

As a kind of image retrieval, re-identification also makes great progress in recent years. By adopting a multi-branch structure, [13] obtains features of different granularities. [14] integrates some current effective tricks and proposes a stronger baseline. On this basis, [15] adds non-local block and GeM pooling to achieve higher accuracy on multiple re-identification datasets. However, it is unclear how these methods work in portrait Thangka retrieval task and how to further improve them particularly for portrait Thangka images.

3   Methodology

3.1   Challenges in Portrait Thangka Image Retrieval

Unlike photographs, Thangka images are artificially drawn with bright colors and artistic decoration, and some figures in Thangka do not have real-world prototypes at all. On the one hand, Thangka images created by different dynasties and different painting genres usually have diverse styles. On the other hand, what makes this task even more challenging is that some figures in Thangka images have multiple incarnations, leading to large intra-class variations. As a consequence, experts often need to combine multiple composition elements to reason about the identity of the figures in Thangka, such as the gesture, religious tools, headdresses, thrones, and even the ride. Therefore, the portrait Thangka image retrieval task puts forward higher requirements on the reasoning ability of retrieval model.

In addition, Thangka images provide a wealth of visual features, but whether one feature can be used to define the identity of figures is uncertain for different figures. For example, color can help identify the identity of the figure (e.g., Bodhisattva Tara) whose color does not change. However, color becomes interference information for the figure who has multiple incarnations of different colors, such as Avalokiteśvara. Therefore, extracting discriminative features that can capture high-level semantic information is critical for accurate retrieval of portrait Thangka images.

3.2   Re-identification Based Portrait Thangka Image Retrieval

We adopt two network structures as our baseline, a global feature learning model named BoT [14] and a local feature model named MGN [13], which achieve state-of-the-art performance in person re-identification task. To further improve their performance on portrait Thangka images, we employ several tricks from the perspectives of ......

Auto Augmentation. Inspired by Neural Architecture Search (NAS), Google proposed a new data augmentation method in [16], called automatic augmentation. In a search space that includes different data enhancement methods, the optimal strategy is found through reinforcement learning and randomly applied to each mini-batch. We use automatic augmentation to preprocess the image to improve the generalization ability of the model.

Instance-Batch Normalization. Instance Normalization learns features that are invariant to appearance changes, such as colors and styles, while Batch Normalization is essential for preserving content-related information and can accelerate training and preserve more discriminative features. Since Thangka images have a variety of painting genres, we employ the Instance-Batch Normalization (IBN) block proposed in [17] to improve the robustness of the model to different painting styles.

Second-Order Attention Block. Inspired by Non-local neural networks, [11] applied the Second-Order Attention mechanism to image retrieval. Specifically, the problem of long-distance information transmission is solved by inserting the Second-Order Attention block in the backbone, so that the network can extract higher-level semantic information. In addition, calculating the similarity of the two parts in the feature map, can help the network focus on more discriminative features and reduce the impact of noise.

Cosine Annealing with Warmup. To maintain the stability of the deep model, we adopt the warmup method in the initial stage of training [14]. A small learning rate at the beginning of training can prevent the model from fitting in the wrong direction, and gradually increasing the learning rate can improve the optimization speed of the model. In the training process, we use cosine annealing to adjust the learning rate to reduce the fluctuation of the model and make the model find the optimal solution as much as possible.

GeM Pooling. The widely-used max-pooling or average pooling cannot capture the domain-specific discriminative features. Generalized-Mean (GeM) pooling [10] provides a flexible way to aggregate the feature map into a single descriptor vector:

$$\text{GeM}\,(f, p) = \left(\frac{1}{N} \sum_{i=0}^{N} f_i^p \right)^{\frac{1}{p}} \tag{1}$$

where p is a learnable parameter. As p increases, the weight of the part with a larger response value in the feature map will become larger. Therefore, p can help the network find a more appropriate aggregation method.

4   Experiments

Dataset and Metrics. We collect 1,870 portrait Thangka images on http://www.datathangka.com/, which contain 85 different figures, including Padmasambhava, Śākyamuni, Mañjuśrī, Cakrasamvara, etc. Further, we divide all images into training set of $1,240$ images and test set of 630 images, which have the same label spaces and no data overlapping. The test set contains 315 query images and 315 gallery images. We use Rank-1 accuracy, Rank-5 accuracy, Rank-10 accuracy, mean Average Precision (mAP), and mINP [15] to evaluate the portrait Thangka image retrieval performance of different models.

Implementation. We first resize input images to 384×128, and use the weights of ResNet-50 pre-trained on ImageNet to initialize the backbone. During the training phase, we choose Adam as the optimizer. As for the learning rate strategy, we give a very small learning rate in the initial training and then gradually linearly increase it to 3.5×10^{-4}, and the minimum learning rate in the cosine annealing process is 1×10^{-7}. We use cosine similarity to measure the distance between feature vectors. All the following experiments are performed on the above portrait Thangka image dataset collected by ourselves (since there is no such dataset in the public domain).

Ablation Study. We conduct ablation studies to discuss and analyze the impact of each trick on the performance of the model. For the model based on global features, we use BoT as the baseline and employ Cosine Annealing with Warmup, Second-Order Attention Block, GeM pooling. We finally obtain 74.29% Rank-1 accuracy, 67.36% mAP and 43.89% mINP by the global feature model, which we call **BoT-Thangka**. For the model based on local features, we apply Auto

Augmentation (Auto Aug), IBN block (IBN), Warmup, Cosine Annealing (CA) and GeM pooling (GeM), and call the obtained model as **MGN-Thangka**. The result is shown in Table 1, which proves that all the above tricks are found to largely improve the retrieval performance. We finally achieve 76.86% Rank-1 accuracy, 69.42% mAP and 45.36% mINP on the above portrait Thangka image dataset.

Table 1. Ablation studies of MGN-Thangka.

MGN	Auto aug	IBN	Warmup	CA	GeM	Rank-1 (%)	mAP (%)	mINP (%)
✓						61.59	54.03	27.39
✓	✓					65.08	56.30	28.50
✓		✓				67.94	56.70	30.28
✓			✓			68.25	59.92	35.32
✓				✓		66.98	60.77	35.98
✓					✓	67.30	58.35	31.06
✓	✓	✓	✓	✓	✓	**76.83**	**69.42**	**45.36**

Compared with Other Methods. We compare BoT-Thangka and MGN-Thangka with some other methods that perform well in person re-identification task, the quantitative results are shown in Table 2. The counterpart methods, BoT [14], AGW [15] and SBS [18], are all based on global features. From the results, we can see that MGN-Thangka obtains the best performance, which suggests that local features play a critical role in portrait Thangka image retrieval. We believe that this is because fine-grained features are critical in distinguishing figures with subtle differences.

Table 2. Quantitative results for the portrait Thangka retrieval task.

	Rank-1 (%)	Rank-5 (%)	Rank-10 (%)	mAP (%)	mINP (%)
BoT (ResNet50) [14]	64.76	79.68	85.40	57.04	29.83
BoT (ResNet50-ibn)	63.81	79.37	86.35	55.78	27.54
AGW (ResNet50) [15]	66.98	82.86	86.67	59.04	33.78
AGW (ResNet50-ibn)	70.79	82.86	87.62	58.80	32.47
SBS (ResNet50) [18]	66.98	82.22	88.57	60.30	38.38
SBS (ResNet50-ibn)	71.75	85.71	89.21	63.28	37.77
BoT-Thangka (ours)	74.29	85.08	89.52	67.36	43.89
MGN-Thangka (ours)	**76.83**	**86.98**	**90.79**	**69.42**	**45.36**

Qualitative Results and Analysis. Some example results obtained by MGN-Thangka are shown in Fig. 2. As can be seen, for the easy query sample in the first row, MGN-Thangka can successfully retrieve all the correct gallery images on top ranks. The query sample in the second row demonstrates that MGN-Thangka can handle color variations to some extent. However, as shown in the third row, MGN-Thangka performs worse when the figure in the query image has very low resolution. These results reveal that portrait Thangka retrieval is a very challenging task.

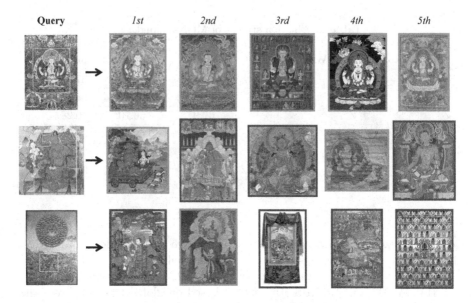

Fig. 2. Qualitative results of MGN-Thangka. The green frame indicates the correct retrieval results, while the red frame indicates the wrong retrieval results. (Color figure online)

Fig. 3. Different cropping methods of portrait Thangka images.

Impact of Image Cropping. In the above experiments, the original portrait Thangka images are used as input. Considering that the figures of interest are only part of the images, we further assess the impact of image cropping on the retrieval performance. Figure 3 shows different cropping methods considered in this experiment, and the corresponding results are summarized in Table 3. From these results, the following observations can be made.

- The best accuracy is obtained by 'Crops' and is obviously better than that obtained by using original images as input. This indicates that the background contains much distracting information with respect to the figure identity.
- Comparing the results of 'Crops' and 'Tight Crops', it can be seen that in addition to the body features, features of religious tools, headdresses, and thrones/rides also provide useful discriminative information for separating one figure from another.
- The results of 'Inverse Crops' demonstrate that the regions surrounding a figure could also have discriminative information, e.g., objects or figures that have co-occurrence relationship with the figure. The challenge is how to more effectively exploit such information.

Table 3. The performance of MGN-Thangka when images cropped in different ways are used as input.

Input	mAP (%)
Original images	69.42
Crops	**75.04**
Tight Crops	74.85
Inverse Crops (O-C)	17.07
Inverse Crops (O-T)	43.92
Inverse Crops (C-T)	40.47

5   Conclusions and Future Work

In this paper, we analyze the characteristics of Thangka images and approach the portrait Thangka image retrieval task from the perspective of re-identification. Furthermore, we investigate the effectiveness of several tricks on this task through ablation studies. We also analyze the impact of different cropping methods on the retrieval performance to study how different features contribute to the re-identification of figures in Thangka images. The results on the portrait Thangka image dataset collected by ourselves demonstrate the challenges in portrait Thangka image retrieval, and it is worth further study to exploit the co-occurrence characteristics of different composition elements in portrait Thangka images.

Acknowledgments. This work was supported by the National Natural Science Foundation of China [NO. 62066042; NO. 61971005], and First-Class Discipline Cultivation Projects of Tibet University (No. 00060704/004).

References

1. Liu, H., Wang, X., Bi, X., Wang, X., Zhao, J.: A multi-feature SVM classification of Thangka headdress. In: 2015 8th International Symposium on Computational Intelligence and Design (ISCID), Hangzhou, China, pp. 160–163. IEEE, December 2015
2. Chen, Y., Liu, X.: Thangka religious tools classification and detection based on HOG+SVM. In: 2019 IEEE 3rd Advanced Information Management, Communicates, Electronic and Automation Control Conference (IMCEC), Chongqing, China, pp. 967–971. IEEE, October 2019
3. Qian, J., Wang, W.: Religious portrait Thangka image retrieval based on gesture feature. In: 2009 Chinese Conference on Pattern Recognition, Nanjing, China, pp. 1–5. IEEE, November 2009
4. Wang, W.: Study of Thangka image retrieval and multimedia presentation management system. In: 2009 Fifth International Conference on Intelligent Information Hiding and Multimedia Signal Processing, Kyoto, Japan, pp. 981–984. IEEE, September 2009
5. Bryan, B., Gong, Y., Zhang, Y., Poellabauer, C.: Second-order non-local attention networks for person re-identification. In: 2019 IEEE/CVF International Conference on Computer Vision (ICCV), Seoul, Korea (South), pp. 3759–3768. IEEE, October 2019
6. Weyand, T., Araujo, A., Cao, B., Sim, J.: Google landmarks dataset v2 – a large-scale benchmark for instance-level recognition and retrieval. In: 2020 IEEE/CVF Conference on Computer Vision and Pattern Recognition (CVPR), Seattle, WA, USA, pp. 2572–2581. IEEE, June 2020
7. Ji, Y.H., et al.: An effective pipeline for a real-world clothes retrieval system (2020)
8. Ge, Y., Zhang, R., Wang, X., Tang, X., Luo, P.: DeepFashion2: a versatile benchmark for detection, pose estimation, segmentation and re-identification of clothing images. In: 2019 IEEE/CVF Conference on Computer Vision and Pattern Recognition (CVPR), Long Beach, CA, USA, pp. 5332–5340. IEEE, June 2019
9. Jegou, H., Douze, M., Schmid, C., Perez, P.: Aggregating local descriptors into a compact image representation. In: 2010 IEEE Computer Society Conference on Computer Vision and Pattern Recognition, San Francisco, CA, USA, pp. 3304–3311. IEEE, June 2010
10. Radenovic, F., Tolias, G., Chum, O.: Fine-tuning CNN image retrieval with no human annotation. IEEE Trans. Pattern Anal. Mach. Intell. **41**(7), 1655–1668 (2019)
11. Ng, T., Balntas, V., Tian, Y., Mikolajczyk, K.: SOLAR: second-order loss and attention for image retrieval. In: Vedaldi, A., Bischof, H., Brox, T., Frahm, J.-M. (eds.) ECCV 2020. LNCS, vol. 12370, pp. 253–270. Springer, Cham (2020). https://doi.org/10.1007/978-3-030-58595-2_16
12. Cao, B., Araujo, A., Sim, J.: Unifying deep local and global features for image search. In: Vedaldi, A., Bischof, H., Brox, T., Frahm, J.-M. (eds.) ECCV 2020. LNCS, vol. 12365, pp. 726–743. Springer, Cham (2020). https://doi.org/10.1007/978-3-030-58565-5_43
13. Wang, G., Yuan, Y., Chen, X., Li, J., Zhou, X.: Learning discriminative features with multiple granularities for person re-identification. In: Proceedings of the 26th ACM International Conference on Multimedia, MM 2018, pp. 274–282. Association for Computing Machinery, New York (2018)

14. Luo, H., Gu, Y., Liao, X., Lai, S., Jiang, W.: Bag of tricks and a strong baseline for deep person re-identification. In: 2019 IEEE/CVF Conference on Computer Vision and Pattern Recognition Workshops (CVPRW), Long Beach, CA, USA, pp. 1487–1495. IEEE, June 2019
15. Ye, M., Shen, J., Lin, G., Xiang, T., Shao, L., Hoi, S.C.H.: Deep learning for person re-identification: a survey and outlook. IEEE Trans. Pattern Anal. Mach. Intell. (2021)
16. Cubuk, E.D., Zoph, B., Mane, D., Vasudevan, V., Le, Q.V.: AutoAugment: learning augmentation strategies from data. In: 2019 IEEE/CVF Conference on Computer Vision and Pattern Recognition (CVPR), Long Beach, CA, USA, pp. 113–123. IEEE, June 2019
17. Pan, X., Luo, P., Shi, J., Tang, X.: Two at once: enhancing learning and generalization capacities via IBN-Net. In: Ferrari, V., Hebert, M., Sminchisescu, C., Weiss, Y. (eds.) ECCV 2018. LNCS, vol. 11208, pp. 484–500. Springer, Cham (2018). https://doi.org/10.1007/978-3-030-01225-0_29
18. He, L., Liao, X., Liu, W., Liu, X., Cheng, P., Mei, T.: FastReID: a Pytorch toolbox for general instance re-identification (2020)

To See Facial Expressions Through Occlusions via Adversarial Disentangled Features Learning with 3D Supervision

Wenxue Yuan, Qijun Zhao[✉], Feiyu Zhu, and Zhengxi Liu

College of Computer Science, Sichuan University, Chengdu, China
qjzhao@scu.edu.cn

Abstract. Facial expression recognition (FER) is still a challenging problem if face images are contaminated by occlusions, which lead to not only noisy features but also loss of discriminative features. To address the issue, this paper proposes a novel adversarial disentangled features learning (ADFL) method for recognizing expressions on occluded face images. Unlike previous methods, our method defines an explicit noise component in addition to the identity and expression components to isolate the occlusion-caused noise features. Besides, we learn shape features with joint supervision of 3D shape reconstruction and facial expression recognition to compensate for the occlusion-caused loss of features. Evaluation on both in-the-lab and in-the-wild face images demonstrates that our proposed method effectively improves FER accuracy for occluded images, and can even deal with noise beyond occlusions.

Keywords: Facial expression recognition · Occlusions · Feature disentanglement · Adversarial learning · Shape features

1 Introduction

Automatic facial expression recognition (FER) has got increasing attention with its widespread applications in plenty of fields, such as human-computer interaction, medical treatment and security. In the past few years, the accuracy of FER has been substantially improved, especially on face images collected in laboratory that are mostly frontal and fully exposed. However, occlusions might frequently occur to faces in real-world scenarios [1,2], resulting in obvious degradation of FER accuracy. This is mainly due to two factors related to occlusions: (i) noisy features extracted from face image regions with occlusions, and (ii) loss of discriminative features in occluded facial regions. Consequently, it is still challenging to recognize expressions in face images contaminated by occlusions.

Existing FER methods that aim to deal with occluded face images can be roughly divided into three categories. Methods in the first category [3] employ patch-based approaches and assign different weights to patches such that the impact of noisy features extracted from patches with occlusions can be alleviated.

© Springer Nature Switzerland AG 2021
J. Feng et al. (Eds.): CCBR 2021, LNCS 12878, pp. 84–91, 2021.
https://doi.org/10.1007/978-3-030-86608-2_10

Methods in the second category [4] first train a FER model using non-occluded face images, and then utilize the model as privilege information to fine-tune another pre-trained FER model using occluded face images.

Instead of learning occlusion-robust feature representations, methods in the last category [5] first complete the face images by recovering the occluded regions, and then use the recovered non-occluded face images to recognize expressions. Although these existing methods achieve promising results, none of them explicitly model occlusion-induced noise or explore additional complementary features.

To further improve FER accuracy, some researchers employ feature disentanglement (FD) for the purpose of separating expression and non-expression features, and they achieve state-of-the-art accuracy on both in-the-lab and in-the-wild data [6,7]. Yet, these FD-based methods do not explicitly consider noisy features, and are thus still limited in handling occluded face images. To enrich features, other researchers propose to extract shape features by using 2D shape descriptors [8] or reconstructed 3D faces [9]. However, they either use hand-crafted feature representations, or fail to jointly optimize 3D face reconstruction and expression feature extraction.

In this paper, we aim to promote the application of FER towards the scenarios of occluded face images by explicitly handling occlusion-induced noise and meanwhile enriching expression features. To this end, we decompose facial features into three components, i.e., identity, expression and noise components, among which expression component describes the identity-independent features of facial expressions while noise component captures the features in face images that are irrelevant to the intrinsic characteristics of facial identity and expression attributes. We implement this feature disentanglement via adversarial learning and joint supervision of multiple tasks. Especially, we use 3D face shape reconstruction as an auxiliary task to supervise the model to learn shape features as complement to texture features. The evaluation results on four benchmark datasets demonstrate the superiority of our proposed method in recognizing facial expressions in images with occlusions or even noise beyond occlusions.

2   Proposed Method

2.1   Overview

Figure 1 shows the overall framework of our proposed method. It mainly consists of three parts for shape feature extraction, texture feature extraction, and expression classification, respectively. Given a face image, respective feature extractors are applied to obtain texture and shape features ($C_{Exp}^T \in R^{29 \times 1}$ and $C_{Exp}^S \in R^{29 \times 1}$), which are then concatenated to form a hybrid feature ($C_{Exp}^{TS} \in R^{58 \times 1}$). Finally, the expression on the input face image is recognized by the expression classifier according to the hybrid feature. In this paper, we simply employ ResNet50 as the texture feature extractor, and a softmax classifier as the expression classifier. To deal with occlusions, inspired by the facial feature disentanglement method in [10], we encode the input face image into three latent representations, i.e., identity component $C_{Id} \in R^{199 \times 1}$, expression component C_{Exp}^{S} and occlusion-included noise component $C_{Occ} \in R^{29 \times 1}$. Among them, the expression component is supposed to be subject-independent and occlusion-robust, and serves as complement to the texture feature. To learn to extract the expression component, we constrain the expression representation to be able to distinguish different expressions as better as possible, and meanwhile the identity and expression representations together to be able to recover (via decoders defined by single fully-connected layer) the non-occluded canonical-view 3D shape of the input face image as precise as possible. To isolate the occlusion-caused noise, we constrain the noise component unable to distinguish different expressions. Below, we first introduce the two key modules in our proposed method, 3D supervised feature disentanglement and adversarial training against occlusion noise, and then specify the learning process to construct a model that can better recognize expressions on occluded faces.

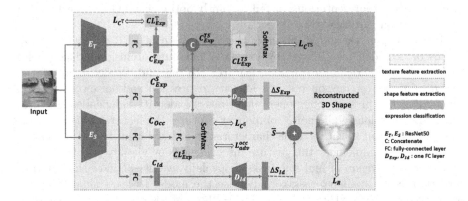

Fig. 1. The framework of our proposed method.

2.2 3D Supervised Feature Disentanglement

The goal of 3D supervised feature disentanglement is to extract expression features in latent shape space as complement to texture features. To implement such disentanglement, following the formulation in [11], we define a 3D face shape as

$$S = \overline{S} + \Delta S_{Id} + \Delta S_{Exp} = \overline{S} + A_{Id}C_{Id} + A_{Exp}C_{Exp}^{S}, \qquad (1)$$

where $\overline{S}$ is the mean 3D face shape, A_{Exp} and A_{Id} represent the identity and expression shape bases, respectively. Given a face image, the coefficients (i.e., the latent expression and identity representations) C_{Exp}^{S} and C_{Id} are obtained via an encoder, and the bases are approximated by respective decoders. To train the involved encoders and decoders, we feed C_{Exp}^{S} to a softmax-based expression classifier CL_{Exp}^{S} to predict the expression on the input face image, and apply 3D reconstruction loss on the obtained 3D face shape and cross-entropy loss on the predicted expression.

2.3   Adversarial Training Against Occlusion Noise

In addition to the identity and expression components, we explicitly separate occlusion noise from other features in the input face image via adversarial learning. Because the noise component is assumed to be irrelevant to facial expressions, it should not be able to distinguish between different expressions. To enforce this constraint on the noise component, we leverage the expression classifier CL_{Exp}^{S} trained during 3D supervised feature disentanglement and carry out adversarial training such that the probabilities generated by the classifier with the noise component as input evenly distribute across all the different expressions. More specifically, to train the encoders when noise component is included, we introduce an $L2$ loss between the predicted expression probabilities and $1/N_{Exp}$ (N_{Exp} is the number of expression classes).

2.4   The Learning Process

To construct the facial expression recognition model of our method, a four-phase learning process is adopted. In the first phase, the shape feature encoder (E_S along with the fully-connected or FC layers for generating latent expression and identity representations) is pre-trained with $L2$ loss on the 300W_LP [12] dataset. In the second phase, we lock the shape feature encoder and train the shape-feature-based expression classifier CL_{Exp}^{S} with cross-entropy loss. In the third phase, we introduce the noise component and re-train the shape feature extractor by using adversarial learning and 3D supervision. Specifically, we lock the shape-feature-based expression classifier CL_{Exp}^{S}, and update the noise-component-included shape feature encoder along with the expression and identity decoders. Finally, an end-to-end training is applied in the fourth phase to update all the blocks except CL_{Exp}^{S} under the following overall loss,

$$L = \lambda_1 L_R + \lambda_2 L_{adv}^{occ} + \lambda_3 L_{C^T} + \lambda_4 L_{C^S} + \lambda_5 L_{C^{TS}}, \tag{2}$$

where L_R is the 3D shape reconstruction loss, L_{adv}^{occ} is the $L2$ loss for adversarial learning of noise component, and L_{C^T}, L_{C^S} and $L_{C^{TS}}$ are cross-entropy losses, respectively, for classification using texture features, shape features and hybrid features. The weights associated with these losses are empirically set as $\lambda_1 = 0.5$, $\lambda_2 = 0.5$, $\lambda_3 = 0.5$, $\lambda_4 = 0.5$ and $\lambda_5 = 1.0$ in our experiments.

It is worth mentioning that the above learning process requires pairs of 2D face images and corresponding ground truth (GT) 3D face shapes as training data. However, GT 3D shapes are not always available for the training images, particularly in-the-wild images. In order to apply our model to the in-the-wild scenarios, we first use in-the-lab data to train the model following the above learning process, and afterwards fine-tune the model with the following two steps. (i) Fine-tune the shape-feature-based expression classifier CL_{Exp}^{S} with in-the-wild face images as in the second learning phase. (ii) Fine-tune the entire model as in the fourth learning phase except that the decoders and 3D shape reconstruction loss are excluded.

3   Experiments

3.1   Datasets and Implementation Details

Three in-the-lab datasets (CK+ [13], MMI [14], Oulu-CASIA [15]) and one in-the-wild dataset (RAF-DB [2]) are used to evaluate our proposed method. **The Extended Cohn-Kanade (CK+) dataset** contains 593 video sequences of 123 subjects with seven types of expressions. Each video sequence shows a shift from neutral expression to the peak expression. **MMI** includes 326 sequences from 32 subjects with each sequence showing the neutral-peak-neutral shift of one of six types of expressions. For both these two datasets, we select one frame of neutral expression and three frames of peak expression from each video sequence as experimental data. **Oulu-CASIA** captures 2,880 video sequences of 80 subjects displaying six types of expressions by using various cameras and lighting sources. In our experiments, we pick the last three peak frames from 480 sequences captured by the VIS system under strong illumination condition. For the above three datasets, ten-fold cross validation is conducted and the average accuracy is reported. **RAF-DB** contains 29,672 face images labelled with basic or compound expressions. We use images with seven basic expressions only, including 12,271 images for training and 3,068 images for testing. All the images are cropped and aligned by Dlib [16].

In order to augment the number of occluded face images, we synthesize occluded images by overlaying various object images (hands, breads, etc.) onto the original non-occluded images in RAF-DB. For CK+, we randomly mask some square regions of varying areas on the face images to generate face images with 8×8 ($R8$), 16×16 ($R16$) and 24×24 ($R24$) occluded regions.

As for the 3D face shape model, we use the mean shape and identity shape bases in BFM2009 [17], and expression shape bases in Facewarehouse [18], resulting in 199-dimensional identity representations and 29-dimensional expression representations. Since the noise component and the expression component share the same classifier in adversarial learning, we set the dimension of noise component as 29 too. For the in-the-lab face images, we utilize the 3D face reconstruction model in [19] to generate the ground truth 3D face shapes. Note that the original non-occluded face images and the corresponding synthetic occluded images share the same ground truth 3D face shapes.

3.2   Results

Results on in-the-lab Data. We first compare our method with state-of-the-art (SOTA) methods for facial expression recognition on occluded images [3,4,20,21] using images with varying occlusion areas that are generated from the CK+ dataset. Results are given in Table 1. As can be seen, our method achieves the best results for the 8×8 and 24×24 occlusion areas, and comparable results for the 16×16 occlusion areas. This proves the effectiveness of our proposed method in conquering the impact of occlusions on facial expression recognition.

Table 1. Recognition accuracy (%) of different methods on CK+ with synthetic occlusions of varying areas.

Methods	R 8	R 16	R 24
WLS-RF [20]	92.20	86.40	74.80
PG-CNN [21]	96.58	95.70	92.86
gACNN [3]	96.58	95.97	<u>94.82</u>
Pan et al. [4]	<u>97.80</u>	**96.86**	94.03
Ours	**97.94**	<u>96.53</u>	**94.89**

Table 2. Recognition accuracy (%) of different methods on three original in-the-lab datasets.

Methods	CK+	MMI	Oulu-CASIA
STM [22]	94.19	75.12	74.59
DTAGN [23]	97.25	70.24	81.46
Lijie et al. [9]	93.30	74.50	-
TRAJ [24]	96.87	-	83.13
Ours	**98.39**	**77.43**	**87.67**

In addition, we also apply our method to the original in-the-lab datasets with comparison to the SOTA accuracy on them. Table 2 summarizes the results. Surprisingly, although the original images in these datasets are free from occlusions, our method overwhelms the counterpart methods on all the three datasets with obvious margins. We believe that this is owing to the fact that factors like illumination and pose variations could essentially result in similar effects of noisy or missing features. The superior performance of our method on these original datasets demonstrates that the proposed adversarial disentangled features learning with 3D supervision can deal with noise beyond occlusions in face images as well.

Table 3. Recognition accuracy of different methods on RAF-DB with synthetic occlusions.

Methods	Accuracy (%)
WGAN [5]	78.35
gACNN [3]	80.54
Pan et al. [4]	81.97
Baseline	76.58
Ours	**82.27**

Table 4. Ablation study results on CK+ with R24 synthetic occlusions.

Texture	Shape	Noise component	Accuracy (%)
✓			93.50
	✓		93.04
	✓	✓	94.13
✓	✓		94.27
✓	✓	✓	**94.89**

Results on in-the-wild Data. The evaluation results on RAF-DB are reported in Table 3. Again, our method achieves the best accuracy among the methods under comparison, thanks to its ability to suppress expression-irrelevant noisy features and meanwhile enhance expression-discriminative features. We also set up a baseline by using the texture feature extractor in Fig. 1 followed by a softmax classifier. As can be seen from Table 3, our method can improve the accuracy of the baseline by about 6%.

Ablation Study. In this experiment, we systematically evaluate the effectiveness of different components in our method by using the CK+ dataset with synthetic occlusions. The results are shown in Table 4, which demonstrate that (i) shape features learned under 3D supervision are effective complementary features to texture features, and (ii) explicitly isolating occlusion-caused noise from facial features does help in recognizing expressions on occluded face images.

4   Conclusion

In this paper, we propose a novel method for facial expression recognition under occlusions. Unlike previous methods, our method introduces an explicit noise component when disentangling facial features and utilizes shape features to complement texture features. We implement the method via adversarial learning and 3D supervision. The state-of-the-art facial expression recognition accuracy achieved by our method on three in-the-lab datasets and one in-the-wild dataset demonstrates that our method not only effectively alleviates the impact of noisy features caused by occlusions and even other factors, but also compensates the lack of discriminative features in occluded regions. In the future, we plan to further improve the method by exploiting attention mechanisms.

Acknowledgment. This work is supported by the National Natural Science Foundation of China (61773270).

References

1. Mollahosseini, A., Hasani, B., Mahoor, M.H.: AffectNet: a database for facial expression, valence, and arousal computing in the wild. IEEE Trans. Affect. Comput. **10**(1), 18–31 (2017)
2. Li, S., Deng, W.: Reliable crowdsourcing and deep locality-preserving learning for unconstrained facial expression recognition. IEEE Trans. Image Proces. **28**(1), 356–370 (2018)
3. Li, Y., Zeng, J., Shan, S., Chen, X.: Occlusion aware facial expression recognition using CON with attention mechanism. IEEE Trans. Image Process. **28**(5), 2439–2450 (2019)
4. Pan, B., Wang, S., Xia, B.: Occluded facial expression recognition enhanced through privileged information. In: Proceedings of the 27th ACM International Conference on Multimedia, pp. 566–573 (2019)
5. Lu, Y., Wang, S., Zhao, W., Zhao, Y.: Wgan-based robust occluded facial expression recognition. IEEE Access **7**, 93594–93610 (2019)
6. Bai, M., Xie, W., Shen, L.: Disentangled feature based adversarial learning for facial expression recognition. In: 2019 IEEE International Conference on Image Processing (ICIP), pp. 31–35. IEEE (2019)
7. Halawa, M., Wöllhaf, M., Vellasques, E., SánchezSanz, U., Hellwich, O.: Learning disentangled expression representations from facial images. arXiv preprint arXiv:2008.07001 (2020)
8. Lekdioui, K., Messoussi, R., Ruichek, Y., Chaabi, Y., Touahni, R.: Facial decomposition for expression recognition using texture/shape descriptors and SVM classifier. Sig. Process. Image Commun. **58**, 300–312 (2017)
9. Li, Jie, Liu, Zhengxi, Zhao, Qijun: Exploring shape deformation in 2D images for facial expression recognition. In: Sun, Zhenan, He, Ran, Feng, Jianjiang, Shan, Shiguang, Guo, Zhenhua (eds.) CCBR 2019. LNCS, vol. 11818, pp. 190–197. Springer, Cham (2019). https://doi.org/10.1007/978-3-030-31456-9_21

10. Liu, F., Zhu, R., Zeng, D., Zhao, Q., Liu, X.: Disentangling features in 3D face shapes for joint face reconstruction and recognition. In: Proceedings of the IEEE Conference on Computer Vision and Pattern Recognition, pp. 5216–5225 (2018)

11. Liu, F., Zhao, Q., Liu, X., Zeng, D.: Joint face alignment and 3d face reconstruction with application to face recognition. IEEE Trans. Pattern Anal. Mach. Intell. **42**(3), 664–678 (2020)

12. Zhu, X., Lei, Z., Liu, X., Shi, H., Li, S.Z.: Face alignment across large poses: a 3D solution. In: 2016 IEEE Conference on Computer Vision and Pattern Recognition (CVPR) (2016)

13. Lucey, P., Cohn, J.F., Kanade, T., Saragih, J., Ambadar, Z., Matthews, I.: The extended cohn-kanade dataset (CK+): a complete dataset for action unit and emotion-specified expression. In: 2010 IEEE Computer Society Conference on Computer Vision and Pattern Recognition-Workshops, pp. 94–101. IEEE (2010)

14. Pantic, M., Valstar, M., Rademaker, R., Maat, L.: Web-based database for facial expression analysis. In: 2005 IEEE International Conference on Multimedia and Expo, pp. 5-pp. IEEE (2005)

15. Zhao, G., Huang, X., Taini, M., othersäInen, M.: Facial expression recognition from near-infrared videos. Image Vis. Comput. **29**(9), 607–619 (2011)

16. Amos, B., Ludwiczuk, B., Satyanarayanan, M., et al.: Openface: a general-purpose face recognition library with mobile applications. CMU Sch. Comput. Sci. **6**(2) (2016)

17. Paysan, P., Knothe, R., Amberg, B., Romdhani, S., Vetter, T.: A 3D face model for pose and illumination invariant face recognition. In: 2009 Sixth IEEE International Conference on Advanced Video and Signal Based Surveillance, pp. 296–301. IEEE (2009)

18. Cao, C., Weng, Y., Zhou, S.: Facewarehouse: a 3D facial expression database for visual computing. IEEE Trans. Visual. Comput. Graph. **20**(3), 413–425 (2013)

19. Zhu, X., Lei, Z., Yan, J., et al.: High-fidelity pose and expression normalization for face recognition in the wild. In: Proceedings of the IEEE Conference on Computer Vision and Pattern Recognition, pp. 787–796 (2015)

20. Dapogny, A., Bailly, K., Dubuisson, S.: Confidence-weighted local expression predictions for occlusion handling in expression recognition and action unit detection. Int. J. Comput. Vis. **126**(2–4), 255–271 (2018)

21. Li, Y., Zeng, J., Shan, S., Chen, X.: Patch-gated CNN for occlusion-aware facial expression recognition. In: 2018 24th International Conference on Pattern Recognition (ICPR), pp. 2209–2214. IEEE (2018)

22. Liu, M., Shan, S., Wang, R., Chen, X.: Learning expressionlets on spatio-temporal manifold for dynamic facial expression recognition. In: Proceedings of the IEEE Conference on Computer Vision and Pattern Recognition, pp. 1749–1756 (2014)

23. Jung, H., Lee, S., Yim, J., Park, S., Kim, J.: Joint fine-tuning in deep neural networks for facial expression recognition. In: Proceedings of the IEEE International Conference on Computer Vision, pp. 2983–2991 (2015)

24. Kacem, A., Daoudi, M., et al.: A novel space-time representation on the positive semidefinite cone for facial expression recognition. In: Proceedings of the IEEE International Conference on Computer Vision, pp. 3180–3189 (2017)

Automatically Distinguishing Adult from Young Giant Pandas Based on Their Call

Yanqiu Zhang[1], Rong Hou[3,4], Longyin Guo[1], Peng Liu[3,4], Shan Zhang[3,4],
Peng Chen[3,4(✉)], and Qijun Zhao[1,2(✉)]

[1] National Key Laboratory of Fundamental Science on Synthetic Vision,
Sichuan University, Chengdu, Sichuan, People's Republic of China
[2] College of Computer Science, Sichuan University, Chengdu, Sichuan,
People's Republic of China
qjzhao@scu.edu.cn
[3] Chengdu Research Base of Giant Panda Breeding, Sichuan Key Laboratory
of Conservation Biology for Endangered Wildlife, Chengdu, Sichuan,
People's Republic of China
[4] Sichuan Academy of Giant Panda, Chengdu 610086, People's Republic of China

Abstract. Knowing the number of adult and young individuals in the giant panda population is of significant in protecting them. Traditionally, this is done by field investigation, which has high cost and low time efficiency. We approach the problem as a two-class soft-biometric recognition task: given a segment that records the call of a giant panda, we aim to classify the giant panda into adult or young. We construct 1,405 call clips of adult giant panda and 285 call clips of young giant panda and propose a framework for vocal-based giant panda age group classification. Based on the framework, we evaluate the effectiveness of various acoustic features and deep neural networks. The results suggest that (i) adult and young giant pandas show different characteristics in high-frequency acoustic features, (ii) it is feasible to automatically distinguish between adult and young giant pandas based on their call with deeply learned features.

Keywords: Age group classification · Acoustic features ·
Soft-biometric · Giant panda · Wildlife conservation

1 Introduction

Age, as a soft biometric trait, has important research significance [1]. There are many literatures about the prediction of human age [2–4]. However, only a few studies on the age prediction of animals. For giant pandas, the age structure is related to the sustainability of the population, so it is very important to know the age of them. Sound is one of the main ways of animal communication [5]. It has the advantages of long transmission distance, strong penetration and rich information. Although there are many literatures on vocal-based age prediction [4,6–8], they are all about human beings. It is of great interests to study vocal-based age prediction of giant pandas.

© Springer Nature Switzerland AG 2021
J. Feng et al. (Eds.): CCBR 2021, LNCS 12878, pp. 92–101, 2021.
https://doi.org/10.1007/978-3-030-86608-2_11

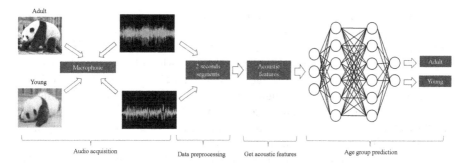

Fig. 1. The call is collected from the Chengdu Research Base of Giant Panda Breeding. We design a framework to predict whether the sound belongs to adult giant panda or young giant panda, so as to analyze the age composition of giant panda.

When using audio signal as the input of network, it is usually necessary to transform the original audio signal into Mel-frequency Cepstral Coefficients (MFCC). MFCC is a feature widely used in automatic speech and speaker recognition. Mel frequency is proposed based on human auditory characteristics. Since human ears are more sensitive to low-frequency signals, MFCC mainly extracts low-frequency information in the signal. In contrast, high-frequency information may play important roles in vocal-based animal communication. Yet, existing literatures almost do not mention how to deal with high-frequency signals of animals. We will for the first time investigate the potential of automatically recognizing the age groups of individual giant pandas (i.e., adult or young) based on their call by using deep neural networks.

We will also study the relative contribution of high-frequency components of the call signal of giant pandas to the age prediction. The rest of this paper is organized as follows. Section 2 briefly introduces related work. Sections 3 and 4, respectively, introduce the dataset and the methods used in this study. Section 5 then presents and analyzes the experimental results. Section 6 finally concludes the paper.

2 Related Work

Due to the increasing awareness of ecological environment protection, researchers began to apply speech recognition algorithms for animals [9]. It is already possible to identify species of birds according to their vocal features [10]. Hendrik et al. constructed a new model to recognize the types of killer whale call, and successfully visualize the feature map [11]. In particular to giant pandas, some researchers proposed a method to recognize individual giant pandas from their call, achieving accuracy of 88.33% on a set of 20 individuals [12]. Others devised a system to automatically predict the mating success of giant pandas based on their call during breeding encounters [13]. However, for both [13] and [12], they do not predict the age of giant pandas, and the subjects are adult giant pandas, and no experiments are conducted on young giant pandas. In [12], the recognition of adult giant panda is not an end-to-end automatic recognition system. The feature of MFCC is extracted in [13], which does not explain the influence of high-frequency information on the speech recognition of giant panda.

The method of determining the age of giant panda is based on chemical signal analysis [14], such as analyzing their excreta. However, it takes a long time for human to collect giant panda's excreta, at which time the chemical signal is to lose effectiveness [15]. So, it is difficult for human to use this information to quickly determine the age groups of the giant panda.

The call of giant pandas contain extremely rich information and giant pandas also have obvious changes in their vocalization [16]. The method of using call for predicting the age has not yet appeared. Based on the above reasons, we use deep learning to predict the age groups of giant pandas by call.

3   Dataset

3.1   Data Acquisition

The data used in this paper are acquired at the Chengdu Research Base of Giant Panda Breeding, by using Shure VP89m, TASCAM DR-100MKII and SONY PCM-D100. The call record is converted from dual channel to single channel, and the sampling rate of single channel call is normalized to 44,100 Hz. There are 1,009 call segments of adult giant pandas, which include the call of both female and male giant pandas. The duration of each call lasts from 0.29 s to 3.25 s. We collect the call from five young giant pandas, and there are 25 calls, each lasting from 5.67 s to 1 minute and 5 s.

3.2   Data Preprocessing

In order to ensure the consistency of data dimensions during training, the original call clips of giant pandas are divided into 2 s clips without overlap, and the segments whose duration is shorter than 2 s are expanded to 2 s via zero-padding on the log-mel spectrum. In this study, we mainly focus on investigating whether the call of giant pandas can reveal their age groups, specifically, young and adult. Therefore, we manually exclude the call clips that are contaminated by other sounds (e.g., human voice or collision sounds between objects). Finally, we obtain 285 call clips of young giant pandas, and 1,405 call clips of adult giant pandas.

Table 1. Duration of call data used in this study.

Age group	Adult	Young
Training data	1,560 s	300 s
Validation data	60 s	90 s
Test data	135.2 s	158.4 s

The overall duration of these call clips are 38.4 min. We divide these data into three subsets, i.e., training, validation and test data. Table 1 summarizes the duration of the call data used in this study.

According to the data acquisition conditions in this study, the call data of young giant pandas have relatively weak background noise, while those of adult ones have some strong background noise (e.g., sound of working air-conditioners). To avoid such bias in the data, we first collect some call data of only background sound appearing in the data of adult giant pandas, and then integrate them into the call of young giant pandas via mixing the signal to enforce that the call data of young and adult giant pandas share similar background noise.

Considering the obvious imbalance between the call data of adult and young giant pandas, we augment the data of young giant pandas by adding Gaussian noise and applying SpecAugment [17]. In SpecAugment, we apply frequency masking by adding a mask with value of 0 to the frequency axis of log-mel spectrum, and time masking by adding a mask with value of 0 to the time axis. After the aforementioned preprocessing of background noise synthesis and augment young giant panda data, the training data for young and adult giant pandas both have 1,280 call clips.

4   Method

We compare three acoustic features, MFCC feature, Pre-emphasis feature and IMFCC feature, by six neural networks to analyze their influence on giant panda age group classification.

4.1   Acoustic Feature

MFCC (Mel-frequency Cepstral Coefficients) is a feature widely used in automatic speech and speaker recognition. It assumes that the human ear is more sensitive to the low-frequency part, which is extracted by triangle mel filter.

IMFCC (Invert Mel-frequency Cepstral Coefficients) is a way to extract high-frequency information in audio data. It uses the inverted triangle mel filter, which is more tightly in the high-frequency information part and can extract more high-frequency information.

Pre-emphasis operation can reduce the loss of high-frequency. The so-called Pre-emphasis is to increase the resolution of high-frequency signal in the original audio signal. This way, in the subsequent extraction of MFCC, the damage of high-frequency signal is reduced and more comprehensive information is obtained.

4.2   Input Feature

Three types of input features are considered in this study. 1) MFCC features F_M extracted directly by triangle mel filter M. 2) The raw signal z with Pre-emphasis H, then triangle mel filter M is used to extract acoustic features, and the extracted features are fused with F_M. The final input feature is multi-scale feature F_P. As shown in formula (1). 3) The original signal z is extracted by invert triangle filter I to get IMFCC features, and then fused with F_M to get multi-scale feature F_I. As shown in formula (2).

$$F_P = \{M(H(z)), F_M\} . \tag{1}$$

$$F_I = \{I(z), F_M\} . \tag{2}$$

4.3 Network Structure

In this paper, six of deep networks are selected for comparative evaluation: AlexNet [18], Xception [19], SENet [20], CRNN [21], Xcep-RNN, and Xcep-RNN-attention. CNN has a very good effect for extracting local features, which helps to extract detailed information from call. However, for voice, the recurrent neural network is more useful because of the characteristics of temporal series data. So, we chose the very typical network in CNN and RNN for experiments.

Xcep-RNN is changing the ordinary convolution of CRNN to depthwise separable convolution, so that the local information extracted from the sample can be realized cross channel interaction and information integration through 1×1 convolution to obtain more comprehensive information. On this basis, the attention [22] is added to obtain more important feature information.

5 Experiments

All the CNN input size is $(180, 32, 1)$, RNN input size is $(180, 32)$. Except for SENet, others batch size are 16, and the SENet is 8. The learning rate is 10^{-3}, and the loss is cross entropy. Each network is trained three times, and 100 epochs each time. The models used in the test are the best three models saved in each network training, and the final evaluation index is the average accuracy of the three models. All experiments are done on Ubuntu, and use the NVIDIA GTX 1070 to help train networks.

5.1 The Effectiveness of Augmentation

We augment the young giant panda call data and experiment the effectiveness of it. The acoustic feature is MFCC. Table 2 shows the result. It obvious to see after augmenting the data, the accuracy of young giant panda has been greatly improved.

Table 2. The effectiveness of augmenting young giant panda data.

Augmentation	Model	AlexNet	Xception	SENet	CRNN	X-RNN	X-RNN-a
No	All	76.88%	78.13%	80.63%	71.25%	71.25%	75.63%
	Adult	91.25%	92.50%	93.75%	81.25%	81.25%	85.00%
	Young	62.50%	63.75%	67.50%	61.25%	61.25%	66.25%
Yes	All	89.38%	90.63%	90.63%	81.88%	81.25%	84.38%
	Adult	97.50%	95.00%	97.50%	83.75%	82.50%	85.00%
	Young	81.25%	86.25%	83.75%	80.00%	80.00%	83.75%

5.2   Compare the Effectiveness of MFCC and Pre-emphasis

The multi-scale feature F_P obtained by this operation will be put into the network for experiment. The experimental results are shown in Table 3.

Table 3. The result of pre-emphasis.

Model	AlexNet	Xception	SENet	CRNN	X-RNN	X-RNN-a
All	87.50%	88.13%	90.63%	82.50%	81.25%	85.63%
Adult	97.50%	95.00%	97.50%	86.25%	85.00%	88.75%
Young	77.50%	81.25%	83.75%	78.75%	77.50%	82.50%

In the Pre-emphasis experiment, the experimental accuracy of CNN is better than that of RNN. The accuracy of SENet is highest for both adult and young pandas, with adult panda prediction accuracy reaching 97.50% and young panda prediction accuracy 83.75%. In order to better observe the experimental results of MFCC and Pre-emphasis, the adult and young giant panda prediction accuracy in the two experiments is respectively made into a line chart, as shown in Fig. 2.

As Fig. 2 shows, for the prediction accuracy of adult giant panda, the high-frequency information obtained by Pre-emphasis is helpful to the prediction of adult giant panda. For the young giant panda, the high-frequency information obtained by Pre-emphasis is not conducive to the prediction of the young giant panda.

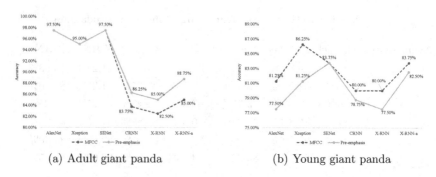

(a) Adult giant panda   (b) Young giant panda

Fig. 2. Prediction accuracy of adult and young giant panda by MFCC and pre-emphasis.

5.3   Compare the Effectiveness of MFCC and IMFCC

The multi-scale feature F_I is put in six deep networks. The results are shown in Table 4.

Table 4. The result of IMFCC.

Model	AlexNet	Xception	SENet	CRNN	X-RNN	X-RNN-a
All	86.25%	86.88%	90.00%	81.25%	83.13%	86.88%
Adult	98.75%	97.50%	97.50%	87.50%	87.50%	92.50%
Young	73.75%	76.25%	82.50%	75.00%	78.75%	81.25%

In this experiment, SENet still works best. Similarly, the experimental results of IMFCC and MFCC are plotted by line chart, as shown in Fig. 3.

Like the Pre-emphasis features, the prediction accuracy of adult giant panda is improved after using IMFCC. The result shows that the young giant panda's prediction accuracy of IMFCC is lower than that of MFCC.

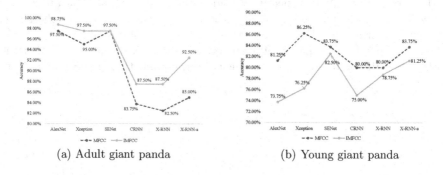

(a) Adult giant panda   (b) Young giant panda

Fig. 3. Prediction accuracy of adult and young giant panda by MFCC and IMFCC.

5.4   Discussion on the Results

Through deep learning to analyze the call of giant pandas, we can effectively recognize the age structure of giant pandas. Pre-emphasis and IMFCC operations are performed on the data to extract the high-frequency information of giant panda call. The experimental results show that both operations can improve the prediction accuracy of adult giant pandas and reduce the prediction accuracy of young giant pandas.

Some literatures can also support our experimental results. These literatures covers not only computer science, but also zoology. The theoretical support of zoological literatures make our results more reliable. The high-frequency information of adult giant panda has certain biological characteristics [12,23], while the high-frequency part of young giant panda is mostly gas noise [24], which is not conducive to the prediction of young giant panda. The research of giant panda age structure prediction based on call is of great application value to the protection and breeding of giant pandas in the wild.

6   Conclusion

We collect a dataset about giant panda call including adult and young, and predict giant panda age groups via their call automatically for the first time. We do experiments on three different acoustic characteristics to analyze the influence of high-frequency signal on giant panda age groups prediction. The results show that it is feasible to automatically distinguish between adult and young giant pandas based on their call with deeply learned features. The age groups prediction of giant pandas based on call is helpful to analyze the age structure of giant pandas in the wild. In the future work, we will try to classify the gender information of giant pandas by their call. We hope to design a set of giant panda attributes detection system based on call.

Acknowledgments. This work was supported by the Chengdu Research Base of Giant Panda Breeding [No. 2021CPB-C01; No. CPB2018-02; No. 2020CPB-C09; No. 2021CPB-B06].

References

1. Anda, F., Becker, B.A., Lillis, D., Le-Khac, N.A., Scanlon, M.: Assessing the influencing factors on the accuracy of underage facial age estimation. In: The 6th IEEE International Conference on Cyber Security and Protection of Digital Services (Cyber Security). (2020)
2. Guo, G., Yun, F., Huang, T.S., Dyer, C.R.: Locally adjusted robust regression for human age estimation. In: IEEE Workshop on Applications of Computer Vision (2008)

3. Hernandez-Ortega, J., Morales, A., Fierrez, J., Acien, A.: Detecting age groups using touch interaction based on neuromotor characteristics. Electr. Lett. **53**(20), 1349–1350 (2017)

4. Li, X., Malebary, S., Qu, X., Ji, X., Xu, W.: iCare: automatic and user-friendly child identification on smartphones. In: the 19th International Workshop (2018)

5. Liuni, M., Ardaillon, L., Bonal, L., Seropian, L., Aucouturier, J.-J.: ANGUS: real-time manipulation of vocal roughness for emotional speech transformations. arXiv preprint arXiv:2008.11241 (2020)

6. Ming, L., Han, K.J., Narayanan, S.: Automatic speaker age and gender recognition using acoustic and prosodic level information fusion. Comput. Speech Lang. **27**(1), 151–167 (2013)

7. Meinedo, H., Trancoso, I.: Age and gender classification using fusion of acoustic and prosodic features. In: Interspeech Conference of the International Speech Communication Association, Makuhari, Chiba, Japan, September 2010

8. Kaushik, M., Pham, V.T., Chng, E.S.: End-to-end speaker height and age estimation using attention mechanism with LSTM-RNN. arXiv preprint arXiv:2101.05056 (2021)

9. Oikarinen, T., Srinivasan, K., Meisner, O., Hyman, J.B., Parmar, S., Fanucci-Kiss, A., Desimone, R., Landman, R., Feng, G.: Deep convolutional network for animal sound classification and source attribution using dual audio recordings. J. Acoust. Soc. Am. **145**(2), 654–662 (2019)

10. Solomes, A.M., Dan, S.: Efficient bird sound detection on the bela embedded system. In: ICASSP 2020–2020 IEEE International Conference on Acoustics, Speech and Signal Processing (ICASSP) (2020)

11. Schröter, H., Nöth, E., Maier, A., Cheng, R., Barth, V., Bergler, C.: Segmentation, classification, and visualization of orca calls using deep learning. In: ICASSP 2019–2019 IEEE International Conference on Acoustics, Speech and Signal Processing (ICASSP), pp. 8231–8235 IEEE (2019)

12. Lu, H.: Analysis and research of giant panda individual identification system based on voiceprint (2019)

13. Yan, W., et al.: Automatically predicting giant panda mating success based on acoustic features. Glob. Ecol. Conserv. **24**, e01301 (2020)

14. White, A.M., Zhang, H.: Chemical communication in the giant panda (ailuropoda melanoleuca): the role of age in the signaller and assessor. J. Zool. **259**(2), 171–178 (2003)

15. Yuan, H., Liu, D., Wei, R., Sun, L., Zhang, S.: Anogenital gland secretions code for sex and age in the giant panda, ailuropoda melanoleuca. Can. J. Zool. **82**(10), 1596–1604(9) (2004)

16. Charlton, B.D., Owen, M.A., Keating, J.L., Martin-Wintle, M.S., Swaisgood, R.R.: Sound transmission in a bamboo forest and its implications for information transfer in giant panda (ailuropoda melanoleuca) bleats. Sci. Rep. **8**(1) (2018)

17. Park, D.S., et al.: Specaugment: a simple data augmentation method for automatic speech recognition. In: Interspeech 2019 (2019)

18. Krizhevsky, A., Sutskever, I., Hinton, G.: Imagenet classification with deep convolutional neural networks. Adv. Neural Inf. Process. Syst. **25**(2) (2012)

19. Chollet, F.: Xception: Deep learning with depthwise separable convolutions. In: 2017 IEEE Conference on Computer Vision and Pattern Recognition (CVPR) (2017)

20. Hu, J., Shen, L., Sun, G.: Squeeze-and-excitation networks. In: Proceedings of the IEEE Conference on Computer Vision and Pattern Recognition, pp. 7132–7141 (2018)

21. Shi, B., Xiang, B., Cong, Y.: An end-to-end trainable neural network for image-based sequence recognition and its application to scene text recognition. IEEE Trans. Patt. Anal. Mach. Intell. **39**(11), 2298–2304 (2016)
22. Vaswani, A., et al.: Attention is all you need. arXiv (2017)
23. Jing Zhu, Z.M.: Estrus calls of giant pandas and their behavioral significance. Curr. Zool. (1987)
24. Cannan Zhao, P.W.: The sound spectrum analysis of calls in the bay giant panda. Discov. Nat. (1988)

Alzheimer's Disease Prediction via the Association of Single Nucleotide Polymorphism with Brain Regions

Yafeng Li, Yiyao Liu, Tianfu Wang, and Baiying Lei[✉]

National-Region Key Technology Engineering Laboratory for Medical Ultrasound, Guangdong Key Laboratory for Biomedical Measurements and Ultrasound Imaging, School of Biomedical Engineering, Health Science Center, Shenzhen University, Shenzhen 518060, China
leiby@szu.edu.cn

Abstract. Imaging genomics is an effective tool in the detection and causative factor analysis of Alzheimer's disease (AD). Based on single nucleotide polymorphism (SNP) and structural magnetic resonance imaging (MRI) data, we propose a novel AD analysis model using multi-modal data fusion and multi-detection model fusion. Firstly, based on the characteristics of SNP data, we fully extract highly representative features. Secondly, the fused data are used to construct fusion features. Finally, according to the characteristics of the fused data, we design a fused prediction model with multiple machine learning models. The model integrates four machine learning models and feeds them into the final XGBoost model for AD prediction. The experimental results show that the data fusion method and the fusion model of multiple machine learning models proposed in this paper can effectively improve the prediction accuracy. Our model can identify AD patients and detect abnormal brain regions and risk SNPs associated with AD, which can perform the association of risk SNPs with abnormal brain regions.

Keywords: Imaging genomics · Alzheimer's disease · Single nucleotide polymorphism · Magnetic resonance imaging · Fusion

1 Introduction

Alzheimer's disease (AD) is a chronic neurodegenerative disease, which is more common in people over 65 years old [1, 2]. Its main clinical manifestations are memory impairment, behavioral disorder and cognitive impairment [3]. According to a report by the Alzheimer's Association (2021), AD is considered to be the sixth leading cause of death in the United States [4]. In addition, there are more than 56 million people with AD worldwide. The number is expected to reach 152 million by 2050 [4], which greatly affects the development of the society. Therefore, in-depth understanding of the pathogenesis of AD is very necessary, accurate early diagnosis will help patients to receive treatment as soon as possible and delay the process of AD.

With the progress and development of imaging technology, scientists began to apply imaging technology for the diagnosis of AD, and achieved great success [5]. Structural

J. Feng et al. (Eds.): CCBR 2021, LNCS 12878, pp. 102–111, 2021.
https://doi.org/10.1007/978-3-030-86608-2_12

magnetic resonance imaging (MRI) is an advanced imaging technique used to measure brain morphometry, which is very sensitive to neurodegeneration. Therefore, MRI can be used to predict the progression of AD [6, 7]. On the other hand, with the development of Genome-wide association study (GWAS), researchers applied this technology in the field of AD and analyzed the related risk genes [8]. Based on the development of imaging technology and genomics, the imaging genomics studying the connection between genes and brain structure and functions are explored by combining two technologies [9].

For multi-modal data in the medical field, how to extract important features from small sample high-dimensional data is quite critical. In terms of gene data, it can extract significant SNP as a feature in the experiment. For example, Huang *et al.* extracted SNP as genetic data from known AD risk genes within the 20 kb range of the risk gene boundary [10]. Bi *et al.* first screened the gene of SNP as a candidate gene, and then extracted the SNP sequence under the gene, and intercepted the extracted SNP according to the set threshold range [11]. Kang *et al.* first performed SNP correlation analysis through GWAS to extract SNPs for disease by relevance [12]. It is found that the SNP mapped by known risk genes as training data is unable to predict potential risk genes and cannot match their own sample population. According to the length of the gene sequence, the potential pathogenic SNP may be omitted.

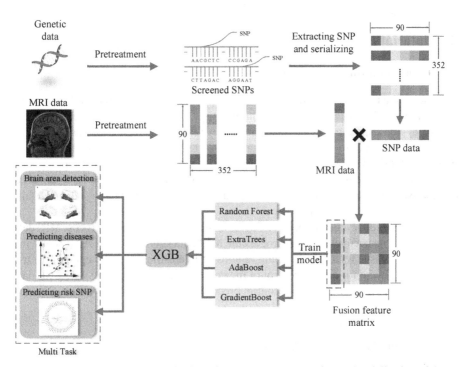

Fig. 1. Our process is roughly divided into three parts: pre-processing and serialization of data, fusion of multimodal data, and prediction and analysis of fusion models.

Gray *et al.* successfully used random forest algorithms for the multi-modal classification of AD [13], which shows that the machine learning algorithm can be effectively used for disease classification. Current research mostly lacks of multimodal data fusion research, predictive solutions, construction and prediction framework. In the recognition of disease-related biomarkers, it is mostly based on the association between genetic variations such as SNP and quantitative trait [14, 15]. Bi *et al.* proposed a new multimodal data fusion training framework for disease prediction and analysis of pathogenic brain regions [16]. However, they all need to ignore the complex one-to-many relationship between a single SNP and multiple brain regions, and thus fails to study the relationship between a single SNP and multiple brain regions.

In order to solve the above problems and challenges, we propose a new multi-modal data fusion multi-detection model fusion framework to study the relationship between a single SNP and multiple brain regions. First of all, we use association analysis in GWAS technology to extract highly relevant SNP as our genetic data to solve the problem of high dimension of genetic data. Secondly, we preprocess gene data, and fuse MRI data through a matrix multiplication. Finally, we build a fusion prediction framework of multiple machine learning models to predict pathogenic brain regions and risk genes. The multimodal data fusion multi-detection model fusion framework of AD is shown in Fig. 1.

2   Material and Methodology

2.1   Data Acquisition and Preprocessing

The data of the research work in this paper come from Alzheimer's Disease Neuroimaging Initiative (ADNI) database (http://adni.loni.usc.edu/). In this study, we use the MRI data of 814 cases in the ADNI1 database, and we find the corresponding gene data of 370 cases according to the data of 814 cases. 370 cases of genetic data are obtained by using Human 610-Quad Bead Chip in ADNI data. According to the preprocessing operation of genetic data, there are 352 cases of data left, of which 300 cases are used as experimental data, and the remaining 52 cases are used as our final test data. Details of the data set are shown in Table 1.

In order to reduce the interference of noise in the experiment, we preprocess MRI data and SNP data respectively. We preprocess the MRI data similar to [17]. After removing 26 cerebellar tissue regions, we obtain regions of interest in 90 brain regions. We use plink [18] software for quality control of the genetic data. We preprocess the SNP data according to [19]. After the quality control procedure, 352 subjects and 499140 SNP are finally retained.

2.2   Construction of Fusion Features

The fusion of multimodal data is a challenging task. Most current studies have performed fusion analysis of genetic and image data by different methods [12, 19], but these studies did not adequately consider the characteristics of genetic and image data. Therefore, in this paper, a new fusion scheme is designed based on the characteristics of genetic

Table 1. Basic information about AD and NC data.

Data	Number	Age (years) (Mean ± SD)	Gender (M/F)	Weight (kg) (Mean ± SD)
AD	160	75.43 ± 7.48	85/75	72.21 ± 13.69
NC	192	75.73 ± 4.88	106/86	76.38 ± 15.34

data and MRI data. We sequence the genetic data and combine the SNP data with the corresponding brain regions, which are more interpretable compared to other methods. The specific integration steps are as follows.

1) We use a chi-square test to analyze the association of the SNP data of the first 300 individuals and extract the first 90 SNP that were highly correlated with disease from them.
2) We extract 90 SNP for all 352 samples and convert the four base information (A, C, G, T) in SNPs into the corresponding numbers (1, 2, 3, 4).
3) We replace the missing allele information on one SNP with 00 to reduce the impact of the missing value in our experiment.
4) We normalize the SNP data to the range of −1 and 1 to better fuse the SNP data and MRI data.
5) We perform a multiplicative fusion operation on the two modal data.

2.3 Model Fusion for Prediction

In this paper, we explore the effect of a single gene on multiple brain regions by extracting single SNP and analyzing them one by one, so as to avoid the effect of multiple genes in the experimental results. The specific steps are as follows.

1) We put 300 cases of fused data into four models trained in Random Forest (RF), Extreme Random Tree (ET), Adaboost (ADA), and Gradient Boosting (GB).
2) The experiment uses 5-fold cross-validation.
3) In this paper, the predicted results of the four models are used as input to train the XGBoost model. Thus, we complete our model fusion training.
4) We use 52 cases data as the test dataset to validate the fusion model.

3 Experimental Results

3.1 Model Performance and Comparison

When tested on the test dataset, the data fusion method and the fusion model based on multiple machine learning models can address the problem of single SNP with multiple brain regions. The prediction accuracy for diseases reached 84.61% on the fused data of 42 single SNP and MRI sequences and 90.38% on the fused data of 48 single SNP and ROI sequences. Based on our experimental results, our model successfully classified SNPs into 42 SNPs with pathogenic risk and 48 SNPs with potential pathogenic risk.

All models in the ablation experiment, except the GB model, are able to distinguish between risk SNPs and common SNPs, which illustrates the effectiveness of our data fusion. Among all models, our model has the highest accuracy in predicting disease under risk SNP, which indicates that the fusion model has good classification performance. The results are shown in Fig. 2.

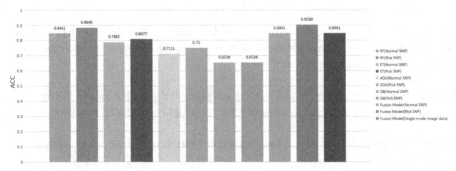

Fig. 2. Comparison of prediction accuracy of different machine learning models. *Normal SNP*: Predicted probability under the fusion of risk-free SNP and MRI data. *Risk SNP*: Predicted probability under the fusion of risk SNP and MRI data. *Single-mode image data*: Predicted probability under unimodal MRI data. *RF*: Random Forest model. *ET*: Extreme Random Tree model. *ADA*: Adaboost model. *GB*: Gradient Boosting model. *Fusion Model*: The fusion model.

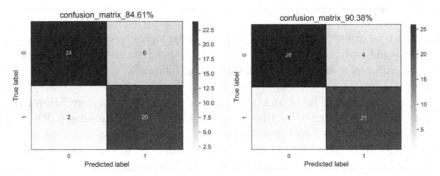

Fig. 3. Multi-detection fusion prediction performance. *0*: NC, *1*: AD. On the left is the predicted probability of the fusion model under the fusion of risk-free SNP and MRI data, and on the right is the predicted probability of the fusion model under the fusion of risk SNP and MRI data.

3.2 Abnormal Brain Regions Prediction

We extract the risk SNP from the fusion model with MRI fusion data features as shown in Fig. 4. The analysis of the fusion data of the SNP with potential pathogenic risk from the multimodal data shows that there are a total of 12 distinct brain abnormal regions. The abnormal regions of the brain are the left region of the hippocampus, the right region of the hippocampus, the left region of the parahippocampal gyrus, the right region of the parahippocampal gyrus, the left region of the inferior temporal gyrus, the right region of the inferior temporal gyrus, the left region of the middle temporal gyrus, the right region of the middle temporal gyrus, the left region of the syrinx, the right region of the syrinx, the left region of the amygdala and the right region of the amygdala. The most obvious abnormalities were found in the left region of the hippocampus, which may reveal that the potential pathogenic risk SNP has a pathogenic effect by significantly affecting the left region of the hippocampus in this brain region.

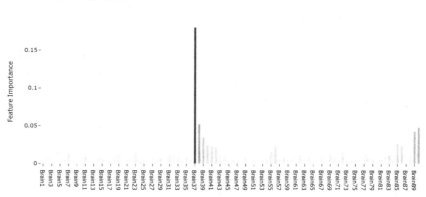

Fig. 4. SNP Feature importance with MRI fusion data. The x-axis indicates the 90 brain regions in the experiment.

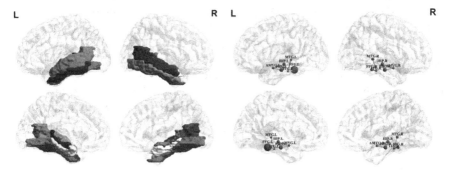

Fig. 5. Schematic diagram of the structure and connectivity of the first 12 abnormal brain regions.

We present the brain regions at potential pathogenic risk for SNP action and the corresponding brain structure connectivity maps on the structural brain map, as shown in Figs. 5 and 6.

3.3 Predicting Risk Genes

Based on the model proposed in this paper, we effectively distinguish between SNP without pathogenic risk and SNP with potential pathogenic risk. Among these 90 SNP,

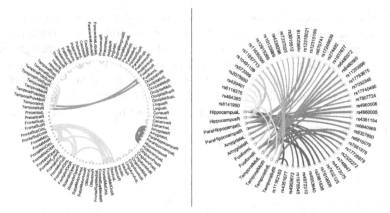

Fig. 6. Left image. The first 12 abnormal brain regions were connected to the circle map. Right image. Schematic representation of the optimal brain region effects of a single SNP. Twelve of the nodes indicate brain regions with obvious abnormalities, and 48 nodes (beginning with rs) indicate SNP with potential pathogenic risk.

42 SNP without pathogenic risk and 48 SNP with potential pathogenic risk were identified. Among the potential pathogenic risk SNP, we learn that 25 SNP are known gene fragments or within 2 kb of the gene by querying the NCBI website (https://www.ncbi. nlm.nih.gov/). For example: rs2075650 on gene TOMM40, rs439401 in the 2 kb range of APOE gene, rs6480565, rs6480572, rs1937677 on gene PRKG1, rs17728979 on gene KIAA0232, etc.

Among these 48 SNP, the pathogenicity has been confirmed in several genomic studies on AD. For example, rs439401 is located in the E2, E4LD cluster of the APOE-APOC1 intergenic region involved in the induction of neuroinflammation and AD [20]. Zhao *et al.* recruited 230 individuals and found that APOC1 and TOMM40 rs2075650 polymorphisms may be independent risk factors of developing AD [21]. In addition, we reflect the brain regions where each SNP acted most strongly on Fig. 7. The brain regions where a single SNP acts preferentially are the left region of the parahippocampal gyrus, the left region of the hippocampus, the left region of the syrinx, the right region of the hippocampus, and the right region of the syrinx.

4   Discussion

4.1   Comparison with Existing Studies

The fusion of multi-modal data for prediction is a common challenge in AD disease diagnosis. In comparison with existing studies, our work focuses on data fusion and overall framework design with the aim of establishing a mapping relationship from genes to brain regions and then from brain regions to genes. Compared with the work of [17], the fusion method of genetic and MRI data proposed in this paper fully takes into account the fact that genetic data usually appear as allelic information, interpolates the missing information, and normalizes the genetic information to be on the same scale as our pre-processed MRI data. Based on the work in this paper, we analyze the brain regions with the strongest single SNP effects and also identify the SNP with the highest association in each brain region.

4.2 Abnormal Brain Regions and Pathogenic Genes

Killiany *et al.* showed that atrophic changes occur within the hippocampus as AD progresses measurable on MRI [22]. The results emphasized the importance of parahippocampal atrophy as an early biomarker of AD [23]. Our experimental results also exactly reflect these abnormal brain regions. According to study [3], neurodegenerative diseases including AD stem from the abnormal accumulation of harmful proteins in the nervous system. The PRKG1 proteins play a vital role in regulating cardiovascular and neuronal functions. The PRKG1 gene regulates the expression of protein kinase, which catalyzes protein phosphorylation. If this gene is mutated, it may lead to abnormal protein phosphorylation, which may lead to abnormal changes in protein activity and eventually to the accumulation of harmful proteins.

4.3 Limitations and Future Work

Although our research work has yielded some good results, the work still has some shortcomings. 1) Small sample size. In future work, we will collect and use as many samples as possible to study the connection between genes and brain regions in depth. 2) The occurrence of disease is multifaceted, and it is not enough to fuse genetic data and imaging data alone. In future work, we will fully consider and fuse patient clinical information, transcriptome and other information in our experiments.

5 Conclusion

In this paper, we have conducted a research work on a multimodal data fusion and multiple machine learning model fusion frameworks for AD. The contributions of this work are as follows. 1) We successfully fuse the image data with gene data, and enable the model to effectively identify SNPs with potential pathogenic risk in subsequent predictive analysis. 2) We build a fusion prediction model with multiple machine learning models, which has good classification performance and a prediction accuracy of 90% for AD diseases. 3) With the features extracted by the model, we detect strong association pairs between single SNP and brain regions. We identify abnormal brain regions and SNP with potential pathogenic risk for AD such as hippocampus, parahippocampal gyrus, rs2075650, rs439401. These research works are important for the diagnosis of AD and multi-dimensional analysis of pathogenic factors.

References

1. Kucmanski, L.S., Zenevicz, L., Geremia, D.S., Madureira, V.S.F., Silva, T.G.d., Souza, S.S.D.: Alzheimer's desease: challenges faced by family caregivers. J. Revista Brasileira de Geriatria e Gerontologia. **196**, 1022–1029 (2016)

2. Khachaturian, Z.S.: Diagnosis of Alzheimer's disease. J. Arch. Neurol. **4211**, 1097–1105 (1985)
3. Mucke, L.: Alzheimer's disease. J. Nat. **4617266**, 895–897 (2009)
4. Association, A.S.: 2021 Alzheimer's disease facts and figures. J. Alzheimer's Dementia **173**, 327–406 (2021)
5. Marchitelli, R., et al.: Simultaneous resting-state FDG-PET/fMRI in Alzheimer disease: relationship between glucose metabolism and intrinsic activity. J. Neuroimage. **176**, 246–258 (2018)
6. McEvoy, L.K., et al.: Alzheimer disease: quantitative structural neuroimaging for detection and prediction of clinical and structural changes in mild cognitive impairment. J. Radiol. **2511**, 195–205 (2009)
7. Vemuri, P., Jack, C.R.: Role of structural MRI in Alzheimer's disease. J. Alzheimer Res. Therapy **24**, 1–10 (2010)
8. Feulner, T., Laws, S., Friedrich, P., Wagenpfeil, S., Wurst, S., Riehle, C., et al.: Examination of the current top candidate genes for AD in a genome-wide association study. J. Mole. Psychiatr. **157**, 756–766 (2010)
9. Hariri, A.R., Drabant, E.M., Weinberger, D.R.: Imaging genetics: perspectives from studies of genetically driven variation in serotonin function and corticolimbic affective processing. J. Biol. Psychiatr. **5910**, 888–897 (2006)
10. Huang, M., Chen, X., Yu, Y., Lai, H., Feng, Q.: Imaging genetics study based on a temporal group sparse regression and additive model for biomarker detection of Alzheimer's Disease. J. IEEE Trans. Med. Imaging 40, 1461–1473 (2021)
11. Bi, X.-A., Hu, X., Wu, H., Wang, Y.: Multimodal data analysis of Alzheimer's disease based on clustering evolutionary random forest. J. IEEE Biomed. Health Inform. **2410**, 2973–2983 (2020)
12. Kang, E., Jang, J., Choi, C.H., Kang, S.B., Bang, K.B., Kim, T.O., et al.: Development of a clinical and genetic prediction model for early intestinal resection in patients with Crohn's disease: results from the IMPACT study. J. J. Clin. Med. **104**, 633 (2021)
13. Gray, K.R., Aljabar, P., Heckemann, R.A., Hammers, A., Rueckert, D., Initiative, A.S.D.N.: Random forest-based similarity measures for multi-modal classification of Alzheimer's disease. J. NeuroImage **65**, 167–175 (2013)
14. Marchetti-Bowick, M., Yin, J., Howrylak, J.A., Xing, E.P.: A time-varying group sparse additive model for genome-wide association studies of dynamic complex traits. J. Bioinform. **3219**, 2903–2910 (2016)
15. Du, L., Liu, K., Zhu, L., Yao, X., Risacher, S.L., Guo, L., et al.: Identifying progressive imaging genetic patterns via multi-task sparse canonical correlation analysis: a longitudinal study of the ADNI cohort. J. Bioinform. **3514**, i474–i483 (2019)
16. Bi, X.-A., Hu, X., Xie, Y., Wu, H.: A novel CERNNE approach for predicting Parkinson's Disease-associated genes and brain regions based on multimodal imaging genetics data. J. Med. Image Anal. **67**, 101830 (2021)
17. Huang, Z., Lei, H., Chen, G., Frangi, A.F., Xu, Y., Elazab, A., et al.: Parkinson's disease classification and clinical score regression via united embedding and sparse learning from longitudinal data. J. IEEE Trans. Neural Netw. Learn. Syst. (2021)
18. Purcell, S., Neale, B., Todd-Brown, K., Thomas, L., Ferreira, M.A., Bender, D., et al.: PLINK: a tool set for whole-genome association and population-based linkage analyses. J. Am. Hum. Gene. **813**, 559–575 (2007)
19. Marees, A.T., de Kluiver, H., Stringer, S., Vorspan, F., Curis, E., Marie-Claire, C., et al.: A tutorial on conducting genome-wide association studies: quality control and statistical analysis. J. Int. Methods Psychiatr. Res. **272**, e1608 (2018)

20. Kulminski, A.M., Shu, L., Loika, Y., He, L., Nazarian, A., Arbeev, K., et al.: Genetic and regulatory architecture of Alzheimer's disease in the APOE region. J. Alzheimer's Dementia Diag. Assess. Dis. Monit. **121**, e12008 (2020)

21. Zhao, T., Hu, Y., Zang, T., Wang, Y.: Integrate GWAS, eQTL, and mQTL data to identify Alzheimer's disease-related genes. J. Front, Gene. **10**, 1021 (2019)

22. Killiany, R., Hyman, B., Gomez-Isla, T., Moss, M., Kikinis, R., Jolesz, F., et al.: MRI measures of entorhinal cortex vs hippocampus in preclinical AD. J. Neurol. **588**, 1188–1196 (2002)

23. Echávarri, C., Aalten, P., Uylings, H.B., Jacobs, H., Visser, P.J., Gronenschild, E., et al.: Atrophy in the parahippocampal gyrus as an early biomarker of Alzheimer's disease. J. Brain Struct. Funct. **215**(3–4), 265–271 (2011)

A Deep Attention Transformer Network for Pain Estimation with Facial Expression Video

Haochen Xu[1,2] and Manhua Liu[1,2(✉)]

[1] Department of Instrument Science and Engineering, School of EIEE,
Shanghai Jiao Tong University, Shanghai 200240, China
{xuhaochen,mhliu}@sjtu.edu.com
[2] The MoE Key Lab of Artificial Intelligence, Artificial Intelligence Institute,
Shanghai Jiao Tong University, Shanghai 200240, China

Abstract. Since pain often causes deformations in the facial structure, analysis of facial expressions has received considerable attention for automatic pain estimation in recent years. This study proposes a deep attention transformer network for pain estimation called Pain Estimate Transformer (PET), which consists of two different subnetworks: an image encoding subnetwork and a video transformer subnetwork. In image encoding subnetwork, ResNet is combined with a bottleneck attention block to learning the features of facial images. In the transformer subnetwork, a transformer encoder is used to capture the temporal relationship among frames. The spatial-temporal features are combined with Multi-Layer Perceptron (MLP) for pain intensity regression. Experimental results on the UNBC-McMaster Shoulder Pain dataset show that the proposed PET achieves compelling performances for pain intensity estimation.

Keywords: Transformer · Attention mechanism · Pain estimation · Facial expression

1 Introduction

In modern medicine and healthcare, automatic pain estimation plays an important role in some clinical diagnoses and treatment applications. Pain level is often estimated by visual observation of patients through health care workers, which suffers from subjective bias. In addition, manual pain estimation does not allow for continuous monitoring of patients. Computer vision and machine learning techniques have been investigated for automatic, objective, and efficient pain estimation to overcome these limitations.

Since the face contains rich information of health conditions, analysis of facial expressions has received considerable attention for automatic pain estimation in recent years. When people suffer from pain, changes in facial expressions are often unconscious. In addition to verbal communication, facial expressions are

J. Feng et al. (Eds.): CCBR 2021, LNCS 12878, pp. 112–119, 2021.
https://doi.org/10.1007/978-3-030-86608-2_13

the most specific and sensitive contactless cues for pain detection and estimation. They can be used as valid indicators of pain and has been widely investigated for automatic pain detection and estimation.

Facial Action Coding System (FACS) was developed for automatic facial expression recognition, which divides facial expressions into different combinations of Action Units (AUs) [1]. AUs refer to the movements of specific facial muscles involved in facial expressions. Some methods were proposed for automatic pain recognition based on the combination of AUs. In these methods, the traditional hand-crafted features such as Histogram of Oriented Gradients (HOG) [2] and Gabor features [3] were extracted from the face images for representation, followed by the classifier such as Support Vector Machines (SVM) [3].

Although the frame-level pain estimation can use spatial features from the face images, sequential facial expression has temporal progression, which is also vital for more accurate pain recognition. Recently deep learning methods, including the Convolutional Neural Networks (CNN) [4,5] and Recurrent Neural Networks (RNN) [6,7] have been proposed to combine the spatial features with the temporal features. In [6], Zhou et al. proposed a Recurrent Convolutional Neural Network (RCNN) in which a recurrent path was added into convolutional layers to estimate pain intensity from videos. However, the public database of face pain expression, such as the UNBC-McMaster Shoulder Pain dataset [13] is too limited to train a deep neural network. Wang et al. proposed to utilize transfer learning from a pre-trained face recognition network for pain estimation regression to address the problem [4]. Rodriguez et al. proposed a Deep Pain model fine-tuning from the Deep Face to extract features from images and fed into a Long Short-Term Memory (LSTM) network to exploit temporal information [7].

Recently, transformer has been successfully investigated to exploit the information of long-range sequential dependency in natural language processing (NLP) [8]. It is also used for machine vision tasks such as image classification, object detection, and segmentation. In [9], Carion et al. proposed a DETR model based on the transformer to realize end-to-end object detection with a fixed number of output detection bounds and classes. In [10], Dosovitskiy et al. proposed Vision Transformer (ViT), which divided an image into 16x16 patches and fed them into a transformer encoder to realize image classification.

Inspired by the success of transformer, we propose a deep attention transformer network for pain estimation with video facial expression, which consists of an image encoding subnetwork and a video transformer subnetwork. First, we build an image encoding subnetwork by combining the Resnet with a bottleneck attention module to extract spatial features. The attention mechanism motivates the network to drop more weight on pain-related ROIs. Second, a transformer subnetwork is built to utilize a transformer encoder to learn the temporal features from the image features. The self-attention mechanism in the transformer helps to capture the complex relations among long sequential features and puts more attention on informative frames. We summarize the contributions of this paper as follows:

1. We propose a ResNet with the learned attention mechanism for extraction of coarse-to-fine spatial features of face images. The attention mechanism can help concentrate the model on the pain-related ROIs for feature extraction.
2. The proposed video transformer subnetwork can capture the temporal features of facial expression video. The self-attention mechanism of transformer can overcome the limitation of the RNN-based methods and modelling the long-range sequence of video.

2 Proposed Method

This section will present the proposed pain estimation algorithm consisting of video facial expression preprocessing, spatial-temporal feature extraction based on deep attention transformer network, and final pain estimation. Figure 1 shows the overview of the proposed deep attention transformer network for pain estimation.

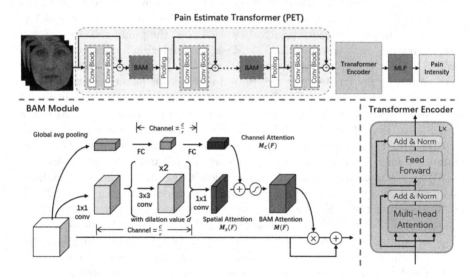

Fig. 1. An overview of the proposed deep attention transformer network on video facial expression for pain estimation. The network consists of BAM-ResNet and a transformer encoder [8] to extract the spatial-temporal features for pain estimation. The illustration of BAM is inspired by [11].

First, we pre-process the sequential images of video with AAM facial landmark detection to locate landmarks on the face. Delaunay triangulation algorithm is used to generate a mask with facial landmarks. The face region is cropped with the mask and then aligned. We divide the input face expression video into many segments to facilitate processing and recognition. Let $D = \{(X_1, Y_1), (X_2, Y_2), \cdots, (X_N, Y_N)\}$ denote N segments of facial expression video where $X_i = \{x_i^1, x_i^2, \cdots, x_i^L\}$ represents the ith video segment consisting of L numbers of image frames and x_i^z denotes the zth frame of the ith segment. $Y_i = \{y_i^1, y_i^2, \cdots, y_i^L\}$ denotes the image labels of the ith video segment where y_i^z is the label of zth image frame. In this work, we use the average of the image labels as the segment label. Thus, the pain estimation is converted to a regression task with the face expression video: $G : X \to H$, where X represents the video segment and H represents the predicted pain intensity of the segment.

Second, we propose a deep attention transformer network for pain estimation called Pain Estimate Transformer (PET), which consists of a frame image encoding subnetwork and a transformer encoder. The overview of our deep attention transformer network is shown in Fig. 1. Motivated by the success of ResNet [12], the image encoding subnetwork is built with the ResNet to extract the spatial features of each face image. We reshape the pre-processed 2D face image into $x_i^z \in \mathbb{R}^{H \times W \times C}$ where (H, W) is the size of the processed image and C is the number of channels. The output feature maps of the tth stage $F_i^{z,t}$ can be represented as:

$$F_i^{z,t} = G_t(x|\{W_i^t\}_{i=1}^{t_N}) \tag{1}$$

where W_i^t denotes the weight matrix of the ith convolutional layer in the tth stage, t_N denotes the number of convolutional layers in the tth stage. The function $G_t(\cdot)$ represents all the convolutional and batch normalization operations in one stage.

In addition, pain information is not evenly located on a facial expression. Previous research based on FACS proposed the Prkachin and Solomon Pain Intensity (PSPI), indicating that pain information is mainly located at brows, eyes, nose wrinkles, and mouth. Instead of using traditional hand-crafted masks, we use learned weights with an attention mechanism to help the network concentrate more on corresponding regions. Inspired by [11], we add a Bottleneck Attention Module (BAM) between every two stages. As shown in Fig. 1, BAM $M(F)$ consists of a Channel Attention $M_C(F)$ and a Spatial Attention $M_S(F)$, which can be represented as:

$$M(F) = \sigma(M_C(F) + M_S(F)) \tag{2}$$

$$M_C(F) = BN(MLP(AvgPool(F))) \tag{3}$$

$$M_S(F) = BN(f_3^{1 \times 1}(f_2^{3 \times 3}(f_1^{3 \times 3}(f_0^{1 \times 1}(F))))) \tag{4}$$

where σ denotes a sigmoid function, BN, $AvgPool$, f represents a batch normalization, Average Pooling and a convolution operation. MLP denotes an MLP with one hidden layer. A dilation value d and a reduction ratio r are used to control the receptive fields and the capacity of the model.

Third, a transformer encoder is added to extract the temporal features of sequential image frames. A standard transformer encoder handles 1D input tensor, for output feature maps of the last stage $F_i^z \in \mathbb{R}^{H_F \times W_F \times C_F}$, where (H_F, W_F, C_F) represent the resolution and channels of the output feature map. We use an Average Pooling to produce 1D tensor $F_i^{z'} \in \mathbb{R}^{C_F}$ and feed them into transformer encoder. As shown in Fig. 1, a standard transformer encoder consists of alternating layers of multi-head attention followed with feed-forward MLP blocks. Every block has a LayerNorm (LN) before them and a residual connection after them. The output feature map of the transformer encoder has the same shape as the input. Finally, an MLP with average pooling is added at the end of the transformer encoder for pain intensity regression.

Finally, for pain intensity regression, an MLP with average pooling is added at the end of the transformer encoder to estimate the output pain intensity value O. The loss function is computed as the mean squared error (MSE) between model output and true label:

$$L = \frac{1}{N} \sum_{i=1}^{N} (G(X_i), Y_i)^2 \tag{5}$$

3   Experimental Results

In this section, we conduct experiments to evaluate the performance of the proposed method with the UNBC-McMaster shoulder pain dataset [13]. The UNBC-McMaster dataset contains 200 videos of facial expression from 25 different subjects. The dataset has 47398 images of size 320×240, which are annotated with PSPI score in the range of 16 discrete pain intensity levels (0–15) using FACS. In the experiment, we follow the same experimental protocol as [14]. There are few images provided for the high pain level. Due to the extremely imbalance among different classes of the dataset, we apply the widely used strategy to reduce the 16 levels into six level: 0(0), 1(1), 2(2), 3(3), 4(4–5), 5(6–15). To prepare the training data, we divide the videos of the UNBC datasets into segments of 48 frames with a stride of 8 frames, resulting in 5361 sequences of data. Preprocessing steps are applied on the original face image as described in Sect. 2. All the face images are reshaped into a size of 224×224. In the implementation, we use ResNet-50 as the base model. The number of layers in the transformer encoder is set to 6. Stochastic Gradient Descent (SGD) is used with a momentum of 0.9 for network training. The initial learning rate is set to 0.001 with a decay of 1e–5. The training epochs are set to 50, and batch size is set to 16.

Leave-one-subject-out (LOSO) cross-validation strategy is used in the experiments. To evaluate the proposed method, we compute the performance measures of Pearson Correlation Coefficient (PCC), Intraclass correlation (ICC), Mean-Squared-Error (MSE), and Mean-Absolute-Error (MAE) for comparison. MSE and MAE are used to evaluate the errors between prediction and ground truth, whereas PCC and ICC are often adapted to measure the linear correlation between the prediction results and ground truths.

The first experiment is to test the effect of sequence lengths of input video segments on the pain estimation performance. The transformer block of our network is to exploit the temporal relationship of the image features for modelling the video segments. Thus, the length of the input video segment may influence the estimation performance of the method. In the experiment, we test the proposed method with different lengths of input video segments. The results

Table 1. Comparison of the pain estimation performances by the proposed method on different sequence lengths of input video segment

Input length	8	16	32	48	64
MSE	0.56	0.51	0.44	**0.40**	0.42

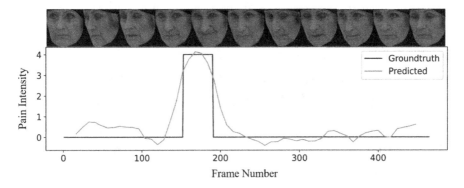

Fig. 2. An example of pain intensity estimation with facial expression video of a subject by the proposed method.

comparison is shown in Table 1. We can see that the proposed method achieves the best performance with the input video segment of 48 frames. Furthermore, Fig. 2 shows an example of pain intensity estimation with our proposed method and the input video segment length set to 48. We can see that the predicated pain intensities by our method are close to the ground truths.

The second experiment is to compare our method with other methods recently published. All the compared methods apply LOSO cross-validation strategy as their experimental protocols. As shown in Table 2, our proposed method achieves promising results when compared with other methods, which explored sequence-based regression tasks with deep learning methods based on RNN and RCNN of different structures. From the results, we can see that our proposed method achieves the best performances of MSE and MAE. The PCC and ICC of our method are also comparable to other methods. Ablation study is conducted to remove the image encoding and video transformer subnetworks from the proposed method to test their performances. We respectively replace the image encoding and video transformer subnetworks with an 1×1 convolutional kernel and an average function to implement the ablation experiments. Results in Table 2 shows that the video transformer subnetwork can obtain temporal information and substantially improve the performance of the model. PET without image encoding subnetwork convergences to a fixed number, which means the model does not work at all.

Table 2. Comparison of the proposed method with other methods and ablation study. IES denotes image encoding subnetwork, and VTS denotes video transformer subnetwork.

Methods	PCC↑	ICC↑	MSE↓	MAE↓
RCNN [6]	0.64	-	-	1.54
Regularization Regression [4]	0.65	-	0.80	0.39
LSTM [7]	0.78	0.45	0.74	0.50
C3D+DFGS+HOG [15]	0.68	-	0.89	-
2pooldeep [16]	0.52	-	1.45	-
Binary Representation [17]	0.81	-	0.69	-
Pain-awareness Regions [18]	0.70	0.55	0.53	0.47
PET without IES	0.03	−0.32	0.10	0.17
PET without VTS	0.43	0.21	0.76	0.66
PET	**0.76**	**0.52**	**0.40**	**0.37**

4   Conclusion

Automatic pain intensity estimation has important applications in disease diagnosis and medical treatments. This paper proposes a deep attention transformer network to learn the spatial and temporal features for pain estimation from facial expression videos. Experimental results and comparison on UNBC-McMaster Shoulder Pain dataset show that the effectiveness of the proposed method for pain estimation.

Acknowledgment. This study was supported in part by National Natural Science Foundation of China (61773263), Shanghai Jiao Tong University Scientific and Technological Innovation Funds (2019QYB02), Shanghai Municipal Science and Technology Major Project (2021SHZDZX0102).

References

1. Ekman, P., Rosenberg, E.L. (eds.): What the Face Reveals: Basic and Applied Studies of Spontaneous Expression Using the Facial Action Coding System (FACS). Oxford University Press, Oxford (1997)
2. Egede, J.O., Valstar, M.: Cumulative attributes for pain intensity estimation. In: Proceedings of the 19th ACM International Conference on Multimodal Interaction (2017)
3. Littlewort, G.C., Bartlett, M.S., Lee, K.: Automatic coding of facial expressions displayed during posed and genuine pain. Image Vis. Comput. 27(12), 1797–1803 (2009)
4. Wang, F., et al. : Regularizing face verification nets for pain intensity regression. In: 2017 IEEE International Conference on Image Processing (ICIP). IEEE (2017)
5. Tavakolian, M., Hadid, A.: Deep spatiotemporal representation of the face for automatic pain intensity estimation. In: 2018 24th International Conference on Pattern Recognition (ICPR). IEEE (2018)

6. Zhou, J., et al.: Recurrent convolutional neural network regression for continuous pain intensity estimation in video. In: Proceedings of the IEEE Conference on Computer Vision and Pattern Recognition Workshops (2016)
7. Rodriguez, P., et al.: Deep pain: exploiting long short-term memory networks for facial expression classification. IEEE Tran. Cybern. 1–11 (2017)
8. Vaswani, A., et al.: Attention is All you Need. In: NIPS (2017)
9. Carion, N., Massa, F., Synnaeve, G., Usunier, N., Kirillov, A., Zagoruyko, S.: End-to-end object detection with transformers. In: Vedaldi, A., Bischof, H., Brox, T., Frahm, J.-M. (eds.) ECCV 2020. LNCS, vol. 12346, pp. 213–229. Springer, Cham (2020). https://doi.org/10.1007/978-3-030-58452-8_13
10. Dosovitskiy, A., et al.: An image is worth 16x16 words: transformers for image recognition at scale. In: ICLR (2021)
11. Park, J., et al.: BAM: bottleneck attention module. In: British Machine Vision Conference (BMVC). British Machine Vision Association (BMVA) (2018)
12. He, K., et al.: Deep residual learning for image recognition. In: Proceedings of the IEEE Conference on Computer Vision and Pattern Recognition (2016)
13. Lucey, P., et al.: Painful data: the UNBC-McMaster shoulder pain expression archive database. In: 2011 IEEE International Conference on Automatic Face and Gesture Recognition (FG). IEEE (2011)
14. Zhao, R., et al.: Facial expression intensity estimation using ordinal information. In: Proceedings of the IEEE Conference on Computer Vision and Pattern Recognition (2016)
15. Wang, J., Sun, H.: Pain intensity estimation using deep spatiotemporal and hand-crafted features. IEICE Trans. Inf. Syst. 101(6), 1572–1580 (2018)
16. Yang, R., et al.: Incorporating high-level and low-level cues for pain intensity estimation. In: 2018 24th International Conference on Pattern Recognition (ICPR). IEEE (2018)
17. Tavakolian, M., Hadid, A.: Deep binary representation of facial expressions: a novel framework for automatic pain intensity recognition. In: 2018 25th IEEE International Conference on Image Processing (ICIP). IEEE (2018)
18. Huang, D., et al.: Pain-awareness multistream convolutional neural network for pain estimation. J. Electr. Imag. 28(4), 043008 (2019)

Cognitive Analysis of EEG Signals Induced by Visual Stimulation of Facial Emotion

Chen Chen and Yuchun Fang$^{(\boxtimes)}$

School of Computer Engineering and Science, Shanghai University, Shanghai, China
ycfang@shu.edu.cn

Abstract. This paper focuses on EEG signals induced by visual stimulation of facial emotion. We mainly research depressed and healthy subjects' cognition to different emotional visual stimulation on the dataset MODMA [1]. We also explore the problem of depression classification based on EEG signals. To solve these problems, we first preprocess EEG signals, and then extracted the LogFbank feature. We propose two methods of Channel Selection and Decision Fusion to analyze EEG signals. The channel selection algorithm considers the correlation between channels and selects the local optimal channel combination. The decision fusion strategy conducts fusion training on the model and improves the generalization of the model. Experimental results demonstrate that our proposed two methods are valid. We find that depressed patients are slower in emotional cognition than healthy controls, and EEG can be used to identify depression.

Keywords: EEG · Visual stimualtion · Facial emotion · Channel selection · Decision fusion

1 Introduction

Electroencephalogram (EEG) is the electrophysiological activity produced by the firing of neurons in the brain [2]. EEG records the changes in electrical waves during brain activity, namely, EEG signals. EEG signals are generally collected from the scalp's surface and can be divided into two types: spontaneous and evoked. Spontaneous EEG signals are produced without external stimulation, while evoked EEG signals are produced under external stimulation. External stimulation is usually sensory stimulation, such as sight and hearing. Evoked EEG signals contain more cognitive characteristics than spontaneous EEG signals.

EEG signals are widely used in emotion recognition due to their high temporal resolution. The EEG data analyzed in emotion recognition is usually evoked. There are many studies adopting different methods to study the problem of emotion recognition based on EEG. In most cases, the EEG data is extracted

© Springer Nature Switzerland AG 2021
J. Feng et al. (Eds.): CCBR 2021, LNCS 12878, pp. 120–127, 2021.
https://doi.org/10.1007/978-3-030-86608-2_14

into features first, and then machine learning or deep learning techniques will be used for analysis.

Zheng et al. [3] focused on the impact of different bands and key channels on emotion recognition, first extracted differential entropy (DE) from EEG signals as a feature, and then trained deep belief networks for emotion recognition. Wang et al. [4] proposed an emotion recognition system based on EEG signals, which extracted features of EEG signals from the time domain and frequency domain, and finally used KNN, MLP, and SVM three classifiers to perform emotion recognition, respectively. Petrantonakis et al. [5] first extracted higher order crossings (HOC) from EEG signals as a feature, and then used the SVM classifier for emotion recognition. Puthankattil et al. [6] used EEG signals to carry out depression recognition research, first extracted relative wavelet energy (RWE) as a feature, and then used artificial neural network (ANN) for depression EEG classification.

In this paper, we focus on EEG signals induced by visual stimulation of facial emotion. Compared with recognizing emotions of the subjects induced by visual stimulation, we research the subject's cognition to emotions of visual stimulation, which is called stimulation recognition. Evoked EEG signals contained in the dataset MODMA we use are recorded from depressed and healthy subjects. Therefore, we separately research the responses of depressed and normal subjects to different emotional visual stimulation. Meanwhile, a study on depression recognition is performed based on EEG signals.

To carry out research, we first preprocess EEG signals, and then extract the LogFbank feature. We propose two methods of Channel Selection and Decision Fusion to analyze EEG signals. The channel selection algorithm can select the local optimal channel combination to reduce the data dimension, thereby saving computing resources. The decision fusion strategy trains multiple single-channel classifiers first, and then trains the fusion classifier, which can effectively improve the accuracy and generalization of the model. Figure 1 shows the flowchart of this paper. XGBoost is selected as the classifier in the experiment.

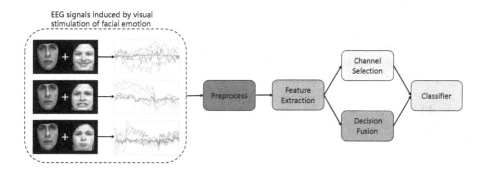

Fig. 1. The flowchart of this paper.

There are two main contributions to our work. First, we discover a new research question from the dataset: studying depression and healthy subjects' cognition to different emotional visual stimulation based on EEG signals. Second, we propose two methods of Channel Selection and Decision Fusion to carry out specific research.

2   Method

2.1   Feature Extraction

MFCC is widely used for the feature representation of speech signals. To apply MFCC to EEG signals, Wang et al. [7] proposed the LogFbank feature, which is a log power spectrum on a non-linear Mel scale of frequency. In this paper, we extract the LogFbank feature of each channel of EEG signals for the feature representation. Figure 2 shows the extraction process of the LogFbank feature.

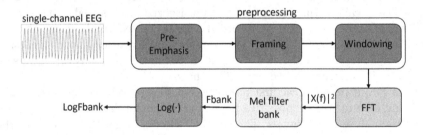

Fig. 2. The extraction process of the LogFbank feature.

First, we preprocess the single-channel EEG data. This process includes three steps: pre-emphasis, windowing and framing. The pre-emphasis process passes signals through a high-pass filter to avoid the attenuation of high-frequency signals. We use a Hamming window, the window length is set to 0.1 s, and the window shift is set to 0.05 s. Then, we use the Fast Fourier Transform (FFT) to calculate the spectrum of each frame of signals, denoted as $X(f)$. Next, we take the modulus square of the spectrum to get the power spectrum, denoted as $|X(f)|^2$. After that, we apply the Mel filter bank $H_K(f)$ to the power spectrum to get the Fbank feature. The Mel filter bank consists of a series of triangle filters. Finally, we take the logarithm of Fbank to obtain LogFbank, defined in Eq. (1).

$$C_{LogFbank}(k) = log\{\sum_{f_{kl}}^{f_{kh}} |X(f)|^2 H_K(f)\}, 1 \leq k \leq K,   (1)$$

where f_{kl} and f_{kh} are the lowest and highest frequency for the k-th filter, and K is the total number of triangle filters. We set K to 10 in this paper.

2.2 Channel Selection

When there are too many channels of EEG signals, the data dimension is very large, which requires a lot of computing resources. Therefore, we propose the channel selection algorithm to select the local optimal channel combination to avoid the above problem.

Let C denote the set containing all channels, S denotes the set of selected channels, N denotes the number of selected channels, and J denotes the evaluation function whose the evaluation index is the classification accuracy. If we want to select the local optimal combination of n channels, the implementation of the channel selection algorithm is as follows:

Step 1: Initialize $C = \{c_1, c_2, \ldots, c_k\}, S = \varnothing, N = 0$;

Step 2: For $\forall\, c_i \in C$, calculate $J(S \cup c_i)$ to find the c_i that can maximize the evaluation function. Set $S = S \cup c_i, C = C\text{-}\{c_i\}, N = N + 1$;

Step 3: If $N > n$, repeat Step 2; otherwise, the algorithm ends and S is output.

2.3 Decision Fusion

Decision fusion is a high-level information fusion method that uses a set of classifiers to provide better and unbiased results. We propose to adopt the decision fusion strategy, mainly for the following two considerations [8]: (1) Due to a large amount of experimental data, if only one classifier is trained, the training process is slow, and the efficiency is low. (2) Decision fusion can effectively improve the performance of the model and make it more generalized. Therefore, we use the decision fusion method to train the first-level classifier for each channel of EEG signals, and then train the second-level fusion classifier.

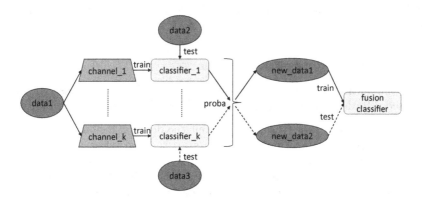

Fig. 3. The implementation details of decision fusion.

Figure 3 shows the implementation details of decision fusion. We divide the data into three parts, one part is used to train k single-channel classifiers, and the other two are used to test these k single-channel classifiers. For each sample in the two test data, testing k classifiers can get k prediction probabilities. We concatenate these probabilities into a k-dimensional feature. In this way, the two test data can form two new data composed of probability features after testing classifiers. For these two new data, one is used for training the fusion classifier and the other is used for testing.

3   Experiments

3.1   Dataset

MODMA. This is a multi-modal dataset provided by Lanzhou University, including EEG and audio data from major depressed disorders (MDD) and healthy controls (HC). We use the 128-electrode EEG signals of 53 subjects recorded under visual stimulation as the experimental data. Among the 53 subjects, 24 are depressed patients and 29 are healthy controls. The stimuli material is facial pictures. Each picture contains two faces, one is emotional and the other is neutral. There are three types of emotional faces: fear, sad, and happy, forming three types of stimuli pairs with neutral faces, which are fear-neutral, sad-neutral and happy-neutral. During the recording of EEG signals, each subject focused on each stimuli pair for 160 trials.

3.2   Data Preprocessing

EEG signals are divided into five frequency bands: delta (1–4 Hz), theta (4–8 Hz), alpha (8–14 Hz), beta (14–31 Hz) and gamma (31–50 Hz) [3]. The data of each subject is divided into 480 segments. Each segment has a duration of 0.8 s, composed of 0.3 s before stimulation and 0.5 s under stimulation. Besides, EEG signals are also processed by independent component analysis (ICA) to eliminate the artifacts.

3.3   Stimulation Recognition

Visual stimulation experiments are designed to study the responses of major depressed disorders (MDD) and healthy controls (HC) to different stimuli pairs.

Analysis of Frequency Bands. We adopt the decision fusion method to perform stimuli pair classification experiments for the two types of subjects. The experimental results are shown in Table 1. Among the five frequency bands, the gamma band achieves the highest accuracy with MDD reaching 97.61% and HC reaching 98.44%. This result corresponds to the characteristics of different frequency bands. When a person is awake or focused, the gamma band in his EEG signals is more pronounced. Obviously, both depressed patients and healthy controls must be awake or attentive during the recording of EEG signals.

Analysis of Subjects. In Fig. 4, we show the detailed results of the three stimuli pairs recognized by depressed subjects and healthy subjects on the gamma band.

Table 1. Accuracy on five frequency bands of two types of subjects.

Bands	MDD	HC
Delta	37.12%	36.12%
Theta	52.12%	51.06%
Alpha	46.88%	46.49%
Beta	41.28%	42.55%
Gamma	**97.61%**	**98.44%**

It demonstrates that, compared with MDD, the response of HC to the three stimuli pairs is relatively more significant. This result is consistent with the conclusion that depression is slower in cognition and processing of emotions than healthy people.

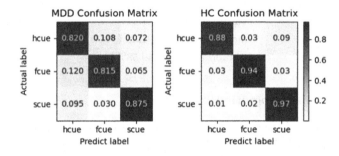

Fig. 4. Confusion matrix of visual stimulation classification results. The three labels (hcue, fcue and scue) respectively represent the three stimuli pairs (happy-neutral, fear-neutral and sad-neutral).

Analysis of Channel Selection. We test the influence of Channel Selection on visual stimulation recognition. Figure 5 shows the changing trend of the classification results of depressed subjects and healthy subjects in the process of selecting 1–8 optimal channels. Obviously, as the number of selected channels increases, the classification accuracy of MDD and HC is increasing, which demonstrates that Channel Selection is valid.

Table 2. Correspondence of 16 electrodes under two standards.

10-20 system	Fp1	Fp2	F3	F4	F7	F8	C3	C4
GSN-128	E22	E9	E24	E124	E33	E122	E36	E104
10-20 system	T3	T4	P3	P4	T5	T6	O1	O2
GSN-128	E45	E108	E52	E92	E58	E96	E70	E83

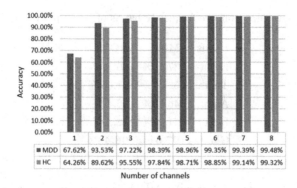

Fig. 5. The result of channel selection.

Table 3. Results of different methods for depression classification.

Method	Accuracy
Feature fusion	83.24%
Channel selection	91.58%
Decision fusion	89.58%

3.4 Depression Recognition

In this section, we conduct depression recognition experiments to explore whether it is possible to determine whether the subject is depressed or healthy based on EEG signals. In these experiments, we do not divide the band of EEG signals, but set the filtering range to 0.3–30 Hz [9].

Referring to the research of depression recognition based on EEG by Akar et al. [10], we select the same 16 electrodes for experiments. They record EEG signals from 16 electrodes according to the international 10–20 system, but our experimental data is recorded following the GSN-128 standard. Table 2 lists the correspondence between these two standards. We adopt the feature fusion strategy to concatenate the feature data of these 16 electrodes for depression recognition. We also adopt our proposed two methods to conduct experiments. The number of selected channels of Channel Selection is set to 16. The results of these three methods are shown in Table 3. Compared with Feature Fusion, achieving an accuracy of 83.24%, Channel Selection and Decision Fusion both improve the results with the accuracy of 91.58% and 89.58%, respectively. Therefore, our proposed two methods are effective.

4   Conclusion

In this paper, we propose two methods: Channel Selection and Decision Fusion. We verify the effectiveness of these two methods in analyzing EEG signals through two experiments of stimulation classification and depression classification. As the number of selected channels increases, the accuracy of stimulation classification continues to improve. Compared with fusing the feature data of 16 electrodes, the two methods of channel selection algorithm and decision fusion strategy achieve better results of depression classification. In addition, by studying the influence of different bands on visual stimulation recognition, we find that the gamma band has the best recognition effect. When studying the responses of depressed subjects and healthy subjects to different stimuli pairs, we find that depressed subjects have a slower cognition of emotions than healthy subjects. EEG can be used for depression recognition effectively.

Acknowledgments. The work is supported by the National Natural Science Foundation of China under Grant No.: 61976132, U1811461 and the Natural Science Foundation of Shanghai under Grant No.: 19ZR1419200.

References

1. Cai, H., et al.: MODMA dataset: a multi-modal open dataset for mental-disorder analysis. arXiv preprint arXiv:2002.09283 (2020)
2. Hu, L., Zhang, Z.: Signal processing and feature extraction. In: Neural Networks and Speech Processing. In: The Springer International Series in Engineering and Computer Science (VLSI), Computer Architecture and Digital Signal Processing), vol. 130. Springer, Boston (2019). https://doi.org/10.1007/978-1-4615-3950-6_6
3. Zheng, W., Lu, B.: Investigating critical frequency bands and channels for EEG-based emotion recognition with deep neural networks. J. Trans. Auton. Ment. Dev. **7**,(3), 162–175 (2015)
4. Wang, X.W., Nie, D., Lu, B.L.: EEG-based emotion recognition using frequency domain features and support vector machines. J. Neural Inf. Process. **7062**, 734–743 (2011)
5. Petrantonakis, P.C., Hadjileontiadis, L.J.: Emotion recognition from EEG using higher order crossings. J. Trans. Inf. Technol. Biomed. **14**(2), 186–197 (2010)
6. Subha, D., Puthankattil, P., Joseph, K.: Classification of EEG signals in normal and depression conditions by ANN using RWE and signal entropy. J. Mech. Med. Biol. **12**, 1240019 (2012)
7. Wang, D., Fang, Y., Li, Y., Chai, C.: Enhance feature representation of electroencephalogram for seizure detection. In: International Conference on Acoustics, Speech and Signal Processing (ICASSP). pp. 1230–1234 (2020)
8. Mangai, U.G., Samanta, S., Das, S., Chowdhury, P.R.: A survey of decision fusion and feature fusion strategies for pattern classification. J. IETE Tech. Rev. **27**, 293–307 (2010)
9. Li, X., et al.: Attentional bias in MDD: ERP components analysis and classification using a dot-probe task. J. Comput. Methods Programs Biomed. **164**, 169–179 (2018)
10. Akar, S.A., Kara, S., Agambayev, S., Bilgiç,M.: Nonlinear analysis of EEGs of patients with major depression during different emotional states. J. Comput. Biol. Med. **67**, 49–60 (2015)

3D Context-Aware PIFu for Clothed Human Reconstruction

Tingting Liao[1,2], Xiangyu Zhu[1,2], Zhen Lei[1,2,3(✉)], and Stan Z. Li[4]

[1] CBSR and NLPR, Institute of Automation, Chinese Academy of Sciences, Beijing, China
{tingting.liao,xiangyu.zhu,zlei}@nlpr.ia.ac.cn
[2] School of Artificial Intelligence, University of Chinese Academy of Science, Beijing, China
[3] Centre for Artificial Intelligence and Robotics, Hong Kong Institute of Science and Innovation, Chinese Academy of Sciences, Hongkong, China
[4] School of Engineering, Westlake University, Hangzhou, China
szli@nlpr.ia.ac.cn

Abstract. In this paper, we propose 3D Context-Aware PIFu to recover 3D clothed human from a single image. Existing implicit function-based models suffer from the unsatisfied robustness to poor pose variations, since they ignore the inherent geometric relationship among 3D points. In this work, we utilize the 3D human model as a strong prior to regularize the reconstruction. With a fitted 3D human model, a global shape is extracted by the Pointnet to handle pose variations, and a local feature is extracted by Graph Convolutional Neural Network (GCNN) to capture geometry details. Besides, to enable the reconstruction network to capture fine-grained geometry on 3D cloth, we propose a multi-view implicit differentiable loss to directly measure the visual effect. Experimental results show that our approach is more robust to pose variations and reconstructs the human body with more details.

Keywords: 3D human reconstruction · Implicit surface reconstruction · Differential rendering

1 Introduction

3D human reconstruction has received considerable attention for its wide application (in AR/VR, games, and virtually try-on). However, it is still challenging to reconstruct high-precision 3D human from a single image due to depth ambiguity, complex poses, and subtle cloth variation. In recent years, implicit representation methods [1–5] have shown promising results since they encode a 3D surface at an infinite resolution to ensure high-fidelity modeling with rich surface details, such as wrinkles and hair. While implicit function is an effective shape representation, it still suffers from two limitations. First, since each point is optimized independently, the trained networks learn overly strong priors on point coordinates but neglect topological information in local areas, which is essential for generating meshes with high-frequency details. Second, such approaches lack robustness to pose variations due to the deficiency of explicit

---

T. Liao and X. Zhu—Equal contributions.

© Springer Nature Switzerland AG 2021
J. Feng et al. (Eds.): CCBR 2021, LNCS 12878, pp. 128–138, 2021.
https://doi.org/10.1007/978-3-030-86608-2_15

human body priors. Approaches that aim to address these limitations can be categorized into two groups.

The first group [1,2,6] mainly focuses on lifting the input image into 3D voxels through a coarse volume loss. Voxelization, however, is inefficient to optimize the model because of the limitation of voxel resolution. The second group [3] relates 3D points with the human body by incorporating body landmarks. For example, [3] computing Radial Basis Function (RBF) distances between points and 57 canonical body landmarks as spatial features. However coarse landmarks are not representative enough to describe the semantic meaning of each point.

In this paper, we propose 3D Context-Aware PIFu to address the above problems, whose overview is shown in Fig. 1. After estimating an initial 3D mesh, a global shape feature is extracted by Pointnet [7] to provide a global (but coarse) description of human pose and shape for each sampled point. Meanwhile, a local feature is further learned by performing GCNN in the neighborhood area. The global and local features are combined to create a 3D semantic field for 3D points so that they are aware of the relative locations to the estimated 3D body. Moreover, to enable the new statistical model of human pose and body shape to capture subtle shape variations on cloth wrinkles, we propose to directly optimize visual effect by comparing the 2D normal and depth map rendered by the implicit field. We evaluate our approach on the task of 3D clothed human reconstruction from a single image, where extensive ablative experiments are conducted to empirically and practically analyze the effectiveness of our method. Both quantitative and qualitative results demonstrate that our method outperforms state-of-the-art human reconstruction methods.

The main contributions of this work are summarized as follows: 1) The Pointnet is employed to model global pose and shape information to improve the robustness against pose variations. 2) GCNN is used to relate queried points with local human mesh to model local geometry information. 3) We extent the implicit differential rendering to a multi-view version, which further refines the fine-grained geometry like cloth wrinkles.

2   Related Work

3D Clothed Human Reconstruction. High fidelity reconstruction of 3D clothed human from a single image is particularly challenging while essential for realism. Great efforts have been made in estimating parametric human bodies [8–11] to recover the 3D human body surface with fine details (e.g., wrinkles and hair). The pioneering work of [12] for the first time proposes to add offsets on the template mesh of SMPL [13] which estimates a naked body without personal details. This also inspired recent works [14–16]. Despite their capability to capture skin-tight clothing, parametric models often fail at more complex topologies such as dresses, skirts, and long hair. Other mesh-based approaches learn to deform a predefined template mesh to target poses. While the use of template meshes is convenient and provides 3D correspondences, it can only model shapes with fixed mesh topology, thus cannot generalize to models with unseen clothes.

In contrast, voxel-based methods have an advantage in reconstructing models with various types of clothes. These approaches [1,2,6,17] represent the 3D output world via a discrete voxel representation, which makes convolution operation possible.

However, this line of works often misses fine-scale details due to the high memory requirement of voxel representation. To address this problem, some progresses [18, 19] have been made by indirectly regressing a continuous implicit function to estimating an occupancy field of the 3D human body. One of the extension works [2–5, 20] is the Pixel-Aligned Implicit Function (PIFu), which utilizes pixel-aligned image features to encode query points for any given 3D location. Despite its ability to produce rich surface details, PIFu still suffers from the feature ambiguity problem and lacks global shape robustness. To overcome this problem, PIFuHD [5] leverages high-resolution images to emboss high-frequency details in a coarse-to-fine manner. Meanwhile, back-side normal is estimated to mitigate the ambiguity problem.

There also exist approaches based on PIFu that incorporate body priors knowledge (e.g., landmark) to facilitate reconstruction. For example, ARCH [3] computes the Radius Basis Function (RBF) distances between each query point and human body landmarks as spatial features to improve their performance. Geo-PIFu [2] utilizes the SMPL model as additional supervision to extract latent voxel features of each query point. More generally, IFNet [1] receives a variety of 3D input such as sparse and dense point clouds, low and high-resolution occupancy grids, which are then encoded as shape features. However, IFNet discretizes the input into voxel grids, leading to undesirable artifacts that may obscure the inherent information of the input.

In contrast, given the point cloud of a human body, our approach directly extracts a global shape descriptor by Pointnet without discretization. Besides, the per-point local feature is also learned by applying GCNN to the point-to-surface neighborhood area. The combination of local geometry and global semantic enables 3D points aware of self-location to the occupancy field.

Differential Rendering. Differential rendering (DR) techniques have been proposed to relate the changes in the observed pixel with that of the 3D models, thus optimize parameters of human representation. Existing methods can be roughly divided into two categories: mesh rasterization based rendering and volume based rendering. OpenDR [21] approximates the rendering process to make it differentiable possible. Another related work is Softrasterizer [22], which extends the traditional rasterization to a soft version, allowing gradients to be computed automatically. However, such approaches require a mesh as input to perform the rendering process, which is not suitable for implicit reconstruction. For volume-based differential rendering, [23] casts a ray from the camera center through the image plane to predict the depth map of the implicit surface. [24] represents each 3D point as a multivariate Gaussian and performs occlusion reasoning with grid discretization and ray tracing. Such methods require an explicit volume to perform occlusion reasoning. Recently, [25] computes the n-order derivative of the implicit filed for each point with central difference approximation, with a focus on reconstructing rigid objects without 3D supervision. In contrast, we extend differential rendering for implicit surface representation to a multi-view version.

3   Method

Our model is based on the Pixel-aligned Implicit Function (PIFu) [4], which is briefly described in Sect. 3.1. We introduce the proposed network structure in Sect. 3.2 and demonstrate multi-view differential rendering loss in Sect. 3.3. Figure 1 provides an overview of our method.

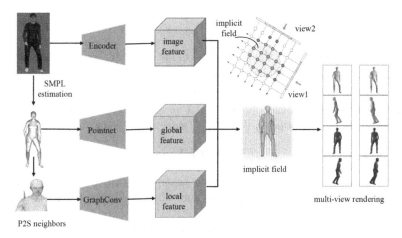

Fig. 1. Overview of our model consisting of three parts: i) global and local feature extraction, ii) implicit surface reconstruction, iii) surface refinement through a multi-view differentiable rendering loss. The 2D illusion of ray-based rendering is shown on the top. Small circle points denote samples, among which red points are mesh interior while the rest are exterior. The mesh surface is in the middle of two adjacent points, with the blue point outside and the red point inside. (Color figure online)

3.1 Pixel-Aligned Implicit Function

The implicit function introduced in [4] assigns a probability to each 3D point. The 3D point inside the target mesh has an occupancy value less than 0.5 and vice versa.

$$\mathcal{F} : \mathbb{R}^3 \rightarrow [0, 1]. \tag{1}$$

Given a point $\mathbf{p} \in \mathbb{R}^3$ and a RGB image $\mathbf{I}$, PIFu models the implicit function as follow:

$$\mathcal{F}(\mathbf{p}, \mathbf{I}) = \mathcal{H}(\varPhi(\mathbf{p}, \mathbf{I}), \mathbf{z}), \tag{2}$$

where $\mathbf{z}$ is the depth value of $\mathbf{p}$, $\varPhi$ is the image feature embedding function, and $\varPhi(\mathbf{p}, \mathbf{I})$ is the pixel aligned image feature. $\mathcal{H}$ is implemented by multi-layer perceptrons (MLP) to regress the probability of 3D points belonging to the target mesh. Once $\mathcal{F}$ is learned, the human occupancy field can be extracted by the Marching Cube algorithm [26], with a threshold of 0.5. However, PIFu has two limitations. First, it does not handle pose variations well due to the lack of body priors, which play an important role in achieving robust 3D reconstruction. Second, PIFu regresses the occupancy value for each sampled point independently, ignoring the inherent correlation between 3D points.

3.2   3D Context-Aware PIFu

To address the above limitations, we utilize the initial body estimated from a given image as a strong prior to regulize the reconstruction. Our model is formulated as:

$$\mathcal{F}(\mathbf{p}, \mathbf{I}, \mathbf{V}) = \mathcal{H}(\Phi(\mathbf{p}, \mathbf{I}), f^g(\mathbf{V}), f^l(\mathbf{p}, \mathbf{V}))), \tag{3}$$

where $\mathbf{V} = \{V_i | i = 1, \ldots, n\}$ is the point cloud of the initial 3D body estimated by [8], f^g and f^l denote the global and local feature respectively.

Global Shape Feature. Given a point cloud $\mathbf{V}$ of the estimated human body, we can extract the global shape feature by Pointnet [7] using the following equation:

$$f^g(\mathbf{V}) = \phi(h(\mathbf{V})), \tag{4}$$

where $h : \mathbb{R}^3 \rightarrow \mathbb{R}^K$ is a multi-layer perceptron (MLP) network and $\phi : \underbrace{\mathbb{R}^K \times \cdots \times \mathbb{R}^K}_{n} \rightarrow \mathbb{R}$ is a max pooling function. The key idea is to learn a mapping $f^g : 2^{\mathbb{R}^N} \rightarrow \mathbb{R}$ from a point cloud to a global feature, with invariance to point order, perturbation, incompletion, and noise. The symmetric property of the max-pooling function makes it possible for ϕ to be invariant to a disordered point cloud. It has been theoretically and experimentally demonstrated that Pointnet tends to summarize a shape by a set of critical points, which provides an overall perspective for 3D points.

Local Geometry Feature. For each sampled point, we find k nearest neighbors (kNN) $\mathbf{V_p} = \{1, \ldots, k\}$, a subset of $\mathbf{V}$ on the initial 3D mesh, and compute the distances to the neighborhood points. A GCNN is performed on the sampled point and the distance to its neighbors to extract the per-point local feature.

$$f^l(\mathbf{p}, \mathbf{V}) = \frac{1}{|\mathbf{V_p}|} \sum_{\mathbf{v}_j \in \mathbf{V_p}} h(\mathbf{p}, \mathbf{D}(\mathbf{p}, \mathbf{v}_j)), \tag{5}$$

where $\mathbf{D}$ is the distance function, h is the graph-convolutional-like operation applied on $\mathbf{p}$ and its neighbors. In particular, this can be implemented by MLP and a mean operation on the dimension of neighbors. The experimental results show that the point-to-surface distance tends to generate a bumpy surface, which is then smoothed by a gaussian blur.

In summary, the local and global features learned from the body priors provide sophisticated semantic information for 3D points, enabling them to have a look at the overall shape and be aware of the relative distances to the occupancy field.

3.3   Multi-view Implicit Rendering

Besides network structure, loss function is also important to capture fine-grained geometry. Inspired by [8], we propose a multi-view rendering loss to optimize the surface based on the previous steps. While recent works [8, 19] have developed differential rendering for implicit representations, they mainly focus on reconstructing generic objects instead of human bodies. In Fig. 1, rays are cast passing through image pixels $\{x_i\}$ under camera views $\{\pi_k\}$. Along each ray, equidistant points are sampled and pass through the network to inference the occupancy probability. Therefore, the silhouette, depth and normal of each pixel can be estimated according to the occupancy values along each ray.

Sihouette. Given a ray $\mathbf{r}$ through image pixel $\mathbf{x}$, the probability of $\mathbf{r}$ hitting the target mesh equals the maximum occupancy value of points along this ray [25]. The silhouette of pixel $\mathbf{x}$ in view π_k can be estimated by:

$$S(\pi_k, \mathbf{x}) = \mathcal{G}(\mathcal{F}(\mathbf{c} + \mathbf{r}(\pi_k, \mathbf{x}) \cdot d_j)_{j=1}^{N_p}), \tag{6}$$

where $\mathbf{c}$ is the camera location; $\mathbf{r}(\pi_k, \mathbf{x})$ is the ray direction; d_j denotes the distance between the camera center and each sampled point along the ray, each containing N_p samples; $\mathcal{G}$ is a max pooling aggregation function.

Depth. After estimating the occupancy probability, we can find an adjacent point pair $(\mathbf{p}_j^{\mathbf{r}}, \mathbf{p}_{j+1}^{\mathbf{r}})$ along ray $\mathbf{r}$ changing from mesh exterior (blue point) to interior (red point).

$$j = \arg\min_j(f(\mathbf{p}_j^{\mathbf{r}}) < \tau \leq \mathbf{p}_{j+1}^{\mathbf{r}})), \tag{7}$$

where $\tau = 0.5$ is the decision threshold. The surface depth is in the interval (d_j, d_{j+1}). We then precisely find the surface depth by evaluating the occupancy value of locations between $(\mathbf{p}_j^{\mathbf{r}}, \mathbf{p}_{j+1}^{\mathbf{r}})$ through the iterative secant method until getting sufficiently close to the surface.

Normal. Assuming $\mathbf{p}_k$ is the point sufficiently close to the mesh surface in view π_k of pixel $\mathbf{x}$, we can approximate its normal using the normalized gradient of function $\mathcal{F}$.

$$\mathbf{N}(\pi_k, \mathbf{x}) = \frac{\delta\mathcal{F}}{\delta\mathbf{p}_k} / \left|\frac{\delta\mathcal{F}}{\delta\mathbf{p}_k}\cdot\right| \tag{8}$$

3.4   Loss Function

The loss function consists of two parts: 3D occupancy loss and 2D reprojection loss.

3D Occupancy Loss. We use the average of mean squared error (MSE) as the occupancy loss.

$$\mathcal{L}_o = \frac{1}{|\mathcal{P}|} \sum_{\mathbf{p}\in\mathcal{P}} \|\mathcal{F}(\mathbf{p}) - \mathcal{F}^*(\mathbf{p})\|_2, \tag{9}$$

where $\mathcal{P}$ is the set of sampled points and $\mathcal{F}^*(\cdot)$ is the ground truth occupancy value corresponding to $\mathcal{F}(\cdot)$.

2D Multi-view Reprojection Loss. We define the multi-view re-projection loss as follow:

$$\mathcal{L}_{\text{sil}} = \frac{1}{K}\frac{1}{|\mathcal{X}|} \sum_k \sum_{x \in \mathcal{X}} \|\mathbf{S}(\pi_k, \mathbf{x}) - \hat{\mathbf{S}}_k(\mathbf{x})\| \tag{10}$$

$$\mathcal{L}_{\text{normal}} = \frac{1}{K}\frac{1}{|\mathcal{X}|} \sum_k \sum_{x \in \mathcal{X}} \|\mathbf{N}(\pi_k, \mathbf{x}) - \hat{\mathbf{N}}_k(\mathbf{x})\| \tag{11}$$

where $\mathbf{S}_k, \mathbf{N}_k$ are the estimated silhouette and normal respectively, and $\hat{\mathbf{S}}_k, \hat{\mathbf{N}}_k$ are the ground truth silhouette and normal map in view π_k respectively.

We only use the occupancy loss to pre-train our model and refine the results with the additional re-projection loss. The total loss function is defined as:

$$\mathcal{L} = \mathcal{L}_o + \lambda_{\text{sil}}\mathcal{L}_{\text{sil}} + \lambda_{\text{normal}}\mathcal{L}_{\text{normal}}. \tag{12}$$

4 Experiments

Our model is trained on the THuman [6] dataset which consists of 6790 scans. We evaluate our method on THuman using 793 subjects unseen in training set and 5 subjects of BUFF [27] dataset.

4.1 Comparison to State-of-the-Art Methods

We compare our method against the state-of-the-art approaches including SPIN [8], DeepHuman [6] and PIFu [4] with three metrics: the average point-to-surface distance (P2S), the Chamfer Distance (CD), and L2 normal. Table 1 shows the comparing results, from which we can observe that our method outperforms PIFu both on THuman and BUFF dataset. Visual results in Fig. 2 demonstrate that our method improves visual fidelity and is more robust with pose variation.

Table 1. Quantitative comparisons of normal, P2S and chamfer errors on THuman and BUFF.

Methods	THuman			BUFF		
	Normal	P2S	Chamfer	Normal	P2S	Chamfer
SPIN [8]	0.4846	1.2345	1.2835	0.3700	0.9287	1.0215
DeepHuman [6]	0.2015	0.4179	0.4250	0.3293	0.8050	0.7627
PIFu [4]	0.3562	1.2335	1.2839	0.1889	0.6472	0.6527
Ours	**0.3328**	**1.1145**	**1.0342**	**0.1892**	**0.6196**	**0.6274**

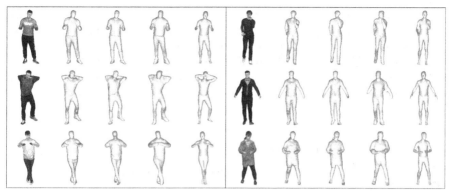

Input   Ours   PIFu   DeepHuman   SPIN   Input   Ours   PIFu   DeepHuman   SPIN

Fig. 2. Qualitative comparisons against state-of-the-art methods [4,6,8] on THuman dataset.

Table 2. Ablative results on THuman.

Method	Normal	P2S	Chamfer
GPIFu	0.1223	0.4739	0.4263
GLPIFu	0.1022	0.3515	0.3308
GLPIFu+R	0.1010	0.3520	0.3296

GT   GPIFu   GLPIFu   GLPIFu+R

Fig. 3. The point to surface distance error maps on the BUFF subject.

5   Ablation Study

We also evaluate our model with several alternatives to assess the factors that contribute to great results. In particular, we evaluate the effectiveness of three main components: the global feature, the local feature, and the multi-view rendering loss. Table 3 provides the ablative results and Fig. 3 presents the geometry, point to surface error visualization using different components, and 2D rendered images. GPIFu is built upon the baseline method PIFu [4] with an additional global feature, while GLPIFu incorporates both global and local features. GLPIFu+R denotes refining the results of GLPIFu by the multi-view rendering loss. When adding the global shape feature, there is a substantial gain compared to PIFu on the THuman dataset. We attribute this to the ability of our model to handle a large variety of poses because the global feature provides an overall perspective for 3D points. By adding the local feature, the figure of three metrics continues to decline. Similarly, the performance becomes better after using the rendering loss. Figure 3 demonstrates a smaller error map and richer geometric details generated by the rendering process (Table 2).

5.1   Performance Analysis

Global Shape Feature. Since the expressiveness of Pointnet is strongly affected by the dimension size of the global feature, we conduct experiments regard to this parameter. Theoretically, the dimension size of the global feature should be greater than the number of critical points. We evaluate three dimensions of 64, 256, 512 in our experiments shown in Table 3. It can be observed that the performance has a slight improvement as the dimension size increases from 64 to 256, followed by a dramatic drop when the dimension up to 512. We also find that the training process is not stable in the early epochs if the dimension size is particularly large. Therefore, we suggest the global feature dimension no greater than 256.

Table 3. Results on the THUman dataset with different size of global shape feature.

Dim	Normal	P2S	Chamfer
64	0.1284	0.4855	0.4357
256	0.1223	0.4739	0.4273
512	0.1603	0.6660	0.5484

Table 4. Results on the THUman dataset using different types of local feature.

	Normal	P2S	Chamfer
P2L	0.1366	0.4397	0.4146
P2L-G	0.1297	0.4351	0.3928
P2S-G	0.1235	0.3594	0.3513

Local Geometry Feature. To validate the effectiveness of our proposed method, we conduct experiments with three different types of local features. Table 4 provides the comparing results on the THuman dataset. P2L computes the distances from query points to landmarks as a local feature. P2L-G performs GCNN on points and landmarks, while P2S-G denotes our proposed local feature extracted by GCNN from points and their point-to-surface neighbors. Results show that P2L tends to ignore some of the parts of the body while P2L-G mitigates this problem to some extent. Compared to P2L-G, P2S-G has a superior performance in terms of three metrics.

6   Discussion and Conclusion

In this paper, we introduce a 3D Context-Aware model for 3D clothed human reconstruction. Our model suggests that human body priors can greatly improve the performance and make the model more robust against pose variations. Experimental results also indicate that the inherent relation between 3D points is vital for implicit surface reconstruction. However, the results of our model are somewhat affected by the initial mesh especially when the pose is not accurately estimated. We will explore this problem in our future research and extension.

Acknowledgements. This work was supported in part by the National Key Research & Development Program (No. 2020AAA0140002), Chinese National Natural Science Foundation Projects #61806196, #61876178, #61976229, #61872367.

References

1. Chibane, J., Alldieck, T., Pons-Moll, G.: Implicit functions in feature space for 3D shape reconstruction and completion. In: 2020 CVPR, pp. 6968–6979 (2020)
2. He, T., Collomosse, J., Jin, H., Soatto, S.: Geo-PIFu: geometry and pixel aligned implicit functions for single-view human reconstruction. In: Conference on Neural Information Processing Systems (NIPS). (2020)
3. Huang, Z., Xu, Y., Lassner, C., Li, H., Tung, T.: ARCH: animatable reconstruction of clothed humans. In: 2020 CVPR, pp. 3090–3099 (2020)
4. Saito, S., Huang, Z., Natsume, R., Morishima, S., Li, H., Kanazawa, A.: PIFu: pixel-aligned implicit function for high-resolution clothed human digitization. In: 2019 IEEE/CVF International Conference on Computer Vision (ICCV), pp. 2304–2314 (2019)
5. Saito, S., Simon, T., Saragih, J., Joo, H.: PIFuHD: Multi-level pixel-aligned implicit function for high-resolution 3D human digitization. In: 2020 IEEE/CVF Conference on Computer Vision and Pattern Recognition (CVPR), pp. 81–90 (2020)
6. Zheng, Z., Yu, T., Wei, Y., Dai, Q., Liu, Y.: Deephuman: 3D human reconstruction from a single image. In: 2019 IEEE/CVF International Conference on Computer Vision (ICCV), pp. 7738–7748 (2019)
7. Charles, R.Q., Su, H., Kaichun, M., Guibas, L.J.: PointNet: deep learning on point sets for 3D classification and segmentation. In: 2017 IEEE Conference on Computer Vision and Pattern Recognition (CVPR), pp. 77–85 (2017)
8. Kolotouros, N., Pavlakos, G., Black, M., Daniilidis, K.: Learning to reconstruct 3D human pose and shape via model-fitting in the loop. In: 2019 IEEE/CVF International Conference on Computer Vision (ICCV), pp. 2252–2261 (2019)
9. Güler, R.A., Kokkinos, I.: HoloPose: holistic 3D human reconstruction in-the-wild. In: 2019 IEEE/CVF Conference on Computer Vision and Pattern Recognition (CVPR), pp. 10876–10886 (2019)
10. Lähner, Z., Cremers, D., Tung, T.: DeepWrinkles: accurate and realistic clothing modeling. In: Ferrari, V., Hebert, M., Sminchisescu, C., Weiss, Y. (eds.) ECCV 2018. LNCS, vol. 11208, pp. 698–715. Springer, Cham (2018). https://doi.org/10.1007/978-3-030-01225-0_41
11. Kanazawa, A., Black, M.J., Jacobs, D.W., Malik, J.: End-to-end recovery of human shape and pose. In: 2018 IEEE/CVF Conference on Computer Vision and Pattern Recognition, pp. 7122–7131 (2018)
12. Alldieck, T., Magnor, M., Xu, W., Theobalt, C., Pons-Moll, G.: Video based reconstruction of 3D people models. In: 2018 IEEE/CVF Conference on Computer Vision and Pattern Recognition (CVPR), pp. 8387–8397 (2018)
13. Loper, M., Mahmood, N., Romero, J., Pons-Moll, G., Black, M.J.: SMPL: a skinned multiperson linear model. ACM Trans. Graph. (TOG) **34**(6), 1–16 (2015)
14. Bhatnagar, B., Tiwari, G., Theobalt, C., Pons-Moll, G.: Multi-garment net: learning to dress 3D people from images. In: 2019 IEEE/CVF International Conference on Computer Vision (ICCV), pp. 5419–5429 (2019)
15. Ma, Q., et al.: Learning to dress 3D people in generative clothing. In: 2020 IEEE/CVF Conference on Computer Vision and Pattern Recognition (CVPR), pp. 6468–6477 (2020)
16. Jiang, B., Zhang, J., Hong, Y., Luo, J., Liu, L., Bao, H.: BCNet: learning body and cloth shape from a single image. In: Vedaldi, A., Bischof, H., Brox, T., Frahm, J.-M. (eds.) ECCV 2020. LNCS, vol. 12365, pp. 18–35. Springer, Cham (2020). https://doi.org/10.1007/978-3-030-58565-5_2
17. Varol, G., et al.: BodyNet: volumetric inference of 3D human body shapes. In: Ferrari, V., Hebert, M., Sminchisescu, C., Weiss, Y. (eds.) ECCV 2018. LNCS, vol. 11211, pp. 20–38. Springer, Cham (2018). https://doi.org/10.1007/978-3-030-01234-2_2

18. Park, J.J., Florence, P., Straub, J., Newcombe, R., Lovegrove, S.: DeepSDF: learning continuous signed distance functions for shape representation. In: 2019 IEEE/CVF Conference on
Computer Vision and Pattern Recognition (CVPR), pp. 165–174 (2019)

19. Liu, S., Zhang, Y., Peng, S., Shi, B., Pollefeys, M., Cui, Z.: Dist: rendering deep implicit
signed distance function with differentiable sphere tracing. In: 2020 IEEE/CVF Conference
on Computer Vision and Pattern Recognition (CVPR), pp. 2016–2025 (2020)

20. Natsume, R., et al.: SiCloPe: silhouette-based clothed people. In: Proceedings of the IEEE
Conference on Computer Vision and Pattern Recognition (CVPR), pp. 4480–4490 (2019)

21. Loper, M.M., Black, M.J.: OpenDR: an approximate differentiable renderer. In: Fleet, D.,
Pajdla, T., Schiele, B., Tuytelaars, T. (eds.) ECCV 2014. LNCS, vol. 8695, pp. 154–169.
Springer, Cham (2014). https://doi.org/10.1007/978-3-319-10584-0_11

22. Liu, S., Chen, W., Li, T., Li, H.: Soft rasterizer: a differentiable renderer for image-based 3D
reasoning. In: 2019 IEEE/CVF International Conference on Computer Vision (ICCV), pp.
7707–7716 (2019)

23. Niemeyer, M., Mescheder, L., Oechsle, M., Geiger, A.: Differentiable volumetric rendering: learning implicit 3D representations without 3D supervision. In: CVPR, pp. 3501–3512
(2020)

24. Insafutdinov, E., Dosovitskiy, A.: Unsupervised learning of shape and pose with differentiable point clouds. In: Bengio, S., Wallach, H., Larochelle, H., Grauman, K., Cesa-Bianchi,
N., Garnett, R., (eds.) Conference on Neural Information Processing Systems (NIPS). Volume 31, Curran Associates, Inc., (2018)

25. Liu, S., Saito, S., Chen, W., Li, H.: Learning to infer implicit surfaces without 3D supervision. In: Advances in Neural Information Processing Systems(NIPS), pp. 8295–8306 (2019)

26. Lorensen, W.E., Cline, H.E.: Marching cubes: a high resolution 3D surface construction
algorithm. ACM SIGGRAPH Comput. Graph. **21**(4), 163–169 (1987)

27. Zhang, C., Pujades, S., Black, M., Pons-Moll, G.: Detailed, accurate, human shape estimation
from clothed 3D scan sequences. In: 2017 IEEE Conference on Computer Vision and Pattern
Recognition (CVPR), pp. 5484–5493 (2017)

Facial Expression Synthesis with Synchronous Editing of Face Organs

Jiangnan Dai(✉)

School of Computer Science and Engineering, Nanjing University of Science
and Technology, Nanjing 210094, China
daijiangnan1997@njust.edu.cn

Abstract. Facial expression synthesis (FES) is to generate a new face
with a desired expression domain. However, in FES field, many current
methods fail to enable relevant facial components to transform simultaneously, which makes the target expression look unnatural. Therefore,
we are purposed to develop a method which can edit main organs synchronously when generating a new expression. Based on this, the global
spatial interaction mechanism is introduced by us which can capture the
long-range dependency between distant positions. Besides, current methods usually suffer from blurs and artifacts around key regions. From the
point of frequency domain, it is probably caused by the distortion of high
frequency information. After this we add a spectrum restriction loss to
original training losses in order to improve the fidelity of generated faces.
Extensive experiments prove our model a great success on two widely-
used datasets: MUG and CASIA-Oulu.

Keywords: Facial expression synthesis · Long-range dependency ·
Frequency domain

1 Introduction

In recent years, FES [1–3] has aroused great concern. It can make modern devices
more convenient for people, such as the personal computer with a more user-
friendly interface, as well as the productions of movies that make people's lives
more colorful. Therefore, it is necessary to synthesize more realistic facial expressions to increase the realism of characters and scenes.

Until very recent, traditional methods mainly include image warping methods. They were based on geometric control [2] and interpolation [3]. Essentially,
they figured out the difference vector between the input and the target expression. The deformation based methods only captured general facial features like
the overall facial shapes, ignoring some concrete details of a normal face. Years
have witnessed the significant progress in GANs [4] in many tasks, such as image
synthesis [5,6], super-resolution [7,8] and face image synthesis [9]. Inspired by
this, a number of GAN-based networks [10–15] were applied to FES tasks. However, there are still some shortcomings in current methods. ExprGAN is able

© Springer Nature Switzerland AG 2021
J. Feng et al. (Eds.): CCBR 2021, LNCS 12878, pp. 139–147, 2021.
https://doi.org/10.1007/978-3-030-86608-2_16

to control the type and intensity of the corresponding facial expression at the same time, but it has a serious overfitting problem. StarGAN [11] and GANimation [13] tend to produce blurs and artifacts especially around regions with great expression changes. Moreover, in these methods, different facial regions did not synchronize with each other when transformed to the target expressions.

In this paper, we aim at developing a method which can edit four main organs synchronously when generating a new expression. For example, when transferring a neural face to a surprised face, not only will the mouth get open, but also the eyes and nose will get changed. Based on this, our model are required to capture remote dependencies directly between any two locations on the input face. However, as for the normal convolution operation, only current receptive field is taken into account, that is to say, the long-range correlation can only be captured when these operations are repeated. By calculating the long-range interaction between any two positions, the Non-Local network [16] captures remote dependency directly. Therefore, inspired by this, we introduce the global spatial interaction mechanism where we make use of the Non-Local module in our network so that the long-range dependency between distant positions on the face can be captured, enabling the generated faces to concentrate on both the global and local information. For the purpose of suppressing the overlapping artifacts and blurs effectively, we additionally add a spectrum restriction loss in the training process to reduce the spectrum distortion inspired by [17]. Experimental results show that when the methods above are blended into our network, the performance can be improved clearly. Our contributions are summarized as follows:

1. We take advantage of the Non-Local module in our model, so as to concentrate on both the global information and local information related to different organs. This is the first time that the global spatial interaction mechanism is used in the field of expression synthesis.
2. We additionally add a spectrum restriction loss so as to penalize spectrum distortions, suppressing the overlapping artifacts and blurs effectively.

2   Proposed Method

We train the generator G to translate an input expression image x into a target expression image $G(x)$ conditioned on a target one-hot label c. The discriminator D adopts the structure of PatchGAN [18] which shares similar functions as StarGAN. Figure 1 and 2 show the overall framework of our proposed network and the structure of the Non-Local block respectively.

2.1   Global Spatial Interaction Mechanism

In our work, since synchronous changes of different facial positions need to be realized when transformed into other facial expressions, conventional methods like StarGAN and GANimation, sometimes lead to the mouth open wide, other regions remaining unchanged. The goal of our work is to realize synchronous changes of different facial positions better.

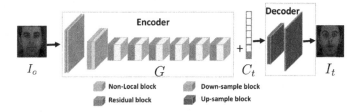

Fig. 1. Framework of our work. $C_t \in R^M$ denotes the target one-hot label, where M is the number of basic expression categories. I_o is the source face and I_t is the target face, both of which are in size of 3 × H × W. Here M, H, and W are set to be 6, 128 and 128 respectively. After six Residual blocks, we concatenate the one-hot label C_t with the immediate output representation to form the tensor with size of $(256 + M)$ × H/4 × W/4.

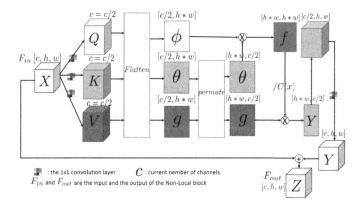

Fig. 2. Structure of the Non-Local block.

Hence, we take advantage of the Non-Local block that can capture remote dependencies directly by computing the interaction between any two locations. This helps further edit relevant organs synchronously when generating a new expression at the pixel level. To be precise, as shown in Fig. 1, we firstly add the Non-Local block at the end of each Down-sample block, in order to encode the input image into a potential feature which reflects relevance between expression-related regions in a more accurate way. Secondly, when added at the end of each Residual block at the middle layer, the Non-Local module is beneficial for modeling mutual features between the input and output. The immediate output representation after the Residual blocks are concatenated with a one-hot expression label c_t in the Decoder, where related areas extracted in the previous stage make corresponding synchronous changes according to the target one-hot label.

The current output is defined as x, the input of the Non-Local block (in Fig. 2). The output of the Non-Local block can be rewritten as:

$$z_i = y_i + x_i, \tag{1}$$

where y_i is given as:

$$y_i = \frac{1}{\mathcal{C}(x)} \sum_{\forall j} f(x_i, x_j) g(x_j), \tag{2}$$

Here i is the index of a certain expression feature map position and j is any index that contains all positions. f is the same as that in [16], computing a pixel-level relationship between i and all other indexes j. This means when transferred to a new expression, j and i will show synchronous changes apparently if they are related to each other. In our work we define f as a dot-product similarity:

$$f(x_i, x_j) = \theta(x_i)^T \phi(x_j). \tag{3}$$

The function g calculates a representation of the feature map x at the position j. The result is finally normalized by $\mathcal{C}(x)$. Here $\mathcal{C}(x) = N$, the number of positions in the feature map x.

2.2   Spectrum Restriction Loss

From the perspective of frequency domain analysis, the generated expression is usually accompanied by blurs and artifacts around key regions, attributed to the distortion of high frequency information. In the spectral power of an image, first we calculate the spectrum feature map by the Discrete Fourier Transform F (seen in Eq. 4) of data $\mathcal{I}$ with size of $X \times Y$, which can be expressed as follows:

$$\mathcal{F}(I)(a, b) = \sum_{x=0}^{X-1} \sum_{y=0}^{Y-1} e^{-2\pi i \cdot \frac{ia}{X}} e^{-2\pi i \cdot \frac{ib}{Y}} \cdot I(x, y), \tag{4}$$

where $a = 0, \cdots, X - 1, \quad b = 0, \cdots, Y - 1$. Then the spectrum distortion is obtained via SD in Eq. 5:

$$SD(k_n) = \int_0^{2\pi} \|\mathcal{F}(I)(k_n \cdot cos(t), k_n \cdot sin(t))\|^2 dt, for \quad n = 0, \cdots, X/2 - 1. \tag{5}$$

Here the binary cross entropy is selected as the loss function $\mathcal{L}_{\text{Spectrum}}$ (seen in Eq. 6), where SD_i^{real} is the mean spectrum representation obtained from real images while SD_i^{out} represents that from the generated images.

$$\mathcal{L}_{\text{Spectrum}} := -\frac{1}{(X/2 - 1)} \sum_{i=0}^{X/2-1} SD_i^{real} \cdot \log(SD_i^{out}) + (1 - SD_i^{real}) \cdot \log(1 - SD_i^{out}) \tag{6}$$

3   Experiment

3.1   Experiment Settings

In our experiment, loss functions are based on StarGAN [11] with same coefficients. In addition, we add the spectrum restriction loss in the end. The coefficient of the spectrum restriction loss is set as $\lambda_{Spec} = 0.1$.

For both the generator and the discriminator, we design our model based on StarGAN [11]. Small changes have been made to the original StarGAN framework in the generator G. The target one-hot label is added to the decoder instead for the reason that after going through too many layers, expression-related information may be lost to a large extent. Secondly, we replace each down-sample stage in the form of ResNet that preserves its down-sampling function.

On **CASIA-Oulu**, we select the last 6 frames of each video on 72 people as the training set and neural faces of 8 people as the test set. On **MUG**, 2603 images with peak expressions on 39 people are chosen to be the training set for trail, while 116 neural faces of 3 people are for test.

In this work, we conduct model evaluation via Peak Signal to Noise Ratio (PSNR) to measure relative realism. Besides, we adopt face verification confidence of which the larger the result is, the higher the possibility they come from the same person is. For the expression classification accuracy, we refer to the face emotion recognition which is also built by Face++ platform. The higher the result is, the higher accuracy the target expression has.

3.2   Comparisons with State-of-Art Methods

For the option of comparative models, we choose StarGAN, AttGAN and ExprGAN. Here we simplify the spectrum restriction loss as Spec and the global spatial interaction mechanism as GSIM. Figure 3 shows our qualitative results on MUG. Compared with previous methods like StarGAN in Fig. 3, our work shows better performance in the changing synchronization as well as the changing range around key areas such as mouth and eyebrow especially when transferring a neural face to a surprised one. Meanwhile, generated faces by our work obtain better average expression accuracy in general (seen in Table 1). Besides, all the three methods above tend to generate far more blurs and artifacts around key regions like eyes and mouth than our method does. Worse still, for ExprGAN, the identity has changed a lot due to its serious overfitting problem. The verification is done using Face++ platform (seen in Table 3), where we compare the input neural faces with the corresponding synthesized ones. As a result, verification confidence by our method is a little lower than that by StarGAN. Maybe it is because happy or surprised faces produce partial deformation that accords with biological characteristics in the training set. But it is far higher than that by ExprGAN. Therefore, above all, our method does well in preserving identity-related features.

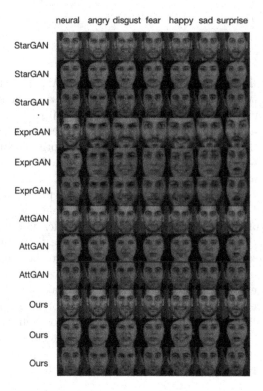

Fig. 3. Qualitatively results of the comparison with state-of-art methods.

Table 1. Average accuracy of facial expressions on MUG by different methods.

Results	Methods		
	StarGAN	AttGAN	Ours
Accuracy	62.014	50.295	**77.82**

Table 2. Ablation results for average accuracy of facial expressions on MUG.

Results	Methods	
	Baseline	Baseline+GSIM
Accuracy	71.17	**72.476**

Table 3. Face identity verification results of our method by Face++ platform.

Method	Confidence ↑
Ours	91.27
ExprGAN	53.33
AttGAN	90.91
StarGAN	**91.85**

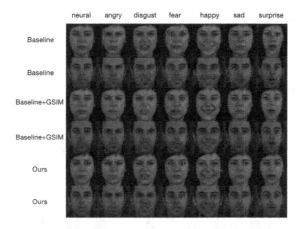

Fig. 4. Qualitative results for the ablation study.

Table 4. Ablation results for expression synthesis realism on MUG.

Methods	PSNR ↑
baseline	26.72
baseline+GSIM	27.49
baseline+GSIM+Spec	**27.74**

3.3   Ablation Study

With regard to the concrete effectiveness of a single module we add, we do some ablation work. Here we simplify the spectrum restriction loss as Spec and the global spatial interaction mechanism as GSIM. Firstly, we exam the ability of the spectrum restriction loss. The reduction of blurs and artifacts can be mainly reflected by the disgusted and surprised faces, such as the damaged ears seen in the last column and the fuzzy mouth in the third column in Fig. 4. In fact, our method outperforms versions without the spectrum restriction loss (in Table 4) quantitatively, probably because the spectrum restriction loss reduces the power spectrum distortion between the real faces and the generated ones, which reduces the blurs and artifacts. Secondly, we report the contribution of GSIM qualitatively and quantitatively (seen in the third and forth rows in Fig. 4 as well as the average expression accuracy (shown in Table 2)). All the results prove that when the Non-Local module is added into our original model, it generally enhances simultaneous changes. Especially when transferred to a surprised face, it emphasizes the importance of synchronization most, which is reflected by the change in the mouth as well as the distance between eyebrows and eyes (seen in the last column in Fig. 4). On the contrary, the surprised face generated without GSIM only shows an apparent change in the range of mouth, other regions remaining nearly unchanged. An explanation might be the Non-Local module, which computes the interaction between any two positions, further extracts the relevance between different regions on the representation in the embedding space. At last, related areas make corresponding synchronous changes according to the target one-hot label.

3.4 Qualitative Results on CASIA-Oulu

Apart from the comparison and ablation study on MUG, we also show the qualitative results on CASIA-Oulu. Apparently, we can see the synchronous changes especially on the surprised face in Fig. 5. In all, our method proves a success on CASIA-Oulu.

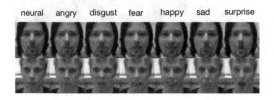

Fig. 5. Qualitative results on CASIA-Oulu.

4 Conclusion

Our proposed method on facial expression synthesis tackles two major issues, one of which is the asynchronous change of different facial positions while the other is reflected by overlapping blurs and artifacts. The experimental results show that the global spatial interaction mechanism proves a good success for generating images with relevant regions consistent to each other. Apart from that, there are fewer blurs and artifacts on the generated face when we balance the power spectrum between the real and the generated images via the novel spectrum restriction loss.

Acknowledgements. We would like to appreciate anonymous reviewers for spending time on our work. This work was supported by the National Natural Science Foundation of China under Grant 62076131.

References

1. Deng, Z., Noh, J.: Computer facial animation: a survey. In: Deng, Z., Neumann, U. (eds.) Data-Driven 3D Facial Animation, pp. 1–28. Springer, London (2008). https://doi.org/10.1007/978-1-84628-907-1_1
2. Liu, Z., Ying, S., Zhang, Z.: Expressive expression mapping with ratio images. In: 28th Annual Conference on Computer Graphics and Interactive Techniques, pp. 271–276. Association for Computing Machinery (2001)

3. Lewis, J.P., Cordner, M., Fong, N.: Pose space deformation: a unified approach to shape interpolation and skeleton-driven deformation. In: 27th Annual Conference on Computer Graphics and Interactive Techniques, pp. 165–172. Association for Computing Machinery (2000)
4. Goodfellow, I., et al.: Generative adversarial networks. In: Advances in Neural Information Processing Systems, pp. 2672–2680. MIT Press (2014)
5. Karras, T., Aila, T., Laine, S., Lehtinen, J.: A unified approach to shape interpolation and skeleton-driven deformation. In: 7th International Conference on Learning Representations, pp. 165–172. Elsevier (2019)
6. Karras, T., Laine, S., Aila, T.: A style-based generator architecture for generative adversarial networks. In: 37th Conference on Computer Vision and Pattern Recognition, pp. 4401–4410. IEEE (2019)
7. Ledig, C., et al.: Photo-realistic single image super-resolution using a generative adversarial network. In: 35th Conference on Computer Vision and Pattern Recognition, pp. 4681–4690. IEEE (2017)
8. Zheng, W., Ye, M., Fan, Y., Xiang, B., Satoh, S.: Cascaded SR-GAN for scale-adaptive low resolution person re-identification. In: 27th International Joint Conference on Artificial Intelligence, pp. 4–11. Morgan Kaufmann (2018)
9. Huang, R., Zhang, S., Li, T., He, R.: Beyond face rotation: global and local perception GAN for photo-realistic and identity preserving frontal view synthesis. In: Computer Society, pp. 2439–2448. IEEE (2017)
10. Mirza, M., Osindero, S.: Conditional generative adversarial nets. In: Computer Science, pp. 2672–2680. IEEE (2014)
11. Choi, Y., Choi, M., Kim, M., Ha, J.W., Choo, J.: StarGAN: unified generative adversarial networks for multi-domain image-to-image translation. In: 36th Conference on Computer Vision and Pattern Recognition, pp. 8789–8797. IEEE (2018)
12. Geng, Z., Cao, C., Tulyakov, S.: 3D guided fine-grained face manipulation. In: 37th Conference on Computer Vision and Pattern Recognition, pp. 9821–9830. IEEE (2019)
13. Pumarola, A., Agudo, A., Martinez, A.M., Sanfeliu, A., Moreno-Noguer, F.: Ganimation: anatomically-aware facial animation from a single image. In: 15th the European Conference on Computer Vision, pp. 818–833. IEEE (2018)
14. Ding, H., Sricharan, K., Chellappa, R.: ExprGAN: facial expression editing with controllable expression intensity. In: 2nd the Association for the Advance of Artificial Intelligence, pp. 748–758. AAAI (2018)
15. Song, L., Lu, Z., He, R., Sun, Z., Tan, T.: Geometry guided adversarial facial expression synthesis. In: 26th ACM International Conference on Multimedia, pp. 627–635. Association for Computing Machinery (2018)
16. Wang, X., Girshick, R., Gupta, A.: Non-local neural networks. In: 36th Conference on Computer Vision and Pattern Recognition, pp. 7794–7803. IEEE (2018)
17. Durall, R., Keuper, M., Keuper, J.: Watch your up-convolution. In: 38th Conference on Computer Vision and Pattern Recognition, pp. 7890–7899. IEEE (2020)
18. Isola, P., Zhu, J.Y., Zhou, T., Efros, A.A.: Image-to-image translation with conditional adversarial networks. In: 34th Conference on Computer Vision and Pattern Recognition, pp. 1125–1134. IEEE (2016)

Multi-lingual Hybrid Handwritten Signature Recognition Based on Deep Residual Attention Network

Wanying Li[1], Mahpirat[2], Wenxiong Kang[3], Alimjan Aysa[1], and Kurban Ubul[1]([⊠])

[1] School of Information Science and Engineering, Xinjiang University, Urumqi, China
kurbanu@xju.edu.cn
[2] Education Office of Xinjiang University, Urumqi, China
[3] School of Automation Science and Engineering, South China University of Technology, Guangzhou, China

Abstract. The writing styles of Uyghur, Kazak, Kirgiz and other ethnic minorities in Xinjiang are very similar, so it is extremely difficult to extract the effective features of handwritten signatures of different languages by hand. To solve this problem, a multi-lingual hybrid handwritten signature recognition method based on deep residuals attention network was proposed. Firstly, an offline handwritten signature database in Chinese, Uyghur, Kazak and Kirgiz was established, with a total of 8,000 signed images. Then, the signature image is pre-processed by grayscale, median filtering, binarization, blank edge removal, thinning and size normalization. Finally, transfer learning method is used to input the signature image into the deep residual network, and the high-dimensional features are extracted automatically by the fusion channel attention for classification. The experimental results show that the highest recognition accuracy of this method is 99.44% for multi-lingual hybrid handwritten signature database, which has a high application value.

Keywords: Multi-lingual · Signature recognition · Transfer learning · Residual network · Attention

1 Introduction

Handwritten signature is a relatively stable and easy to obtain biological behavior characteristic gradually formed in human's acquired living habits. It is widely used in finance, public security, justice and administration and other fields, and is one of the important ways of personal identity authentication. Many domestic and foreign researchers have studied signature recognition technology [1–6].

Xinjiang has been a multi-ethnic region since ancient times. In recent years, researchers have made in-depth research on handwritten signature recognition technology of Uyghur, Kazak and other ethnic minorities. In literature [7–9], Kurban Ubul extracted the global center point feature, local center point feature, ETDT feature and

© Springer Nature Switzerland AG 2021
J. Feng et al. (Eds.): CCBR 2021, LNCS 12878, pp. 148–156, 2021.
https://doi.org/10.1007/978-3-030-86608-2_17

density feature of Uyghur signature respectively, and studied Uyghur handwritten signature recognition technology. Mo Longfei [10] used discrete curvelet transform for Uyghur and Kirgiz signature images to extract the energy features and multi-scale block local binary mode is combined to form new signature feature.

Considering the existence of multi-lingual hybrid handwritten signature recognition problem in Xinjiang, in this paper, based on deep learning, an exploratory research on multi-lingual hybrid handwritten signature recognition technology is conducted. The self-built hybrid signature database of Chinese, Uyghur, Kazak and Kirgiz are pre-processed and input into ResNet50, a residual network which was added the channel attention module SE (squeeze-and-excitation) [11]. Through the method of transfer learning, a high recognition rate is obtained for multi-lingual offline handwritten signatures.

2 Related Theories

2.1 Transfer Learning

Transfer learning [12] is a kind of machine learning method in the field of artificial intelligence. It can solve the problems of small amount of annotated data, long training time, low generalization performance and personalized requirements.

ImageNet [13] is the largest image recognition database in the world, with more than 14 million images available for recognition. Considering that the images of ImageNet's large-scale database are all images of natural scenes, which are greatly different from the self-built multi-lingual handwritten signature images, and the scale of the self-built database is limited, this paper adopts the idea of transitive transfer learning [14] to carry out knowledge transfer based on the network model. Firstly, transfers between the ImageNet database and the large-scale public GPDS Synthetic English signature database, and then transfers between the GPDS Synthetic and the multi-lingual signature database. Finally, the recognition results of hybrid four languages handwritten signatures are obtained.

2.2 SE-ResNet

The SE (squeeze-and-excitation) module is a channel attention mechanism that focuses on the relationship between channels and can automatically learn the important weights of different channel features. The SE module takes the convoluted feature map as input. First, using an adaptive average pooling operation to obtain the global feature of the channel (Eq. 1). The excitation operation consists of two full connection layers and the Sigmoid activation function to obtain the relationship and weight between different channels (Eq. 2). Finally, the channel weight obtained is multiplied and weighted with the original feature through Scale operation to obtain the final output feature with channel attention (Eq. 3).

$$Z_c = F_{sq}(u_c) = \frac{1}{H \times W} \sum_{i=1}^{H} \sum_{j=1}^{W} u_c(i,j) \qquad (1)$$

$$S = F_{ex}(Z, W) = \sigma(g(Z, W)) = \sigma(W_2 \delta(W_1 Z)) \tag{2}$$

$$\tilde{X}_c = F_{scale}(u_c, S_c) = S_c \cdot u_c \tag{3}$$

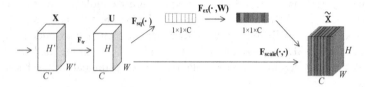

Fig. 1. The squeeze-and-excitation module structure.

Z_c is the global feature of the cth channel in the convolutional layer, u_c is the output of the cth channel in the convolutional layer, H and W are the size of the feature map. S represents the weight of C feature graphs in U. σ represents the Sigmoid activation function, δ represents the ReLU activation function, W_1 and W_2 are the parameter matrix, and X_c is the output of the cth channel in the SE layer. F_{tr} stands for a convolution or a set of convolutions (Fig. 1).

ResNet can not only solve the difficult training problem caused by network depth, but also complete the task with accuracy far higher than other traditional network models. Resnet has two branches, the residual function and the identity mapping of the input. After simple addition operation of these two branches, the nonlinear transformation of ReLU activation function is carried out to form a complete residual module. The network structure formed by the stack of multiple residual models is called "residual network".

In order to extract the deep features that can better express the signature characteristics in the multi-lingual signature image, considering the influence of less training samples on the depth of the network and the amount of computation, this paper selects the ResNet50 network to build the multi-lingual handwritten signature recognition model, which contains 49 convolutional layers and 1 fully connected layer.

SE applications are very flexible and can be easily embedded into ResNet, ResNext, Inception, and other networks for integration. After the fusion, the number of parameters of the model is only increased by about 10%, but the performance is significantly improved.

2.3 Focal Loss

Focal Loss [15] is a loss function commonly used in the field of target detection, which can be used to solve the problems of unbalanced category ratio and uneven difficult and easy samples. Focal Loss has two main parameters, α and γ. The α parameter is used to alleviate the problem of unbalanced category proportion, while the γ parameter solves the problem of unbalanced difficult and easy samples. In the binary classification problem, the formula for focus loss is as follows (Eq. 4). Wherein, p_t is the probability estimate of the category. Different from the target detection field, in the multi-classification task, the α parameter of Focal Loss has no role and can only adjust the multiple of the overall Loss value.

$$FL_{\text{loss}} = -\alpha_t (1 - p_t)^\gamma \log(p_t) \tag{4}$$

Considering that Uyghur, Kazak and Kirgiz are very similar in their writing styles, this paper uses Cross Entropy and Focal Loss as loss functions respectively, conducts comparative experiments by adjusting the γ parameters of Focal Loss.

3 Database and Pre-processing

3.1 Signature Database

GPDS Synthetic [16] is a large English public handwritten signature database, which contains a total of 192,000 images of 4000 people (each person has 24 real signatures and 24 generated forged signatures), which can be used for the research of handwritten signature identification and recognition. In order to improve the recognition rate and speed of multi-lingual handwritten signatures, the real signatures of 4000 people in the GPDS Synthetic database were extracted, and a total of 96000 signature images were transferred and learned.

The self-built multi-lingual offline handwritten signature database consists of three steps: acquisition, scanning and segmentation. The collection of multi-lingual handwritten signature images is that the signers write their names in the form of Chinese, Uyghur, Kazak and Kirgiz on the collection template paper printed with A4 paper and with 21 rectangular boxes in the same day. A Lenovo M7400 scanner was used to scan with 300 dpi and BMP image format, which was cropped with Photoshop software and stored in a numbered sequence on the computer. By removing the signatures which cannot be experimented manually, the multi-lingual handwritten signature offline database is established by using images of four languages, including Chinese, Uyghur, Kazak and Kirgiz, with 100 people in each language, 20 signatures in each people, and a total of 8000 signature samples (Fig. 2).

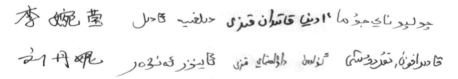

Fig. 2. Samples of self-built multi-lingual signature database.

3.2 Pre-processing

There are some problems in the GPDS Synthetic database and the self-built multi-lingual database, such as discrete noise, irrelevant background, different handwriting thickness and large blank edge. Therefore, it is necessary to preprocessing the signature image before recognizing the signature image written by hand.

In this paper, the weighted average method is used to gray the signed image, the median filter is used to remove the irrelevant noise, and the OTSU method is used to binarize the signed image and remove the background of the signed image. The boundary of signature handwriting is determined by scanning method, and the blank area outside the signature is clipped. Use the Skeletonize package to extract the signature handwriting skeleton and refine the handwriting. Finally, normalize the size of all the signed images and change the size of the image to 224 * 224. Through these preprocessing operations, not only the storage space and calculation amount of the signature image can be reduced, but also the influence of irrelevant factors on signature recognition can be reduced to a large extent (Fig. 3).

(a)original image   (b)filter image

(c)Binary image   (d)thinning image

Fig. 3. Pre-processing result.

4 Training and Classification

The video card model of the experimental computer in this paper is NVIDIA Quadro M4000, with 8 GB of video memory, Intel(R) Xeon(R) CPU E5–1603 V4@2.80 GHz, and 16 GB of memory. Using PyCharm Community Edition 2020.3.3x64 on Windows 10 64-bit system, multi-lingual handwritten signature recognition based on transfer learning and SE-ResNet50 is implemented.

The experimental process first involves one transfer between the large-scale ImageNet database and the public GPDS Synthetic signature database, and then a second transfer between the GPDS Synthetic signature database and the self-built multi-lingual signature database. All experiments in the GPDS database have trained 50 epochs, and all experiments in the multi-lingual database have trained 20 epochs, with a learning rate of 0.0001, batch size is 32, and the Adam optimizer is adopted.

4.1 GPDS Signature Recognition

For the GPDS synthetic signature database, the training set and the test set are divided in a ratio of 75%:25% for experiments, that is, 18 signatures of each person were used for training, 6 for testing, a total of 72000 signatures for training and 24000 signatures for testing. The Cross Entropy was used as the loss function, and the weights of all the convolutional layers and the fully connected layers in the pre-training model were fine-tuned to compare the ResNet50 model and the SE-ResNet50 model.

By analyzing the experimental results, the accuracy of ResNet50 and SE-ResNet50 reaches 98.15% and 98.97% respectively, which proves that SE-ResNet50 is a more effective signature recognition method.

4.2 Multi-lingual Signature Recognition

For the multi-lingual signature database which mixed Chinese, Uyghur, Kazak and Kirgiz were divided into the training set and test set in a ratio of 80%:20%, that is, 16 signatures of each person were used for training, 4 for testing, a total of 6400 signatures for training and 1600 signatures for testing. Cross Entropy and Focal Loss were used as loss functions, ReLU were used as activation function, and all convolutional layer and fully connected layer weights were fine-tuned for the optimal model of GPDS database test results (Fig. 4).

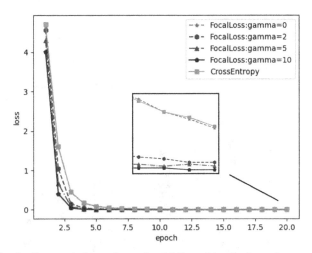

Fig. 4. Changes in loss values of multi-lingual handwritten signatures.

In the contrast experiment of adjusting the gamma parameter of Focal Loss, γ is tested with 0, 2, 5, 10 respectively. When γ equals 0, the loss decreases approximately to the Cross Entropy, and the larger the γ, the faster the loss decreases. Through several comparative experiments, the highest recognition result of multi-lingual offline handwritten signature is 99.44%. Reasons for achieving such a high recognition accuracy may include the fact that the signature data is too clean and similar (Table 1).

The handwritten signatures mixed with Chinese, Uyghur, Kazak and Kirgiz were tested and the recognition accuracy of each language was calculated. As can be seen from the following figure, the recognition accuracy of the five models for Chinese is basically stable, with a small fluctuation between 99.25%–99.75% and the average recognition accuracy is 99.625%. For Uyghur and Kazak, different models and parameters have a great influence on the recognition accuracy. The recognition accuracy of Uyghur is

Table 1. Multi-lingual handwritten signature recognition results.

Loss function	Train accuracy	Test accuracy
CrossEntropy	100.00%	**99.44%**
FocalLoss:gamma = 0	100.00%	**99.44%**
FocalLoss:gamma = 2	100.00%	99.19%
FocalLoss:gamma = 5	100.00%	98.75%
FocalLoss:gamma = 10	100.00%	98.75%

between 98.75% and 99.75%, the average recognition accuracy is 99.292%, while that Kazak is between 98.25% and 99.75% the average recognition accuracy is 99.00%. Kirgiz is more difficult to recognize than the other three languages, the recognition accuracy is between 98.25% and 99.75%, the average recognition accuracy is 98.625% (Fig. 5).

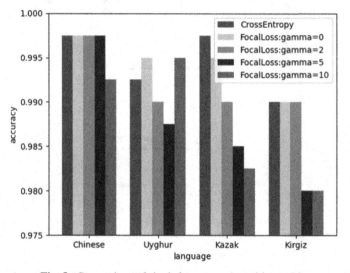

Fig. 5. Comparison of single language recognition result.

5 Conclusion

Up to now, no researchers have mixed handwritten signatures of Chinese, Uyghur, Kazak and Kirgiz. In this paper, a multi-lingual hybrid handwritten signature recognition method based on deep residuals attention network is proposed. Using the method, the highest recognition accuracy of GPDS synthetic database (4000 people) is 98.97%, and the highest recognition accuracy of multi-lingual database (300 people) is 99.44%.

Experimental results show that this method can effectively recognize signatures for these four languages.

However, there are still the following problems in this paper: the signature data collected is too clean and similar, the signature quantity of each person is too small, and it needs to be retrained if new personal identity is added.

The main idea of the follow-up work is to improve the structure of the network model, so that it can be applied to the multi-lingual handwritten signature database with a smaller number and a wider category, so as to further improve the recognition accuracy of offline handwritten signature.

Acknowledgment. This work was supported by the National Science Foundation of China under Grant (No. 61862061, 61563052, 61163028), and the Graduate Student Scientific Research Innovation Project of Xinjiang Uygur Autonomous Region under Grant No. XJ2020G064.

References

1. Hadjadji, B., Chibani, Y., Nemmour, H.: An efficient open system for offline handwritten signature identification based on curvelet transform and one-class principal component analysis. Neurocomputing **26**(22), 66–77(2017)
2. Alik, N., et al.: Large-scale offline signature recognition via deep neural networks and feature embedding. Neurocomputing **359,** 1–14 (2019)
3. Singh, N.: An efficient approach for handwritten devanagari character recognition based on artificial neural network. In: 2018 5th International Conference on Signal Processing and Integrated Networks (SPIN) (2018)
4. Aravinda, C.V., et al.: Signature recognition and verification using multiple classifiers combination of Hu's and hog features. In: 2019 International Conference on Advanced Mechatronic Systems (ICAMechS) IEEE (2019)
5. Younesian, T., et al.: Active transfer learning for Persian offline signature verification. In: 2019 4th International Conference on Pattern Recognition and Image Analysis (IPRIA) (2019)
6. Xiaoqing, M.A., Sang, Q.: Handwritten signature verification algorithm based on LBP and deep learning. Chin. J. Quant. Electr. **34**, 23–31 (2017)
7. Ubul, K., et al.: Uyghur off-line signature recognition based on local central line features. In: Zhou, J., et al. (eds.) Biometric Recognition. CCBR 2017. Lecture Notes in Computer Science, vol. 10568. Springer, Cham (2017). https://doi.org/10.1007/978-3-319-69923-3_80
8. Ubul, K., et al.: Multilingual Offline Handwritten Signature Recognition Based on Statistical Features. Springer, Cham (2018)
9. Ubul, K., et al.: Uyghur offline signature recognition based on density feature. Comput. Eng. Des. (in Chinese) **37**(08), 2200–2205 (2016)
10. Mo, L.F., et al.: Off-Line handwritten signature recognition based on discrete curvelet transform. In: Sun, Z., He, R., Feng, J., Shan, S., Guo, Z. (eds.) Biometric Recognition. CCBR 2019. Lecture Notes in Computer Science, vol. 11818. Springer, Cham (2019). https://doi.org/10.1007/978-3-030-31456-9_47
11. Jie, H., Li, S., Gang, S.: Squeeze-and-excitation networks. In: 2018 IEEE/CVF Conference on Computer Vision and Pattern Recognition (CVPR) IEEE (2018)
12. Pan, S.J., Qiang, Y.: A Survey on transfer learning. IEEE Trans. Knowl. Data Eng. **22**(10), 1345–1359 (2010)
13. Jia, D., et al.: ImageNet: A large-scale hierarchical image database. In: Proceedings of IEEE Computer Vision & Pattern Recognition, pp. 248–255 (2009)

14. Tan, B., et al.: Transitive transfer learning. In: ACM SIGKDD International Conference on Knowledge Discovery & Data Mining ACM (2015)
15. Lin, T.Y., et al.: Focal Loss for dense object detection. IEEE Trans. Patt. Anal. Mach. Intell. **99,** 2999–3007 (2017)
16. Ferrer, M.A., Díaz-Cabrera, M., Morales, A.: Synthetic off-line signature image generation. In: 6th IAPR International Conference on Biometrics IEEE (2013)

Traumatic Brain Injury Images Classification Method Based on Deep Learning

Shaojie Zhang, Taiyang Cao, and Haifeng Zhao[✉]

Anhui Provincial Key Laboratory of Multimodal Cognitive Computation, School of Computer Science and Technology, Anhui University, Anhui 230601, China
zhangshaojie@ahu.edu.cn, caotaiyang@stu.ahu.edu.cn

Abstract. Computed tomography (CT) images of traumatic brain injury (TBI) rely heavily on physicians' experience in the diagnosis and the accuracy is limited. This paper will introduce a computer aided diagnosis (CAD) algorithm that will help doctors classify CT images of TBI and determine whether there is damage. In the CAD algorithm, we propose a brand new neural network structure based on Convolutional Neural Network (CNN) according to actual requirements. The proposed new neural network is called VGG-SE-PCR, which is composed of the traditional convolutional neural network VGG-S, the squeeze and excitation module SE and pixel-wise correlation retaining module PCR. It can adaptively select features from different brain CT images, and retain the correlation information between pixels. In addition, we adopt the strategy of transfer learning to solve the problem of insufficient datasets and avoid local optima. The method has been verified on 636 brain CT images, and achieved classification accuracy of 89.3%. Additionally, the effectiveness of SE module and PCR module is verified through the ablation experiments. In comparison with other state-of-the-art methods, our method has better performance on diagnostic accuracy based on CT images of TBI patients.

Keywords: Traumatic brain injury · Computed tomography · Convolutional neural network · Transfer learning

1 Introduction

TBI [1] is a serious injury with extremely high morbidity, rapid changes in injuries, and the highest fatality rate. According to statistics, there are 300 cases per 100000 people worldwide each year, with a fatality rate as high as 15%, accounting for 85% of all trauma mortality rates. The annual number of TBI patients in the United States accounts for 2% of the total population, and medical expenses are as high as 56.3 billion dollars. In China, TBI has become the leading cause of disability and death among young people, and its mortality rate has exceeded hot spots such as tumors, cardiovascular and cerebrovascular diseases. There are about 600,000 patients with TBI every year, and about 100,000 of them die. Therefore, research on TBI diagnostic technology has become a serious problem in academia [2].

© Springer Nature Switzerland AG 2021
J. Feng et al. (Eds.): CCBR 2021, LNCS 12878, pp. 157–164, 2021.
https://doi.org/10.1007/978-3-030-86608-2_18

Due to the diverse and complex characteristics of TBI images, professional doctors are required to screen one by one. Doctors are prone to visual fatigue after long hours of work, so it is inevitable that missed diagnosis and misdiagnosis will occur. Therefore, in recent years, using computer-aided technology to process TBI images and to assist doctors in diagnosis have become the main stream to improve the level of TBI treatment. Deep learning has made breakthrough progress in processing images, and also in processing medical images. Deep learning has been extensively and deeply researched in the fields of lung cancer [3], and its diagnostic accuracy has reached more than 76%. It does not require the operator to have the expertise to identify cancer. It replaces the artificial extraction by automatically extracting the effective features of CT images to classify. For example, Ahmed [4] uses transfer learning of convolutional neural networks and classifies brain tumors together with fully connected (FC) layers. Our TBI classification is more difficult than brain tumor classification, because the TBI's injury site is not as easy to observe as the tumor injury site.

Compared with other medical images, CT images of TBI are multi-layered, and slices are taken every 5 mm, so the content of neighboring slices obtained from the same patient of TBI varies greatly. However, existing neural networks based on CNN usually have fixed parameters after training and cannot process such CT images properly. And the feature map after the convolution layer is directly sent to the fully connected layer, which will cause the loss of information between pixels. In order to solve these two problems, we propose a new VGG-SE-PCR method based on deep learning. According to the input CT images of different TBI, the network adaptively selects features, and retains the correlation between image pixels, the parameters and the number of connections are greatly reduced, the complexity of network is also reduced, and therefore it has strong robustness. Through experimental verification of 636 brain CT images provided by the partner hospital, our method is superior to the state-of-art deep learning methods.

2 Methods

The structure of the VGG-SE-PCR network proposed in this paper is shown in Fig. 1, and the related symbol description is shown in Fig. 2. The network is constructed based on VGG-S [5] and consists of three parts. The first part (Part1) is similar to VGG-S. It includes five convolutional layers and three maximum pooling layers. The size of the TBI image is adjusted to 224 × 224 and sent to the network. It firstly passes through the convolution layer and after a layer of convolution operations, enter the ReLU layer for activation, and then put the results into the maximum pooling layer (Convolutional neural networks are prone to over-fitting after multiple convolutions, so adding a pooling layer after convolution can effectively save resources and speed up training). And then send the output result to the second layer. The following layers accomplish similar operations, which are not repeated here. This part is to extract features from the input TBI image.

The second part (Part 2) uses the SE [6] module. Because the resolution of CT images of TBI is low, which is taken every 5 mm slice by slice, neighboring slices result in greatly different pictures. The image has high flexibility, and the network with fixed parameters is not suitable for processing TBI images, so we chose the SE module. The third part (Part3) is the PCR module. If the output after the convolution layer is directly connected to the fully connected layer, it will cause the loss and incompleteness of the correlation information between the image pixels. Therefore, instead of straightening the obtained features directly, we send them to the global average pooling layer [7] after a layer of convolution, and then connect with the fully connected layer softmax [8] function for the CT images of the brain (damage or non-damage) classification. In addition, we adopt a transfer learning strategy to train the VGG-SE-PCR network, which can learn more complex features in TBI images.

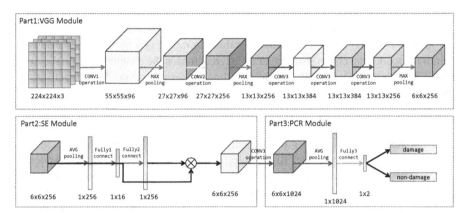

Fig. 1. The VGG-SE-PCR module. The input of VGG-SE-PCR is a CT image of the brain. First, the image passes through five convolutional layers and three pooling layers. Then, the obtained feature maps are transferred to the SE module, which can adaptively select the most relevant feature maps. Finally, the feature maps with different weights are transferred to the PCR module for brain image classification.

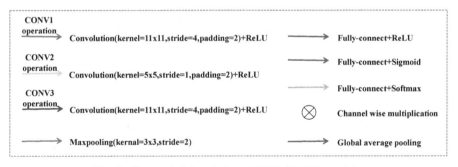

Fig. 2. The symbol description of VGG-SE-PCR module.

2.1 The SE Module

As illustrated in Fig. 3, the SE module is composed of space squeeze and channel excitation. We represent the input feature as $U = [u_1, u_2, \ldots, u_c]$, $U \in \mathbb{R}^{W \times H \times C}$, the feature U is the first squeeze operated, and the global average pooling is used for spatial compression, which $z \in \mathbb{R}^C$ is generated by shrinking U in the spatial dimension W × H, where the c-th element of z is calculated by the following formula:

$$z_c = \frac{1}{W \times H} \sum_{i=1}^{W} \sum_{j=1}^{H} u_c(i,j). \tag{1}$$

Then z is transformed to s:

$$s = \sigma(W_2\delta(W_1z)). \tag{2}$$

Where δ refers to the ReLU function and σ refers to the Sigmoid function. $W_1 \in \mathbb{R}^{\frac{C}{r} \times C}$, $W_2 = \mathbb{R}^{C \times \frac{C}{r}}$ (the dimensionality reduction ratio r is a hyperparameter). This operation encodes the channel dependence and reactivates the channel. The final output of the SE module is obtained by readjusting the transformed output U with activation, which is expresses as:

$$\widehat{U} = sU = [s_1u_1, s_2u_2, \ldots, s_cu_c]. \tag{3}$$

In our network, the number of channels input to the SE module C = 256, we set r = 16. By introducing the SE module to explicitly model the interdependence between channels, our network can learn global features, emphasize important features, and suppress unimportant features, given channels different weights. Therefore, network adaptive feature selection can be achieved, and will be enhanced with the development of network learning.

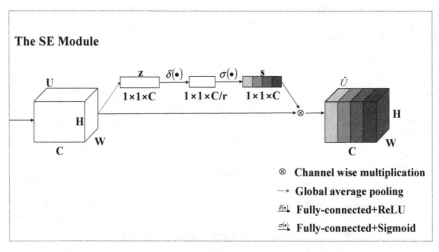

Fig. 3. The SE module. The colors on different channels represent different weights.

2.2 The PCR Module

In CNN, the features obtained by a series of convolutions are sent to the fully connected layer for classification. However, straightening the features in the FC layer will lose the correlation information between pixels, and the radiologist needs to combine the global information of the brain image when diagnosing TBI. So we made the following changes: (1) after weighting the features of the SE module, replace the first FC layer with a convolutional layer, which can further refine the features to obtain more accurate features. (2) We do not straighten the features directly into a vector, but adopt a global average pooling layer, which can effectively retain the correlation information between pixels. And adaptive parameters can avoid overfitting in this layer, which is very important in TBI classification. (3) Finally, we use the FC layer and the softmax function to classify the brain CT images. The dimension of input features is 1024 and the dimension of the output features is 2 (damage or non-damage).

2.3 Network Training

During the training phase, the labels of the input brain CT image (damage or non-damage) are known. Based on these labels, we use softmax for binary classification to obtain the results. The principle of softmax classifier:

$$p_c = \frac{e^{z_c}}{\sum_{d=1}^{c} e^{z_d}}.$$ (4)

z is the input vector, c is the dimension of the vector, and p is the probability of being classified into a certain category.

Given M samples $X = \{x_i\}_{i=1}^{M}$ from Q classes, the correspondent label is expressed as $Y = \{y_i\}_{i=1}^{M}$ and $y_i \in \{1,2,\ldots Q\}$. For classification, the objective loss function of the training network is defined as the cross-entropy error between the predicted values and the correct labels:

$$loss = -\sum_{1=1}^{M} \sum_{q=1}^{Q} J(y_i,q)\log(p^q(x_i)).$$ (5)

with an indicator function J defined as:

$$J(y_i,q) = \begin{cases} 1, y_i = q \\ 0, y_i \neq q \end{cases}.$$ (6)

Gradient descent algorithm [9] is used to update the network parameters to minimize the loss. In the training phase, we adopt the strategy of transfer learning, because training from scratch is a difficult and time consuming process that requires a large amount of labeled training data and powerful computing resources [10]. We use the weights of pre-trained neural networks with the same architecture to initialize the weights on the network layer [11]. The pre-training network is originally trained on the ImageNet Large Scale Visual Recognition Challenge (ILSVRC) [12] dataset. This process is called fine-tuning, and it has been successfully used in many applications [13]. The weight of the pre-trained network is transferred to the network that we want to train. The last fully connected layer has many nodes, and these nodes depend on the number of classes we classify (damaged or non-damaged), so we set Q = 2. Before training we rescale the image to 224 × 224. After the training network reaches its optimal state on ImageNet dataset, we use CT images of TBI to fine-tune the network [14]. The transfer learning [15] strategy avoids random initialization which may lead to undesirable local minimums, solves the problem of insufficient datasets, and improves the classification accuracy of TBI.

3 Experiments and Results

We collect 636 CT images of the brain from the partner hospital. The labels of these images (damage or non-damage) are marked and confirmed by a professional radiologist. Figure 4 illustrates CT images of the brain with and without damage respectively. Among these brain CT images, 306 are non-damaged images and 330 are damaged images. Before sending them to the network for training, the image size is adjusted to 224 × 224. Taking into account the problem of insufficient training data set, we expand the data. We flip, invert and rotate each image in the range of ($-20°$, $+20°$), as a result, we get 1320 brain images with damage and 1224 without damage.

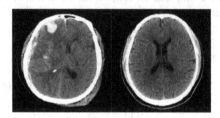

Fig. 4. The damaged brain CT image (left), the non-damaged brain CT image (right).

Sensitivity and specificity are used to evaluate experiments or models of classification, and are widely used measurement standards in medical field. The higher the sensitivity, the less likely the damaged to be missed. The higher the specificity, the less likely the non-damaged to be misdiagnosed. In our experiments, we defined non-damaged as a positive sample, and damaged is marked as a negative sample. Our experimental results use these three indicators: accuracy, sensitivity and specificity, the evaluation results are summarized in Table 1.

Table 1. Evaluation results with different structures. Ac (%) I Sn (%) I Sp (%): mean accuracy, sensitivity, specificity.

Structure	No transfer learning	Transfer learning
VGG-S	84.0l85.7l82.5	86.7l92.9l81.2
VGG-SE	86.2l90.5l82.5	87.6l94.8l81.2
VGG-PCR	86.4l91.4l82.1	88.0l95.7l82.1
VGG-SE-PCR	86.2l91.9l81.2	**89.3l98.6l82.9**

First of all, we conduct an ablation experiment on our network structure. We set up the original VGG-S, VGG-SE, VGG-PCR and VGG-SE-PCR, and we also adopt two methods (with or without transfer learning) to train our network. We find that the network model add with transfer learning converge faster during training, and achieve better results in the diagnosis of brain CT images. Our proposed model achieves the highest accuracy (accuracy, sensitivity, specificity are 89.3%, 98.6%, 82.9%). The accuracy of VGG-SE and VGG-PCR is higher than that of VGG-S, indicating the effectiveness of SE and PCR modules. Sensitivity indicators are of great significance. The increase in sensitivity means that the rate of missed diagnosis can be reduced. As more patients with TBI can be found early detection and early treatment can be achieved. Therefore, sensitivity is a more critical indicator than specificity. So the specificity is slightly lower than the sensitivity is acceptable.

Table 2. Classification results produced by different methods. The three metrics are accuracy (Ac), Sensitivity (Sn), and Specificity (Sp).

Method	Ac (%)	Sn (%)	Sp (%)
LeNet-5	86.4	92.4	81.2
CNN-Brain	85.3	89.0	80.4
VGG-SE-PCR	**89.3**	**98.6**	**82.9**

In the second stage, we conduct a comparative experiment. LeNet-5 [16] is a network used to recognize handwritten digits in major banks. Its network model is relatively simple and the recognition accuracy is high. At present, this kind of network is widely used in many fields such as pattern recognition and license plate character recognition. CNN-Brain method is proposed by Li [17] as a new deep convolutional neural network, which not only improves the classification accuracy, but also is a successful attempt in brain CT images. In order to test our network performance, we compare LeNet-5 and CNN-Brain with our network VGG-SE-PCR. The evaluation results are summarized in Table 2. The results show that our method achieves the best results in accuracy, sensitivity and specificity.

4   Conclusions

In this paper, a deep convolutional neural network VGG-SE-PCR is proposed to classify the CT images of traumatic brain injury, which is composed of VGG-S, SE module and PCR module. Based on the fact that the input brain CT image is sliced every 5 mm, and neighboring slices are dramatically different, which means the image has high flexibility, we choose the SE module for adaptive feature selection. Feature selection through the SE module can selectively emphasize useful information features and suppress less useful features. Doctors in the radiology department must use the global features of the brain to diagnose whether the brain is damaged, so we use the PCR module to reduce the loss or incompleteteness of correlation information between pixels. With the help of these two modules, we have achieved the best results in both the ablation experiment and the comparative experiment with two latest methods. In addition, in our network, the strategy of adopting transfer learning has proved to be effective.

In future work, we will collect more datasets, work on more effective feature selection modules, and build more efficient networks to achieve better classification results. At the same time, we will further explore the detection of TBI images, and strive to develop a computer aided system which will combine automatic detection, diagnosis and report generation of CT images to provide better medical services for more people.

Acknowledgments. This work was supported in part by the National Natural Science Foundation of China (No.61876002, 62076005).

References

1. Carney N.A.: Guidelines for the management of severe traumatic brain injury. VI. Indications for intracranial pressure monitoring. J. Neurotrauma. **24** (supplement 1), 1–106 (2007)
2. Huang, Q., Zhang, F., Li, X.: Machine learning in ultrasound computer-aided diagnostic systems: a survey. BioMed. Res. Int. 2018, 5137904 (2018)
3. Yang, J., Geng, C., Wang, H., et al.: Histological subtype classification of lung adenocarcinoma in low-resolution CT images based on DenseNet. J. Zhejiang Univ. (Engineering and Technology Edition) **53**(06), 151–157 (2019)
4. Ahmed, K.B., Hall, L.O., Goldgof D.B., et al.: Fine-tuning convolutional deep features for MRI based brain tumor classification. In: SPIE Medical Imaging. Society of Photo-Optical Instrumentation Engineers (SPIE) Conference Series (2017)
5. Paul, R., Hawkins, S.H., Schabath, M.B., et al.: Predicting malignant nodules by fusing deep features with classical radiomics features. J. Med Imaging. **5**(1), 1 (2018)
6. Hu, J., Shen, L., Albanie, S., et al.: Squeeze-and-excitation networks. J. IEEE Trans. Patt. Anal. Mach. Intell. (99), 7132–7141 (2017)
7. Lin, M., Chen, Q., Yan, S.: Network in network. In: International Conference on Learning Representations (2014)
8. Brown, P.F., Pietra, V.J.D., Souza, P.V.D., et al.: Class-based n-gram models of natural language. J. Comput. Lingust. **18**(4), 467–479 (1992)
9. Ruder, S.: An overview of gradient descent optimization algorithms. arXiv preprint arXiv: 1609.04747 (2016)
10. Ma, J., Wu, F., Zhu, J., et al.: A pre-trained convolutional neural network based method for thyroid nodule diagnosis. J. Ultrasonics. **73**, 221–230 (2017)
11. Chi, J., Walia, E., Babyn, P., Wang, J., Groot, G., Eramian, M.: Thyroid nodule classification in ultrasound images by fine-tuning deep convolutional neural network. J. Digit. Imaging **30**(4), 477–486 (2017). https://doi.org/10.1007/s10278-017-9997-y
12. Russakovsky, O., et al.: Imagenet large scale visual recognition challenge. Int. J. Comput. Vis. **115**(3), 211–252 (2015)
13. Razavian, A.S., Azizpour, H., Sullivan, J., Carlsson, S.: CNN features off-the-shelf: an astounding baseline for recognition. ArXiv14036382 Cs (2014)
14. Zhang, G., Zhu, D., Liu, X., et al.: Multi-scale pulmonary nodule classification with deep feature fusion via residual network. J. Ambient Intell. Hum. Comput. (2018)
15. Pan, S.J., Yang, Q.: A survey on transfer learning. J. IEEE Trans. Knowl. Data Eng. **22**(10), 1345–1359 (2010)
16. Lecun, Y., Bottou, L.: Gradient-based learning applied to document recognition. J. Proc. IEEE. **86**(11), 2278–2324 (1998)
17. Li, W.: Research on brain CT image classification based on deep learning. Comput. Methods Program. Biomed. **138,** 49–56 (2017)

Palatal Rugae Recognition via 2D Fractional Fourier Transform

Jinbo Wei[1], Hong Shangguan[1(✉)], Qiang Luo[1], Xiong Zhang[1], Bing Li[2], and Zhigang Jia[1]

[1] School of Electronic Information Engineering, Taiyuan University of Science and Technology, Taiyuan 030024, China
shangguan_hong@tyust.edu.cn
[2] Stomatology Hospital, Shanxi Medical University, Taiyuan 030001, China

Abstract. Palatal rugae is a new type of biological feature that is suitable for forensic identification in special environments. This work proposes to perform palatal rugae recognition via 2D fractional fourier transform (FrFT). Firstly, since FrFT is superior in the time-frequency analysis of non-stationary signals, we extract the time-frequency characteristics of palatal rugae profiles using 2D FrFT; Secondly, we achieve feature dimensionality reduction by constructing feature vector utilizing the discrete cosine transform (DCT) coefficients, which show the greatest discriminative power; Finally, we use support vector machine (SVM) to perform classification and recognition. In addition, we perform weighted fusion of the recognition results obtained by using different single order fractional domain amplitude spectrum to obtain a better final result. In particular, each weight parameter value is determined by calculating the contribution rate to recognition of each fractional domain amplitude spectrum. Experimental results show that the proposed method is effective.

Keywords: Palatal rugae · Fractional fourier transform · Discrete cosine transform · Support vector machine

1 Introduction

Biometric indicators used in forensic identification should be uniqueness, universality, permanence, collectability and identifiability [1]. The commonly used biometric indicators in forensic identification technology include teeth, craniofacial morphology, fingerprints, palm prints, iris, DNA, etc. [2, 3], however they still suffer from economic, security and environmental limitations in some special environments, such as fire, chemical corrosion or external trauma. As shown in Fig. 1, Palatal rugae [4] is heritable, stable, unique, high temperature resistant and corrosion resistant [5, 6]. Taking into account the particularity of forensic identification application background, as an auxiliary feature, palatal rugae may become a key factor in the identification of victims in a specific case. Although this kind of application opportunities are few, even the success of an individual case is still of great significance for forensic identification.

© Springer Nature Switzerland AG 2021
J. Feng et al. (Eds.): CCBR 2021, LNCS 12878, pp. 165–173, 2021.
https://doi.org/10.1007/978-3-030-86608-2_19

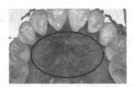

Fig. 1. Schematic diagram of palatal ruage

In early research works, palatal ruage recognition is mainly realized by manual recognition, which relies on the experience of forensic experts. Professor Li's research team first using image recognition technology to realize palatal ruage recognition [5, 6]. In 2020, Zhang et al. [7] realized the real 3D palatal ruage automatic recognition for the first time, and proposed a 3D palatal ruage recognition method based on cyclic spectrum analysis. However, It needs to reduce the 3D data to one dimension gradually in the process of feature extraction, which increases the complexity of the algorithm. Based on their work, we proposes a 2D FrFT-based palatal rugae recognition method. Becouse the upper jaw edge curve in the palatal rugae profile image sequence has rich features in the time-frequency domain, this work extracts feature vectors by performing 2D-FrFT [8–10] on the entire palatal rugae profile image after isometric slicing. The direct feature extraction from 2D slice data reduces the complexity of the algorithm, and improve the feature extraction and utilization efficiency of the recognition system. The contributions of this work can be summarized as following:

Data Augmentation. This work producted a dataset containing images with defects on the basis of the existing palatal rugae profile image dataset containing only standard images.

Feature Dimensionality Reduction. This work achieves feature selection by discriminative power analysis (DPA). We performed DCT on the FrFT amplitude spectrum of palatal rugae profile image, and selected the DCT coefficients which has the maximum DP value as the optimal eigenvector, to ensure the recognition ability while reducing the dimensionality.

Classification. This work propose to consider the contribution rate to recognition of each order fractional domain amplitude spectrum, and to perform weighted fusion of the recognition results obtained by using different single order fractional domain amplitude spectrum to obtain a better final result. In particular, each weight parameter value is determined by calculating the contribution rate to recognition of each fractional domain amplitude spectrum.

2 The Proposed Palatal Rugae Recognition System

As shown in Fig. 2, the proposed recognition system is composed of three modules: image preprocessing, feature extraction and classification. Firstly, to remove the interference of background, the obtained 2D palatal rugae profile images should be preprocessed by binary method in the image preprocessing module. Secondly, in the feature extraction module, we construct the training set and the test set respectively. In the training process, we utilize 2D FrFT and DCT-DPA to perform feature extraction and feature dimensionality reduction, and then construct the feature vector dictionary for SVM by using the optimal eigenvector. In the test process, we construct the feature vector dictionary by utilizing the output DCT coefficients corresponding to the optimal eigenvector during training. Finally, in the classification module, through calculating the contribution rate of each order fractional domain amplitude spectrum, we construct the weight parameter dictionary, and vote on the five SVM classification results obtained by using different single order fractional domain amplitude spectrum to obtain the final result. Figure 3 shows the different fractional amplitude spectrums and phase spectrums of a palatal rugae profile image. It can be seen that with the increase of the order of FrFT, the contour information and texture information of the original palatal rugae profile image are mainly reflected in the fractional amplitude spectrums.

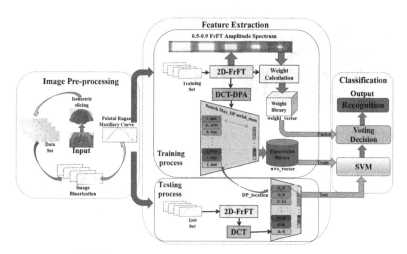

Fig. 2. The proposed palatal rugae recognition system

Figure 4(a) shows a DCT coefficients image obtained by performing DCT on an fractional amplitude spectrum of palatal rugae profile image. It can be observed that, the main information of the DCT coefficients image, that is, the low-frequency information is distributed in the upper left corner of the image, while the high-frequency information is concentrated in the lower right corner of the image. A key issue that needs to be considered is how to effectively extract DCT coefficients. Commonly used methods [11] include matrix extraction method and Zig-Zag method two kinds, as shown in Fig. 4(b) and Fig. 4(c), the shaded part in the image are the selected DCT coefficients. The two traditional methods are not advisable for palatal rugae recognition. This is because different DCT coefficients' contribution to recognition are different. This work achieves feature vector selection by discriminative power analysis (DPA), and we select DCT coefficient whose DP value is the greatest as the feature vector. To make the DCT coefficient at a certain position get a large DP value, the following two conditions should

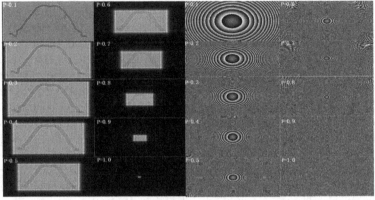

(a) The fractional amplitude spectrums   (b) The fractional phase spectrums

Fig. 3. Different fractional amplitude and phase spectrums of a palatal rugae profile image.

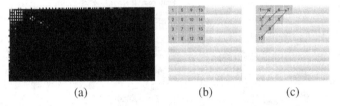

(a)   (b)   (c)

Fig. 4. (a) The DCT coefficients image of a fractional amplitude spectrum of the palatal rugae profile image; (b) the matrix extraction method (c) zig-zag.

be met: ① the variance between classes is large enough; ② the within-class variance is small enough. If the DCT coefficient matrix X of a fractional amplitude spectrum of palatal rugaes with a size of M × N is:

$$
X = \begin{bmatrix} x_{11} & x_{12} & \cdots & x_{1N} \\ x_{21} & x_{22} & \cdots & x_{2N} \\ \vdots & & \vdots & \vdots \\ x_{M1} & x_{M2} & \cdots & x_{MN} \end{bmatrix}_{M \times N}
\tag{1}
$$

Assuming that there are C-type objects in the palatal rugae training set, and each type of object has S training samples, there are a total of C × S training samples. The discriminative power of each coefficient x_{ij} can be obtained by the following method:

Calculation Method of the DP Values of DCT Coefficients

Step1: The DCT coefficients in the training set are recombined to form moments:

$$A_{ij} = \begin{bmatrix} x_{ij}(1, 1) & x_{ij}(1, 2) & \cdots & x_{ij}(1, C) \\ x_{ij}(2, 1) & x_{ij}(2, 2) & \cdots & x_{ij}(2, C) \\ \vdots & \vdots & \vdots & \vdots \\ x_{ij}(S, 1) & x_{ij}(S, 2) & \cdots & x_{ij}(S, C) \end{bmatrix}_{S \times C}$$

Step2: Calculate the mean variance of all classes: V_{ij}^W

Step3: Calculate the variance of all training samples: V_{ij}^B

Step4: Estimate the discrimination value at the location:

$$D(i, j) = V_{ij}^B \Big/ V_{ij}^W, \ 1 \le i \le M, 1 \le j \le N$$

In this paper, we utilize SVM to classify and recognize the palatal rugae feature vectors obtained after dimensionality reduction. By analyzing the characteristics of the fractional domain amplitude spectrums of each order, it can be found that when the order is in the range of [0.5, 1.5], the time-frequency characteristics are abundant; and because the FrFT is symmetrical when the order is between 0–1.0 and when the order is between 1.0–2.0, this work calculates the fusion weighted values of different recognition results by calculating the recognition contribution of the fractional amplitude spectrums with an order of 0.5–0.9 (step size 0.1). The weight parameter value calculation method is as follows: ① Perform FrFT on the palatal rugae profile image to obtain the fractional domain amplitude spectrums under different orders, and then put together the fractional domain amplitude spectrum features of the same order to form a new training set, denoted as $T_i(i = 1, 2, \cdots, M)$; ② If $X_i = [x_{i1}, x_{i2}, \cdots, x_{iN}]$ is the N fractional amplitude spectrums in the $i\text{-}th$ training set, calculate the euclidean distance between each fractional amplitude spectrum image x_{ij} in the first training set and other fractional amplitude spectrum images in the same training set, and find the k nearest vectors. Then count the number of samples in the same class as the vector in these k vectors, denoted by k_{ij}. The weight parameter value of the $i\text{-}th$ training set can be obtained by Formula (2), After normalization, the final weight parameter value can be obtained:

$$\varpi_i = 1 \Big/ Nk \sum_{j=1}^{N} k_{ij} \tag{2}$$

$$\omega_i = \varpi_i \big/ \varpi_1 + \varpi_2 + \cdots + \varpi_M \tag{3}$$

③ Perform weighted statistics on the SVM classification results under each order to obtain the final classification results. The possibility that the image to be recognized belongs to the category is as follows:

$$P_c(f) = 1 \Big/ M \sum_{i=1}^{M} \omega_i q_i^c, \quad q_i^c = \begin{cases} 1, f_i \in c_i \\ 0, f_i \notin c_i \end{cases} \tag{4}$$

The final result is:

$$Recognition(f) = \underset{c}{\mathrm{argmax}}(p_c) \tag{5}$$

3 Experimental Results and Analysis

To verify the effectiveness of the proposed method, we constructed a palatal rugae profile image database with defects based on the standard palatal rugae profile image database constructed by Zhang et al. [7]. As shown in Fig. 5, two kinds of palatal rugae defects are simulated in the constructed database. Figure 5(a) and (b) are standard palatal rugae profile images with complete maxillary edge curve data. Figure 5(c) is a simulated data loss caused by the missing scan of the scanner, and the data of the upper jaw edge curve in the profile image of the palatal rugae is lost in this case. Figure 5(d) is a simulated situation where the palatal rugae area of the collected object is affected by the pathological changes. Although the data of the smoothed palatal rugae profile image is complete, part of it is fake data. The standard palatal rugae profile image database includes images of 91 individuals, and 5 groups of palatal rugae profile images for each person, and 40 profile images for each palatal rugae sample, and 18200 images in total. The defective palatal rugae profile image database includes images of 91 individuals, and 10 groups of palatal rugae profile images for each person, of which the first 5 groups are datas from the standard database, and the last 5 groups are datas with defects, and 36400 images in total.

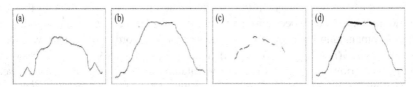

Fig. 5. Schematic diagram of defective samples in the palatal rugae profile image database with defects.

After 2D FrFT, we can obtain the fractional domain amplitude spectrums of each palatal rugae profile image. Since the obtained feature vector suffer from data redundancy and the dimensional disaster of feature vectors, it is necessary to study the feature vector construction scheme. Table 1 shows the feature vector dimensions obtained using different feature vector construction schemes. The different schemes used are labeled as follows: ID#1 construct the feature vector by cascading 40 amplitude spectrums directly; ID#2: construct the feature vector by cascading the ROIs; ID#3 construct the feature vector by cascading the mean and variance values of the 40 amplitude spectrums; Respectively, ID#4–ID#7 not block and divide the ROIs of the 40 amplitude spectrums into 2×2, 3×3 and 4×4 blocks, and construct the feature vector by cascading the mean and variance values of each blocks. Figure 6 shows the recognition results obtained by using different feature vector construction schemes and different fractional orders. It can be seen that when the fractional order $p = 1$, that is, when it is in the frequency domain, the obtained recognition accuracy rate performs poor. However, good recognition accuracy rate can be obtained in the fractional domain, and the highest recognition accuracy rate can be obtained by using scheme ID#2, and it even reaches 91.2% when the fractional order $p = 0.9$. This proves that using 2D FrFT which containing rich time-frequency information to construct feature vectors has great advantages.

Table 1. Dimensions of different feature vector construction schemes under different orders

p	0.5	0.6	0.7	0.8	0.9
ID#1	2184000	2184000	2184000	2184000	2184000
ID#2	931840	671840	408000	200080	65880
ID#3	80	80	80	80	80
ID#4	80	80	80	80	80
ID#5	320	320	320	320	320
ID#6	720	720	720	720	720
ID#7	1280	1280	1280	1280	1280

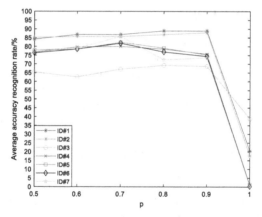

Fig. 6. The recognition results obtained by using different feature vector construction schemes and different fractional orders.

Figure 7 shows the recognition results obtained by using different methods. It can be seen from Fig. 7(a) that the average recognition accuracy rate of the proposed algorithm is always higher than that of the matrix extraction method and zig-zag method under the condition of selecting the same number of features, and the experimental results are also better than the classical dimensionality reduction schemes (PCA and LDA) in the standard palatal rugae database. It can be seen from Fig. 7(b) that the robustness of the proposed method is much higher than that of other methods, and the average recognition accuracy rate reaches more than 91%, which is also much higher than that of classical methods. In addition, when the feature dimension is greater than 40, the method in this paper achieves the same recognition rate as that in literature [7], but uses fewer feature dimensions.

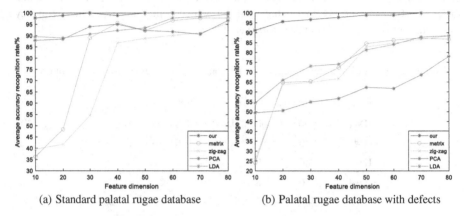

(a) Standard palatal rugae database   (b) Palatal rugae database with defects

Fig. 7. The recognition rate of different algorithms

4   Conclusions and Prospects

In this paper, DCT is utilized to compress the fractional domain amplitude spectrum features, and the DPA method is adopted to select the best DCT coefficients, which solves the problem of feature vector redundancy. In order to make full use of the fractional amplitude spectrums, we perform weighted fusion of the recognition results obtained by using different single order fractional domain amplitude spectrum to obtain a better final result. Experiment results prove the reliability of the proposed algorithm. However, there are still some areas to be improved and studied in future: (1) The existing standard database is made by isometric slicing, and the future research can focus on using non-uniform slicing to reduce the complexity of 3D palatal rugae data. The number of slices should be larger on areas where the palatal rugaes are densely distributed; and the number of slices should be reduced on areas where the palatal rugaes are sparsely distributed. (2) There are a lot of independent loop operations in the algorithm. CUDA acceleration algorithm can be used to further improve the execution speed of the algorithm.

Acknowledgments. This work was supported by Shanxi Key Laboratory of Advanced Control and Equipment intelligence (Grant No. 201805D111001).

References

1. Jain, A., Hong, L., Pankanti, S.: Biometric identification. Commun. ACM **43**(2), 90–98 (2000)
2. Jain, A.K., Nandakumar, K., Ross, A.: 50 years of biometric research: accomplishments, challenges, and opportunities. Pattern Recogn. Lett. **79**, 80–105 (2016)

3. Patil, M.S., Patil, S.B., Acharya, A.B.: Palatine rugae and their significance in clinical dentistry: a review of the literature. J. Am. Dent. Assoc. **139**(11), 1471–1478 (2008)
4. Mustafa, A.G., Allouh, M.Z., Alshehab, R.M.: Morphological changes in palatal rugae patterns following orthodontic treatment. J. Forensic Leg. Med. **31**, 19–22 (2015)
5. Bing, L., Wu, X.P., Feng, Y., et al.: Palatal rugae for the construction of forensic identification. Int. J. Morphol. **32**(546), 546–550 (2014)
6. Wu, X.P., Han, J.N., Fen, P., et al.: Application of palatal rugae morphology in forensic identification. Int. J. Morphol. **34**(2), 510–513 (2016)
7. Zhang, X., Luo, Q., Shangguan, H., et al.: Three-dimensional palatal rugae recognition based on cyclic spectral analysis. Biomed. Sig. Process. Control **68**, 102718 (2021)
8. Ozaktas, H.M., Barshan, B.: Convolution, filtering, and multiplexing in fractional Fourier domains and their relation to LFM and wavelet transforms. J. Opt. Soc. Am. A **11**(2), 547–559 (1993)
9. Barbu, M., Kaminsky, E.J., Trahan, R.E.: Fractional Fourier transform for sonar signal processing. In: Proceedings of OCEANS 2005 MTS/IEEE, vol. 2, pp. 1630–1635 (2005)
10. Martone, M.: A multicarrier system based on the fractional Fourier transform for time-frequency selective channels. IEEE Trans. Commun. **49**(6), 1011–1020 (2001)
11. Zhonghua, L., Jun, Y., Zhong, J.: An adaptive face recognition method for Gabor image feature extraction and weight selection. Acta Photonica Sin. **40**(004), 636–641 (2011)

Hand Biometrics

Fusion of Partition Local Binary Patterns and Convolutional Neural Networks for Dorsal Hand Vein Recognition

Kefeng Li[(✉)], Quankai Liu, and Guangyuan Zhang

School of Information Science and Electric Egineering, Shandong Jiaotong University,
Jinan, China

Abstract. Although deep learning algrithms have outstanding performance in biometrics and been paid more and more attention, triditional features for should not be ignored. In this paper, fusion of partition local binary patterns (PLBP) and convolutional neural networks (CNNs) is investigated in three schemes. In serial fusion (SF) method, PLBP feature is extracted and reshaped as the input of CNNS. Decision fusion (DF) carries out the PLBP with nearest neighour classifer and CNNs seperatelly and weighted fuses the results. For feature fusion (FF), PLBP feature is reshaped and weighted fused with the feature map of CNNs. To examine the proposed methods, NCUT data set with 2040 images from 204 hands is augmented using PCA. The results indicate that when the PLBP and CNNs are merged in FF scheme with weights of 0.2 and 0.8, our fusion method reaches a state-of-the-art recognition rate of 99.95%.

Keywords: Dorsal hand vein recognition · PLBP · CNNs · Fusion

1 Introduction

Hand vein patterns have attracted growing attention in recent years. As the dorsal hand vein (DHV) is located beneath the skin, it is hard to be duplicated and damaged. And the capture of DHV images are less intrusive and more user friendly [1] and [2].

The acquisition of hand vein images using near IR (NIR) imaging has been studied in [3–6] and [7]. By now, there some valid DHV databases, such as NCUT database [3] and FYO database [7]. In this work, NCUT database is adopted to examine the proposed methods. It contains 2,040 images from 102 individuals in which 52 are female and 50 are male. Ten images of each hand were captured for every individual. Some image samples in the database are illustrated in Fig. 1.

In early years, some traditional features were proposed to work on DHV recognition. Watershed transformation was used to extract Feature Points of Vein Patterns (FPVP) in [8]; triangulation was proposed in [9]; Scale-invariant feature transform (SIFT) in [10]; local binary pattern (LBP) were studied in [3, 11–13] and [14]. The recent advances in deep learning are leading to significant changes also in the biometric. CNNs were investigated in [15] and [16], some typical deep learning models were applied for DHV

© Springer Nature Switzerland AG 2021
J. Feng et al. (Eds.): CCBR 2021, LNCS 12878, pp. 177–184, 2021.
https://doi.org/10.1007/978-3-030-86608-2_20

Fig. 1. Sample images in NCUT database

recognition in [17], some classic neuro networks are evaluated 2D and 3D palm vein recognition[18]. But seldom research on the fusion of traditional feature and deep learning method. In this paper, the PLBP feature is fused with CNNs in three schemes: SF, DF and FF.

2   Related Works

2.1   Data Argument

As there are just 10 images for each hand in NCUT database, it is not ideal to adopt deep learning method. So that data argument is necessary. An enlargement method based on double PCA was proposed by us in [19]. The basic structure of this method is shown in the Fig. 2.

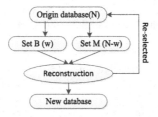

Fig. 2. Basic structure of the data argument

The origin database is divided into two sets, feature set B and projection set M. Then the reconstruction is carried out by merging the information from both sets to get new images. In this work, 240 new samples of each hand are reconstructed and combined with original images together to form a new database with 10200 images totally.

2.2   PLBP

Local Binary Patterns (LBP) provides an efficient rotation-invariant texture descriptor. Partition Local Binary Patterns (PLBP) was previously proposed and improved by the authors in [3] and [13].

To extract PLBP feature, each vein image is scaled to M and divided into N non-overlapping rectangular regions as shown in Fig. 3.

After partition, $LBP_{8,2}^{riu2}$ (rotation invariant uniform patterns calculated from 8 sampling points on a circle of radius 2) features are extracted from each sub images and connected together to form the PLBP feature. The feature histogram of 64 sub-images is shown in Fig. 4.

Fig. 3. Rectangular partition

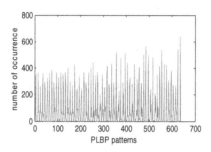

Fig. 4. PLBP feature histograms of 64 sub-images

2.3 CNNs

A typical architecture of CNNs is structured as a series of stages. In this work, the architecture is summarized in Fig. 5 and the details are listed in Table 1 [15]. It contains 11 learned layers—4 convolutional, 4 pooling and 3 fully-connected.

Table 1. The components of the CNNs

layer		Kernel size	stride
Convolutional layer	1	5*5*1	1
	3	5*5*32	1
	5	3*3*64	1
	7	3*3*128	1
Max pooling layer	2,4,6,8	2*2	\
Fully-connected layers	9,10	1024	\
	11	512	\

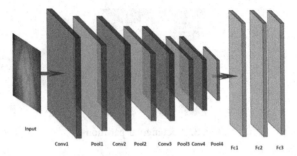

Fig. 5. The architecture of our CNNs

3 Fusion of PLBP and CNNs

The fusion of PLBP and CNNs is investigated in three schemes: serial fusion (SF), decision fusion (DF) and feature fusion (FF).

3.1 SF

The flowchart of the SF method is shown in Fig. 6. As the PLBP feature extracted from the image is a 1 * 640 dimension vector, it should be reshaped to a feature image.

Here, we use H_i denotes the LBP histogram of the ith sub-image.

$$H_i = [h_{i,1} \ h_{i,2} \ \cdots \ h_{i,10}] \ (i = 1, 2, \ldots, N) \tag{1}$$

As the $h_{i,10}$ is the statistics of the other pattern except the 9 rotation invariant uniform patterns, it could be omitted without influence of representation of the sub-image. The rest 9 items could be reshaped as:

$$H_i^r = \begin{bmatrix} h_{i1} & h_{i2} & h_{i3} \\ h_{i4} & h_{i5} & h_{i6} \\ h_{i7} & h_{i8} & h_{i9} \end{bmatrix} \tag{2}$$

Then the reshaped histograms of sub-images are connected to form a 24 * 24 dimensions PLBP feature image as follows:

$$Feature\_plbp = \begin{bmatrix} H_1^r & \cdots & H_8^r \\ \vdots & \ddots & \vdots \\ H_{57}^r & & H_{64}^r \end{bmatrix} \tag{3}$$

The PLBP feature images are input to the trained CNNs to do the recognition work.

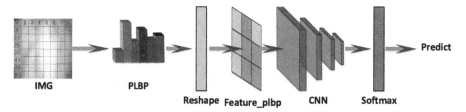

Fig. 6. The diagram of SF

3.2 DF

DF scheme is realized as the gram shown in Fig. 7. The images are input to the trained CNNs and get the prediction results *pCNN*. At the same time, PBLP features are calculated the L2 distance with the register features, followed by normalization to *[0, 1]* as the result *pPLBP*. Then the two probabilities are fused to *pFusion* as follow:

$$pFusion = \alpha \times pPBLBP + (1 - \alpha) \times pCNN \tag{4}$$

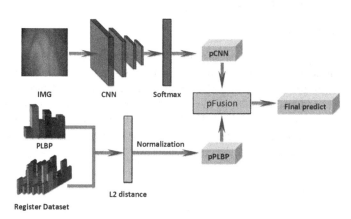

Fig. 7. The diagram of DF

3.3 FF

FF approach is described in Fig. 8. The PLBP feature is reshaped to the PLBP feature image *Feature_plbp* using the Eq. (1)–(3). And the PLBP feature image is fused to the CNNs feature map *Feature_img* as Eq. (5). The combined feature map *Feature_mixed* is sent to the fully-connected layers.

$$Feature\_mixed = \alpha \times Feature\_plbp + (1 - \alpha) \times Feature\_img \tag{5}$$

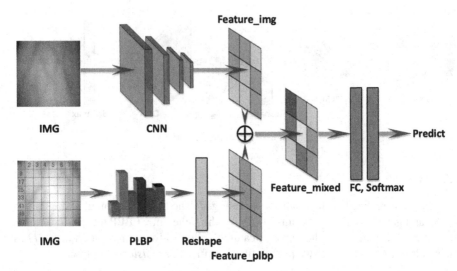

Fig. 8. The diagram of FF

4   Experiments and Results

4.1   Data Preparation

To train and examine the effectiveness of the CNNs for hand-dorsa vein recognition, the NCUT hand-dorsa vein dataset and the enlarged dataset is selected [19]. The enlarged database contains 204 hands with 250 samples for each hand. The dataset was divided into training set and test set. 80% of the samples were adopted to train the model. The left ones were used to validate the model. 5 images of each hand in the training set are randomly selected and the mean vectors of the PLBP features extracted from them are considered as the register feature for each hand.

4.2   Fusion of PLBP and CNNs

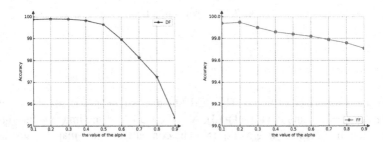

Fig. 9. The influence of fusion weight α for DF and FF

For the DF and FF approach, the fusion factor α controls the performance of the models. In order to explore a suitable value, multiple experiments are carried out with the parameters growth of 0.1. From the results shown in Fig. 9, when α is set to 0.2, both the DF and FF perform best with the recognition rates (RR) of 99.9% and 99.95%.

We compare our best results, with the top ones reported on the same database using different experimental algorithms. As shown in Table 2. The FF scheme achieves the state-of-the-art recognition rates when the weights of PLBP and CNNs are 0.2 and 0.8 respectively.

Table 2. Comparison with other methods on NCUT database

Method	Year	Recognition rate
PLBP [11]	2010	90.88%
WPLBP [12]	2011	98.63%
OMGs + SIFT [10]	2012	99.02%
MPLBP [13]	2015	98.83%
VGG-16 [17]	2016	99.31%
WSM [20]	2016	99.31%
GDRKG + SIFT + MtSRC [21]	2015	99.74 ± 0.07%
CNNs [15]	2018	99.61%
PLBP + CNNs:SF	2021	99.88%
PLBP + CNNs:DF	2021	99.9%
PLBP + CNNs:FF	2021	99.95%

5 Conclusions

In this paper, we discuss the fusion of PLBP and CNNs in three approaches. Fusion feature in FF scheme can achieves the state-of-the-art recognition rates when the weights of PLBP and CNNs are 0.2 and 0.8 respectively, clearly demonstrating the feasibility and superiority of fusion of tridational feature and deep learning for this issue.

References

1. Ding, Y., Zhuang, D., Wang, K.: A study of hand vein recognition method. In: IEEE International Conference on Mechatronics and Automations, pp. 2106–2110 (2005)
2. Delac, K., Grgic, M.: A survey of biometric recognition methods. In: 46th International Symposium Electronics in Marine, pp. 184–193 (2004)
3. Wang, Y., Li, K., Cui, J.: Hand-dorsa vein recognition based on partition local binary pattern. In: 10th International Conference on Signal Processing, pp. 1671–1674 (2010)
4. Zhao, S., Wang, Y., Wang, Y.: Biometric verification by extracting hand vein patterns from low-quality images. In: Proceedings of the Fourth International Conference on Image and Graphics, pp. 667–671 (2007)

5. Cross, J.M., Smith, C.L.: Thermo graphic imaging of the subcutaneous vascular network of the back of the hand for biometric identification. In: Proceedings IEEE 29th Annual International Carnahan Conference Security Technology, pp. 20–35 (1995)

6. Wang, L., Leedham, G.: Near- and far-infrared imaging for vein pattern biometrics. In: Proceedings IEEE International Conference Video Signal Based Surveillance, pp. 52–57, Sydney, November 2006

7. Toygar, Ö., Babalola, F.O., Bitirim, Y.: FYO: a novel multimodal vein database with palmar, dorsal and wrist biometrics. IEEE Access **8**(1), 82461–82470 (2020)

8. Zhou, B., Lin, X.R., Jia, H.B.: Application of multiresolutional filter on feature extraction of palm-dorsa vein patterns. J. Comput. Aided Des. Comput. Graph. **18**(1), 41–45 (2006)

9. Kumar, A., Prathyusha, K.V.: Personal authentication using hand vein triangulation and knuckle shape. IEEE Trans. Image Process. **18**(9), 2127–2136 (2009)

10. Wang, Y., Zhang, K., Shark, L.-K.: Personal identification based on multiple keypoint sets of dorsal hand vein images. IET Biometrics **3**(4), 234–245 (2014)

11. Wang, Y., Li, K., Cui, J., Shark, L.-K., Varley, M.: Study of hand-dorsa vein recognition. In: Huang, D.-S., Zhao, Z., Bevilacqua, V., Figueroa, J.C. (eds.) ICIC 2010. LNCS, vol. 6215, pp. 490–498. Springer, Heidelberg (2010). https://doi.org/10.1007/978-3-642-14922-1_61

12. Wang, Y., et al.: Hand-dorsa vein recognition based on coded and weighted partition local binary patterns. In: International Conference on Hand-based Biometrics (ICHB 2011) (2011)

13. Li, K., Zhang, G., Wang, Y., Wang, P., Ni, C.: Hand-dorsa vein recognition based on improved partition local binary patterns. In: Yang, J., Yang, J., Sun, Z., Shan, S., Feng, J. (eds.) CCBR 2015. LNCS, vol. 9428, pp. 312–320. Springer, Cham (2015). https://doi.org/10.1007/978-3-319-25417-3_37

14. Achban, A., Nugroho, H.A., Nugroho, P.: Wrist hand vein recognition using local line binary pattern (LLBP). In: 5th International Conference on Science and Technology (ICST) (2020)

15. Li, K., Zhang, G., Wang, P.: Hand-dorsa vein recognition based on deep learning. In: 2018 International Conference on Security, Pattern Analysis, and Cybernetics (SPAC), pp. 203–207, Jinan (2018)

16. Kuzu, R.S., Maiorana, E., Campisi, P.: Vein-based biometric verification using densely-connected convolutional autoencoder. IEEE Sig. Process. Lett. **27**, 1869–1873 (2020)

17. Li, X., Huang, D., Wang, Y.: Comparative study of deep learning methods on dorsal hand vein recognition. In: You, Z. (ed.) CCBR 2016. LNCS, vol. 9967, pp. 296–306. Springer, Cham (2016). https://doi.org/10.1007/978-3-319-46654-5_33

18. Jia, W., et al.: A performance evaluation of classic convolutional neural networks for 2D and 3D palmprint and palm vein recognition. Int. J. Autom. Comput. **18**, 18–44 (2021)

19. Li, K., Zhang, G., Wang, Y., Wang, P., Ni, C.: Enlargement of the Hand-dorsa vein database based on PCA reconstruction. In: You, Z. (ed.) CCBR 2016. LNCS, vol. 9967, pp. 288–295. Springer, Cham (2016). https://doi.org/10.1007/978-3-319-46654-5_32

20. Li, X., et al.: Hand dorsal vein recognition by matching width skeleton models. In: International Conference on Image Processing (ICIP) (2016)

21. Zhang, R., et al.: Improving feature based dorsal hand vein recognition through random keypoint generation and fine-grained matching. In: IAPR International Conference on Biometrics (ICB), pp. 326–333 (2015)

Pose-Specific 3D Fingerprint Unfolding

Xiongjun Guan, Jianjiang Feng[(⊠)], and Jie Zhou

Department of Automation, Beijing National Research Center for Information
Science and Technology, Tsinghua University, Beijing 100084, China
guanxj17@mails.tsinghua.edu.cn, {jfeng,jzhou}@tsinghua.edu.cn

Abstract. In order to make 3D fingerprints compatible with traditional
2D flat fingerprints, a common practice is to unfold the 3D fingerprint
into a 2D rolled fingerprint, which is then matched with the flat fingerprints by traditional 2D fingerprint recognition algorithms. The problem with this method is that there may be large elastic deformation
between the unfolded rolled fingerprint and flat fingerprint, which affects
the recognition rate. In this paper, we propose a pose-specific 3D fingerprint unfolding algorithm to unfold the 3D fingerprint using the same
pose as the flat fingerprint. Our experiments show that the proposed
unfolding algorithm improves the compatibility between 3D fingerprint
and flat fingerprint and thus leads to higher genuine matching scores.

Keywords: Fingerprint · Distortion · Registration · 3D fingerprint
unfolding

1 Introduction

Fingerprint is one of the most widely used biometric traits because it is very
stable, easy to collect and highly distinctive. Up to now, 2D fingerprint images
obtained by contact-based sensors are the dominating fingerprint image type [1].
However, the quality of 2D fingerprint images is affected by factors such as skin
deformation and skin humidity. Compared with 2D fingerprints, 3D fingerprints
are not deformed, less affected by dry or wet fingers, and hygienic, since they
are acquired in a non-contact manner [2]. Due to this advantage, a number of
3D fingerprint sensing technologies have been proposed [3,4,11].

Since existing fingerprint databases contain mainly 2D fingerprints and 2D
fingerprint sensors are very popular, new 3D fingerprint sensors need to be compatible with 2D fingerprint sensors. Considering that 3D fingerprint sensors
are expensive and large, a common application scenario is using a 3D sensor
for enrollment and a 2D sensor for recognition. For compatibility, enrolled 3D
fingerprints are usually unfolded into 2D rolled fingerprints [3–12], which are
then matched to query flat fingerprints by traditional 2D fingerprint recognition
technology.

Generally, there are two types of 3D fingerprint unfolding methods: parametric method and non-parametric method. The parametric method uses a hypo-
thetical geometric model to approximate the 3D shape of the finger. In these

© Springer Nature Switzerland AG 2021
J. Feng et al. (Eds.): CCBR 2021, LNCS 12878, pp. 185–194, 2021.
https://doi.org/10.1007/978-3-030-86608-2_21

methods, 3D fingerprints are projected into a parametric model. Commonly used parametric models include cylinders [3–5], spheres [6,7], and deformable cylinders [8,9]. In addition, there are methods to determine the parameters by analyzing the curvature of the fingerprint [10]. Most of these methods use axially symmetric parametric models. However, since the finger is irregular, these models do not fully conform to the shape of the fingers. This will cause additional deformation when unfolding. The non-parametric method does not assume the shape of the finger. These methods first smooth the surface of the finger and then unfold it according to the surface curvature [11,12]. Because of special shape of finger, it cannot be spread out on a plane without tearing. In addition, the deformation of the fingerprint is related to its pressing pose, and the pose of the query fingerprint is not known in advance. Therefore, there is large deformation between the unfolded fingerprint and the query fingerprint when the 3D fingerprint is unfolded in the enrollment stage. This will result in false non-matches.

The problem of fingerprint distortion can also be solved in the recognition stage. In order to deal with the skin deformation problem, researchers have proposed various deformable registration algorithms and matching algorithms tolerant to skin distortion [13–17], which are however designed for 2D fingerprints. Since there is no explicit consideration of 3D finger shape during registration or matching, non-mated fingerprints may appear similar after unreasonable deformable registration, which may result in false matches.

In this paper, we propose a pose-specific 3D fingerprint unfolding algorithm to unfold the 3D fingerprint using the same pose as the flat fingerprint, with the aim of reducing deformation between unfolded fingerprint and flat fingerprint. We collected a database of mated 2D and 3D fingerprints and performed matching experiments on it. Experiments show that pose difference is a very important cause for fingerprint deformation and genuine matching score can be greatly improved by pose-specific unfolding.

2   Proposed Method

Figure 1 shows the complete process of the proposed pose-specific 3D fingerprint unfolding algorithm. The algorithm first unfolds the 3D fingerprint using the normal pose, next estimates the specific pose of the query flat fingerprint by minutiae matching, then unfolds the 3D fingerprint using the estimated pose, and finally applies a simple 2D fingerprint registration method. The two unfolding algorithms are the same and the only difference is that the pose of the 3D fingerprint is adjusted during the second unfolding. In the following we describe the unfolding and 3D pose estimation steps, since other steps are very basic or based on existing techniques. We use "unfolding" to represent the specific step as well as the whole algorithm. Its meaning should be clear based on the context.

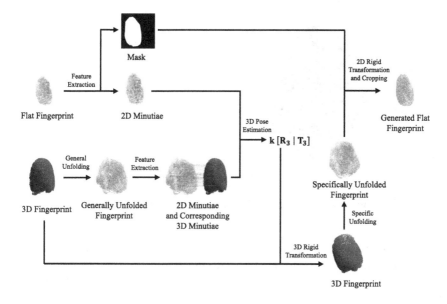

Fig. 1. Flowchart of the proposed pose-specific 3D fingerprint unfolding.

2.1   Unfolding

General 3D model rendering techniques are not suitable for generating high quality fingerprint images from 3D point cloud for two reasons. Firstly, in 3D model rendering, the light-dark relationship is usually obtained by setting the light source, which is difficult to unify the brightness in different areas of a fingerprint image. Secondly, affected by the position of the light source, rendered bright area (fingerprint ridge) will be out of phase with real flat fingerprints. The previous method of generating fingerprints from point clouds [11] calculates the surface depth by fitting the smooth surface of the finger. This method may overfit and cause the ridge line to be uneven. Therefore, we propose an algorithm to get unfolded rolled fingerprints using local point sets from finger point clouds, including two steps: point cloud visualization and unfolding.

Visualization. The texture of a flat fingerprint is produced when the finger is in contact with the sensor plane. Generally speaking, the more prominent the ridge line, the deeper the fingerprint texture. The visualization method in this work simulates this property, takes the neighborhood around each point in the point cloud as the partial surface, and calculates the depth of the point relative to the surface.

The schematic diagram of point cloud visualization is shown in Fig. 2. Let V be the point set of the 3D finger. For a point p in V, the neighborhood point X is defined as

$$X = \{x_i \mid x_i \in V \text{ and } \|x_i - p\| < r\}, \tag{1}$$

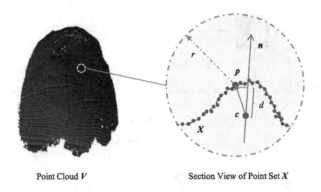

Point Cloud V Section View of Point Set X

Fig. 2. Schematic diagram of the visualization method.

where r is the maximum distance from any points in X to p. We set the point center as the mean of all the points in X, denoted as c. Let n be the normal vector of the point set X computed by principal component analysis (PCA). The surface depth of p relative to X is then computed as

$$d = (p - c)^T n. \tag{2}$$

For each point in the 3D finger, we use the normalized surface depth d_n as the pixel value which is computed as

$$d_n = \frac{d - d_{min}}{d_{max} - d_{min}}, \tag{3}$$

and project it to the imaging plane, where d_{max} and d_{min} are determined from the depth d of all point cloud. The comparison between the visualized result and the real flat fingerprint is shown in Fig. 3.

Unfolding. We use the arc length between two points in the point cloud as the coordinates of the unfolded fingerprint. Let (x, y, z) be the point cloud coordinates and $(u, v, 0)$ be the unfolded fingerprint coordinates. The unfolding relationship of the direction of u is defined as

$$\frac{\partial u}{\partial x} = \sqrt{1 + (\frac{\partial z}{\partial x})^2} \, , \quad \frac{\partial u}{\partial y} = \sqrt{1 + (\frac{\partial z}{\partial y})^2}, \tag{4}$$

and the relationship of v is the same.

Figure 4 shows the comparison of the visualization results of point clouds of two fingers of different poses before and after unfolding. The area with a large tilt relative to the observation plane can be effectively flattened.

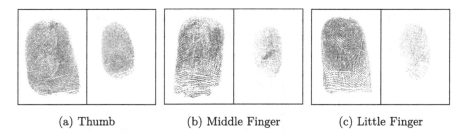

(a) Thumb   (b) Middle Finger   (c) Little Finger

Fig. 3. Visualization results of 3D point clouds (left) and real flat fingerprints (right) in each subfigure. Image quality is similar, while the former has a larger area. There is perspective distortion in the visualization result which will be removed by unfolding step.

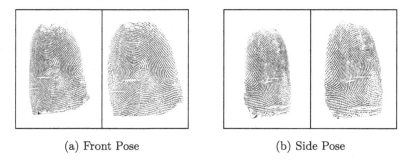

(a) Front Pose   (b) Side Pose

Fig. 4. Visualization results of point clouds of two fingers of different poses before (left) and after (right) unfolding.

2.2   3D Pose Estimation

The 3D pose estimation step conducts global rigid transformation between the 3D fingerprint and the flat fingerprint. Minutiae from each unfolded rolled fingerprint and flat fingerprint are extracted using VeriFinger [19]. MCC minutia descriptor [18], which is a state-of-the-art minutiae descriptor, is used to compute similarity between all possible minutiae pairs. Then we use spectral clustering method [20] to find corresponding minutiae pairs. Since the corresponding 3D minutiae of 2D minutiae in the unfolded rolled fingerprint are known, we obtain correspondences between 3D minutiae and 2D minutiae in the flat fingerprint.

Given mated 3D/2D minutiae pairs, we estimate a 3D rigid transformation to minimize the average distance of minutia pairs under orthogonal projection. For a minutiae point (x, y, z) and its projection coordinates (u, v), the relationship is given as

$$
\begin{bmatrix} u \\ v \\ 0 \end{bmatrix} = \begin{bmatrix} 1 & 0 & 0 \\ 0 & 1 & 0 \\ 0 & 0 & 0 \end{bmatrix} \left(k \begin{bmatrix} \boldsymbol{R_3} \mid \boldsymbol{t_3} \end{bmatrix} \begin{bmatrix} x \\ y \\ z \\ 1 \end{bmatrix} \right),
\tag{5}
$$

where k is the scaling parameter, R_3 and t_3 denote the rotation matrix and translate matrix of the rigid transformation in 3D. This estimation method needs at least 6 matching points.

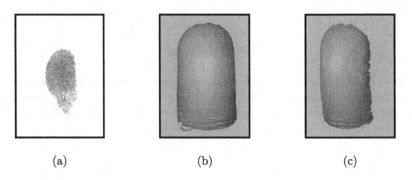

(a)   (b)   (c)

Fig. 5. Illustration of 3D pose estimation. (a) A real flat fingerprint. (b) Corresponding finger point cloud in the original pose. (c) Corresponding finger point cloud in the same pose as the flat fingerprint.

Figure 5 shows an example of transformed 3D fingerprint using 3D pose estimation results. We run the unfolding algorithm again on the transformed 3D fingerprint to obtain the pose-specific rolled fingerprint.

3   Experiment

3.1   Database

Due to the lack of databases containing high quality finger point clouds and corresponding flat fingerprints, we collected a database for this study. The finger point clouds were captured by using a commercial structured light 3D scanner, while the corresponding 2D flat fingerprints at multiple poses were captured with a Frustrated Total Internal Reflection (FTIR) fingerprint sensor. 3D point clouds of 150 fingers and 1200 corresponding flat fingerprints (8 images per finger) were used in experiments. Finger data were collected from people aged 20 to 30, including 13 males and 2 females. Ten fingers were collected for each person.

3.2   Matching Score

The purpose of 3D fingerprint unfolding is to improve the compatibility of 3D fingerprints and flat fingerprints, that is, to improve the matching score between them. We match the results of two unfolding algorithms with the same flat fingerprint, and the relative level of the matching score (VeriFinger [19] is used to calculate the matching score) can reflect the performance of unfolding algorithms. Due to high fingerprint quality in the database, genuine match scores

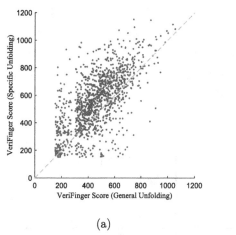

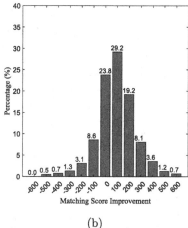

(a)   (b)

Fig. 6. The effect of different unfolding methods on genuine matching scores. (a) The VeriFinger matching score of unfolded fingerprints after general unfolding (X-axis) and specific unfolding (Y-axis). The red dotted line indicates that the scores obtained by the two methods are the same. (b) Histogram of matching score improvement from general pose to specific pose.

are much higher than impostor match scores and genuine matches and impostor matches are totally separable. Therefore, we use the improvement of genuine matching score as an indicator of unfolding quality.

Two unfolded fingerprints are cropped before computing VeriFinger matching scores according to the segmentation map of the real flat fingerprint to avoid the influence of redundant areas. According to Fig. 6, we can see that most of the matching performance are improved after pose-specific unfolding and only a small part of the fingerprint matching scores slightly drop. The curve shows that unfolding in a specific pose will have a better performance than unfolding directly. We analyzed the cases where pose-specific unfolding failed and found that in these cases, 3D pose estimation is inaccurate due to very small number of matching minutiae between 3D fingerprint and flat fingerprint.

3.3 Deformation Field

We estimate the deformation field between flat fingerprints and unfolded fingerprints with general pose and specific pose to directly measure the performance of the unfolding algorithm. We use the matching minutiae of the unfolded fingerprint and the flat fingerprint as control points and estimate the deformation field through thin plate spline interpolation.

Five representative examples are given in Fig. 7. Each row corresponds to a pair of 3D and 2D flat fingerprints. These examples show that the improvement of the matching score is closely related to reduction of fingerprint distortion: when fingerprint distortion is greatly reduced, the matching score improves very much; when fingerprint distortion is almost unchanged, the matching score hardly improves. The comparison also proves that pose-specific unfolding does greatly reduce fingerprint deformation caused by different finger poses. It should be noted that the different finger poses are only part of the factors that cause deformation. Therefore, the deformation will only be relatively reduced but will not disappear completely by using the proposed unfolding algorithm.

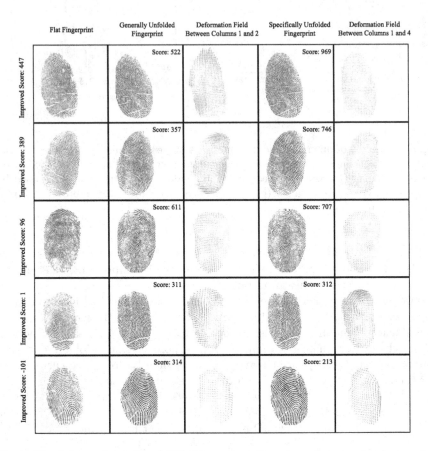

Fig. 7. The deformation fields and VeriFinger matching scores between flat fingerprints and unfolded fingerprints with general pose and specific pose. Longer arrows indicate larger deformation.

3.4 Efficiency

The average times of major steps of the proposed unfolding algorithm are reported in Table 1. We ran the algorithm on a PC with 2.50 GHz CPU. All functions are implemented in MATLAB except for minutiae extraction which is performed using VeriFinger. The total time for the proposed unfolding algorithm is about 14 s. Since the fingerprint pairs have to be matched twice and the image size is large (900 pixel × 900 pixel), the feature extraction and matching part is time-consuming. Compared with general unfolding, our method requires additional steps for 3D pose estimation, 3D rigid transformation and specific unfolding, which take about 6.8 s.

Table 1. Speed of major steps of the proposed unfolding algorithm.

Step	Time (s)
General unfolding	3.08
Feature extraction	2.17
3D pose estimation	2.23
3D rigid transformation	1.44
Specific unfolding	3.12
2D rigid transformation and cropping	2.32

4 Conclusion

There are significant modal differences between 3D fingerprints and 2D fingerprints. To address this compatibility problem, existing algorithms focus on unfolding 3D fingerprints in the enrollment stage without considering the pose of the query fingerprint. In this paper, we propose a novel pose-specific 3D fingerprint unfolding algorithm. By unfolding the 3D fingerprint in a specific pose, the deformation is effectively reduced which improves the matching score with the real flat fingerprint. Meanwhile, our current method still has some shortcomings. The algorithm is slow and needs to be performed for each query fingerprint. Larger dataset should be collected to understand the performance on fingerprints of various poses and quality. In addition, the pressing force will also cause the deformation of the fingers, which are not considered. We plan to address the above limitations in the future.

Acknowledgments. This work was supported in part by the National Natural Science Foundation of China under Grant 61976121.

References

1. Maltoni, D., Maio, D., Jain, A.K., Prabhakar, S.: Handbook of Fingerprint Recognition. Springer, London (2009). https://doi.org/10.1007/978-1-84882-254-2
2. Kumar, A.: Individuality of 3D fingerprints. In: Contactless 3D Fingerprint Identification. ACVPR, pp. 109–119. Springer, Cham (2018). https://doi.org/10.1007/978-3-319-67681-4_8
3. Chen, Y., Parziale, G., Diaz-Santana, E., Jain, A.K.: 3D touchless fingerprints: Compatibility with legacy rolled images. In: Biometrics Symposium: Special Session on Research at the Biometric Consortium Conference, pp. 1–6. IEEE (2006)

4. Zhao, Q., Jain, A., Abramovich, G.: 3D to 2D fingerprints: unrolling and distortion correction. In: International Joint Conference on Biometrics (IJCB), pp. 1–8. IEEE (2011)
5. Labati, R.D., Genovese, A., Piuri, V., Scotti, F.: Quality measurement of unwrapped three-dimensional fingerprints: a neural networks approach. In: International Joint Conference on Neural Networks (IJCNN), pp. 1–8. IEEE (2012)
6. Wang, Y., Lau, D.L., Hassebrook, L.G.: Fit-sphere unwrapping and performance analysis of 3D fingerprints. Appl. Opt. **49**(4), 592–600 (2010)
7. Anitha, R., Sesireka, N.: Performance improvisation on 3D converted 2D unraveled fingerprint. IOSR J. Comput. Eng. (IOSR-JCE) **16**(6), 50–56 (2014)
8. Wang, Y., Hassebrook, L.G., Lau, D.L.: Data acquisition and processing of 3-D fingerprints. IEEE Trans. Inf. Forensics Secur. **5**(4), 750–760 (2010)
9. Labati, R.D., Genovese, A., Piuri, V., Scotti, F.: Fast 3-D fingertip reconstruction using a single two-view structured light acquisition. In: IEEE Workshop on Biometric Measurements and Systems for Security and Medical Applications (BIOMS), pp. 1–8. IEEE (2011)
10. Dighade, R.R.: Approach to unwrap a 3D fingerprint to a 2D equivalent. University of Maryland, Master Thesis (2012)
11. Fatehpuria, A., Lau, D.L., Hassebrook, L.G.: Acquiring a 2D rolled equivalent fingerprint image from a non-contact 3D finger scan. In: Biometric Technology for Human Identification III. Volume 6202, International Society for Optics and Photonics, vol. 62020C (2006)
12. Shafaei, S., Inanc, T., Hassebrook, L.G.: A new approach to unwrap a 3-D fingerprint to a 2-D rolled equivalent fingerprint. In: IEEE 3rd International Conference on Biometrics: Theory, Applications, and Systems (BTAS), pp. 1–5. IEEE (2009)
13. Bazen, A.M., Gerez, S.H.: Fingerprint matching by thin-plate spline modelling of elastic deformations. Pattern Recogn. **36**(8), 1859–1867 (2003)
14. Ross, A., Shah, S., Shah, J.: Image versus feature mosaicing: a case study in fingerprints. In: Biometric Technology for Human Identification III. Volume 6202, International Society for Optics and Photonics, vol. 620208 (2006)
15. Cheng, X., Tulyakov, S., Govindaraju, V.: Minutiae-based matching state model for combinations in fingerprint matching system. In: CVPR Workshop on Biometrics, pp. 92–97 (2013)
16. Si, X., Feng, J., Yuan, B., Zhou, J.: Dense registration of fingerprints. Pattern Recogn. **63**, 87–101 (2017)
17. Cui, Z., Feng, J., Li, S., Lu, J., Zhou, J.: 2-D phase demodulation for deformable fingerprint registration. IEEE Trans. Inf. Forensics Secur. **13**(12), 3153–3165 (2018)
18. Cappelli, R., Ferrara, M., Maltoni, D.: Minutia cylinder-code: a new representation and matching technique for fingerprint recognition. IEEE Trans. Pattern Anal. Mach. Intell. **32**(12), 2128–2141 (2010)
19. Neurotechnology Inc., VeriFinger. http://www.neurotechnology.com
20. Leordeanu, M., Hebert, M.: A spectral technique for correspondence problems using pairwise constraints. In: International Conference on Computer Vision (ICCV) (2005)

Finger Vein Recognition Using a Shallow Convolutional Neural Network

Jiazhen Liu[1], Ziyan Chen[1], Kaiyang Zhao[1], Minjie Wang[1], Zhen Hu[1],
Xinwei Wei[1], Yicheng Zhu[1], Yuncong Yu[1], Zhe Feng[1], Hakil Kim[2],
and Changlong Jin[1(✉)]

[1] School of Mechanical, Electrical and Information Engineering, Shandong
University, Weihai, China
{liujiazhen,celinechan,kenyonz,minjiewang,zhenhu,vanessa_wei,
yuncongyu,zhefeng}@mail.sdu.edu.cn, cljin@sdu.edu.cn
[2] School of Information and Communication Engineering, INHA University,
Incheon, Korea
hikim@inha.ac.kr

Abstract. Deep learning-based finger vein recognition (FVR) can be
classified as either a closed-set architecture (CS-architecture) or an open-
set architecture (OS-architecture) based on the system output. The CS-
architecture has limited practicality due to its closure, and the OS-
architecture has limited generalization ability due to its challenging convergence. To improve the practicality and performance of deep learning-
based FVR, we hypothesize that a shallow convolutional neural network
is suitable for FVR based on the observation of the difference between
face recognition and FVR. Consequently, we design a shallow network
with three convolutional blocks and two fully connected layers that
can be efficiently applied for both CS-architecture and OS-architecture.
Moreover, an improved interval-based loss function is used to extract
discriminative large-margin features. The proposed network has excellent performance, verified by extensive experiments on publicly available
databases.

Keywords: Additive margin loss · Closed-set · Finger vein
recognition · Open-set and shallow convolutional neural network

1 Introduction

In recent years, although the leading biometric technologies (e.g., fingerprint,
face, and iris) have been widely applied in practice, they are threatened by
forged features. However, the demand for the security of identity authentication
has increased in modern society. Developing a safe but high-performing biometric
technology is essential. Finger vein (in contrast to fingerprint, iris, and face) is
a new, widely studied type of biometrics that has emerged in the past decade.
It has attracted researchers' attention due to its anti-counterfeiting, invisibility,
ease of use, and other excellent characteristics. Furthermore, with the emergence

© Springer Nature Switzerland AG 2021
J. Feng et al. (Eds.): CCBR 2021, LNCS 12878, pp. 195–202, 2021.
https://doi.org/10.1007/978-3-030-86608-2_22

of powerful deep learning, more researchers have introduced deep learning into finger vein recognition (FVR) [1–9].

Deep learning-based FVR can be classified as either closed-set architecture (CS-architecture) [1,10–12] or open-set architecture (OS-architecture) [2–9,13–19] based on the system output.

1. **CS-architecture:** CS-architecture uses a Softmax layer to output the specified category [1,10–12] of the input sample in one forward propagation. It recognizes trained categories only, and the extended system requires complicated retraining. The practicality of the CS-architecture is limited.
2. **OS-architecture:** In contrast to CS-architecture, the OS-architecture outputs the feature map [3,9,14,16,19] or dimension-reduced vector [2,5,7,8,18] of an input sample, or the comparison result of the difference/composite image [4,6,13,15] of two input samples.

We designed a shallow CNN that can achieve a CS-architecture and OS-architecture in one framework. The CS-architecture of our model is mainly for experimental usage, which is used to illustrate that the shallow network has sufficient feature extraction capability. The proposed network consists of three convolutional blocks and two fully connected (FC) layers. In the OS-architecture, the improved interval-based loss function enables the proposed network to learn discriminative large-margin features and fulfill the role of clustering similar feature vectors while dispersing different feature vectors.

2   Related Work

In this era of deep learning, FVR can be classified into two classes: 1) conventional algorithm-based FVR and 2) deep learning-based FVR. Before 2017, research on FVR focused on conventional algorithms in recent years, and shifted to deep learning-based algorithms. Since the Repeated Line Tracking (RLT) algorithm was developed in 2004, many effective conventional methods have been developed for FVR. They can be broadly classified into two classes: 1) vein pattern extraction-based and 2) and non-vein pattern extraction-based.

Due to strong feature extraction ability, more researchers are focusing on how to use an artificial neural network to identify finger veins. The OS-architecture FVR uses a CNN to match two finger vein images. Whether the two samples belong to the same category is determined by a matching score. Therefore, the equal error rate (EER (%)) is adopted as the performance evaluation standard for the OS-architecture. Two approaches can be used to generate a matching score: 1) combining two samples into one sample as an input to the CNN and 2) using the CNN to extract features and calculating the similarity between those features as matching scores for recognition.

For the first OS-architecture approach, Hong et al. [13] used difference images, which were obtained by reducing the corresponding pixels of two finger-vein images, as the input to a VGG16-based CNN. Wan Kim et al. [15] proposed finger vein and finger shape multimodal biometrics based on a deep CNN, which also used difference images for FVR. Song et al. [6] researched a method using composite images—less susceptible to noise compared to using difference images—as the input to a deep dense CNN (DENSENET). In addition to the combination of input images, Fang et al. [4] presented a two-stream network to integrate the original image. For the second OS-architecture approach, Lu et al. [5] used a CNN model pre-trained on ImageNet to develop a CNN-based local descriptor termed CNN competitive order (CNN-CO) that can exploit discriminative pattern features for FVR. Qin et al. [3] used a method based on a combination of known state-of-the-art hand-crafted segmentation techniques to obtain label data. Similarly, Jalilian et al. [19] proposed a method focused on the direct extraction of actual finger-vein patterns from near-infrared finger images without any specific pre- or post-processing using semantic segmentation CNNs. Yang et al. [9] proposed a method termed FV-GAN to perform finger vein extraction. Apart from pattern features, features of dimensionality reduction are also frequently adopted. Xie and Kumar [8] introduced several CNN models and supervised discrete hashing for finger vein authentication. Hu et al. [14] proposed a template-like matching strategy while extracting features with spatial information to address rotation and translation. Tang et al. [7] constructed a Siamese structure combined with a modified contrastive loss function.

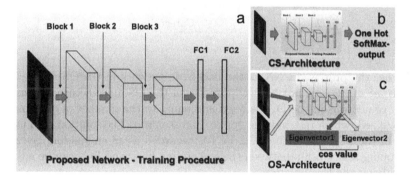

Fig. 1. Proposed framework, a) the proposed network in the training procedure, b) the proposed network used in CS-architecture, and c) the proposed network used in OS-architecture.

3   Proposed Method

Figure 1 depicts the proposed framework, in which Fig. 1a illustrates the shallow CNN framework, taking the region of interest (ROI) image as the input. Figure 1b and 1c are the use of Fig. 1a in the CS-architecture and OS-architecture, respectively. For the input size, the raw ROIs, with different sizes from two open databases, are all resized to 80×80 pixel images, which ensures that the proposed shallow CNN can extract sufficient features and have a faster forward propagation speed. The proposed framework requires only the ROI image without any preprocessing. The proposed framework can switch between the CS-architecture and OS-architecture merely by changing the loss function. The specific structure and parameters are depicted in Table 1.

Table 1. Proposed shallow CNN framework

	Layer type	#Filters	Output	Filter size	#Stride
	Input Layer	–	$80 \times 80 \times 1$	–	–
CNN Block1	Conv1 (Relu)	24	$80 \times 80 \times 24$	3×3	1×1
	MaxPool1	1	$16 \times 16 \times 24$	5×5	5×5
	BN1	–	$16 \times 16 \times 24$	–	–
CNN Block2	Conv2 (Relu)	48	$16 \times 16 \times 48$	3×3	1×1
	MaxPool2	1	$8 \times 8 \times 48$	2×2	2×2
	BN2	–	$8 \times 8 \times 48$	–	–
CNN Block3	Conv3 (Relu)	48	$8 \times 8 \times 48$	3×3	1×1
	MaxPool3	1	$4 \times 4 \times 48$	2×2	2×2
	BN3	–	$4 \times 4 \times 48$	–	–
FC1	FC1 (Relu)	–	512×1	–	–
	DropOut	Rate = 0.2	512×1	–	–
FC2	FC2	–	Categories $\times 1$	–	–

We use the proposed CNN as the backbone network in the OS-architecture. The output of FC2 cannot be used directly in the OS-architecture because the number of neurons in the FC2 is fixed and equal to the number of categories to be recognized, which restricts the application scenario. The solution is to use the output of the FC1 rather the FC2. FC1 is regarded as an embedding layer, and the mapping relationship between the embedding layer and FC2 can be adjusted by modifying the loss function.

First, we use the output f of the FC1 and the weight W and bias b between FC1 and FC2 to represent the output result z of the FC2 layer: $z = \sum W \cdot f + b$. According to the product $a \cdot b = \|a\| \cdot \|b\| \cdot \cos \theta_{a,b}$, the loss function is as follows:

$$\mathcal{L} = -\frac{1}{n} \sum_{i=1}^{n} \log \frac{e^{\|W_{y_i}\| \cdot \|f_i\| \cos(\theta_{y_i}) + b_{y_i}}}{\sum_{j=1}^{c} e^{\|W_j\| \|f_i\| \cos(\theta_j) + b_j}}, \tag{1}$$

where c and y_i are the number of categories in training and the label value of the i-th sample, respectively. The original loss function constrains the relationship between f and W in terms of angle and distance. Because the optimization involves both angle and distance, it is challenging to quantify the optimization result. Furthermore, if this loss function only constrains the relationship either for angle or distance, we can quantify the similarity between the features of two samples, which leads to the recognition method no longer relying on labels. The intention is to aggregate features of the same categories. Inspired by AMSoftmax [20], we removed the constraint on distance in the loss function. Set the weight w to 1 and the bias b to 0.

Based on this improvement, the loss function will only optimize the cosine distance. Correspondingly, the model's classification boundary for category i and j is the cosine distance as $\cos(\theta_i) = \cos(\theta_j)$, where θ is the angle between the feature and weight vector. However, removing the optimization of the distance in the loss function will degrade optimization performance. To enhance the effect of the loss function, an interval parameter m must be added. As depicted in Fig. 2, the dotted line represents the classification boundary. Subtracting a positive margin on one side of boundary can make the decision more favorable to the other side. It increases the penalty of the loss function, which strengthens the cohesion of homogeneous samples. Moreover, we add a scaling factor s to avoid the gradient vanishing problem. After these adjustments, the loss function is improved as follows:

$$\mathcal{L}_{AMS} = -\frac{1}{n}\sum_{i=1}^{n}\log\frac{e^{s\cdot\left(\cos\theta_{y_i}-m\right)}}{e^{s\cdot\left(\cos\theta_{y_i}-m\right)}+\sum_{j=1,j\neq y_i}^{n}e^{s\cdot\cos\theta_j}}. \tag{2}$$

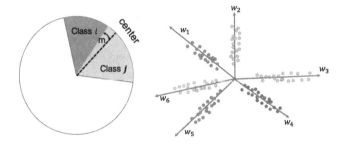

Fig. 2. Classification boundary and optimization results.

The loss function enables each category of samples mapped to a region with a small angle to the weight vector of the corresponding label. Furthermore, increasing the angle between different weight vectors will increase the angle between non-homogeneous samples improving the accuracy of feature mapping. To achieve this goal, we add a regularization term. Assume that W is the weight matrix between FC1 and FC2. Due to the previous constraint $\|w\| = 1$, the weight vectors and weight matrix satisfy

$$W_i^T \cdot W_j = \cos\left(\theta_{W_i W_j}\right), \tag{3}$$

and take the exponent of e to the result:

$$P = e^{\sum_{i=1}^{c}\sum_{j=1}^{c}W_i^T \cdot W_j}. \tag{4}$$

Add P to the loss function. The smaller the value of P, the higher the overall angle summation between w and the more dispersed the feature distribution. The final loss function we propose for the OS-architecture can be expressed as:

$$\mathcal{L}_f = \mathcal{L}_{AMS} + \varepsilon \cdot P. \tag{5}$$

Operations such as regularization can be further added to improve the model's generalization ability. Using the improved interval-based loss function to optimize the proposed network and the output of FC1 obtained by forwarding propagation produces the feature vectors. The similarity between two input samples is obtained by measuring the cosine value of the feature vectors, resulting in open-set recognition.

4   Experiments

To validate the performance of the proposed framework, some experiments were conducted on two publicly available databases, SDUMLA [21] and MMCBNU [22]. SDUMLA consists of 3,816 samples, 636 categories from 106 subjects, while MMCBNU consists of 6000 samples, 600 categories from 600 subjects. The performance indicator we used is equal error rate (EER), indicating the point at which false reject rate and false accept rate are equal. The input images are region of interesting provided by database itself.

Table 2. Experimental results of the finger-vein database (EER (%))

Database	EER	Method
SDUMLA	5.70	Siamese CNN [7]
	3.91	Difference image [13]
	2.45	Semantic Segmentation [19]
	2.35	Composite Image [6]
	2.34	Multimodal Biometric Recognition [15]
	2.29	Proposed
MMCBNU	0.79	FV-Net [7]
	0.47	Proposed
	0.30	FV-Net [14]

We extract representative results from related literature and compare them with our results under similar test protocols. Our algorithm's performance is state-of-the-art compared with that of the others, as shown in Table 2, which confirms the feasibility of the proposed algorithm.

Table 3 presents the parameter size and run-time comparison. The average time for the proposed CNN to run an image independently was 2.48 ms, which

Table 3. Run-time and parameter size comparison (ms); testing on Ubuntu 18.04, using Nvidia GeForce GTX2080 GPU, Intel Core E5-2610.

	VGG16	VGG19	RESNET50	DENSENET	Proposed
Run-time	5.24	6.02	11.21	51.98	**2.48**
Parameter size	18M	29M	27M	13M	**0.7M**

is significantly faster than other deep neural networks. Compared with the existing algorithm, the proposed algorithm has a higher recognition rate and faster recognition speed.

Thus the experiments verified the proposed hypothesis, illustrating shallow CNNs can achieve excellent performance and strong practicability. Furthermore, in our another experiment, we tried adding other finger vein databases as training set. The performance of the model trained in this way can be further improved, which became the focus of our next research.

5 Conclusion

In this paper, we design a shallow network with three convolutional blocks and two fully connected layers that can be efficiently applied for both CS-architecture and OS-architecture of FVR. An improved interval-based loss function is used to extract discriminative large-margin features. The proposed network has excellent real-time performance, which enables easy retraining, having high practicability.

Acknowledgements. This work is supported by the Natural Science Foundation of Shandong Province, China (No. ZR2014FM004).

References

1. Das, R., Piciucco, E., Maiorana, E., Campisi, P.: Convolutional neural network for finger-vein-based biometric identification. IEEE Trans. Inf. Forensics Secur. **14**(2), 360–373 (2019)
2. Kang, W., Liu, H., Luo, W., Deng, F.: Study of a full-view 3D finger vein verification technique. IEEE Trans. Inf. Forensics Secur. **15**, 1175–1189 (2020)
3. Qin, H., El-Yacoubi, M.A.: Deep representation-based feature extraction and recovering for finger-vein verification. IEEE Trans. Inf. Forensics Secur. **12**(8), 1816–1829 (2017)
4. Fang, Y., Wu, Q., Kang, W.: A novel finger vein verification system based on two-stream convolutional network learning. Neurocomputing **290**, 100–107 (2018)
5. Lu, Y., Xie, S., Wu, S.: Exploring competitive features using deep convolutional neural network for finger vein recognition. IEEE Access **7**, 35113–35123 (2019)
6. Song, J.M., Kim, W., Park, K.R.: Finger-vein recognition based on deep DenseNet using composite image. IEEE Access **7**, 66845–66863 (2019)
7. Tang, S., Zhou, S., Kang, W., Wu, Q., Deng, F.: Finger vein verification using a Siamese CNN. IET Biometrics **8**(5), 306–315 (2019)

8. Xie, C., Kumar, A.: Finger vein identification using convolutional neural network and supervised discrete hashing. Pattern Recogn. Lett. **119**, 148–156 (2019)
9. Yang, W., Hui, C., Chen, Z., Xue, J., Liao, Q.: V-GAN: finger vein representation using generative adversarial networks. IEEE Trans. Inf. Forensics Secur. **14**(9), 2512–2524 (2019)
10. Radzi, S., Hani, M., Bakhteri, R.: Finger-vein biometric identification using convolutional neural network. Turk. J. Electr. **24**, 1863–1878 (2016)
11. Fairuz, S., Habaebi, M.H., Elsheikh, E.M.A., Chebil, A.J.: convolutional neural network-based finger vein recognition using near infrared images. In: 2018 7th International Conference on Computer and Communication Engineering (ICCCE), pp. 453–458 (2018)
12. Hou, B., Yan, R.: Convolutional auto-encoder based deep feature learning for finger-vein verification. In: IEEE International Symposium on Medical Measurements and Applications (MeMeA) 2018, pp. 1–5 (2018)
13. Hong, H.G., Lee, M.B., Park, K.R.: Convolutional neural network-based finger-vein recognition using NIR image sensors. Sensors **17**(6), 1297 (2017)
14. Hu, H., et al.: FV-Net: learning a finger-vein feature representation based on a CNN. In: 2018 24th International Conference on Pattern Recognition (ICPR), pp. 3489–3494 (2018)
15. Kim, W., Song, M.J., Park, R.K.: Multimodal biometric recognition based on convolutional neural network by the fusion of finger-vein and finger shape using near-infrared (NIR) camera sensor. Sensors **18**(7), 2296 (2018)
16. Jalilian, E., Uhl, A.: Enhanced segmentation-CNN based finger-vein recognition by joint training with automatically generated and manual labels. In: 2019 IEEE 5th International Conference on Identity, Security, and Behavior Analysis (ISBA), pp. 1–8 (2019)
17. Yi, D., Lei, Z., Liao, S., Li, S.Z.: Learning face representation from scratch. Computer Science (2014)
18. Su, K., Yang, G., Yang, L., Li, D., Su, P., Yin, Y.: Learning binary hash codes for finger vein image retrieval. Pattern Recogn. Lett. **117**, 74–82 (2019)
19. Jalilian, E., Uhl, A.: Finger-vein recognition using deep fully convolutional neural semantic segmentation networks: the impact of training data. Presented at the 2018 IEEE International Workshop on Information Forensics and Security (WIFS) (2018)
20. Wang, F., Cheng, J., Liu, W., Liu, H.: Additive margin softmax for face verification. IEEE Signal Process. Lett. **25**(7), 926–930 (2018)
21. Yin, Y., Liu, L., Sun, X.: SDUMLA-HMT: a multimodal biometric database. In: Sun, Z., Lai, J., Chen, X., Tan, T. (eds.) CCBR 2011. LNCS, vol. 7098, pp. 260–268. Springer, Heidelberg (2011). https://doi.org/10.1007/978-3-642-25449-9_33
22. Lu, Y., Xie, S.J., Yoon, S., Wang, Z., Park, D.S.: An available database for the research of finger vein recognition. In: 2013 6th International Congress on Image and Signal Processing (CISP), vol. 01, pp. 410–415 (2013)

Finger Crystal Feature Recognition Based on Graph Convolutional Network

Zihao Zhao$^{(\boxtimes)}$, Ziyun Ye, Jinfeng Yang, and Haigang Zhang

Institute of Applied Artificial Intelligence of the Guangdong-Hong Kong-Macao Greater Bay Area, Shenzhen Polytechnic, Shenzhen 518055, China
{zhzhao,yeziyun2020,jfyang,zhanghg}@szpt.edu.cn

Abstract. Finger biometrics have been widely used in human identity recognition. The effective combination of finger multimodal features can greatly improve the security and reliability of recognition. This paper proposes a crystal structure graph model to perform fusion and recognition for finger prints, finger veins and finger knuckle prints. First, the block division method and the Steerable filter are used to generate graph node from trimodal images. Then, these nodes are connected into a cube-shaped crystal graph. This crystal graph combines the three modal features of the finger. Next, a Graph Convolutional Network model is built to identify and classify these crystal graphs. This model can update the graph nodes, so as to make a global representation of the crystal graph. In the experiments, the recognition accuracy of the finger crystal graph model exceeds 90%.

Keywords: Finger crystal graph · Biometric recognition · Finger trimodal · Graph Convolutional Network · Feature fusion

1 Introduction

Through continuous innovation, biometric recognition has been deeply integrated with the current social and economic development [1,2]. At present, the available human biometrics can be divided into physiological characteristics and behavior characteristics [3,4]. To improve the accuracy, universality and reliability of identity recognition, it is necessary to apply multi biometrics to jointly describe and express the identity of a person [5]. Finger carries three modal features: finger print (FP), finger kunckle print (FKP), and finger vein (FV), which can effectively overcome the general personality factors such as individual height, wearing makeup, ambient light, and viewing angle changes. Therefore, the finger-based multimodal biometric fusion recognition technology has important significance.

In recent years, many fusion recognition methods of finger multimodal features have been proposed. Li et al. [6] proposed the multimodal finger recognition method (FV and FKP) based on hash learning feature representation. Daas et al.

© Springer Nature Switzerland AG 2021
J. Feng et al. (Eds.): CCBR 2021, LNCS 12878, pp. 203–212, 2021.
https://doi.org/10.1007/978-3-030-86608-2_23

[7] proposed a deep learning based FV and FKP multimodal biometric recognition systems. Wang et al. [8,9] first proposed FP, FKP and FV trimodal feature fusion and recognition methods by Convolutional Neural Network (CNN) or local coding algorithm. Zhang et al. [10] explored the description of finger trimodal features based on graph theory, and proposed the reasonable fusion framework. These finger multimodal feature fusion recognition methods are limited by the primary and secondary relationship of different modalities, and cannot effectively deal with the feature deformation caused by size normalization. To realize the representation and recognition of finger global features, this paper proposes an organic fusion recognition method based on the Graph Convolutional Network (GCN).

GCN acts on the graph structure directly. It has been more and more widely used in various fields such as social networks, knowledge graphs, recommendation systems and even life sciences [11,12]. Many GCN derivative models have made breakthroughs in graph analysis algorithms. Kipf et al. [13] had delicately designed a method of extracting features from graph data, so as to perform node classification, graph classification, and link prediction on the graph data. To improve the performance and generalization ability of GCN, Velickovic et al. proposed the Graph Attention Networks (GAT) model [14]. GAT uses the attention mechanism to assign different weights to different neighbor nodes. Ying et al. proposed the DiffPool model [15], which is a differentiable graph pooling model. It can generate a hierarchical representation of the graph, and can be combined with various graph neural network architectures in end-to-end manner. Self-Attention Graph Pooling (SAGPool) [16] uses the self-attention mechanism to determine the deletion and retention of nodes, and obtains better graph classification performance on the benchmark dataset.

GCN has excellent performance in graph analysis and can be applied in the recognition of finger multimodal crystal graphs. First, we divide the original FP, FV and FKP images into regular blocks, and generate feature nodes through the Steerable filter. Then, we formulate the connection rules between the nodes, and get the regular cubic crystal structure graph data. This crystal graph highly integrates the three modal features of the finger. Next, an improved SAGPool model is constructed to perform the recognition of crystal graphs. After convolution, pooling and readout operations, a highly abstract feature representation of the crystal graph can be obtained. The basic architecture of the proposed method is shown in Fig. 1. We perform some comparative experiments to verify the effectiveness of this method, and achieve a classification accuracy higher than 90% on the self-built trimodal database.

The main contributions of our work is highlighted below: a. We propose a novel concept of crystal graph structure to realize the representation and recognition of finger trimodal features. b. Based on the finger trimodal database, our improved GCN model can achieve a great classification accuracy.

The rest of this paper is organized as follows. Section 2 introduces the construction method of finger trimodal crystal graph. In Sect. 3, the improved GCN model for crystal graph classification is presented in detail. The experimental results are discussed and analyzed in Sect. 4. Finally, conclusions are drawn in Sect. 5.

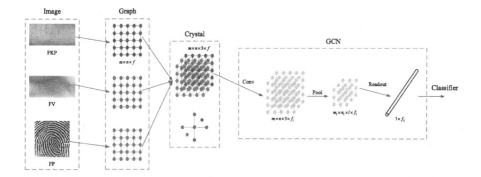

Fig. 1. The flow chart of the proposed method. m, n and l are the size of the graph, f is the length of node feature. Conv is used for updating node features, the convolution kernel is in diamond shape. Pool is used for node deletion and retention. The node features can be aggregated into graph global feature by readout.

2   Crystal Graph Construction Method

In this Section, we introduce the construction method of finger trimodal crystal graph. Based on original FV, FP, FKP images, we extract node feature through block division and the Steerable filter. Then, the unimodal graph is obtained by setting the neighbor counts of each node. Finally, we splice and merge the graphs corresponding to different modalities to obtain the final crystal graph.

2.1   Node Generation

The original captured trimodal images contain many noise, which cannot be used for graph node generation. We should make necessary preprocessing for these images. First, we extract the region of interest (ROI) from original images using inter-phalangeal joint prior method [17]. Then, the Gabor filter is used to enhance features of FV, FP and FKP. The frequency and direction of the Gabor filter are similar to the human visual system, and it is particularly suitable for image texture representation and discrimination. To further eliminate the influence of background noise and texture thickness, we binarize and skeletonize the image. Finally, all images are adjusted into the same size.

Next, the sliding window method is used to evenly divide the image into a $M \times N$ block matrix. The detailed calculation method of block number is,

$$M \times N = \frac{a}{m} \times \frac{b}{n}, \tag{1}$$

where a and b are the image width and height, the m and n are the window width and height. There are no overlapping areas between blocks. These image blocks are the base of graph nodes. Each image block has unique texture information. This process is shown in Fig. 2. To represent the blocks as available feature information, we apply the Steerable filter. Steerable filter is a common tool for image processing, especially with good performance when analyzing the curve structure of the image. The calculation formula of Steerable filter is,

$$h^\theta(x, y) = \sum_{j=1}^{N} k_j(\theta) f^{\theta_j}(x, y), \tag{2}$$

where h^θ is Steerable filter, x and y is the size of filter (image block size), θ is angle of Steerable filter, $k(\theta)$ is interpolation function, $f(x, y)$ is arbitrary filter function, N is number of basic filters, θ_j is the rotation angle of the basic filter in the basic filter group. We perform Steer filtering on the blocks, extract the texture energy in the direction of 0–360°, and get a 360 length vector, which is expressed as the feature of the block. These feature vectors with a length of 360 are the feature nodes corresponding to the image blocks.

Fig. 2. Schematic diagram of image block division.

2.2 Graph Generation and Crystal Generation

In computer science, a graph is a collection of nodes connected by a series of edges. Graphs are used to store data with a M - N logical relationship. With the generation of trimodal feature nodes, we construct unimodal graph by setting neighbor number for each node. As shown in Fig. 3, the image is transformed to some nodes. Assuming that node 0 is a randomly selected target node, its adjacent first-order neighbors can be set to 4 or 8. Since there are no overlapping areas when dividing image blocks, the correlation between nodes 1, 3, 6, 8 in Fig. 3(b) and node 0 is low. Further considering the storage space and computational complexity, we decide to set the effective neighbor number of each node to 4, and the direction is up, down, left, and right. It should be noted that if the node at graph edge, the number of its neighbors is 3, and the number of neighbors of the node at corner is 2. We connect the single modal nodes according to the above rules, and the corresponding modal graph structure data will be generated.

Based on the generated three unimodal graphs, we can construct a crystal structure graph data to characterize the trimodal features of the finger. The graphs of the FV, FP and FKP are in same size. So, we randomly superimpose the graphs of the three modes to form a regular cubic crystal. In chemistry, crystals are composed of particles such as molecules, atoms, and ions. Here, these particles are replaced by different nodes. Each node is connected to adjacent nodes above and below. Each crystal graph contains three layers of FV, FP and

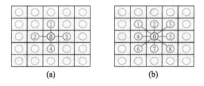

Fig. 3. Node neighbor connection rules. (a) means 4 neighbors, (b) means 8 neighbors.

FKP. Different modal graphs are randomly superimposed, which can increase the diversity of the data and enhance the representativeness of the crystal graph feature. Each node in the center layer of the crystal has 6 first-order neighbors, and the number of first-order neighbors for nodes located at the edges and vertices is reduced. Figure 4 shows a crystal graph in $10 \times 10 \times 3$ size, which is a suitable crystal graph size. Another better size is $20 \times 20 \times 3$. The proposed crystal contains FP, FV and FKP feature of the finger, which is helpful for subsequent research on the global representation of finger biometrics.

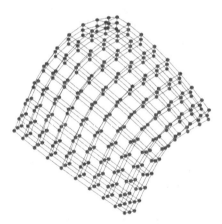

Fig. 4. The visualization result of crystal graph, which is drawn by Python NetworkX.

3   Crystal Graph Classification Model

Based on the finger trimodal crystal graph data, we construct a suitable GCN to perform feature reduction and node optimization. After multiple iterations of training, it is possible to realize the aggregation of the node feature to the crystal graph feature, thereby obtaining a feature vector that can represent the entire finger.

3.1   Graph Convolutional Network

GCN extends the convolution operation from traditional data (such as images) to graph data. The core idea is to learn a function mapping $f(\cdot)$, through the node v_i in the graph, it can aggregate its own features x_i and its neighbor features x_j to generate new representation of node v_i. The general linear function of the convolutional layer is,

$$H^{l+1} = f(H^l, A), \tag{3}$$

where l is layer, $H^0 = X$ is the first input layer, A is adjacency matrix, $X \in R^{N \times F}$, N is the node number, F is the feature length. The difference between different GCN models lies in the implementation of $f(\cdot)$. The GCN model can continuously update the node features through the convolutional layer, and finally realize the classification prediction of the node.

To perform the classification of graph, we also need to add pooling layers and readout layers to the GCN model. Graph data usually contains a large number of nodes. These nodes need to be comprehensively considered during training, and only important nodes are retained. The GCN pooling layer is mainly implemented by sorting the nodes, and then taking top k nodes. After convolution and pooling, the remaining nodes need to be aggregated to obtain the feature representation of the graph. The current readout layer is mostly based on simple operations such as summation and average. Therefore, in order to avoid diluting the features of important nodes, the number of input nodes in the readout layer should not be too much, which also reflects the importance of the pooling layer. Next, we use the global graph feature output by the readout layer as input, and the graph can be classified through a classifier.

3.2   The Improved SAGPool Model

To adapt the crystal graph classification task, we choose and improve the SAG-Pool, which with excellent performance. SAGPool is the first method to use self-attention for graph pooling. Here, the model architecture contains three convolutional layers, three pooling layers, three readout layers and a classifier (as shown in Fig. 5).

SAGPool uses the graph convolution to get the self-attention score. So the result of this pooling is based on the features and topology of the graph. The calculation formula of the convolutional layer is,

$$h^{(l+1)} = \sigma(\widetilde{D}^{-\frac{1}{2}} \widetilde{A} \widetilde{D}^{-\frac{1}{2}} h^{(l)} \Theta), \tag{4}$$

where $\Theta \in R^{F \times F'}$, F and F' respectively represent the input feature dimension and output feature dimension of the $l+1$ layer, σ is ReLU activation function.

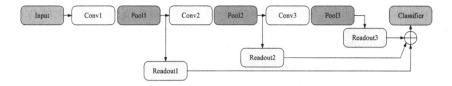

Fig. 5. The architecture of the SAGPool model.

$\widetilde{A}$ is adjacency matrix includes node itself, $\widetilde{D}$ is degree matrix of each node in $\widetilde{A}$. $\widetilde{D}^{-\frac{1}{2}}\widetilde{A}\widetilde{D}^{-\frac{1}{2}}$ is used to normalize $\widetilde{A}$. The score Z of self-attention is calculated as,

$$Z = \sigma(\widetilde{D}^{-\frac{1}{2}}\widetilde{A}\widetilde{D}^{-\frac{1}{2}}X\Theta_{att}), \qquad (5)$$

where X is feature matrix, $\Theta_{att} \in R^{F\times 1}$. The model retains nodes according to the score Z and obtains the index. The model obtains a new feature matrix and adjacency matrix according to the index. The readout layer aggregates node features by concatenating the mean and maximum of all nodes. Its output feature X_{out} is,

$$X_{out} = \text{ave}(x_i) \parallel \max(x_i), i \in [1, N], \qquad (6)$$

where N is the node number, x_i is the feature of the i-th node, $\parallel$ is concatenating operation.

The specific model parameters are as follows. The feature dimension of the hidden layer is 90. The node retention rate of the pooling layer is 0.5, 0.4 and 0.25 respectively. The classifier includes 3 layer, the number of neurons in each layer is 1024.

4 Experiments

To verify the effectiveness of the proposed method, we conduct three experiments. First, we compare the influence of crystal graph structure, node feature dimension, and network parameters on the classification results. Next, we compare the performance of some different GCN models. Finally, we compare the model recognition results obtained from different modal fusion graphs.

The currently public finger biometric databases only contain one or two modalities, and there is no database with FV, FP, and FKP. The research team establishes a finger trimodal database, which contains 100 categories of corresponding FV, FP, FKP images, and each category has ten image samples. We conduct experiments based on this database, using a NVIDIA RTX2070 GPU graphics card. First, we compare the differences of various crystal structures and GCN model parameters. Crystal structures contain node number and feature length. Model parameters contain node feature length in hidden layer, node retention ratio of the pooling layer and neuron number in the classifier. In order to reduce the required memory, we adopt the sparse matrix format. The node features are normalized before model training. The learning rate is set to 0.002 and the training epoch is 300. The ratio of training set to test set is 8:2. The experimental results are presented in Table 1.

Table 1. Parameter comparison experimental results.

Node	Feature	Hidden	Ratio	Classifier	Accuracy
$10 \times 10 \times 3$	90	64	0.5,0.5,0.5	512	62.27%
$10 \times 10 \times 3$	90	64	0.5,0.4,0.3	512	65.11%
$10 \times 10 \times 3$	360	64	0.5,0.5,0.5	512	74.06%
$10 \times 10 \times 3$	360	90	0.5,0.5,0.5	1024	75.63%
$10 \times 10 \times 3$	360	90	0.5,0.4,0.3	1024	77.80%
$10 \times 10 \times 3$	360	128	0.5,0.4,0.3	1024	76.39%
$20 \times 20 \times 3$	90	64	0.5,0.4,0.3	512	83.04%
$20 \times 20 \times 3$	360	90	0.5,0.4,0.3	1024	88.42%
$20 \times 20 \times 3$	360	90	0.5,0.4,0.25	1024	**90.28%**
$20 \times 20 \times 3$	360	128	0.5,0.4,0.25	1024	86.16%

From the results in Table 1, it can be found that different crystal structure has a greater impact on the algorithm, and the parameters of the GCN model have less impact. With the increase of the node number and feature dimension in the crystal graph, the experimental results have improved significantly. When the node distribution of each modal graph is set to 20×20, it can more specifically reflect the uniqueness of biometrics. At the same time, the feature of 360 length is better than 90 length. To avoid too much memory and too sparse node features, we did not further try more node distribution. Due to the limited performance of the GCN model in the graph classification task at this stage (the classification accuracy of public data sets is around 80%), even if we adaptively optimize the model, we still fail to achieve a particularly ideal accuracy. The loss curve of the model training process is shown in Fig. 6 (The 9-th experiment).

In addition, our model is also compared with other models, and the results are recorded in Table 2. It can be found that the two models (GCN and GAT) without the pooling layer do not work well. The DiffPool and SGAPool models with the pooling layer can achieve higher accuracy. In addition, our improvements have further improved the performance of the SAGPool on the finger trimodal crystal graph database. If only one of FV, FP, FKP is used to train the graph classification model, the final classification accuracy rate is around 70%, which shown in Table 3. This also proves that fusing the three modal graphs into a crystal graph can improve the recognition ability of the model, thus demonstrating the effectiveness of our method.

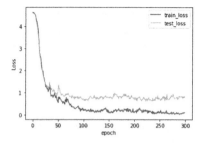

Fig. 6. The loss curve of the model training process.

Table 2. Model comparison experimental results.

Model	GCN	GAT	DiffPool	SAGPool (ori)	SAGPool (ours)
Accuracy	57.44%	63.18%	79.03%	84.80%	90.28%

Compared with state-of-the-art approaches, the method proposed in this paper still has great potential for improvement in accuracy. With the expansion of the training database, we believe that the accuracy will be greatly improved. In the actual feature recognition, our method is based on the crystal graph data and does not directly input the original image, so the confidentiality of personal privacy information has been improved. This is also the main advancement of the proposed method.

Table 3. Comparative experimental results of different modal graphs.

Modal	FP	FV	FKP	FV+FKP	FV+FKP+FP
Accuracy	77.82%	69.51%	66.04%	84.85%	90.28%

5   Conclusions

This paper proposed a novel method of finger trimodal feature fusion recognition. First, FV, FP, FKP images were fused into a crystal structure graph to obtain the global feature of the finger. To perform recognition and classification of this graph, we applied the SAGPool model. By adjusting the graph structure and model structure, we had achieved a classification accuracy over 90%. Although the accuracy was not particularly ideal, our work proposed a new solution for finger multimodal feature recognition, especially in data confidentiality and feature globality. In future work, we will explore a more scientific method of node connection in crystal graph, and a more effective GCN model algorithm.

Acknowledgments. This work was supported in part by the National Natural Science Foundation of China under Grant 62076166 and 61806208, in part by the General Higher Education Project of Guangdong Provincial Education Department under Grant 2020ZDZX3082.

References

1. Vandana, Kaur, N.: A study of biometric identification and verification system. In: International Conference on Advance Computing and Innovative Technologies in Engineering (ICACITE), Greater Noida, India, pp. 60–64 (2021)
2. Li, S., Zhang, B., Zhao, S., et al.: Local discriminant coding based convolutional feature representation for multimodal finger recognition. Inf. Sci. **547**, 1170–1181 (2021)
3. Fan, C., Peng, Y., Cao, C., et al.: GaitPart: temporal part-based model for gait recognition. In: IEEE/CVF Conference on Computer Vision and Pattern Recognition (CVPR), Seattle, USA, pp. 14213–14221 (2020)
4. Yang, J., Zhang, X.: Feature-level fusion of fingerprint and finger-vein for personal identification. Pattern Recogn. Lett. **33**(5), 623–628 (2012)
5. Devi, R., Sujatha, P.: A study on biometric and multi-modal biometric system modules, applications, techniques and challenges. In: 2017 Conference on Emerging Devices and Smart Systems (ICEDSS), Tamilnadu, India, pp. 267–271 (2017)
6. Li, S., Zhang, B., Fei, L., et al.: Joint discriminative feature learning for multimodal finger recognition. Pattern Recogn. **111**, 107704 (2021)
7. Daas, S., Yahi, A., Bakir, T., et al.: Multimodal biometric recognition systems using deep learning based on the finger vein and finger knuckle print fusion. IET Image Process. **14**(15), 3859–3868 (2020)
8. Wang, L., Zhang, H., Yang, J.: Finger multimodal features fusion and recognition based on CNN. In: IEEE Symposium Series on Computational Intelligence (SSCI), Xiamen, China, pp. 3183–3188 (2019)
9. Li, S., Zhang, H., Shi, Y., et al.: Novel local coding algorithm for finger multimodal feature description and recognition. Sensors **19**(9), 2213 (2019)
10. Zhang, H., Li, S., Shi, Y., et al.: Graph fusion for finger multimodal biometrics. IEEE Access **7**, 28607–28615 (2019)
11. Zhao, L., Song, Y., Zhang, C.: T-GCN: a temporal graph convolutional network for traffic prediction. IEEE Trans. Intell. Transp. Syst. **21**(9), 3848–3858 (2020)
12. Wu, Z., Pan, S., Chen, F., et al.: A comprehensive survey on graph neural networks. IEEE Trans. Neural Netw. Learn. Syst. **32**(1), 4–24 (2021)
13. Kipf, T.N., Welling, M.: Semi-supervised classification with graph convolutional networks. In: 5th International Conference on Learning Representations (ICLR), Toulon, France (2017)
14. Velickovic, P., Cucurull, G., Casanova, A., et al.: Graph attention networks. In: 6th International Conference on Learning Representations (ICLR), Vancouver, Canada (2018)
15. Ying, Z., You, J., Morris, C., et al.: Hierarchical graph representation learning with differentiable pooling. In: 32nd Conference on Neural Information Processing Systems (NIPS), Montreal, Canada, pp. 4805–4815 (2018)
16. Lee, J., Lee, I., Kang, J.: Self-attention graph pooling. In: 36th International Conference on Machine Learning (ICML), Long Beach, USA, pp. 3734–3743 (2019)
17. Yang, J., Wei, J., Shi, Y.: Accurate ROI localization and hierarchical hyper-sphere model for finger-vein recognition. Neurocomputing **328**, 171–181 (2019)

Signatured Fingermark Recognition Based on Deep Residual Network

Yongliang Zhang[1], Qiuyi Zhang[1], Jiali Zou[1], Weize Zhang[2(⊠)], Xiang Li[1], Mengting Chen[1], and Yufan Lv[3]

[1] College of Computer Science and Technology, Zhejiang University of Technology, Hangzhou 310023, China
[2] College of Education, Zhejiang University of Technology, Hangzhou 310023, China
zwz@zjut.edu.cn
[3] Institute of Forensic Science, Ministry of Public Security, Beijing 100038, China

Abstract. Traditional fingerprint recognition methods based on minutiae have shown great success on for high-quality fingerprint images. However, the accuracy rates are significantly reduced for signatured fingermark on the contract. This paper proposes a signatured fingermark recognition method based on deep learning. Firstly, the proposed method uses deep learning combined with domain knowledge to extract the minutiae of fingermark. Secondly, it searches and calibrates the texture region of interest (ROI). Finally, it builds a deep neural network based on residual blocks, and trains the model through Triplet Loss. The proposed method achieved an equal error rate (EER) of 0.0779 on the self-built database, which is far lower than the traditional methods. It also proves that this method can effectively reduce the labor and time costs during minutiae extraction.

Keywords: Signatured fingermark · Weak label · Residual block · Triplet Loss

1 Introduction

Fingerprint recognition has become one of the most mature and widely used biometric technologies. For high-quality fingerprint images, the automatic fingerprint identification system (AFIS) has almost perfect performance. However, high-quality images cannot be obtained in practical applications, due to factors such as the collection environment and equipment. The signatured fingermark studied in this paper in such a case.

As shown in Fig. 1, signature fingermark images are usually in low-quality. During the collection process, uneven distribution of inkpads and pressing force will cause problems such as ridge lines adhesion and images incomplete. The written instruments used for fingermark may have different colors and contain other noises. This greatly affects the accuracy of fingermark recognition. However, fingerprint recognition is widely used in civil and economic dispute cases. Especially in China, the method of fingerprinting with signature is often used in contracts, IOUs and other written instruments with legal effects. This reflects the necessity of research on signatured fingermark recognition.

© Springer Nature Switzerland AG 2021
J. Feng et al. (Eds.): CCBR 2021, LNCS 12878, pp. 213–220, 2021.
https://doi.org/10.1007/978-3-030-86608-2_24

In the existing literature, it is found that there are few relevant researches on signatured fingermark. We investigate some other low-quality fingerprint image recognition methods for reference. A. A. Paulino [1] proposed a latent fingerprint recognition based on AFIS, which combined the manually marked minutiae with the automatically extracted minutiae to improve the accuracy of the potential full fingerprint matching. However, the manual marking method consumes too much labor cost and time cost. WANG Ya-ni [2] proposed a convolutional neural network-based recognition algorithm for low-quality fingerprints, which used the Poincare formula to calculate the singular points of the fingerprint image as anchor points to cut the original image and the refined image and send them together to the net. A. R. Patil [3] proposed a fingerprint recognition system for Infants and Toddlers, which used the core point to determine the ROI. And it used the improved Gabor filter to derive the proper finger codes for recognition. However, the singular points are often difficult to extract from signatured fingermark. Fingerprint minutiae will be a better choice. The FingerNet used to extract fingerprint minutiae was proposed in Literature [4]. Y. Tang proved that their method has better minutiae extraction ability in scenes with blurred ridges and noisy backgrounds. And the deep residual learning [5] showed excellent performance on ImageNet2015.

Therefore, this paper proposes a fingermark recognition method based on deep residual network called FR-DRN algorithm. It consists of two parts: extracting fingermark minutiae based on FingerNet, and implementing fingermark recognition based on deep residual learning. The main contributions of this paper are enumerated as follows: combining the octantal nearest-neighborhood structures (ONNS) which was developed in our earlier studies to make weak labels. And use them to train fingerprint minutiae extraction algorithms. This work greatly reduces labor and time costs and improves the efficiency of minutiae extraction; Building a residual network based on the residual block to extract deep texture features, which improves the accuracy of fingermark matching.

This paper is organized as follows: the methods of making weak labels and the deep residual network is introduced in Sect. 2. In Sect. 3, experiment is carried out based on the self-built signatured fingermark database and the results are analyzed in detail. Conclusion is given in Sect. 4.

Fig. 1. Signatured fingermark images obtained from the contract.

2 FR-DRN Algorithm

Motivated by the favorable performance of deep residual network, the FR-DRN is proposed for signatured fingermark. In this section, FingerNet is firstly implemented to extract minutiae. Then, image blocks are cut according to minutiae. Furthermore, the deep residual network constructed is used to realize fingermark recognition.

2.1   Extract Fingerprint Minutiae

We reference fingerNet and combine our own ideas to complete the following work.

The first step is to register rolling fingerprints and signatured fingermarks. Firstly, establish a database containing signatured fingermarks and rolling fingerprints. They are in one-to-one correspondence. The traditional algorithm of minutiae extraction is used to extract the minutiae of the two respectively, and the minutiae matching algorithm based on ONNS is used to find the corresponding minutiae pairs of the two, and the affine transformation matrix of the rolling fingerprint is established according to them. Then, affine transformation is used to register the rolling fingerprint to the signatured fingermark, and the registered rolling fingerprint and minutiae are obtained.

The second step is to make segmentation mask labels, minutiae weak labels and orientation field weak labels. Hand-made segmentation mask labels for signatured fingermark and rolling fingerprint, and used to train a fully convolutional neural network. Use the network to divide the signatured fingermark and the rolling fingerprint, and obtain the overlapping fingerprint area. The minutiae of the rolling fingerprint in the overlap area are used as the minutiae weak label. Then, calculating the orientation field of the segmented rolling fingerprint using the method proposed in literature [6]. Use it as the orientation field weak label corresponding to the signatured fingermark.

The registered rolling fingerprint is used to generate weak labels for the minutiae and orientation fields of the fingermark. Compared with hand-made strong labels, this process does not require manual labeling, which greatly improves efficiency and saves labor costs and time costs.

The last step is to use FingerNet to calculate the orientation field and minutiae. The final rendering is shown in Fig. 2.

Fig. 2. From left to right are the original image, segmentation mask, predicted orientation field, and predicted minutiae

2.2   Processing Training Sample and Normalization

After obtaining the minutiae of an image, normalize the orientation of the minutiae to the same angle by rotating the image with each minutia as the center. Cutting the image block size of w × w pixels as the training sample after orientation normalization. Before cutting, comparing the block which to be cut with the segmentation mask. If the area of the foreground is less than 50% of the entire block, the block will be discarded to ensure the robustness of the image block. Finally, the image blocks from the same minutia are classified into the same category, which is used as the category label of the training sample.

Rotating all image blocks by four smaller angles, such as $-3°$, $3°$, $-6°$ and $6°$. This not only ensures the diversity of the samples, but also improves the generalization ability of the model and prevents the model from overfitting.

2.3 Convolutional Neural Network Based on Residual Block

The convolutional neural network built in this paper is composed of a series of residual blocks in series to extract the high-order features of the image. The basic residual block is shown in Fig. 3 (left). Each convolutional layer is followed by a Batch Normalization layer which is not shown in the figure. The depth of the feature template may change after each pooling layer. A 1×1 convolutional layer is added when the depth changes in order to keep the input and output depths of the residual block consistent. The improved structure is shown in Fig. 3 (right).

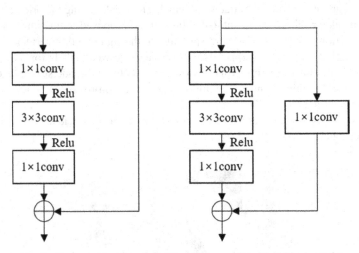

Fig. 3. Basic residual block (*left*) and improved residual block (*right*)

Since the number of parameters of the model is not large, and the method of expanding the sample has been able to solve the problem of model overfitting when making samples, dropout is not used in the training process. The overall network structure is shown in Fig. 4. The input image size is 114×114. After a 3×3 convolutional layer, 4 pooling layers and 13 residual blocks operation, 256 7×7 feature maps are obtained. And then get a 1024-dimensional vector output after going through the fully connected layer.

The network uses Triplet Loss [7] for training. The main feature of the Triplet Loss method is that: the sample is input in the form of a triplet during the training process. Each triplet is constructed as follows: randomly select a sample from the training sample, which is called the reference sample I_i^a, and then randomly select a positive sample I_i^p that comes from the same label as I_i^a. And the negative sample that belongs to a different category from I_i^a is called I_i^n. The three samples form a triplet $\left(I_i^a, I_i^p, I_i^n\right)$. During training, 3 features (x_i^a, x_i^p, x_i^n) are obtained after each triple is input into the network, and the entire network parameters are adjusted by solving the following loss function and using the gradient descent method:

$$Loss = argmin \sum_i \left(\left\| x_i^a - x_i^p \right\|_2^2 - \left\| x_i^a - x_i^n \right\|_2^2 + threshold \right)_+. \tag{1}$$

$(x)_+$ means $max(x, 0)$, $\left\| x_i^a - x_i^p \right\|_2^2$ represents the Euclidean distance between I_i^a and I_i^p, $\left\| x_i^a - x_i^n \right\|_2^2$ represents the Euclidean distance between I_i^a and I_i^n, the *threshold* is set to 1 in this network. The purpose of network training is to shorten the distance between I_i^a and I_i^p, while expanding the distance between I_i^a and I_i^n, that is to meet:

$$\left\| x_i^a - x_i^p \right\|_2^2 + threshold < \left\| x_i^a - x_i^n \right\|_2^2. \tag{2}$$

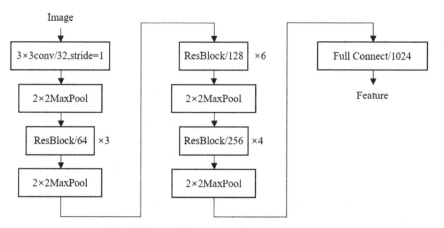

Fig. 4. Convolutional neural network structure

3   Experiment

3.1   Dataset

We have built a signatured fingermark database to verify the recognition performance of the proposed FR-DRN algorithm, since there is no public database of signatured fingermark.

The signatured fingermark database is divided into two parts: training set and test set. The training set is collected by 87 people. Everyone collects 6 fingers and 6 images of each finger, totaling 3132 fingermark images. The test set is collected by 30 people. Everyone collects 6 fingers and 5 images of each finger, totaling 900 fingermark images. Scanning the collected images and cutting them to obtain single finger image with a resolution of 500 dpi.

3.2 Experiment Evaluation Metrics

During the test experiment, each fingerprint image is compared with all other images in the test set. Then we calculate the scores and rank them from highest to lowest. Finally, statistical results are used to measure the performance of this algorithm. The statistical results to measure the performance of the algorithm use the internationally accepted fingerprint matching algorithm evaluation index. We use the following indicators:

- False Acceptance Rate (FAR). The probability that two fingerprint images from different fingers are incorrectly judged to be from the same finger.
- False Rejection Rate (FRR). The probability that two fingerprint images from the same finger are incorrectly judged to be from different fingers.
- Equal Error Rate (EER). When the false acceptance rate and the false rejection rate are the same, EER is equal to FAR and FRR.
- FAR (0.0001). When FAR is 0.0001, its value is equal to FRR.
- Match Rate (MR). MR1 represents the accuracy of Top1.

3.3 Experiment Results and Analysis

There is no research work on recognition algorithm for signatured fingermark at present. In order to verify the effectiveness of the deep learning recognition algorithm proposed in this paper on the signatured fingerprint database, we use the traditional fingerprint recognition algorithm to conduct a comparative experiment. A fingerprint image recognition algorithm based on minutiae [8] developed by the project team in the early stage won the first prize in the fingerprint recognition competition of the 2nd China Biometric Recognition Contest in 2014. This shows that the algorithm has good performance for fingerprints with higher image quality and has a certain recognition value.

The following comparative experiments were carried out on the signatured fingermark database:

- Algorithm 1: It uses traditional methods to extract fingermark minutiae, and then uses fingerprint image recognition algorithm based on minutiae for recognition.
- Algorithm 2: It uses FingerNet to extract fingermark minutiae, and then uses fingerprint image recognition algorithm based on minutiae for recognition.
- Algorithm 3 (FR-DRN): It uses FingerNet to extract fingermark minutiae, and then uses the deep learning algorithm proposed in this paper for recognition.

The experimental results of the above three algorithms on the signatured fingermark database are shown in Table 1, and the receiver operating characteristic curve (ROC) is shown in Fig. 5.

The experimental results show that:

1. It can be seen from Table 1 that Algorithm 1 is inferior to Algorithm 2. It proves that for signatured fingermark, extracting minutiae based on FingerNet has obvious advantages, which reflects the importance of introducing FingerNet.

Table 1. Experimental results of three algorithms on the signatured fingermark database

Algorithm	EER	FAR (0.0001)	MR1
Algorithm 1	0.2263	0.4398	62.03
Algorithm 2	0.1693	0.3260	73.67
Algorithm 3 (FR-DRN)	0.0779	0.3746	79.19

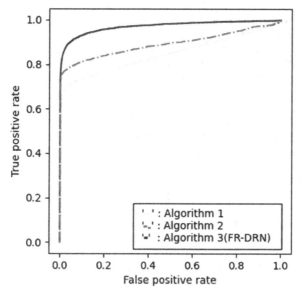

Fig. 5. ROC curve of signatured fingermark database

2. It can be seen from Table 1 that Algorithm 2 is inferior to Algorithm 3. It is proved that the deep learning recognition method proposed in this paper has better performance than the traditional fingerprint recognition method for the signatured fingermark.

In summary, combining FingerNet and the recognition method in this paper can improve the accuracy of signatured fingermark recognition to a certain extent.

4 Conclusion

There are shortcomings of low accuracy and poor robustness in recognize signatured fingermark by using traditional methods. This paper introduces FR-DRN that combines FingerNet, and convolutional neural network based on residual block which improves the recognition accuracy of signatured fingermark to a certain extent. In order to further improve the recognition accuracy, this paper believes that the next step can be considered to remove the signature from the image before recognizing.

Acknowledgement. This work was supported by the Public welfare project of Zhejiang Science and Technology Department under Grant LGF18F030008.

References

1. Paulino, A.A., Jain, A.K., Feng, J.: Latent fingerprint matching: fusion of manually marked and derived minutiae. In: 2010 23rd SIBGRAPI Conference on Graphics, Patterns and Images, pp. 63–70 (2010). https://doi.org/10.1109/SIBGRAPI.2010.17
2. Wang, Y.-N., Wu, Z.-D., Zhang, J.-W.: Low-quality-fingerprint identification based on convolutional neural network (Chinese). Commun. Technol. **50**(06), 1276–1280 (2017)
3. Patil, A.R., Rahulkar, D., Modi, C.N.: Designing an efficient fingerprint recognition system for infants and toddlers. In: 2019 10th International Conference on Computing, Communication and Networking Technologies (ICCCNT), pp. 1–7 (2019). https://doi.org/10.1109/ICCCNT 45670.2019.8944342
4. Tang, Y., Gao, F., Feng, J., Liu, Y.: FingerNet: an unified deep network for fingerprint minutiae extraction. In: 2017 IEEE International Joint Conference on Biometrics (IJCB), pp. 108–116 (2017). https://doi.org/10.1109/BTAS.2017.8272688
5. He, K., Zhang, X., Ren, S., Sun, J.: Deep residual learning for image recognition. In: 2016 IEEE Conference on Computer Vision and Pattern Recognition (CVPR), pp. 770–778 (2016). https://doi.org/10.1109/CVPR.2016.90
6. Ratha, N.K., Chen, S., Jain, A.K.: Adaptive flow orientation-based feature extraction in fingerprint images. Pattern Recogn. **28**(11), 1657–1672 (1995)
7. Schroff, F., Kalenichenko, D., Philbin, J.: FaceNet: a unified embedding for face recognition and clustering. In: 2015 IEEE Conference on Computer Vision and Pattern Recognition (CVPR), pp. 815–823 (2015). https://doi.org/10.1109/CVPR.2015.7298682
8. Zhang, Y., Fang, S., Zhou, B., Huang, C., Li, Y.: Fingerprint match based on key minutiae and optimal statistical registration. In: Sun, Z., Shan, S., Sang, H., Zhou, J., Wang, Y., Yuan, W. (eds.) CCBR 2014. LNCS, vol. 8833, pp. 208–215. Springer, Cham (2014). https://doi.org/10. 1007/978-3-319-12484-1_23

Dorsal Hand Vein Recognition Based on Transfer Learning with Fusion of LBP Feature

Gaojie Gu[1], Peirui Bai[1(✉)], Hui Li[1], Qingyi Liu[1], Chao Han[1], Xiaolin Min[1], and Yande Ren[2]

[1] College of Electronic Information Engineering, Shandong University of Science and Technology, Qingdao 266590, China
[2] Department of Radiology, Affiliated Hospital of Qingdao University, Qingdao 265000, Shandong, China

Abstract. Traditionally, training an end-to-end convolutional neural network (CNN) requires sufficient samples and time cost in dorsal hand vein recognition. In addition, the local features are easy to be lost. Aiming to overcome these shortcomings, a method that fuses features of local binary patterns (LBP) into the ResNet-50 framework using transfer learning is proposed in this paper. Firstly, the texture features encoded by the LBP operator and the pre-processed images are fused. Then, the fused features are input into the ResNet-50 network in a way of transfer learning. Two kinds of vein recognition experiments are carried out to validate the performance of the proposed method, i.e. personal recognition and gender recognition. Dorsal hand vein dataset includes 1928 images collected from left and right hand of 97 volunteers. The experimental results demonstrated that the proposed method achieved superior performance than the classical feature training.

Keywords: Dorsal hand vein recognition · Gender recognition · Transfer learning · Local binary pattern · ResNet-50 network

1 Introduction

Recently, dorsal hand vein recognition become an important and favorite branch in the field of biometric recognition [1]. The dorsal hand vein recognition has several attracting advantages compared to the traditional biometric recognition. First, the vein pattern is unique as the vein network of each person, even the right and left hand of the same person, is different. Second, the vein image is collected from the location under the skin of a living subject that is not easy to be forged. Third, the collection of vein image is contactless and non-invasive.

The critical step of the dorsal hand vein recognition is how to extract and express the features effectively. One popular manner is to take advantage of the shape descriptor to disclose the differences between different vein patterns. For example, the location and

© Springer Nature Switzerland AG 2021
J. Feng et al. (Eds.): CCBR 2021, LNCS 12878, pp. 221–230, 2021.
https://doi.org/10.1007/978-3-030-86608-2_25

angle of short straight vectors [2], endpoints and crossing points [3], local and global geometric structure extractor [4] etc. However, the manual feature descriptors are subjective measurements in essence. They usually depend heavily on the controlling parameters selection and require suitable pre-processing methods. Recently, deep features collected by the deep learning techniques show promising prospect in dorsal hand vein recognition [5, 6]. The most common deep learning network is the convolutional neural network (CNN), which can be employed in a pre-trained style or a transfer learning style [7, 8]. More recently, there emerged a trend that combing both hand-drafted features and deep features to enhance the accuracy and robustness of biometric recognition [9, 10]. Motivated by this strategy, we proposes a method to fuse LBP features into the ResNet-50 framework in a transfer learning style. The main work and contributions are as follows:

(1) The texture features encoded by LBP are input into the ResNet-50 network, and transfer learning is adopted to improve the recognition rate and robustness.
(2) Two kinds of application scenarios are designed to confirm the performance of the proposed method, i.e. the personal recognition and the gender recognition.
(3) A customized dataset including 1928 dorsal hand vein images is established. Different groups are designed in terms of the recognition task, such as images of gender, images of left and right hand etc.

This paper is organized as follows. The second section introduces briefly the background of the proposed method that includes the principles of the LBP operator and the ResNet network. The third section details the proposed method. The experiments and discussions are presented in the fourth section. Finally, conclusion remarks are drawn in the last section.

2 Background

2.1 Local Binary Patterns

The local binary pattern is an operator that describes the texture feature of an image [11]. It has several desirable characteristics such as high computational efficiency, strong discriminated ability and simple expression. Assume a 3×3 LBP operator, the gray values of the 8 adjacent pixels will be determined in terms of the comparison results with that of the central pixel. That is, taking the gray value of the central pixel as a threshold, the gray value of the adjacent pixels will be set as 1 if the value is greater than the threshold value. Otherwise, the value is set as 0. A demonstration of LBP operation is illustrated in Fig. 1. The operation can be formulated as follows:

$$\text{LBP}(x_c, y_c) = \sum_{p=0}^{7} 2^p \cdot S(i_p - i_c) \tag{1}$$

where (x_c, y_c) denotes the coordinate of the center pixel. i_c and i_p denotes the gray value of the center pixel and the neighboring pixel respectively. S denotes the sign function which can be expressed as follows:

$$S(x) = \begin{cases} 1 & x \geq 0 \\ 0 & x < 0 \end{cases} \tag{2}$$

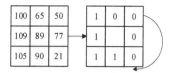

Fig. 1. A demonstration of LBP operation

2.2 ResNet Network Using Transfer Learning

Transfer learning is a learning strategy which aims at improving the performance of target learners on target domains by transferring the knowledge contained in different but related source domains [12]. Owning to its advantages such as less requirement of sufficient data and training time, etc., transfer learning has been applied in medical image classification [13–15]. The transfer learning can be implemented in various deep learning models, e.g. convolutional neural network [16, 17], recurrent neural network [18]. Usually, fine-tuning [19–21] can solve common classification problem in transfer learning by transferring the weight from a pre-trained network to a new network. A common fine-tuning operation is to replace the last fully connected layer of the pre-trained CNN with a new fully connected layer. The number of nodes in new fully connected layer depends on the number of classes in the dataset. Then a new pattern classifier is trained.

The ResNet is a deep learning network which addresses the network degradation by introducing a deep residual learning framework [22]. It uses the residual unit structure as shown in Fig. 2. Assuming the input is x and the learned feature is H(x), the residual unit of the learned feature can be expressed as $F(x) = H(x) - x$. The formulation of $F(x) + x$ can be realized by feed forward neural networks with shortcut connections. The residual unit structure can avoid the feature loss of the convolutional layer during information transmission. It has been demonstrated that the ResNet network can extract more features that are suitable for applying in medical image classification [23, 24].

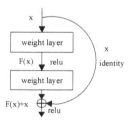

Fig. 2. Basic residual block

In order to reduce the number of parameters, a three-layer residual unit called a bottleneck is introduced in the ResNet-50 architecture as shown in Fig. 3. The first 1×1 filter and the second 3×3 filter are designed to reduce the dimension. The third 1×1 filter is designed to increase the dimension. In this paper, the pre-trained ResNet-50 network is transferred to recognize dorsal hand vein patterns adopting fine-tuning strategy.

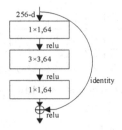

Fig. 3. A bottleneck block in ResNet-50

3   The Proposed Method

The block diagram of the proposed dorsal hand vein recognition method is illustrated in Fig. 4. There are five steps in the flow chart.

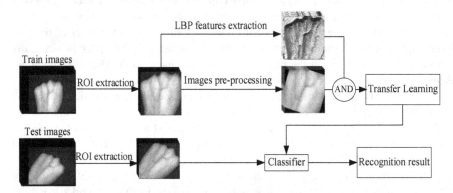

Fig. 4. Block diagram of the proposed dorsal hand vein recognition method

First, the ROI images of the dorsal hand are obtained by cropping the bounding box [25]. Background noise and irrelevant information are removed by this operation. Second, LBP features of ROI are extracted which are rotation invariant and gray-scale invariant [11]. LBP features represent mainly the local features and the edge features as well as present the direction of the dorsal hand vein patterns. This processing operation reduces the interference of uncertainty such as imbalanced illumination. Third, a pre-processing of dorsal hand vein is carried out to determine the center point of ROI images. By taking this center point, the size of the images is cropped to 224 × 224. Then, image enhancement and data enhancement are implemented by changing brightness and rotating randomly.

Subsequently, the LBP features and the original ROI images are input into the ResNet-50 network, which has been trained on the ImageNet dataset. The VeinNet is obtained by ResNet-50 transfer learning as shown in Fig. 5, the parameters of the ResNet-50 network are initialized first, then the parameters are updated by training and further adapted to the vein dataset. The VeinNet consists of seven parts, including the input layer, five convolution stages and the output layer. Each convolution block contains a bottleneck in stage 2 to 5 described in Fig. 5. Five convolution filters can extract lots of features. The full connection layer of the ResNet-50 is replaced by a linear layer, and a Softmax classification layer is acted as an output layer.

Finally, the Softmax classifier [26] is used for classifying the vein patterns and obtaining the recognition results. In statistics, the Softmax classifier is derived from the classification of logistic regression by judging the input data and output results. In Softmax, the loss function mainly adopts the form of cross-entropy loss. The purpose of the loss function is to measure the error between the ground-truth and the predicted results.

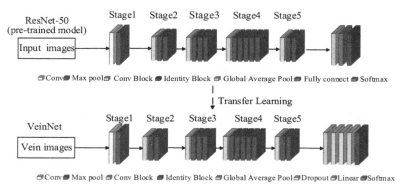

Fig. 5. The proposed VeinNet obtained by transfer learning of ResNet-50

4   Experiments and Discussion

Two kinds of vein recognition are carried out to validate the performance of the proposed method, i.e. personal recognition and gender recognition. The images of both right and left hand are collected from 97 different subjects (55 males and 42 females) using a commercial infrared device DF-300. The infrared wavelength is 850 nm. Figure 6 demonstrates six example dorsal hand vein images collected from different views. The direction of collection includes random rotation to the right ($-30°$, $30°$) (Fig. 6(a)), forward (Fig. 6(b)), and random rotation to the left ($-30°$, $30°$) (Fig. 6(c)). In each direction, 5 images are captured and stored.

ROI extraction is implemented using MATLAB R2016a. Other experiments are implemented using Python. Experimental environment is i5-9300H CPU and GeForce GTX 1650 GPU and Pytorch framework. The optimizer adopts the SGD method. The initial learning rate is set to 0.001. The default values of training parameters such as batch size, momentum, and epoch are set as 16, 0.9, 50 respectively.

4.1   Personal and Gender Recognition Based on the Original Database

In personal recognition experiments, the training set contains 970 images (5 forward images of each subject). The validation set contains 388 images (randomly selected 2

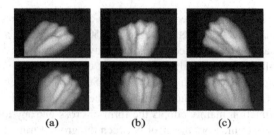

(a)   (b)   (c)

Fig. 6. Six example near infrared images of dorsal hand vein

images for each subject). The test set includes 557 images. The experimental results are shown in Table 1. It can be seen that the recognition rate by fusing the LBP features is 65.71%, which is 3.05% higher than that of using the original ROI images. It confirms the efficiency to enhance the recognition rate by presenting more useful information about the dorsal hand vein. It also validates the possibility of transferring the knowledge of the ImageNet into the dorsal hand vein recognition. The recognition rate of LBP images is greatly affected by noise, so the experiment of using single LBP image is not considered in the experiment.

Table 1. Personal and gender recognition rates of different input images based on the original database

Input images	Personal recognition rate	Gender recognition rate
LBP	2.8%	19.8%
ROI	62.66%	94.56%
ROI + LBP	65.71%	94.74%

In gender recognition experiments, the labels are classified into four categories i.e. male left dorsal hand vein, male right dorsal hand vein, female left dorsal hand vein, and female right dorsal hand vein. The training set and the validation set contains 970 and 388 images respectively. 570 test images are randomly selected from the remaining images. The image pre-processing is same as the personal recognition. The experimental results are shown in Table 1. It can be seen that the recognition rate of gender can achieve 94.56% and 94.74% using ROI images and ROI + LBP images respectively, which are apparently higher than that of personal recognition. Obviously, this is because the number of personal recognition categories is much higher than gender recognition. However, the gender recognition rate using fused features is slightly higher than that of using the original ROI images. It implies that the insufficient samples and original image quality limit the performance for gender recognition.

4.2   Personal and Gender Recognition Based on the Image Enhancement and Data Augmentation

In order to improve the recognition performance, this section further investigates the schemes from two points of view, i.e. image enhancement and data augmentation. As shown in Fig. 7, the first column (Fig. 7(a)) illustrates two ROI images cropped by center cropping processing. Figure 7(b) shows the images after image enhancement processing. Figure 7(c) shows the images obtained by random rotation within (−30°, 30°), which are employed to augment the dataset. Figure 7(d) shows the images obtained by the both processing.

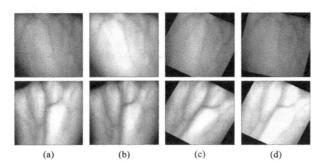

(a)   (b)   (c)   (d)

Fig. 7. Demonstration of image enhancement and data augmentation of two dorsal hand vein images

The recognition results corresponding to the above experiments based on the image enhancement and data augmentation are shown in Table 2. In personal recognition experiments, the first experiment is designed through increasing the ratio of brightness and contrast of images by 30%. The experimental results listed in the first row and the previous two columns are 64.99% and 65.88% respectively, which are 2.33% and 0.17% higher than the corresponding results in Table 1. In the second row, the recognition rates of data augmentation listed in the previous two columns are 87.97% and 90.31% respectively, which are 25.31% and 24.6% higher than the corresponding results in Table 1. It reflects that the number of images have significant influence to the recognition rate than that of image enhancement, although image enhancement is also benefit to improve the recognition rate. If both image enhancement and data augmentation are adopted, the recognition rates can be further improved to 90.31% and 92.28% respectively. The experimental results confirm that both image enhancement and data augmentation are effective means to improve the recognition performance of personal recognition.

In gender recognition experiments, similar experimental schemes are conducted. The recognition rates listed in the third and fourth columns in Table 2 are 92.10% and 94.82%, 92.36% and 95.26%, 94.84% and 97.19% respectively, which corresponding to three pre-processing schemes i.e. image enhancement, data augmentation, and combination of them. It is interesting to observe that the improvement effect is very limited for the gender recognition by adopting the three pre-processing schemes and ROI images. Slight improvements are achieved by adopting the three pre-processing schemes and ROI +

LBP images, that can be observed from the results listed in the fourth column in Table 2. It may be due to the very limited target categories in gender recognition. Therefore, it is still an attractive issue to find factors that are effective to enhance the recognition rate of gender recognition.

For personal and gender recognition, Table 3 shows the recognition accuracy of transfer learning in Alex-Net, VGG16, Resnet-50 and VeinNet models. The parameter settings of the model is the same as that of VeinNet. It is observed that the proposed system achieves the highest results in transfer learning. The proposed approaches give better results compared to other methods.

Table 2. Personal and gender recognition rates of different input images based on image enhancement and data augmentation

Scheme	Personal recognition rate		Gender recognition rate	
	ROI	ROI + LBP	ROI	ROI + LBP
Image enhancement	64.99%	65.88%	92.10%	94.82%
Data augmentation	87.97%	90.31%	92.36%	95.26%
Image enhancement + data augmentation	90.31%	92.28%	94.84%	97.19%

Table 3. The recognition accuracy of transfer learning in different methods

Methods/Tasks	Personal recognition rate	Gender recognition rate
AlexNet	46.84%	76.84%
VGG16	31.23%	81.40%
ResNet-50	90.31%	94.84%
VeinNet	92.28%	97.19%

5 Conclusion

A novel dorsal hand vein recognition method is proposed by using transfer learning on ResNet-50 network. The recognition performance improves significantly by fusing the LBP feature with the traditional ROI feature. Two kinds of recognition experiments are conducted to validate the performance of the proposed method by applying it to personal recognition and gender recognition respectively. Otherwise, the schemes of performance enhancement are investigated simultaneously. The experimental results demonstrate that an obvious enhancement in recognition rate when introducing the dorsal hand vein texture feature and adopting image enhancement and data augmentation to personal recognition. However, these factors show limited capability to enhance the performance of gender recognition. The future study mainly focus on two related topics based on the results and analysis in this paper. First, how to enhance the efficiency of knowledge transferring in gender recognition, modifying the architecture of deep learning network or optimal fusing deep and hand-crafted features? Second, what is the effective means to integrate the gender recognition into the framework of the personal recognition, and how to enhance the recognition performance through this way?

Acknowledgement. This work was supported in part by the National Natural Science Foundation of China under Grant 61471225.

References

1. Uhl, A., Busch, C., Marcel, S.: Handbook of Vascular Biometrics. Springer, Cham (2020). https://doi.org/10.1007/978-3-030-27731-4
2. Kumar, A.: Personal authentication using hand vein triangulation and knuckle shape. IEEE Trans. Image Process. **38**(9), 2127–2136 (2009)
3. Hu, Y.P., Wang, Z.Y.: Hand vein recognition based on the connection lines of reference point and feature point. J. Infrared Phys. Technol. **62**(2), 110–114 (2014)
4. Huang, D., Zhu, X.R.: Dorsal hand vein recognition via hierarchical combination of texture and shape clues. J. Neurocomput. **214**, 815 (2016)
5. Weng, L., Li, X., Wang, W.: Finger vein recognition based on deep convolutional neural networks. In: CISP-BMEI (2020)
6. Wan, H., Lei, C.: Dorsal hand vein recognition based on convolutional neural networks. In: BIBM (2017)
7. Al-Johania, N.A., Elrefaei, L.: Dorsal hand vein recognition by convolutional neural networks: feature learning and transfer learning approaches. J. Int. J. Intell. Eng. Syst. **12**(3), 171–178 (2019)
8. Pan, Z., Wang, J.: Hand-dorsa vein recognition based on selective deep convolutional feature. J. IEICE Trans. Inf. Syst. **E103**D(6), 1423–1426 (2020)
9. Kuang, H.L., Zhong, Z.H., Liu, X.H.: Palm vein recognition using convolution neural network based on feature fusion with HOG feature. In: ICSGEA (2020)
10. Wang, Y.D., Huang, S.Y.: Identification of heterogeneous hand vein based on LBP and multi-level structure. Comput. Meas. Control **03**, 47 (2017)
11. Ojala, T.: A comparative study of texture measures with classification based on feature distributions. Pattern Recogn. **29**, 51 (1996)
12. Zhuang, F.Z., Qi, Z.Y.: A comprehensive survey on transfer learning. In: Proceedings of the IEEE (2021)
13. Liang, H., Fu, W.L.: A survey of recent advances in transfer learning. In: ICCT (2019)
14. Niu, S.T., Liu, Y.X., Wang, J.: A decade survey of transfer learning (2010–2020). IEEE Trans. Artif. Intell. **1**, 151 (2020)
15. Xu, J.H., Dong, X.Y.: A survey of transfer learning in breast cancer image classification. In: IICSPI (2020)
16. Ribani, R., Marengoni, M.: A survey of transfer learning for convolutional neural networks. In: SIBGRAPI-T (2019)
17. Wang, J., Wang, G., Zhou, M.: Bimodal vein data mining via cross-selected-domain knowledge transfer. IEEE Trans. Inf. Forensics Secur. **13**, 733 (2017)
18. Tang, Z.Y., Wang, D., Zhang, Z.Y.: Recurrent neural network training with dark knowledge transfer. In: ICASSP (2016)

19. Tajbakhsh, N.: Convolutional neural networks for medical image analysis: full training or fine tuning? IEEE Trans. Med. Imag. **35**(5), 76 (2016)
20. Zhou, Z.W.: Fine-tuning convolutional neural networks for biomedical image analysis: actively and incrementally. In: Proceedings IEEE Computer Society Conference on Computer Vision and Pattern Recognition (2017)
21. Kamble, R.M.: Automated diabetic macular edema (DME) analysis using fine tuning with Inception-Resnet-v2 on OCT images. In: IECBES (2018)
22. He, K.M., Zhang, X.Y., Ren, S.Q.: Deep residual learning for image recognition. In: CVPR (2016)
23. Youssef, T.A., Aissam, B., Khalid, D.: Classification of chest pneumonia from x-ray images using new architecture based on ResNet. In: ICECOCS (2020)
24. Demir, A., Yilmaz, F., Kose, O.: Early detection of skin cancer using deep learning architectures: Resnet-101 and Inception-v3. In: TIPTEKNO (2019)
25. Singh, A., Goyal, H.: Human identification based on hand dorsal vein pattern using BRISK and SURF algorithm. In: IJEAT (2020)
26. Xu, J., Yin, J.: Kernel least absolute shrinkage and selection operator regression classifier for pattern classification. Comput. Vis. **7**, 55 (2013)

An Improved Finger Vein Recognition Model with a Residual Attention Mechanism

Weiye Liu, Huimin Lu$^{(\boxtimes)}$, Yupeng Li, Yifan Wang, and Yuanyuan Dang

School of Computer Science and Engineering, ChangChun University of Technology,
Changchun 130102, Jilin, China
{2201903014,2202003028,2202003035}@stu.ccut.edu.cn, {luhuimin,
dangyuanyuan}@ccut.edu.cn

Abstract. Deep learning-based Biometric authentication has become one of the most popular research subjects in the field of Computer Vision. In this paper, we propose a novel model architecture for finger vein recognition based on an improved residual attention network. First, we squeeze the size of the original network to adapt to the training data scale. Then, to prevent excessively repeated operations of linear extraction, we introduce the Inception unit to replace some residual units in the original model. The multi-branch structure can learn vein features from different aspects. Besides that, with the attention block, primary vein patterns can be extracted and the bottom-up, top-down structure activates feature maps with learned attention weights. The experimental results show that our model acquires 98.58% and 97.54% accuracy on two public datasets, respectively. Compared with state-of-the-art models, the proposed model has fewer parameters and better performance.

Keywords: Finger vein recognition · Biometrics · Deep learning · Attention mechanism · Inception module

1 Introduction

Finger vein recognition, as the 2nd-generation of Biometric identification technology, has drawn worldwide attention. Compared with other commonly-used bio-features such as fingerprint, face, and palmprint, finger vein has the unique characteristics of living authentication, internal features, and high security. The first paper about finger vein recognition was proposed in 2000, by Kono et al. [1]. In the next decades, more studies about finger vein recognition have appeared. In 2004, Miura et al. [2] proposed the Repeated Line Tracking (RLT) method and extracted completed finger vein patterns. In 2007, Miura et al. [3], again, proposed the Maximum Curvature (MC) method for vein extraction. Nowadays, the RLT and MC have become the two most typical methods of finger vein extraction.

Earlier, in this field, traditional machine learning based recognition methods were the mainstream. These methods generally contain the following steps: image preprocessing, feature extraction, feature matching, and recognition. Image preprocessing needs to

© Springer Nature Switzerland AG 2021
J. Feng et al. (Eds.): CCBR 2021, LNCS 12878, pp. 231–239, 2021.
https://doi.org/10.1007/978-3-030-86608-2_26

locate the finger Region of Interest (ROI) that contains abundant and available vein patterns. The ROI can not only eliminate redundant information such as background noises but also reduce the image sizes to speed the subsequent processing. Also, feature extraction is another key step. How to devise novel extraction algorithms to obtain integral and available vein features that people are difficult to distinguish, has become crucial.

In recent years, with the wave of deep learning developments, CNN-based methods have been the hotspot in finger vein recognition. Benefitting from the self-learning ability of neural network, vein features can be extracted and identified with fewer manual interventions. However, several problems still need to be solved. For instance, how to learn features effectively with limited images and avoid overfitting problems, it is worthy of notice.

To solve the aforementioned issues, we introduce an improved finger vein recognition model based on a residual attention network [4]. The proposed model has fewer trainable parameters and a smaller size. It shortens the period of model recognition and does not impact the model performance. Moreover, the newly introduced Inception unit [5] could learn features from aspects and raise the recognition accuracy further.

2 Related Works

In general, different conventional finger vein recognition methods usually generate varied results. With different quality images that are affected by different elements, such as uneven illuminations, blurred veins, complex backgrounds, and rotations, the traditional methods need to be designed accordingly. On the contrary, deep learning-based methods learn features and global information of images effortlessly with a large amount of training data. Compared with conventional methods, end-to-end learning methods are more robust against different quality images.

Since 2016, CNN-based methods have grown remarkably. Ahmad Radzi et al. [6] used a four-layer CNN architecture to recognize a 50-class dataset. It only includes convolutional layers, pooling layers, and dense layers. Das et al. [7] proposed a CNN model for finger vein recognition based on four public databases. The correct identification rates on all databases were beyond 95%. Except for the above self-designed pure CNN models, some mature models can be modified and transferred to finger vein recognition. Hong et al. [8] performed a pre-trained VGG-16 model. After fine-tuning, a true-false image pair was inputted into the model. Then the model outputs binary classification results. The pre-trained models rely on excellent learning capabilities, with different tasks, simply adjusting structures can achieve feature learning. Kyoung et al. [9] used a two-branch DenseNet-161 architecture to recognize composite vein images. They first adopted ROI extraction and segmentation to acquire vein texture and vein shape images, respectively. Then they constituted these two types of images and delivered them to the model. The model finally outputted two different feature maps. A score-level fusion method was applied to connect the maps and the softmax layer calculated the matching score.

With years of developments, attention mechanism [10] has stepped from the field of NLP (Natural Language Processing) into CV (Computer Vision) [11–14]. In different tasks (Object Detection [11], Image Segmentation [12], Image Classification [13, 14], etc.), the attention mechanism exhibits excellent performance. In 2017, Wang et al. [4] proposed a residual attention network. In this model, the attention module was pluggable. Through stacking it repeatedly, the depth of the network can be increased. Moreover, the two-branch architecture guided the learning of features in each position. The attention residual learning method ensured features deliver to deeper layers without gradients vanishing during backpropagation. Some large-scale datasets such as ImageNet and Cifar-100, have a large amount of samples and features. This deep network can learn these features effectively.

3   Proposed Method

3.1   Model Architecture

The architecture of the proposed network is shown in Fig. 1. The whole structure of the network consists of the input layer, preprocessing layer, Attention Block, postprocessing layer, and the output layer. The preprocessing layer consists of a convolution layer and a maxpooling layer. Before getting into the output layer, the feature maps generated from the Attention Block will enter an Inception unit. Then it follows one maxpooling layer and two convolution layers. When reaching the flatten layer, two-dimensional feature maps are flattened one-dimensional feature vectors. The dense layer receives these vectors and the softmax function maps them into probability distribution of [0, 1]. Finally, the output layer generates N class probabilities of all samples.

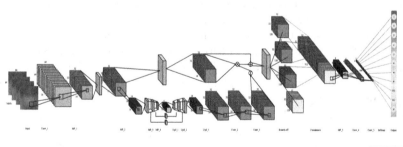

Fig. 1. The architecture of the proposed network

3.2   Residual Attention Block

The body of the model is the Residual Attention Block (RAB). It contains two branches: the Trunk Branch and the Soft Mask Branch. The Trunk Branch consists of two residual units. This branch extracts vein patterns from input feature maps. The Soft Mask Branch adopts the hourglass network [15], the bottom-up structure learns global vein information and then squeezes the feature maps into the smallest sizes (4 × 4 pixels in our model). Another top-down structure expands the down-sampling features, and a sigmoid layer normalizes them into the range of [0, 1].

3.3 Attention Residual Learning

To maintain the richness of vein patterns and make sure that the model could learn vein features adequately, we still use the attention residual learning:

$$H(x) = (T(x)*M(x)) + T(x) = (1 + M(x))*T(x). \tag{1}$$

$T(x)$ denotes the features generated from the Trunk Branch, it includes the main vein patterns. $M(x)$ denotes the features generated from the Soft Mask Branch. It ranges from 0 to 1 after a sigmoid layer. These normalized features of $M(x)$ can be seen as weights. The weight at each position can grant the attention importance to the corresponding feature of $M(x)$. When $M(x)$ closes to 0, the RAB learned vein features $H(x) = T(x)$, which means the vein patterns will not lose and the model can learn.

4 Experiments

4.1 Datasets

In our experiments, we use two publicly available finger vein datasets: the FV-USM [16] and the MMCBNU_6000 (MMCBNU for short) [17]. The FV-USM dataset was funded by Universiti Sains Malaysia. It contains 123 subjects. For each subject, 4 fingers were provided. Each finger was captured 6 times for one session. Thus, from two sessions, a total of 5904 (123 × 4 × 6 × 2) finger vein images were obtained. Each image is stored in "JPG" format, and has a size of 640 × 480 pixels. Some samples are shown in Fig. 2(a). The MMCBNU dataset was built by Chonbuk National University, South Korea. It includes 100 participants and each of them provides 6 fingers. Each finger was collected 10 times and it has 6000 (100 × 6 × 10) finger vein images ("BMP", 480 × 640 pixels). Some samples of MMCBNU are shown in Fig. 2(b).

These two datasets all provide finger vein ROI images. To eliminate the impacts of background noises, uneven illuminations, and finger rotations, we employ the ROI images for recognition with our model. More details of the used datasets are described in Table 1.

4.2 Comparison Experiments

To prove the performance of the proposed model, we implement ample experiments and compare it with several state-of-the-art models and traditional methods. LeNet-5, the first typical CNN model, was proposed by Lecun et al. [18] in 1998. The ResNet-50 was proposed by He et al. [19]. It has 49 convolution layers, 2 pooling layers, and an *fc* layer. With the proposed residual learning, model depth can extend tremendously. Different from the CNN architecture, the Capsule Network [20] introduces a novel layer named capsule. This layer extracts object features and combines more available information

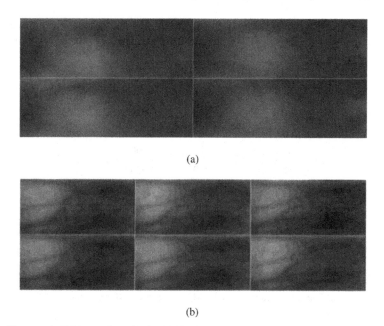

(a)

(b)

Fig. 2. Finger vein ROI samples of a single finger in datasets of (a) FV-USM and (b) MMCBNU

Table 1. Details description of used two public finger vein datasets

Dataset	Subject	Session	Fingers per subject	Images per finger	Total images	Original size
FV-USM	123	2	4	6	5904	640 × 480
MMCBNU	100	1	6	10	6000	480 × 640

such as relative positions and rotations. The CNN model in [7] is designed simply, but the parameter amount in each convolution layer is still huge. The Vision Transformer (ViT) model was proposed in 2020, by Dosovitskiy et al. [21]. This is the first attempt to use Transformer for image classification. Except for deep learning models, we also compared the model with some effective traditional methods, LBP [22] and 2DPCA [23]. The experimental results are shown in Table 2.

The results indicate that with a small size and fewer parameters, our model reaches the best accuracy, all beyond 97% on two datasets. For FV-USM, it captured images from two sessions. Thus, the vein images of a single finger contain more available features and the model can extract vein patterns precisely. Table 3 shows the comparison of the model performance on FV-USM with different sessions. The recognition results verify our hypothesis as well. In the MMCBNU dataset, each finger has 10 images, but they were captured from one session. Between the images, more redundant information exists that the model could not learn effectively.

Table 2. Accuracy of different methods on two public datasets. For the FV-USM dataset, 8 samples for training and 4 for testing. For the MMCBNU dataset, 6 for training and 4 for testing.

Method	Accuracy	
	FV-USM	MMCBNU
LBP	0.8469	0.8213
2DPCA	0.9499	-
LeNet-5	-	0.9000
ResNet-50	0.9852	0.9567
CapsNet	-	0.9580
CNN [7]	0.9753	-
ViT	0.9522	0.9513
Proposed model	**0.9858**	**0.9754**

Table 3. Accuracy on FV-USM dataset with different sessions

Session	Training	Test	Accuracy
Sess. 1	4	2	0.9644
Sess. 2	4	2	0.9817
All	8	4	0.9858

4.3 Performance Analysis

In our model, many residual units were implemented to extract vein features. Each residual unit consists of three subunits, and each subunit involves three layers: a convolution layer, a BN (BatchNormalization) layer, and a ReLU layer. The shortcut connection transmits original vein features to hinder layers, so the model can learn features completely. During model training, with an appropriate batch size setting (we set as 128), the model converges at a fast speed, and the losses are reduced to a minimal value with residual learning. Figure 3 shows the value changes of training accuracy and losses on two datasets.

Another advantage of our model is that the scale is relatively small, it has less trainable parameters. For each epoch, the time consumption and computed resources can decrease, but the model performance is still kept on a high level. For most compact embedded devices, the volumes and hardware resources are limited, so it is hard to afford many deep neural networks with massive parameters and large memories. Figure 4 shows that compared with some state-of-the-art recognition models, the proposed model has relatively few parameters (about 5.85M). Fewer parameters mean less memory footprint and faster recognition speed. For our model, the recognition time of per image is less than 10 ms (5.59 ms per FV-USM image, 7.08 ms per MMCBNU image). Thus, it is a good choice to apply our model to some mobile scenes.

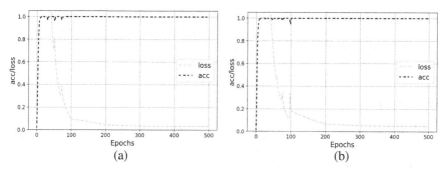

Fig. 3. Value changes of training accuracy and losses on (a) FV-USM and (b) MMCBNU

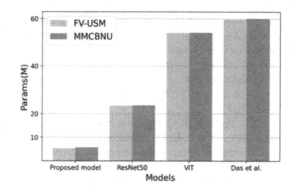

Fig. 4. Comparisons of parameter scales of different models

5 Conclusion

In this paper, we propose an improved finger vein recognition model. To fit the scale of existing public finger vein datasets, we compress the original residual attention network to medium size. Then we discard some layers and introduce the Inception structure to make the model learn features from different scales. To prove the proposed model, some experiments are performed on two public datasets. We select several typical traditional methods and advanced neural networks to compare. Results show that the proposed model possesses good recognition performance with fewer parameters.

In the following studies, we will further improve the model and make it express higher recognition rates with more datasets. Besides, 3D biometric recognition is a popular research field. Such as 3D palmprint and palm vein recognition, has emerged many functional recognition models [24, 25]. Similarly, studies about 3D finger vein recognition [26] have increased gradually in recent years. It is another work we will partake in the future.

Acknowledgments. This research is sponsored by the Key R&D Program of Science and Technology Development Plan of Jilin Province of China (No. 20200401103GX); the Key Program of

Science and Technology Research during the 13th Five-Year Plan Period, the Educational Department of Jilin Province of China (No. JJKH20200680KJ, and No. JJKH20200677KJ); and the National Natural Science Foundation of China (No. 61806024).

References

1. Kono, M.: New method for the identification of individuals by using of vein pattern matching of a finger. In: Proceedings of Fifth Symposium on Pattern Measurement, pp. 9–12 (2000)
2. Miura, N., Nagasaka, A., Miyatake, T.: Feature extraction of finger-vein patterns based on repeated line tracking and its application to personal identification. Mach. Vision. Appl. **15**(4), 194–203 (2004)
3. Miura, N., Nagasaka, A., Miyatake, T.: Extraction of finger-vein patterns using maximum curvature points in image profiles. IEICE Trans. Inf. Syst. **90**(8), 1185–1194 (2007)
4. Wang, F., Jiang, M., Qian, C.: Residual attention network for image classification. In: Proceedings of the IEEE Conference on Computer Vision and Pattern Recognition, pp. 3156–3164 (2017)
5. Szegedy, C., Ioffe, S., Vanhoucke, V., et al.: Inception-v4, inception-resnet and the impact of residual connections on learning. In: Proceedings of the AAAI Conference on Artificial Intelligence, pp. 1–12 (2017)
6. Radzi, S.A., Hani, M.K., Bakhteri, R.: Finger-vein biometric identification using convolutional neural network. Turk. J. Electr. Eng. Comput. Sci. **24**(3), 1863–1878 (2016)
7. Das, R., Piciucco, E., Maiorana, E., et al.: Convolutional neural network for finger-vein based biometric identification. IEEE Trans. Inf. Forensics Secur. **14**(2), 360–373 (2019)
8. Hong, H.G., Lee, M.B., Park, K.R.: Convolutional neural network-based finger-vein recognition using NIR image sensors. Sensors **17**(6), 1–21 (2017)
9. Non, K.J., Choi, J., Hong, J.S., et al.: Finger-vein recognition based on densely connected convolutional network using score-level fusion with shape and texture images. IEEE Access **8**(1), 96748–96766 (2020)
10. Bahdanau, D., Cho, K., Bengio, Y.: Neural machine translation by jointly learning to align and translate. arXiv preprint arXiv:1409.0473 (2014)
11. Cao, J., Chen, Q., Guo, J., et al.: Attention-guided context feature pyramid network for object detection. arXiv preprint arXiv:2005.11475 (2020)
12. Fu, J., Liu, J., Tian, H., et al.: Dual attention network for scene segmentation. In: Proceedings of the IEEE Conference on Computer Vision and Pattern Recognition, pp. 3146–3154 (2019)
13. Woo, S., Park, J., Lee, J.Y., et al.: CBAM: Convolutional block attention module. In: Proceedings of the European Conference on Computer Vision, pp. 3–19 (2018)
14. Hu, J., Shen, L., Sun, G., et al.: Squeeze-and-excitation networks. In: Proceedings of the IEEE Conference on Computer Vision and Pattern Recognition, pp. 7132–7141 (2018)
15. Newell, A., Yang, K., Deng, J.: Stacked hourglass networks for human pose estimation. In: Proceedings of the European Conference on Computer Vision, pp. 483–499 (2016)
16. Asaari, M.S.M., Suandi, S.A., Rosdi, B.A.: Fusion of band limited phase only correlation and width centroid contour distance for finger based Biometrics. Expert. Syst. Appl. **41**(7), 3367–3382 (2014)
17. Lu, Y., Xie S.J., Yoon, S., et al.: An available database for the research of finger vein recognition. In: Proceedings of 6th IEEE International Congress on Image and Signal Processing (CISP), pp. 410–415 (2013)
18. LeCun, Y., Bottou, L., Bengio, Y., et al.: Gradient-based learning applied to document recognition. P IEEE. **86**(11), 2278–2324 (1998)

19. He, K., Zhang, X., Ren, S., et al.: Deep residual learning for image recognition. In: Proceedings of the IEEE Conference on Computer Vision and Pattern Recognition. pp. 770–778 (2016)
20. Sabour, S., Frosst, N., Hinton, G.E.: Dynamic routing between capsules. arXiv preprint arXiv: 1710.09829 (2017)
21. Dosovitskiy, A., Beyer, L., Kolesnikov, A., et al.: An image is worth 16×16 words: Transformers for image recognition at scale. arXiv preprint arXiv:2010.11929 (2020)
22. Ojala, T., Pietikainen, M., Maenpaa, T.: Multiresolution gray-scale and rotation invariant texture classification with local binary patterns. IEEE Trans. Pattern Anal. **24**(7), 971–987 (2002)
23. Yang, J., Zhang, D., Frangi, A.F., et al.: Two-dimensional PCA: a new approach to appearance-based face representation and recognition. IEEE Trans. Pattern Anal. **26**(1), 131–137 (2004)
24. Jia, W., Gao, J., Xia, W., et al.: A performance evaluation of classic convolutional neural networks for 2D and 3D palmprint and palm vein recognition. Int. J. Autom. Comput. **18**(1), 18–44 (2021)
25. Jia, W., Xia, W., Zhao, Y., et al.: 2D and 3D palmprint and palm vein recognition based on neural architecture search. Int. J. Autom. Comput. **18**(3), 377–409 (2021)
26. Kang, W., Liu, H., Luo, W., et al.: Study of a full-view 3D finger vein verification technique. IEEE Trans. Inf. Forensics Secur. **15**, 1175–1189 (2019)

A Lightweight CNN Using HSIC Fine-Tuning for Fingerprint Liveness Detection

Chengsheng Yuan[1,2(✉)], Jie Chen[1,2], Mingyu Chen[1,2], and Wei Gu[1,2(✉)]

[1] Engineering Research Center of Digital Forensics, Ministry of Education, Nanjing University of Information Science and Technology, Nanjing, China
{003234,201983290263,201983290123,001788}@nuist.edu.cn
[2] School of Computer and Software, Nanjing University of Information Science and Technology, Nanjing, China

Abstract. As an individual's unique biometric, fingerprints are widely used for identification. In recent years, attacks based on forged fingerprints have caused many hidden security risks. Therefore, the detection of forged fingerprints is significant, and fingerprint liveness detection is proposed. Methods based on neural networks have achieved great results, but most of the proposed networks have excessive parameters to meet the needs of practical applications. To this end, this paper designs a lightweight CNN model, whose parameters of the model is only 58 kb, for fingerprint liveness detection. Also, spatial pyramid pooling layer (SPP) is introduced to the networks to enable our network to handle fingerprint images of any size. Meanwhile, this paper propose a HSIC fine-tuning algorithm to initial the parameters of our network before backpropagation, which improves the performance of the network. Experimental results significantly surpass the existing performance, achieving ACE of 2.875 on LivDet 2011 and 1.91 on LivDet 2013.

Keywords: Fingerprint liveness detection · CNN · Fine-tuning · LivDet

1 Introduction

With the continuous development of multimedia technology, private information is also under great threat when people enjoy the convenience brought by technology. How to effectively protect personal privacy has become an urgent problem to be solved. Numerous work has been done in academia to solve these problems. Among them, the technology based on biometrics has become a popular means of information protection for its particularity and uniqueness.

Among all the biometrics features, fingerprints are unique, immutable, and universal, and are widely used in various identity authentication systems. But the security of fingerprint identification systems has always been challenged by fake fingerprints. Fake fingerprints can be made from a variety of available and

© Springer Nature Switzerland AG 2021
J. Feng et al. (Eds.): CCBR 2021, LNCS 12878, pp. 240–247, 2021.
https://doi.org/10.1007/978-3-030-86608-2_27

inexpensive materials, such as gelatin, silica gel, wood glue and plasticine. Therefore, detecting whether fingerprints are forged is of great significance to personal information security [1]. In order to solve the spoofing attack problem of forged fingerprints, fingerprint liveness detection technology is proposed. The research on fingerprint activity detection is mainly divided into two categories, one is based on hardware facilities, and the other is based on software [2]. The hardware-based method is to add additional sensors to the fingerprint detection device to extract human biological characteristics, such as body temperature, blood flow, pulse, smell and other information [3]. The software-based method uses an algorithm to analyze the characteristics of the acquired fingerprint image to determine whether the fingerprint is true or false. Consider that there is no need for other sensors, the liveness of fingerprint images is detected through image processing technology, so software-based methods are more cost-effective and easy to upgrade.

Compared with the traditional manual feature extraction method, many excellent fake fingerprint detection schemes are obtained through the learning ability of neural network. The convolutional neural network (CNN) [4] can extract higher-dimensional fingerprint semantic features compared with traditional manual methods. However, most networks using CNN have a very deep number of layers, which will consume a lot of memory and time to train, and there is a certain overfitting phenomenon. What's more, the parameter amount of the trained network is too large, which also leads to the excessive cost of deployment on the mobile terminal.

Meanwhile, many fingerprints liveness detection systems based on the CNN method must be input with a fixed size, but fingerprint images collected by fingerprint sensors in actual application scenarios may have different sizes. In order to meet the input requirements, many systems directly adopt resizing or cropping methods, but this will cause the loss of key features extracted by the sensor, resulting in large differences in the learned features and poor fingerprint liveness detection performance.

In order to solve the above problems, this paper proposes a lightweight CNN-SPP [5] fingerprint liveness detection network based on fine-tuning using Hilbert-Schmidt independence criterion (HSIC) [6]. Spatial pyramid pooling layer (SPP-Net) is also added to solve the problem that the network cannot input fingerprint images of different sizes. What's more, considering that the amount of data in the LivDet 2011 and 2013 [7,8] used is too little, the CNN is prone to overfitting. This paper utilizes HSIC to fine-tune the initial parameters of the network to reduce the overfitting phenomenon of the network. The main contributions of this paper are concluded as follows:

- SPP-Net is introduced to our lightweight CNN. SPP-Net allows our network to perform multi-scale input while improving performance and enhancing the robustness of our network. Meanwhile, high-performance lightweight network are more suitable to put into mobile terminal.
- Use HSIC to fine-tune our network parameters before training. The fine-tuned network performs better in the experiment than the non-fine-tuned one. HSIC

fine-tuning alleviates the overfitting problem of the network, especially when facing the fingerprint dataset is not adequate.

The rest of this paper is as follows: We introduce our network and the HSIC fine-tuning algorithm used in the second section. The third section will show the details and results of our experiment. Finally, the conclusion will be given.

2   Proposed Methods

In this section, a convolutional neural network using pyramid pooling is specailly designed for fingerprint liveness detection. The CNN network is not only lightweight but also has excellent performance. Meanwhile, the amount of data in the LivDet dataset is very small, and the use of backpropagation is easy to overfit which will make the performance poor. To this end, we propose a method of fine-tuning the parameters by HSIC, which effectively reduces the problem of network over-fitting and improves the performance of the proposed network.

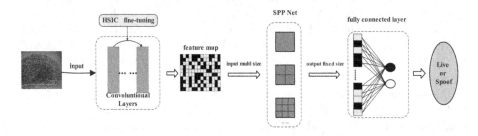

Fig. 1. The flow chart of our proposed method

2.1   Model Structure

In response to the problem of the general CNN being too large, we build a neural network with only two convolutional layers and a fully connected layer for testing. The test results show that although the network has a good fitting effect on the training dataset, the performance on the testing dataset is very poor, and the over-fitting phenomenon is very serious, especially on Biometrika and Italdata. Obviously, using a neural network with an overly simple structure will greatly reduce the amount of parameters and training costs, while it is hard to learn the optimal classification boundary between fake and real fingerprints.

In order to simultaneously solve the problem of poor performance of the lightweight CNN and the need to input fixed-size images, SPP-Net is introduced in this paper. It is added after the convolution operation being completed, the extracted feature maps of different sizes are divided into the same number of blocks and then pooled, and finally the features of the same size are extracted and directly input to the fully connected layer as the Fig. 1 shows. SPP-Net can also segment the same feature map at different levels to perform multi-scale feature extraction. This can alleviate the over-fitting phenomenon of convolutional neural network to a certain extent and improve the performance of CNN. In addition, this paper uses both average pooling and maximum pooling in SPP-Net, so that the global features of the fingerprint can be paid attention to during training, and the local features will not be lost [9].

2.2 HSIC Fine-Tuning

HSIC, like mutual information, can be used to measure the independence between two variables. But unlike mutual information, HSIC does not need to calculate the probability density of two variables, but directly converts it into a sampling form. Its manifestation is as follows:

$$
\begin{aligned}
HSIC(X,Y) = {} & E_{(x_1,y_1)\sim p(x,y),(x_2,y_2)\sim p(x,y)}[K_X(x_1,x_2)K_Y(y_1,y_2)] \\
& + E_{x_1\sim p(x),x_2\sim p(x),y_1\sim p(y),y_2\sim p(y)}[K_X(x_1,x_2)K_Y(y_1,y_2)] \quad (1) \\
& - 2E_{(x_1,y_1)\sim p(x,y),x_2\sim p(x),y_2\sim p(y)}[K_X(x_1,x_2)K_Y(y_1,y_2)]
\end{aligned}
$$

where K_X, K_Y is kernel function, E is the expecation about X and Y. Transform formula 1 into the matrix form of unbiased estimation and simplified as shown in the formula 2:

$$
HSIC(X,Y) = \frac{1}{(n-1)^2}Tr(K_X J K_Y J) \quad (2)
$$

Algorithm 1. HISC fine-tuning method

Input: n:number of data, m:batch size, L:number of layers, Z_i:the output of i-th layer and the intput of (i+1)-th layer, T_i:the i-th layer, X_i:the i-th batch data, *iteration*:the epoches of backpropagation, θ_i:the parameters of i-th layer
Output: Model after HSIC fine-tuning and backpropagation
  for i in range($1,\lfloor\frac{n}{m}\rfloor$) **do**
    $Z_0 = X_i$
    for j in range(1,L) **do**
      $Z_j = T_{j-1}(Z_{j-1})$
      $g_j = \nabla_{\theta_j}(nHSIC(Z_j,X_i) - \beta nHSIC(Z_j,Y_i))$
      $\theta_j = \theta_j - \alpha g_j$
    end for
  end for
  for i in range(1,*iteration*) **do**
    backpropagation;
  end for

---

where $J = I - \frac{1}{n}$, I is N-order identity matrix. Furthermore, we use normalized HSIC (nHSIC) as the formula used in the algorithm.

$$
nHSIC(X,Y) = Tr(\tilde{K}_X \tilde{K}_Y) \quad (3)
$$

where $\tilde{K}_X = \overline{K_X}(\overline{K_X} + \varepsilon n I_n)^{-1}$, $\overline{K_X}$ means centered kernel matrix. And the $\tilde{K}_Y$ is same. So the fine-tuning goal can be described as formula 4.

$$Z_i^* = \arg\min_{Z_i}(nHSIC(Z_i, X) - \beta nHSIC(Z_i, Y)) \tag{4}$$

Combined with formula 3 and 4, the HSIC fine-tuning method is shown in Algorithm 1. Gaussian function is used as the kernel function.

3   Experiments

In this section, we first introduce the datasets and evaluation metrics. Then, we test the characteristics of the HSIC algorithm on a simple CNN. Finally, we conduct experiments on the performance of our proposed fine-tuning method and network.

Table 1. Details of LivDet 2011 and LivDet 2013

Dataset	Sensor (Acronym)	Image size	Training (Live/Spoof)	Testing (Live/Spoof)
LivDet2011	Biometrika (Bio)	312×372	1000/1000	1000/1000
	Digital (Dig)	355×391	1004/1000	1000/1000
	Italdata (Ita)	640×480	1000/1000	1000/1000
	Sagem (Sag)	352×384	1008/1008	1000/1036
LivDet2013	Biometrika (Bio)	312×372	1000/1000	1000/1000
	Italdata (Ita)	640×480	1000/1000	1000/1000
	CrossMatch (Cro)	800×750	1250/1000	1250/1000
	Swipe (Swi)	208×1500	1221/979	1153/1000

3.1   Datasets and Evaluation Metrics

The datasets we use are LivDet 2011 and 2013 to test our method. The details of the two datasets are shown in Table 1. We also use small-angle rotation, flipping, zooming, and brightness enhancement methods to enhance the dataset to improve the robustness of the CNN.

Average Classification Error (ACE) is the average of the misclassification rate of real fingerprints and the misclassification rate of fake fingerprints. Formula 5 and 6 is the evaluation metrics.

$$ACE = \frac{F_{fake} + F_{live}}{2} \tag{5}$$

F_{fake} is the misclassification rate of spoof fingerprints and F_{live} is the misclassification rate of live fingerprints. Average Classification Accuracy(ACA) is defined as formula 6:

$$ACA = 1 - ACE \tag{6}$$

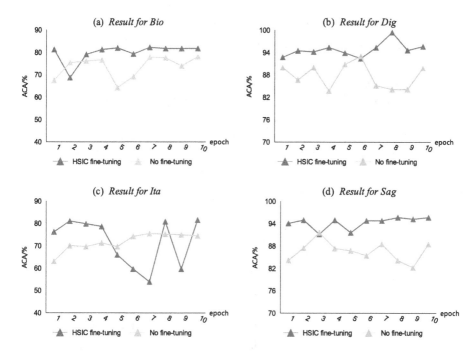

Fig. 2. The ACA of two layer CNN compared with only backpropagation on LivDet 2011

3.2 Experiment on Lightweight CNN-SPP Net

First, HSIC fine-tuning algorithm is used to test LivDet 2011 on the two-layer CNN proposed in Sect. 2.1, and the results are shown in Fig. 2. The relusts after HSIC fine-tuning not only converge faster than those without fine-tuning, but the best performance is also better to a certain extent. The phenomenon shows that HSIC fine-tuning algorithm is less likely to fall into a local minimum, and the ability to find the global optimal solution is stronger than BP, and HSIC's understanding of fingerprint features is more reasonable, alleviate the overfitting problem of the network.

Then train the proposed lightweight CNN-SPP net on LivDet 2011 and 2013, and compare the results of using HSIC fine-tuning and not using. Meanwhile, the training results are compared with the results of other papers. The results are shown in Tables 2 and 3.

After adding the SPP-Net to the simple CNN, the algorithm can process multi size fingerprint images and the performance is greatly improved. The ACA on LivDet2011's Sagem improves nearly 4% from the Fig. 2 and Table 2. And comparing with methods without HSIC fine-tuning, our method's ACE improves 2.15 on LivDet 2011 and 0.9 on LivDet 2013. Especially ACE on LivDet 2011's Ita and LivDet 2013's CrossMatch improves greatly, that improves 5.2% and 3.87%.

Table 2. ACE for LivDet 2011

Method	LivDet 2011				
	Biometrika	Digital	Italdata	Sagem	Average
BSIF [10]	6.8	13.65	**3.55**	4.86	7.22
WLBPD [11]	5.65	4.1	11.85	2.25	5.96
LCPD [12]	4.9	4.2	11	2.7	5.7
CNN-VGG [4]	5.2	3.2	8	1.7	4.52
CNN-Alexnet [4]	5.6	4.6	9.1	3.1	5.6
Only BP	5.6	2.05	10.3	2.15	5.025
BP+HSIC	**3.5**	**1.35**	5.1	**1.55**	**2.875**

Table 3. ACE for LivDet 2013

Method	LivDet 2013				
	Biometrika	Italdata	CrossMatch	Swipe	Average
HIG-BP [13]	3.9	28.76	1.7	14.4	12.19
WLBPD [11]	**0.4**	0.95	-	4.31	-
SURF [14]	5.75	6.08	4.6	4.6	5.26
CNN-VGG [4]	1.8	**0.4**	**3.4**	3.7	2.325
CNN-Alexnet [4]	1.9	0.5	4.7	4.3	2.85
Only BP	1.55	0.75	8.4	**0.56**	2.815
Proposed Approach	1.4	0.6	4.53	1.11	**1.91**

4   Conclusions

We propose a lightweight CNN network with SPP-Net and train it after HSIC fine-tuning, which achieves the state-of-the-art results for fingerprint liveness detection with less parameters. The fine-tuning algorithm we proposed can improve the performance of CNN when the overfit phenomenon occuors, which help the CNN escape from the local minimum and find the global optimal solution. What's more, the proposed CNN-SPP network only has the parameters of 58 kb. Our future work is futher improving the performance with least cost and studying the robustness of our network against unkown spoof fingerprints.

Acknowledgment. This work is supported by the National Key R&D Program of China under grant 2018YFB1003205; by the Jiangsu Basic Research Programs-Natural Science Foundation under grant BK20200807; by the Research Startup Foundation of NUIST 2020r015; by the Canada Research Chair Program and the NSERC Discovery Grant; by the Priority Academic Program Development of Jiangsu Higher Education Institutions (PAPD) fund; by the Collaborative Innovation Center of Atmospheric Environment and Equipment Technology (CICAEET) fund, China.

References

1. Marasco, M., Ross, A.: A survey on antispoofing schemes for fingerprint recognition systems. ACM Comput. Surv. (CSUR), **47**(2), 1–36 (2014)
2. Zhang, Y., Pan, S., Zhan, S., Li, Z., Gao, M., Gao. C.: Fldnet. light dense CNN for fingerprint liveness detection. IEEE Access **8**, 84141–84152 (2020)
3. Reddy, P.V., Kumar, A., Rahman, S,M,K., Mundra, T.S.: A new antispoofing approach for biometric devices. IEEE Trans. Biomed. Circ. Syst. **2**(4), 328–337 (2008)
4. Nogueira, R.F.: de Alencar Lotufo, R., Campos, R.: Machado. fingerprint liveness detection using convolutional neural networks. IEEE Trans. Inf. Forens. Secur. **11**(6), 1206–1213 (2016)
5. He, K., Zhang, X., Ren, S., Sun. J.: Spatial pyramid pooling in deep convolutional networks for visual recognition. IEEE Trans. Patt. Anal. Mach. Intell. **37**(9), 1904–1916 (2015)
6. Gretton, A., Bousquet, O., Smola, A., Schölkopf, B.: Measuring statistical dependence with hilbert-schmidt norms. In: Jain, S., Simon, H.U., Tomita, E. (eds.) ALT 2005. LNCS (LNAI), vol. 3734, pp. 63–77. Springer, Heidelberg (2005). https://doi.org/10.1007/11564089_7
7. Yambay, D., Ghiani, L., Denti, P., Marcialis, G.L., Roli, F., Schuckers, S.: . Livdet 2011–fingerprint liveness detection competition 2011. In: 2012 5th IAPR International Conference on Biometrics (ICB), pp. 208–215. IEEE (2012)
8. Ghiani, L., Yambay, D., Mura, M., Tocco, S., Marcialis, G.L., Roli, F., Schuckers, S.: Livdet 2013 fingerprint liveness detection competition 2013. In: 2013 International Conference on Biometrics (ICB), pp. 1–6. IEEE (2013)
9. Yu, D., Wang, H., Chen, P., Wei, Z.: Mixed pooling for convolutional neural networks. In: Miao, D., Pedrycz, W., Ślęzak, D., Peters, G., Hu, Q., Wang, R. (eds.) RSKT 2014. LNCS (LNAI), vol. 8818, pp. 364–375. Springer, Cham (2014). https://doi.org/10.1007/978-3-319-11740-9_34
10. Ghiani, L., Hadid, A., Marcialis, G.L., Roli, F.: Fingerprint liveness detection using binarized statistical image features. In: 2013 IEEE Sixth International Conference on Biometrics: Theory, Applications and Systems (BTAS), pp. 1–6. IEEE (2013)
11. Yuan, C., Sun, X., Lv, R.: Fingerprint liveness detection based on multi-scale LPQ and PCA. China Commun. **13**(7), 60–65 (2016)
12. Gragnaniello, D., Poggi, G., Sansone, C., Verdoliva, L.: Local contrast phase descriptor for fingerprint liveness detection. Patt. Recogn. **48**(4), 1050–1058 (2015)
13. Gottschlich, C., Marasco, E., Yang, A.Y., Cukic, B.: Fingerprint liveness detection based on histograms of invariant gradients. In: IEEE International Joint Conference On Biometrics, pp. 1–7. IEEE (2014)
14. RDubey, R.K., Goh, J., Vrizlynn, L.L.: Thing. fingerprint liveness detection from single image using low-level features and shape analysis. IEEE Trans. Inf. Foren. Secur. **11**(7), 1461–1475 (2016)

An Efficient Joint Bayesian Model with Soft Biometric Traits for Finger Vein Recognition

Liping Zhang[1,2,3,4], Linjun Sun[1,2,3,4], Xiaoli Dong[1,2,3,4], Lina Yu[1,2,3,4],
Weijun Li[1,2,3,4(✉)], and Xin Ning[1,2,3,4(✉)]

[1] Institute of Semiconductors, Chinese Academy of Sciences, Beijing 100083, China
{zliping,sunlinjun,dongxiaoli,yulina,wjli,ningxin}@semi.ac.cn
[2] Beijing Key Laboratory of Semiconductor Neural Network Intelligent Sensing
and Computing Technology, Beijing 100083, China
[3] School of Microelectronics, University of Chinese Academy of Sciences,
Beijing 100049, China
[4] Cognitive Computing Technology Joint Laboratory, Wave Group,
Beijing 100083, China

Abstract. In this work, we propose an efficient joint Bayesian model that expanded with soft biometric traits for finger vein recognition, which is different from the existing mainstream finger vein recognition methods that extract features from the region of interest (ROI) of finger vein images. First, a two-branch convolutional neural networks (CNNs) is designed to extract feature simultaneously from finger shape images and ROI vein images, respectively, the aim of which is to extract more information from different parts of fingers. Then, two different features are fused by concatenating. Finally, a joint Bayesian recognition loss is used to train the proposed two-branch CNN which is to promote intra-class variance minimization and inter-class variation maximization. Further, in our framework, a end-to-end learning method of CNNs and joint Bayesian recognition loss is achieved to optimize the parameters. Experiments performed on two public finger vein databases demonstrate that the proposed model is efficient and achieves better performance than state-of-the-art methods.

1 Introduction

In recent years, the technology of biometrics has developed rapidly. Finger vein recognition is a new biometric technology that uses the hemoglobin from the finger vein to absorb the near-infrared light and compose a finger vein image. Compared with other biometrics, finger vein information is more secure and stable. In other words, it is not easily duplicated owing to the fact that it is hidden inside the finger. However, due to the instability of illumination and acquisition environment, finger vein recognition performance has been constrained in practical applications.

© Springer Nature Switzerland AG 2021
J. Feng et al. (Eds.): CCBR 2021, LNCS 12878, pp. 248–258, 2021.
https://doi.org/10.1007/978-3-030-86608-2_28

Currently, the main methods of finger vein recognition consist of extracting features from the region of interest (ROI) of the finger vein [1–5]. The advantage is that this can accurately locate the main information of veins according to the position of the joint and the edge of the finger [6,7]. However, the information of the finger edge and shape is ignored. If the original finger vein image is used for feature extraction, other problems arise, such as complex background information, noise, finger rotation and offset. To address the above issues, a few researchers have used soft biometric traits [8] of the finger to assist finger vein recognition. These soft biometric traits include finger back texture [9], width of finger [10], fingertip angle [11], intensity of finger vein background [12]. However, the method by using the width of finger as soft biometrics ignores the continuity of finger contour and inflection point information. The method using fingertip angle as soft biometric can only be used on specific finger vein data sets, because some finger vein database images do not collect finger tip information, so the method is not universal. The intensity distribution of finger vein background largely depends on the external light, which will lead to the instability of soft biometrics, and it is not easy to separate the foreground and background information of fingers. In this work, we use the shape information of finger as soft biometrics and combining finger vein information to improve the recognition performance, and a two-branch CNNs is proposed to extract the soft biometric traits and vein features of fingers.

In CNNs, loss function plays an important role in deep learning [13–15]. Moreover, a good loss function can improve the performance of a convolutional neural network (CNN) model. Softmax loss [13] is the most commonly used classified loss function at present. However, the performance of the Softmax loss function is poor in reducing intra-class variation. To solve this issue, Many loss functions were proposed to provide a margin strategy that makes the classification boundary more compact [15,16]. Moghaddam et al. [17] proposed a Bayesian method for face verification and achieved good performance. To better consider inter-class variation, Chen et al. [18] proposed a joint Bayesian method for face verification to consider the difference of inter-class and extra-class. Motivated by the joint Bayesian verification, this study proposes a joint Bayesian recognition loss take into consideration the relation of samples and identity so as to achieve end-to-end learning of CNNs and joint Bayesian recognition loss. Firstly, the finger shape image and ROI vein image are obtained through segmentation and ROI detection [7]. Then, the ROI vein image and finger shape image are input into two-branch CNNs in order to extract features. Finally, a joint Bayesian recognition loss is proposed so as to classify fusion features. The experimental procedure is shown in Fig. 1.

The remainder of this paper is organized into five sections. Section 2 describes the background, while Sect. 3 explains the method. Section 4 presents datasets and experimental results, and Sect. 5 summarizes key conclusions.

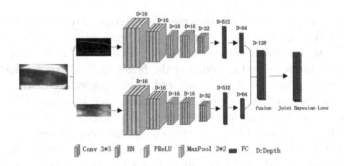

Fig. 1. Architecture of the proposed framework.

2   Background

2.1   Soft Biometric Traits

Soft biometric traits [8] are those characteristics that provide some information about the individual but lack the distinctiveness and permanence necessary in order to sufficiently differentiate between any two individuals. Soft biometric traits [19] have been under extensive investigation and research in recent years. [20] proposed a fusion of fingerprint and body weight and fat measurements to support fingerprint biometric recognition. [21] presented a method for geometric gait recognition with stride length and height, whereas [22] exploited gender, ethnicity, and facial marks to improve the performance of face recognition.

Some researchers have used soft biometric traits [8] of the finger to assist finger vein recognition. [9] introduced a method for improving robustness by using finger-dorsal texture as a soft biological trait and combining finger vein information. [23] proposed the width of the phalangeal joint as a soft biometric trait to increase robustness and assist finger vein recognition. [10,24] proposed using the information of finger width as a soft biometric trait in finger vein recognition. The width of the finger is mainly calculated in a horizontal direction, and then a spectrogram or matrix is formed. [11] proposed the width of the finger and the fingertip angle as new soft biometric traits for finger vein recognition. [12] exploited the intensity distribution of finger vein background as a soft biometric trait generated from the vein image.

2.2   Joint Bayesian Verification

To better explain the methods and improvements proposed in this study, the joint Bayesian verification method [18] will be first briefy introduced. In this setting, the presentation of relevant sample features is affected by two factors: identity and intra-class variations. A sample feature is represented by two independent Gaussian variables

$$x = \mu + \varepsilon, \tag{1}$$

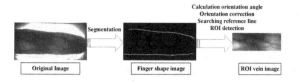

Fig. 2. The flowchart of data preprocessing.

where x is the sample feature vector, μ is its identity, and ε represents intra-class variations. The μ and ε are distributed independently as $N(0, S_\mu)$ and $N(0, S_\varepsilon)$, respectively. S_μ and S_ε are the between-class and within-class covariance, which can be estimated by an EM method.

Let H_I be the intra-class hypothesis that samples x_1 and x_2 belong to the same class, and let H_E be the extraclass hypothesis that two samples belong to different classes. The joint distributions $p(x_1, x_2 | H_I)$ and $p(x_1, x_2 | H_E)$ are, respectively, zero-mean Gaussians with covariance matrices

$$\begin{bmatrix} S_\mu + S_\varepsilon & S_\mu \\ S_\mu & S_\mu + S_\varepsilon \end{bmatrix}, \tag{2}$$

$$\begin{bmatrix} S_\mu + S_\varepsilon & 0 \\ 0 & S_\mu + S_\varepsilon \end{bmatrix}, \tag{3}$$

The log-likelihood ratio is the following:

$$r(x_1, x_2) = log\frac{p(x_1, x_2 | H_I)}{p(x_1, x_2 | H_E)} = x_1^T A x_1 + x_2^T A x_2 - 2x_1^T G x_2, \tag{4}$$

where

$$A = (S_\mu + S_\varepsilon)^{-1} - (F + G), \tag{5}$$

$$\begin{bmatrix} F + G & G \\ G & F + G \end{bmatrix} = \begin{bmatrix} S_\mu + S_\varepsilon & S_\mu \\ S_\mu & S_\mu + S_\varepsilon \end{bmatrix}^{-1}. \tag{6}$$

The ratio can be used to measure the probability of similarity between two samples.

3   The Proposed Method

3.1   Data Preprocessing

This is a brief introduction of acquisition of ROI vein images and finger shape images. The main purpose of edge detection is to get the shape of the finger in order to distinguish the foreground and background. In [7], a simplified Statistical Region Merging (SSRM) with dynamical adjustment of precision parameter is proposed to segment the finger body and background area. Then novel Directional Linkage Clustering Method (DLCM) is used to improve the accuracy of finger edge detection. Further, the direction correction of the finger foreground image is made, the joint line is located, and the candidate box is selected in order to get ROI vein images. The flowchart of data processing is shown in Fig. 2.

3.2   Network Structure

Two-branch networks are used without sharing weights so as to extract the features of the finger shape and the features of the ROI vein. The two-branch networks are used here in the same network structure. The network of branch CNNs includes five convolutional layers, five PReLU layers, four Maxpooling layers, and two fully connected layers. The fusion feature vector is formed by the feature connection extracted by two networks. The finger shape images and ROI vein images are of size 60×128.

3.3   Joint Bayesian Recognition Loss

This paper proposes a joint Bayesian recognition loss. This new method is inspired by the joint Bayesian method [18], for face verification. Verification means getting the joint Bayesian probability score between two samples, and recognition means calculating the Bayesian probability score of the sample and the class agent. The feature vector is denoted as x, while is its identity. The μ and x are distributed independently as $N(0, S_\mu)$ and $N(0, S_\mu + S_\varepsilon)$. The joint distributions $p(x, \mu | H_I)$ and $p(x, \mu | H_E)$ are, respectively, zeromean Gaussians with covariance matrices shown in Eq. 8 and Eq. 9.

The log-likelihood ratio is as follows:

$$r(x, \mu) = log \frac{p(x, \mu | H_I)}{p(x, \mu | H_E)} = x^T D x + \mu^T F \mu - 2x^T F \mu, \tag{7}$$

where

$$D = (S_\mu + S_\varepsilon)^{-1} - F. \tag{8}$$

The joint Bayesian recognition loss is:

$$L_{JBS} = - \sum_{i=1}^{C} y_i \log \frac{e^{r(x, \mu_i)}}{\sum_{j=1}^{c} e^{r(x, \mu_j)}}. \tag{9}$$

S_μ and S_ε are two unknown covariance matrices which can be obtained from the data, and the EM method is used to update them. For details of the EM algorithm, please refer to references [18].

3.4   Joint Bayesian Model

In this study, the finger shape images and ROI vein images are first obtained by segmentation and ROI interception. Then, the ROI vein images and finger shape images are input into two-branch networks so as to extract features. Finally, a joint Bayesian recognition loss is proposed for measuring the probability and loss of the fusion feature. The architecture of the proposed framework is shown in Fig. 1. Table 1 shows the overall training process of the joint Bayesian model.

Table 1. Efficient training process of joint Bayesian model.

Input:
The finger vein images are divided into finger shape images and ROI vein images. The finger shape images and ROI vein images are respectively passed through the branch CNNs and output features, and then connected into fusion features $\{x_{ij}\}$; The number of classes n; The number of samples of the ith; class m_i; The total number of the samples of all classes k.
Output:
The CNNs model parameters and joint Bayesian recognition loss parameters $\{S_\mu; S_\varepsilon\}$.
Joint Bayesian Model Learning:
1): Initialize CNNs parameters and $\{S_\mu; S_\varepsilon\}$.
2): Training CNNs and updating parameters of CNNs.
3): Calculate the expectation of the variables of each class (E-step) when epoch equals joint Bayesian update stones: $$F=S_\varepsilon^{-1},$$ $$D= (S_\mu+S_\varepsilon)^{-1} - F,$$ $$G = -(m_iS_\mu + S_\varepsilon)^{-1}S_\mu S_\varepsilon^{-1},$$ $$E\left[\mu_i\right] = S_\mu(F + m_iG)\sum_j x_{ij},$$ $$E\left[\varepsilon_{ij}\right] = S_\varepsilon F x_{ij} + S_\varepsilon G \sum_j x_{ij}.$$
4): Update the joint Bayesian recognition loss parameter (M-step): $$S_\mu = \frac{1}{n}\sum_i E\left[\mu_i\mu_i^T\right],$$ $$S_\varepsilon = \frac{1}{k}\sum_{i,j} E\left[\varepsilon_{ij}\varepsilon_{ij}^T\right].$$
5): Repeat step 3) and step 4) until convergence.
6): Update the F, G, D.
7): Update the joint Bayesian model.

4 Experimental and Results

Datasets. The method was used on two public finger vein datasets. The MMCBNU_6000 [25] database includes 6,000 images of 100 volunteers and their 6 fingers, with 10 images of each finger. The SDUMLA database [26] includes 106 subjects with 6 fingers per subject, which is a total of 3816 images. To train the CNN, we simply chose the first 8 samples of each subject in MMCBNU_6000 and the first 4 samples of each subject in SDUMLA as training samples. The reason we chose 8 and 4 is to ensure that each subject in both databases has two positive imposter test samples. First, the recognition performance of different features was compared. When the input data is a finger shape image or an ROI vein image, the network structure was the respective branch network in Fig. 1. When the finger shape image and ROI vein image were used as input data at the same time, finger shape images and ROI vein images were used as the input data of each branch network, respectively. The branch networks are shown in Fig. 1. The loss function is the Softmax function.

Table 2. Genuine acceptance rate (GAR@EER) of different inputs on the test datasets.

Input	MMCBNU_6000	SDUMLA
Soft	86.25%	69.42%
ROI	98.75%	96.07%
ROI & Soft	**99.42%**	**98.27%**

In the table, Soft represents finger shape images as input images; ROI represents ROI vein images as input images; ROI &Soft represents finger shape images and ROI vein images as input images.

Table 3. Genuine acceptance rate (GAR@EER) of joint Bayesian model with various loss functions on ROI & soft of the test dataset.

Loss function	MMCBNU_6000	SDUMLA
Softmax	99.42%	98.27%
Center+Softmax	99.58%	98.43%
ASoftmax	99.67%	98.51%
AMSoftmax	99.75%	98.66%
Joint Bayesian recognition	**99.83%**	**99.06%**

Implementation Details. This work employed an SGD optimizer with a momentum of 0.9 and weight decay of 0.0001. The batch size was 64 and the learning rate started at 0.001. The training finished at 300 epochs. All the experiments were performed under the following configuration: an NVIDIA GeForce GTX 1080, a CPU running at 2.66 GHz with 16 GB memory, and a Linux system. The CNNs and loss functions were implemented using the PyTorch framework.

4.1   Comparison Between Different Inputs

First, experiments are carried out to test the recognition performance with different input. When the input image is finger shape image or ROI vein image, the network structure adopts the corresponding branch network in Fig. 1 to test the recognition performance of the model. Table 2 tabulates the results. As can be seen in Table 2, ROI of finger vein can be used for identification independently, and the recognition performance is satisfactory. The shape of the finger has a

Table 4. EER% comparison with the state-of-the-art algorithms on the different datasets.

Method	MMCBNU_6000	SDUMLA
LLBP [27]	–	2.65
Gabor filter [12, 28]	2.42	2.58
Repeated line tracking [29]	5.74	5.85
Maximum curvature [29]	2.69	3.65
ASAVE [27]	0.62	1.39
PG-Gabor [29]	0.71	1.35
Weighted vein code indexing [2]	0.42	0.99
Two-channel deep-learning framework [30]	0.20	0.94
HOPGR [31]	0.70	–
Our proposed method	**0.17**	**0.94**

certain distinction but it lack the distinctiveness in order to sufficiently differentiate between any two individuals. The proposed method that combines finger shape features and ROI vein features performs better than Soft and ROI, which proves its effectiveness.

4.2 Comparison Between Different Loss Function

Then, the performance of the proposed joint Bayesian recognition loss function was compared with that of classical loss functions. Finger shape images and ROI vein images were used as input data of each branch network, respectively.

The results in Table 3 show that the performance of the proposed joint Bayesian recognition loss function is better than it is the case with other loss functions on the MMCBNU_6000 dataset and the SDUMLA dataset. The joint Bayesian recognition loss function not only minimizes intra-class variation and maximizes inter-class variation but also successfully integrates the relationship between samples and class agents.

4.3 Comparison with the State-of-the-Art Methods

Finally, the performance of this method was compared with the method of finger vein recognition on MMCBNU_6000 dataset and the SDUMLA dataset. The comparison methods include LLBP, Gabor filter, repeated line tracking, maximum curvature, ASAVE, PG-Gabor, weighted vein code indexing, HOPGR and two-channel deep-learning framework. The results are shown in Table 4.

The results in Table 4 show that the proposed method is superior to most state-of-the-art methods on two datasets. On SDUMLA dataset, the proposed method achieves equivalent performance with the two-channel deep-learning framework [30]. However, the SUDMLA database has only one imposter test sample in [30], the ratio of number of training samples to number of test samples is 5:1, and the ratio of the number of training samples to the number of test samples in our paper is 4:2.

The simultaneous training of joint Bayesian recognition loss and CNNs greatly improves the training process and ensures that the parameters of CNNs and joint Bayesian recognition loss are optimized at the same time. Experimental results also demonstrate the effectiveness of the proposed joint Bayesian model.

5   Conclusion

This study proposed a joint Bayesian model that fuses ROI vein features and soft biometric traits in order to increase the amount of information for finger vein recognition. The features extracted by two-branch networks were firstly fused in order to improve the performance of recognition. Then, a joint Bayesian recognition loss based on the joint Bayesian verification method was proposed, and an end-to-end trainable framework was established in order to optimize model parameters. Experiments on public finger vein datasets showed that the proposed joint Bayesian recognition loss function performs better than the current prevailing loss functions and demonstrated the effectiveness of the joint Bayesian model. A future step is to consider adding some margin strategies to the joint Bayesian loss function in order to make the classification boundary more compact.

Acknowledgment. This work is supported by the National Natural Science Foundation of China (Grant No. 61901436) and the Key Research Program of the Chinese Academy of Sciences (Grant No. XDPB22).

References

1. Kang, W., Liu, H., Luo, W., Deng, F.: Study of a full-view 3d finger vein verification technique. IEEE Trans. Inf. Forensics Secur. **15**, 1175–1189 (2019)
2. Yang, L., Yang, G., Xi, X., Su, K., Chen, Q., Yin, Y.: Finger vein code: from indexing to matching. IEEE Trans. Inf. Forensics Secur. **14**(5), 1210–1223 (2018)
3. Zhang, Y., Li, W., Zhang, L., Ning, X., Sun, L., Lu, Y.: Adaptive learning gabor filter for finger-vein recognition. IEEE Access **7**, 159821–159830 (2019)
4. Zhang, L., Li, W., Ning, X., Dong, X., Liu, W.: A finger vein recognition method based on histogram of oriented lines and (2D)2FPCA. J. Comput. Aid. Des. Comput. Graph. **30**(2), 6 (2018)
5. Yang, J., Shi, Y., Jia, G.: Finger-vein image matching based on adaptive curve transformation. Pattern Recogn. **66**, 34–43 (2017)
6. Yang, J., Wei, J., Shi, Y.: Accurate ROI localization and hierarchical hyper-sphere model for finger-vein recognition. Neurocomputing **328**, 171–181 (2019)
7. Gao, Y., Wang, J., Zhang, L.: Robust ROI localization based on image segmentation and outlier detection in finger vein recognition. Multimedia Tools Appl. **79**, 20039–20059 (2020)

8. Jain, A.K., Dass, S.C., Nandakumar, K.: Can soft biometric traits assist user recognition? In: Biometric Technology for Human Identification, vol. 5404, pp. 561–572. International Society for Optics and Photonics (2004)

9. Yang, W., Yu, X., Liao, Q.: Personal authentication using finger vein pattern and finger-dorsa texture fusion. In: Proceedings of the 17th ACM International Conference on Multimedia, pp. 905–908 (2009)

10. Kim, W., Song, J.M., Park, K.R.: Multimodal biometric recognition based on convolutional neural network by the fusion of finger-vein and finger shape using near-infrared (NIR) camera sensor. Sensors 18(7), 2296 (2018)

11. Asaari, M.S.M., Rosdi, B.A.: A single finger geometry recognition based on widths and fingertip angles (WFTA). In: MVA, pp. 256–259 (2013)

12. Kang, W., Lu, Y., Li, D., Jia, W.: From noise to feature: exploiting intensity distribution as a novel soft biometric trait for finger vein recognition. IEEE Trans. Inf. Forensics Secur. 14(4), 858–869 (2018)

13. Sun, Y., Wang, X., Tang, X.: Deep learning face representation from predicting 10,000 classes. In: Proceedings of the IEEE Conference on Computer Vision and Pattern Recognition, pp. 1891–1898 (2014)

14. Sun, L., Li, W., Ning, X., Zhang, L., Dong, X., He, W.: Gradient-enhanced softmax for face recognition. IEICE Trans. Inf. Syst. 103(5), 1185–1189 (2020)

15. Wang, F., Cheng, J., Liu, W., Liu, H.: Additive margin softmax for face verification. IEEE Signal Process. Lett. 25(7), 926–930 (2018)

16. Liu, W., Wen, Y., Yu, Z., Li, M., Raj, B., Song, L.: SphereFace: deep hypersphere embedding for face recognition. In: Proceedings of the IEEE Conference on Computer Vision and Pattern Recognition, pp. 212–220 (2017)

17. Moghaddam, B., Jebara, T., Pentland, A.: Bayesian face recognition. Pattern Recogn. 33(11), 1771–1782 (2000)

18. Chen, D., Cao, X., Wipf, D., Wen, F., Sun, J.: An efficient joint formulation for Bayesian face verification. IEEE Trans. Pattern Anal. Mach. Intell. 39(1), 32–46 (2016)

19. Nixon, M.S., Correia, P.L., Nasrollahi, K., Moeslund, T.B., Hadid, A., Tistarelli, M.: On soft biometrics. Pattern Recogn. Lett. 68, 218–230 (2015)

20. Ailisto, H., Vildjiounaite, E., Lindholm, M., Mäkelä, S.M., Peltola, J.: Soft biometrics-combining body weight and fat measurements with fingerprint biometrics. Pattern Recogn. Lett. 27(5), 325–334 (2006)

21. Moustakas, K., Tzovaras, D., Stavropoulos, G.: Gait recognition using geometric features and soft biometrics. IEEE Signal Process. Lett. 17(4), 367–370 (2010)

22. Park, U., Jain, A.K.: Face matching and retrieval using soft biometrics. IEEE Trans. Inf. Forensics Secur. 5(3), 406–415 (2010)

23. Yang, L., Yang, G., Yin, Y., Xi, X.: Exploring soft biometric trait with finger vein recognition. Neurocomputing 135, 218–228 (2014)

24. Kang, B.J., Park, K.R.: Multimodal biometric method based on vein and geometry of a single finger. IET Comput. Vision 4(3), 209–217 (2010)

25. Lu, Y., Xie, S.J., Yoon, S., Wang, Z., Park, D.S.: An available database for the research of finger vein recognition. In: 2013 6th International Congress on Image and Signal Processing (CISP), vol. 1, pp. 410–415. IEEE (2013)

26. Yin, Y., Liu, L., Sun, X.: SDUMLA-HMT: a multimodal biometric database. In: Sun, Z., Lai, J., Chen, X., Tan, T. (eds.) CCBR 2011. LNCS, vol. 7098, pp. 260–268. Springer, Heidelberg (2011). https://doi.org/10.1007/978-3-642-25449-9_33

27. Yang, L., Yang, G., Yin, Y., Xi, X.: Finger vein recognition with anatomy structure analysis. IEEE Trans. Circuits Syst. Video Technol. 28(8), 1892–1905 (2017)

28. Kumar, A., Zhou, Y.: Human identification using finger images. IEEE Trans. Image Process. **21**(4), 2228–2244 (2011)
29. Yang, L., Yang, G., Wang, K., Liu, H., Xi, X., Yin, Y.: Point grouping method for finger vein recognition. IEEE Access **7**, 28185–28195 (2019)
30. Fang, Y., Wu, Q., Kang, W.: A novel finger vein verification system based on two-stream convolutional network learning. Neurocomputing **290**, 100–107 (2018)
31. Zhang, L., Li, W., Ning, X., Sun, L., Dong, X.: A local descriptor with physiological characteristic for finger vein recognition. In: 2020 25th International Conference on Pattern Recognition (ICPR), pp. 4873–4878. IEEE (2021)

A Novel Local Binary Operator Based on Discretization for Finger Vein Recognition

Chengcheng Zhao, Huimin Lu$^{(\boxtimes)}$, Yupeng Li, Weiye Liu, and Ruoran Gao

School of Computer Science and Engineering, ChangChun University of Technology, Changchun, Jilin 130102, China
{2202003113,2202003028,2202003047}@stu.ccut.edu.cn,
luhuimin@ccut.edu.cn

Abstract. It is well known that since the binary sequence and weights of the local binary operator are obtained based on local features, the local binary operator has a good description of local texture features. These algorithms have been widely used in finger vein feature extraction. However, this type of algorithm is less effective in describing the global information of the image. In this paper, we propose a new method called Discrete Binary Pattern (DBP) for obtaining binary sequences and weights. This method obtains the DBP code by calculating the mean and standard deviation in the local region of pixels and combining them efficiently, then the combined data is used as the basis to obtain the binary sequence and weight of DBP. This method overcomes the poor extraction of global image information by local binary operators. To test the effectiveness of the algorithm, we compared DBP with other representative local binary operators on three finger vein datasets, FV-USM, UTFVP, and SDUMLA. The EER of DBP achieves state-of-the-art performance in the three databases, and its AUC value is stable above 0.90 in experimental data. The accuracy of DBP is equal to the performance of LDP algorithm, but its time complexity is better than that of LDP algorithm.

Keywords: Discrete binary pattern · Finger vein feature extraction · Main texture feature · Binarization · Dispersion

1 Introduction

As an important method of feature extraction, Local Binary Pattern (LBP) has been widely used and has shown great brilliance in the first generation of biometric identification systems [1]. Ojala et al. were the first to judge and evaluate the performance of LBP by using the Kurbach discriminant method based on sample distribution and prototype distribution [2]. Over the years, many improved algorithms and related applications based on LBP 2 began to emerge, such as Linear Local Binary Pattern (LLBP) [3], Local Gradient Pattern (LGP) [6], Gradient Directional Pattern (GDP) [5], Local Directional Pattern (LDP) [4], Local Optimal Oriented Pattern (LOOP) [7], and Uniform Local Binary Pattern (ULBP) [8]. The original LBP operator is defined as taking the center pixel of the window as the threshold to be compared with the gray values of 8

© Springer Nature Switzerland AG 2021
J. Feng et al. (Eds.): CCBR 2021, LNCS 12878, pp. 259–266, 2021.
https://doi.org/10.1007/978-3-030-86608-2_29

adjacent pixels within a 3 × 3 neighborhood. If the surrounding pixel value is greater than the center pixel value, the position of the pixel point is marked as 1; otherwise, it is 0.

In this way, 8-pixel values in a 3 × 3 neighborhood can be compared to produce 8 bits of binary number (usually converted to decimal as LBP code, a total of 256 kinds), which is the LBP value of the pixel point in the center of the window, and is used to reflect the texture information of region [7]. LDP [7] is an improved local pattern descriptor by using the Kirsch masks to add the directional component. LLBP [3] is an improved version of LBP. The neighborhood taken by LLBP is no longer 3 × 3, but is a horizontal (vertical) component, centered on a certain pixel point. LBP codes in both horizontal and vertical directions are calculated and fused. LGP [6] calculates the binary code by considering the pairwise relationship between neighborhood pixels. LOOP adds the characteristics of rotation invariance based on LBP and LDP [2, 7], while ULBP [8] is an improvement based on LBP, which takes into account the "0, 1 hop" characteristic of binary mode of image features in LBP, and thus achieves the effect of noise reduction by filtering out part of "0, 1 hop".

The above algorithms have been widely used in finger vein feature extraction, but they have an inherent disadvantage. As a binary algorithm, such as LDP, LBP and ULBP, to ensure the number of image feature information and the accuracy of recognition, the filter kernel is set as small as possible, generally 3 × 3, so these algorithms only have a good extraction effect on local texture features. However, for smaller masks, the noise features will be mixed with local texture features due to the interference of noise. Because of these characteristics, these algorithms cannot be used to extract main texture features.

In this paper, we propose a new method called Discrete Binary Pattern (DBP) for obtaining binary sequences and weights in finger vein images. This method obtains the DBP code by calculating the mean and standard deviation in the local region of pixels and combining them efficiently. This method overcomes the poor extraction of global image information by local binary operators.

2 Related Work

Literature [10] proposed a binarization method based on local domain space. This method uses local region information as a source of threshold values, and calculates the mean and variance of all pixels in the $R \times R$ domain space. Then, the mean and variance are effectively combined as the threshold for binarization. This method works very well for binarization after optimizing the threshold value. Therefore, we believe that pixel dispersion information, such as the mean and variance within a local region, can describe the global pixel gradient variation of an image well. So, we think we can extract global image information by dispersing information.

Through experiments, [4–6] et al. have proved that the local binary descriptor has a better extraction effect for local texture features. However, we can clearly see by the feature images of the local binary operator that they are composed of some discontinuous pixel blocks, so they cannot describe the global pixel gradient variation of the image very well.

To solve these problems for local binary operators, we propose a new algorithm. We effectively combine the standard deviation and mean values in the local domain space (we call it pixel dispersion), Then this information is used to obtain the DBP binary sequence and the weights of the binary sequence. We will give a detailed explanation of the algorithm below.

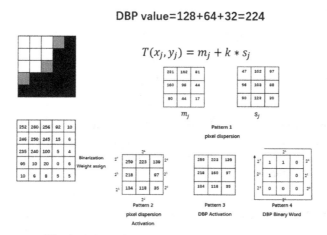

Fig. 1. Schematic diagram of DBP (when $k = 0.6$)

3 Method

We define i_c as the intensity value of a pixel (x_c, y_c) in an $m \times n$ domain space in image. Then we calculate the mean and standard deviation of the pixels in each $m \times n$ domain space separately. As shown in Fig. 1, we set $m = 3$ and $n = 3$, then the standard deviation and mean in this region can be expressed as:

$$m_j = \frac{\sum_{c=0}^{n} i_c}{n} \tag{1}$$

$$s_j = \sqrt{\frac{\sum_{c=0}^{n} (m_i - i_c)^2}{n}} \tag{2}$$

where the subscript j denotes the mean and standard deviation in the j-th domain space. Then, we define a bias k for the standard deviation s_j to reduce the effect of image noise during feature extraction. Then the pixel dispersion $T(x_j, y_j)$ can be defined as:

$$T(x_j, y_j) = m_j + k * s_j \tag{3}$$

where (x_i, y_i) is the position of the pixel dispersion corresponding to the i-th domain space. The dispersion distribution T_{Guided} is finally obtained by extracting the pixel dispersion T in each $m \times n$ region in turn.

We assume that p_c is the intensity of the dispersion (x_c, y_c) in the dispersion distribution graph T_{Guided}, p_n $(n = 0, ..., 7)$ is the intensity of a pixel in the 3×3 neighborhood of (x_c, y_c) excluding the center pixel p_c. Let p_k be the k-th dispersion intensity value, then we set the binary sequence element to 1 when p_k is greater than p_c, and 0 in other cases. By the above method, we get the binary sequence of DBP. Then, we use the dispersion p_k sequence number w_k ($k = 0,...,7$) as the weights of the elements on the binary sequence corresponding to p_k. Finally, we calculate the DBP code, and the BDP values for the pixels (x_c, y_c) are as follows:

$$BDP(x_c, \ y_c) = \sum_{n=0}^{7} s(p_k) * 2^{w_n} \tag{4}$$

$$s(p_k) = \begin{cases} 1, & \text{if } p_k > p_c \\ 0, & \text{others} \end{cases} \tag{5}$$

The proposed method effectively combines the main texture information with local texture information. Thus, it not only substantially improves the feature extraction capability of the local binary operator, but also enhances the robustness of the local binary operator to noise (Table 3).

Table 1. Recognition accuracy of the algorithms on the three datasets (%)

Algorithms	SDUMLA	FV-USM	UTFVP
LLBP [3]	73	52.2	30
LBP [2]	56	48	70
ULBP [8]	67	57	80
LDP [4]	90	72	90
DBP	**90**	**72**	**90**
LOOP [7]	50	54	62.5
LGP [6]	85	65	87.5
GDP [5]	26	16	35

Table 2. EER of the algorithms on the three datasets

Algorithms	SDUMLA	FV-USM	UTFVP
LLBP [3]	0.097	0.153	0.148
LBP [2]	0.064	0.063	0.165
ULBP [8]	0.061	0.072	0.154
LDP [4]	0.046	0.066	0.109
DBP	**0.042**	**0.063**	**0.095**
LOOP [7]	0.082	0.068	0.157
LGP [6]	0.050	0.063	0.12
GDP [5]	0.088	0.132	0.167

Table 3. AUC of the algorithms on the three datasets

Algorithms	SDUMLA	FV-USM	UTFVP
LLBP [3]	0.944	0.909	0.876
LBP [2]	0.955	0.964	0.880
ULBP [8]	0.956	0.951	0.888
LDP [4]	0.963	0.991	0.920
DBP	0.965	**0.993**	**0.922**
LOOP [7]	0.943	0.952	0.910
LGP [6]	**0.967**	0.962	0.923
GDP [5]	0.951	0.929	0.886

4 Experiments

To verify the effectiveness of the proposed algorithm, we compare it with other representative local binary algorithms on three public finger vein datasets: FV-USM, UTFVP, and SDUMLA.

For the FV-USM and SDUMLA datasets, we chose 40 classifications, and used four images from six samples in the database as the training set, and two other images as the verification set, respectively. For UTFVP with a small number of samples, to reduce the impact of a large data throwing on the classification of the classifier, we chose 20 categories, and used two images of four samples from each category as the training set, and another two images as the validation set.

For the AUC and EER, 120 classifications of data from the three datasets were selected for measurement.

The FV-USM finger vein dataset was collected from 123 participants, including 83 men and 40 women, each one providing 4 fingers, for a total of 492 finger vein images. Each finger was sampled six times, resulting in six finger vein images, and each image with a size of 300×100 pixels and a depth of field of 8 bits. The database also contains ROI images that have already been captured and can be used directly.

The SDUMLA finger vein library includes 106 participants, each person providing three fingers - index, middle, and ring - and each finger was captured six times to form six finger vein images. Each image is 320×240 pixels in size.

The UTFVP finger vein database includes 60 participants, 44 males and 16 females, each one providing a total of 6 categories for the left and right hands including index, middle, and ring fingers. Each finger includes 4 finger vein images, and each image with a size of 672×380 pixels.

We tested the accuracy, EER, and AUC values of each algorithm on the three datasets using SVM. From Table 1, we can see that the proposed algorithm has a higher accuracy than other algorithms and is on par with LDP algorithm. However, the time complexity of the proposed algorithm in this paper is 20% better than the LDP algorithm. DBP performs better than other algorithms because it effectively extracts both local texture features and global image information. At the same time, the DBP algorithm has a

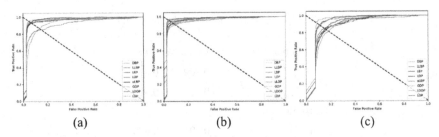

Fig. 2. ROC curves of each dataset ((a): FV-USM; (b): SDUMLA; (c): UTFVP)

good time complexity due to the small complexity of the mean and standard deviation calculation. GDP has the worst performance on the three datasets because the GDP algorithm is based on the Sobel descriptor, which is less descriptive for weak edge features such as finger veins. LOOP has a high recognition rate for small fine-grained images, but for other images, like finger vein images, it is not very good.

As can be seen from Table 2, the EER of the LGP and LDP algorithms considering the neighborhood pixel distribution are relatively high, which indicates that the information on the neighborhood pixel distribution is particularly important. The EER of the proposed algorithm DBP is significantly better than that of LBP and its improved algorithm, and it is also better than that of the improved algorithm LDP. This shows that the description of the classification accuracy of DBP is closer to the actual situation. The experiment also proves the advantage of DBP in the accuracy test. Meanwhile, the AUC value of DBP algorithm was not the best on each dataset, however, it is the most stable of all the algorithms tested. ROC curves for each dataset are shown as Fig. 2. From Fig. 2, we can see that all ROC curves of DBP are stable above 0.9, which further reflects that the accuracy of the proposed algorithm on these three datasets is closer to the real situation.

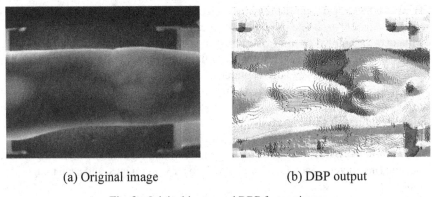

(a) Original image   (b) DBP output

Fig. 3. Original image and DBP feature image

To evaluate the robustness of the proposed algorithm for finger vein data and its effectiveness in the representation of main texture features, we tested the accuracy, EER, and AUC values of each algorithm on three datasets, respectively. The results are shown

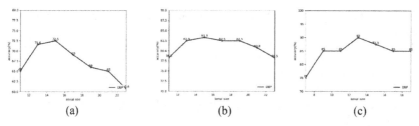

Fig. 4. The accuracy of the proposed algorithm under different kernal size

in Fig. 2. DBP feature extraction effect is shown in Fig. 3. Through the experiments, we found that the DBP algorithm has good robustness to all the tested datasets by adjusting the k-factor and the mask size of the algorithm. As shown in Fig. 4, after the experimental analysis, for FV-USM and SDUMLA, the best results are achieved when k is 0.6 and the kernal size is 15×15, while for UFTVP, the best results are achieved when the kernal size is 13×13. Morever, We selected 1288 image samples for further accuracy test on the LFW (Labeled Faces in the Wild) face dataset, and the recognition accuracy reached 81.37%. It is proved that the proposed algorithm is still effective on other dataset.

5   Conclusion

In this paper we proposed a new Discrete Binary Pattern (DBP), which further enhances the robustness of local binary descriptors to noise and enhances the ability of extracting global information of image. We compared its performance with the current representative local binary operators and their variants on several public finger vein datasets, and the result shows that the proposed algorithm is effective.

As a local binary operator, DBP can deal with the problem of weak edge feature extraction more deeply. Next, we plan to further improve the effectiveness of DBP by enhancing the representation of global image information.

Acknowledgments. This research is sponsored by the Key R&D Program of Science and Technology Development Plan of Jilin Province of China (No. 20200401103GX); the Key Program of Science and Technology Research during the 13th Five-Year Plan Period, the Educational Department of Jilin Province of China (No. JJKH20200680KJ, and No. JJKH20200677KJ); and the National Natural Science Foundation of China (No. 61806024).

References

1. Pujol, F.A., Jimeno-Morenilla, A., Sanchez-Romero, J.L.: Face recognition using a hybrid SVM–LBP approach and the Indian movie face database. Curr. Sci. **113**(5), 974–977 (2017)
2. Ojala, T., Pietikinen, M., Harwood, D.: Performance evaluation of texture measures with classification based on Kullback discrimination of distributions. In: Proceedings of ICPR (1994)
3. Rosdi, B.A., Shing, C.W., Suandi, S.A.: Finger vein recognition using local line binary pattern. Sensors **11**(12), 11357–11371 (2011)

4. Lee, E.C., Jung, H., Kim, D.: New finger biometric method using near infrared imaging. Sensors **11**(3), 2319–2333 (2011)
5. Ahmed, F.: Gradient directional pattern: a robust feature descriptor for facial expression recognition. Electron. Lett. **48**(19), 1203–1204 (2012)
6. Mohammad, S.I.: Local gradient pattern - a novel feature representation for facial expression recognition. J. AI Data Min. **2**(1), 33–38 (2014)
7. Chakraborti, T., McCane, B., Mills, S., Pal, U.: LOOP descriptor: local optimal-oriented pattern. IEEE Signal Process. Lett. **25**(5), 635–639 (2018)
8. Ming, Y., Wang, G., Fan, C.: Uniform local binary pattern based texture-edge feature for 3D human behavior recognition. PLoS ONE **10**(5), e0124640 (2015)
9. Hu, N., Ma H., Zhan, T.: Finger vein biometric verification using block multi-scale uniform local binary pattern features and block two-directional two-dimension principal component analysis. Optik **208**(30), 163664 (2018)
10. Niblack, W.: An introduction to digital image processing. In: Advances in Computer Graphics Vi, Images: Synthesis, Analysis, & Interaction. Prentice-Hall International, Japan (1986)

A Generalized Graph Features Fusion Framework for Finger Biometric Recognition

Hongxu Qu[1,2], Haigang Zhang[1(✉)], Jinfeng Yang[1], Zhitao Wu[2], and Liming He[3]

[1] Institute of Applied Artificial Intelligence of the Guangdong-Hong Kong-Macao Greater Bay Area, Shenzhen Polytechnic, Shenzhen 518055, China
{zhanghg,jfyang}@szpt.edu.cn
[2] College of Electronical and Information Engineering, University of Science and Technology Liaoning, Anshan 114051, China
[3] Shenzhen Mould-tip Injection Technology Company Limited, Shenzhen 518107, China

Abstract. The finger contains three compact biological features named fingerprint, finger-vein, and finger-knuckle-print. How to effectively integrate the biological characteristics of the three modalities is the key to improve the feature expression ability of the fingers. However, the scale inconsistency and feature expression differences of different modal images seriously limit the effectiveness of finger features fusion. In this paper, a new theoretical framework for finger multimodal feature fusion and recognition is explored, where graph convolutional neural network is the main network backbone. Converting the pixel and texture features of finger biometric modalities into graph structure data can eliminate the feature fusion restriction. We propose two feature fusion strategies: competitive fusion and eigenvector centrality fusion. The competitive fusion aims to fuse graph by connecting nodes with similar feature importance, where the eigenvector centrality fusion connects nodes with similar structural importance to fuse graph. The experimental results show that the fusion method proposed in this paper can achieve better performance in finger biometric recognition.

Keywords: Finger multimodal · Graph convolutional neural network · Feature fusion

1 Introduction

Fingers contain rich biometric information, and the unimodality of finger, especially fingerprint (FP), has been widely used in the field of biometric identifi-

This work was supported in part by the National Natural Science Foundation of China under Grant 61806208, in part by the General Higher Education Project of Guangdong Provincial Education Department under Grant 2020ZDZX3082, in part by the Rural Science and Technology Commissioner Project of Guangdong Provincial Science and Technology Department under Grant KPT20200220.

© Springer Nature Switzerland AG 2021
J. Feng et al. (Eds.): CCBR 2021, LNCS 12878, pp. 267–276, 2021.
https://doi.org/10.1007/978-3-030-86608-2_30

cation. Research in recent years has shown that finger-vein (FV) and finger-knuckle-print (FKP) both have excellent ability of identification [17]. Compared with other biometric carriers, finger features are relatively portable to obtain. Recently, finger unimodal biometrics encounters some technical difficulties. Every biometric trait has some theoretical upper bound in terms of its discrimination capability [2]. For example, FP and FKP both have the problem of vulnerability, loss and defilement, which significantly affects the stability of finger recognition [12]. Therefore, finger multimodal biometrics has received extensive attention [3]. Besides, exploring finger trimodal fusion recognition has the following technical advantages in implementation: (1) It is easy to collect the finger trimodal features since they are located tightly. (2) The finger's trimodal features are supplementary in identity representation. For example, FV can judge the living body. However, FP and FKP cannot. The feature images of FP and FKP are very clear, but the FV feature images are slightly worse. (3) FV, FP, and FKP have similar texture features, which lays the foundation for the development of unified image processing technology.

At present, finger trimodal fusion recognition still has two difficulties: (1) Image scale inconsistency [6]. The reason is that the trimodal features of finger have different characteristic shapes. The selection of the image scale during the feature collection process determined by the shape of characteristic. The straightforward scale normalization is easy to destroy image structure information. (2) Lack of a general feature expression method to extract the trimodal features of finger into a unified feature space. We are inspired by graph theory and aim to explore a method to express finger features with graph structure data, and construct a feature fusion framework based on graph convolutional neural networks (GCNs).

In this paper, a generalized fusion framework based on graph convolutional neural networks has been proposed for finger trimodal recognition. The main contributions of this work are as follows: (1) We utilize simple linear iterative clustering (SLIC) superpixel segmentation algorithm [15] to abstract finger trimodal feature into graph structure data. (2) We propose two new graph fusion methods named competitive fusion and eigenvector centrality fusion. Competitive fusion and eigenvector centrality fusion focus on node features and structural features respectively to deal with different types of graph structure data. (3) We design a parallel graph convolutional neural network structure to solve the problem of the uneven number of nodes in the finger trimodal graph cause by the inconsistency of the finger trimodal scale.

2   Related Work

2.1   Finger Fusion Recognition

Multimodal biometric fusion operation is carried out on four levels: pixel level, feature level, decision level, matching score level [1]. The fusion at pixel level refers to direct manipulation of input images. It is unstable and infeasible to make fusion for the multimodal biometrics of fingers at pixel level [6]. The fusion at matching score level and decision level are based on the matching score and recognition results of unimodal respectively. Ref. [17] shows related research on finger multimodal fusion recognition at the decision level. The fusion at feature level aims to express feature information more accurately by performing a series of processing on the biometric images. Ref. [6–8,17] introduce some finger multimodal fusion methods at feature level. It is worth noting that the development of deep learning provides new ideas for finger biometric multimodal fusion. Ref. [11] proposed a convolutional neural network framework for finger trimodal fusion and recognition.

2.2 Graph Convolutional Neural Network

Graph is composed of a number of given nodes and edges connecting pairs of nodes. As an image description method, nodes represent the information of different areas of image, and the edges represent the relationshape between different areas. The traditional convolution operations are not applicable to graph structured data. Therefore, researchers have introduced GCNs. The development of GCNs are divided into spatial and spectral domain. Spatial convolution is to perform convolution directly on the graph. Spectral convolution define convolution kernel at spectral domain and then convert back to the spatial domain by fourier transform. Ref. [9,20] proposed some influential models of spatial convolution, such as GraphSAGE, etc. Ref. [13,18] proposed the main models of spectral convolution, such as ChebNet, etc. With the development of GCNs, they are applied in many fields, such as computer vision [10], chemistry and biology [5], etc.

2.3 Graph Feature Extraction and Recognition

In the past few years, relevant scholars have put forward a global biometrics expression based on the graph model and achieve better results. Graph based global biometric expression can effectively solve the problem of inconsistencies in multimodal feature space of finger. Ref. [4] represented a blood vessel biometric sample of retina, palm vein and FV as a spatial graph. Minutiae points are selected as nodes of the graph, and blood vessel connections as edge sets. However, the image details are unstable, and image enhancement may produce false nodes. Ref. [22] proposed a method of constructing weighted triangulation graph based on feature similarity, and verified that the weighted graph can describe the FV feature well and has good recognition performance. Ref. [6] used triangulation graphs to express the feature information of FV, FP and FKP, and proposed two fusion frameworks to achieve better performance.

3   Multimodal Biometrics Fusion Framework

In this section, we introduce the graph fusion framework for finger trimodal recognition as shown in Fig. 1.

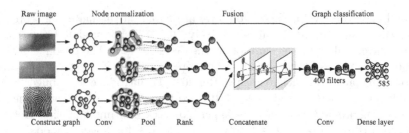

Fig. 1. The Schematic diagram of finger trimodal fusion recognition framework. Three input raw images are constructed as graph, and graphs are passed through parallel graph convolutional neural network. Then we sort nodes within every graph and fuse graphs together. Finally train the graph classification network.

3.1 Construction of Graphs

A weighted graph with N nodes can be expressed as $\mathbf{G} = (\mathbf{V}, \mathbf{E}, \mathbf{W})$, where $\mathbf{V} = \{v_i, v_2, ...v_N\}$ is the node set, $\mathbf{E} = \{e_{ij}\}$ represents the edge set, and $\mathbf{W}$ represents the weighted matrix of the edges, $w_{ij} \in \mathbf{W}$ is the weight of edge e_{ij}, The feature matrix is represented by $\mathbf{X} \in \mathbb{R}^{N \times F}$, $x_i \in \mathbb{R}^F$ is defined as the feature vector of the i-th node, and F is the dimension of the feature.

Here we use the SLIC-based method to select nodes and extract node features. The original images have been divide into many superpixel block by the SLIC. Each block forms a node. The node features are described as pixel intensity value and centroid coordinates. Similarity between nodes as the edge weight. Firstly, SLIC method converts the original image to the CIELAB color space, where the brightness, color value (L, a, b) and space coordinates (x, y) of each pixel compose a five dimensional vector (L, a, b, x, y). We set k initial cluster centers $c_i = [l_i, a_i, b_i, x_i, y_i]^\mathrm{T}$ in the image. Each pixel will be assigned to a cluster center. Then the color distance d_c and the spatial distance d_s between the searched pixel and the cluster are combined to obtain the final distance D:

$$d_c = \sqrt{(l_j - l_i)^2 + (a_j - a_i)^2 + (b_j - b_i)^2} \tag{1}$$

$$d_s = \sqrt{(x_j - x_i)^2 + (y_j - y_i)^2} \tag{2}$$

$$D = \sqrt{(d_c/N_c)^2 + (d_s/N_s)^2} \tag{3}$$

where $N_s = \sqrt{N/k}$ is the maximum spatial distance within the class, N is the total number of pixels, and N_c is the maximum color distance. N_c is set to a constant to balance the relative importance between color similarity and spatial similarity.

Each super pixel block is constructed as a node. The pixel intensity value $M_{sp} = \sum_{n-1}^{N_i} p_n/255N_i$, and centroid coordinates $C_{sp} = (x_i, y_i)/S_{max}$, where N_i represents the total number of pixels in the i-th superpixel block, p_n is the pixel value of each pixel, and S_{max} is the maximum image size. Since these two features have different scales, standardization processing is used here to obtain the final node features $x_i = [M_{sp}, C_{sp}]$.

The pixel intensity and the position information are combined together to determine the similarity of nodes. Therefore, the weight between nodes can be obtained by the similarity between node features:

$$s_{ij} = exp(-\frac{\|x_i - x_j\|_2^2}{\sigma^2}) \tag{4}$$

where s_{ij} is the similarity between node features, x_i and x_j are the feature vector of node i and j respectively, σ is a constant value between 0 and 1. Then, we construct K-nearest neighbor graph.

3.2 Node Normalization

In the process of graph fusion, the graph with different sizes will greatly affect the fusion of finger trimodal features. We construct a parallel graph convolutional neural network. Each branch included the graph convolution layer and pooling layer. Graph convolution layer extract local substructure features. We use DIFFPOOL [16] to normalize the number of nodes in the graph. DIFFPOOL is a differentiable graph pooling module, which uses a graph neural network to extract information, and then uses another graph neural network to obtain the assignment matrix. Assignment matrix indicates how much weight each node in the upper layer is assigned to the nodes in the next layer. Each branch network has the same network structure shown in Fig. 2.

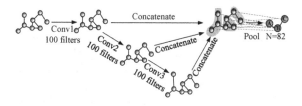

Fig. 2. The structure of a branch of the parallel graph convolutional neural network.

3.3 Fusion Frameworks

In this section, we propose two fusion frameworks of finger trimodal features.

Competitive Fusion. In graphs composed of different finger modalities, each node has different feature and structural information. In other words, each node plays a different role in the graph. In order to fuse finger trimodal graph effectively, a natural idea is to merge nodes that play similar roles. However, between graphs of different modalities, nodes that play similar role are not in a one-to-one correspondence in the original node sequence. To fuse nodes with similar role, the nodes need to be sorted according to certain rule, which can extract certain characteristics of nodes.

The graphs that we construct have a set of nodes, $\mathbf{X} = \{\boldsymbol{x}_1, \boldsymbol{x}_2, ..., \boldsymbol{x}_N\}$, $\boldsymbol{x}_i \in \mathbb{R}^F$. $\mathbf{A} \in \mathbb{R}^{N \times N}$ is the adjacency matrix, where N is the number of nodes, F is the number of features in each node. The competitive fusion framework pays attention to the feature information of nodes. We design a rule to rank the feature importance of nodes:

$$s = rank(\sum_{j=1}^{F} rank(\boldsymbol{x}^j)) \tag{5}$$

where $rank()$ is the rank operation that can return the sequence of the elements within input vector. $\boldsymbol{x}^j$ represents features of all nodes in channel j. $\boldsymbol{s}$ is the new sequence of nodes obtained by the competitive fusion framework. Then the finger trimodal graphs can be integrated according to the obtained sequence $\boldsymbol{s}$.

Then, we use the resulting arrangement sequence to perform graph fusion. We take FV and FP as an example:

$$\mathbf{X}_{fusion} = \mathbf{X}_{fv}(\boldsymbol{s}_1) || \mathbf{X}_{fp}(\boldsymbol{s}_2) \tag{6}$$

$$\mathbf{A}_{fusion} = \mathbf{A}_{fv}(\boldsymbol{s}_1) + \mathbf{A}_{fp}(\boldsymbol{s}_2) \tag{7}$$

where $||$ is the connect operation, $\mathbf{X}_{fv}(\boldsymbol{s}_1)$ represents the node feature matrix of FV sorted by $\boldsymbol{s}_1$, and $\mathbf{X}_{fp}(\boldsymbol{s}_2)$ represents the node feature matrix of FP sorted by $\boldsymbol{s}_2$. $\mathbf{X}_{fusion}$ is the node feature matrix after fusion. $\mathbf{A}_{fv}(\boldsymbol{s}_1)$ and $\mathbf{A}_{fp}(\boldsymbol{s}_2)$ represent the adjacency matrices of FV and FP after sorting. $\mathbf{A}_{fusion}$ is the adjacency matrix after fusion.

Eigenvector Centrality Fusion. We are inspired by the work of Bonacich [14] and the eigenvector centrality use for node sorting. Eigenvector centrality is a statistical way of measuring a node's role in a graph. The node degree is not necessarily sufficient to measure the importance of a node in a graph. Because the node degree does not consider the importance of neighbors, so we use a more powerful method which is known as eigenvector centrality. Different from node degree, eigenvector centrality takes into account of how influential a node's neighbors are. Then the node's eigenvector centrality e_i is defined as a recurrence relation in which the node's centrality is proportional to the average centrality of its neighbors:

$$e_i = \frac{1}{\lambda} \sum_{j \in V} a_{ij} e_j \tag{8}$$

where a_{ij} represents the relation between node i and node j. If node i is not connected to node j, then $a_{ij} = 0$. We can rewrite Eq. (8) in matrix form:

$$\lambda e = \mathbf{A} e \tag{9}$$

The centrality vector e is the eigenvector of the adjacency matrix $\mathbf{A}$ associated with the eigenvalue λ. From Eq. (9), we can see that eigenvector centrality can express the structural information of the node. It is wise to choose the largest eigenvalue in absolute value of matrix $\mathbf{A}$ as λ. Based on virtue of Perron-Frobenius theorem, this choice guarantees the following desirable property: if $\mathbf{A}$ is irreducible, then the eigenvector solution e is both unique and positive.

One perspective of eigenvector centrality is that it ranks the likelihood that a node is visited on a random walk of infinite length on the graph. This view can be illustrated that we can use power method to solve the eigenvector centrality problem [21].

$$e^{(t+1)} = \mathbf{A}e^{(t)} \tag{10}$$

After obtaining the eigenvector centrality, we can sort the centrality for each node. From another perspective, this also sort nodes based on their structural importance. So that nodes with similar structural information can be fused.

$$s = rank(e) \tag{11}$$

where s is the new ordering of nodes obtained by the eigenvector centrality strategy. We can repeat the operation of the matrix connection.

4   Experimental Results

In this section, we present the experimental results of the proposed graph fusion frameworks for finger trimodal recognition. In our homemade finger trimodal database [6], there are 17550 images in total from 585 fingers. Each modality collects 5850 pictures. For one finger of one category, we collect 10 images. The training set, validation set, and test set are allocated at a ratio of 8:1:1.

4.1   Unimodal Recognition

Here we verify the recognition results of the three modalities respectively. In the experiment, the structure and parameters of the graph neural network are shown in Fig. 2. We choose the softmax as the classifier. The loss function is negative Log Likelihood Loss. The optimizer is Adam. Each training batch has 24 samples. Learning rate is set to 0.0001.

The number of superpixel numbers of the SLIC algorithm for the establishment of a graph is an important parameter. Different superpixel numbers will result in the different number of nodes in the graph, which will have an impact on the performance of finger trimodal recognition. Table 1 shows experiment results of different number of the superpixel. We can see that the graph convolutional neural network has achieved good results in the recognition of finger single modality. Especially for FV recognition, the accuracy rate reached 99.4% at 200sp. It can be concluded from the result that choosing 200sp or 300sp can provide the better performance for each modality. In the following trimodal fusion experiment, we will choose 200sp to achieve better performance.

Table 1. Recognition accuracy for finger unimodal recognition.

Pattern	100sp	200sp	300sp	400sp	500sp
FV (%)	97.4	99.4	98.9	98.5	98.1
FKP (%)	95.2	98.5	98.1	98.7	97.9
FP (%)	93.5	93.6	93.9	92.0	91.8

4.2 Trimodal Fusion Recognition

This section shows the performance of finger trimodal recognition under different fusion strategies. The training parameters are consistent in the experiment of unimodal recognition. To verify the stable and robust performance of the fusion frameworks, we add two types of noises: feature noise and structure noise with 0 as the mean and 1 as the variance. Firstly, we compare the competitive fusion framework and eigenvector centrality fusion framework with the direct connection fusion with data without noise. Connection fusion use the original node sequence to fuse. In addition, we conduct some comparison experiments between the proposed fusion methods and two fusion strategies in this paper. We select score fusion and input fusion, and put them under the backbone of the graph convolutional neural network to do experiments. Input fusion constructs trimodal into graph with the same scale, and fuse them before sending them to network [6]. Figure 3(a) shows the ROC curve of the five fusion strategies. We can see the proposed fusion frameworks have better performance.

Then, we use the data with noise for training, and compare the stability of competitive fusion and eigenvector centrality fusion under different types of data sets. Figure 3(b) and Fig. 3(c) show the ROC curve. Under the data set containing feature noise, the performance of direct connection fusion and competitive fusion become a bit worse. The performance of score fusion and input fusion is greatly affected by feature noise. Because competitive fusion strengthens the node feature and offset the feature noise to a certain extent. The performance of competitive fusion is stronger than that of direct connection fusion. Eigenvector centrality fusion focuses on mining structural features, which avoids the feature noise of the graph in the fusion process. So the eigenvector centrality fusion can achieve better performance. Similarly, competitive fusion has better performance under the data set with structure noise. Table 2 presents the accuracy and EER which prove the above analysis.

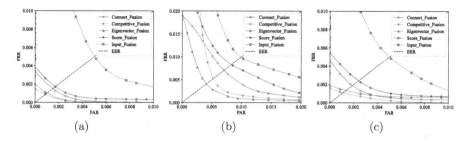

Fig. 3. ROC curve under different noise. (a) Data without noise. (b) Data with feature noise. (c) Data with structure noise.

Table 2. Comparison results for the trimodal biometrics under different noise.

Fusion method	Without noise		With feature noise		With structure noise	
	EER (10^{-2})	Acc (%)	EER (10^{-2})	Acc (%)	EER (10^{-2})	Acc (%)
Input fusion [6]	0.43	96.1	0.95	82.4	0.53	94.6
Score fusion [19]	0.15	99.4	0.84	94.1	0.18	97.4
Connect fusion	0.13	99.4	0.71	93.4	0.17	98.1
Competitive fusion	0.06	99.6	0.45	95.3	0.10	99.1
Eigenvector fusion	0.04	99.7	0.33	98.5	0.11	98.9

5 Conclusion

In this paper, two generalized graph fusion frameworks are provided to get more stabile and better recognition performance. These two methods are considered from the perspective of graph features and graph structure, so as to adapt to different data sets. A weighted graph construction method based on SLIC has been established, which can solve the problem of feature space does not match. In experiment, a homemade finger trimodal dataset has been applied to demonstrate the better performance of the proposed method.

References

1. Jain, A.K., Ross, A., Prabhakar, S.: An introduction to biometric recognition. IEEE Trans. Circ. Syst. Video Technol. **14**(1), 4–20 (2004)
2. Jain, A.K., Ross, A.: Multibiometric systems. Commun. ACM **47**(1), 34–40 (2004)
3. Ross, A., Jain, A.: Information fusion in biometrics. Pattern Recogn. Lett. **24**(13), 2115–2125 (2003)
4. Arakala, A., Davis, S.A., Hao, H., Horadam, K.J.: Value of graph topology in vascular biometrics. IET Biom. **6**(2), 117–125 (2017)
5. Dai, H., Li, C., Coley, C.W., Dai, B., Song, L.: Retrosynthesis prediction with conditional graph logic network. arXiv preprint arXiv:2001.01408 (2020)
6. Zhang, H., Li, S., Shi, Y., Yang, J.: Graph fusion for finger multimodal biometrics. IEEE Access **7**, 28607–28615 (2019)

7. Yang, J., Zhong, Z., Jia, G., Li, Y.: Spatial circular granulation method based on multimodal finger feature. J. Electr. Comput. Eng. 1–7 (2016)
8. Yang, J., Zhang, X.: Feature-level fusion of fingerprint and finger-vein for personal identification. Pattern Recogn. Lett. **33**(5), 623–628 (2012)
9. Gilmer, J., Schoenholz, S.S., Riley, P.F., Vinyals, O., Dahl, G.E.: Neural message passing for quantum chemistry. In: International Conference on Machine Learning, pp. 1263–1272. PMLR (2017)
10. Chen, J., Pan, L., Wei, Z., Wang, X., Ngo, C.-W., Chua, T.-S.: Zero-shot ingredient recognition by multi-relational graph convolutional network. In: Proceedings of the AAAI Conference on Artificial Intelligence, vol. 34, pp. 10542–10550 (2020)
11. Wang, L., Zhang, H., Yang, J.: Finger multimodal features fusion and recognition based on CNN. In: 2019 IEEE Symposium Series on Computational Intelligence (SSCI), pp. 3183–3188. IEEE (2019)
12. Singh, M., Singh, R., Ross, A.: A comprehensive overview of biometric fusion. Information Fusion **52**(i), 187–205 (2019)
13. Defferrard, M., Bresson, X., Vandergheynst, P.: Convolutional neural networks on graphs with fast localized spectral filtering. In: Advances in Neural Information Processing Systems (NIPS), pp. 3844–3852 (2016)
14. Bonacich, P.: Power and centrality: a family of measures. Am. J. Sociol. **92**(5), 1170–1182 (2012)
15. Achanta, R., Shaji, A., Smith, K., Lucchi, A., Fua, P., Süsstrunk, S.: SLIC super-pixels compared to state-of-the-art superpixel methods. IEEE Trans. Pattern Anal. Mach. Intell. **34**(11), 2274–2282 (2012)
16. Ying, R., Morris, C., Hamilton, W.L., You, J., Ren, X., Leskovec, J.: Hierarchical graph representation learning with differentiable pooling. In: Advances in Neural Information Processing Systems, December 2018, pp. 4800–4810 (2018)
17. Khellat-Kihel, S., Abrishambaf, R., Monteiro, J.L., Benyettou, M.: Multimodal fusion of the finger vein, fingerprint and the finger-knuckle-print using Kernel Fisher analysis. Appl. Soft Comput. J. **42**, 439–447 (2016)
18. Kipf, T.N., Welling, M.: Semi-supervised classification with graph convolutional networks. In: 5th International Conference on Learning Representations, ICLR 2017 - Conference Track Proceedings, pp. 1–14 (2017)
19. Patil, V.H., Dhole, S.A.: An efficient secure multimodal biometric fusion using palm print and face image. Int. J. Appl. Eng. Res. **11**(10), 7147–7150 (2016)
20. Hamilton, W.L., Ying, R., Leskovec, J.: Inductive representation learning on large graphs. arXiv preprint arXiv:1706.02216 (2017)
21. Hamilton, W.L.: Graph representation learning. In: Synthesis Lectures on Artificial Intelligence and Machine Learning, vol. 14, no. 3, pp. 1–159 (2020)
22. Ye, Z., Yang, J., Palancar, J.H.: Weighted graph based description for finger-vein recognition. In: Zhou, J., et al. (eds.) CCBR 2017. LNCS, vol. 10568, pp. 370–379. Springer, Cham (2017). https://doi.org/10.1007/978-3-319-69923-3_40

A STN-Based Self-supervised Network for Dense Fingerprint Registration

Yang Yu, Haixia Wang$^{(\boxtimes)}$, Yilong Zhang, and Peng Chen

College of Computer Science and Technology, Zhejiang University of Technology,
Hangzhou, China
hxwang@zjut.edu.cn

Abstract. Dense fingerprint registration in the preprocessing stage plays a vital role in the subsequent fingerprint fusion, mosaic, and recognition. However, the existing conventional methods are limited by handcraft features, while the methods based on deep learning lack a large amount of ground truth displacement fields. To overcome these limitations, we propose a self-supervised learning model to directly output densely registered fingerprints. With a spatial transformation network (STN) connected after fully convolutional network (FCN), image deformation interpolation can be achieved to obtain the registered image. Self-supervised training is achieved by maximizing the similarity of images, without the need for ground truth displacement fields. We evaluate the proposed model on publicly available datasets of internal-external fingerprint image pairs. The results demonstrate that the accuracy of the model is comparable to that of the conventional fingerprint registration while executing orders of magnitude faster.

Keywords: Fingerprint registration · Self-supervised · Convolutional networks

1 Introduction

Fingerprint-based personal identification has been used since centuries ago, owning to their distinctiveness and stability [1]. In the process of fingerprint recognition, fingerprint registration has been widely applied and become a key step. For conventional fingerprints, registration pre recognition helps to increase the recognition accuracy [2]. With skin distortion and aging, internal fingerprints [3] which are measured under the skin, are complement to conventional external fingerprints. Internal fingerprint and external fingerprint registration is conducive to the subsequent fingerprint matching, fusion, stitching and so on [4].

Fingerprint registration refers to the effect of removing distortion by estimating the geometric transformation between two fingerprints [4]. This is an important and difficult stage before fingerprint recognition. According to the effect of fingerprint registration, the existing registration techniques can be roughly divided into sparse-coarse registration and dense-fine registration. Although a variety of registration alignment algorithms have been proposed, dense-fine registration remains an unresolved and challenging problem [5]. Most previous fingerprint registration algorithms used matching minutiae pairs or

© Springer Nature Switzerland AG 2021
J. Feng et al. (Eds.): CCBR 2021, LNCS 12878, pp. 277–286, 2021.
https://doi.org/10.1007/978-3-030-86608-2_31

other features and the corresponding spatial transformation model to realize image registration [6, 7]. However, these methods are obviously limited by the number of minutiae or feature points. The fingerprint minutiae distribution is often sparse and uneven, and it is difficult to extract reliable minutiae from low-quality fingerprints. Therefore, we usually call these methods sparse-coarse fingerprint registration methods. In contrast to them, dense-fine registration refers to finding the pixel-level displacement between two fingerprints directly by some methods, without relying on sparse feature points.

Undoubtedly, it is a great challenge for fingerprint images to find the pixel-level deformation field directly. Firstly, fingerprints are different from ordinary images. They are formed by numerous simple lines (valleys and ridges). This makes fingerprints have strong local self-similarity. Thus it is difficult to find the true mate among many highly similar non-mated regions. Secondly, noise will lead to changes in ridge patterns. This makes it possible to miss the true mate. Faced with these difficult challenges, some traditional-based registration methods [8–10] have provided better registration results in recent years. However, in the case of high fingerprint distortion and poor fingerprint quality, the registration performance of these algorithms is still limited. Inspired by the achievements of deep learning in the field of stereo matching and medical image registration, some researchers currently proposed to use deep learning architecture to solve fingerprint dense-fine registration [11–13]. To train an end-to-end network, they need sufficient pairs of mated fingerprints and corresponding dense displacement filed. Unfortunately, acquiring a large size of ground truth data of displacement fields from challenging mated fingerprints manually is a gigantic task. To solve this problem, we combine STN network [14] with convolution network. It can replace the network's demand for a large number of true deformation field data by self-learning the similarity between paired fingerprint images. The main contributions of this paper are as follows:

1) A self-supervised learning model is proposed to directly output densely registered fingerprints in an end-to-end manner.
2) The self-supervised network training mode combines FCN and STN to replace a large number of complicated manual truth labeling processes.

The rest of this paper is organized as follows: Sect. 2 introduces the related fingerprint registration works, Sect. 3 describes the details of the proposed approach and Sect. 4 reports the experiments evaluated. Finally, we draw our conclusion in Sect. 5.

2 Related Work

2.1 Sparse Minutiae Registration of Fingerprints

A number of approaches for minutia-based registration have been proposed in the previous literatures. Zhao et al. [6] presented a minutia-based fingerprint registration method that considers local and global structures. The use of both the local and global transformation parameters makes their algorithm be able to tolerate, to some extent, the nonlinear deformation. In the follow-up research, Thin-plate spline (TPS) model was introduced to deal with the elastic distortion of fingerprints [15], and it is still widely used in recent years. Literatures [5, 9, 11] combined the matching feature point pairs obtained by traditional methods with TPS as the initial coarse registration step of the proposed algorithm. Paulino et al. [7] used a robust alignment algorithm (descriptor-based Hough transform) to align fingerprints and measures similarity between fingerprints by considering both minutiae and orientation field information. However, these methods are sensitive to ridge skeleton error, which is very common in poor quality fingerprints [12].

2.2 Dense Pixel-Level Registration of Fingerprints

In order to optimize sparse-coarse registration based on minutiae pairs, Si et al. [8] put forward the concept of dense fingerprint registration for the first time. They proposed a novel dense fingerprint registration algorithm, which consists of a composite initial registration step and a dual-resolution block-based registration step. However, the calculation of image correlation is very time consuming. Cui et al. [9] developed a phase-based fingerprint registration method by extending the method of phase demodulation from communication area. They use fingerprint patterns that look like two-dimensional cosine waves, which is a very interesting idea. The fly in the ointment is that the algorithm is still obviously limited by the low quality of fingerprints. In 2019, Lan et al. [10] presented a model-based non-rigid fingerprint registration by combining orientation fields with the traditional model-based method. The following year, aiming at solving the situation that both translation and deformation exist at the same time, they presented a combined registration algorithm based on correlation and the orientation field [16]. Yu et al. [3] also used digital correlation of images for dense-fine registration of fingerprints collected by multi-sensors. In the last two years, deep learning methods have been gradually introduced into the field of fingerprint registration. Cui et al. [11, 12] used displacement regression network to directly regress displacement from fingerprint image. Gu et al. [13] trained a Siamese network to estimate the geometric transformation. The method based on deep learning can greatly improve the speed. However, the existing methods are based on supervised learning and need a lot of ground truth data, which is undoubtedly difficult to obtain.

3 Proposed Registration Method

The flowchart of the proposed method is shown in Fig. 1. Compared with supervised learning, the registration method based on self-supervised learning only needs to provide fingerprints pairs and does not need labels (i.e. real displacement fields) when training learning networks. With the introduction of STN [14], CNN has the ability of spatial transformation. It can be inserted into the existing convolutional neural network structure. STN is directly connected to the deep learning network, and the input image is deformed by the obtained displacement field to obtain the registered image. During training, the loss function value is calculated by using the registered image and the reference image, and it is propagated back and optimized continuously.

3.1 Registration Network

The registration network is mainly divided into regression network, grid generator and sampler.

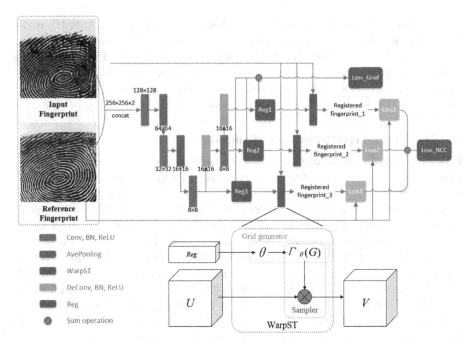

Fig. 1. Flowchart of the proposed method. (Color figure online)

The regression network uses a fully convolutional network structure. The inputs of the network are the image to be registered and the reference image, which are concatenated into a two-channel image. In order to retain the size of the feature map, all convolutional layers use edge padding. In the network, four convolutional layers are applied as shown by the blue modules in Fig. 1; each contains a convolution with a kernel size of 3 × 3 and a stride of 2, a batch normalization and a ReLU activation. Each of the first two convolutional layers is followed by an average-pooling layer to expand the receptive field of the network. Each of the last two convolutional layers is followed by a deconvolutional layer with a kernel size of 3 × 3 and a stride of 2. There are three regression layers presented in this network to predict the spatial transformation parameters. They are after the last two convolutional layers and the last deconvolutional layer, respectively. Each regression layer consists of a convolution with a kernel size of 3 × 3, a stride of 1, and an output channel of 2. Thus, the outputs of the network are three sets of spatial transformation parameters, whose scales are 8 × 8, 8 × 8, and 16 × 16. We use three regression layers to achieve multi-resolution fingerprint image registration. Among them, 8 × 8 registration point pairs are relatively sparse (learning coarse registration). In contrast, 16 × 16 is relatively dense (learning fine registration).

The output of each regression layer is input into the corresponding WarpST module together with the image to be registered. Each WarpST module consists of a grid generator and a sampler. The grid generator constructs each set of spatial transformation parameters into a sampling grid. The sampling grid represents a spatial mapping relationship between the registered image and the reference image. The size and interval of the sampling grid are determined by the input image and the spatial transformation parameters. Based on the different sampling grid, the sampler registers the images using bicubic interpolation. U is the image to be registered, and V is the image after registration.

3.2 Loss Function

The loss is weighted by three sets of spatial transformation losses, which includes normalized cross-correlation loss and smoothing loss:

$$L = \sum_{i=1}^{3} \lambda_i (L_{ncc} + L_{smooth}). \tag{1}$$

In our experiment, λ_1, λ_2, and λ_3 are set to 0.7, 0.2 and 0.1 respectively.

The normalized cross-correlation loss L_{ncc} is obtained from the between the reference image T and the registered image R. The formula is defined as follows:

$$L_{ncc} = \frac{\frac{1}{mn} \sum_{i=1}^{m} \sum_{j=1}^{n} (T_{x,y}(i,j) - \overline{T}_{x,y})(R(i,j) - \overline{R})}{\sqrt{\frac{1}{mn} \sum_{i=1}^{m} \sum_{j=1}^{n} (T_{x,y}(i,j) - \overline{T}_{x,y})^2} \sqrt{\frac{1}{mn} \sum_{i=1}^{m} \sum_{j=1}^{n} (R(i,j) - \overline{R})^2}}, \tag{2}$$

where $\overline{T}_{x,y}$ and $\overline{R}$ represent the respective image means, m and n refer to the image width and height respectively.

The smoothing loss L_{smooth} is calculated from the gradient of the spatial transformation parameters by the regression network.

$$L_{smooth} = \sum \left(\left| \nabla^x (M_{reg}) \right|_1 + \left| \nabla^y (M_{reg}) \right|_1 \right), \tag{3}$$

where M_{reg} is the regression map of the network output. ∇^x and ∇^y represents the gradient of regression map in the x direction and y direction. $| \ |_1$ represents a norm between them.

4 Experiments and Results

The experiments are performed on a computer with an Intel Core CPU i9-10900X and a NVIDIA GeForce GTX2080Ti with 11G memory. The training and evaluating of network are based on the Tensorflow 1.13.1.

4.1 Dataset

In order to evaluate the performance of the proposed approach, we used the dataset in reference [3]. In this paper, they first proposed a multi-sensor fingerprint registration method for TIR and OCT. In order to adapt to the training of the network, the effective fingerprint area of 500 * 500 size is firstly intercepted from the original data set, and then compressed into an image of 256 * 256 size by the imresize function of Matlab. Among them, TIR fingerprint refers to the fingerprint collected by traditional pressing optics. OCT fingerprint refers to the internal fingerprint under finger skin obtained based on optical coherence tomography (OCT) [17, 18]. OCT fingerprint is affected by acquisition equipment and acquisition methods, and there is a relative deformation between OCT fingerprint and TIR fingerprint acquired synchronously. For this reason, they put forward a registration algorithm based on generative adversarial network and digital image correlation for dense registration of two types of fingerprints. The data we use in the experiments comes from the fingerprint pairs registered by this method. This set of data is chosen because the goal of fine registration in this paper is for the complete fusion of internal and external fingerprints. Other fingerprint databases are also suitable for this network after coarse registration. Notably, the experimental fingerprint pairs with relative deformation are obtained by the following operations on the basis of the above data.

Firstly, 110 pairs of data are selected from total internal reflection fingerprint and optical coherence tomography fingerprint. Among them, 70 groups were used as the initial data of the training set, and 40 groups were used as tests. Then, some simulated deformation fields are randomly generated and added to TIR fingerprint images to increase the generation of deformed fingerprint pairs. The construction of the simulated deformation field can be realized by uniformly sampling the TIR fingerprint image data of 256 * 256 sizes at 16 * 16 coordinate points, and then automatically and randomly adjusting the abscissa and ordinate values of these coordinate points. In addition to this form of data augmentation, any fingerprint pair without huge deformation can also be used to train and test the network.

These simulated deformed fingerprint pairs were used for two experiments. For the first experiment in Sect. 4.3.1, to verify the registration effect between deformed TIR and OCT fingerprints. OCT fingerprints are taken as the reference images and the deformed TIR fingerprint as the input image to be registered. Each of these 70 TIR fingerprints contains 60 kinds of deformation fields, with a total of 4200 kinds of deformation fields (4200 sets of training data). For the test data set, each of the 40 fingerprints contains 14 kinds of deformation fields, including 560 kinds of deformation fields (560 sets of test data). And for the experiment in Sect. 4.3.1, to verify the registration effect between registration between deformed TIR and standard TIR fingerprints (original TIR fingerprint before deformation). Similarly, we used 2100 kinds of deformation fields as training sets and 280 kinds as test sets.

4.2 Training Parameters

The Adadelta is utilized optimizer to train our networks and the initial learning rate lr are set to 0.0001. The batch size is 10 and the input size of network is 256 × 256. We train the network with 250 epochs and select the best evaluation model.

4.3 Results

The proposed registration method is compared with a non-rigid dense-fine fingerprint method (OFD) [10] and the method proposed in [3]. We evaluate the image similarity of reference fingerprints and the registered fingerprints to side reflect the registration accuracy. Two indicators, structural similarity index (SSIM) [19] and correlation coefficient (CC) [20] are adopted. Their values close to 1 lead to high similarity. Fingerprint matching is not the main goal of this paper. The purpose of this paper is to propose an end-to-end self-supervised network with fine registration to prepare for the subsequent fingerprint fusion.

4.3.1 Registration Between Deformed TIR and OCT Fingerprints

Simulated and real deformed fingerprint pairs are used to carry out two experiments in this part. Firstly, the simulated deformed fingerprint pairs are used to carry out the following first experiment. This group of data comes from the data augmentation method mentioned in Sect. 4.1. OCT fingerprints are taken as reference images, and register TIR fingerprint with various deformation fields to be close to OCT fingerprint. Some of their registration results of TIR and OCT fingerprints are shown in Fig. 2. The quantitative values of SSIM and CC are show in Table 1. Obviously, the network designed in this paper can realize fingerprint distortion correction, and the registration accuracy is similar to OFD algorithm. Note that the average running time of our algorithm is only 0.016 s, which is about one-tenth of that of OFD algorithm. Figure 3(a) further shows the image correlation coefficient distributions by these registration methods.

Table 1. Registration accuracy

Method	Similarity indicator	
	SSIM	CC
No registration	0.5710	0.5749
Lan et al. [10] (OFD)	0.7306	0.7360
Proposed method	**0.7271**	**0.7328**

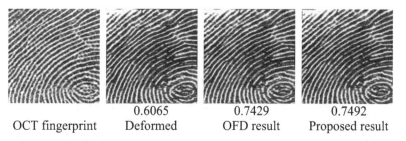

	0.6065	0.7429	0.7492
OCT fingerprint	Deformed	OFD result	Proposed result

Fig. 2. Registration results and (the values below are CC values).

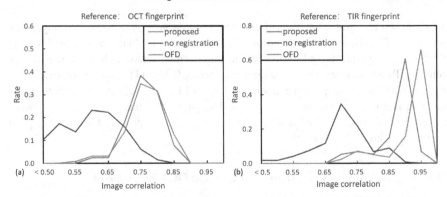

Fig. 3. Image correlation coefficient distributions of the algorithms for (a) deformed TIR and OCT fingerprints; (b) deformed TIR and standard TIR fingerprints.

Secondly, the fingerprint with real deformation field is used to test the generalization ability of the model. In this group of experiments, the network model trained by the above experiments is used and the parameters are fixed. Then 600 sets of internal and external fingerprint pairs after coarse registration by GAN + F-DIC + OR method mentioned in reference [3] are used to test the model.

The proposed method is compared with the combination of GAN and two-step registration method proposed in [3]. Table 2 shows the results of comparative experiments. Note that, in this experiment, the external fingerprint (TIR fingerprint) is regarded as the reference image while the OCT fingerprint is used as the image to be registered, which is different with the training setting. This proves the generalization ability of the proposed network.

Table 2. Registration accuracy

Method	Similarity indicator	
	SSIM	CC
No registration	0.5194	0.5335
Yu et al. [3]	0.5919	0.6137
Proposed method	**0.5942**	**0.6162**

4.3.2 Registration Between Deformed TIR and Standard TIR Fingerprints

Even after correction by algorithm [3], there are still differences between OCT fingerprint and TIR fingerprint due to different acquisition sensors and insufficient registration accuracy. In order to show the registration effect of the algorithm more concretely, we conducted the second experiment. In this experiment, TIR fingerprint without deformation field is used as reference image. We use network and OFD algorithm to achieve the effect of distortion removal as much as possible. The registration results are shown in Fig. 4. Figure 3(b) shows the image correlation coefficient distributions under the experimental conditions. Obviously, OFD algorithm is superior to this algorithm under this experimental condition. However, the performance of this algorithm may be improved by increasing the amount of training data, the deformation field and adjusting the number of training iterations.

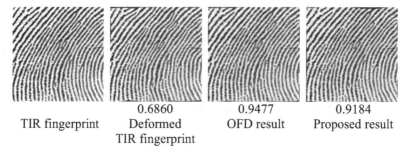

| TIR fingerprint | 0.6860
Deformed
TIR fingerprint | 0.9477
OFD result | 0.9184
Proposed result |

Fig. 4. Registration results (the values below are CC values).

5   Conclusion

In this paper, we propose a self-supervised learning model to achieve dense registration of fingerprints. STN-based network can be conncccted to the end of deep learning network, and transform the input image according to the regression displacement field, so as to realize self-supervised network registration. This method does not need a large amount of ground truth displacement field data. Compared with the existing fingerprint dense-fine registration, their registration performance is equivalent, but the speed is several orders of magnitude higher. However, our algorithm still has some shortcomings. Because of its unsupervised nature, it needs more training data to improve its learning ability. Only in this way can we obtain better and higher registration accuracy. Future research includes the improvement of network performance and the design of coarse-to-fine registration with network.

Acknowledgments. This work was supported in part by Natural Science Foundation of Zhejiang Province under Grant LY19F050011, National Natural Science Foundation of China under Grant 61976189, 61905218, 62076220, and Fundamental Research Funds for the Provincial Universities of Zhejiang under grant RF-C2019001.

References

1. Lee, H.C., Gaensslen, R.E. (eds.): Advances in Fingerprint Technology. Elsevier, New York (1991)
2. Novikov, S.O., Ushmaev, O.S.: Effect of elastic deformation registration in fingerprint identification. Pattern Recognit. Image Anal. **16**(1), 15–18 (2006)
3. Yu, Y., Wang, H., Chen, P., et al.: A new approach to external and internal fingerprint registration with multisensor difference minimization. IEEE Trans. Biometrics Behav. Identity Sci. **2**(4), 363–376 (2020)
4. Maltoni, D., Maio, D., Jain, A.K., Prabhakar, S.: Handbook of Fingerprint Recognition. Springer, London (2009). https://doi.org/10.1007/978-1-84882-254-2
5. Cui, Z., Feng, J., Zhou, J.: Dense fingerprint registration via displacement regression network. In: 2019 International Conference on Biometrics (ICB), pp. 1–8. IEEE (2019)
6. Zhao, D., Su, F., Cai, A.: Fingerprint registration using minutia clusters and centroid structure 1. In: 18th International Conference on Pattern Recognition (ICPR 2006), Hong Kong, pp. 413–416 (2006)
7. Paulino, A.A., Feng, J., Jain, A.K.: Latent fingerprint matching using descriptor-based Hough transform. IEEE Trans. Inf. Forensics Secur. **8**(1), 31–45 (2013)
8. Si, X., Feng, J., Yuan, B., Zhou, J.: Dense registration of fingerprints. Pattern Recognit. **63**, 9252–9260 (2017)
9. Cui, Z., Feng, J., Li, S., Lu, J., Zhou, J.: 2-D phase demodulation for deformable fingerprint registration. IEEE Trans. Inf. Forensics Secur. **13**(12), 3153–3165 (2018)
10. Lan, S., Guo, Z., You, J.: A non-rigid registration method with application to distorted fingerprint matching. Pattern Recognit. **95**, 48–57 (2019)
11. Cui, Z., Feng, J., Zhou, J.: Dense fingerprint registration via displacement regression network. In: Proceedings International Conference Biometrics (ICB), pp. 1–8, June 2019
12. Cui, Z., Feng, J., Zhou, J.: Dense registration and mosaicking of fingerprints by training an end-to-end network. IEEE Trans. Inf. Forensics Secur. **99**, 1 (2020)
13. Gu, S., Feng, J., Lu, J., Zhou, J.: Latent fingerprint registration via matching densely sampled points. IEEE Trans. Inf. Forensics Secur. **16**, 1231–1244 (2021)
14. Jaderberg, M., Simonyan, K., Zisserman, A., et al.: Spatial transformer networks. In: Advances in Neural Information Processing Systems, pp. 2017–2025 (2015)
15. Bazen, A.M., Gerez, S.H.: Fingerprint matching by thin-plate spline modelling of elastic deformations. Pattern Recognit. **36**(8), 1859–1867 (2003)
16. Lan, S., Guo, Z., You, J.: Pre-registration of translated/distorted fingerprints based on correlation and the orientation field. Inf. Sci. **520**, 292–304 (2020)
17. Sun, H., Zhang, Y., Chen, P., et al.: Synchronous fingerprint acquisition system based on total internal reflection and optical coherence tomography. IEEE Trans. Instrum. Meas. **69**(10), 8452–8465 (2020)
18. Ding, B., Wang, H., Chen, P., et al.: Surface and internal fingerprint reconstruction from optical coherence tomography through convolutional neural network. IEEE Trans. Inf. Forensics Secur. **16**(99), 685–700 (2020)
19. Zhou, W., Bovik, A.C., Sheikh, H.R., Simoncelli, E.P.: Image quality assessment: from error visibility to structural similarity. IEEE Trans. Image Process. **13**(4), 600–612 (2004)
20. Madhuri, G.S., Gandhi, M.P.I.: Image registration with similarity measures using correlation techniques - a research study. In: Proceedings of ICCIC, pp. 1–4 (2015)

An Arcloss-Based and Openset-Test-Oriented Finger Vein Recognition System

Zhenxiang Chen, Wangwang Yu, Haohan Bai, and Yongjie Li[✉]

School of Life Science and Technology, University of Electronic Science and Technology of China, Chengdu 610054, China
liyj@uestc.edu.cn

Abstract. Finger vein recognition has advantages that can't be replaced by other biometrics. Our designed system employs the feature vectorization pattern and multiple strategies, such as Arcloss, image enhancement designed in this paper and luminance-inversion data augmentation. Compared with the other algorithms using classifiers, this system is open-set testable and doesn't require additional computer resource for new category registration, which is more in line with practical application requirements. The recognition rate of this system is up to 99.8% in closed-set test on two public databases, and the recognition rate keeps acceptable when the training samples are reduced. The recognition rate can reach about 95% in cross open-set test. This paper also proposes two optimal threshold determination strategies to determine whether a category is registered or not.

Keywords: ArcLoss · Open-set test · Feature vectorization

1 Introduction

Finger vein identification has two modes of testing, one is to identify new samples of the trained categories, called closed-set test. The other is to identify new samples of untrained categories after they are registered, called open-set test. Open-set test is more in line with the practical application requirements, the categories of closed-set test have been trained, so the recognition is easier. In contrast, open-set test is more difficult.

In the following we only review some resent deep learning based finger vein recognition algorithms because their performances are better than that of the traditional algorithms. For example, a binary classification network was used to design a finger vein verification network [1]. The given two images are sent into the network at the same time, and the network outputs 0 or 1, where 0 represents imposter matching and 1 represents genuine matching. The use of multiple classifiers to design finger vein recognition algorithms is the most widely used strategy in literature, and most of the existing methods only focus

© Springer Nature Switzerland AG 2021
J. Feng et al. (Eds.): CCBR 2021, LNCS 12878, pp. 287–294, 2021.
https://doi.org/10.1007/978-3-030-86608-2_32

on closed-set test. For example convolutional networks or auto-encoder networks were used to extract features from finger vein images, which were then sent into a linear layer classifier [2–4] or a SVM classifier [5]. A shallow network was used for further learning of the features before being put into the classifier [6]. The method of SVM classifier with one against one strategy requires multiple classifiers, which need to be trained again after new categories are added. Of course, it can't work well for open-set test. In addition, new category registration requires additional computer resources. There is also a risk of leakage of category information during data transferring.

The use of feature vectorization pattern for recognition can achieve the purpose of open-set test. The model discards the classifier and the network is only used for feature vector extraction, then a distance metric is used to measure the similarity between the feature vectors. This mode doesn't require computer resources for new categories registration. The latest research in finger vein recognition [7] starts to focus on open-set test by using this pattern.

In addition, the accuracy and robustness of finger vein recognition algorithms need to be improved. Just as the methods proposed in literature [2,3], their accuracies decrease rapidly as the training sample number of categories decreases.

This paper is open-set test oriented, focusing on obtaining a feature vector with high generalization capability using a feature vectorization model, and We fully tested the system on two public datasets, SDUMLA and FVUSM, as well as on a self-built joint dataset with closed-set and open-set. Ablation tests were performed to demonstrate the effectiveness of the adopted strategy. The computation efficiency was also tested.

2 Methods

2.1 Image Pre-processing

ROI Extraction. We use the method proposed in the paper [8] for region of interest(ROI) extraction, which is then resized to $128 * 256$ pixels.

Image Enhance. We use the contrast-limited adaptive histogram enhancement (CLAHE) and the enhancement process proposed in the literature [9] to improve the contrast between the blood vessels and the background as much as possible, and the whole enhancement process is as follows:
Input: ROI image
*Step*1: Normalization and Gamma correction
*Step*2: Unsharp masking based on Gaussian filtering
*Step*3: CLAHE
*Step*4: Median filtering
We set $c = 1$, $\gamma = 2$ in Gamma correction. The size of Gaussian blur kernel is $[4, 4]$ in unsharp masking. The number of blocks in CLAHE is $[8, 8]$ and the contrast restriction parameter is 0.1.

2.2   Process and Strategy for Training and Testing of Feature Extraction Networks

The flow chart of training and testing the feature extraction network in this work is shown in Fig. 1, where the feature extraction network is the residual network Resnet18 [10], added with batch normalization operation, and the activation function Relu is replaced with PRelu.

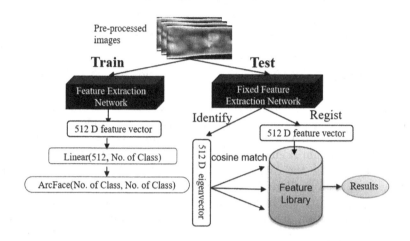

Fig. 1. The proposed flow chart of system training and testing

In the training phase, we first perform brightness-inversion data augmentation at first so that the number of samples in the training category becomes twice as large as before. Data augmentation with random angular rotation within 6° and small random up/down/left/right panning is also performed. Several examples of image augmentation are shown in Fig. 2. The input batch size for training is 256. The input image is turned into a 512-dimensional feature vector after senting into the feature extraction network, which is mapped to an indicator vector on the angular space after passing through the layers linear layer and Arcface layer in turn, the dimensionality of the indicator vector is the number of categories. We next use this indicator vector to calculate the ArcLoss [11] and then update the network parameters by using a stochastic gradient descent algorithm with 0.9 for momentum, 10^{-5} for regularization, and 0.1 for the learning rate. ArcLoss is recognized as the optimal loss function in metric learning, which is written as:

$$L_{arc} = -\frac{1}{N} \sum_{i=1}^{N} \log \frac{e^{s \cdot (\cos(\theta_{yi}+m))}}{e^{s \cdot (\cos(\theta_{yi}+m))} + \sum_{j=1, j \neq y_i}^{n} e^{s \cdot \cos \theta_j}} \tag{1}$$

where $\cos\theta_j$ represents the feature vector after normalizing the features and weights, and $\cos\theta_j$ multiplied by the parameter s represents the distribution of the feature vector over a hypersphere of radius s. m is the boundary penalty added to the angle θ_j. We set, $s = 32$ and $m = 0.5$. ArcLoss is optimized directly in the angular space, which has the good ability of intra-class aggregation and inter-class separation.

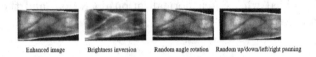

Enhanced image   Brightness inversion   Random angle rotation   Random up/down/left/right panning

Fig. 2. Image augmentation schematic

In the testing phase, we first perform a registration process to build a feature database. For recognition, the obtained feature vector is compared with the feature vector of each categories in the features database by calculating the cosine distance, so that we get a similarity vector, and then each value in the similarity vector is compared with a threshold value to determine the category of the input image. If the maximum similarity is greater than the threshold, category of the input is judged to be the category corresponding to the maximum similarity, and if the maximum similarity is less than the threshold, the input category is judged to be unregistered. In this paper, we adopt two methods for the best threshold determination, one is to choose the threshold corresponding to equal error rate, which guarantees the maximum verification accuracy. The second is to pass the similarity vector through Softmax, which enlarges the gap between the intra-class and inter-class matching similarities, and then the threshold value can be taken as 0.5. In this work, the network is trained for a total of 100 epochs, and we take the best test performance to report.

3   Results and Analysis

The specific information of the four public databases used in this work is shown in Table 1, and we treat each finger as a category. Figure 3(a) shows the examples of ROI images of the four public databases, and Fig. 3(b) shows the image enhancement results of different steps.

Table 1. Information of the four public databases used in this work

Database	Subjects	No. of fingers	Images/per finger	Sessions	Image size	Total images
SDUMLIA	106	6	6	1	320 * 240 pxl	3816
SCUT	100	6	6	1	288 * 640 pxl	3600
FV-USM	123	4	12	2	640 * 480 pxl	5904
VERA	110	2	2	1	665 * 250 pxl	440

As for the evaluation metrics, ACC represents the accuracy rate when judging the input category as the category corresponding to the maximum value of the similarity vector, and EER represents the equal error rate.

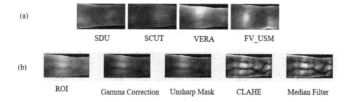

Fig. 3. Example of preprocessing. (a) ROI image show, (b) Image enhancement change process

3.1 Closed-Set Test

Closed-Set Test on SDUMLA. Table 2 compares the closed-set test performance on the SDUMLA dataset. Table 3 shows the closed-set test performance comparison when trained with different number of images on the SDUMLA dataset.

FV_USM Dataset Characteristics and Closed-Set Test on This Library. The FV_USM dataset is collected in two sessions, characterized by a serious center rotation difference between the samples of two sessions, as shown in Fig. 4. Table 4 shows the closed-set test on the FV_USM. It can be seen that for the case of two sessions, our method is superior to the compared methods. When trained with four images from each sessions and testing with the remaining two images from each sessions, the accuracy is up to 99.90%. This result shows that the central rotation problem can be solved if the training set contains samples with different central rotations of each category.

Table 2. Closed-set test on SDUMLA

Database	Methods	ACC	ERR
	Das et al. 2019 [2]	98.90%	/
SDUMLA Library	Yang et al. 2019 [12]	/	0.94%
Training Set:5 images	Zhang et al. 2019 [13]	/	1.09%
Test:remaining 1 image	Boucherit et al. 2020 [3]	99.48%	/
	Hou et al. 2020 [5]	99.78%	0.21%
	Ours	99.84%	0.15%

Table 3. Closed set test with different No. of images trained on SDUMLA

Database	Methods	Training 1	Training 2	Training 3	Training 4	Training 5
SDUMLA	Das et al. 2019 [2]	75.25%	77.99%	80.27%	97.48%	98.90%
	Hou et al. 2020 [3]	65%	66%	84.64%	89.88%	99.48%
	Ours	92.10%	92.61%	94.86%	99.69%	99.84%

Table 4. Closed-set test on the FVUSM

Methods	FV_USM Two sessions		
	Training 1 Test 6	Training 6 Test 6	Training 4*2 Test 2*2
Das et al. 2019 [2]	72.97%	/	98.58%
Boucherit et al. 2020 [3]	70.10%	81.71%	96.15%
Ours	88.18%	92.79%	99.90%

3.2 Open-Set Test

Open-Set Test and Computation Efficiency Evaluation on Joint Database. The open-set is divided into training set and test set by categories. In order to have enough categories, the SDUMLA (636 * 6), the SCUT (600 * 6) and the VERA (220 * 2) database were combined into a joint database in this work. Where VERA was expanded by 3 times to achieve category sample balance. The joint database contains 1456 categories with 6 images per category. The training set and test set was randomly assigned by categories in the ratio of 7:3, and the recognition rate is 97.24% (Table 5). The computation time for verification is 50 ms for our system, on an Intel Core i7-8700 CPU @3.20 GHz desktop PC with 32.0 GB of RAM.

Database-Cross Open-Set Test. Database-cross test is a more rigorous open-set test. We trained on the SDUMLA database and tested the two sessions of the FV_USM database separately, and the test accuracy can reach about 95% on average (Table 6).

3.3 Mixed Open-Set Test and Closed-Set Test on SDUMLA

Table 7 shows the mixed open-set test and closed-set test on the SDUMLA. We registered all the categories, and the similarity was calculated between the input

Class:024_2

(a) first Session   (b) second Session

Fig. 4. Severe center rotation discrepancy in FV-USM

Table 5. Open set recognition performance on joint libraries

Database	Test Set	ACC	EER	Time
Joint library (7:3)	Login:436 * 1	97.24%	1.57%	(30+20) ms
Training set:1020 * 6	Identify:436 * 5			

Table 6. Library-cross open-set test

Training	Regist	Testing	ACC
SDUMLA 636 * 5	SDUMLA 1st image	SDUMLA 636 * 1	99.84%
	FV_USM 1 Sessions 1st image	FV_USM 1st 492 * 5	94.88%
	FV_USM 2 Sessions 1st image	FV_USM 2 Sessions 492 * 5	96.87%

and all the categories during open-set test and closed-set test. The recognition rate of open-set test is 98.75%, indicating that our network doesn't recognize the untrained categories as one of the trained categories.

3.4 Ablation Test

We have performed closed-set ablation tests on the SDUMLA database and open-set ablation tests on the joint database to verify the effectiveness of each policy, and the results are shown in Table 8.

Table 7. Mixed open-set and closed-set test on SDUMLA

Dataset	Methods	Test set	ACC
SDUMLA (9:1)	Baseline: Resnet18	set_1:572 * 1	98.25%
Training set: 572 * 5		set_2:64 * 5	92.19%
Regist set: 636 * 1	Ours	set_1:572 * 1	99.65%
		set_2:64 * 5	98.75%

Table 8. Ablation test

Marking of steps	Database	Test set	Methods	ACC
			A	97.33%
	SDUMLA Library	Login:636 * 1	A+B	97.80%
A: Resnet	Training Set 636 * 5	Regist:636 * 1	A+B+C	99.06%
B: Bright-inversion expansion			A+B+C+D	99.84%
C: Image Enhancement			A	89.00%
D: ArcFace	Joint library	Regist:435 * 1	A+B	91.00%
	Training set 1020 * 6	Identify:436 * 5	A+B+C	95.00%
			A+B+C+D	97.24%

4 Conclusion

The proposed system can be easily registered and used to recognize untrained categories. We have done sufficient experiments to prove that this system has good performance in open-set test and closed-set test, with good robustness.

The ablation experiments show that ArcLoss, the image enhancement, and brightness-inversion data expansion are effective for the finger vein feature vectorization task. In addition, we conclude that the central rotation problem can be solved if the training set contains samples with different central rotations for each category. In the mixed open-set test and closed-set test, we demonstrate the feasibility of feature vectorization, where our network doesn't recognize the untrained categories as one of the trained categories.

References

1. Hong, H.G., Lee, M.B., Park, K.R.: Convolutional neural network-based finger-vein recognition using NIR image sensors. Sensors **17**(6), 1297 (2017)
2. Das, R., Piciucco, E., Maiorana, E., et al.: Convolutional neural network for finger-vein-based biometric identification. IEEE Trans. Inf. Forensics Secur. **14**(2), 360–373 (2019)
3. Boucherit, I., Zmirli, M.O., Hentabli, H., Rosdi, B.A.: finger vein identification using deeply-fused convolutional neural network. J. King Saud Univ. Comput. Inf. Sci. (2020)
4. Zhao, D., Ma, H., Yang, Z., Li, J., Tian, W.: Finger vein recognition based on lightweight CNN combining center loss and dynamic regularization. Infrared Phys. Technol. **105**, 103221 (2020)
5. Hou, B., Yan, R.: Convolutional autoencoder model for finger-vein verification. IEEE Trans. Instrum. Meas. **69**(5), 2067–2074 (2019)
6. Hou, B., Yan, R.: Convolutional auto-encoder based deep feature learning for finger-vein verification. In: IEEE International Symposium on Medical Measurements and Applications (MeMeA), pp. 1–5. IEEE (2018)
7. Ou, W.F., Po, L.M., Zhou, C., Rehman, Y.A.U., Xian, P.F., Zhang, Y.J.: Fusion loss and inter-class data augmentation for deep finger vein feature learning. Expert Syst. Appl. **171**, 114584 (2021)
8. Lee, E.C., Lee, H.C., Park, K.R.: Finger vein recognition using minutia-based alignment and local binary pattern-based feature extraction. Int. J. Imag. Syst. Technol. **19**(3), 179–186 (2009)
9. Zidan, K.A., Jumaa, S.S.: An Efficient Enhancement Method for Finger Vein Images Using Double Histogram Equalization (2020)
10. He, K., Zhang, X., Ren, S., Sun, J.: Deep residual learning for image recognition. In: Proceedings of the IEEE Conference on Computer Vision and Pattern Recognition, pp. 770–778 (2016)
11. Deng, J., Guo, J., Xue, N., Zafeiriou, S.: Arcface: additive angular margin loss for deep face recognition. In: Proceedings of the IEEE/CVF Conference on Computer Vision and Pattern Recognition, pp. 4690–4699 (2019)
12. Yang, W., Hui, C., Chen, Z., Xue, J.H., Liao, Q.: FV-GAN: finger vein representation using generative adversarial networks. IEEE Trans. Inf. Forensics Secur. **14**(9), 2512–2524 (2019)
13. Zhang, Y., Li, W., Zhang, L., Ning, X., Sun, L., Lu, Y.: Adaptive learning Gabor filter for finger-vein recognition. IEEE Access **7**, 159821–159830 (2019)

Different Dimension Issues in Deep Feature Space for Finger-Vein Recognition

Yiqi Zhong[1], Jiahui Li[1], Tingting Chai[1(✉)], Shitala Prasad[2], and Zhaoxin Zhang[1(✉)]

[1] Faculty of Computing, Harbin Institute of Technology, Harbin, China
{170150237,2190400505}@stu.hit.edu.cn
{ttchai,zhangzhaoxin}@hit.edu.cn
[2] Institute of Infocomm Research, A*STAR, Singapore, Singapore
shitala@ieee.org

Abstract. Hand-crafted approaches were the dominating solutions and recently, more convolutional neural network (CNN)-based methods have been proposed for finger-vein recognition. However, the previous deep learning methods usually designed the network architecture with increasing layers and parameters, which incurs device memory issues and processing speed issues. Although many researchers have devoted to design image enhancement algorithms to improve the recognition performance of hand-crafted methods, it is interesting to investigate whether deep learning method can achieve satisfactory performance without image enhancement. This paper focuses on two different dimension issues: lightweight CNN design and the impact of image enhancement on deep learning methods. The experimental results demonstrate that the proposed method LFVRN is comparable or superior to the prior competition winners. In addition, image enhancement is validated not inevitable for the proposed lightweight CNN model LFVRN.

Keywords: Finger-vein recognition · CNN-based method · Network architecture design · Image enhancement

1 Introduction

Finger-vein equips the ability of providing trustworthy solutions for identity verification contending with spoof and replay attack because the subcutaneous vascular tissues are almost invisible to the naked eyes, hard to acquire without the subjects' cooperation [1–3]. Besides, the image quality of finger-vein is less

All authors contribute equally.
The authors would like to express their sincere gratitude to Associate Prof. Adams Wai-Kin Kong and Dr. Wojciech Michal Matkowski for their comments and advices some time ago.

J. Feng et al. (Eds.): CCBR 2021, LNCS 12878, pp. 295–303, 2021.
https://doi.org/10.1007/978-3-030-86608-2_33

susceptible to non-ideal acquisition conditions owing to the application of NIR light in real vein imaging [4]. Although CNN-based methods provide prominent baseline for finger-vein recognition, there is still room for accuracy and efficiency improvement due to one of the three major limitations. First, the recognition performance is sensitive to the design of CNN architecture. Second, the hyperparameters, such as learning rate, batch size and iterations are difficult to be set as standard values, which may change for different datasets. Third, large-scale networks are hard to train, not only will they result in the decline of learning efficiency, but also will bring out over-fitting. In contrast, small-scale networks are more efficient and have better generalization ability, but too shallow networks would lead to under-fitting [5].

To address the mentioned drawbacks and weakness, the lightweight finger-vein recognition network (LFVRN) is developed to perform high-efficiency finger-vein recognition, whilst exploring the impact of image enhancement on deep learning method in the filed of finger-vein. Overall, the main contributions of this work can be summarized as:

- A lightweight CNN model of 4.93 million parameters using partial pre-trained MobileNetV2 plus customized auxiliary block is designed to simplify the training process and implement high-performance finger-vein recognition. The proposed CNN model 'LFVRN' achieves desirable performance in comparison with other deep learning methods.
- The impact of image enhancement is surveyed via exhaustive comparative experiments by using Automatic color enhancement (ACE) algorithm [6] and Contrast Limited Adaptive Histogram Equalization (CLAHE) algorithm [7]. The experimental results on HKPU [1], FV-USM [8], SDUMLA [9] and UTFVP [10] validate that image enhancement is much more necessary for the existing pre-trained deep learning models. With negligible accuracy rise, it is not necessary for the proposed LFVRN method.

2   Related Work

The explosive growth in deep model size and computation cost accounts for new challenges on how to efficiently deploy deep learning models on various hardware platforms. Training a specialized network from scratch requires considerable computational resources, including time, energy, financial and environmental costs (giving rise to CO_2 emission as much as five cars' lifetime) [11]. Research on deep learning is striving to miniaturize neural networks. While ensuring the accuracy of deep models, the volume is smaller and the speed is faster. Many lightweight CNNs were proposed to improve the hardware efficiency, such as MobileNets [12,13], which make it possible for mobile terminals and embedded devices to run CNN models. Inspired by the high-effect of lightweight CNN and it saves natural resources well due to the ease of training, our emphasis is to explore small-scale CNN model by combing pre-trained convolutional layers and elaborately-designed assistant network block for efficient finger-vein recognition.

Furthermore, image enhancement plays an important role in renovating sample quality including noise elimination, illumination equalization and texture sharpening, which in turn improves the accuracy of biometrics [14–16]. However, these methods are observed to suffer from multiple steps, which makes the whole recognition process tedious and time-consuming. Driven by the remarkable learning capability of CNN from raw image, we are devoted to investigate the impact and necessity of image enhancement on CNN-based finger-vein recognition methods.

3   Methodology and Network Topology

3.1   Finger-Vein ROI Extraction

Different ROI extraction protocols are applied for different finger-vein databases. FV-USM provides segmented ROI images, which can be directly used as the input data, while for HKPU database, we capitalize on the provided binary mask to implement finger segmentation. Subsequent processing steps are in line with the algorithm designed for SDUMLA and UTFVP. Driven by [17–19], the two masks [18] are used to detect upper and lower boundary to segment finger region for SDUMLA. Then, the phalangeal joints location and image alignment [17,19] are used for both HKPU and SDUMLA.

The height of ROI image is determined by the strategy proposed in [19] as shown in Fig. 1. Note that the resulting ROI images inevitably has small background pixels, unsharp texture, exposure and rotation. In this work, there is no further refinement operation for texture enhancement because CNNs are believed robust to the above-mentioned non-ideal situations. ROI images are resized to 64 × 192 pixels where 64 and 192 represent the width and height of the ROI, respectively. Specially, the original images in SDUMLA have three color channels while others have one channel.

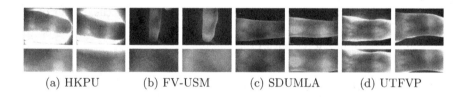

(a) HKPU   (b) FV-USM   (c) SDUMLA   (d) UTFVP

Fig. 1. Finger-vein images and the corresponding ROI images

3.2   Network Topology of LFVRN

The lightweight network with excellent classification ability as the backbone is the top priority. LFVRN crops pre-trained MobileNetV2 after the seventh bottleneck, followed by a dropout layer (Dropout1), a convolution layer (Conv), a batch normalization layer (BNorm), a ELU layer (ELU), a dropout layer

(Dropout2) and a fully connected layer (FC). LFVRN is trained with finger-vein ROI images in end-to-end fashion, which fine-tunes partial structure of pre-trained MobileNetV2 model and trains the assistant block from scratch. Figure 2 shows the architecture of LFVRN and the details of LFVRN are provided as follows.

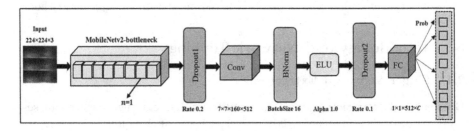

Fig. 2. Network architecture of LFVRN

- The input layer is fed with finger-vein image of size $224 \times 224 \times 3$. The segmented ROI image of size 64×192 is padded with itself and resized into 224×224. Every three ROI images can form a square input image. For one-channel image, the input can be automatically converted into three-channel image by concatenation.
- The layers from pre-trained MobileNetV2 model transform the input image into $7 \times 7 \times 160$. The parameter n of the sixth bottleneck block is set to 1.
- In the assistant block, the dropout rates of Dropout1 and Dropout2 are separately set to 0.2 and 0.1. Conv has 512 convolutional filters of size $7 \times 7 \times 160$. The batch size of BNorm is set to 16. The assistant block transforms the output of the last hidden layer into $1 \times 1 \times 512$.
- FC has C convolutional filters of size $1 \times 1 \times 512$, generating the output of size $1 \times 1 \times C$. C represents the number of finger-vein classes. *CrossEntropyLoss* is used as loss function for back propagation.

4   Experiments and Results

Each finger of an individual is considered as a class. In case of databases having two sessions, the first session is used for training while the second session is used for testing. Whereas, the databases with only one session are evenly divided into two halves for each class. As for finger-vein classes with odd images, the extra one image is placed in the training set. The deep learning methods VGG16 [20], ResNet50 [21], MobileNetV2 and ShuffleNetV2 and LFVRN with ArcFace loss (LFVRN_Arc) [22] are considered for comparison. LFVRN with CrossEntropy loss is expressed as LFVRN_CE in the following part. The learning rates of VGG16, ResNet50, MobileNetV2, ShuffleNetV2, LFVRN_Arc and LFVRN_CE are set to $1e^{-3}$, $1e^{-2}$, $1e^{-2}$, $1e^{-2}$, $5e^{-3}$ and $1e^{-2}$, respectively. The batch size of all deep learning models is set to 16. The training epoch of LFVRN_Arc, LFVRN_CE and other pre-trained deep models is set to 60, 200 and 400, respectively.

4.1   Finger-Vein Recognition Using Original Images

Finger-Vein Identification. As performance metrics, we considered Rank-1 correct identification rate (the higher, the better, abbreviated as CIR). Table 1 lists the CIR results of LFVRN and other compared methods on the considered databases. The **first** and second best experimental results are highlighted in bold and underline, respectively. As shown in Table 1, LFVRN_CE and LFVRN_Arc generally outperforms other deep learning approaches with the margin of over 10% CIR and LFVRN_CE performs the best compared with other deep learning methods.

Table 1. Comparison of CIR between LFVRN and other compared methods on the considered Finger-vein databases (%).

Networks	HKPU	FV-USM	SDUMLA	UTFVP
VGG16	66.67	64.36	83.96	80.28
ResNet50	51.90	81.13	77.73	49.44
MobileNetV2	54.84	84.96	83.49	51.39
ShuffleNetV2	40.79	78.76	74.53	40.42
LFVRN_Arc	<u>92.54</u>	<u>97.02</u>	<u>96.91</u>	**98.61**
LFVRN_CE	**96.98**	**98.58**	**97.75**	**98.61**

Finger-Vein Verification. As performance metrics, we considered Equal Error Rate (the lower, the better, abbreviated as EER). Table 2 summarizes the EER results of LFVRN_CE, LFVRN_Arc and other deep learning methods on four considered databases. It can be seen that LFVRN_CE achieves the lowest EER values of 1.90%, 0.61% on HKPU and FV-USM, the second lowest EER values of 1.42% and 0.83% on SDUMLA and UTFVP. For SDUMLA and UTFVP, LFVRN_Arc performs the best with lowest EER values, which shows that LFVRN is effective and superior to cope with finger-vein recognition problem.

4.2   Comparison of Time Efficiency

Table 3 gives the time efficiency comparison of the proposed LFVRN and other deep learning models. All experiments were executed in Python 3.8.8 with Pytorch 1.7.0 using a system with Intel(R) Core(TM) i7-9700K CPU @3.60 GHz, 16 GB RAM, and NVIDIA RTX 2060 SUPER 8 GB GPU card. The mean execution time represents the average running time for testing one finger-vein image

Table 2. Comparison of EER between LFVRN and other compared methods on the considered Finger-vein databases (%).

Networks	HKPU	FV-USM	SDUMLA	UTFVP
VGG16	8.10	9.68	4.40	4.44
ResNet50	12.26	4.61	4.84	20.56
MobileNetV2	7.62	3.35	4.12	11.94
ShuffleNetV2	13.81	5.81	5.81	20.22
LFVRN_Arc	2.86	1.02	**1.26**	**0.28**
LFVRN_CE	**1.90**	**0.61**	1.42	0.83

Table 3. Time efficiency analysis between LFVRN and other compared methods.

Networks	No. of parameters	Mean execution time
VGG16	136.00 M	**5.84 ms**
ResNet50	24.38 M	12.31 ms
MobileNetV2	2.77 M	11.70 ms
ShuffleNetV2	1.69 M	12.32 ms
LFVRN_Arc	5.67 M	10.69 ms
LFVRN_CE	4.93 M	10.27 ms

from the four considered databases. As can be seen from Table 3, LFVRN_CE model performs the second fastest but the number of model parameters is greatly reduced in comparison with VGG16.

4.3   Finger-Vein Recognition Using Enhanced Images

In [23], the authors point out that the image enhancement has no effect on deep learning methods and even decreases the recognition accuracy. However, there is some weakness in [23], which can be summarized as: (1) The accuracy improvement on HKPU (from 71.11% to 96.55%) and FV-USM (from 72.92% to 98.58%) is achieved by mixing two sessions of finger-vein images, which is not fit with normal practice in the field of biometrics. (2) The image enhancement claim for CNN-based finger-vein recognition is verified by using CLAHE algorithm, which is not persuasive due to mixing sessions, only one enhancement algorithm. Also, there are incongruent CMC trends on SDUMLA and UTFVP that contradicts the conclusion.

In this paper, we split training and testing sets avoiding mixing different sessions of finger-vein images. Also, two different image enhancement algorithms ACE and CLAHE are considered for the validation. Table 4 and 5 display the CIR and EER of LFVRN and other compared deep learning models on HKPU, FV-USM, SDUMLA and UTFVP. It can be seen from Table 1, 2, 4 and 5, the two enhancement algorithms have different effects on the experimental results.

On the whole, ACE boosts finger-vein recognition by promoting the CIR and bringing down the EER, while the CLAHE has the opposite impact on finger-vein recognition. This indicates that enhancement algorithms do not necessarily produce more efficient texture pattern for deep learning models. With large accuracy promoting between original data and ACE data on the compared models, the image enhancement is highly necessary for baseline lightweight CNN models. The CIR and EER improvements of LFVRN are no more than 0.60% and 0.20%, so the image enhancement is not indispensable for well-designed CNN-based finger-vein recognition method.

Table 4. Comparison of CIR and EER between LFVRN and other compared methods using ACE data (%).

Networks	HKPU		FV-USM		SDUMLA		UTFVP	
	CIR	EER	CIR	EER	CIR	EER	CIR	EER
VGG16	79.76	4.76	84.35	4.07	82.23	4.87	74.03	6.11
ResNet50	78.41	3.33	91.02	2.64	77.04	7.86	53.61	17.50
MobileNetV2	85.40	3.24	90.31	2.64	86.64	4.16	67.22	6.94
ShuffleNetV2	55.32	8.10	86.89	4.27	75.84	5.98	42.78	17.22
LFVRN_Arc	94.68	1.90	98.14	0.81	95.60	1.57	98.33	0.69
LFVRN_CE	97.14	1.90	99.09	0.41	97.27	1.42	99.03	0.69

Table 5. Comparison of CIR and EER between LFVRN and other compared methods using CLAHE data (%).

Networks	HKPU		FV-USM		SDUMLA		UTFVP	
	CIR	EER	CIR	EER	CIR	EER	CIR	EER
VGG16	60.79	8.53	62.74	5.03	80.61	5.03	75.56	5.46
ResNet50	73.57	6.19	88.48	7.18	77.25	7.86	52.64	17.04
MobileNetV2	76.43	3.81	91.16	4.32	82.02	4.16	70.42	6.98
ShuffleNetV2	71.75	6.19	89.43	5.60	79.98	5.98	52.92	14.44
LFVRN_Arc	95.24	1.79	97.12	2.04	93.71	1.57	93.71	1.39
LFVRN_CE	96.59	1.43	98.37	2.67	97.22	1.42	97.22	1.81

4.4   Qualitative Analysis of Deep Models

As shown in Table 1 and 2, LFVRN exhibits quite stable and high performance accuracy, whereas the compared approaches show obvious accuracy variations on different finger-vein databases. The superiority of LFVRN lies in the powerful feature extraction ability of CNN and the dedicated assistant block plays an important role in achieving desirable recognition performance for all the databases. If the well-designed assistant block is removed from LFVRN, the model will significantly degrades its performance in terms of CIR and EER. It can be found from Table 1 and 2, there is a significant accuracy gap between pre-trained MobileNetV2 and LFVRN, even though LFVRN adopts partial MobileNetV2 as the backbone for feature extraction. The reason for the poor finger-vein recognition performance of pre-trained models is the over-fitting problem caused by small-scale finger-vein data, as well as the large image differences between finger-vein database and ImageNet. The experimental results prove that LFVRN is efficient and promising.

5 Conclusion

This paper introduces LFVRN model of 4.93M parameters to achieve promising finger-vein biometrics in terms of identification and verification, respectively. LFVRN is simple and easy to train. The absence of well-designed dedicated assistant block on the top lead to desirable recognition accuracy and time efficiency in comparison with other deep learning models. Furthermore, We explore better understanding the role of image enhancement in deep learning based finger-vein recognition. The experimental results prove that ACE algorithm can significantly boost recognition performance for baseline lightweight CNN models, while almost all methods show accuracy decline by using CLAHE. With inappreciable accuracy promotion, image enhancement is not indispensable for LFVRN method.

References

1. Kumar, A., Zhou, Y.: Human identification using finger images. IEEE Trans. Image Process. **21**(4), 2228–2244 (2012)
2. Menott, D., et al.: Deep representations for iris, face, and fingerprint spoofing detection. IEEE Trans. Inf. Foren. Sec. **10**(4), 864–879 (2015)
3. Noh, K.S.: A study on the authentication and security of financial settlement using the finger vein technology in wireless internet environment. Wirel. Pers. Commun. **89**(3), 761–775 (2016)
4. Zharov, V., Ferguson, S., Eidt, J., Howard, P., Fink, L., Waner, M.: Infrared imaging of subcutaneous veins. Lasers Surgery Med. **34**(1), 56–61 (2004)
5. Zhao, D., Ma, H., Yang, Z., Li, J., Tian, W.: Finger vein recognition based on lightweight CNN combining center loss and dynamic regularization. Infrared Phys. Technol. **105**, 1–10 (2020)
6. Getreuer, P.: Automatic color enhancement ACE and its fast implementation. Image Process. On Line **2**, 266–277 (2012)
7. Zuiderveld, K.: Contrast Limited Adaptive Histograph Equalization. Graphic Gems IV. Academic Press Professional, San Diego, pp. 484–485 (1994)
8. Asaari, M.S.M., Suandi, S.A., Rosd, B.A.: Fusion of band limited phase only correlation and width centroid contour distance for finger based biometrics. Expert Syst. Appl. **14**(2), 360–373 (2014)

9. Yin, Y., Liu, L., Sun, X.: SDUMLA-HMT: a multimodal biometric database. In: Sun, Z., Lai, J., Chen, X., Tan, T. (eds.) CCBR 2011. LNCS, vol. 7098, pp. 260–268. Springer, Heidelberg (2011). https://doi.org/10.1007/978-3-642-25449-9_33

10. Ton, B.T., Veldhuis, R.N.J.: A high quality finger vascular pattern dataset collected using a custom designed capturing device. In: International Conference Biometrics (ICB), pp. 1–5 (2013)

11. Cai, H., Gan, C., Wang, T., Zhang, Z., Han, S.: Once-for-All: train one network and specialize it for efficient deployment. In: International Conference Learning Representations (ICLR), pp. 1–15 (2020)

12. Sandler, M., Howard, A., Zhu, M., Zhmoginov, A., Chen, L.: MobileNetV2: inverted residuals and linear bottlenecks. In: IEEE/CVF Conference Computing Vision Pattern Recognition (CVPR), pp. 4510–4520 (2018)

13. Howard, A., et al.: Searching for MobileNetV3. In: IEEE/CVF Conference Computing Vision (ICCV), pp. 1314–1324 (2019)

14. Chen, L., Wang, J., Yang, S., He, H.: A finger vein image-based personal identification system with self-adaptive illuminance control. IEEE Trans. Instrum. Meas. **66**(2), 6859–6887 (2017)

15. Syarif, M.A., Ong, T.S., Teoh, A.B.J., Tee, C.: Enhanced maximum curvature descriptors for finger vein verification. Multimedia Tools Appl. **76**(5), 6859–6887 (2016). https://doi.org/10.1007/s11042-016-3315-4

16. Qin, H., EI-Yacoubi, M. A.: Deep representation for finger-vein image-quality assessment. IEEE Tran. Circuits Syst. Video Technol. **28**(8), 1677–1693 (2018)

17. Wang, J., Shi, Y.: Finger-vein ROI localization and vein ridge enhancement. Pattern Recogn. Lett. **33**, 1569–1579 (2012)

18. Lee, E.C., Lee, H.C., Park, K.R.: Finger vein recognition using minutia-based alignment and local binary pattern-based feature extraction. Int. J. Imag. Syst. Tech. **19**(3), 179–186 (2009)

19. Yang, L., Yang, G., Yin, Y., Xiao, R.: Sliding window-based region of interest extraction for finger vein images. Sensors **13**(3), 3799–3815 (2013)

20. Simonyan, K., Zisserman, A.: Very deep convolutional networks for large-scale image recognition, In: International Conference Learning Representation (ICLR), pp. 1–14 (2015)

21. He, K., Zhang, X., Ren, S., Sun, J.: Deep residual learning for image recognition. In: International Conference Computing Vision and Pattern Recognition (CVPR), pp. 770–778 (2016)

22. Deng, J., Guo, J., Xue, N., Zafeiriou, S.: ArcFace: additive angular margin loss for deep face recognition. In: IEEE/CVF Conference Computing Vision Pattern Recognition (CVPR), pp. 4690–4699 (2019)

23. Das, R., Piciucco, E., Maiorana, E., Campisi, P.: Convolutional neural network for finger-vein-based biometric identification. IEEE Trans. Inf. Foren. Sec. **14**(2), 360–373 (2019)

Facial Biometrics

Holistic Co-occurrence Prior
for High-Density Face Detection

Qixiang Geng and Dong Liang[✉]

College of Computer Science and Technology, Nanjing University of Aeronautics
and Astronautics, Nanjing 211106, People's Republic of China
liangdong@nuaa.edu.cn

Abstract. Though object detection has made tremendous strides, small
object detection remains one of the challenges. Aggregating information
from context becomes a natural choice for the detection of small objects
with appearance degradation. This paper discusses how to properly utilize high-level contextual prior knowledge to enhance the capabilities of
anchor-based detectors for small and crowded face detection. We propose density-aware face co-occurrence prior for inferred box harmonization. Specifically, We mine the face spatial co-occurrence information on
the holistic view according to the density estimation. We also collect
a challenging face detection dataset - Crowd Face, to provide adequate
samples to prominent the bottleneck of detecting crowded faces. We integrate our proposed method with the anchor-based detectors and test
it on benchmarked datasets (WIDER FACE and Crowd Face). Experiments indicate it obviously enhances the performance of existing face
detectors in crowd scenes. Especially for the detectors with poor inferring performance, the improvements of the detectors integrated with the
proposed scheme are obvious. Our approach is plug-and-play and model-
independent, which could be integrated into the existing anchor-based
detectors without extra learning.

Keywords: Face detection · Crowded scene · Density-aware ·
Co-occurrence prior

1 Introduction

Robust face detection in the open world is an ultimate component to handle
various facial-related problems. Due to the promising development of deep Convolutional Neural Networks, face detection has made tremendous progress in
recent years [1–3]. Renewed detection paradigms [4,5], strong backbone [6–8]
and large scale dataset [9] jointly push forward the limit of face detection to
approach humans' cognition. In video surveillance, since the faces are usually
far away from the surveillance camera, small face detection in crowded scenes is
a challenging problem with practical needs.

The central issue of small and occluded face detection in crowded scenes is
the appearance degradation caused by shallow resolution. Therefore, aggregating

© Springer Nature Switzerland AG 2021
J. Feng et al. (Eds.): CCBR 2021, LNCS 12878, pp. 307–315, 2021.
https://doi.org/10.1007/978-3-030-86608-2_34

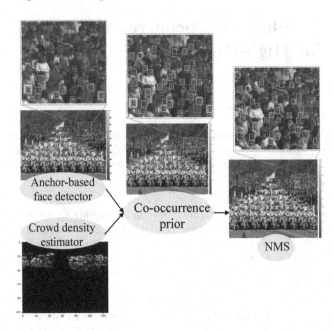

Fig. 1. The architecture of the proposed method. According to crowd density estimation, face co-occurrence prior increases true positives of the inferred face boxes.

information from context becomes a natural choice. [10–12] reviewed contextual information and analyzed its role for challenging object detection in empirical evaluation. [13] shows that humans detecting objects that violate their standard context take longer and make more errors. For face detection, [6,14] focus on low-level context to detect small faces and [5] demonstrates that both contextual information and scale-variant representations are crucial. Similarly, [15] pools ROI features around faces and bodies for detection. The contextual information of faces is usually employed in the low-level context via a different receptive field of feature maps. We find that the roughly head counting information is also valuable for face detection.

In this paper, we explore the spatial distribution of faces on the whole image as high-level contextual information to detect the hard samples, which we call *co-occurrence* prior. In our previous researches, we proposed a series of background modeling methods based on co-occurrence prior to obtain stable context information between pixels for video foreground segmentation [16–23]. Inspired by this, in this paper, we try to introduce the co-occurrence prior to hard face detection to improve the utilization efficiency of scene spatial information. According to the density map which can reflect the head location and offer spatial distribution of faces, we propose a universal strategy before the standard non-maximum suppression (NMS) formula in anchor-based detectors, which could be independent of a specific training strategy. Face co-occurrence prior harmonizes the outputs of a detector according to crowd density estimation. It enhances the sensitivity and specificity of the detector via increasing true positives. Figure 1 illustrates the proposed detection framework. We also collect a challenging face detection dataset with tiny faces - Crowd Face, to provide adequate samples to further prominent the bottleneck of detecting crowded faces.

2   Face Co-occurrence Prior Based on Density Map

Crowd Density Map. A density map is widely used in crowd analysis since it can exhibit the headcount, locations and their spatial distribution. Given a set of N training images $I_{i1 \leq i \leq N}$ with corresponding ground-truth density maps D_i^{gt}, density map estimation learns a non-linear mapping $\mathcal{F}$ that maps an input image I_i to an estimated $D_i^{est}(I_i) = \mathcal{F}(I_i)$, that is as similar as D_i^{gt} in terms of L_2 norm. To each image I_i, we associate a set of 2D points $P_i^{est} = \{P_{i,j}\}_{1 \leq j \leq C_i}$ that denote the position of each human head, where C_i is the headcount in image I_i. The corresponding estimated density map D_i^{est} is obtained by a total probability formula via convolving it with a Gaussian kernel $\mathcal{N}^{est}(p \mid \mu, \sigma^2)$. We have $\forall p \in I_i$,

$$D_i^{est}(p \mid I_i) = \mathcal{F}(p \mid I_i) = \mathcal{F}[\sum_{j=1}^{C_i} \mathcal{N}^{gt}(p \mid \mu = P_{i,j}, \sigma^2)], \tag{1}$$

where μ and σ represent the mean and standard deviation of the normal distribution.

For each head point $P_{i,j}$ in a given image, denoting the distances to its K nearest neighbors as $\{d_k^{i,j}\}_{(1 \leq k \leq K)}$. The average distance is therefore

$$\overline{d^{i,j}} = \frac{1}{K} \sum_{k=1}^{K} d_k^{i,j}. \tag{2}$$

Although the crowd density map cannot directly show the head's size, in a high-density crowd scene, since the individuals are densely distributed, it can roughly represent the head size. The head size is approximately equal to the distance between two neighboring individuals' centers in crowded scenes. The density estimate network we used is CAN [24]. It can accurately estimate the crowd density map, especially when perspective effects are strong.

Co-occurrence of Homogeneous Faces. In a crowd scene, many faces are assigned low confidence scores by the detector since the face appearance is scarce and inadequate, resulting in failure to detect them. Therefore, we utilize the co-occurrence of faces to make more sensitive detection when the face is ambiguously or marginally visible in a crowd scene. Face co-occurrence here refers to the co-occurrence of homogeneous faces. Specifically, as mentioned earlier, the head size in a high-density crowd scene is approximately equal to the distance between two neighboring heads. Therefore, we can observe that in the local region around

---

Algorithm 1: Face co-occurrence prior for inferred box harmonization

---

Data: $\mathcal{B} = \{b_{x,y}\}$, $\mathcal{S} = \{s_{x,y}\}$, $\mathcal{A} = \{A_i^n\}$, D_i^{est}, γ, s_t,
$\mathcal{B}$ is the list of initial inferred boxes, $\mathcal{S}$ contains corresponding inferred scores,
A_i^n is the list of different density areas, D_i^{est} is the estimated density map.

for $b_{x,y}$ in $\mathcal{B}$ do
   $BS_{x,y} \leftarrow size(b_{x,y})$
   for $\mathcal{B}$ in A_i^n do
      $a_i^n \leftarrow size(A_i^n)$; $\widehat{Z}_i^n \leftarrow \sum_{p \in A_i^n} D_{est}(p|A_i^n)$;
      $\rho_i^n = \widehat{Z}_i^n / a_i^n$
      if $s_{x,y} \geqslant s_t$ then
         $m \leftarrow m + 1$; $BS_{sum}^n \leftarrow BS_{sum}^n + BS_i$
      $BS_{avg}^n \leftarrow BS_{sum}^n / m$

for $b_{x,y}$ in $\mathcal{B}$ do
   if $b_{x,y}$ in A_i^n then
      if $(1 - \gamma)BS_{avg}^n \leq BS_{x,y} \leq (1 + \gamma)BS_{avg}^n$ then
         $s_{x,y} = \sigma[D_{i(x,y)}^{est}(p \mid b_{x,y})\rho_i^n]s_{x,y} + s_{x,y}$

---

each head, the size of the face is approximately the same size. So, if the scores of many faces dominate in a local region, it is reasonable that some inferred boxes which are similar to the sizes of these faces have a high probability of being faces. According to the co-occurrence prior, we increase the scores of real faces with low scores after a detector's inferring phase.

Hence, we need to design a mechanism to reconcile and intervene face detection in high-density regions (small face regions), and give up interventions for low-density regions. As mentioned earlier, the density map presents how heads distribute in terms of the pixel intensity of the map. So, we propose a co-occurrence face strategy based on density map, as illustrated in Algorithm 1. We send the image into the density estimate network to get the density map D_i^{est} first. We define a dense grid on image I_i, and produce blocks $\mathcal{A} = \{A_i^n\}$ with 50% overlapping to minimize border effects, where n is the number of blocks. The number of people in different blocks is estimated by integrating over the values of the predicted density map as follows,

$$\widehat{Z}_i^n = \sum_{p \in A_i^n} D_i^{est}(p \mid A_i^n). \tag{3}$$

We calculate the density of each corresponding block and record it as ρ_i^n.

$$\rho_i^n = \widehat{Z}_i^n / a_i^n, \tag{4}$$

where a_i^n is the area of region A_i^n. There are two constraints to filter the inferred box for reconciliation. (1) In the corresponding high-density block, if the score of an inferred box $s_{x,y}$ exceeds the score threshold s_t, the inferred box could be a true human face. Then, the average size of all the high score faces is calculated and recorded as BS_{avg}^n, which tells us the size of faces that appear in the region. (2) These boxes with the size between $(1 - \gamma, 1 + \gamma)BS_{avg}^n$ are further filtered out as the inferred box for reconciliation and the inferred boxes whose scores are ultimately lower than the original threshold will be deleted. The reconciliation formula is as follows,

$$s_{x,y} = \sigma[D_{i(x,y)}^{est}(p \mid b_{x,y})\rho_i^n]s_{x,y} + s_{x,y}, \tag{5}$$

where σ is the Sigmoid function, $b_{x,y}$ is the inferred box and $s_{x,y}$ is the corresponding confidence score. In this way, we increase the scores of real faces which have low confidence scores.

3   Experimental Evaluation

3.1   Dataset Preparation and Experimental Setting

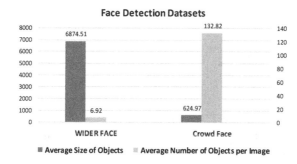

Fig. 2. Comparison of benchmark dataset WIDER FACE and our Crowd Face dataset. Two quantities are measured for each dataset: average size of objects (blue plots) and average number of objects per image (orange plots). (Color figure online)

WIDER FACE. In face detection literature, a widely used benchmark is WIDER FACE [9]. WIDER FACE contains 32203 images with 393793 faces, of which 40% are used for training, 10% for validation, and 50% for testing. According to the detection rate, the validation data are divided into three classes: "easy", "medium", and "hard".

Crowd Face. Considering the proposed solution in this paper is mainly for low-resolution and obscured face detection in crowd scenes, we have prepared a harder dataset - Crowd Face. There are 34 images with 10731 annotated faces, and the maximum number of faces on an image is 1001. As illustrated in Fig. 2, compared with WIDER FACE, each image in Crowd Face has smaller faces and more faces, as shown in Fig. 4.

Experimental Setting. In our experiments, we compare many different settings of parameters, and finally set $s_t = 0.5$, $\gamma = 0.1$. The models we used to verify our proposed methods are HR [5], S^3FD [25], LFFD [26], CAHR [20], EXTD [27], PyramidBox [28], DSFD [2] and TinaFace [3]. All the models we used in the experiments are trained with the WIDER FACE training set and tested on the WIDER FACE validation set and Crowd Face.

3.2 Ablation Experiments with Peer Comparision

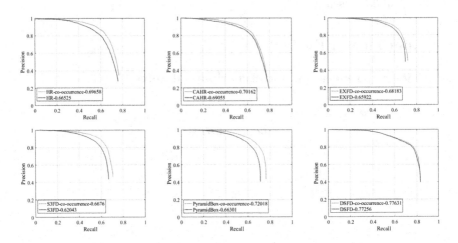

Fig. 3. P-R curves of density-aware face co-occurrence, compared with the original models (HR, CAHR, EXTD, S^3FD, PyramidBox, DSFD).

Table 1. Performance of the proposed method integrated to existing face detectors and tested on WIDER FACE and Crowd Face datasets.

Dataset	WIDER FACE - easy		WIDER FACE - medium		WIDER FACE - hard		Crowd face	
Method	Orignal	Proposed	Orignal	Proposed	Orignal	Proposed	Orignal	Proposed
LFFD [26]	0.873	0.873	0.861	**0.862**	0.750	**0.756**	0.601	**0.632**
HR [5]	0.925	0.925	0.911	**0.912**	0.816	**0.821**	0.665	**0.697**
CAHR [20]	0.928	0.928	0.912	0.912	0.832	**0.839**	0.691	**0.701**
EXTD [27]	0.921	0.921	0.911	0.911	0.846	**0.850**	0.659	**0.682**
S^3FD [25]	0.945	0.945	0.934	**0.935**	0.853	**0.855**	0.620	**0.668**
PyramidBox [28]	0.960	0.960	0.948	0.948	0.888	**0.890**	0.663	**0.720**
DSFD [2]	0.966	0.966	0.957	0.957	0.905	**0.906**	0.773	**0.776**
TinaFace [3]	0.963	0.963	0.956	**0.957**	0.930	**0.932**	0.771	**0.781**

Fig. 4. Comparison of the proposed approach integrated into HR detector (cyan ellipses) and the original HR (magenta rectangles) in crowd scenes. (Color figure online)

Test on WIDER FACE. In this part, we first test the performance of our proposed method on WIDER FACE. As is shown in Table 1, we integrate our co-occurrence prior to several anchor-based detectors including the state-of-the-art ones, and compare their Average Precision (AP) performance with the original detectors on the WIDER FACE dataset. Table 1 shows that the proposed approach integrating within all face detectors have better performance than the original methods in WIDER FACE-hard set. Especially for the detectors with poor inferring performance, the improvements of the detectors integrated with the proposed scheme are obvious. Although our method is designed for high-density crowd scenes, and WIDER FACE **easy** and **medium** set contains few crowd scene images, our method does not degrade result on the two subsets.

Test on Crowd Face. In order to further verify the performance of our proposed method in crowd scenarios, we test it on Crowd Face. As shown in Table 1 (the right part), all the state-of-the-art anchor-based detectors enhance the performance after integrating our method compared with their original detectors. As illustrated in Fig. 3, Precision-Recall curves show that our method has higher AP performance than original detectors around 0.3–5.7%, indicates the capability of the proposed approach in challenging situations. Figure 4 shows the comparison of the proposed method integrated within HR [5] (cyan ellipses) and original HR (magenta rectangles) in crowd scenes, where the proposed approach helps the detector find more true faces in crowd scenes.

4 Conclusion

We propose a general approach by utilizing high-level spatial contextual information according to density estimation. Our proposed density-aware co-occurrence prior can detect more true faces and make sense to detect low resolution faces in the crowded challenge. The proposed method does not require any extra training and is simple to implement. In the future, we will further explore richer context information to solve low-resolution face detection in crowded scenes.

References

1. Zhu, J., Li, D., Han, T., Tian, L., Shan, Y.: ProgressFace: scale-aware progressive learning for face detection. In: Vedaldi, A., Bischof, H., Brox, T., Frahm, J.-M. (eds.) ECCV 2020. LNCS, vol. 12351, pp. 344–360. Springer, Cham (2020). https://doi.org/10.1007/978-3-030-58539-6_21
2. Li, J., Wang, Y., Wang, C.: DSFD: dual shot face detector. In: CVPR (2019)
3. Zhu, Y., Cai, H., Zhang, S., Wang, C., Xiong, Y.: TinaFace: strong but simple baseline for face detection. In: arXiv (2020)
4. Lin, T., Dollár, P., Girshick, R., He, K., Hariharan, B., Belongie, S.: Feature pyramid networks for object detection. In: CVPR (2017)
5. Hu, P., Ramanan, D.: Finding tiny faces. In: CVPR (2017)
6. Liu, W., et al.: SSD: single shot multibox detector. In: Leibe, B., Matas, J., Sebe, N., Welling, M. (eds.) ECCV 2016. LNCS, vol. 9905, pp. 21–37. Springer, Cham (2016). https://doi.org/10.1007/978-3-319-46448-0_2
7. Ren, S., He, K., Girshick, R.B., Sun, J.: Faster r-cnn: Towards real-time object detection with region proposal networks. In: IEEE Transactions on Pattern Analysis and Machine Intelligence. (2017)
8. Lin, T., Goyal, P., Girshick, R., He, K., Dollár, P.: Focal loss for dense object detection. IEEE Trans. Pattern Anal. Mach. Intell. **50**, 2980 (2017)
9. Yang, S., Luo, P., Loy, C.C., Tang, X.: Wider face: a face detection benchmark. In: CVPR (2016)
10. Oliva, A., Torralba, A.: The role of context in object recognition. In: Trends in Cognitive Sciences (2007)
11. Wolf, L., Bileschi, S.M.: A critical view of context. Int. J. Comput. Vis. **69**, 251 (2006)
12. Divvala, S.K., Hoiem, D.W., Hays, J., Efros, A.A., Hebert, M.: An empirical study of context in object detection. In: CVPR (2009)
13. Biederman, I., Mezzanotte, R.J., Rabinowitz, J.C.: Scene perception detecting and judging objects undergoing relational violations. In: Cognitive Psychology (1982)
14. Zhang, S., Zhu, X., Lei, Z., Wang, X., Shi, H., Li, S.Z.: Detecting face with densely connected face proposal network. In: CCBR (2018)
15. Zhu, C., Zheng, Y., Luu, K., Savvides, M.: CMS-RCNN: contextual multi-scale region-based CNN for unconstrained face detection. In: Bhanu, B., Kumar, A. (eds.) Deep Learning for Biometrics. ACVPR, pp. 57–79. Springer, Cham (2017). https://doi.org/10.1007/978-3-319-61657-5_3
16. Liang, D., Hashimoto, M., Iwata, K., Zhao, X., et al.: Co-occurrence probability-based pixel pairs background model for robust object detection in dynamic scenes. Pattern Recogn. **48**, 134 (2015)

17. Liang, D., Kang, B., Liu, X., Sun, H., Zhang, L., Liu, N.: Cross scene video foreground segmentation via co-occurrence probability oriented supervised and unsupervised model interaction. In: ICASSP (2021)
18. Liang, D., Liu, X.: Coarse-to-fine foreground segmentation based on co-occurrence pixel-block and spatio-temporal attention model. In: ICPR (2021)
19. Wu, T., et al.: Score-specific non-maximum suppression and coexistence prior for multi-scale face detection. In: ICASSP (2019)
20. Wu, T., Liang, D., Pan, J., Kaneko, S.: Context-anchors for hybrid resolution face detection. In: ICIP (2019)
21. Liang, D., Kaneko, S., Sun, H., Kang, B.: Adaptive local spatial modeling for online change detection under abrupt dynamic background. In: ICIP (2017)
22. Zhou, W., Kaneko, S., Hashimoto, M., Satoh, Y., Liang, D.: Foreground detection based on co-occurrence background model with hypothesis on degradation modification in dynamic scenes. Signal Process. **160**, 66 (2019)
23. Xiang, S., Liang, D., Kaneko, S., Asano, H.: Robust defect detection in 2D images printed on 3D micro-textured surfaces by multiple paired pixel consistency in orientation codes. IET Image Process. **14**, 3373 (2020)
24. Liu, W., Salzmann, M., Fua, P.: Context-aware crowd counting. In: CVPR (2019)
25. Zhang, S., Zhu, X., Lei, Z.: S^{3}FD: single shot scale-invariant face detector. In: ICCV (2017)
26. He, Y., Xu, D., Wu, L.: LFFD: a light and fast face detector for edge devices. In: arXiv (2019)
27. Yoo, Y., Han, D., Yun, S.: EXTD: extremely tiny face detector via iterative filter reuse. In: arXiv (2019)
28. Tang, X., Du, D.K., He, Z.: PyramidBox: a context-assisted single shot face detector. In: ECCV (2018)

Iris Normalization Beyond Appr-Circular Parameter Estimation

Zhengquan Luo[1,2], Haiqing Li[3], Yunlong Wang[2(✉)], Zilei Wang[1], and Zhenan Sun[2]

[1] University of Science and Technology of China, Hefei, Anhui, China
[2] Center for Research on Intelligent Perception and Computing, National Laboratory of Pattern Recognition, Institute of Automation, Chinese Academy of Sciences, Beijing, China
yunlong.wang@cripac.ia.ac.cn
[3] IriStar Technology Co., Ltd., Tianjin 300457, China

Abstract. The requirement to recognize the iris image of low-quality is rapidly increasing with the practical application of iris recognition, especially the urgent need for high-throughput or applications in covert situations. The appr-circle fitting can not meet the needs due to the high time cost and non-accurate boundary estimation during the normalization process. Furthermore, the appr-circular hypothesis of iris and pupil is not entirely established due to the squint and occlusion in non-cooperative environments. To mitigate this problem, a multi-mask normalization without appr-circular parameter estimation is proposed to make full use of the segmented masks, which provide robust pixel-level iris boundaries. It bridges the segmentation and feature extraction to recognize the low-quality iris, which is thrown directly by the traditional methods. Thus, the complex samples with no appr-circular iris or massive occlusions can be recognized correctly. The extensive experiments are conducted on the representative and challenging databases to verify the generalization and the accuracy of the proposed iris normalization method. Besides, the throughput rate is significantly improved.

Keywords: Normalization · Iris recognition · Segmentation

1 Introduction

The application of iris recognition is rapidly developed, which is ubiquitous in access control [1], payment, security check-in, and so on. Especially, the high throughput or the covert situations urge higher requirements to the advance on iris recognition methods, which need to handle low-quality images at higher speed. Due to the non-cooperative environment of covert situations, the low quality mainly reflects in serious gaze deviation, compound blur factors, intricate occlusions, and specular reflections. The high-throughput demand not only means less time cost to deal with one single iris but also means correct recognition of low-quality iris images, which are thrown directly by the traditional recognition system.

© Springer Nature Switzerland AG 2021
J. Feng et al. (Eds.): CCBR 2021, LNCS 12878, pp. 316–324, 2021.
https://doi.org/10.1007/978-3-030-86608-2_35

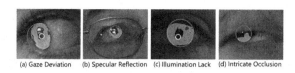

(a) Gaze Deviation   (b) Specular Reflection   (c) Illumination Lack   (d) Intricate Occlusion

Fig. 1. The examples from UBIRIS.v2 [5] with error appr-circular parameter estimation in non-cooperative environment.

The normalization of the iris bridges the segmentation/localization and the feature extraction, which resists the negative influence of iris size changing and pupillary dilation as one essential part of the iris recognition system [6]. The common normalization methods employ the appr-circular parameter estimation to determine the inner/outer boundaries of the iris. It is usually found that the erroneous estimation may hinder the correct recognition, although accurate segmented masks are obtained. The reason is that the shape of the iris in image acquisition tends to be miscellaneous at a distance. Moreover, the appr-circular hypothesis of iris and pupil is violated due to the serious gaze deviation. These make it infeasible to estimate appr-circular parameters. The brute-force estimation gets the wrong appr-circular parameter of the low-quality images from non-cooperative environments, leading to the incorrect recognition of the wrong normalized iris area. Specifically, the well-known Wilde's circular Hough Transform [3] finds the optimum parameters for circle fitting, and Daugman's integro-differential operator [2] finds the strongest intensity over the circle parameter space. These widely applied methods all require that the iris or pupil should have a clear and separable boundary without much occlusion or blur, which can not be met. For example, Fig. 1 shows some samples with deviative estimation results from the UBIRIS.v2 [5].

To solve these problems, a novel iris normalization method beyond appr-circular parameter estimation is proposed in this paper. It employs three segmentation masks as input: the pupil mask, the iris outer boundary mask, and the mask of effective iris areas. With the development of CNN-based iris segmentation methods, one robust pixel-based iris segmentation can approximate the iris's boundaries even in low-quality iris images without parameter estimation. The previous work [7] verifies that three separate masks can provide more robust and accurate inter/outer boundaries than a single mask due to the introduction of the spatial prior. In order to correct the uncertain boundary of the segmentation methods, the smooth and continuous constraints of iris boundaries are introduced as spatial prior [8], improving the robustness of masks. Then, the centre of the effective iris area mask is applied as the start point. A cluster of polar rays is emitted around evenly from it. The sampling line segment is defined by the intersections of each ray crossing the pupil mask and iris outer mask. Overall, the segmented iris and the mask of the effective iris area are normalized in the polar domain. There is no extra parameter estimation during the entire normalization process, which reduces the time cost. The Multi-mask normalization makes full use of the segmented masks of low-quality iris, which is not accurate or appr-circular.

The extensive experiments are conducted on representative and challenging databases such as CASIA.v4-distance [4] and UBIRIS.v2 [5]. The results show that the iris recognition employing the pioneer normalization can reach SOTA accuracy. What more, the failure-to-enroll rate can be reduced to 0% on CASIA.v4-distance and 0.29% on UBIRIS.v2. It means that the throughput rate is significantly improved by the multi-mask normalization method.

2   Related Work

The well-known rubber sheet as iris normalization model is proposed by Daugman [2]. Then, several iris normalization methods [10,11] based on

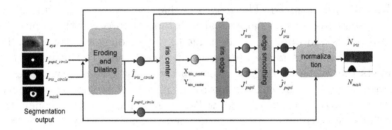

Fig. 2. The input of the normalization is the iris image and three segmented masks. The effective iris centre is calculated after eroding, dilating and hole filling. Then, the first-order smoothing is performed. Finally, the iris image and the effective area mask are normalized according to the mapping relationship.

non-linear sampling are proposed. However, with the rapid development of CNN-based iris segmentation methods, the gap between segmentation and normalization of iris recognition is enlarged. To bridge this gap, the circular Hough transforms [3] is introduced, and there are some similar methods [12,13]. However, the time cost of complex calculation and the low-quality factors in non-cooperative environments hinder localization performance. The region clustering [14] is applied to narrow the parameter search range. Viterbi algorithm [15] is applied to find coarse low-resolution contours with few noisy gradients points. Considering the boundaries or iris are not strictly circular, some flexible curve shapes are employed by some works, such as elliptic contours [16] and active geodesic contours [17]. Alternatively, Our work focus on iris normalization beyond appr-circular parameter estimation.

3   Technical Details

The multi-mask normalization does not need the parameterized appr-circular fitting as the input. Instead, the raw iris image and three masks, including the iris mask, the pupil mask, and the mask of the effective area, are fed to the proposed iris normalization method. These masks are the pixel-level binary results of the iris segmentation process. The recent state-of-art segmentation network can provide robust inter/outer iris boundaries beyond traditional localization methods. However, the uncertainty of border classification is the common issue of segmentation methods. To mitigate the degradation, the smooth and continuous constraints of iris boundaries in the physiological structure are introduced as spatial prior [8], improving the accuracy of the iris boundary. In details, the morphologically eroding and dilating are employed to eliminate noise points and amend missing points of the iris mask and the pupil mask.

Specifically, $I_{iriscircle}$ and $I_{pupilcircle}$ are the iris binary outer mask and pupil binary mask. Multiple morphological operations, including erosion, dilation, and hole filling, are repeated on $I_{iriscircle}$ and $I_{pupilcircle}$, until only one connected region is left in the image, to get new $\hat{I}_{iriscircle}$ and $\hat{I}_{pupilcircle}$. Then, the center of the effective area of $\hat{I}_{iriscircle}$ is applied as the center point $(X_{iriscenter}, Y_{iriscenter})$ of the normalization process. Next, according to the number of polar coordinates expansion, a cluster of polar rays are emitted around evenly from the centre. After that, the sampling line segment is defined by the intersections of each ray crossing the pupil mask and iris outer mask. $\left(J_{pupil}^i, J_{iris}^i \right)$ represents the distance from the inner to the outer using the centre point at the angle i:

$$J_{pupil}^i = max\left\{ dis_p | \hat{I}_{pupilcircle}(X_{pupil}, Y_{pupil}) = 1 \right\} \qquad (1)$$

$$J_{iris}^i = max\left\{ dis_p | \hat{I}_{iriscircle}(X_{iris}, Y_{iris}) = 1 \right\} \qquad (2)$$

where $X_{pupil} = X_{pupilcenter} + dis_p * cosi, Y_{pupil} = Y_{pupilcenter} + dis_p * sini$, $X_{iris} = X_{iriscenter} + dis_p * cosi, Y_{iris} = Y_{iriscenter} + dis_p * sini$. After that, the boundary values are smoothed to be aligned with the continuous physiological structure. The first order boundary smoothing is employed instead of image smoothing because the most distinguishing feature of the iris image is extracted from the clear texture. Image smoothing wipes out the discriminative information and blurs the details of the iris texture.

Finally, each polar coordinate ray from the iris centre is sampled uniformly between the two boundaries of the iris boundaries. The iris image and iris mask are normalized according to the relationship between the raw image and polar coordinates image. The mapping of the coordinate relationship is:

$$N_{iris}(i, j) = I_{eye}(X, Y) \qquad (3)$$

$$N_{mask}(i, j) = I_{mask}(X, Y) \qquad (4)$$

$$X = X_{iriscenter} + \left[\frac{j}{N} * \left(\hat{J}_{iris}^i - \hat{J}_{pupil}^i \right) + \hat{J}_{pupil}^i \right] * cos\left(\frac{2\pi i}{M} \right) \qquad (5)$$

$$Y = Y_{iriscenter} + \left[\frac{j}{N} * \left(\hat{J}_{iris}^i - \hat{J}_{pupil}^i \right) + \hat{J}_{pupil}^i \right] * sin\left(\frac{2\pi i}{M} \right) \qquad (6)$$

where the N, M represent that the normalized image size is $N * M$. The whole normalization method is shown in Fig. 2.

4   Experiments and Analysis

4.1   Databases

Two representative and challenge iris databases are employed to verify the superiority of the multi-mask normalization.

CASIA-Distance [4] contains 2567 partial face images from 142 subjects. The capturing at-a-distance employs a long-range camera in near-infrared illumination (NIR). Two iris images were manually cropped from each partial face. The resolution is 640 × 480. Then, the off-the-shelf segmentation/localization models and the iris feature extraction model as UniNet is applied to ensure the fairness of comparison with other normalization methods. The details are shown in the subsection of recognition experiments.

UBIRIS.v2 [5] contains 11102 images from 259 subjects. The acquisition equipment is a Canon EOS 5D camera, and the images were captured as subjects were on-the-move and at-a-distance under visible illumination (VIS). Thus, the non-cooperative environments lead to complex low-quality factors of iris. Figure 1 shows the examples of the segmentation and the localization of some selected iris images. Other settings are the same as the CASIA-Distance [4].

4.2   Evaluations

The performance of iris recognition is evaluated by verification and identification. The failure-to-enroll rate (FTE) is taken into account to evaluate the performance of normalization methods.

Failure-to-Enroll Rate (FTE). The FTE is the percentage of images that failed to be enrolled in the entire database. It can be understood as the feature extraction of the iris image failed due to the error in previous processes.

Decidability Index (DI). The DI is firstly proposed by Daugman [2], which measures the separation between the genuine and impostor distributions. It is defined as:

$$DI = \frac{\mu_G - \mu_I}{\sqrt{\frac{1}{2}\left(\sigma_G^2 + \sigma_I^2\right)}} \tag{7}$$

where μ_G, μ_I, σ_G^2, and σ_I^2 are the means and standard deviations of the genuine (G) and impostor (I) dissimilarity scores.

DET Curve. Detection Error Trade-off (DET) curve shows all operating points, which is FRR versus FAR. FRRs are compared at FAR = 1%, 0.1%, 0.01% and 0.001%. Equal Error Rate (EER), i.e. FRR = FAR, as a well-known metric for biometrics, where lower value means better performance.

Rank-N Accuracy. Rank-N identification accuracy is defined as the number of hit times versus the number of total probe images. The hit sample means the same identity appears in the first N queries of the descending score order. The Rank-1, Rank-5, Rank- 10 accuracy are displayed, and the Cumulative Match Characteristic (CMC) curve is plotted.

4.3   Recognition Experiments

Table 1. The recognition results of CASIA-distance [4] database. The iris segmentation methods are Hough transform [3] (**H**) and IriSegNet [7] (**S**). The normalization methods are rubber sheet [2] (**R**) and our Multi-mask (**M**). For example, **H_R** means the recognition results of Hough-transform localization and rubber sheet normalization combination. Iris feature extraction employs UniNet [9], which is a recent SOTA method.

	FTE	DI	EER	Rank-1	Rank-5	Rank-10	FRR@ FAR = 1%	FRR@ FAR = 0.1%	FRR@ FAR = 0.01%	FRR@ FAR = 0.001%
H_R	3.91	0.7547	21.88	84.27	89.50	91.27	36.93	76.8	93.2	99.98
H_M	0.37	1.8255	18.36	84.34	89.23	90.07	47.36	92.97	99.82	100.00
S_R	0.41	2.4585	4.83	97.57	98.51	98.77	7.41	12.17	18.87	28.94
S_M	0.00	3.6931	4.39	98.21	98.92	99.08	7.19	12.64	19.80	30.42

Table 2. The recognition results of the UBIRIS.v2 [5] database verify the generalization in the cross-spectral situation of Multi-mask normalization.

	FTE	DI	EER	Rank-1	Rank-5	Rank-10	FRR@ FAR = 1%	FRR@ FAR = 0.1%	FRR@ FAR = 0.01%	FRR@ FAR = 0.001%
S_R	1.71	0.4879	39.40	4.48	12.15	17.31	93.12	98.39	99.71	99.97
S_M	0.29	0.7293	29.36	37.44	54.24	59.84	71.54	84.01	91.77	97.35

To verify the effectiveness of the proposed iris normalization method, extensive experiments of iris recognition are conducted on CASIA-Distance [4] and UBIRIS.v2 [5] databases. The localization employs Hough Transform [3] and IriSegNet [7], and the normalization employs rubber sheet [2] and our Multi-mask methods.

For details, the Hough Transform [3], as a well-known localization method, can provide parameters of circle estimation. The input is the eye part image, and the output is the parameter of the iris inner/outer boundaries. The IriSeg-Net [7], as a pioneer iris segmentation method, can provide three segmented masks. The inner/outer circle parameters are estimated from two masks via the Hough Transform. The rubber sheet [2], as a widely used iris normalization method, employs the appr-circular parameters to normalized the iris and the mask. The rubber sheet and our multi-mask normalization both normalized the raw image and effective iris area mask to 512 * 64 templates. Besides, to create the input of the multi-mask normalization, the iris mask and pupil mask can be generated by simple operation according to the circle parameters only when the Hough Transform is employed as localization. In addition, the UniNet [9] is applied as a feature extraction network that employs the off-the-shelf model. The Hamming distance is used as the measurement to calculate the matching score.

Considering that the FTEs of methods combination are different, a 512 * 64 all-zero feature and mask are generated for the failed images joining the final recognition to ensure the fairness of the comparison.

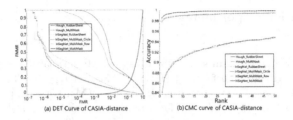

(a) DET Curve of CASIA-distance   (b) CMC curve of CASIA-distance

Fig. 3. The DET curve and the CMC curve of iris recognition on CASIA-Distance [4] database.

The recognition result in Table 1 shows that the multi-mask normalization is better than rubber sheet [2] no matter the localization is Hough Transform [3] or IriSegNet [7] in CASIA-Distance [4]. The FTE drops to 0%, which means all images can throughput the system. However, the disadvantages of FRR may be caused by the through of many low-quality iris images. Besides, the results in Table 2 are terrible due to the cross-spectral setting of the experiment. However, the FTE and EER are significantly reduced by the multi-mask normalization compared with the rubber sheet [2]. Figure 4 visually shows the contribution of multi-mask normalization to improving the distinguishability of features. The DET curve and the CMC curve in Fig. 3 represent the advantage of our methods.

Table 3. The ablation study verifies that the performance of multi-mask normalization surpasses appr-circular parameter estimation methods on CASIA-Distance [4]. Furthermore, the morphological operation can improve the performance.

	Appr-circular estimation	No-parameter estimation	Morphological operation	FTE	DI	EER	Rank-1	FRR@ FAR = 1%
S_M_Circle	✓			0.00	3.4373	4.56	97.86	13.32
S_M_Raw		✓		0.00	3.447	4.43	98.04	7.26
S_M		✓	✓	0.00	3.6931	4.39	98.21	7.10

4.4   Ablation Study

Table 3 shows the results of the ablation study that iris recognition in CASIA-Distance [4] employed the multi-mask normalization in different settings. Besides, the IrisSegNet [7] is applied as the segmentation model, and UniNet [9] is employed as the feature extraction model. It validates the advantage of the multi-mask setting without appr-circular parameter estimation of our normalization, which outperforms the appr-circular parameter estimation. The introduction of morphological operation as spatial prior can further improve the recognition performance. Figure 3 visually demonstrate the advantages of the proposed methods.

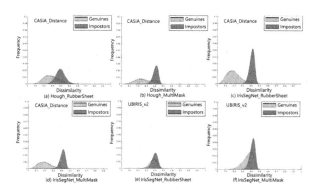

Fig. 4. The dissimilarity distribution of the recognition results. (a), (b), (c), (d) represent the distribution of CASIA-Distance [4], and (e), (f) show the results of UBIRIS.v2. It represents the multi-mask normalization can improve distinguishability.

5   Conclusion

In this paper, a multi-mask without appr-circular parameter estimation normalization is proposed to bridge the segmentation and feature extraction of iris recognition. The recognition performance is improved due to the low-quality iris can be correctly recognized. Our method can normalize irides of arbitrary shape. The full use of the robust segmented masks can make up the negative influence of the error localization of the iris in the non-cooperative environment. Besides, the extra time cost of the localization to the iris inner/outer boundaries is reduced. Thus, the throughput rate is significantly enhanced for the entire recognition process. The extensive experiments on the representative and challenge database verify the robustness and accuracy of our normalization methods. In the future study, we will focus on the learnable iris normalization methods without parameter estimation, which can be incorporated into the CNN model to build an end-to-end iris recognition system.

References

1. Sequeira, A.F., et al.: PROTECT multimodal DB: fusion evaluation on a novel multimodal biometrics dataset envisaging border control. In: Proceedings of International Conference of the Biometrics Special Interest Group (BIOSIG), pp. 1–5, September 2018
2. Daugman, J.G.: High confidence visual recognition of persons by a test of statistical independence. IEEE Trans. Pattern Anal. Mach. Intell. **15**(11), 1148–1161 (1993)
3. Wildes, R.P.: Iris recognition: an emerging biometric technology. Proc. IEEE **85**(9), 1348–1363 (1997)
4. BI Test: Casia.v4 Database. http://www.idealtest.org/dbDetailForUser.do?id=4. Accessed Feb 2020
5. Proenca, H., Filipe, S., Santos, R., Oliveira, J., Alexandre, L.A.: The UBIRIS.v2: a database of visible wavelength iris images captured on the-move and at-a-distance. IEEE Trans. Pattern Anal. Mach. Intell. **32**(8), 1529–1535 (2010)

6. Vyas, R., Kanumuri, T., Sheoran, G., Dubey, P.: Recent trends of ROI segmentation in iris biometrics: a survey. Int. J. Biom. **11**(3), 274 (2019)
7. Wang, C., Muhammad, J., Wang, Y., et al.: Towards complete and accurate iris segmentation using deep multi-task attention network for non-cooperative iris recognition. IEEE Trans. Inf. Forensics Secur. **15**, 2944–2959 (2020)
8. Hofbauer, H., Jalilian, E., Uhl, A.: Exploiting superior CNN-based iris segmentation for better recognition accuracy. Pattern Recogn. Lett. **120**, 17–23 (2019)
9. Zhao, Z., Kumar, A.: Towards more accurate iris recognition using deeply learned spatially corresponding features. In: Proceedings of the IEEE International Conference on Computer Vision, pp. 3809–3818 (2017)
10. Yuan, X., Shi, P.: A non-linear normalization model for iris recognition. In: Li, S.Z., Sun, Z., Tan, T., Pankanti, S., Chollet, G., Zhang, D. (eds.) IWBRS 2005. LNCS, vol. 3781, pp. 135–141. Springer, Heidelberg (2005). https://doi.org/10.1007/11569947_17
11. Tomeo-Reyes, I., Ross, A., Clark, A.D., Chandran, V.: A biomechanical approach to iris normalization. In: 2015 International Conference on Biometrics (ICB), pp. 9–16. IEEE (2015)
12. Zhao, Z., Kumar, A.: A deep learning based unified framework to detect, segment and recognize irises using spatially corresponding features. Pattern Recogn. **93**, 546–557 (2019)
13. Kerrigan, D., Trokielewicz, M., Czajka, A., Bowyer, K.W.: Iris recognition with image segmentation employing retrained off-the-shelf deep neural networks. In: Proceedings of the International Conference on Biometrics (ICB), pp. 1–7, June 2019
14. Proença, H., Alexandre, L.A.: Iris segmentation methodology for non-cooperative recognition. IEE Proc.-Vis. Image Sig. Process. **153**(2), 199–205 (2006)
15. Sutra, G., Garcia-Salicetti, S., Dorizzi, B.: The Viterbi algorithm at different resolutions for enhanced iris segmentation. In: Proceedings of the 5th IAPR International Conference on Biometrics (ICB), pp. 310–316, March 2012
16. Banerjee, S., Mery, D.: Iris segmentation using geodesic active contours and Grab-Cut. In: Huang, F., Sugimoto, A. (eds.) PSIVT 2015. LNCS, vol. 9555, pp. 48–60. Springer, Cham (2016). https://doi.org/10.1007/978-3-319-30285-0_5
17. Shah, S., Ross, A.: Iris segmentation using geodesic active contours. IEEE Trans. Inf. Forensics Secur. **4**(4), 824–836 (2009)

Non-segmentation and Deep-Learning Frameworks for Iris Recognition

Wenqiang Wu, Ying Chen$^{(\boxtimes)}$, and Zhuang Zeng

Nanchang Hangkong University, Nanchang, China

Abstract. Traditional iris recognition algorithms and data-driven iris recognition generally believe that the iris recognition process should be divided into a series of sub-processes which makes the iris recognition process more complex. Furthermore, each sub-process relies on specific algorithm which greatly increases the computational complexity of the overall framework of the model. The work proposes an end-to-end iris recognition algorithm based on deep learning. We encourage the reuse of feature and increase the interaction information across channels with the aim of improving the accuracy and robustness of iris recognition, at the same time, to some extent, reducing the complexity of the model. Related experiments are conducted in three publicly available databases, CASIA-V4 Lamp, CASIA-V4 Thousand and IITD. The results showed that non-process-based iris algorithm that we proposed consistently outperforms than several classical and advance iris recognition methods.

Keywords: Non-process · End-to-End iris recognition · Deep learning

1 Introduction

Iris recognition, in the field of biometric identification, is considered as the most secure and promising identification method owing to uniqueness, high security and non-contact nature [1]. With the outbreak of the new crown pneumonia epidemic in 2020, contacting biometric identification methods bring many challenges to identity information authentication, including fingerprint recognition and mask face recognition, iris recognition has more advantages in this case for comprehensive advantages and characteristics. Currently, the accuracy and robustness of iris recognition, with the continuous maturation and development of deep learning techniques have significantly improved [4]. However, most of them divide the process of iris recognition into a series of isolated unit modules which brought some challenges to the iris recognition process. First of all, since each sub-process is independent with each other, the cumulative error generated by each unit module will eventually affect the accuracy. Secondly, because each module needs to be trained separately, the computational effort increases significantly, leading to a further increase in the overall module size of iris recognition. There are few studies on iris recognition methods for direct recognition of the original iris image currently. There are two contributions in this paper.

© Springer Nature Switzerland AG 2021
J. Feng et al. (Eds.): CCBR 2021, LNCS 12878, pp. 325–334, 2021.
https://doi.org/10.1007/978-3-030-86608-2_36

(1) An end-to-end iris recognition network (ETENet) is proposed. Without performing the submodules of unit such as preprocessing, iris segmentation and data augmentation, the work directly takes the captured raw iris image as the input to the network model for recognition for feature extraction and recognition. Through a series of demonstrations, end-to-end network that our proposed still outperforms most of the better performing algorithms.

(2) The algorithm is designed for encourage feature reuse and cross-channel interaction, with the aim of extracting robust real-valued feature templates in a stable manner and achieving more accurate template matching. Some ablation experiments are conducted to test the effectiveness of the dense connection-based and channel-attention mechanisms.

2   Related Work

Segmentation and classification are considered as one of the most important tasks in the field of computer vision, and after more than 30 years of development, the research on iris recognition under restricted states is becoming more and more mature [2]. Currently, there are two categories of algorithms, iris recognition algorithms based on traditional methods and deep-learning.

2.1   Iris Recognition Algorithms Based on Traditional Methods

Daugman [3] firstly proposed feature extraction of the normalized iris image using Gabor filter, then the extracted iris features were binarized, and finally the matching score between two iris feature templates was calculated using Hamming distance. The Gabor or log-Gabor filter is relatively coarse in its ability to extract iris features. Therefore, Sun and Tan [11] first proposed to use multileaf differential filtering for feature extraction of iris images and obtained rich iris feature templates. Chen [1] used the SIFI method to extract to iris features, then processed the extracted iris features according to the sub-features strategy, and finally fused and effectively improved the iris recognition accuracy in the region selected by the sub-features

2.2   Iris Recognition Algorithms Based on Deep Learning

Zhao Zhe and Ajay Kumar [4] proposed a framework combining deep learning to study the iris domain problems and achieved superior experimental results than traditional methods. Wang K et al. [5] based on deep learning framework can accurately extract iris feature texture information in different spectra and achieve robust cross-spectral iris recognition. Hugo Proenca [2] proposed a segmentation-free and non-holistic deep learning framework for iris recognition, however, there is still room for improvement in the accuracy and robustness of this algorithm. Kuo Wang and Ajay Kumar [10] proposed a segmentation-free and non-holistic deep learning framework for iris recognition. However, the algorithm still has room for improvement in iris recognition accuracy and robustness.

Kuo Wang and Ajay Kumar et al. [10] effectively combined the eyelash feature information around the eye region with the feature texture information of the iris to improve the accuracy and robustness of iris recognition at long distances.

3 Proposed Method

The proposed framework of iris recognition algorithm, as shown in Fig. 1, is based on non-process, in other words, iris recognition is independent of processes such as iris segmentation, image enhancement and normalization. First of all, we employ the original iris images as the input to the iris classification model for feature learning during the training phase. And then, we employ the trained model to extract the features of the original iris image and generate the corresponding feature templates. Finally we calculate the matching score of the templates to complete the end-to-end iris recognition process.

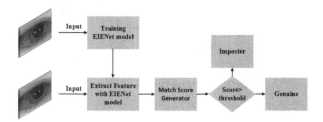

Fig. 1. End-to-end iris recognition framework.

3.1 ETENet

The proposed network in this paper fully draws the advantages and features of deep learning networks such as DenseNet [12] and ECA-Net [13], which perform well in computer vision. As shown in Fig. 2, the ETENet network mainly consists of a 5×5 convolutional layer, 6 layers of ETE block, 6 layers of connection layer, a global average pooling layer and a fully connected layer.

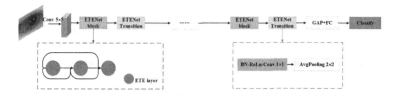

Fig. 2. The structure of ETENet.

The structure of ETElayer is shown in Fig. 3. First of all, a global averaging layer (GAP) is performed for a given input X to obtain the feature matrix of $1 \times 1 \times C$. As shown in Eq. 1, where Uk, W and H denote the k dimensional, length and width of the feature matrix respectively.

$$Z = GAP(U_K) = \frac{1}{W \cdot H} \sum_{i=1}^{N} \sum_{j}^{H} U_K(i, j) \tag{1}$$

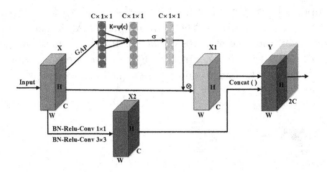

Fig. 3. The structure of ETElayer.

As shown in Eq. 2 and Eq. 3, we perform a one-dimensional convol to capture the inter-channel interaction information and learn the channel adaptive weight values, and then assign to X to get X1 after activation by the ReLu function. K is determined by the channel number adaptive mapping function (c), c is the channel dimension, and the values of α and γ are set to 2 and 1 respectively.

$$W = \sigma(Conv1D(Y)) \tag{2}$$

$$K = \psi(C) = \left| \frac{\log_2 C}{\gamma} + \frac{\alpha}{\gamma} \right|_{odd} \tag{3}$$

The BN layer emerged mainly to solve the problem of keeping the training and test sets independently and identically distributed in machine learning. If the distribution of the input is not stable, that is, the distribution of the input gradually moves towards the two ends of the nonlinear function, then the training will be difficult to converge. However, we can pull the input distribution back to a normal distribution with a mean of 0 and a variance of 1 by introducing BN. In this way, it can generate a more obvious gradient in the back propagation, and is easier to converge and effectively alleviate the problem of the disappearance of the gradient. We use BN-ReLu-Conv1 $\times$ 1 and BN-ReLu-Conv3 $\times$ 3 at Bottleneck and get X2, and finally stitch X1 and X2 together by Concating to form the new output Y. The equation of BN is shown in Eq. 4, and formula of activation function of ReLu is shown in Eq. 5.

$$\alpha^k = \gamma^k \cdot \frac{\chi^k - E(\chi^k)}{\sqrt{Var[\chi^k]}} + \beta^k \tag{4}$$

$$F(X) = Max(0, x) \tag{5}$$

The structure of ETE Block is shown in Fig. 4. According to the captured cross-channel interaction information with the dense connection mechanism, each layer will additionally acquire the features of Bottleneck layer and finish the stitching in dimensions by Concating. Therefore, the feature information of different dimensions can be learned in the forward propagation stage, and for this purpose, we perform a series of ablation experiments on the dataset to verify the role and impact of ETE Block. The structure of ETENET is shown in Table 1.

Table 1. Detailed layer-wise structure of ETENET.

Name	Layer type	Number of stride/filter	Output size
InputConv1	Convolution 5 × 5	2 × 2/64	128 × 64 × 64
ETE block 1	ETE layer X2	1 × 1/48	128 × 64 × 160
Transition layer 1	BN-Relu-Conv 1 × 1 Average pooling 2 × 2	1 × 1/160 2 × 2	64 × 32 × 160
ETE block 2	ETE layer X2	1 × 1/48	64 × 32 × 256
Transition layer 2	BN-Relu-Conv 1 × 1 Average pooling 2 × 2	1 × 1/256 2 × 2	32 × 16 × 256
ETE block 3	ETE layer X2	1 × 1/48	32 × 16 × 352
Transition layer 3	BN-Relu-Conv 1 × 1 Average pooling 2 × 2	1 × 1/352 2 × 2	16 × 8 × 352
ETE block 4	ETE layer X2	1 × 1/48	16 × 8 × 448
Transition layer 4	BN-Relu-Conv 1 × 1 Average pooling 2 × 2	1 × 1/448 2 × 2	8 × 4 × 448
ETE block 5	ETE layer X2	1 × 1/48	8 × 4 × 544
Transition layer 5	BN-Relu-Conv 1 × 1 Average pooling 2 × 2	1 × 1/544 2 × 2	4 × 2 × 544
ETE block 6	ETE layer X2	1 × 1/48	4 × 2 × 640
Transition layer 6	BN-Relu-Conv 1 × 1 Average pooling 2 × 2	1 × 1/640 2 × 2	2 × 1 × 640
GAP	Global average pooling		1 × 1 × 640
FC	Fully connected		Class numbers

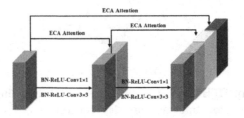

Fig. 4. The structure of ETE block.

4   Experiments and Results

The work choosed false acceptance rate (FAR), true acceptance rate (TAR) and equal error rate (EER) as the performance level evaluation metrics. Meanwhile, we drew the corresponding observer operating characteristic (ROC). In order to ensure the fairness of the experimental comparison, we conducted a series of experiments on three publicly available iris datasets, CASIA-V4 Lamp, CASIA-V4 Thousand and IITD, according to the requirements of comparison literature and verified that model proposed in this paper has higher accuracy and robustness.

4.1   Dataset

CASIA Iris Image Database V4 Lamp (CA4L) [8] used different illuminations to acquire iris images of the same subject with 411 subjects and 16,212 iris images for the whole dataset. Since the left and right eyes of each subject were divided into different categories, the whole dataset had a total of 822 categories of images. In order to reflect the fairness of the experiment, we divided the dataset according to the comparative literature [2,6]. CASIA Iris Image Database V4 Thousand (CA4T) [8]used NIR to acquire 1000 subjects' iris images 10 images for each subject's left and right eyes, and divided them into different classes, therefore, the whole dataset had 2000 classes and 20,000 iris images. The first 5 iris images of each class were used for training, and the remaining 5 were used for testing, so the training and testing sets were 10,000 images each. IITD [9]collected 224 iris images from 224 subjects using NIR, 10 images per subject, and unlike the previous two datasets, this dataset does not differentiate between additional categories for the left and right eyes, so the total number of 224 categories in the dataset is 2240. The ratio of the validation and test sets was set to 3:1:1, and the number of iris images was 1344, 448, and 448 respectively. The detailed parameters of the dataset are shown in Table 2.

4.2   Experimental Environment and Parameters

The experimental environment is as follows. CPU: Intel (R) Xeon(R) Gold CPU @ 2.30 GHz 2.29 GHz, GPU: NVIDIA GeForce RTX 2080 Ti 11 GB, Memory:

Table 2. The detailed parameters of the dataset.

Property	CA4L	CA4T	IITD
Number of class	822	2000	224
Number of images	16212	20000	2240
Number of train	4090	10000	1344
Number of val			448
Number of test	4090	10000	448
Image size	640×480 pixels	640×480 pixels	320×240 pixels
Input size of image	160×120 pixels	160×120 pixels	160×120 pixels

64.0 GB. Excessive batchsize can effectively save the time of network training and speed up the convergence of the model, however, it will increase the computational space of the computer. On the other hand, too small batchsize will easily cause the loss function value to oscillate back and forth. Considering the hardware equipment constraints, the optimal value of the hyperparameter batchsize is set to 8. At the same time, the initial value of the learning rate is 0.0001 and the number of iterations is 200. In order to prevent the model from overfitting due to its dependence on the dataset, we use the same hyperparameters in training all datasets, as shown in Fig. 5.

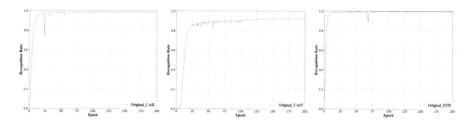

Fig. 5. Rank curves of validation dataset.

4.3   Comparison with Other Experiments

We used ETENet to extract iris features and normalized the extracted features and to obtain the corresponding real-valued feature matrix by the function of Softmax, the size of feature matrix was numclasses (numclasses refer to the number of validation set classes). CA4L contains 4,090 genuine pairs and 3,357,890 imposter pairs. CA4T contains 10,000 genuine pairs and 19,990,000 imposter pairs. IITD contains 448 genuine pairs and 99,904 imposter pairs. To verify the excellent performance of our proposed algorithm, we select the algorithm that performs better on these three datasets for comparison, with EER as the comparison metric. The ROC curves of this set of comparison experiments are shown in Fig. 6, and ETENet shows very excellent performance compared with other algorithms. As shown in Table 3, the accuracy of our proposed algorithm is significantly better than the other algorithms for all three data sets when FAR = 0.001. The EER values are less than 0.1% in both datasets, CA4L and IITD, which indicates that the algorithm has strong generalization and robustness.

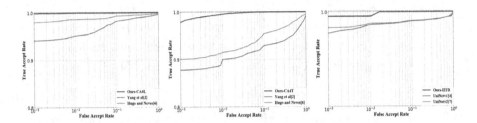

Fig. 6. ROC curves compared to other advanced methods.

Table 3. Results compared to other advanced methods.

Datasets	Approach	TAR (FAR = 0.001)	EER
CA4L	Proposed method	99.87%	0.07%
	Hugo and Neves [2]	99.21%	0.60%
	Yang et al. [6]	93.07%	2.80%
CA4T	Proposed method	98.11%	0.63%
	Hugo and Neves [2]	92.84%	3.00%
	Yang et al. [6]	87.13%	3.50%
IITD	Proposed method	99.77%	0.02%
	UniNet [4]	98.97%	0.76%
	UniNet.v2 [7]	99.18%	0.68%

4.4   Impact of ETENet Block

To verify the impact of dense connectivity and channel attention mechanisms in ETENet blocks on ETENet networks, we have done relevant ablation experiments on three publicly available datasets. We remove dense joins and cross-channel interactions in the ETE block with the same data set and hyperparameters. As shown in Fig. 7 and Fig. 8, accuracy significantly decrease after removing and the convergence of the function is also relatively slow. At the same time, the eer values on all three databases are more than 2.0%. The difference between the comparison results is very obvious (Table 4).

Table 4. Comparative results of ablation experiments.

Datasets	ETENet block	TAR (FAR = 0.001)	EER
CA4L	Yes	99.87%	0.07%
	No	89.91%	2.71%
CA4T	Yes	98.11%	0.63%
	No	69.78%	5.23%
IITD	Yes	99.77%	0.02%
	No	94.86%	2.19%

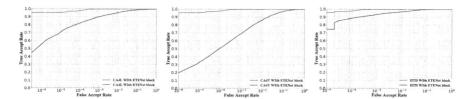

Fig. 7. ROC curves of ablation experiment.

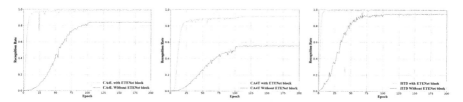

Fig. 8. Rank curves of ablation experiment.

5   Conclusion

This paper proposes that the end-to-end iris recognition algorithm that based on deep learning can still show excellent performance without the process of iris segmentation, data addition and normalization. Compared with other advanced methods, it has higher matching accuracy and stronger robustness. To a certain extent, reducing the dependence of sub-modules can lower the space complexity required by the model and the cumulative error generated by the cumbersome pretreatment process on the overall framework, which is conducive to the better application of iris recognition in lightweight applications. At the same time, the original iris image contains both iris and non-iris regions, and how the non-iris regions will affect iris recognition should be a question for further work.

Acknowledgments. This work is supported by the National Natural Science Foundation of China under Grants 61762067.

References

1. Chen, Y.: Research on Iris Localization and Recognition Algorithm. Jilin University, Changchun (2014)
2. Proenca, H., Neves, J.C.: Segmentation-less and non-holistic deep-learning frameworks for iris recognition. In: Proceedings of the IEEE/CVF Conference on Computer Vision and Pattern Recognition Workshops (2019)
3. Daugman, J.: How iris recognition works. In: The Essential Guide to Image Processing, pp. 715–739. Academic Press (2009)
4. Zhao, Z., Kumar, A.: Towards more accurate iris recognition using deeply learned spatially corresponding features. In: Proceedings of the IEEE International Conference on Computer Vision, pp. 3809–3818 (2017)
5. Wang, K., Kumar, A.: Cross-spectral iris recognition using CNN and supervised discrete hashing. Pattern Recogn. **86**, 85–98 (2019)
6. Yang, G., Zeng, H., Li, P., et al.: High-order information for robust iris recognition under less controlled conditions. In: 2015 IEEE International Conference on Image Processing (ICIP), pp. 4535–4539. IEEE (2015)
7. Zhao, Z., Kumar, A.: A deep learning based unified framework to detect, segment and recognize irises using spatially corresponding features. Pattern Recogn. **93**, 546–557 (2019)
8. CASIA-IRIS-V4 Iris Image Database Version 4.0 (CASIA-IRIS-V4-IrisV4)
9. IITD Iris Database. http://www.comp.polyu.edu.hk/~csajaykr/IITD
10. Wang, K., Kumar, A.: Periocular-assisted multi-feature collaboration for dynamic iris recognition. IEEE Trans. Inf. Forensics Secur. **16**, 866–879 (2020)
11. Sun, Z., Tan, T.: Ordinal measures for iris recognition. IEEE Trans. Pattern Anal. Mach. Intell. **31**(12), 2211–2226 (2008)
12. Huang, G., Liu, S., Van der Maaten, L., et al.: CondenseNet: an efficient DenseNet using learned group convolutions. Im: Proceedings of the IEEE Conference on Computer Vision and Pattern Recognition, pp. 2752–2761 (2018)
13. Wang, Q., Wu, B., Zhu, P., et al.: ECA-Net: efficient channel attention for deep convolutional neural networks. In: CVF Conference on Computer Vision and Pattern Recognition (CVPR). IEEE (2020)

Incomplete Texture Repair of Iris Based on Generative Adversarial Networks

Yugang Zeng, Ying Chen$^{(\boxtimes)}$, Huimin Gan, and Zhuang Zeng

Nanchang Hangkong University, Nanchang, China

Abstract. A PGGAN-based iris image restoration framework for autonomously restoring obscured iris information regions in iris images is proposed in the paper. First, to stabilize the training, the paper introduces the fade-in operation in the training phase of resolution doubling, so that the resolution increase can be smoothly transitioned. Simultaneously, the deconv network is removed, and conv + upsample is used instead, so that the generated model avoids the checkerboard effect. Second, the paper uses white squares to mask the real image to mimic the iris image with light spots in real scenes and obtains the restored image by network restoration. Finally, we use the restored image and the incomplete image as two input classes of the same recognition network, which proves the true validity of the restored image. The results of extensive comparative experiments on publicly available IITD datasets show that the proposed restoration framework is feasible and realistic.

Keywords: Iris repair · Iris recognition · GAN

1 Introduction

Iris recognition is considered to be the safest and the most promising biometric identification method due to its advantages of uniqueness, stability, and non-contact [1]. During the COVID-19 epidemic, contact fingerprint recognition and face recognition under masks have brought difficulties to identity authentication. In this case, iris recognition technology has more advantages. However, with the popularity of mobile sampling devices, a large number of iris images with external reflections are captured and used for iris recognition, resulting in a decrease in recognition accuracy. As shown in Fig. 1, due to the reflection of the glasses and the external light source, a large number of effective information areas of the iris are blocked by the light spots. Hence, how to effectively restore the occluded iris area to improve the accuracy of iris recognition is of great research significance.

At present, few scholars have done research on iris image restoration and enhancement. Recently, generative adversarial networks (GAN) have shown excellent performance in image generation. The unique adversarial training method of GAN greatly improves the quality of the generated images. Therefore, the application of GAN to iris images restoration have great research prospects.

J. Feng et al. (Eds.): CCBR 2021, LNCS 12878, pp. 335–345, 2021.
https://doi.org/10.1007/978-3-030-86608-2_37

Fig. 1. Examples of common images of missing iris information

2   Related Work

2.1   Traditional Image Restoration Methods

Ballester et al. [2] proposed a method for propagation based on iso-illumination lines. Bertalmio [3] first introduced the partial differential equation (PDE) algorithm to the field of image restoration. Chan [4] improved the TV model and proposed the fast optimal transfer algorithm (FOTA). Zhang et al. [5] combined the TV model with fractional derivatives and proposed a fractional order TV model. The above described are diffusion-based image restoration methods, which use a gradual smoothing transition from the edges to the center, allowing the smoothing to be preferentially dispersed to the area to be repaired. However, this type of method can only effectively fill small or narrow missing areas, and is not ideal for filling larger areas.

2.2   Deep Learning Image Restoration Methods

Pathak et al. [6] first proposed the application of CNNs to image inpainting. They proposed the context encoder (CE) structure and the use of adversarial training [7] to learn image features while returning missing parts in the image. Zhao et al. [8] proposed an image complementation method for context encoder that uses adversarial loss to complement missing regions of the image. An importance-weighted context loss considering the proximity to the corrupted region was used in [9]. Yu et al. [10] proposed a network with a two-stage network convolutional network and a contextual attention layer. Liu et al. [11] proposed a nested GAN for facial embedding. Yang et al. [12] proposed an optimization method based on GAN. Chen et al. proposed a method for iris data enhancement based on GAN [13]. These methods have better self-directed learning capabilities than traditional methods. However, these methods suffer from the problem of discontinuity between missing and non-missing regions, obvious repair traces, coarse visual effects and lack of pixel consistency on high-resolution images. The main contributions of this paper are as follows:

- An iris image restoration framework based on PGGAN is proposed to autonomously complete the missing iris information in the iris image. The unique progressive training method of PGGAN is very effective for generating fine and high-definition iris textures.
- This paper uses the single variable principle to vary the size and position of the occlusion site in turn, and uses all types of images from each group of experiments as the input class of the same recognition network. The experimental results show that the restored images show substantial improvement in visual and in all metrics.

3 Method of This Paper

Progressive growing of GANs (PGGAN) [14] adopts the idea of progressive training, which stabilizes the training of GAN by gradually increasing the resolution of the generated image. This progressive nature allows training to first discover the large-scale structure of the image distribution, and then shift attention to finer and finer scale details, rather than learning all scales at the same time. Therefore, PGGAN is very suitable for generating fine and high-resolution images such as iris texture.

3.1 Network Architecture

The datasets used in this paper are all two-dimensional images. As shown in Fig. 2, the network training starts with a 4 × 4 pixels low spatial resolution discriminator. As the training progresses, layers are gradually added to the generator and discriminator, thus increasing the spatial resolution of the generated images. Due to the limited hardware resources, the k value is set to 256 pixels.

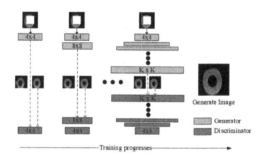

Fig. 2. Network training progresses

Generator Structure. The structure of the generator in this paper is shown in Fig. 3. The input block defines a Dense layer that has enough activations to create a given number of 4 × 4 feature maps. The raw discriminator layers from 8 × 8 resolution to k × k resolution consist of an upsampling layer and two 3 × 3 convolutions, which are followed by the Leaky Relu activation function and the pixelnorm method immediately after the convolution operation.

The pixelnorm layer has no trainable weights. It normalizes the feature vectors in each pixel to unit length and applies them after the convolution layer in the generator, which prevents the signal amplitude from spiraling out of control during training and stops the signal from escalating. The specific mathematical formula is as follows, C is the number of feature mappings, the value of each pixel (x, y) on the C channel is normalized to a fixed length, a is the input tensor, b is the output tensor, and ϵ is the value that prevents division by zero.

$$b_{x,y} = \frac{a_{x,y}}{\sqrt{\frac{1}{C} \sum_{C}^{j=0} a_j^{x,y} + \epsilon}} \tag{1}$$

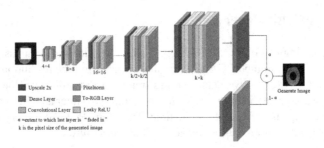

Fig. 3. Generator structure diagram

Each time the existing resolution training is completed, a new set of layers is added to double the resolution. To prevent the sudden addition of a new top layer from impacting the pre-existing bottom layer, the top layer is "fading in" linearly. The specific structure is shown in Fig. 4.

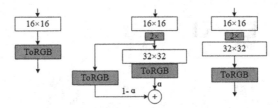

Fig. 4. Generator fading in structure diagram

Discriminator Structure. The structure of the discriminator used in this paper is shown in Fig. 5. The input image first passes through the from-RGB layer. From-RGB projects the feature vector to the RGB color and performs the opposite operation to to-RGB. When training the discriminator, input real images to match the current resolution of the network. The discriminator layer from $k/2 \times k/2$ resolution to 8×8 resolution is composed of two 3×3 convolutional layers and a down-sampling layer. The last layer consists of Minibatch stddev, a 3×3 convolution, a 4×4 convolution and a fully connected layer.

During the training process, the discriminator fading in a new input layer to support a larger input image, then inserts a new layer block and down-samples the output of the new block. After down-sampling, the output of the new block and the output of the old input processing layer are combined using a weighted average, where the weight is controlled by the hyperparameter α. The specific process is shown in Fig. 6.

Meanwhile, the discriminator uses minibatch standard deviation in the output block to help distinguish "real" training data batches from "fake" generation batches. This encourages the generator to generate more variations so that the statistics computed in the generated batches are more similar to those in the training data batches.

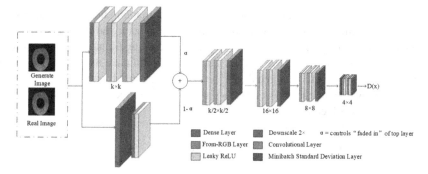

Fig. 5. Structure diagram of the discriminator

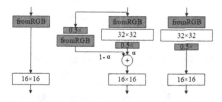

Fig. 6. Discriminator fading in structure diagram

3.2 Evaluation Index

Peak Signal-to-Noise Ratio (PSNR) and Structural Similarity (SSIM) are proposed in [15] to reflect the true degree of the generated image and are an objective standard for evaluating the image. Meanwhile, false accept rate (FAR), true accept rate (FRR), equal error rate (EER), ROC, and CMC curves are used to evaluate the recognition performance of iris images before and after repair in this paper.

4 Experiments and Results

4.1 Description of Databases and Hardware Environment

IITD iris database [16] having 2240 iris images with 320×240 pixels and the corresponding ground truth (GT) images proposed in [17] are employed in our paper. In the experiment, the logical AND operation result images between original and corresponding GT images are recognized as real images. The sample images employed in our experiment are shown in Fig. 7.

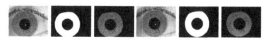

Fig. 7. Examples of the original image, the corresponding GT image, and the real image

In the experiment, the real image is preprocessed into 256×256 pixels. The IITD dataset consists of 224 classes, and the 1st and 6th sheets of each class serial number were used as the test set, for a total of 448 sheets. The remaining ones were used as the training set, totaling 1792 sheets. The ratio of the training set to the test set is 8:2.

In our experiment, Tensorflow is used as the deep learning framework. The learning rate of this network model is set to 0.002. The batch size of each iteration is set to 16. Meanwhile, setting the gradient penalty in the WGAN-GP loss function to stabilize the gradient also ensures that $G(z)$ is close to x while $D(G(z))$ does not exceed $D(x)$, and improves the network convergence probability.

4.2 Experimental Program and Result Analysis

Figure 8 shows the experimental process and results of a 128 × 128 occlusion white block. To form an effective contrast effect with the restored iris image, we choose (64, 64) as the masking origin to obtain the mutilated image shown in Fig. 8(b). It can be seen from the figure that the repair effect of the repaired image is quite obvious.

(a)real image   (b)incomplete image   (c)restored image

Fig. 8. Examples of three types of images

We calculate the PSNR and SSIM values of the real and incomplete images, the real image and the restored image of this group of experiments, as shown in Table 1. The PSNR and SSIM values in the table are the average values of 448 images in the test set. It can be seen from the table that the PSNR value of the real image and the restored image has reached 20.220 db, which is 155% higher than the PSNR value of the incomplete image, and the SSIM value has also been improved.

Table 1. PSNR and SSIM when the occlusion size is 128 × 128

Real image comparison	Number of test sets	PSNR	SSIM
Incomplete image	448	7.919	0.630
Restored image	448	**20.220**	**0.670**

To further illustrate the effectiveness of restored images, this paper recognizes the above three types of images. In order to ensure the universality of the experimental conclusions, the recognition network is Alexnet [18]. In the recognition experiments, the batch size is set to 16, the epoch is set to 200, the learning rate is set to 0.0001.

The experiment data of the recognition experiment is same as the repair experiment but expanded 5 times.

Figure 9 shows the ROC curve of the incomplete and restored image in the same recognition network. It can be seen that when the FAR value is less than 1, the restored curve is always higher than the incomplete curve, which shows the recognition effect of the restored image is obviously better than that of the incomplete image and the proposed method is very feasible for repairing the incomplete iris image.

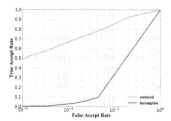

Fig. 9. ROC curve of the incomplete and restored image under the same recognition network

In order to explore the image restoration effect of the network under different occlusion sizes, this paper again selects the (64, 64) coordinate point as the occlusion origin and sets 64×64 and 32×32 white blocks respectively for occlusion. Figure 10 respectively shows the experimental process and results. From the naked eye only, the repaired image in (B) has a slightly finer iris texture than the repaired image in (A), and the repair effects of the two types of images are not much different.

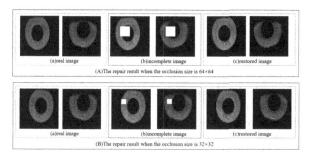

Fig. 10. Examples of restoration effects of two types of images

Similarly, calculate the PSNR and SSIM values for the two types of images in the two sets of experiments and the real images, as shown in Table 2. From the table that the PSNR values in the two experiments have been greatly improved, and SSIM has also been improved. The analysis shows that since SSIM compares the luminance, contrast, and structure of two types of images, the iris images used in this experiment are grayscale images and the pixel values of the iris texture are very close to each other, so the SSIM values calculated from the restored images are still very close compared to the SSIM values of the incomplete images, although they are improved.

Table 2. PSNR and SSIM values of the two types of images

Real image comparison	Number of test sets	PSNR	SSIM
Incomplete image under 64 × 64	448	12.564	0.722
Restored imageunder 64 × 64	448	**23.015**	**0.749**
Incomplete image under 32 × 32	448	17.188	0.766
Restored imageunder 32 × 32	448	**26.221**	**0.775**

Figure 11 shows the ROC curves derived from two sets of experiments for two types of images with the same recognition network model described above. (a) and (b) are the ROC curves of the restored and incomplete image when the size of the occluded white block is 64 × 64 and 32 × 32, respectively. When the FAR value is less than 1, the restored curves of the two images are always much larger than the incomplete curve. Compared with (a), the distance between the two curves in (b) is smaller. It can be seen that the smaller the occlusion of the white block, the closer the recognition effect of the restored image and the incomplete image.

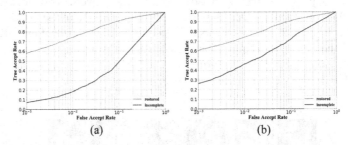

(a)   (b)

Fig. 11. ROC curves of the two types of images in the two sets of experiments

Figure 12(a) shows the ROC curves obtained from the restored images of the above three sets of experiments under the same recognition network. The figure shows that the recognition effect of the restored image when the occlusion size is 128 × 128 is lower than that the size is 64 × 64 and 32 × 32. The recognition effect of the restored image at 64 × 64 and 32 × 32 is very close, which shows that the network has a better ability to learn iris texture information and can repair incomplete iris images well.

Figure 12(b) shows the ROC curves of restored images obtained in the recognition network when the occlusion origin is (64, 64), (64, 128), (128, 64), (128, 128), and the size of occlusion white blocks are 64 × 64 respectively. It can be seen from the figure that the recognition effects of the restored images obtained under the four different positions are very similar. It can be seen that the network in this paper has a good repair effect on the missing iris information in different positions. An example of a specific restored image is shown in Fig. 13. Only from the naked eye, the repairing effects of the four types of restored images are almost the same.

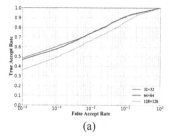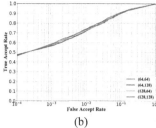

(a)   (b)

Fig. 12. (a) is the ROC curve of the repaired image when the size of the white block is different under the same position, (b) is the ROC curve diagram of the restored image when the white blocks of the same size are occluded in different positions.

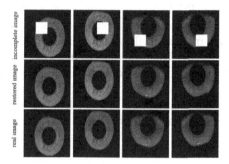

Fig. 13. Display of repair effects in different positions

To confirm the authenticity of the restored region, this experiment fills 50 times Gaussian noise for the information missing region of the mutilated image under the masked white block size of 128×128, and thus obtains the noisy image as shown in Fig. 14. Similarly, the noisy image is input into the same recognition network described above to obtain the ROC curve as shown in Fig. 15. From the figure that the recognition effect of noisy images is improved relative to that of incomplete images. This is because the pixel value of 50 times gaussian noise is very close to the iris texture and the black background of the image, and not easily detectable by the network. The pixel value of the white square in the incomplete image is much larger than the iris texture, and it is easy to be learned as a feature. However, in Fig. 15, the recognition effect of restored images is much higher than that of noisy images. In summary, the restored image obtained by the method is real and effective.

Fig. 14. Noisy image with missing area filled with 50 times gaussian noise

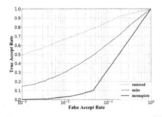

Fig. 15. The ROC curve of the restored, noise, and incomplete images with the size of the occluded white block of 128×128

5   Conclusion

This paper proposes a novel PGGAN-based iris image restoration framework, which is used to repair incomplete iris images and has a good repairability. The paper sets up comparative experiments from multiple angles to demonstrate the feasibility, effectiveness, and authenticity of this method. The paper notices that PGGAN's progressive training method is very suitable for generating fine images such as iris texture. In the future, combining GAN with iris image restoration is a good development direction. However, the follow-up development of this work is also challenging. How to achieve complete unsupervised autonomous restoration of broken iris images in real scenes without GT images is a difficult problem that needs to be overcome.

Acknowledgments. This work is supported by the National Natural Science Foundation of China under Grants 61762067.

References

1. Chen, Y., et al.: An adaptive CNNs technology for robust iris segmentation. IEEE Access **7**, 64517–64532 (2019)
2. Ballester, C., et al.: Filling-in by joint interpolation of vector fields and gray levels. IEEE Trans. Image Process. **10**(8), 1200–1211 (2001)
3. Bertalmio, M., Bertozzi, A.L., Sapiro, G.: Navier-stokes, fluid dynamics, and image and video inpainting. In: Proceedings of the 2001 IEEE Computer Society Conference on Computer Vision and Pattern Recognition, CVPR 2001. IEEE, vol. 1, pp. I–I (2001)
4. Chan, R.H., Wen, Y.W., Yip, A.M.: A fast optimization transfer algorithm for image inpainting in wavelet domains. IEEE Trans. Image Process. **18**(7), 1467–1476 (2009)
5. Zhang, Y., et al.: A class of fractional-order variational image inpainting models. Appl. Math. Inf. Sci. **6**(2), 299–306 (2012)
6. Pathak, D., et al.: Context encoders: Feature learning by inpainting. In: Proceedings of the IEEE Conference on Computer Vision and Pattern Recognition (2016)
7. Goodfellow, I.J., Pouget-Abadie, J., Mirza, M., et al.: Generative adversarial networks. arXiv preprint arXiv:1406.2661 (2014)
8. Zhao, J.B., Mathieu, M., Goroshin, R., et al.: Stacked what where auto-encoders. arXiv:1506.02351 (2016)
9. Yeh, R.A., et al.: Semantic image inpainting with deep generative models. In: Proceedings of the IEEE Conference on Computer Vision and Pattern Recognition (2017)

10. Yu, J., Lin, Z., Yang, J., Shen, X., Lu, X., Huang, T.S.: Generative image inpainting with contextual attention. arXiv preprint (2018)
11. Liu, J., Jung, C.: Facial image inpainting using multi-level generative network. In: 2019 IEEE International Conference on Multimedia and Expo (ICME). IEEE, pp. 1168–1173.s (2019)
12. Yang, C., et al.: High-resolution image inpainting using multi-scale neural patch synthesis. In: Proceedings of the IEEE Conference on Computer Vision and Pattern Recognition (2017)
13. Chen, Y., Liu, Z.S.: Research on iris data enhancement method based on GAN. Inf. Commun. 214(10), 36–40 (2020)
14. Karras, T., Aila, T., Laine, S., et al.: Progressive growing of GANs for improved quality, stability, and variation. arXiv preprint arXiv:1710.10196 (2017)
15. Wang, Z., Bovik, A.C., Sheikh, H.R., Simoncelli, E.P.: Image quality assessment: from error visibility to structural similarity. Trans. Imgage. Proc. 13(4), 600–612 (2004)
16. IITD iris database. http://www.comp.polyu.edu.hk/~csajaykr/IITD/Database_Iris.html
17. Hofbauer, H., et al.: A ground truth for iris segmentation. In: 2014 22nd International Conference on Pattern Recognition. IEEE (2014)
18. Krizhevsky, A., Sutskever, I., Hinton, G.E.: ImageNet classification with deep convolutional neural networks. In: NIPS, pp. 1106–1114 (2012)

Deepfakes Detection Based on Multi Scale Fusion

Peng Sun[1]($\boxtimes$), ZhiYuan Yan[1], Zhe Shen[2], ShaoPei Shi[3], and Xu Dong[1]

[1] Criminal Investigation Police University of China, Shenyang 110854, Liaoning, China
[2] Shenyang Aerospace University, Shenyang 110136, Liaoning, China
[3] Key Lab of Forensic Science, Ministry of Justice, Shanghai, China

Abstract. Generative adversarial networks (GANs) and deep learning technologies pose a great threat to public security. The traditional forgery and tampering detection methods are difficult to use for the detection of such images or videos. In this paper, based on the deep learning method, the deep neural network is used to extract, fuse and classify the higher dimensional space-time features of the input image and sequence frame in the spatial and temporal dimensions, and a kind of automatic deepfakes detection technology based on multi-dimensional space-time information fusion is proposed. In the spatial dimension, using the spatial learning ability of convolutional neural network (CNN), the feature pyramid (FPN) is fused to the feature map extracted by the backbone feature extraction network for up sampling and weighted fusion. According to the results of higher dimensional feature fusion classification, deepfakes are detected.

Keywords: Deepfakes · Multi scale fusion · Deep learning · Computer vision

1 Introduction

The rapid development of artificial intelligence technology has profoundly changed the world. While providing various conveniences for people's lives, it also brings many new security risks. One of the most typical is the fake face changing technology. Using this technology, we can easily and quickly forge a large number of realistic face changing videos, followed by the spread of false news on the network and illegal and criminal activities involving face changing videos. With the help of highly developed Internet, the potential threat of these face changing videos to social public security is difficult to accurately estimate. The "face changing" video incidents of spoofing political figures and public figures emerge in endlessly, causing very bad negative effects, and even indirectly leading to the military coup in Gabon. At present, there are three kinds of common fake face changing tools: Face2Face, FaceSwap and deepfakes. Among them, deepfakes enables the network to learn the deeper features of the target face in the video, and can match the subtle movements and expression changes of the face. Compared with other deep face changing tools, deepfakes is more mature and reliable. With the emergence of the generation of confrontation neural network model by GANs, various kinds of false face changing technologies based on GANs are constantly proposed. Based

© Springer Nature Switzerland AG 2021
J. Feng et al. (Eds.): CCBR 2021, LNCS 12878, pp. 346–353, 2021.
https://doi.org/10.1007/978-3-030-86608-2_38

on deepfakes, a new false face changing tool FaceSwap GAN was obtained by adding resistance loss and perception loss. In this technology, anti loss is used as a discriminator to make the generated face changing video closer to the replaced video. The introduction of perceived loss can make the direction of eye rotation more realistic, so that the output face changing video has higher quality.

How to deal with the huge impact of deepfakes and its derivative technology on public security has become a major problem faced by governments and academia. In order to effectively control the potential impact of false face changing technology, domestic and foreign scholars have carried out face changing video detection research. Facebook and Microsoft have also jointly held a global deepfakes detection competition to promote the development of detection technology. Based on supervised learning, this paper uses different types of deep neural networks to extract, fuse and classify high-dimensional spatio-temporal features of faces in video in spatial and temporal dimensions, and proposes a kind of automatic false face detection method based on multi-dimensional spatio-temporal information fusion.

2 Relative Work

Early human face tampering methods introduced obvious tampering traces and facial distortion in forged images or videos. It can be detected by the method of detecting the characteristics of human blink, or according to the inconsistency of diffuse reflection information in the pupil of both eyes in the false face. Literature [8] uses human head posture, face key point distribution and other real face biometrics to detect tampering traces in video. Because the improved deepfakes method no longer relies on artificial means for face splicing and replacement, but uses CNN, GANs and other deep learning methods to carry out deep forgery and tampering, which makes the detection of false faces in deepfakes fall into trouble again. With more and more AI labs at home and abroad, such as Alibaba and Google, paying attention to the problem of deep forgery video image detection, the academic research on deep forgery video detection has gradually developed from traditional detection to deep detection.

The existing detection methods based on deep learning are mainly divided into two categories. One is to detect a single image, that is, to extract the spatial dimension information from the image directly by CNN. This method can capture the local features of each image to a certain extent, and let convolutional neural network learn the distribution of true and false face features through big data driven method. Among them, literature [3] uses Xception network for pre training to achieve good detection rate on a single data set, Afchar et al. [10] builds a shallow CNN network to learn the micro features of true and false faces, and Nguyen et al. [11] builds their own capsule network architecture to classify the features extracted by VGG network. This kind of CNN based method shows high detection rate in a single tampering method. But at the same time, there are many defects, such as relying on a specific data set and the algorithm of generating false face, the most important is that it is unable to judge the subtle changes of the two frames in the tampered video stream.

The second is based on image sequence detection, which introduces the recurrent neural network (RNN) on the basis of CNN. References [5, 6] use a CNN to extract intra frame features, followed by a time aware RNN network to capture inter frame inconsistency caused by face change. When the feature vectors from CNN are introduced into RNN to extract the time dimension features, we can learn the coherence between the image sequences, such as the frequency of blinking, the amplitude of mouth movement, the continuity and smoothness of the head movement, that is, the evolution of the character's action with the time dimension. A large number of researchers have proved that this method is more effective than single frame image detection. Therefore, this paper also adopts the second kind of method. However, there are still two problems in this kind of method. One is that we only need the output results of RNN in the last layer, and the output results of all layers in the middle are redundant, resulting in a lot of parameter "waste". In this regard, reference [12] proposed that attention mechanism, namely long-term and short-term memory network (LSTM), can be added to RNN to make neural network pay more attention to some interesting parts and reduce the amount of model parameters.

In this paper, we focus on the problem of strong video compression in the mainstream deepfakes detection method and the poor effect of face detection for different scales and resolutions. Experiments on a large number of Celeb-DF datasets and Faceforensics++ datasets containing strong compression and multi-scale multi-resolution face video and images show that the robustness and accuracy of the proposed method are better than the current mainstream deepfakes detection algorithm to a certain extent.

3   Our Method

3.1   Method Flow

As shown in Fig. 2, the workflow of our neural network model based on multi-scale feature fusion is presented. It is composed of four parts: 1. Firstly, the face region is extracted and cropped by Dlib face detection algorithm, and then the cropped image is rotated and aligned; 2. The aligned image is transferred to CNN to extract the spatial dimension features; 3. The high-dimensional feature map obtained by CNN is pooled and then transferred to LSTM to extract sequence features and inter frame changes; 4. The output of the last layer of LSTM is passed through the full connection layer, and dropout is added after the full connection layer to resist over fitting. Finally, Softmax function is used to output the neural network classification results.

3.2   Spatial Feature Extraction

The existing literature and comparative experiments show that CNN + LSTM framework can effectively fuse the spatial and temporal features of video. The most suitable CNN network for feature extractor is ResNet50, which has good performance in this framework. However, ResNet50 network can't directly extract the multi-scale features of the image, which leads to the problem of poor face detection effect for different scales and resolutions. Resnet50 + FPN (feature pyramid) originated from the object detection task in computer vision. In the mainstream target detection algorithms based on anchor, such as Faster R-CNN, the detection effect of small objects is not very good. This is

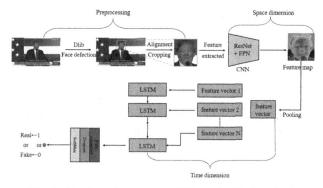

Fig. 2. The detection process of this method is described.

because the small target itself has very little pixel information, which is very easy to lose in the process of down sampling, resulting in the network can't learn its spatial dimension characteristics well. Therefore, at present, more and more target detection algorithms begin to join FPN structure to fuse different scale pixels and semantic information, so that the network can learn more features and information. After the size of the input image is continuously compressed through the convolution layer, the up sampling and feature fusion are carried out. Finally, the feature vector after feature fusion is output, that is, the feature extraction in the spatial dimension is completed, and then the feature vector is introduced into LSTM to further learn the temporal dimension features. This paper introduces the feature pyramid model on the basis of ResNet50 network structure. The specific network model architecture after introducing the feature pyramid model is shown in Fig. 3.

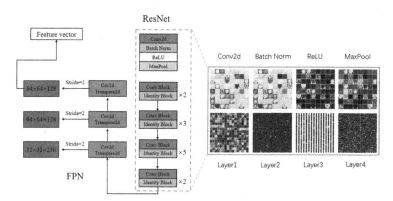

Fig. 3. ResNet50 + FPN network structure for spatial feature extraction.

The output feature vector of the last layer of the network is up sampled, and the feature vector of the penultimate layer is weighted and fused, and so on, the width and height of the final feature vector is 64. By introducing the FPN structure based on

ResNet50, the network can extract the spatial features of the input image at different scales.

3.3 Time Feature Extraction

Through CNN, we can extract the features of the spatial dimension of the image, but so far we have not considered that there may be close connections between the two frames in the middle of the video stream, and these connections are likely to be the breakthrough to detect deepfakes. The authors of literature [5, 6] have also verified this view through many experiments. In order to add the time series to the neural network, it is necessary to send the high-dimensional eigenvectors finally obtained by CNN into RNN (recurrent neural network). The input of a certain layer in RNN can be considered as the joint action of this frame and the previous frame, that is, the previous moment and the next moment are considered at the same time. However, there is a problem in using RNN alone, that is, the number of parameters is too large, because RNN only outputs the results of the last layer, while the outputs of many middle layers are not used, resulting in a large number of parameter redundancy. Therefore, it is very important to add an attention mechanism to limit the output of neural network, that is, LSTM. LSTM is a kind of time cycle neural network, which is widely used in the detection of time series, such as voice and video. LSTM network has a variety of variants, such as self-attention mechanism [13], two-way attention mechanism [14], and currently very popular, recently referred to the computer vision task of multi attention mechanism [15]. This paper will quantitatively evaluate the effect of different attention mechanism models on deepfakes detection through experiments. Through CNN, we can extract the features of the spatial dimension of the image, but so far we have not considered that there may be close connections between the two frames in the middle of the video stream, and these connections are likely to be the breakthrough to detect deepfakes. The authors of literature [5, 6] have also verified this view through many experiments. In order to add the time series to the neural network, it is necessary to send the high-dimensional eigenvectors finally obtained by CNN into RNN (recurrent neural network). The input of a certain layer in RNN can be considered as the joint action of this frame and the previous frame, that is, the previous moment and the next moment are considered at the same time. However, there is a problem in using RNN alone, that is, the number of parameters is too large, because RNN only outputs the results of the last layer, while the outputs of many middle layers are not used, resulting in a large number of parameter redundancy. Therefore, it is very important to add an attention mechanism to limit the output of neural network, that is, LSTM. LSTM is a kind of time cycle neural network, which is widely used in the detection of time series, such as voice and video. LSTM network has a variety of variants, such as self-attention mechanism [13], two-way attention mechanism [14], and currently very popular, recently referred to the computer vision task of multi attention mechanism [15]. This paper will quantitatively evaluate the effect of different attention mechanism models on deepfakes detection through experiments.

4 Experimental Results and Analysis

4.1 Deepfakes Datasets

For the deepfakes dataset, Rssler has developed Faceforensics++ [3]. Most of the data are from real videos on YouTube, but the face changing effect is obvious. Obvious tampering traces can be seen at the splicing of two images. On this basis, Jiang, L. and others open source deepforensis-1.0 dataset [16], which is more realistic than the former. Celeb DF and DFDC dataset [17, 18] improve the problems of low resolution and color inconsistency of synthetic face to a certain extent, and the content quality is higher. Therefore, we choose celeb DF dataset with better tampering effect, Combined with the self-built data set, the network model is trained. Finally, the model performance is evaluated and tested in the most popular dataset of Faceforensics++ Table 1 summarizes the most mainstream data sets of deepfakes, as well as their advantages and disadvantages.

4.2 Analysis of Experimental Results

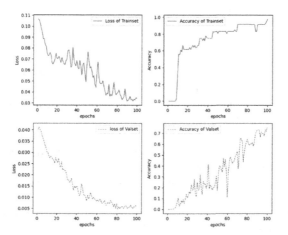

Fig. 4. Visual display of model training results.

In the experiment, ResNet50 is used as the Backbone to extract the features, learn the spatial dimension features of the image, delete the full connection layer of resnet50, transfer the output of the network to the FPN network, then connect the LSTM through the FPN, and finally output the classification and recognition results through a full connection layer, and add dropout to resist over fitting. After the training, the results are visualized, and the loss of classification is decreasing and converging, and finally tends to be stable; On the other hand, the accuracy of the model increases with the number of iterations. Figure 4 shows the time evolution of the accuracy and loss of our model in the training set and validation set after 100 generations of training.

4.3 Model Performance Comparison

This paper uses the general accuracy to quantitatively evaluate the performance of the model. The accuracy rate represents the classification accuracy rate on the verification set after the model converges, and the quantitative description is: the number of correct classifications on the verification set/the total number of verification sets. We prove that the performance of Deepfakes detection algorithm can be improved to a certain extent through multi-scale fusion.

Table 1. The comparison among different models.

Model/Dataset	Celeb-DF (accuracy %)	FaceForensics++ (accuracy %)
ResNet50	60.3	63.1
ResNet50 + LSTM	68.9	76.4
Xception	75.3	79.7
ResNet50 + FPN + LSTM	86.2	90.8

5 Conclusion

Aiming at the problems of strong video compression and poor face detection results for different scales and resolutions in mainstream deepfakes detection methods, this paper proposes a deep forgery and tamper detection technology based on multi-scale fusion. After introducing ResNet50 + FPN + LSTM structure to fuse spatial and temporal features of video, experiments are carried out on Celeb-DF dataset and Faceforensics++ dataset including strong compression and multi-scale and multi-resolution face video and image. The results show that the robustness and accuracy of model detection are better than the current mainstream deep fakes detection algorithm to a certain extent.

Acknowledgments. This work was supported by Technical Research Program of Ministry of Public Security (2020JSYJC25), Open Project of Key Laboratory of Forensic Science of Ministry of Justice (KF202014), Young scientific and technological talents breeding project of Liaoning Provincial Department of Education (JYT2020130) , Innovative Talents Support Program of Liaoning Province.

References

1. Bi, X., Wei, Y., Xiao, B., Li, W., Ma, J.: Image forgery detection algorithm based on cascaded convolutional neural network. J. Electron. Inf. Technol. **41**(12), 2987–2994 (2019)
2. Matern, F., Riess, C., Stamminger, M.: Exploiting visual artifacts to expose deepfakes and face manipulations. In: 2019 IEEE Winter Applications of Computer Vision Workshops (WACVW). IEEE (2019)
3. Rssler, A., Cozzolino, D., Verdoliva, L., Riess, C., Thies, J., Niener, M.: FaceForensics++: Learning to Detect Manipulated Facial Images (2019)

4. Faceswap-GAN. https://github.com/shaoanlu/faceswap-GAN
5. Guera, D., Delp, E.J.: Deepfakes video detection using recurrent neural networks. In: 15th IEEE International Conference on Advanced Video and Signal Based Surveillance (AVSS). IEEE (2018)
6. Sabir, E., Cheng, J., Jaiswal, A., AbdAlmageed, W., Masi, I., Natarajan, P.: Recurrent convolutional strategies for face manipulation detection in videos. Interfaces (GUI) **3**(1) (2019)
7. Li, Y., Chang, M.C., Lyu, S.: In Ictu Oculi: exposing AI generated fake face videos by detecting eye blinking. In: 2018 IEEE International Workshop on Information Forensics and Security (WIFS). IEEE (2018)
8. Yang, X., Li, Y., Lyu, S.: Exposing deep fakes using inconsistent head poses. In: ICASSP 2019 - 2019 IEEE International Conference on Acoustics, Speech and Signal Processing (ICASSP). IEEE (2019)
9. Yang, X., Li, Y., Qi, H., Lyu, S.: Exposing GAN-synthesized faces using landmark locations. In Proceedings of the ACM Workshop on Information Hiding and Multimedia Security, pp. 113–118. (2019)
10. Afchar, D., Nozick, V., Yamagishi, J., Echizen, I.: MesoNet: a compact facial video forgery detection network. In: 2018 IEEE International Workshop on Information Forensics and Security (WIFS). IEEE (2018)
11. Nguyen, H.H., Yamagishi, J., Echizen, I.: Capsule-forensics: using capsule networks to detect forged images and videos. In: ICASSP 2019 - 2019 IEEE International Conference on Acoustics, Speech and Signal Processing (ICASSP). IEEE (2019)
12. Hochreiter, S., Schmidhuber, J.: Long short-term memory. Neural Comput. **9**(8), 1735–1780 (1997)
13. Zhao, H., Jia, J., Koltun, V.: Exploring self-attention for image recognition (2020)
14. Dong, Y., Fu, Y., Wang, L., Chen, Y., Li, J.: A sentiment analysis method of capsule network based on BiLSTM. EEE Access **8**(99), 37014–37020 (2020)
15. Han, K., Wang, Y., Chen, H., Chen, X., Tao, D.: A survey on visual transformer (2020)
16. Jiang, L., Wu, W., Li, R., Qian, C., Chen, C.L.: DeeperForensics-1.0: A Large-Scale Dataset for Real-World Face Forgery Detection (2019)
17. Dolhansky, B., Howes, R., Pflaum, B., Baram, N., Ferrer, C.C.: The deepfake detection challenge (DFDC) preview dataset (2019)
18. Li, Y., Yang, X., Sun, P., Qi, H., Lyu, S.: Celeb-DF: A New Dataset for DeepFake Forensics (2019)

Balance Training for Anchor-Free Face Detection

Chengpeng Wang[2], Chunyu Chen[1], Siyi Hou[1], Ying Cai[3], and Menglong Yang[1,2(✉)]

[1] School of Aeronautics and Astronautics, Sichuan University, Chengdu, China
mlyang@scu.edu.cn
[2] Wisesoft Inc., Chengdu, China
[3] College of Electronic and Information, Southwest Minzu University, Chengdu, China

Abstract. Large-scale variations on face detection make the performance of the model hard to improve. In this paper, we propose a novel balance training method for anchor-free face detection. Firstly, we propose a data augmentation called crop-mosaic to provide scale continuous, balance and controllable Gtboxes. Secondly, we design a density balance scale assignment strategy to divide the scale matching range for different scale faces. Thirdly, we introduce a scale normalization loss for comparing training performance with each levels. The proposed methods are implemented on Caffe. Extensive experiments on popular benchmarks WIDER FACE demonstrate that the performance of model training based on Mobilenet-v1 is close to the state-of-the-art face detectors.

Keywords: Face detection · Anchor-free · Data augmentation

1 Introduction

Face detection is a fundamental step of face recognition system. The Viola-Jones face detector [1] which is regarded as a landmark real-time detector appeared as early as a decade ago, it uses cascade classifiers, adaBoost algorithm and Harr-like handcraft feature. With the development of deep learning, face detection has made great progress [4–9, 11].

However, face detection is still a difficult task which needs to solve various variations on scale, occlusion, pose, illumination, blurry, makeup, expression and so on in the unconstrained environments. Especially large-scale variations [9] from several pixels to thousands of pixels. A scale balance distribution sampling should be pro-posed to fed faces with different scales into the network. Meanwhile, multi-scale feature pyramids should match appropriate proportion of samples at different levels for balance supervision [10]. By adjusting the anchor distribution and IoU threshold, various anchor-based matching strategies can achieve balanced sampling, while anchor-free method is difficult to achieve this requirement through a single setup without these strategies.

We propose a series of related approaches to achieve large scale balance training. Firstly, we introduce a new data augmentation method called crop-mosaic to generate ground-truth bounding boxes (Gtbox) with continuous scale distribution. While it can

J. Feng et al. (Eds.): CCBR 2021, LNCS 12878, pp. 354–364, 2021.
https://doi.org/10.1007/978-3-030-86608-2_39

control the proportion of different scale faces in a mini-batch. Secondly, we used the density balance scale assignment strategy to divide the scale matching range for different scale faces, which make each Gtbox match feature positions balance. Thirdly, we introduce a scale normalization loss for estimating and comparing performance with each level. According to the loss, the weights of different scale samples are tuned to make the training scale balance.

2   Related Work

2.1   Scale Balance Data Augmentation

The early SSD sampling [2] random crop original image to generate face samples with different scales. PyramidBox++ sampling method [14] specifies a Gtbox of different scales as the center, and crop on the original graph. CSP [20] adopt the similar strategy in PyramidBox [5] to increase the proportion of small faces. yolo-v4 introduce a new method called mosaic [15], which mixes 4 training images into one image for increasing the number of small objects. Stitcher [16] resized images into smaller components and then stitched into the same size to regular images which contain inevitable smaller objects. These methods are random and uncontrollable to change the samples scale distribution which fed into the network for training at the same time (in a mini-batch).

2.2   Anchor Free Detection

Early one-stage detector yolo-v1 [3] didn't use anchor for Gtbox matching, it divides the input image into an S × S grid. The grid cell which contains the center of a Gtbox is responsible for detecting that object. Densebox [21] label a filled circle located in the center of a face bounding box as positive region, predicts distance from positive location to left-top and right-bottom corners of the bounding box. CenterNet [22] assign the center pixel of a bounding box as positive and regress size from the point. FCOS [19] limit the range of bounding box as positives and directly regress four distances from all positive locations. Center-ness is used to down-weight the low-quality bounding boxes predicted by a location far from the center of an object. Fovea box [18] use Scale Assignment and Object Fovea to limit the range of positives on feature pyramidal levels and learn a transformation that maps the networks localization at cell (x, y) in the feature maps to the Gtbox. CSP [20] assign the location where an object's center point falls as positive which Similar to yolo-v1, other location surrounding the positive are defined as negatives with a Gaussian mask to reduce the ambiguity.

3   Proposed Methods

Figure 1 shows the pipeline of the algorithm which is a classic one stage detection framework, and the common feature fusion module LFPN and feature enhancement module RFB are integrated. Inspired by the ATSS [12] and PAA [13], we utilize a probabilistic-based label assignment. We directly regress the distance between the edge of the bounding box and location (x, y) which is similar to FCOS [19].

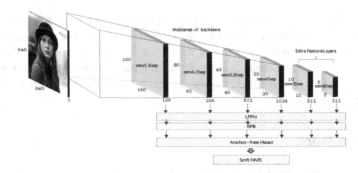

Fig. 1. Framework

For balance training, we first propose a quality sample augmentation in Sect. 3.1. Then we utilize a scale assignment method to balance the matching the Gtboxes of various scales and feature points in Sect. 3.2. In Sect. 3.3, we use scale normalization loss to supervise the training of each feature levels and adjust the proportion of samples matching to each levels.

3.1 Crop-Mosaic Sample Augmentation

In order to make the model be able to deal with various scales of face and have the similar optimal performance, samples of various scales need to be balance fed into training balance at the same time, the original image sequence is difficult to obtain ideal samples in each batch.

We randomly set cropbox on the original image to obtain the training image, in order to avoid truncation of Gtbox by the cropbox border, the range of vertex coordinates of the cropbox does not overlap with that of all Gtbox edges. At the same time, avoiding the overlapping judgment of cropbox edge and Gtbox edge greatly reduce the sampling time in training.

We use WIDER FACE [23] database as the training set, which has a small number of large-scale faces. The image after cropping which is directly used for training will obtain the scaled up Gtbox, in this case, n = 1 in Eq. 1. WIDER FACE has a large number of small face samples, but most of them are concentrated in some images, and the distribution is uneven in the image sequence. Inspired by mosaic [15] method, we construct small face sample artificially. Mosaic data augmentation stitches to four different together images in which the size of Gtboxes is random and difficult to control. We generate n^2 (n = 2 or 3) crop boxes with different scales from an original image, then resize them to the same size (w, h) and splice them into one image, so that the scale range of face Gtboxes in this image can be wider and the distribution is balanced, as shown in Fig. 2. We will make a quantitative analysis in Sect. 4.2.

$$w = \sum_{i=1}^{n^2} w_i/n^2 \quad n \in \{1, 2, 3\}$$
$$h = \sum_{i=1}^{n^2} h_i/n^2 \quad n \in \{1, 2, 3\}$$

(1)

During training, each training image fed into the batch is randomly sample by one of the following options:

1. an original input image
2. four images cropped from the original input image that the maximum Jaccard overlap with the original image is 0.3 0.4 0.6 or 0.7
3. a mosaic image with n^2 cropped images (n = 2)
4. a mosaic image with n^2 cropped images (n = 3)

(a) Original image   (b) Crop-Mosaic image

Fig. 2. Crop-mosaic data augmentation from one pic

Adjusting the proportion of these optins can control the distribution of samples of different scales. Figure 5(a)(b) shows two different sample distributions.

3.2 Density Balance Scale Assignment

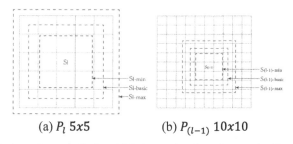

(a) P_l 5x5   (b) $P_{(l-1)}$ 10x10

Fig. 3. (a) (b) Scale assignment limits which feature level can be matched by Gtbox of various sizes

Generally, the anchor-free method matches the feature points and the Gtbox according to their position relationship. If the feature points of all feature levels are included, the large Gtbox will contain more feature points than the small Gtbox.

Inspired by the scale assignment in foveabox [18], we set the corresponding basic scale (S_{basic}) for each feature level, enlarge or narrow the scope of S_{basic} ranging from

S_{min} to S_{max}. According to the Eq. 2, when $\eta = \sqrt{2}$, the scale is divided as shown in Fig. 3, $S_{(l-1)max} = S_{l-min}$, The scale space is divided into L continuous disjoint subspaces.

On feature level P_l, the resolution is k^2 and $S_l = 1/k^2$. **We propose the feature matching density D_l** to quantify that Gtbox can match how many feature points in the feature level P_l and D_{all} indicates that in all feature levels. If different S_{gtbox} has similar D_{all}, the assignment is fair to any size of Gtbox. As shown in Table 1, $\eta = \left(\sqrt{2}\right)^n$. When n = 1, each feature level has the same feature density distribution, but the number of feature points can be matched is less. When n = 3, the number of feature points that can be matched by large-size Gtbox increases, while the number of feature points that can be matched by small-size Gtbox decreases, resulting in the unbalanced matching.

The experimental results in paper [18]. Table 2 show that $\eta = 2$ has the best performance. The experimental results in Fig. 4 of paper [17] show that the feature response of a certain scale target will concentrate on the adjacent feature level. We abandoned the scales far away from $S_{l-basic}$ and set $\eta = 2$, which takes into account the balance and quantity of sample matching.

It can be seen from Table 1 that when n is large, the number of feature points that can be matched by small Gtbox and large Gtbox will be greatly different. When $l = 1$, there is no P_{l-1}, P_{l-2}, Gtbox can only match to feature points in P_l, P_{l+1}, P_{l+2} which make small Gtboxes are relatively lack of matching samples. This is one of the reasons why small targets are difficult to detect.

$$
\begin{aligned}
S_{l-basic} &= 16 \cdot S_l \\
S_{l-min} &= S_{l-basic}/\eta^2 \\
S_{l-max} &= S_{l-basic} \cdot \eta^2 \\
S_{gtbox} &\in \left[S_{l-basic}/\eta^2, S_{l-basic} \cdot \eta^2\right] \\
D_l &= S_{gtbox}/S_l
\end{aligned}
\tag{2}
$$

3.3 Scale Normalization Loss

Face detector needs to deal with faces with large scale changes at the same time, and the feature levels matched with different scale faces need to achieve the close detection performance. Focal loss adjusts the weight of all samples according to the loss. However, the weights of samples with same loss but different scales cannot be distinguished.

We utilize the $SN\_Loss\_L_i$ (Eq. 3) to evaluate the model performance in level L_i without focal loss. According to this, the weights of samples in different levels are assigned. $N_{Gtbox\_L_i}$ is the total number of Gtboxes matched by level L_i, $Lconf_j\_L_i$ is the softmax loss over two classes on level L_i, the range of j is all positive and negative samples of the level L_i.

During the training, we sum and normalize the loss of samples matching to different levels. Due to density balance scale assignment in Sect. 3.2, we can simply divide by Gtboxes number to achieve normalization. We find that when the number of samples of different scales in each layer is distributed in equal proportion, the $N\_Loss\_L_1$ is the largest, to $SN\_Loss\_L_6$ decreasing in turn. We consider that the feature extraction of

Table 1. Matching density in each feature levels when η is different.

η	S_{gtbox}	D_{l-2}	D_{l-1}	D_l	D_{l+1}	D_{l+2}	D_{all}
$\sqrt{2}$	$[S_{min}, S_{mid}]$	/	/	[8, 16]	/	/	[8, 16]
	$[S_{mid}, S_{max}]$	/	/	[16, 32]	/	/	[16, 32]
$\left(\sqrt{2}\right)^2$	$[S_{min}, S_{mid}]$	/	[8 × 4, 16 × 4]	[8, 16]	/	/	[40, 80]
	$[S_{mid}, S_{max}]$	/	/	[16, 32]	[16/4,32/4]	/	[20, 40]
$\left(\sqrt{2}\right)^3$	$[S_{min}, S_{mid}]$	[8 × 4 × 4, 16 × 4 × 4]	[8 × 4, 16 × 4]	[8, 16]	[8/4,16/4]	/	[170, 340]
	$[S_{mid}, S_{max}]$	/	[16 × 4, 32 × 4]	[16, 32]	[16/4,32/4]	[(16/4)/4, (32/4)/4]	[85, 170]

small face is deficiency (the Gtbox area is small and the feature level is shallow), and the supervision of training the level is relatively insufficient, so training smaller face detection level need more samples. Using the sample augmentation with controllable scale and quantity in Sect. 3.1, we adjust the proportion of different sampling options to control the proportion distribution of samples in different levels. It is equivalent to adjusting the weight of different levels of samples, so that the $SN\_Loss\_L_i$ of each level can keep close value during training. We will make a concrete analysis in Sect. 4.2.

$$SN\_Loss\_L_i = \sum_j Lconf_j\_L_i / N_{Gtbox\_L_i} \qquad (3)$$

4 Experiments

4.1 Dataset

We use the WIDER FACE dataset to train our face detector and perform evaluations on the validation and test sets.

4.2 Implementation Details

Baseline
We build our face detector baseline based on SSD [2].

We use Mobilenet-v1 as the backbone to ensure that it can be trained and applied on ordinary equipment. The backbone is initialized by pre-trained model on the ImageNet classification task. Add extra feature layers after backbone and use 320^2 as network input to construct a 5-level feature pyramid with size of $80^2\ 40^2\ 20^2\ 10^2\ 5^2$. We use the data augmentation described in Sect. 3.1. Options 1–3 are random fed into batch. We use hard example mining in SSD, The proportion of positive and negative is 1:3. During inference, the prediction boxes with score above 0.005 go through soft NMS to generate final results.

Optimization

Our models are trained on 4 NVIDIA GTX 1080ti GPUs. batch_size is 1, iter_size is 16, mini_batch (=batch_size * iter_size) is 16. We use SGD with 0.9 momentum. base_lr is set to 0.001 and decreased 10X at iteration 70k, the training ended at 120k iterations. Our experiments are implemented on caffe-ssd. All the codes and trained models will be available in the future.

Analysis Crop-Mosaic

Table 2 shows an image sequence in training set. Horizontal coordinate is image serial number, and longitudinal coordinate is feature level. The number of samples in each feature level of each image is counted. **In order to update the parameters of each feature level in a balanced way during back propagation, each level should have samples in one batch**. In theory, if any size sample can be cropped out from an original image, the need of training can be satisfied if batch_size is set to 1. However, due to the uncontrollable size of the Gtboxes in original image, it is difficult to achieve this. We can only optimize the sampling method to try to make the batch_size as small as possible to ensure that each level has enough samples. In this way it is no longer necessary to use expensive GPUs for training.

Table 2. Sample distribution in a batch

level	image sequence in one batch																sum
	1	2	3	4	5	6	7	8	9	10	11	12	13	14	15	16	
P5	0	1	0	0	0	0	1	0	0	0	0	0	0	0	0	0	2
P4	0	0	0	0	1	0	1	1	1	0	0	0	0	1	0	0	5
P3	0	0	0	0	0	1	3	0	0	1	9	5	0	1	0	2	22
P2	0	0	0	0	0	3	1	0	0	0	11	0	6	2	0	0	23
P1	2	0	1	3	0	1	0	0	0	0	1	0	2	0	0	0	10

We define $Interval_{zero}$ for the image sequence with zero consecutive samples for each level (Take Table 2 for example, there are three $Interval_{zero}$ in the green background of level P5, P3, P1 and the valuse are 4, 2, 1). **The distribution of the variable can evaluate the quality of the sampling program.** Figure 4 shows the statistical curve of $Interval_{zero}$ in different feature levels after training 1000 iterations. Horizontal ordinate is the value of $Interval_{zero}$, longitudinal coordinates is the number of $Interval_{zero}$ when $Interval_{zero} = N$. Area ratio under the curve can reflect the probability that there are no samples in the P_i level in a mini-batch when the batch_size is set to N. In our experiment, we set N(batch_size) = 16 to ensure that each layer has samples with high probability. The smaller the value of N, the better the sampling procedure. From the comparison of Fig. 5(a)(b), it can be seen that the proportion of $Interval_{zero}$ with lower value are increased by crop mosaic sample augmentation.

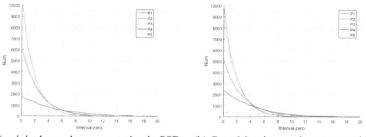

(a) original sample augmentation in SSD   (b) Crop-Mosaic sample augmentation

Fig. 4. $Interval_{zero}$ statistics for each level

Analysis Scale Normalization Loss

Different data augmentation constructs different training sample distribution. Sample set A uses the method described in Sect. 3.1 with option 1–3, counts the number of Gtboxes matched by different feature levels separately. The proportion distribution after normalization is shown in Fig. 5(a), From the bottom to the top level, the number of samples decreases step by step. Figure 5(c) shows the SN_Loss curve when training with sample set A. with the iteration, the loss of each level can be stabilized to a balanced value. In Fig. 5(b), sample set B only selects option 2 when sampling, two images cropped from the original input image that the maximum jaccard overlap with the original image is 0.2 or 0.8, which makes the sample proportion of each level close to the same. Due to random cropping, the data augmentation is difficult to generate large Gtbox which make samples in level P_i are relatively less. Figure 5(d) shows that the SN_Loss of the lower level is larger than that of the higher level, and the decline is slower. In this way, it is easy to find that sample set A is a better distribution.

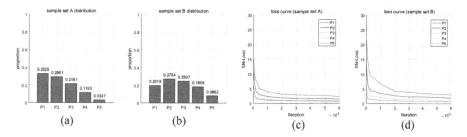

Fig. 5. Training sample distribution and their loss curve

Comparisons to the State-of-the-Arts

High resolution of the lowest feature level is helpful to detect face with smaller size. Add another extra feature layer to the baseline and change the network input to 640^2, a 6-level feature pyramid with size of 160^2 80^2 40^2 20^2 10^2 5^2 can be constructed Sect. 3.2. Data augmentation described in Options 1–4 is random fed into batch.

Figure 6 shows the evaluation results between ours and CSP which are both anchor-free based for single-scale testing. CSP adopts ResNet-50 as backbone, training on 8

GPUs with 2 images per GPU. Ours adopts Mobilenet-v1 as backbone, training on 4 GPUs with 1 image per GPU. However, the results show that our performance is close to CSP.

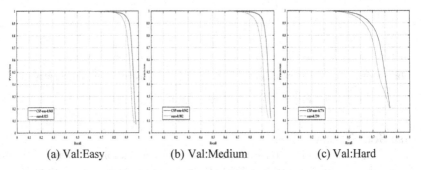

(a) Val:Easy   (b) Val:Medium   (c) Val:Hard

Fig. 6. Precision-recall curves on WIDER FACE validation sets

Most of the faces in hard validation set are very small, the detection rate is affected by the resolution of the bottom level of the feature pyramid. People always use multiscale testing to increase the resolution at the bottom of the feature level. Considering the uncontrollable factors of multi-scale testing, it is difficult to form an effective comparison because of the great influence on the evaluation results. We simply use the **single model for single-scale testing**. As shown in Table 3, the performance of many other methods are lower than original papers. Our method we trained with lightweight network on the common equipment also achieved more ideal performance.

Table 3. Performance comparisons on the WIDER FACE validation set

Method	Backbone	Easy	Medium	Hard
Retinaface	ResNet-50	0.951	0.943	0.844
SRN [24]	ResNet-50	0.93	0.873	0.713
CSP	ResNet-50	0.948	0.942	0.774
DSFD [7]	ResNet-152	0.951	0.942	0.851
SSH [4]	VGG-16	0.921	0.907	0.702
EXTD	Mobilenet-v1	0.851	0.823	0.672
Ours	Mobilenet-v1	0.923	0.902	0.739

5   Conclusion

In this work, a balance training method is presented for anchor-free face detection. We propose a data augmentation called crop-mosaic to provide sacle balance Gtboxes. In order to evaluate the efficiency of sampling procedure quantitatively we introduce a zero-sample interval statistical method. The statistical results can be used as reference for setting the batchsize. We design a density balance scale assignment strategy for Gtboxes matching. Lastly, we introduce a scale normalization loss for balance training with each levels. Experiments showed that the proposed methods achieved excellent detection performance without consuming a large number of GPUs for training.

Acknowledgments. This work was supported in part by the National Natural Science Foundation of China under Grant U1933134, in part by the Sichuan Science and Technology Program under Grant 2018JY0602 and Grant 2018GZDZX0024, and in part by the Fund of Sichuan University under Grant 2018SCUH0042.

The Fundamental Research Funds for the Central Universities, Southwest Minzu University (2020PTJS27004).

References

1. Viola, P.A., Jones, M.J.: Rapid object detection using a boosted cascade of simple features. In: CVPR (2001)
2. Liu, W., et al.: SSD: single shot MultiBox detector. In: Leibe, B., Matas, J., Sebe, N., Welling, M. (eds.) ECCV 2016. LNCS, vol. 9905, pp. 21–37. Springer, Cham (2016). https://doi.org/10.1007/978-3-319-46448-0_2
3. Redmon, J., Divvala, S., Girshick, R., Farhadi, A.: You only look once: unified, real-time object detection. In: CVPR (2016)
4. Najibi, M., Samangouei, P., Chellappa, R., Davis, L.S.: SSH: Single stage headless face detector. In: Proceedings of IEEE International Conference on Computer Vision (ICCV) (2017)
5. Tang, X., Du, D.K., He, Z., Liu, J.: PyramidBox: a context-assisted single shot face detector. In: Ferrari, V., Hebert, M., Sminchisescu, C., Weiss, Y. (eds.) ECCV 2018. LNCS, vol. 11213, pp. 812–828. Springer, Cham (2018). https://doi.org/10.1007/978-3-030-01240-3_49
6. Zhang, S., Zhu, X., Lei, Z., Shi, H., Wang, X., Li, S.Z.: FaceBoxes: a CPU real-time face detector with high accuracy. In: International Joint Conference on Biometrics (2017)
7. Li, J., et al.: DSFD: dual shot face detector. In: CVPR (2019)
8. Zhang, B., et al.: ASFD: automatic and scalable face detector. arXiv preprint arXiv:2003.11228 (2020)
9. Zhu, J., Li, D., Han, T., Tian, L., Shan, Y.: ProgressFace: scale-aware progressive learning for face detection. In: Vedaldi, A., Bischof, H., Brox, T., Frahm, J.-M. (eds.) ECCV 2020. LNCS, vol. 12351, pp. 344–360. Springer, Cham (2020). https://doi.org/10.1007/978-3-030-58539-6_21
10. Ming, X., Wei, F., Zhang, T., Chen, D., Wen, F.: Group sampling for scale invariant face detection. In: CVPR (2019)
11. Zhang, S., Zhu, X., Lei, Z., Shi, H., Wang, X., Li, S.Z.: S3FD: single shot scale-invariant face detector. In: ICCV (2017)
12. Zhang, S., Chi, C., Yao, Y., Lei, Z., Li, S.Z.: Bridging the gap between anchor-based and anchor-free detection via adaptive training sample selection. In: CVPR (2020)
13. Kim, K., Lee, H.S.: Probabilistic anchor assignment with IoU prediction for object detection. In: Vedaldi, A., Bischof, H., Brox, T., Frahm, J.-M. (eds.) ECCV 2020. LNCS, vol. 12370, pp. 355–371. Springer, Cham (2020). https://doi.org/10.1007/978-3-030-58595-2_22
14. Li, Z., Tang, X., Han, J., Liu, J., He, R.: PyramidBox++: high performance detector for finding tiny face. arXiv preprint arXiv:1904.00386 (2019)

15. Bochkovskiy, A., Wang, C.-Y., Liao, H.-Y.M.: YOLOv4: optimal speed and accuracy of object detection. arXiv preprint arXiv:2004.10934 (2020)
16. Chen, Y., et al.: Stitcher: feedback-driven data provider for object detection. arXiv preprint arXiv:2004.12432 (2020)
17. Zhu, B., et al.: AutoAssign: differentiable label assignment for dense object detection. arXiv preprint arXiv:2007.03496 (2020)
18. Kong, T., Sun, F., Liu, H., Jiang, Y., Li, L., Shi, J.: FoveaBox: beyond anchor-based object detector. IEEE Trans. Image Process. **29**, 7389–7398 (2020)
19. Tian, Z., Shen, C., Chen, H., He, T.: FCOS: fully convolutional one-stage object detection. In: ICCV (2019)
20. Liu, W., Hasan, I., Liao, S.: Center and scale prediction: a box-free approach for pedestrian and face detection. In: CVPR (2019)
21. Huang, L., Yang, Y., Deng, Y., Yu, Y.: DenseBox: unifying landmark localization with end to end object detection. arXiv preprint arXiv:1509.04874 (2015)
22. Zhou, X., Wang, D., Krähenbühl, P.: Objects as points. arXiv preprint arXiv:1904.07850v2
23. Yang, S., Luo, P., Loy, C.C., Tang, X.: WIDER FACE: a face detection benchmark. In: CVPR (2016)
24. Chi, C., Zhang, S., Xing, J., Lei, Z., Li, S.Z.: Selective refinement network for high performance face detection. In: AAAI (2019)

One-Class Face Anti-spoofing Based on Attention Auto-encoder

Xiaobin Huang, Jingtian Xia, and Linlin Shen$^{(\boxtimes)}$

Computer Vision Institute, School of Computer Science and Software Engineering,
Shenzhen University, Shenzhen 518060, China
{huangxiaobin2017,xiajingtian2018}@email.szu.edu.cn,
llshen@szu.edu.cn

Abstract. Face anti-spoofing (FAS) is crucial to defense spoofing attack against face recognition system. Most of existing methods use a large number of attack samples to train the classification model, which requires high computational and labelling costs. It's also not flexible to collect large number of attack sample each time a new attack model is invented. To address the issue, we propose an Attention Auto-Encoder (AAE) based one-class FAS model in this paper. As only real face samples are required for training, the generalization capability of our method can be significantly improved. In addition, for FAS tasks, attention-based model can filter out irrelevant information and pay attention to consistent feature of genuine face. We use reconstruction error and the latent layer of AAE network to calculate the spoofness score to evaluate the proposed approach. Comprehensive experiments on CASIA-FASD and REPLAY-ATTACK databases show that our method achieves superior performance on cross-dataset testing, i.e., 20.0% and 26.9% HTER is achieved. The results suggest that our method is much more robust against attack patterns not available in the training set.

Keywords: Face anti-spoofing · Attention auto-encoder · One-class · Loss function · Spoofness score

1 Introduction

With the wide use of intelligent device, face recognition system, due to its convenience and high accuracy, has become a ubiquitous technology in both industry application and commercial products, such as phone unlock and access control etc. However, face recognition system can be easily attacked by print attack, video attacks and 3D mask attack, for its insensitivity to genuine face and fake ones. To tackle this problem, face anti-spoofing (FAS) is drawing more and more attentions. Some supervised methods, like Texture-based models and CNN based models, have been proposed. Texture-based models attempt to extract handcrafted features, e.g., LBP [1], SIFT [2] and HoG [3], and input them into a traditional classifier, e.g., SVM and LDA, to make a binary decision. CNN based methods [4–6] utilize deep learning network and softmax loss to learn spoofing features.

© Springer Nature Switzerland AG 2021
J. Feng et al. (Eds.): CCBR 2021, LNCS 12878, pp. 365–373, 2021.
https://doi.org/10.1007/978-3-030-86608-2_40

Though supervised methods, requiring large scale training data to cover as many attack patterns as possible, are effective for FAS tasks, their performances are limited by the following problems: in real-word applications, when attacks not covered in training data are present, the performance of detector will significantly drop. As a result, the spoofing detector needs to be trained using a large number of new attack samples, which requires high computational and labelling costs. To increase the generalization capability of spoofing detector, we propose in this paper an attention based one-class model for this purpose, which only requires real face samples for training.

One-class model, also known as unary classification model, tries to identify objects of a specific class among all other objects. The model manages to form the space of positive samples and recognize negative samples by judging if the sample belongs to the space. Besides, it only utilizes positive samples to train the model. i.e., when a new attack pattern appears, the model can recognize this attack without seeing in advance the new attack data. [7, 8] are the first attempts on one-class FAS, they regard FAS as an outlier detection problem for live faces. However, they use handcrafted features such as LBP to represent live faces, which were shown to be less effective.

Attention-based model used in deep learning aims to pay attention to important region of images and feature maps. The attention-based model used in FAS tasks can filter out irrelevant information and pay attention to consistent feature of genuine faces. What's more, attention-based detector can focus on the face information and ignore background information, the generalization capability of the detector can thus be improved. [9] applies the attention-based model to the FAS for the first time, but it applies the attention mechanism to the network channel, not to the image.

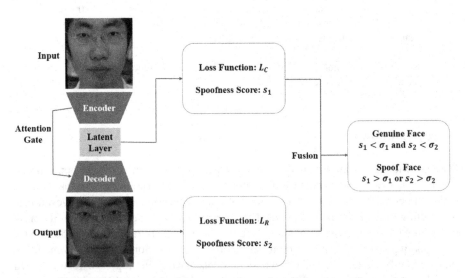

Fig. 1. The framework of the proposed one-class face anti-spoofing model.

As shown in Fig. 1, we propose a one-class face anti-spoofing method based on the attention auto-encoder (AAE). First, we use an auto-encoder with attention gates to reconstruct the face images and extract the latent features of the faces. In this paper, we use data containing only genuine faces as the training set to train this AAE. In order to obtain the latent feature and the reconstructed image of the face, we use the center loss L_c and the mean square error L_R as the loss function in the latent layer and output layer of the AAE, respectively. Then, based on the output of the latent layer and output layer of the AAE, the spoofness scores s_1 and s_2 are designed. Finally, we input test sample and get the spoofness scores. When both scores are less than the thresholds, the sample is judged as a geniune face, otherwise it is judged as a spoof face.

2 The Proposed Method

In this section, we introduce the structure of the AAE, the loss functions used by the network, and the spoofness scores for distinguishing genuine and spoof faces in details.

2.1 Attention Auto-encoder

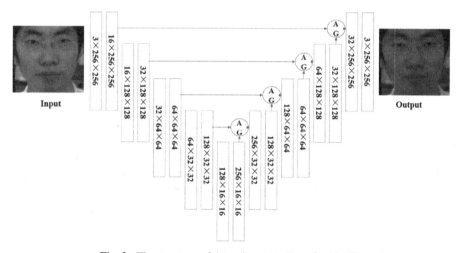

Fig. 2. The structure of Attention Auto-Encoder (AAE).

Figure 2 shows the structure of the AAE. As shown in the Fig, AAE contains 1 encoder, 1 decoder and 4 Attention Gates (AGs). The input of the encoder is a genuine face image with size $3 \times 256 \times 256$, and the output of the encoder and the decoder is the latent layer with size $256 \times 16 \times 16$ and the reconstructed image with size $3 \times 256 \times 256$, respectively. The encoder contains 10 convolutional layers and 4 down-pooling layers, and the decoder contains 4 AGs and 8 convolutional layers. The center loss and the spoofness score s_1 are applied to the latent layer, the reconstruction loss and the spoofness score s_2 are applied to the output layer.

Figure 3 shows the structure of the AG. The AG in the figure is the first attention gate of the network, that is, the bottom attention gate in Fig. 2. The two inputs, Input1 and Input2, of the AG come from the Encoder and the Decoder respectively. Firstly, it performs convolution on Input1 and upsampling on Input2, so that the network gets two feature maps of the same size. Then, it connects the 1 × 1 convolutional layer after two feature maps and sums them. Finally, it performs ReLU activation, 1 × 1 convolution and sigmoid activation on the summed feature map, and then performs dot multiplication with the matrix obtained after upsampling on Input2, to obtain the Hadamard product, which is the output of the AG.

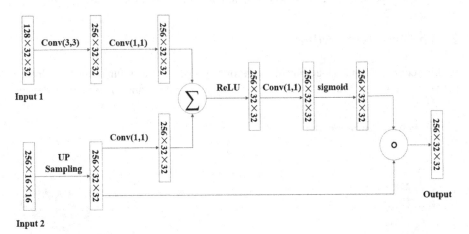

Fig. 3. The structure of Attention Gate (AG).

In attention gate, weight matrix, which implements the attention mechanism, is built by three 1 × 1 convolutional layers. By multiplying the feature map with the weight matrix, we can obtain the correlation between the map and the target. Our purpose of using the attention mechanism is to learn the importance of each pixel to the target, focus on the area related to the target and ignore the irrelevant areas.

2.2 Reconstruction Loss and Center Loss

The entire network training process is divided into two stages. In the first stage, we only apply the reconstruction loss L_R in the output layer to make the output image of the network similar to the input image as much as possible. The formula of L_R is as follows:

$$L_R = \frac{1}{2} \sum_{i=1}^{m} \|F_{AAE}(x_i) - x_i\|_2^2 \tag{1}$$

where x_i is the input of the network, $F_{AAE}(x_i)$ is the output of the network, m is the number of the sample.

In the second stage, the center loss is applied to in the latent layer of the network to make the encoder extract the same features from different real faces. The formula of L_C is as follows:

$$L_c = \frac{1}{2} \sum_{i=1}^{m} \|c - F_E(x_i)\|_2^2 \tag{2}$$

$$c = \frac{1}{m} \sum_{i=1}^{m} F_E(x_i) \tag{3}$$

where $F_E(x_i)$ is the output of the encoder, c is the average of $F_E(x_i)$.

In the second stage, L_R and L_c are applied to the network at the same time, the formula of the total loss function L is as follows:

$$L = L_R + \lambda L_c = \frac{1}{2} \sum_{i=1}^{m} \|F_{AAE}(x_i) - x_i\|_2^2 + \frac{\lambda}{2} \sum_{i=1}^{m} \|c - F_E(x_i)\|_2^2 \tag{4}$$

where λ is the hyperparameter to adjust the ratio of L_C to L_R.

As the loss function of the network, L constrains the output layer and the latent layer at the same time, which can not only reconstruct the real face images, but also extract the common deep features from the real face images.

2.3 Spoofness Score

After training the AAE, two spoofness scores are designed to detect spoofing faces. Based on L_c, the first spoofness score s_1 is calculated using the output of latent layer, as follows:

$$s_1 = \frac{1}{N_L} \sqrt{\sum_{j=1}^{N_L} \left[\frac{\sum_{k=1}^{H_L} \sum_{l=1}^{W_L} c(j,k,l)}{H_L * W_L} - \frac{\sum_{k=1}^{H_L} \sum_{l=1}^{W_L} F_E(x,j,k,l)}{H_L * W_L} \right]^2} \tag{5}$$

where N_L, H_L, W_L is the number of channels, the height and the width of output of the latent layer, and j, k and l are the coordinates of each pixel of latent feature map, x is the test sample.

Firstly, the latent feature map is converted into a feature vector by average pooling. Then, we calculate the L2 distance between the vector of the test sample and the center of genuine faces. s_1 thus represents the difference between the deep feature of test sample and genuine faces.

Based on the L_R, the second spoofness score s_2 is calculated using the feature map of output layer, as below:

$$s_2 = \frac{1}{N_O * H_O * W_O} \sqrt{\sum_{j=1}^{N_O} \sum_{k=1}^{H_O} \sum_{l=1}^{W_O} \left[x(j, k, l) - F_{AAE}(x, j, k, l)\right]^2} \tag{6}$$

where N_O, H_O, W_O is the number of the channels, the height and the width of the output feature map. s_2 thus represents the difference between the reconstructed image and the original image of the test sample.

The smaller s_1 and s_2, the larger probability the test sample will be genuine. We set two thresholds σ_1 and σ_2. When $s_1 < \sigma_1$ and $s_2 < \sigma_2$, the test sample is judged to be genuine, otherwise it is judged to be spoof. Both σ_1 and σ_2 are obtained through experiments.

3   Experiments

3.1   Datasets

In this paper, the experiments were conducted on two databases, i.e. CASIA-FASD database [10] and REPLAY-ATTACK database [11]. The CASIA-FASD database contains 600 genuine and spoof videos of 50 subjects, i.e. 12 videos (3 genuine and 9 spoof) for each subject. This database has 3 kinds of imaging qualities and 3 kinds of attacks, i.e. the warped photo attack, the cut photo attack and video attack. The training set and the testing set consist of 20 subjects (60 genuine videos and 180 spoof videos) and 30 subjects (90 genuine videos and 270 spoof videos), respectively. The Idiap REPLAY-ATTACK database consists of 1200 videos recordings of both real-access and attack attempts of 50 different subjects. The training set, the validation set and the testing set consist of 15 subjects, 15 subjects and 20 subjects, respectively. Three types of attacks, i.e. printed photograph, mobile phone and tablet attacks, are available.

3.2   Performance Metrics

In our experiment, the testing performances on the databases are evaluated with the ACC (accuracy), ACER (Average Classification Error Rate) and HTER (Half Total Error Rate). The ACER is the half of the sum of the APCER (Attack Presentation Classification Error Rate) and the BPCER (Bonafide Presentation Classification Error Rate). The HTER is the half of the sum of the FAR (False Acceptance Rate) and the FRR (False Rejection Rate).

3.3   Experimental Settings

We first obtains each frame of image from video, detects faces on each frame through MTCNN [12], and then aligns and scales the size of face images to 256×256. Finally, all the face images are input into the network and classified as real or spoofing faces.

This experiment was implemented on Keras. In the first training stage, the network is optimized with RMSPROP under a mini-batch size of 4, the initial learning rate is 0.0001, the epoch is 200; in the second training stage, the initial learning rate is 0.00001, the epoch is 300, others remain unchanged.

3.4   Results

Firstly, we do an ablation experiment and compare different spoofness scores. Table 1 showed the comparison of different methods using different spoofness scores on the CASIA-FASD. As shown in Table 1, the method of using AAE network structure is better than that using AE, which shows that the attention mechanism has played a role in the network so that the network can extract better features. In addition, we found that fusing the two spoofness scores can get the best ACER. When single spoofness score is applied, s_2 is better than s_1.

Table 1. Results of different methods using different spoofness scores on the CASIA-FASD.

Spoofness score	Method	ACC (%)	ACER (%)
s_1	AE	79.72	23.15
	AAE	80.56	22.41
s_2	AE	80.83	21.29
	AAE	81.94	19.11
Fusion	AE	81.39	18.89
	AAE	**83.89**	**16.85**

Secondly, we compare the performance of different methods when test set and training set have the same attack pattern. Table 2 shows the results of different methods on CASIA-FASD database. In Table 2, ResNet-18 is a benchmark method for supervised learning, and AAE is our one-class method. As shown in Table 2, the performance of supervised learning is much better than the one-class method. When the training set and the test set have the same attack pattern, the data distribution of the training set is very similar to the test set, so the classification boundary found on the training set by supervised learning can be well fitted to the test set. The training set of one-class method does not have negative samples, so the classification boundary found by this method is not as good as the supervised method.

Table 2. Performance comparison of different methods on CASIA-FASD when the attack patterns of the training set and the test set are the same.

Train	Test	Method	ACC (%)	ACER (%)
Genuine face, Photo attack	Genuine face, Photo attack	**Resnet-18**	**95.19**	**5.56**
Genuine face		AAE	83.61	15.56
Genuine face, Video attack	Genuine face, Video attack	**Resnet-18**	**96.11**	**3.89**
Genuine face		AAE	81.67	18.33

Thirdly, we compare the performance of different methods when the test set and the training set have different attack patterns. Table 3 shows the performance comparison of different methods on CASIA-FASD. From Table 3, we conclude that, for supervised learning, when the training set and the test set have different attack patterns, the performance is worse than that of the one-class method. When the training set and the test set use different attack patterns, the data distribution of the training set and the test set is different, so the classification boundary found on the training set by supervised learning cannot well fit the test set. When a certain attack pattern not available in the training set is presented, the supervised method cannot correctly classify the attack pattern. On the contrary, the one-class method is still able to detect the spoof faces, based on the learned boundary of the positive samples.

Table 3. Performance comparison of different methods on CASIA-FASD when the attack patterns of the training set and the test set are different.

Train	Test	Method	ACC (%)	ACER (%)
Genuine face, Photo attack	Genuine face, Video attack	Resnet-18	71.11	28.89
Genuine face		**AAE**	**81.67**	**18.33**
Genuine face, Video attack	Genuine face, Photo attack	Resnet-18	78.52	24.72
Genuine face		**AAE**	**83.61**	**15.56**

Finally, we perform a cross-database testing between the CASIA-FASD and Replay-Attack databases. As shown in Table 4, our method achieves the best performance. Since the shooting scenes and acquisition equipment in the two databases are different, the results of cross-database testing for general supervised methods on these two databases are not good enough. Our method uses the attention mechanism to minimize the influence of background, image quality and other factors, so it can achieve better results than others.

Table 4. The result of different methods on cross database testing between the CASIA-FASD and REPLAY-ATTACK databases.

Methods	HTER (%)			
	Train	Test	Train	Test
	CASIA FASD	REPLAY ATTACK	REPLAY ATTACK	CASIA FASD
CNN [13]	48.5		45.5	
STASN [14]	31.5		30.9	
FaceDs [6]	28.5		41.1	
Depth + RPPG [15]	27.6		28.4	
Our method	**20.0**		**26.9**	

4 Conclusion

This paper proposed a one-class face anti-spoofing method based on AAE network, which uses attention auto-encoder to learn the distribution of real faces. Our approach was tested by using CASIA-FASD and REPLAY-ATTACK databases. The results show that, when encountering novel attack patterns not available in the training set, our method has a better ability to discriminate genuine and spoof face.

Acknowledgements. This work is supported by Natural Science Foundation of China under grants no. 91959108.

References

1. de Freitas Pereira, T., Anjos, A., De Martino, J.M., Marcel, S.: LBP − TOP based counter-measure against face spoofing attacks. In: Park, J.-I., Kim, J. (eds.) ACCV 2012. LNCS, vol. 7728, pp. 121–132. Springer, Heidelberg (2013). https://doi.org/10.1007/978-3-642-37410-4_11

2. Komulainen, J., Hadid, A., Pietikainen, M.: Context based face anti-spoofing. In: IEEE International Conference on Biometrics: Theory, Applications and Systems, pp. 1–8 (2014)

3. Patel, K., Han, H., Jain, A., et al.: Secure face unlock: spoof detection on smartphones. IEEE Trans. Inf. Forensics Secur. 11(10), 2268–2283 (2016)

4. Atoum, Y., Liu, Y., Jourabloo, A., et al.: Face anti-spoofing using patch and depth-based CNNs. In:IEEE International Joint Conference on Biometrics, pp. 319–328. IEEE (2017)

5. Feng, L., Po, L., Li, Y., et al.: integration of image quality and motion cues for face anti-spoofing: a neural network approach. J. Vis. Commun. Image Represent. 38, 451–460 (2016)

6. Jourabloo, A., Liu, Y., Liu, X.: Face de-spoofing: anti-spoofing via noise modeling. In: Proceedings of the European Conference on Computer Vision, pp. 290–306 (2018)

7. Arashloo, S., Kittler, J., Christmas, W.: An anomaly detection approach to face anti-spoofing detection: a new formulation and evaluation protocal. IEEE Access 5, 13868–13882 (2017)

8. Boulkenafet, Z., Komulainen, J., Li, L., et al.: OULU-NPU: a mobile face presentation attack database with real-world variations. In: IEEE International Conference on Automatic Face & Gesture Recognition, pp. 612–618 (2017)

9. Chen, H., Hu, G., Lei, Z., et al.: Attention-based two-stream convolutional networks for face spoofing detection. IEEE Trans. Inf. Forensics Secur. 15, 578–593 (2019)

10. Zhang, Z., Yan, J., Liu, S., et al.: A face anti-spoofing database with diverse attacks. In: IAPR International Conference on Biometrics, pp. 26–31 (2012)

11. Chingovska, I., Anjos, A., Marcel, S.: On the effectiveness of local binary patterns in face anti-spoofing. In: Proceedings of the International Conference of Biometrics Special Interest Group, pp. 1–7 (2012)

12. Zhang, K., Zhang, Z., Li, Z., et al.: Joint face detection and alignment using multitask cascaded convolutional networks. IEEE Sig. Process. Lett. 23(10), 1499–1503 (2016)

13. Yang, J., Lei, Z., Li, S.: Learn convolutional neural network for face anti-spoofing. https://arxiv.org/abs/1408.5601

14. Yang, X., Luo, W., Bao, L., et al.: Face anti-spoofing: model matters, so does data. In: IEEE/CVF Conference on Computer Vision and Pattern Recognition, pp. 3502–3511 (2019)

15. Liu, Y., Jourabloo, A., Liu, X.: Learning deep models for face anti-spoofing: binary or auxiliary supervision. In: IEEE/CVF Conference on Computer Vision and Pattern Recognition, pp. 389–398 (2018)

Full Quaternion Matrix and Random Projection for Bimodal Face Template Protection

Zihan Xu, Zhuhong Shao[✉], Yuanyuan Shang, and Zhongshan Ren

College of Information Engineering, Capital Normal University, Beijing, China
{2181002009,zhshao,5528,renzs}@cnu.edu.cn

Abstract. Considering that the information representation among multimodal biometric is complementary and the necessity of privacy-sensitive information protection over cloud and Internet of Things, this paper presents a secure template protection algorithm for bimodal face images using full-type quaternion generic polar complex exponential transform and random projection. The bimodal face images are firstly encoded into a full quaternion matrix and quaternion generic polar complex exponential transform is used for generating primary features. Then sparse random projection is followed aiming at making the fused features non-invertibility and be able to reissued. In additionally, the generalized discriminant analysis is employed to reduce dimension of the selected features. Experimental results obtained on three face datasets have demonstrated that the proposed method presents good recognition performance in comparison with other existing methods, while it can ensure the secrecy and privacy of facial images.

Keywords: Cancelable face template · Multi-biometric features · Quaternion generic polar complex exponential transform · Sparse random projection

1 Introduction

Currently, facial images have been widely used to unlock mobile phones, cash registers at supermarkets and passing access control at rail stations. However, facial characteristics are irreplaceable and facial images imply some personal sensitive information, such as age, healthcare or financial records. Studies have revealed that biometric information without handled manner may be accessed by adversaries for malicious intention. Therefore, the security and privacy in biometric based identity authentication systems have become a significant concern [1, 2].

To secure biometric template, several schemes including biometric cryptosystems, cancelable biometrics, Homomorphic Encryption and visual cryptography based methods were investigated. Among them, the first two categories have more reliability [3]. For example, Shen et al. [4] introduced a face block scrambling recognition (FBSR) method based on deep convolutional neural network (CNN), where the Arnold was employed for scrambling. However, the Arnold transform is periodic and the CNN model requires a certain amount of training samples and computational costs for better performance. In contrast, cancelable template strategy can secure face images with a high level. Once

© Springer Nature Switzerland AG 2021
J. Feng et al. (Eds.): CCBR 2021, LNCS 12878, pp. 374–383, 2021.
https://doi.org/10.1007/978-3-030-86608-2_41

the face template is leaked, alternative one can be generated and reissued. For remote multi-server environment, biometric authentication framework using cancelable biometrics and secret sharing was studied in [5]. Soliman et al. [6] selected the scale invariant feature transform to extract the facial features and they were subsequently encrypted with the double random phase encoding technique.

Furthermore, it is expected that the combination of multimodal biometric is able to enhance the reliability of biometric system [7]. Gomez-Barrero et al. [8] introduced a cancelable template generation scheme based on Bloom Filter which can fuse templates with different sizes. Kaur et al. [9] proposed a template protection method using random distance method (RDM) which is appropriate for unimodal and multimodal biometric recognition systems. It not only guarantees a non-invertible transform but also reduces half amount of data. Chang et al. [10] put forward a multi-biometric authentication approach used bit-wise encryption scheme, which can make the recognition performance of protected and unprotected systems equal.

This paper aims to develop a cancelable template protection approach for bimodal face images. The contributions of this paper are: (1) A framework for multimodal face recognition using quaternion transform is proposed. (2) The proposed full-type quaternion generic polar complex exponential transform can effectively extract features of bimodal face and improve recognition accuracy. (3) The random projection strategy is applied to make the algorithm satisfy revocability with little influence on the accuracy.

The remainder of this paper is arranged as follows. The Sect. 2 presents the proposed scheme in detail. In Sect. 3, a series of experiments performed on three multi-biometric datasets are conducted to demonstrate the feasibility and security of the proposal. Some conclusions are drawn in Sect. 4.

2   Proposed Method

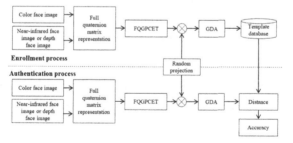

Fig. 1. Flowchart of the proposed algorithm.

In this section, a novel cancelable recognition approach is proposed for bimodal face. The face images of different modalities are integrated into a full quaternion matrix, where the features are extracted by using the full-type quaternion generic polar complex exponential transform (FQGPCET). Followed by random projection, the property of non-invertibility is achieved. Finally, the generalized discriminant analysis (GDA) dimension reduction technique is further used. Figure 1 demonstrates the flowchart of the proposed algorithm.

2.1 Enrollment Process

The enrollment process consists of multimodal fusion, cancelable template generation and dimension reduction.

(1) Let $I_c(x, y)$ and $I_d(x, y)$ be two face images with the same size $m_1 \times n_1$, they are first precoded into a full quaternion matrix $I_f(x, y)$ as

$$I_f(x, y) = I_d(x, y) + iI_{c,R}(x, y) + jI_{c,G}(x, y) + kI_{c,B}(x, y) \tag{1}$$

where $I_c(\cdot)$ and $I_d(\cdot)$ are color face and another modality, $I_{c,R}(\cdot), I_{c,G}(\cdot), I_{c,B}(\cdot)$ are the RGB components of I_c respectively.

Next, the quaternion generic polar complex exponential transform (QGPCET) [11] is generalized to full-type, which is employed for extracting primary features. Mathematically, the definition and fast computation of the FQGPCET is given as,

$$H_{nms}^L(I_f) = \int_0^1 \int_0^{2\pi} \sqrt{\frac{sr^{s-2}}{2\pi}} e^{-\mu 2n\pi r^s} e^{-\mu m\theta} I_f(r, \theta) r dr d\theta = A_{nms}'^L + B_{nms}'^L i + C_{nms}'^L j + D_{nms}'^L k \tag{2}$$

and

$$\begin{cases} A_{nms}'^L = \text{Re}(H_{nms}(I_d)) - \frac{1}{\sqrt{3}}[\text{Im}(H_{nms}(I_{c,R})) + \text{Im}(H_{nms}(I_{c,G})) + \text{Im}(H_{nms}(I_{c,B}))] \\ B_{nms}'^L = \text{Re}(H_{nms}(I_{c,R})) + \frac{1}{\sqrt{3}}[\text{Im}(H_{nms}(I_d)) + \text{Im}(H_{nms}(I_{c,G})) - \text{Im}(H_{nms}(I_{c,B}))] \\ C_{nms}'^L = \text{Re}(H_{nms}(I_{c,G})) + \frac{1}{\sqrt{3}}[\text{Im}(H_{nms}(I_d)) + \text{Im}(H_{nms}(I_{c,B})) - \text{Im}(H_{nms}(I_{c,R}))] \\ D_{nms}'^L = \text{Re}(H_{nms}(I_{c,B})) + \frac{1}{\sqrt{3}}[\text{Im}(H_{nms}(I_d)) + \text{Im}(H_{nms}(I_{c,R})) - \text{Im}(H_{nms}(I_{c,G}))] \\ H_{nms} = \frac{2\pi}{M^2} \sum_{u=0}^{M-1} \sum_{v=0}^{M-1} f[r_u, \theta_v] \sqrt{\left(\frac{u}{M}\right)^{s/2-1} \Big/ 2\pi s} e^{-j2n\pi \frac{u}{M}} e^{-j2m\pi \frac{v}{M}} \end{cases} \tag{3}$$

where H_{nms} is the QGPCET with order n, repetition m and basis parameter s, $\mu = (i+j+k)/\sqrt{3}$ is an unit pure quaternion, $\text{Re}(\cdot)$ and $\text{Im}(\cdot)$ are the real and imaginary component of a complex number respectively, M is up-sampling parameter, $f[r_u, \theta_v]$ is the discretization of $f(r, \theta)$.

(2) To make the FQGPCET features revocable, random projection is applied to $H_{nms}^L(I_f)$. This strategy is realized by using a sparse random projection matrix R in which the elements are all distributed independently and identically following the distribution,

$$R_{i,j} = \sqrt{3} \begin{cases} 1, \text{ with probability } \frac{1}{6} \\ 0, \text{ with probability } \frac{2}{3} \\ -1, \text{ with probability } \frac{1}{6} \end{cases} \tag{4}$$

where $R_{i,j}$ represents the entries of sparse random projection matrix. Since the size of $H_{nms}^L(I_f)$ is $(2n+1) \times (2n+1)$, the size of the sparse random projection matrix R is set to $d \times (2n+1)$ and the projected feature matrix W_f is calculated by,

$$W_f = R H_{nms}^L (I_f) \tag{5}$$

Subsequently, W_f is transferred to a real matrix as,

$$w = [vect(W_{f,1}), vect(W_{f,2}), vect(W_{f,3}), vect(W_{f,4})] \tag{6}$$

where $vect(\cdot)$ represents a function mapping a matrix $W_f \in \mathbb{R}^{d \times (2n+1)}$ to a vector with length of $d(2n+1)$ and $\{W_{f,1}, W_{f,2}, W_{f,3}, W_{f,4}\}$ are respectively the real part and three imaginary parts of W_f.

(3) Suppose that $\{w_1, w_2, \cdots, w_{M_1}\}$ are M_1 training vectors with N_1 kinds of data which derives from the training fusion features after random projection and ϕ is a non-linear mapping function which maps w into a high-dimensional space, the between-class scatter B and within-class scatter V are computed as,

$$
\begin{cases}
B = \dfrac{1}{M_1} \sum_{p=1}^{N_1} n_p \sum_{q=1}^{n_p} (w_{pq}) \left(\sum_{r=1}^{n_p} w_{pr} \right)^{\mathrm{T}} \\
V = \dfrac{1}{M_1} \sum_{p=1}^{N_1} \sum_{q=1}^{n_p} \phi(w_{pq}) \phi^{\mathrm{T}}(w_{pq})
\end{cases}
\tag{7}
$$

where n_p is the size of the p-th class, w_{pq} is the q-th vector in the p-th class and T is transposition. Generalized discriminant analysis (GDA) aims to solve the problem,

$$v_1 = \arg\max_{v_1} \frac{v_1^{\mathrm{T}} B v_1}{v_1^{\mathrm{T}} V v_1} \tag{8}$$

There exists coefficients a_i satisfying,

$$v_1 = \sum_{i=1}^{M_1} a_i \phi(w_i) \tag{9}$$

The projection of a vector w_i on the l-th eigenvector v_1^l can be calculated by,

$$v_1^l \phi(w_i) = \sum_{j=1}^{M_1} a_j^l \phi(w_j) \phi(w_i) = \sum_{j=1}^{M_1} a_j^l k(w_j, w_i) \tag{10}$$

where $k(w_j, w_i)$ is a kernel function and a_j^l denotes the j-th coefficient of the l-th eigenvector. Here the polynomial function is chosen and defined as,

$$k(w_j, w_i) = (w_j \cdot w_i)^{d_1} \tag{11}$$

where · denotes dot product of two vectors, d_1 is the order of the polynomial function and is set to 2. The eigenvectors corresponding to the first $l(l \leq N_1 - 1)$ largest eigenvalues are finally selected to compose the projection matrix $V = [v_1^1, v_1^2, \cdots, v_1^l]$ and the projection of w_i in the GDA space is computed as,

$$y_{tr,i} = V^T \phi(w_i) \tag{12}$$

2.2 Authentication Process

When there are individuals that need to be authenticated, the query template is generated in a similar way with token. Then it is matched with the reference template stored in database. Suppose that the tested features are $y_{te,j}(j = 1, 2, \cdots, M_2)$, the matching is performed using cosine distance,

$$l = \frac{y_{tr,i} \cdot y_{te,j}}{|y_{t,i}||y_{v,j}|} \tag{13}$$

where the operator $|\cdot|$ denotes the modulus of vector.

3 Experimental Results

To evaluate the feasibility and validity of the proposed method, a series of experiments are performed on three face datasets. The Lab2 dataset [12] contains visible light and near-infrared face images of 50 subjects and there are 20 images in each modality for each individual. The CASIA NIR-VIS dataset [13] consists of visible light and near-infrared face images, which includes 5576 images of 474 subjects. The number of face images for a single modality of each individual ranges from 4 to 12. The IIIT-D RGB-D face database [14] collects 9162 face images from 106 subjects. The number of images for a single modality of each subject varies from 11 to 254. In experiments, all face images are cropped according to eye position and resized to 64 × 64 pixels.

3.1 Recognition Results

In this subsection, the influence of up-sampling parameter, basis parameter, transform order, compression degree and the number of eigenvectors on recognition results is tested. In the experiments, the recognition accuracy is obtained by changing a factor being tested while the rest are fixed. For each subject in the three datasets, the numbers of images in both modalities chosen randomly for training are respectively set at 4, 3 and 4.

Firstly, to find out the desirable up-sampling parameter M, the other parameters are set at $n = 15, s = 2, d = (2n + 1) \times 60\%$ and $l = 40$. As shown in Fig. 2, it is clearly that the recognition accuracy rises with the increase of M. This attributes to the fact that the up-sampling parameter determines the computational accuracy of the FQGPCET. However, when the up-sampling parameter reaches a certain value, the extracted features by the FQGPCET is enough to produce desirable recognition accuracy and the increase of M hardly bring further improvement. Figure 3 presents the recognition accuracy under varying s and M is set at 100, it can be observed that for all three datasets, the accuracy increases when s varies from 0.5 to 2 and reaches the peak value, and then decreases. With $M = 100$ and $s = 2$, the recognition accuracy with different order n is shown in Fig. 4, we can observe that with the increase of order n, the recognition accuracy becomes larger gradually. When the order n is more than 15, the accuracy begins to decline.

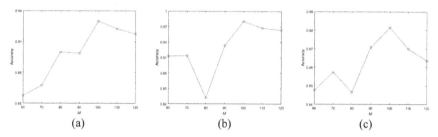

Fig. 2. Recognition accuracy with different M: (a) Lab2 (b) CASIA and (c) IIIT-D.

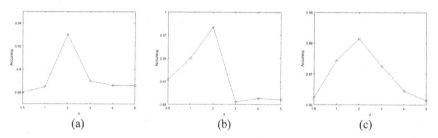

Fig. 3. Recognition accuracy with different s: (a) Lab2 (b) CASIA and (c) IIIT-D.

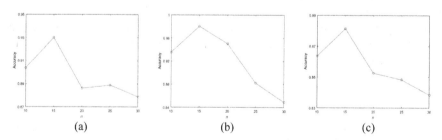

Fig. 4. Recognition accuracy with different n: (a) Lab2 (b) CASIA and (c) IIIT-D.

Next, the influence of compression degree on recognition accuracy is explored by changing d, where it is set at $d = k(2n+1)$. The other parameters are fixed to $M = 100$, $s = 2$, $n = 15$ and $l = 40$. From the results provided in Fig. 5, it is apparently that with the increase of k, the accuracy continues to improve on the whole. The accuracy achieves the maximum when k is equal to 60%.

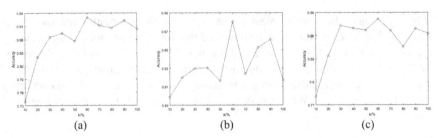

Fig. 5. Recognition accuracy with different compression degrees: (a) Lab2 (b) CASIA and (c) IIIT-D.

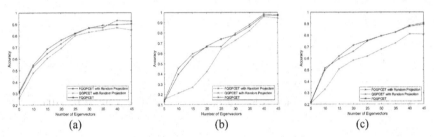

Fig. 6. Recognition accuracy with different number of eigenvectors: (a) Lab2 (b) CASIA and (c) IIIT-D.

Finally, recognition accuracy with the relation of the number of eigenvectors is evaluated when the other parameters are set at $M = 100$, $s = 2$, $d = (2n + 1) \times 60\%$ and $n = 15$. It can be seen from Fig. 6 that with the increase of the number of eigenvectors, the recognition accuracy by using QGPCET and FQGPCET improves continually and reaches a maximum at a certain amount. In addition, the recognition accuracy by using the proposed FQGPCET effectively enhanced in comparison with using QGPCET. This result is due to the combination of another modality of face, which makes the feature information more discriminative. More significantly, the employment of random projection seems to have no effect on the recognition accuracy. To obtain the trade-off between accuracy and time consumption, the number of eigenvectors is set at 40 on Lab2 and CASIA datasets and 45 on IIIT-D dataset.

3.2 Analysis of Security

In order to quantitatively evaluate the correlation between different feature templates, the correlation index (CI) is calculated as,

$$CI = \left| \frac{\sum (T_1 - \overline{T}_1) \sum (T_2 - \overline{T}_2)}{\sqrt{\sum (T_1 - \overline{T}_1)^2 \sum (T_2 - \overline{T}_2)^2}} \right| \tag{14}$$

where $\{T_1, T_2\}$ denotes two templates, $\{\overline{T}_1, \overline{T}_2\}$ represents their average values and $|\cdot|$ is the modulus operation.

In this experiment, 50 subjects in per dataset were randomly selected. For each subject, a set of bimodal face images were randomly selected and 6 feature templates were generated with different random projection matrices. From the results of CI values presented in Fig. 7, it can be observed that the average CI of per subject and dataset are less than 0.09. Small value of CI denotes little correlation between different templates and one cannot use the leaked template to crack the updated face recognition system which verifies the revocability.

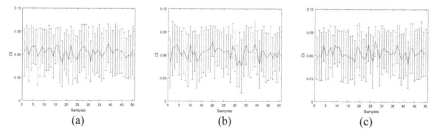

(a)   (b)   (c)

Fig. 7. The results of CI: (a) Lab2 (b) CASIA and (c) IIIT-D.

3.3 Comparison with Other Methods

To further demonstrate the superiority of the proposed algorithm, the recognition accuracy, precision, recall and F_{score} are compared with those by using the FBSR method, the RDM method and the Bloom Filter method. For the proposed algorithm, the parameters when using the Lab2 and CASIA datasets are set at $M = 100$, $s = 2$, $n = 15$, $d = (2n + 1) \times 60\%$, $l = 40$ and when using the IIIT-D dataset are set at $M = 100$, $s = 2$, $n = 15$, $d = (2n+1) \times 60\%$, $l = 45$. The parameters of the other three algorithms respectively refer to [4, 8, 9].

As demonstrated in Table 1 and Fig. 8, the proposed method achieves best performance on Lab2 and IIIT-D datasets compared to other methods and gets comparable performance on CASIA dataset. The proposed FQGPCET can fuse different face modalities effectively and result in the desirable performance. In general, these results have validated the reliability of the proposed algorithm.

Table 1. Comparison results of different methods

Dataset	Methods	Accuracy	Precision	Recall	F_{score}
Lab2	RDM [9]	90.75	92.24	90.75	90.46
	Bloom Filter [8]	92.25	93.13	92.25	92.21
	FBSR + GrayFace [4]	84.25	85.36	84.25	84.09
	FBSR + Near-Infrared Face [4]	82.38	83.89	82.38	82.14
	The proposed	93.00	93.63	93.00	92.94

(continued)

Table 1. (*continued*)

Dataset	Methods	Accuracy	Precision	Recall	F_{score}
CASIA	RDM [9]	83.82	76.27	79.54	76.30
	Bloom Filter [8]	99.85	99.89	99.86	99.86
	FBSR + Gray Face [4]	92.68	93.47	93.41	92.28
	FBSR + Near-Infrared Face [4]	74.30	77.13	74.58	72.45
	The proposed	98.02	98.33	98.25	97.98
IIIT-D	RDM [9]	83.76	83.09	87.58	82.41
	Bloom Filter [8]	85.33	85.94	83.70	83.09
	FBSR + GrayFace [4]	81.81	81.07	80.65	78.58
	FBSR + FaceDepth [4]	70.07	65.01	66.82	63.15
	The proposed	90.33	86.29	87.67	85.86

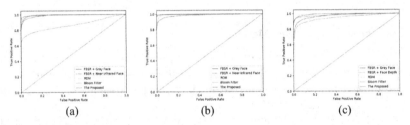

(a)   (b)   (c)

Fig. 8. ROC plots of different methods: (a) Lab2 (b) CASIA and (c) IIIT-D.

4   Conclusion

This paper investigates a secure bimodal face template using full-type quaternion generic polar complex exponential transform and random projection. The feasibility and reliability of the proposal is experimentally verified and compared with other techniques under different modalities. The results have demonstrated the combination of bimodal face is beneficial to improve the recognition accuracy. It also shows that the method in this paper satisfies non-invertibility, revocability, and diversity. Future work will concentrate on developing lightweight deep convolutional neural network for automatic extraction of multimodal face features.

References

1. Chamikara, M.A.P., Bertok, P., Khalil, I., Liu, D., Camtepe, S.: Privacy preserving face recognition utilizing differential privacy. Comput. Secur. 97, 101951 (2020)
2. Shahreza, H.O., Marcel, S.: Towards protecting and enhancing vascular biometric recognition methods via biohashing and deep neural networks. IEEE Trans. Biomet. Behav. Identity Sci. 3(3), 394–404 (2021)

3. Sarkar, A., Singh, B.K.: A review on performance, security and various biometric template protection schemes for biometric authentication systems. Multimed. Tools Appl. **79**, 27721–27776 (2020)

4. Shen, W., Wu, Z., Zhang, J.: A face privacy protection algorithm based on block scrambling and deep learning. In: 2018 International Conference on Cloud Computing and Security, pp. 359–369 (2018)

5. Kaur, H., Khanna, P.: Privacy preserving remote multi-server biometric authentication using cancelable biometrics and secret sharing. Fut. Gener. Comput. Syst. **102**, 30–41 (2020)

6. Soliman, R.F., et al.: Double random phase encoding for cancelable face and iris recognition. Appl. Opt. **57**(35), 10305–10316 (2018)

7. Babamir, F.S., Kırcı, M.: A multibiometric cryptosystem for user authentication in client-server networks. Comput. Netw. **181**, 107427 (2020)

8. Gomez-Barrero, M., Rathgeb, C., Li, G., Ramachandra, R., Galbally, J., Busch, C.: Multi-biometric template protection based on bloom filters. Inf. Fusion **42**, 37–50 (2018)

9. Kaur, H., Khanna, P.: Random distance method for generating unimodal and multimodal cancelable biometric features. IEEE Trans. Inf. Foren. Secur. **14**(3), 709–719 (2019)

10. Chang, D., Garg, S., Hasan, M., Mishra, S.: Cancelable multi-biometric approach using fuzzy extractor and novel bit-wise encryption. IEEE Trans. Inf. Foren. Secur. **15**, 3152–3167 (2020)

11. Yang, H., Qi, S., Niu, P., Wang, X.: Color image zero-watermarking based on fast quaternion generic polar complex exponential transform. Signal Process. Image Commun. **82**, 115747 (2020)

12. Xu, Y., Zhong, A., Yang, J., Zhang, D.: Bimodal biometrics based on a representation and recognition approach. Opt. Eng. **50**(3), 037202 (2011)

13. Li, S., Yi, D., Lei, Z., Liao, S.: The CASIA NIR-VIS 2.0 face database. In: IEEE Conference on Computer Vision and Pattern Recognition Workshops, pp. 348–353 (2013)

14. Goswami, G., Bharadwaj, S., Vatsa, M., Singh, R.: On RGB-D face recognition using Kinect. In: IEEE Sixth International Conference on Biometrics: Theory, Applications and Systems, pp. 1–6 (2013)

Kinship Verification via Reference List Comparison

Wenna Zheng[1] and Junlin Hu[2(✉)]

[1] College of Information Science and Technology, Beijing University of Chemical Technology, Beijing, China
[2] School of Software, Beihang University, Beijing, China
hujunlin@buaa.edu.cn

Abstract. Kinship verification based on facial images has attracted the attention of pattern recognition and computer vision community. Most of existing methods belong to supervised mode, in which they need to know the labels of training samples. In this paper, we adapt an unsupervised method via Reference List Comparison (RLC) for kinship verification task, which does not use external data or data augmentation. Specifically, we obtain a reference list by calculating the similarities of a probe image and all the images in the reference set. Given two probe face images, their similarity is reflected by the similarity of the two ordered reference lists. Experimental results on the KinFaceW-I and KinFaceW-II datasets show the effectiveness of RLC approach for kinship verification.

Keywords: Kinship verification · Unsupervised learning · Similarity

1 Introduction

The goal of kinship verification is to determine whether two persons have a kin-relationship. Although appraisal of DNA is the most accurate way to accomplish this, this process is costly and is not applicable in many situations, such as facing human trafficking and looking for missing persons. The research in psychology and cognitive sciences [1] has shown that the human face is an important clue for kinship verification.

In the past decade, a lot of work about kinship verification have proposed. These methods can be roughly divided into three types: feature-based, metric learning-based and deep learning-based methods. Feature-based methods [2–4] dedicate to mine or construct informative and discriminative features as face descriptors to feed classifiers such as SVM and KNN. Metric learning-based methods [5–10] enhance the discrimination of face images by learning feature embedded subspaces. In these subspaces, discrepancy of intraclass samples (with kinship) is decreased while discrepancy of interclass samples (without kinship) is increased. Deep learning-based methods [11–13] resort to learning algorithms and deep convolutional networks to look for the most efficient encoding way. The similarity of latent features encoded by networks is further measured to

© Springer Nature Switzerland AG 2021
J. Feng et al. (Eds.): CCBR 2021, LNCS 12878, pp. 384–391, 2021.
https://doi.org/10.1007/978-3-030-86608-2_42

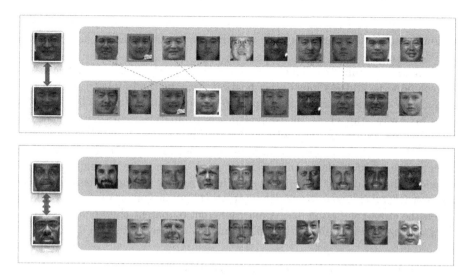

Fig. 1. The basic idea of RLC method. The top two lines are positive sample pairs and the bottom two lines are negative sample pairs.

determine the verification results. Most of the existing methods aim to address kinship verification in an supervised way.

In this paper, we exploit an unsupervised approach, called Reference List Comparison (RLC), to study the problem of kinship verification. Figure 1 shows the basic idea of RLC method for kinship verification. RLC approach firstly computes the similarities between a probe image and all images in reference set and sorts them to get a reference ordered list. The similarity of an image pair is measured by the location permutation between the two reference ordered lists. According to the fact that persons with kinship relations are more similar than those without kin-relationship and an observation that sorted reference lists are similar for similar people [14], so reference lists can be treated as a clue to verify kinship relations. Experiments on KinFaceW-I and KinFaceW-II [5] datasets demonstrate the efficacy of RLC method for kinship verification.

2 Related Work

Existing kinship verification methods can be intuitively divided into three types: feature-based, metric learning-based and deep learning-based. Feature-based method developed earlier than the other two types. Fang et al. [2] firstly propose a kinship verification approach, where they use a pictorial structures model to identify the main facial low-level features and combine them into a feature vector to feed KNN and SVM classifier. Yan et al. [3] propose a prototype-based discriminative feature learning method and its multi-view mode to learn multiple mid-level features to improve the verification performance. Aliradi et al. [4]

introduce a face and kinship verification system that uses discriminative information based on the exponential discriminant analysis (DIEDA) and multiple scale descriptors.

For metric learning-based methods, Lu et al. [5] firstly introduce metric learning technique to address kinship verification. This method aims to learn a distance metric to push intra-class samples to be close and pull inter-class samples to be far away. Yan et al. [6] propose a discriminative multi-metric learning method which jointly learns multiple distance metrics with multiple extracted features. Hu et al. [8] propose a large margin multi-metric learning framework to make use of multiple features. Liang et al. [9] propose a weighted graph embedding-based metric learning approach to capture the intra-class compactness and interclass separability. Zhou et al. [12] design a coupled DNN which models the cross-generation discrepancy inherent on parent-child pairs and facilitates deep metric learning with limited amount of labeled kinship data.

3   Reference List Comparison Method

In this section, we introduce the unsupervised reference list comparison method for kinship verification. We first describe the computation process of similarity between two reference lists. Then, we employ two similarity measurements: structural similarity (SSIM) [15] and cosine similarity.

3.1   Comparison of Reference Lists

We firstly divide all the images in dataset into two sets. One is reference set while the other is probe set. We compute the similarity between each image in a pair (P_A, P_B) of probe set and all images in the reference set and get two reference lists (L_A, L_B). The two reference lists are sorted in descending order by similarity and each of them is regarded as a signature of the corresponding image in the pair. Some of subjects contained in the two ordered reference lists are partly repetitive but their locations are different due to the differences between images. Based on this, we calculate the location permutation distance of two reference lists to implicitly measure the similarity between the two probe images. We use the measure proposed by Jarvis and Patrick [16] to quantify the permutation distance between two reference lists. Specifically, for N subjects in a reference set, let $\tau_A(n)$ (or $\tau_B(n)$) denote the position of subject n in the sorted list L_A (or L_B). The subjects in the front part of a sorted reference list are more similar to the corresponding probe image. Therefore, we only take the first k subjects into account. The formula of the measurement is

$$R(L_A, L_B) = \sum_{j=1}^{N} |k + 1 - \tau_A(j)| \times |k + 1 - \tau_B(j)|, \tag{1}$$

where k is a hyper-parameter and we set it to different values to evaluate the effectiveness of the method in the experiment. $R(L_A, L_B)$ is the RLC score of the two probe images P_A and P_B.

3.2 Similarity Measure

Considering human faces are structured and facial images in datasets are highly aligned, we choose SSIM [15] to measure the similarity of two facial images. SSIM, which considers lightness, contrast and structure information jointly, is widely used for measuring the difference between a distorted image and an original image and measuring content consistency between two images. Computation of SSIM is patch-wise. Specifically, a $k \times k$ window is set to traverse a whole image by a sliding way with fixed step size. Given an image patch X with sizes of H and W, its average intensity μ_X and intensity variance σ_X is computed as:

$$\mu_X = \frac{1}{HW} \sum_{i=1}^{H} \sum_{j=1}^{W} X(i,j), \tag{2}$$

$$\sigma_X = \left(\frac{1}{HW-1} \sum_{i=1}^{H} \sum_{j=1}^{W} (X(i,j) - \mu_X)^2 \right)^{\frac{1}{2}}, \tag{3}$$

where μ_X is used for measuring lightness and σ_X is used for measuring contrast.

Given another image patch Y with average intensity μ_Y and intensity variance σ_Y, the covariance σ_{XY} of X and Y is computed as:

$$\sigma_{XY} = \frac{1}{HW-1} \sum_{i=1}^{H} \sum_{j=1}^{W} (X(i,j) - \mu_X)(Y(i,j) - \mu_Y). \tag{4}$$

Then SSIM of X and Y is computed by:

$$SSIM(X,Y) = \frac{(2\mu_X\mu_Y + c_1)(2\sigma_{XY} + c_2)}{(\mu_X^2 + \mu_Y^2 + c_1)(\sigma_X^2 + \sigma_Y^2 + c_2)}, \tag{5}$$

where c_1 and c_1 are two positive constants. SSIM between two images is the average SSIM of all image patches.

Cosine Similarity is a widely used method to measure similarity between feature vectors. It computes the cosine of angle between two vectors to represent similarity. The formula is as:

$$cos(x_1, x_2) = \frac{\sum_{i=1}^{d} x_{1i} x_{2i}}{\left(\sum_{i=1}^{d} x_{1i}^2 \right)^{\frac{1}{2}} \left(\sum_{i=1}^{d} x_{2i}^2 \right)^{\frac{1}{2}}}, \tag{6}$$

in which $x_1 \in \mathbb{R}^d$ and $x_2 \in \mathbb{R}^d$ represent two vectors. We use cosine similarity to measure the similarity of HOG, LBP and DSIFT features between the probe image and the reference set.

4   Experiments

We evaluate the unsupervised RLC method on KinFaceW-I and KinFaceW-II datasets, which are the most commonly used in kinship verification task.

4.1   Datasets

The images in KinFaceW-I and KinFaceW-II datasets were all collected from Internet, including some celebrities and their parents or children. The difference of the two datasets is that face images with kinship relations collected from various photos in KinFaceW-I and from the same photo in KinFaceW-II. There are four kinds of kin relationship in KinFaceW, i.e., Father-Son (F-S), Father-Daughter (F-D), Mother-Son (M-S) and Mother-Daughter (M-D). There are 156, 134, 116 and 127 pairs of kinship images for F-S, F-D, M-S and M-D in KinFaceW-I dataset, and there are 250 pairs of kinship images for each kin relation in KinFaceW-II. The resolution of each image is 64×64.

4.2   Evaluation Metrics

Accuracy is the most common metrics in the kinship verification task. Given the similarity values of all image pairs in the dataset, we sort these values and traverse them. For each value, we see it as a threshold. If the similarity value of an image pair is lower or higher than the threshold, the sample is classified as the negative (without kinship) or the positive (with kinship). After this process, the number of True Positive (TP) and True Negative (TN) are obtained and the accuracy is computed as follows:

$$Accuracy = \frac{TP + TN}{N}. \tag{7}$$

4.3   Experimental Settings

For each dataset, we use 5-fold cross validation. The image pairs in each dataset are divided into 5 groups with same capacity. In each group, the number of positive samples (with kinship) and negative samples (without kinship) are same. One of these groups is set as a probe set and the others are set as a reference set. After obtaining all similarities of the images in a probe set, the probe set is set to another group. Finally, we can obtain similarities of all image pairs.

4.4   Ablation Studies

Feature Settings. SSIM is originally computed based on image intensity. We replace the image intensity with HOG, the features extracted by LBP and the features extracted by DSIFT respectively to evaluate the effects. The average value, variance and covariance in SSIM are computed based on the above features. In this experiment, we consider the first 100 subjects in similarity lists, namely, k is set to 100. As shown in Table 1, SSIM computed by image intensity is higher than the others.

Table 1. Accuracies (%) of different feature settings on KinFaceW-I dataset.

Feature	F-S	F-D	M-S	M-D	Mean
Original image	80.8	72.1	69.4	70.5	73.2
HOG	61.5	57.9	60.0	63.4	60.7
LBP	58.4	57.5	63.0	61.5	60.1
DSIFT	59.6	59.7	58.2	63.8	60.3

Table 2. Accuracies (%) of different measures on KinFaceW-I dataset.

Feature	SSIM	Cosine similarity
HOG	60.7	74.5
LBP	60.1	70.0
DSIFT	60.3	73.6

Measure Settings. We use SSIM and cosine similarity to measure the similarity between image pairs and between features constructed by HOG, LBP and DSIFT of image pairs. In this experiment, k is also set to 100. As shown in Table 2, using cosine similarity as similarity measure is much better than SSIM in terms of the three features. Compared to Table 1, the accuracy of using HOG based cosine similarity is better than that of original image based SSIM.

Hyper-parameter Settings. We explore the best setting of k, which decides how many subjects in reference lists should be considered. k is to 100, 50, 25, 20, 10 to evaluate the accuracy. The similarity between images is computed by SSIM based on original image. As shown in Table 3, when k is set to 10 and 20, the list cannot be used as an effective identifier of image so the accuracy is low. The accuracy is relatively stable when k is at least set to 25.

Table 3. Accuracies (%) of different k on KinFaceW-I dataset.

k	F-S	F-D	M-S	M-D	Mean
100	80.8	72.1	69.4	70.5	73.2
50	81.7	70.9	69.8	72.8	73.8
25	82.1	69.8	69.8	71.6	73.3
20	80.2	67.2	68.5	71.6	71.9
10	71.5	62.3	63.3	70.0	66.8

4.5   Comparison with Other Methods

We compare RLC method with SILD [17] method using LBP and HOG features on KinFaceW-I and KinFaceW-II datasets, as shown in Tables 4 and 5. For the KinFaceW-I dataset, the accuracy of RLC method is better than SILD method. For the KinFaceW-II dataset, the accuracy of RLC + SSIM using original image is lower than that of method using LBP and HOG features. Experimental results on both KinFaceW-I and KinFaceW-II datasets show that RLC is better than SILD method using the same feature.

Table 4. Accuracies (%) of different methods on the KinFaceW-I dataset.

Method	F-S	F-D	M-S	M-D	Mean
SILD (LBP) [17]	76.9	69.1	64.2	66.6	69.2
SILD (HOG) [17]	79.5	70.9	67.7	72.8	72.7
RLC + CS (LBP)	78.8	68.3	63.8	68.9	70.0
RLC + CS (HOG)	81.7	72.8	69.8	73.6	74.5
RLC + SSIM	80.8	72.1	69.4	70.5	73.2

Table 5. Accuracies (%) of different methods on the KinFaceW-II dataset.

Method	F-S	F-D	M-S	M-D	Mean
SILD (LBP) [17]	75.4	66.6	70.6	66.0	69.6
SILD (HOG) [17]	74.2	66.6	70.6	67.0	69.6
RLC + CS (LBP)	75.6	71.2	70.8	66.2	71.0
RLC + CS (HOG)	77.2	71.2	69.8	67.4	71.4
RLC + SSIM	75.2	66.0	68.0	67.0	69.1

5   Conclusion

In this paper, we address kinship verification task by exploiting an unsupervised reference list comparison (RLC) method. The similarity of an image pair is represented by the distance between two reference lists. Each list is sorted by the similarity between the probe image and the reference set. We use SSIM and cosine similarity to measure the similarity of images. Experiments on KinFaceW-I and KinFaceW-II datasets are conducted to show the effectiveness of RLC for kinship verification.

Acknowledgments. This work was supported by the Beijing Natural Science Foundation under Grant 4204108.

References

1. DeBruine, L.M., Smith, F.G., Jones, B.C., Roberts, S.C., Petrie, M., Spector, T.D.: Kin recognition signals in adult faces. Vision. Res. **49**(1), 38–43 (2009)
2. Fang, R., Tang, K.D., Snavely, N., Chen, T.: Towards computational models of kinship verification. In: IEEE International Conference on Image Processing, pp. 1577–1580. IEEE (2010)
3. Yan, H., Lu, J., Zhou, X.: Prototype-based discriminative feature learning for kinship verification. IEEE Trans. Cybernet. **45**(11), 2535–2545 (2014)
4. Aliradi, R., Belkhir, A., Ouamane, A., Elmaghraby, A.S.: DIEDA: discriminative information based on exponential discriminant analysis combined with local features representation for face and kinship verification. Multimedia Tools Appl., 1–18 (2018)
5. Lu, J., Zhou, X., Tan, Y.P., Shang, Y., Zhou, J.: Neighborhood repulsed metric learning for kinship verification. IEEE Trans. Pattern Anal. Mach. Intell. **36**(2), 331–345 (2013)
6. Yan, H., Lu, J., Deng, W., Zhou, X.: Discriminative multimetric learning for kinship verification. IEEE Trans. Inf. Forensics Secur. **9**(7), 1169–1178 (2014)
7. Hu, J., Lu, J., Yuan, J., Tan, Y.-P.: Large margin multi-metric learning for face and kinship verification in the wild. In: Cremers, D., Reid, I., Saito, H., Yang, M.-H. (eds.) ACCV 2014. LNCS, vol. 9005, pp. 252–267. Springer, Cham (2015). https://doi.org/10.1007/978-3-319-16811-1_17
8. Hu, J., Lu, J., Tan, Y.P., Yuan, J., Zhou, J.: Local large-margin multi-metric learning for face and kinship verification. IEEE Trans. Circuits Syst. Video Technol. **28**(8), 1875–1891 (2017)
9. Liang, J., Hu, Q., Dang, C., Zuo, W.: Weighted graph embedding-based metric learning for kinship verification. IEEE Trans. Image Process. **28**(3), 1149–1162 (2018)
10. Hu, J., Lu, J., Liu, L., Zhou, J.: Multi-view geometric mean metric learning for kinship verification. In: IEEE International Conference on Image Processing, pp. 1178–1182 (2019)
11. Hu, J., Lu, J., Tan, Y.P.: Discriminative deep metric learning for face verification in the wild. In: IEEE Conference on Computer Vision and Pattern Recognition, pp. 1875–1882 (2014)
12. Zhou, X., Jin, K., Xu, M., Guo, G.: Learning deep compact similarity metric for kinship verification from face images. Inf. Fusion **48**, 84–94 (2019)
13. Li, W., Lu, J., Wuerkaixi, A., Feng, J., Zhou, J.: Reasoning graph networks for kinship verification: from star-shaped to hierarchical. IEEE Trans. Image Process. **30**, 4947–4961 (2021)
14. Schroff, F., Treibitz, T., Kriegman, D., Belongie, S.: Pose, illumination and expression invariant pairwise face-similarity measure via Doppelgänger list comparison. In: International Conference on Computer Vision, pp. 2494–2501 (2011)
15. Wang, Z., Bovik, A.C., Sheikh, H.R., Simoncelli, E.P.: Image quality assessment: from error visibility to structural similarity. IEEE Trans. Image Process. **13**(4), 600–612 (2004)
16. Jarvis, R.A., Patrick, E.A.: Clustering using a similarity measure based on shared near neighbors. IEEE Trans. Comput. **100**(11), 1025–1034 (1973)
17. Lu, J., et al.: The FG 2015 kinship verification in the wild evaluation. In: IEEE International Conference and Workshops on Automatic Face and Gesture Recognition, pp. 1–7 (2015)

Face Attribute Estimation with HMAX-GCNet Model

Zeyuan Deng[1,2], Yuchun Fang[1(✉)], and Yaofang Zhang[1]

[1] School of Computer Engineering and Science, Shanghai University,
Shanghai, China
ycfang@shu.edu.cn
[2] School of Computer Science and Engineering, NorthEastern University,
Shenyang, China

Abstract. With the development of biomedicine, more and more computational models inspired by biological vision system have emerged. The HMAX model (Hierarchical Model and X) based on the visual pathway of the cerebral cortex is one of the classic calculation models. The model has achieved remarkable results in several coarse-grained recognition tasks. In this paper, the use of this model in fine-grained attribute prediction is studied. We propose a new image patch extraction method consisting of the distribution characteristics of face attributes. Graph convolutional neural networks are used to learn the relationship between attributes, which is embedded in the HMAX features. Compared with traditional HMAX, our prediction model performs better on face attribute estimation, with an improvement of 3%.

Keywords: HMAX model · Graph convolutional neural network · Face attribute estimation

1 Introduction

The biological vision system has a complex and superior hierarchical structure, which can accurately obtain over 80% of the external information. It can also track the target in real-time, and provide reliable recognition results [1]. So it is a hot topic to explore the mechanism behind collecting and processing information in specific areas of the biological cerebral cortex. The HMAX model [2,3] is one of the classic calculation models. This model has been widely used in coarse-grained tasks such as target object recognition in recent years and has achieved outstanding recognition results.

Since traditional HMAX deals with global target detection and recognition tasks, all pixels are treated equally when extracting image patches from the C1 layer response vector. For the fine-grained face attribute prediction task studied in this paper, we first divide the face and face attributes into five parts according to different regions and proposed a new extraction method according to the characteristics of the face region. Considering the symmetry of human faces, we

© Springer Nature Switzerland AG 2021
J. Feng et al. (Eds.): CCBR 2021, LNCS 12878, pp. 392–399, 2021.
https://doi.org/10.1007/978-3-030-86608-2_43

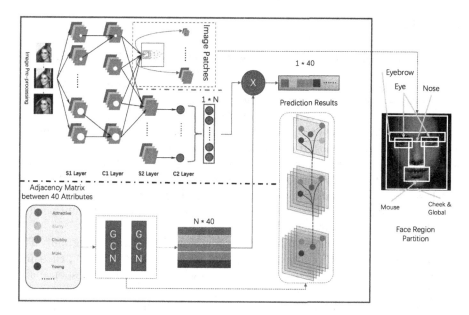

Fig. 1. Overview of the proposed HMAX-GCNet Model. The input of the model is the face image. The model is mainly divided into upper and lower layers. The lower layer of the model is the GCNet module, which is mainly to learn the relationship between attributes and embed it in the upper layer of HMAX features. The upper layer of the model is the HMAX module, and the process is mainly divided into image patch extraction and feature vector calculation. The image patch is cut and spliced from the C1 layer. The partition of face region is shown on the right, which the extraction process will be referred to. Here we take mouth as an example. When calculating the image HMAX feature, the RBF unit in the S2 layer will use the image patch extracted above.

also try feasible dimensionality reduction methods to improve recognition performance. The current mainstream classifiers, such as SVM, AdaBoost, etc., are also used in the experiment. In addition, the different attributes of the attribute prediction task have mutual influences. So we introduce the graph machine neural network [4] to explore this relationship, which is embedded in the HMAX feature vector. We propose the HMAX-GCNet model illustrated by Fig. 1. After that, to further improve the quality of the sample image, we preprocess the image based on the semantic information to improve the overall prediction effect further.

The contributions of our work are as follows:

1. Considering the particularity of the distribution of face attributes, we propose a method of extracting face attribute-specific image patches. It enables the model to have better recognition performance on attribute prediction tasks.
2. We propose the HMAX-GCNet prediction model. This model uses the graph convolutional neural network to learn the relationship between different face attributes. The learned related information is embedded in HMAX features.

2   Related Work

2.1   Robust Object Recognition with Cortex-Like Mechanisms

The HMAX model [3] imitates the brain's visual cortex, which is a layered structure consisting of multiple layers of superficial cells and complex cells. HMAX is divided into S1 (simple cell), C1 (complex cell), S2, C2.

S1 layer: This layer will process the input grayscale images in parallel to obtain the response vector. It uses a Gabor filter, which can reasonably simulate receiving and processing simple cells in the brain's visual cortex.

C1 Layer: This layer corresponds to the complex cells of the visual cortex, which shows the invariance of tolerance to image orientation rotation and size scaling. The main operation of this layer on the image is the maximum pooling operation on the adjacent size response graph.

S2 layer: This layer is the radial basis function (RBF) processing unit. The response vector of each S2 unit is the spatial Euclidean distance (i.e., the similarity between the two) calculated from the newly input C1 layer response and the specific image patches obtained by the previous operation.

C2 layer: This layer performs maximum global pooling on all scales and directions of the entire S2 layer to calculate the response. The calculation process only retains the value of the best match in the result, representing the probability value of each image patch appearing in the test image.

2.2   Research Status of HMAX Model

Zhao et al. [5] used the edge detection and extraction algorithm of non-classical receptive fields. It can reduce the influence of complex background on the recognition task, which improves the recognition accuracy.

Zhu et al. [6] proposed to use the wavelet transform to decompose sliced pictures and then use the SVDP algorithm for feature extraction. This method has a good scale and direction invariance.

3   Method

3.1   Attribute Distribution Characteristics

The human face mainly consists of 5 critical areas (Eyebrows, Eye, Nose, Mouse, Cheek & Global) and 70 key points. The critical point setting refers to CMU's open-source OpenPose [7,8]. We divide the face attributes according to different regions, as shown in Table 1. For example, arched eyebrows should have a strong correlation with eyebrows, which should have nothing to do with the characteristics of the mouth.

Table 1. CelebA attribute classification

Face area	Related face attributes
Eyebrows	Arched eyebrows, bushy eyebrows
Eye	Bags under eyes, eyeglasses, narrow eyes
Nose	Big nose, high cheekbones, pointy nose
Mouse	Big lips, mouth slightly open, goatee, mustache, no beard, smiling, wearing lipstick
Cheek and global	5_o_Clock_Shadow, attractive, bald, bangs, black hair, blond hair, blurry, brown hair, chubby, double chin, gray hair, heavy makeup, male, oval face, pale skin, receding hairline, rosy cheeks, sideburns, straight hair, wavy hair, wearing earrings, wearing hat, wearing necklace, wearing necktie, young

3.2 HMAX-GCNet Model

We discover that attributes are not only geographically specific but also have mutual influences between different attributes. So we use a graph convolutional neural network to learn the relationship between attributes. In the initialization phase, we use the GloVe word embedding method to represent the attribute nodes and calculate the probability that the attributes appear together to form the required adjacency matrix of the GCN network.

$$H^{(l+1)} = \delta \left(\widetilde{D}^{-\frac{1}{2}} \widetilde{A} \widetilde{D}^{-\frac{1}{2}} H^l W^l \right) \tag{1}$$

$$\mathcal{L} = -\frac{1}{n} \Sigma \left(y_n \times \ln x_n + (1 - y_n) \times \ln(1 - x_n) \right) \tag{2}$$

The propagation formula between GCN networks is as Eq. 1. Among them, δ is the nonlinear activation function, $\widetilde{D}$ is the degree matrix, $\widetilde{A}$ is the adjacency matrix of the relationship graph, H^l is the node feature of the first layer of the model, and W^l is the parameter that needs to be learned in the first layer of the model. The prediction result $\hat{y}$ is the calculated product of W and x, where W is the parameter that the lower layer needs to learn, and x is the HMAX feature of the extracted image.

We use $\hat{y}$ to predict the attribute >0 considers the attribute exists, and <0 considers the attribute does not exist. The task belongs to multi-label classification, so we use BCEWithLogitsLoss (Eq. 2) as the loss function. The x_n is the prediction result, and x_n is the true label.

4 Experiment

4.1 Dataset

CelebA (CelebFaces Attribute) [9]. The Chinese University of Hong Kong provides this dataset openly. It collects 202,599 images from 10,177 stars. The original size is 178 pixels × 218 pixels. This dataset belongs to a binary classification problem with multiple labels.

4.2   Implementation Details

Image Preprocessing. Since the CelebA data set is intercepted from various websites and magazines through crawlers, we find that the quality of the image data is not ideal, and the background of some images may even seriously affect the main body information of the face. So in order to standardize the image and improve the sample quality, we design the following preprocessing operations respectively. We place the face image in the center of the image based on the key points, and fill the border with black to make the image square. In addition, we extract the main body based on the semantic information of the image and remove unnecessary background content.

Construction of Image Patches. The design angle of the original model is coarse-grained, so it treats all areas of the face equally and does not fully consider the distribution area of the features. Here we experimented with different extraction strategies. We randomly selected 20 images to form image patches based on the critical points marked in the region. Considering the symmetry of the face, we tried to use the left half of the face instead of the whole face to speed up the performance. In order to locate the hairstyle area, we used the chin and the tip of the nose as reference points for regional positioning. In addition, we also set different numbers of patches.

4.3   Relationship Between Image Patches and Attributes

In the experiment, the image patch used in the S2 layer consists of five regions. Each picture is calculated with these five regional patches, and each of these five response vectors is assigned a weight value. Here we define the weight as the contribution of the patch in the area to the current attribute. A linear classifier is trained to fine-tune the weight of patches. Table 2 shows the strong correlation between face attributes and regional image patches. The result of the experiment is in line with expectations and also in line with our perceptions.

Table 2. Regional contribution ranking

Attr.	No. 1	No. 2	No. 3	No. 4	No. 5
Mouth slightly open	Mouse	Cheek	Nose	Eye	Eyebrow
Smiling	Mouse	Eye	Eyebrow	Cheek	Nose
Arched eyebrows	Eyebrow	Eye	Cheek	Nose	Mouse
Big nose	Nose	Mouse	Cheek	Eye	Mouse
Wearing lipstick	Mouse	Cheek	Nose	Eye	Eyebrow

4.4   Ablation Study

The image patches extraction method can affect the final recognition effect, so we try seven different extraction methods. By analyzing the Table 3, we can get the following conclusions.

Table 3. Comparison with different HMAX model

Extract randomly	Num of patches	Half face or whole face	Include hair	Use GCNet	Image preprocessing	Accuracy
√	–	–	–	–	–	83.7%
×	4	Half	×	×	×	84.4%
×	4	Whole	×	×	×	84.6%
×	4	Whole	√	×	×	84.9%
×	8	Whole	√	×	×	85.6%
×	8	Whole	√	√	×	86.0%
×	8	Whole	√	√	√	**86.7%**

In the competition between half-face patches and whole-face patches, the overall accuracy rate is only reduced by 0.2%, while the calculation amount is reduced by half. In addition, the size number of the patch will directly affect the overall accuracy. A larger patch means a larger receptive field so that the overall accuracy rate will be relatively higher. When we embed the interrelationships between attributes in features, the expressive ability of feature vectors is enhanced. Moreover, through the preprocessing operation, the background interference to the prediction is removed, and finally, a 3% performance improvement is obtained compared with the traditional method.

4.5   Comparison with Other Methods

Table 4 shows the prediction results of several state-of-the-art methods on the CelebA dataset in recent years. All comparison experiments' training set and test set follow the 180K test set and 20K test set. We assume that pre-training may improve a specific overall accuracy rate, so in the analysis process, we hold the opinion that the prediction performance of the HMAX-GCNet model exceeds that of some deep learning methods in recent years. We find that the prediction models [10–12] performance is not as good as our method. The performance gap is mainly caused by whether the relationship between different attributes is considered. Compared with Method [13,14], there is a big gap between the depth and complexity of our prediction model. The model in Method [13] uses five convolutional layers and two fully connected layers, and Method [14] uses three convolutional layers and two fully connected layers. The difference in model structure makes the prediction accuracy have a particular gap. In addition, our prediction model does not have additional pre-training data, so compared with method two pre-trained on CASIA-WebFace, there is still a 5% prediction gap (Fig. 2).

Table 4. Comparison with other methods for forecasting problems

Method	Pretraining strategy	Accuracy
FaceTracker [10]	Without pre-training	81.1%
PANDA [11]	Using pre-trained DPM model [15]	85.4%
CTS-CNN [12]	Pre-train model on WebFace	86.6%
LNets+ANet [16]	Pre-train model on ILSVRC and CelebA	87.3%
MCNN-AUX [14]	Without pre-training	91.3%
HFAE [13]	Pre-train model on CASIA-WebFace	**92.6%**
Ours	Without pre-training	86.7%

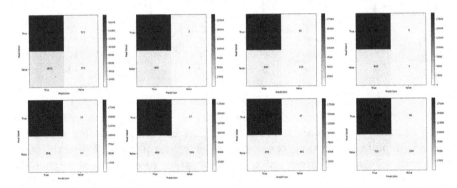

Fig. 2. Confusion matrix for CelebA face attribute prediction. The horizontal and vertical coordinates of the confusion matrix are both [correct, wrong].

5   Conclusion and Outlook

We propose an image patch extraction method based on the distribution characteristics of face attributes, and the experiments prove that the attributes have regional characteristics. In addition, the graph convolutional neural network is used to learn the relationship between attributes and embed it into the feature vector. The HMAX-GCNet prediction model is proposed in the article. We show the confusion matrix of 8 attributes in CelebA dataset in Fig. 2. Compared with the traditional HMAX model, the overall prediction performance of face attributes is improved by 3%.

Further, we can improve the structure of the HMAX model, consider whether it is possible to add the S3 layer, C3 layer... to deepen the calculation model and strengthen the feature expression ability of the entire model.

Acknowledgments. The work is supported by the National Natural Science Foundation of China under Grant No.: 61976132, U1811461 and the Natural Science Foundation of Shanghai under Grant No.: 19ZR1419200.

References

1. Moeller, S., Nallasamy, N., Tsao, D.Y., Freiwald, W.A.: Functional connectivity of the macaque brain across stimulus and arousal states. J. Neurosci. **29**(18), 5897–5909 (2009)
2. Riesenhuber, M., Poggio, T.: Hierarchical models of object recognition in cortex. Nat. Neurosci. **2**(11), 1019–1025 (1999)
3. Serre, T., Wolf, L., Bileschi, S., Riesenhuber, M., Poggio, T.: Robust object recognition with cortex-like mechanisms. IEEE Trans. Pattern Anal. Mach. Intell. **29**(3), 411–426 (2007)
4. Kipf, T.N., Welling, M.: Semi-supervised classification with graph convolutional networks. arXiv preprint arXiv:1609.02907 (2016)
5. Zhao, H.-W., Cui, H.-R., Dai, J.-B., Zang, X.-B.: Contour detection based on HMAX model and non-classical receptive field inhibition. J. Jilin Univ. (Eng. Technol. Edn.) **42**(1), 128–133 (2012)
6. Zhu, C., Song, S., Yang, S.: HMAX model based on brain-like face recognition algorithm. J. Tianjin Univ. Technol., page 01 (2018)
7. Cao, Z., Simon, T., Wei, S.-E., Sheikh, Y.: Realtime multi-person 2d pose estimation using part affinity fields. In: Proceedings of the IEEE Conference on Computer Vision and Pattern Recognition, pp. 7291–7299 (2017)
8. Cao, Z., Hidalgo, G., Simon, T., Wei, S.-E., Sheikh, Y.: OpenPose: realtime multi-person 2d pose estimation using part affinity fields. IEEE Trans. Pattern Anal. Mach. Intell. **43**(1), 172–186 (2019)
9. Liu, Z., Luo, P., Wang, X., Tang, X.: Deep learning face attributes in the wild. In: Proceedings of International Conference on Computer Vision (ICCV), December 2015
10. Kumar, N., Belhumeur, P., Nayar, S.: FaceTracer: a search engine for large collections of images with faces. In: Forsyth, D., Torr, P., Zisserman, A. (eds.) ECCV 2008. LNCS, vol. 5305, pp. 340–353. Springer, Heidelberg (2008). https://doi.org/10.1007/978-3-540-88693-8_25
11. Zhang, N., Paluri, M., Ranzato, M., Darrell, T., Bourdev, L.: PANDA: pose aligned networks for deep attribute modeling. In: Proceedings of the IEEE Conference on Computer Vision and Pattern Recognition, pp. 1637–1644 (2014)
12. Zhong, Y., Sullivan, J., Li, H.: Face attribute prediction using off-the-shelf CNN features. In: 2016 International Conference on Biometrics (ICB), pp. 1–7. IEEE (2016)
13. Han, H., Jain, A.K., Wang, F., Shan, S., Chen, X.: Heterogeneous face attribute estimation: a deep multi-task learning approach. IEEE Trans. Pattern Anal. Machine Intell. **40**(11), 2597–2609 (2017)
14. Hand, E.M., Chellappa, R.: Attributes for improved attributes: a multi-task network for attribute classification. arXiv preprint arXiv:1604.07360 (2016)
15. Zhang, N., Farrell, R., Iandola, F., Darrell, T.: Deformable part descriptors for fine-grained recognition and attribute prediction. In: Proceedings of the IEEE International Conference on Computer Vision, pp. 729–736 (2013)
16. Liu, Z., Luo, P., Wang, X., Tang, X.: Deep learning face attributes in the wild. In: Proceedings of the IEEE International Conference on Computer Vision, pp. 3730–3738 (2015)

Wavelet-Based Face Inpainting with Channel Relation Attention

Huiwen Shao and Yunlian Sun[(✉)]

School of Computer Science and Engineering, Nanjing University of Science and Technology, Nanjing 210094, China
{shaohuiwen,yunlian.sun}@njust.edu.cn

Abstract. As the underlying characteristic distribution differs among different frequencies, existing face inpainting methods on RGB domain can cause some artificial boundaries and blurred details when the masks are large. To reduce this interference, we propose to inpaint face images in wavelet domain with two branches to capture global structure topology and local detailed texture separately. Meanwhile, we adopt the channel relation attention module to learn different weights for different feature channels, with the aim of ensuring the consistency between structure and texture features. In addition, a new wavelet loss is designed to constrain the generated wavelet coefficients closer to the ground truth. Experimental results on CelebA-HQ and Helen datasets demonstrate that our Wavelet Prediction Network outperforms current state-of-the-art face inpainting techniques both qualitatively and quantitatively, especially when handling face images with large masks.

Keywords: Face inpainting · Wavelet domain · Channel attention

1 Introduction

Image inpainting is proposed to virtually fill in the missing pixels, making the inpainted image realistic. It has wide applications for repairing damaged images, removing objects and editing contents. A branch of image inpainting known as face inpainting, is challenging since no similar patches could be copied from known areas when facial features are occluded. To break out the limitation, learning-based methods become the mainstream approaches. Initially, the Context Encoder [3] proposed by Pathak proved strong effect of GAN [4] on image inpainting. Based on GAN, many learning-based methods explored semantic and structural priors to assist with inpainting process [5–8], commonly using two-stage framework [1,9–11]. EdgeConnect used the edge map got by canny operator as the structure information [1], while StructureFlow took edge-preserved smooth image as prior which retained sharp edge and low-frequency structure [10]. Besides, the gradient map adopted by Yang remained the edge information and high-frequency texture [11]. Considering the uniqueness of human face, symmetry [12,13], facial UV map [14], landmarks [15] and depth information [16] were introduced to make the inpainting results more authentic.

© Springer Nature Switzerland AG 2021
J. Feng et al. (Eds.): CCBR 2021, LNCS 12878, pp. 400–409, 2021.
https://doi.org/10.1007/978-3-030-86608-2_44

Fig. 1. Inpainting results of different approaches on celebA-HQ test set with large mask areas. (a) Input is Ground Truth with mask. (b) EdgeConnect [1]. (c) Rethinking [2]. (d) Our method. (e) Ground Truth.

However, these prior-based methods just utilize incompletely separated frequency information as priors in RGB domain, rarely in frequency domain [17,18]. As the underlying characteristic distribution of different frequencies is different, directly processing on the RGB image will lead to artificial boundaries and blurred textures, especially for large masks. We thus propose to conduct face inpainting in frequency domain. As shown in Fig. 1, compared to the EC [1] and Rethink [2] methods with large masks, our frequency-based approach generates more coherent context and authentic texture, looking visually pleasant.

In our method, we first introduce the Discrete Wavelet Transform (DWT) to inpaint in frequency domain [19]. A face image is decomposed to one low-frequency and three high-frequency sub-bands through DWT. As is well-known, low-frequency features could represent structure information and high-frequency features represent texture information. Inspired by this idea, to avoid the interference caused by different frequencies, we develop a framework with two branches to extract structure and texture features separately. Besides, in [20], the tight relationship between structure and texture of object was characterized as coherence prior because only the coherence prior can determine the whole semantic content of image ultimately. Since the channel attention module has been used in image restoration task [21], we thus exploit the relations obtained by the channel relation attention module to keep the consistency of the extracted features [22]. Based on above motivations, we propose our Wavelet Prediction Network for face inpainting. The main contributions are summarized as following points:

(1) Introducing the DWT, we propose a wavelet-based framework with global branch to extract structure topology and local branch to extract detailed texture.
(2) To build communication among extracted features, we adopt the channel relation attention module to capture the global information itself and

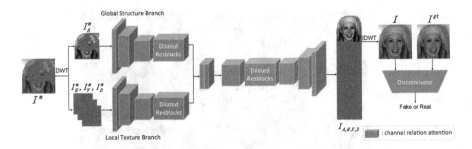

Fig. 2. The pipeline of our Wavelet Prediction Network.

pairwise correlations with different frequencies information, which is suitable to guarantee the consistency between structure and texture features.

(3) We design a wavelet loss for predicted wavelet coefficients to constrain accurate frequency information. Experimental results show that our approach outperforms state-of-the-art face inpainting techniques, especially for large masks.

2   Method

2.1   Wavelet Transfer

By selecting appropriate filters, the wavelet transform can greatly reduce or remove the correlation among different features. Since the Haar wavelet is enough to learn different frequencies information, we choose the 2-D fast wavelet transform (FWT) in this paper [23]. Through the low-pass and high-pass filters of FWT, the face image is decomposed to four sub-bands representing approximation (A), horizontal (H), vertical (V) and diagonal (D) information.

2.2   Network Architecture

Let I^{gt} be the ground truth image, I^m be the masked image and I be the restored image. Through FWT, the four frequency sub-bands of ground truth can be denoted as $I_A^{gt}, I_H^{gt}, I_V^{gt}, I_D^{gt}$ whose resolutions are half of I^{gt}. For image I^m and image I, the notations are analogous except for the superscripts. Figure 2 presents the framework of our Wavelet Prediction Network, which includes a generator to inpaint masked image and a discriminator for adversarial training.

Generator. Through DWT, we consider the low-frequency sub-band I_A^m as input of global structure branch and concatenate the rest high-frequency sub-bands I_H^m, I_V^m, I_D^m as input of local texture branch. Two branches have the same architecture but don't share parameters, consisting of one convolution with large receptive field, two down-sample layers and four dilated residual blocks. Then we concatenate the structure and texture features and reweigh their feature channels

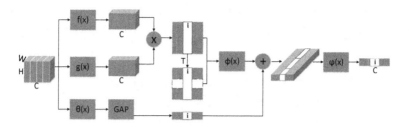

Fig. 3. Diagram of the channel relation attention module. "T" means the transpose of the matrix and "+" means concatenation operation. Red box means $R_c(i,:)$, blue box means $R_c(:,i)$ and orange box represents global information. (Color figure online)

with channel relation attention module. Followed by four dilated residual blocks and decoders, generator outputs the complete wavelet coefficients. In the end, these coefficients are inversely reconstructed into a restored face image I through the Inverse Discrete Wavelet Transformation (IDWT) [24].

Discriminator. We use the 70×70 PatchGAN with spectral normalization as our discriminator structure to classify the results in RGB domain [25]. The image I is deemed to fake training data while image I^{gt} to real training data.

2.3 Channel Relation Attention

The channel relation attention module was first proposed in [22] for person re-identification. It stacks the pairwise correlations/affinities with different feature channels and the feature channel itself to learn the attention. In this paper, we adopt it to strengthen the communication of different frequency features.

As illustrated in Fig. 3, channel relation attention views a feature tensor $X \in \mathbb{R}^{C \times H \times W}$ as C feature nodes. At each channel, feature node $x_i \in R^d$ $(i = 1, \cdots, C)$ is a $d = H \times W$-dimensional feature map. The pairwise relation $r_{i,j}$ of node i and node j is computed using dot-product affinity as follows:

$$r_{i,j} = f(x_i)^T g(x_j) , \qquad (1)$$

where $f(\cdot)$ and $g(\cdot)$ are two embedding functions, T means the transpose of the matrix. Then, all the relations corresponding to the ith feature node in the affinity matrix $R_c \in \mathbb{R}^{C \times C}$ are stacked as a relation vector $r_i \in [R_c(i,:), R_c(:,i)] \in \mathbb{R}^{2C}$ to represent the pairwise relations of feature node x_i. Next, to exploit the global information, the feature itself x_i is concatenated with the relation vector r_i to get the channel relation feature y_i, which is defined as:

$$y_i = [pool_c(\theta_s(x_i)), \phi_s(r_i)] , \qquad (2)$$

where $pool_c(\cdot)$ is the global average pooling (GAP) operation to reduce the dimension to 1, $\theta_s(\cdot)$ and $\phi_s(\cdot)$ denote two embedding functions. In this paper,

Table 1. Quantitative evaluation results on CelebA-HQ test set with irregular masks. ↑ indicates higher is better while ↓ indicates lower is better. All results are cited from [26] except for Rethink which is re-implemented by ourselves with publicly available code.

	10–20%	20–30%	30–40%	40–50%	50–60%	Metrics
CA [27]	28.52	25.08	22.64	20.62	18.43	PSNR↑
EC [1]	31.88	28.31	25.81	23.67	20.82	
Rethink [2]	32.76	29.39	26.80	24.80	21.75	
GAIN [26]	**32.92**	**29.53**	27.17	25.13	22.49	
Ours	32.24	29.43	**27.24**	**25.47**	**22.75**	
CA [27]	0.954	0.910	0.855	0.788	0.683	SSIM↑
EC [1]	0.977	0.951	0.916	0.868	0.770	
Rethink [2]	0.981	0.961	0.934	0.899	0.815	
GAIN [26]	**0.982**	**0.963**	0.939	0.906	0.836	
Ours	0.980	0.962	**0.940**	**0.911**	**0.844**	
CA [27]	1.45	2.54	3.84	5.43	7.88	l_1 (%)↓
EC [1]	**0.86**	1.64	2.55	3.67	5.79	
Rethink [2]	0.96	**1.44**	2.04	2.74	4.23	
GAIN [26]	**0.86**	1.49	2.18	3.03	4.58	
Ours	1.09	1.52	**2.01**	**2.60**	**3.80**	

all embedding functions are a spatial 1×1 convolutional layer followed by Batch Normalization (BN) and ReLU activation to reduce the calculation. Finally, the ultimate channel relation attention value a_i of feature node x_i is written as:

$$a_i = \varphi(y_i) = Sigmoid(W_2 ReLU(W_1 y_i)) , \tag{3}$$

where W_1 shrinks the channel dimension with a ratio and W_2 transforms the channel dimension to 1 by 1×1 convolution followed by BN.

2.4   Wavelet Loss

To guarantee the accurate predictions from frequency domain, we adopt the corresponding wavelet loss for four sub-bands (A, H, V, D), defined as:

$$
\begin{aligned}
L_{A,H,V,D} &= \|I_{A,H,V,D} - I^{gt}_{A,H,V,D}\|_1 , \\
L_{wav} &= \lambda_1 L_A + \lambda_2 L_H + \lambda_3 L_V + \lambda_4 L_D ,
\end{aligned}
\tag{4}
$$

where $\lambda_i (i = 1, \cdots, 4)$ is a tradeoff parameter. In the meantime, to enhance the similarity between generated image I and ground truth I^{gt}, we introduce the reconstruction loss L_{re} (L_1 loss) to keep the semantic information, perceptual loss L_{per} [29] to improve the high-level details and adversarial loss L_{adv} (MSE loss [28]) for adversarial training. The overall training loss is computed as:

$$L_{total} = \lambda_w L_{wav} + \lambda_r L_{re} + \lambda_{adv} L_{adv} + \lambda_p L_{per} , \tag{5}$$

where λ_w, λ_r, λ_{adv} and λ_p are the tradeoff parameters. After fine tuning the value of parameters, we found that the impact brought by different parameters is small. Thus, referring to the other work in face inpainting, we set $\lambda_i(i = 1, \cdots, 4) = 1$, $\lambda_w = 1$, $\lambda_r = 1$, $\lambda_{adv} = 0.1$, $\lambda_p = 0.1$ in our experiment.

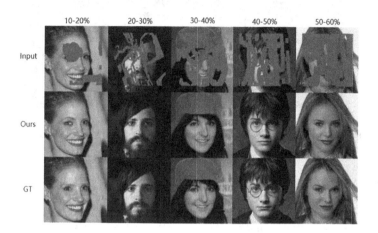

Fig. 4. Inpainting results on CelebA-HQ test set with irregular masks.

3 Experiments

3.1 Experimental Setup

We evaluate the performance of our methods on CelebA-HQ [30] and Helen [31] datasets with irregular masks [32]. Both datasets are following the standard partition. For CelebA-HQ ,to reduce the data fluctuation brought by irregular mask, we take 2000 face images from original 2993 test images in sequence as final test set. During training, we employ the data augmentation such as flipping to stable the learning. Our model is optimized by the Adam optimizer with a learning rate of 2×10^{-4}. The image size is 256×256 and the batchsize is 16.

3.2 Comparison

Quantitative Comparisons. We introduce the PSNR, SSIM and l_1 loss as our evaluation metrics. Table 1 shows our result compared to four current state-of-the-art methods: CA [27], EC [1], GAIN [26] and Rethink [2]. We can see that our method outperforms the existing methods for large masks. For the small mask areas (10–20% and 20–30%), our results are slightly inferior. We guess the reason is that the model pays too much attention on global structure features. When the occlusion is small, the global topology is easy to capture while the effect of high-frequency texture details is suppressed. A better hyper-parameters setting may improve the performance.

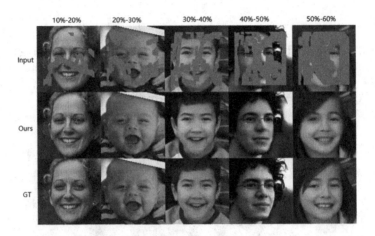

Fig. 5. Inpainting results on Helen test set with irregular masks.

Qualitative Comparisons. Figure 1 shows some samples from different methods on CelebA-HQ test set with large mask areas. When the occluded area is large, other methods generate inconsistent and blurred context, specially for eyes and hairs. With irregular masks, We present some examples of our method on CelebA-HQ test set in Fig. 4 and Helen test set in Fig. 5. All results of our approach are coherent in semantic context and boundary, looking more authentic.

3.3   Abaltion Study

To demonstrate the contributions of wavelet transform and channel attention, we conduct several ablation studies on CelebA-HQ test set with 20–30% mask area. As two branches can increase the number of parameters, we first verify two contributions without two branches. All the residual blocks in our experiments are a 32×32 spatial dimension map. Besides, to study the effect of channel attention in wavelet domain, we only replace it with $1 \times 1conv$ fusion. All the results shown in Table 2 prove our contributions.

Table 2. Evaluations of ablation study on CelebA-HQ test set with 20–30% mask area.

Two-branches	Wavelet-transform	Channel-attention	PSNR ↑	SSIM ↑	$l_1(\%)$ ↓
–	✓	–	28.63	0.955	1.76
–	–	✓	28.51	0.955	1.90
✓	✓	$1 \times 1conv$	29.30	0.961	1.55
✓	✓	✓	**29.43**	**0.962**	**1.52**

4   Conclusion

We propose a novel inpainting method in wavelet domain. To avoid the interference, we acquire the global structure topology and local detailed texture with two branches. The channel relation attention module is taken to reweigh the acquired structure and texture features and keep them consistent. Experimental results show that our method achieves better performance than current state-of-the-art for large masks.

Acknowledgements. We would like to appreciate anonymous reviewers for spending time on our work. This work was supported by the National Natural Science Foundation of China under Grant 62076131.

References

1. Nazeri, K., Ng, E., Joseph, T., Qureshi, F.Z., Ebrahimi, M.: EdgeConnect: generative image inpainting with adversarial edge learning. ArXiv Preprint ArXiv:1901.00212. (2019)
2. Liu, H., Jiang, B., Song, Y., Huang, W., Yang, C.: Rethinking image inpainting via a mutual encoder-decoder with feature equalizations. In: Vedaldi, A., Bischof, H., Brox, T., Frahm, J.-M. (eds.) ECCV 2020. LNCS, vol. 12347, pp. 725–741. Springer, Cham (2020). https://doi.org/10.1007/978-3-030-58536-5_43
3. Pathak, D., Krahenbuhl, P., Donahue, J., Darrell, T., Efros, A.A.: Context encoders: feature learning by inpainting. In: 2016 IEEE Conference on Computer Vision and Pattern Recognition, pp. 2536–2544 (2016)
4. Goodfellow, I.J., et al.: Generative adversarial networks. Adv. Neural Inf. Process. Syst. **3**, 2672–2680 (2014)
5. Yu, J., Lin, Z., Yang, J., Shen, X., Lu, X., Huang, T.: Free-form image inpainting with gated convolution. In: 2019 IEEE/CVF International Conference on Computer Vision, pp. 4470–4479 (2019)
6. Li, J., He, F., Zhang, L., Du, B., Tao, D.: Progressive reconstruction of visual structure for image inpainting. In: 2019 IEEE/CVF International Conference on Computer Vision, pp. 5962–5971 (2019)
7. Song, L., Cao, J., Song, L., Hu, Y., He, R.: Geometry-aware face completion and editing. In: Proceedings of the AAAI Conference on Artificial Intelligence, vol. 33, pp. 2506–2513 (2019)
8. Liao, H., Funka-Lea, G., Zheng, Y., Luo, J., Kevin Zhou, S.: Face completion with semantic knowledge and collaborative adversarial learning. In: Jawahar, C.V., Li, H., Mori, G., Schindler, K. (eds.) ACCV 2018. LNCS, vol. 11361, pp. 382–397. Springer, Cham (2019). https://doi.org/10.1007/978-3-030-20887-5_24
9. Zhang, Z., Zhou, X., Zhao, S., Zhang, X.: Semantic prior guided face inpainting. In: Proceedings of the ACM Multimedia Asia, pp. 1–6 (2019)
10. Ren, Y., Yu, X., Zhang, R., Li, T.H., Liu, S., Li, G.: StructureFlow: image inpainting via structure-aware appearance flow. In: 2019 IEEE/CVF International Conference on Computer Vision, pp. 181–190 (2019)
11. Yang, J., Qi, Z., Shi, Y.: Learning to incorporate structure knowledge for image inpainting. In: Proceedings of the AAAI Conference on Artificial Intelligence **34**, 12605–12612 (2020)

12. Li, X., Hu, G., Zhu, J., Zuo, W., Wang, M., Zhang, L.: Learning symmetry consistent deep CNNs for face completion. IEEE Trans. Image Process. **29**, 7641–7655 (2020)

13. Yan, B., Lin, Q., Tan, W., Zhou, S.: Assessing eye aesthetics for automatic multi-reference eye in-painting. In: 2020 IEEE/CVF Conference on Computer Vision and Pattern Recognition, pp. 13509–13517 (2020)

14. Deng, J., Cheng, S., Xue, N., Zhou, Y., Zafeiriou, S.: UV-GAN: adversarial facial UV map completion for pose-invariant face recognition. In: 2018 IEEE/CVF Conference on Computer Vision and Pattern Recognition, pp. 7093–7102 (2018)

15. Yang, Y., Guo, X.: Generative landmark guided face inpainting. In: Peng, Y., et al. (eds.) PRCV 2020. LNCS, vol. 12305, pp. 14–26. Springer, Cham (2020). https://doi.org/10.1007/978-3-030-60633-6_2

16. Yuan, X., Park, I.K.: Face de-occlusion using 3d morphable model and generative adversarial network. In: 2019 IEEE/CVF International Conference on Computer Vision, pp. 10062–10071 (2019)

17. Wang, J., et al.: Image inpainting based on multi-frequency probabilistic inference model. In: Proceedings of the 28th ACM International Conference on Multimedia, pp. 1–9 (2020)

18. Roy, H., Chaudhury, S., Yamasaki, T., Hashimoto, T.: Image inpainting using frequency-domain priors. J. Electron. Imaging **30**, 23016 (2021)

19. Daubechies, I.: The wavelet transform, time-frequency localization and signal analysis. IEEE Trans. Inf. Theory **36**, 961–1005 (1990)

20. Liao, L., Xiao, J., Wang, Z., Lin, C.W., Satoh, S.: Image inpainting guided by coherence priors of semantics and textures. In: 2020 IEEE/CVF Conference on Computer Vision and Pattern Recognition, pp. 6539–6548 (2020)

21. Wang, D., Tang, H., Pan, J., Tang, J.: Learning a tree-structured channel-wise refinement network for efficient image deraining. In: 2021 IEEE International Conference on Multimedia and Expo, pp. 1–6 (2021)

22. Zhang, Z., Lan, C., Zeng, W., Jin, X., Chen, Z.: Relation-aware global attention for person re-identification. In: 2020 IEEE/CVF Conference on Computer Vision and Pattern Recognition, pp. 3186–3195 (2020)

23. Mallat, S.G.: A theory for multiresolution signal decomposition: the wavelet representation. IEEE Trans. Pattern Anal. Mach. Intell. **11**, 674–693 (1989)

24. Liu, P., Zhang, H., Lian, W., Zuo, W.: Multi-level wavelet convolutional neural networks. IEEE Access **7**, 74973–74985 (2019)

25. Isola, P., Zhu, J.Y., Zhou, T., Efros, A.A.: Image-to-image translation with conditional adversarial networks. In: 2017 IEEE Conference on Computer Vision and Pattern Recognition, pp. 5967–5976 (2017)

26. Zhang, J., et al.: GAIN: gradient augmented inpainting network for irregular holes. In: Proceedings of the 27th ACM International Conference on Multimedia, pp. 1870–1878 (2019)

27. Yu, J., Lin, Z., Yang, J., Shen, X., Lu, X., Huang, T.S.: Generative image inpainting with contextual attention. In: 2018 IEEE/CVF Conference on Computer Vision and Pattern Recognition, pp. 5505–5514 (2018)

28. Mao, X., Li, Q., Xie, H., Lau, R.Y., Wang, Z., Smolley, S.P.: Least squares generative adversarial networks. In: 2017 IEEE International Conference on Computer Vision, pp. 2813–2821 (2017)

29. Johnson, J., Alahi, A., Fei-Fei, L.: Perceptual losses for real-time style transfer and super-resolution. In: Leibe, B., Matas, J., Sebe, N., Welling, M. (eds.) ECCV 2016. LNCS, vol. 9906, pp. 694–711. Springer, Cham (2016). https://doi.org/10.1007/978-3-319-46475-6_43

30. Karras, T., Aila, T., Laine, S., Lehtinen, J.: Progressive growing of GANs for improved quality, stability, and variation. In: 6th International Conference on Learning Representations (2017)
31. Ding, X., Wang, L.: Facial landmark localization. In: Li, S., Jain, A. (eds.) Handbook of Face Recognition, pp. 305–322. Springer, London (2011). https://doi.org/10.1007/978-0-85729-932-1_12
32. Liu, G., Reda, F.A., Shih, K.J., Wang, T.-C., Tao, A., Catanzaro, B.: Image inpainting for irregular holes using partial convolutions. In: Ferrari, V., Hebert, M., Sminchisescu, C., Weiss, Y. (eds.) ECCV 2018. LNCS, vol. 11215, pp. 89–105. Springer, Cham (2018). https://doi.org/10.1007/978-3-030-01252-6_6

Monocular 3D Target Detection Based on Cross-Modal and Mass Perceived Loss

Jingang Chen[1,2,3], Fengsui Wang[1,2,3(✉)], Furong Liu[1,2,3], and Qisheng Wang[1,2,3]

[1] School of Electrical Engineering, Anhui Polytechnic University, Wuhu 241000, China
fswang@ahpu.edu.cn
[2] Anhui Key Laboratory of Detection Technology and Energy Saving Devices, Wuhu 241000, China
[3] Key Laboratory of Advanced Perception and Intelligent Control of High-End Equipment, Ministry of Education, Wuhu 241000, China

Abstract. In recent years, the monocular 3D target detection algorithm based on pseudo-LiDAR has achieved great accuracy improvement on the KITTI data set. However, due to the large amount of noise contained in the point cloud obtained by depth estimation, the detection accuracy is affected. In this paper, we propose a monocular 3D target detection network that adaptively fuses image and pseudo-LiDAR information, and realizes quality perception of the prediction boxes. First, we propose an adaptive feature fusion mechanism, which uses the attention mechanism to achieve effective fusion of different modal information, to improve the precision of target detection. Then, to gain awareness about the quality of the forecast box, we propose to construct an independent 3D detection box confidence prediction network, and put forward a quality perception loss to train the confidence prediction network. Finally, the experimental verification on the KITTI data set shows that the proposed algorithm is higher than that of other algorithms.

Keywords: Machine vision · 3D target detection · Cross-modal feature fusion · Perceived loss of quality

1 Introduction

In recent years, CNN-based 3D target detection technology has developed rapidly. Since 3D target detection technology needs to provide accurate position and attitude information of the target in 3D space, most 3D target detection algorithms adopt LiDAR to obtain accurate point cloud information of the target in space, such as PointNet++ [1]. Although these detection techniques have a good performance, they rely heavily on expensive point cloud information collected by LiDAR sensor. In order to solve the problem of cost, scholars proposed to detect 3D targets from monocular images. However, due to the lack of depth information in monocular images, the accuracy of monocular 3D target detection is restricted. In order to reduce the performance gap between the image-based and the LiDAR-based method, Wang [2] et al. proposed a monocular 3D target detection algorithm based on pseudo-LiDAR. By combining prior knowledge such as geometric

© Springer Nature Switzerland AG 2021
J. Feng et al. (Eds.): CCBR 2021, LNCS 12878, pp. 410–418, 2021.
https://doi.org/10.1007/978-3-030-86608-2_45

constraints with CNN, the depth map is predicted from the monocular image and projected into the 3D space. Although the depth data can effectively help the understanding of 3D scenes, there is still a large gap between the depth information predicted from the monocular image and the LiDAR signal due to the large amount of noise.

In this paper, we present a monocular 3D target detection algorithm based on cross-modal feature fusion and quality awareness loss. First, relying only on the pseudo-LiDAR information containing a lot of noise will lead to the problem of missed detection and false detection, so we put forward a kind of based on attention mechanism across the modal characteristics of the fusion network, through the use of advanced 2D detection network extraction image color and semantic features, then use the attention mechanism to realize the point cloud features and image feature fusion. Secondly, to solve the problem of lack of quality perception of 3D detection box, a confidence prediction network and quality perception loss of 3D bounding box were proposed.

2 Related Works

At present, monocular 3D target detection is mainly divided into two method:

Images Based: Early monocular 3D target detection networks, for example, Deep3DBox [7] and SSD-6D [8], built a set of equations by using geometric constraint relations, which were based on the projection of 3D target boxes onto images and would be close to the 2D detection boxes. In the detection algorithm of GS3D [9], a mature 2D detection network is used to recover a 3D bounding box for each predicted 2D target box. M3D-RPN [10] estimates both 2D and 3D detection boxes. But due to the lack of depth information, there is still a large performance gap compared with LiDAR signals with accurate depth information.

Pseudo-LiDAR Based: Another way of monocular 3D target detection is to use the depth map as the network input. For example, Pseudo-LiDAR [11] first converts the depth map into the form of 3D point cloud, and then provides the pseudo-LiDAR to the 3D detection network, effectively improving the detection accuracy. PatchNet [6] verified the influence of data representation on 3D detection, and further improved the performance of 3D detector by converting pseudo point cloud data into picture coordinate form and combining with mature 2D CNN technology. But due to the large amount of noise in the pseudo point cloud, the problem of missed detection may exist only depending on the information provided by the pseudo point cloud.

3 Proposed Method

In this section, a monocular 3D target detection network based on cross-modal and perceived loss is proposed. We will first introduce the overall framework, then the implementation of each part, and finally introduced the deployment details of the entire network.

3.1 Network Frameworks

The structure of the monocular 3D target detection algorithm proposed in this paper is shown in Fig. 1. It can be divided into two parts:

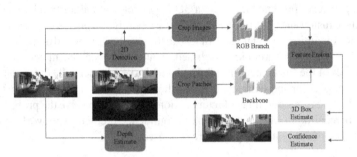

Fig. 1. Overall network framework

(1) **Data processing stage.** Firstly, 2D detection network is used to obtain 2-D bounding box of each target from monocular images, and depth estimation network DORN [12] is used to recover the depth map of monocular images. Secondly, internal and external parameters of the camera are used to calculate the spatial position coordinates of each 2D detection target and integrate them into the image representation. Finally, the spatial position coordinates and RGB images of each target are obtained as the input of the subsequent 3D detection network.

(2) **3D target detection stage.** Firstly, we use the pre-trained Darknet53 network as the image feature extraction branch, from RGB image extracted color, semantic and other information, secondly by cross-modal fusion module implements different modal characteristics of fusion, Finally, three confidence prediction branches of 3D bounding boxes were constructed, which were optimized by quality awareness loss function, and the confidence of each predicted 3D bounding box was recalculated.

3.2 Cross-Modal Feature Fusion Network

Since the depth map calculated by the depth estimation network has many noises, which seriously affect the subsequent 3D detection and regression tasks.We propose an adaptive feature fusion network, its network structure is shown in Fig. 2. The whole network includes two modules, RGB image feature extraction module and adaptive cross-modal feature fusion module. Firstly, this module conducts up-sampling processing on the image of the target region, and the target region is restored to 256×256 size through linear interpolation. Secondly, image features are extracted by Darknet53, Point cloud features and image features are shown in Eq. 1.

$$D = \left\{ s | s \leftarrow [P_{xyz}(m), F_{rbg}(n)], m \in B, n \in B' \right\} \tag{1}$$

Where m and n are the pseudo-LiDAR and image features corresponding to the target region respectively, and P_{xyz} and F_{xyz} are the output of point cloud feature extraction branch and image feature extraction branch respectively.

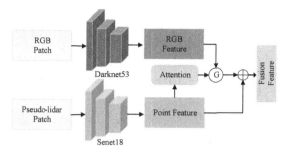

Fig. 2. Cross-modal feature fusion network

Finally, the weight G is obtained by using the attention mechanism for the point cloud features, and shown in Eq. 2, then in order to achieve the fusion of different modal features, the point cloud features and the weighted image features are added to each pixel.

$$G = \partial\left[f\left(P_{xyz}^{avg} + P_{xyz}^{max}\right)\right] * P_{xyz} \tag{2}$$

Where, f is the nonlinear activation function, P_{xyz}^{avg} and P_{xyz}^{max} is the max pooling and average pooling for point cloud feature P_{xyz}, and ∂ is the Sigmoid activation function.

3.3   3D Quality Perception Loss

In 3D detection task, to predict 3D quality perception test box is very important, because our final evaluation index is AP score for all predicted frame's confidence after sorting again calculation, and the driven based on 2D monocular 3D target detection, depends only on the 2D confidence. Therefore, In this paper, an independent 3D quality perception branch was redesigned to output the confidence of the predictive bounding box. By measuring the IOU between the predictive bounding box of the target and the real tag as well as the distance between the center point, the bounding box with higher quality scored higher.

3.3.1   Perceived Quality Loss

In this paper, by studying the IOU between the prediction boxes and the ground truth boxes and the Euclidean distance between their central coordinates, we designed the quality perceived loss L_{conf} to optimize the confidence score.

The mass loss function L_{conf} is shown in Eq. 3, where T_i represents the IOU between the real boxes and the prediction boxes in Eq. 4, K represents the distance from its center in Eq. 5, C_i^{3D} represents the prediction confidence score. Through the quality perceived loss, the final confidence score of each prediction box is directly related to the test result, and the corresponding quality perceived confidence is predicted for each prediction surrounding box respectively.

$$L_{conf} = (1 - T_i) \log C_i^{3D} - T_i \log(1 - C_i^{3D}) \tag{3}$$

$$T_i = e^{-(iou+k)} \tag{4}$$

$$\begin{cases} k = e^{-d} \\ d = \sum_i (x_i - x'_i)^2 + (y_i - y'_i)^2 + (z_i - z'_i)^2 \end{cases} \tag{5}$$

3.3.2   Quality Perception Network Structure

As shown in Fig. 3, we establish confidence predict branch of three parallel, which is consistent with the structure of each branch, and each branch outputs a prediction confidence.

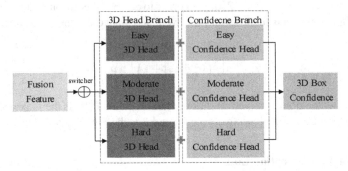

Fig. 3. 3D confidence prediction network

4   Experimental Results and Analysis

The experimental data set of this paper is KITTI, which contains 7481 training pictures and 7352 test pictures. Since the truth data of the test set is not officially provided, the training set is divided into 3712 pictures as the training set and 3769 pictures as the test set. Referred to the evaluation system in article [13], this paper only used the average interpolation accuracy of 11 points as the evaluation index in most previous work.

4.1   The Experimental Results and Analysis

This paper mainly verifies the effectiveness and advantages of the algorithm from the following aspects, the experimental results are shown in Table 1. Ours baseline is PatchNet [6].

(1) Ours1 verifies the effectiveness of our proposed cross-channel feature fusion network.
(2) Ours2 verifies the effectiveness of our proposed 3D quality awareness loss.

Table 1. The experimental results (IOU = 0.7) (in %)

Method	BEV detection			3D detection		
	Easy	Moderate	Hard	Easy	Moderate	Hard
Baseline [6]	44.4	29.1	24.1	35.1	22.0	19.6
Ours1	45.34	29.45	24.39	35.24	22.10	19.74
Ours2	51.09	34.56	28.77	40.41	26.92	23.55
Ours3	**52.68**	**35.58**	**29.29**	**42.19**	**27.70**	**23.90**

(3) Ours3 means to conduct joint training on the adaptive cross-modal fusion module and the quality perceived loss and confidence prediction branch in the baseline model.

As can be seen from Table 1, compared with the baseline model PatchNet, the final algorithm in this paper improved by 7.09, 5.70 and 4.30 points respectively under Easy, Moderate and Hard standards, which greatly improved the detection accuracy of the monocular 3D target detection algorithm.

4.2 Compare with Other Advanced Algorithms

In order to further verify the advance of the proposed algorithm, this paper compared the performance of several advanced monocular 3D target detection algorithms, such as Pseudo-LiDAR, AM3D and the baseline model of this paper, in the KITTI evaluation set, the experimental results are shown in Table 2.

Table 2. Comparison of performance of different algorithms in Average Precision (AP3D) (in %)

Method	Data	IOU = 0.5			IOU = 0.7		
		Easy	Moderate	Hard	Easy	Moderate	Hard
Mono3D [14]	Mono	25.19	18.20	15.52	2.53	2.31	2.31
Deep3DBox [7]	Mono	27.04	20.55	15.88	5.85	4.10	3.84
Pseudo-LiDAR [11]	Mono	66.3	42.3	38.5	28.2	18.5	16.4
AM3D [5]	Mono	68.86	49.19	42.24	32.23	21.09	17.26
PatchNet [6]	Mono	70.43	48.80	41.92	35.1	22.0	19.6
DDMP-3D[15]	Mono	–	–	–	31.14	23.12	19.45
Ours	Mono	**76.90**	**55.94**	**47.92**	**42.19**	**27.70**	**23.90**

As can be seen from Table 2, the algorithm proposed in this paper is state-of-art performance in the monocular 3D target detection task.Compared with the baseline model PatchNet and the latest method DDMP-3D, our method has better performance in detection accuracy.

4.3 Visual Qualitative Analysis

Figure 4 shows the visualization of network prediction results, in which the green bounding box represents the truth value, the red bounding box represents the prediction box of the algorithm in this paper, and the values on each prediction bounding box represent the confidence of the 3D bounding box output by the network.

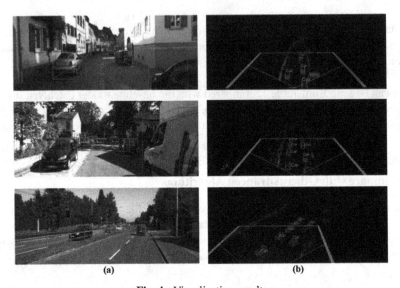

(a)   (b)

Fig. 4. Visualization results

It can be intuitively seen from the visualization figure that the prediction result of the algorithm in this paper is very accurate for the target at a short distance. However, when the target is far away, although the turning angle and size can be predicted, there is still a large deviation in the spatial position, which is also easy to cause the problem of false detection and leak detection for the occlusion and truncation objects.

5   Conclusions

In this paper, we propose a monocular 3D target detection algorithm based on cross-modal and mass awareness loss. in order to get more precision of target characteristics for 3D object detection task, we propose an adaptive cross-modal feature fusion network, which uses attention mechanism to achieve adaptive fusion between RGB features and point cloud features. In addition, based on the current monocular surrounded by 3D target detection algorithm is lack of 3D frame quality perception problem, put forward a kind of 3D surround box quality loss function, the IOU between the prediction box and the ground truth and the distance from the center were used as the monitoring signal, optimize 3D confidence predict network. Through verification on the KITTI data set, it can be seen the detection accuracy of the proposed algorithm has been greatly improved.

Acknowledgments. This work was supported by the Natural Science Foundation of the Anhui Higher Education Institutions of China (Grant No. KJ2019A0162), the Natural Science Foundation of Anhui Province, China (Grand No. 2108085MF197 and Grand No.1708085MF154), and the Open Research Fund of Anhui Key Laboratory of Detection Technology and Energy Saving Devices, Anhui Polytechnic University (Grant No. DTESD2020B02).

References

1. Qi, C.R., Yi, L., Su, H., et al.: PointNet++: deep hierarchical feature learning on point sets in a metric space. arXiv preprint arXiv:1706.02413 (2017)
2. Wang, Y., Chao, W.L., Garg, D., et al.: Pseudo-lidar from visual depth estimation: bridging the gap in 3D object detection for autonomous driving. In: Proceedings of the IEEE/CVF Conference on Computer Vision and Pattern Recognition, pp. 8445–8453 (2019)
3. Ku, J., Mozifian, M., Lee, J., et al.: Joint 3D proposal generation and object detection from view aggregation. In: 2018 IEEE/RSJ International Conference on Intelligent Robots and Systems (IROS), pp. 1–8. IEEE (2018)
4. Qi, C.R., Liu, W., Wu, C., et al.: Frustum PointNets for 3D object detection from RGB-D data. In: Proceedings of the IEEE Conference on Computer Vision and Pattern Recognition, pp. 918–927 (2018)
5. Ma, X., Wang, Z., Li, H., et al.: Accurate monocular 3D object detection via color-embedded 3D reconstruction for autonomous driving. In: Proceedings of the IEEE/CVF International Conference on Computer Vision, pp. 6851–6860 (2019)
6. Ma, X., Liu, S., Xia, Z., Zhang, H., Zeng, X., Ouyang, W.: Rethinking pseudo-lidar representation. In: Vedaldi, A., Bischof, H., Brox, T., Frahm, J.-M. (eds.) ECCV 2020. LNCS, vol. 12358, pp. 311–327. Springer, Cham (2020). https://doi.org/10.1007/978-3-030-58601-0_19
7. Mousavian, A., Anguelov, D., Flynn, J., et al.: 3D bounding box estimation using deep learning and geometry. In: Proceedings of the IEEE conference on Computer Vision and Pattern Recognition, pp. 7074–7082 (2017)
8. Kehl, W., Manhardt, F., Tombari, F., et al.: SSD-6D: making RGB-based 3D detection and 6d pose estimation great again. In: Proceedings of the IEEE International Conference on Computer Vision, pp. 1521–1529 (2017)
9. Li, B., Ouyang, W., Sheng, L., et al.: GS3D: an efficient 3D object detection framework for autonomous driving. In: Proceedings of the IEEE/CVF Conference on Computer Vision and Pattern Recognition, pp. 1019–1028 (2019)
10. Brazil, G., Liu, X.: M3D-RPN: monocular 3D region proposal network for object detection. In: Proceedings of the IEEE/CVF International Conference on Computer Vision, pp. 9287–9296 (2019)
11. Qiu, J., Cui, Z., Zhang, Y., et al.: DeepLiDAR: deep surface normal guided depth prediction for outdoor scene from sparse lidar data and single color image. In: Proceedings of the IEEE/CVF Conference on Computer Vision and Pattern Recognition, pp. 3313–3322 (2019)
12. Fu, H., Gong, M., Wang, C., et al.: Deep ordinal regression network for monocular depth estimation. In: Proceedings of the IEEE Conference on Computer Vision And Pattern Recognition, pp. 2002–2011 (2018)

13. Geiger, A., Lenz, P., Urtasun, R.: Are we ready for autonomous driving? The KITTI vision benchmark suite. In: 2012 IEEE Conference on Computer Vision and Pattern Recognition, pp. 3354–3361. IEEE (2012)
14. Simonelli, A., Bulo, S.R., Porzi, L., et al.: Disentangling monocular 3D object detection. In: Proceedings of the IEEE/CVF International Conference on Computer Vision, pp. 1991–1999 (2019)
15. Wang, L., Du, L., Ye, X., et al.: Depth-conditioned dynamic message propagation for monocular 3D object detection. In: Proceedings of the IEEE/CVF Conference on Computer Vision and Pattern Recognition, pp. 454–463 (2021)

Low-Quality 3D Face Recognition with Soft Thresholding

Shudi Xiao[1], Shuiwang Li[2], and Qijun Zhao[1(✉)]

[1] College of Computer Science, Sichuan University, Chengdu, China
`xiaoshudi@stu.scu.edu.cn`, `qjzhao@scu.edu.cn`
[2] College of Information Science and Engineering, Guilin University of Technology, Guilin, China

Abstract. 3D face recognition has developed rapidly in the past decade for its robustness to large variations of illumination and pose. Plenty of researches in the past have been done based on high-quality 3D faces, which, however, have limitations in real applications because of expensive 3D scanners and high computational cost. Recently, low-quality 3D face recognition is attracting increasing attention because of its lower acquisition cost and faster acquisition speed, making it easier to generalize in practice. However, identity feature in low-quality 3D face data is easily damaged by massive noise, leading to very low accuracy in face recognition. To deal with this problem, we propose a trainable Soft Thresholding Module (STM) to explicitly recover 3D faces from highly noised inputs, which is different from existing methods that either use untrainable preprocessing techniques or implicitly learn robust feature representations. Experimental results show that the proposed method is effective and achieves state-of-the-art performance in low-quality 3D face recognition.

Keywords: 3D face recognition · Soft thresholding module · Low-quality

1 Introduction

With the development of deep learning techniques and the release of many big 2D face datasets [1,2], 2D face recognition (FR) has achieved great success [3,4] and has been widely applied in the real world. However, 2D FR systems are still vulnerable to lighting, makeup, races, etc. In contrast to 2D FR, 3D FR depends on the geometric shape of the face, which is quite robust to large variations of illumination and pose and protects the FR system from makeup, presentation attacks, and so on. During the past two decades, 3D FR solutions [5,6] have achieved high accuracies in many 3D face datasets and benchmarks, e.g. FRGC v2 [8], Bosphorus [9]. However, it should be noted that most 3D FR studies focus on high-quality 3D face captured by very expensive 3D scanners, and the acquisition of data cannot meet the requirement of real-time, which makes 3D FR far from practical applications. Recently, the popularization of consumer depth

© Springer Nature Switzerland AG 2021
J. Feng et al. (Eds.): CCBR 2021, LNCS 12878, pp. 419–427, 2021.
https://doi.org/10.1007/978-3-030-86608-2_46

cameras such as Kinect and RealSense, makes it possible to obtain depth data at an affordable price and a very high frame rate. But the quality of the data captured by these kinds of sensors is really low-quality. In Fig. 1, we visualize the feature maps from the output of the first convolution of the Led3d [11] network, which is a SOTA backbone in low-quality 3D FR. As can be seen, the geometric shapes of 3D faces that reflect identity information are severely damaged by massive noise. For dealing with this problem, existing methods either use untrainable preprocessing techniques [11] or implicitly learn feature representations robust to noise [12]. However, these methods are unsatisfactory in removing this noise and recovering accurate geometric shapes, which we consider very crucial for 3D face recognition.

Motivated by the success of soft thresholding in signal denoising [13], which filters the noise close to 0 with the learned threshold, in this paper, we proposed a trainable soft thresholding module (STM) to explicitly recover 3D faces from highly noised inputs. The proposed module is then used to construct a novel network for low-quality 3D FR. The experimental results show that the proposed soft thresholding module is effective in removing noise and recovering geometric shapes and that our approach achieves state-of-the-art performance in low-quality 3D face recognition.

The rest of this paper is organized as follows. Section 2 introduces the related work in low-quality 3D FR and soft thresholding. Section 3 describes the details of the proposed method. Section 4 reports the qualitative and quantitative results. Finally, we present the conclusion in Sect. 5.

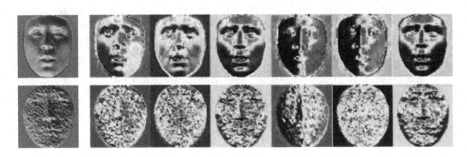

Fig. 1. Visualization of normal map and features of high-qualiy and low-quality 3D face. The first row is the high quality normal map and the corresponding six feature maps with the highest response. The second row is the low-quality normal map and the corresponding six highest-response feature maps. These feature maps are computed by the network proposed in [11].

2   Related Work

Low-Quality 3D FR. Early studies on low-quality 3D FR are mainly traditional methods, such as ICP [10], PCA [7], which get promising results. However, the subjects they used are very limited and the performances of these methods drop significantly in large-scale datasets with abundant challenging scenarios, such as Lock3DFace [10] and Extended-Multi-Dim [18]. With the advent of Lock3DFace [10], and Extended-Multi-Dim [18], there have been some methods based on deep learning one after another. For instance, Hu et al. [18] proposed three strategies to train low-quality depth-based face recognition models with the help of high-quality depth data. Mu et al. [11] proposed a novel lightweight deep network and a series of data augmentations to achieve the best performance in the Lock3DFace dataset compared with four state-of-the-art CNNs [14–17]. Zhang et al. [12] used complex probability models to learn flexibly distributional representation and infer the clean feature from the posterior. However, none of these methods effectively deals with the noise presented in low-quality 3D faces. In this work, we propose to handle the noise in the process of feature extraction in a trainable manner, which improves the performance in low-quality 3D FR as our experiments show.

Soft Thresholding. In the past, the soft thresholding method was often used as a critical step in signal denoising methods [19,20]. Typically, the original signal is transformed to an insignificant domain and then features close to zero are converted to zero using soft thresholding. Traditional wavelet thresholding methods use hand-designed filters to transform useful information into very positive or negative features and noisy information into near-zero features. Designing such a filter requires a lot of experience, which is very challenging. With the arrival of deep learning, we can automatically learn to get a good filter by the gradient descent algorithm of deep learning. In the latest work, Zhao et al. [13] achieve high fault diagnosing accuracy by embedding soft thresholds in their network, the input of which is highly noised vibration signals. However, no one has tried to use soft thresholding for low-quality 3D FR denoising before, and we use it for the first time for low-quality 3D FR tasks and verify the effectiveness of the method through experiments.

3   Proposed Method

In this section, we will introduce the network architecture and the soft thresholding module (STM) of our approach in detail.

3.1   Network Architecture

The network architecture of our method is shown in Fig. 2. The input to our network is a normal map of the 3D shape, which is calculated as in [21]. Our network consists of five CNN blocks with three jump connections, which is similar to the one proposed in [11]. Each CNN block is composed of a 3×3 convolution layer, a batch normalization layer, a ReLU activation layer and a 3×3 max pooling layer with stride 2. To relieve the impact of noise and recover the 3D face, we add a soft threshold module after the first CNN block. And then, we use the BN-Dropout-FC-BN structure to get the final 512-D embedding feature,

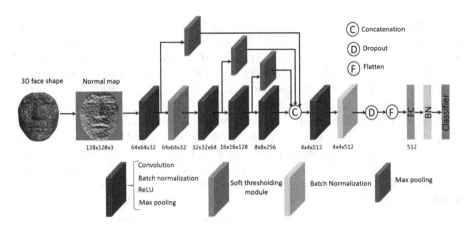

Fig. 2. Network architecture of the proposed method.

which will be delivered to a Fully-Connected layer of classifiers to predict the probability of belonging to each class. Note that BN and FC denote, respectively, the batch normalization layer and the fully-connected layer.

3.2   Soft Thresholding Module

The results shown in Fig. 1 demonstrate that the noise response is relatively small compared to the valid high response region. If the noise is not processed, it will be mixed with helpful information and affect the 3D face recognition. We propose for the first time a soft thresholding module for denoising in low-quality 3D face recognition. Figure 3 shows the proposed soft thresholding module (STM). Our goal is to relieve the impact of noise on feature extraction with this module. We first feed the input features through the convolutional, BN, ReLU, and convolutional layers, respectively, to make the noise as close to 0 as possible. Then, we use absolute operations and the GAP layer to obtain a one-dimensional vector that serves as a threshold for each channel. After that, this one-dimensional vector is propagated to the FC and Sigmoid layers to get a scaling parameter used to make the soft threshold not too large, which is a very important step in the whole module. After that, we apply the threshold to reduce the noise in each channel of the feature map. The function of the soft thresholding process can be expressed as:

$$f = \begin{cases} x - \tau & x > \tau \\ 0 & -\tau \leq x \leq \tau \\ x + \tau & x < -\tau \end{cases} \tag{1}$$

where x is the input feature, f is the output feature, and τ is the threshold for every feature map. τ is a positive parameter because of the sigmoid function. The process of soft thresholding is trainable, and the derivative of output on input is either one or zero.

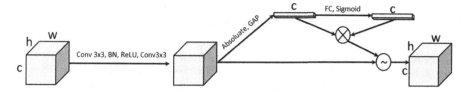

Fig. 3. Framework of the proposed soft thresholding module.

4 Experiments

In this section, we conduct extensive experiments to evaluate the effectiveness of the proposed method and compare it with state-of-the-art methods. The datasets, settings, protocols, and experimental results are described in detail in the following.

4.1 Datasets

Lock3DFace [10] is a comprehensive low-quality 3D face dataset, which is collected by Kinect V2. It includes 5671 videos of 509 Chinese subjects. Each subject has neutral (NU), expression (FE), occlusion (OC), pose (PS), and time (TM) subsets, respectively.

Extended-Multi-Dim [18] is the largest dataset with color and corresponding low-quality depth images captured by RealSense and high-quality 3D face shapes scanned by high-quality 3D scanner. It contains about 3027 videos of 902 objects with expression and pose variations.

Bosphorus [9] is a high-quality dataset of 4666 3D faces and 105 subjects, with variations in expression, occlusion, and pose.

FRGC v2 [8] contains 4007 high-quality 3D faces of 466 subjects, with expression changes.

4.2 Quantitative Evaluation

Protocol and Results on Lock3DFace. For a fair comparison, we follow the close-set protocol and data process pipeline presented in [11] for training and testing. For each subject in Lock3DFace, six frames are sampled with an equal interval from the first neutral-frontal depth videos for training, and the other videos are divided into four test subsets (FE, OC, PS, and TM). In the test phase, all frames are extracted in each video for independent processing, and the entire video labels are predicted by simply voting. Our model is pre-trained on the combination of FRGC v2 and Bosphorus and then fine-tuned on Lock3DFace.

Table 1 shows the recognition results of our approach and six state-of-the-art methods. As can be seen, our method achieves the highest average accuracy of 59.03%, which proves the effectiveness of our method. Specifically, our method

Table 1. Rank-1 identification rates (%) on Lock3DFace with different methods. **FE**: facial expression; **OC**: occlusion; **PS**: pose; **TM**: time; **AVG**: average.

Methods	FE	OC	PS	TM	AVG
VGG16 [14]	79.63	36.95	21.70	12.84	42.80
ResNet34 [15]	62.83	20.32	22.56	2.07	32.23
Inception-V2 [16]	80.48	32.17	33.23	12.54	44.77
MobileNet-V2 [17]	85.38	32.77	28.30	10.60	44.92
Led3D [11]	86.94	48.01	37.67	26.12	54.28
Zhang et al. [12]	**92.38**	**49.3**	43.34	31.80	58.68
Ours	89.88	45.32	**47.04**	**38.76**	**59.03**

significantly surpasses the second place method proposed by [12] with gains of 3.70% and 6.96% in PS and TM subsets, respectively.

Protocol and Results on Extended-Multi-Dim. We conduct the open-set experiment as [18]. The training data consists of 299k processed depth images of size 128×128 of 430 objects. The test data consists of two subsets: test set A and test set B. Test set A contains 256k images of 275 objects, and test set B contains 60K images of 228 objects. Table 2 shows the recognition accuracies of our approach and five state-of-the-art methods following the same protocol of this dataset. As can be seen, our proposed method achieves the highest accuracies in all subsets. Remarkably, our method significantly outperforms the second place method Led3D [11] in the tests Pro.-A-PS1, Pro.-A-PS2, Pro.-A-Avg, and Pro.-B, with improvements of 16%, 17.8%, 8.7% and 7.5%, respectively.

Table 2. Rank-1 identification rates (%) on Extended-Multi-Dim with different methods. **Pro** denotes probe or test set. **NU**: neutral expression; **FE**: facial expression; **PS1**: pose1; **PS2**: pose2.

Methods	Pro.-A-NU	Pro.-A-FE	Pro.-A-PS1	Pro.-A-PS2	Pro.-A-Avg	Pro.-B
ResNet34 [15]	94.6	90.8	67.2	49.6	80.4	70.3
Inception-V2 [16]	90.6	86.5	57.3	41.4	74.6	64.5
MobileNet-V2 [17]	90.8	83.9	58.1	39.9	73.6	64.3
Hu et al. [18]	94.2	90.7	60.8	42.3	80.0	66.4
Led3D [11]	96.2	94.8	67.9	47.2	81.8	71.6
Ours	**98.8**	**97.2**	**83.9**	**65.0**	**90.5**	**79.1**

Ablation Study. We use Lock3dFace to evaluate the effectiveness of our proposed method. Specifically, we evaluate the proposed STM according to whether it is incorporated or not and how it is plugged into the network architecture. The resulted models are denoted by model A, B, C, and D, respectively. Model A is the baseline without the addition of the STM, and the other models are obtained by placing the STM between different convolution blocks. Table 3 summarizes the recognition accuracies of all these models. As can be seen, compared with the baseline network A, all models with STM have different degrees of improvement in performance, which proves the effectiveness of our method for improving recognition accuracy in low-quality 3D FR. It can also be seen that the best result is achieved by placing the STM after the first CNN block. We think that the noise will be mixed with valuable features and is difficult to filter out in deeper layers. So We choose to put the STM after the first CNN block as our proposed model.

Table 3. Ablation study. Rank-1 identification rates (%) on Lock3DFace of our proposed network. **Block1-block2** denotes the STM is placed between the first CNN block and the second CNN block in our network. And so are the others.

Methods	block1-block2	block2-block3	block3-block4	Lock3DFace				
				FE	OC	PS	TM	AVG
A				88.72	43.73	41.91	36.09	56.50
B	✓			**89.88**	45.32	**47.04**	**38.75**	**59.03**
C		✓		89.81	**46.22**	45.96	37.28	58.71
D			✓	88.79	44.32	44.48	32.10	56.65

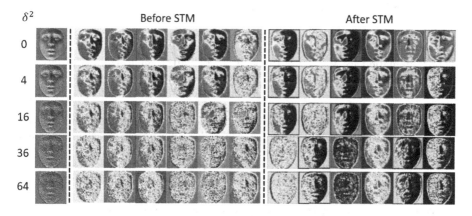

Fig. 4. Visualization of features before and after the soft threshold module. δ^2 denotes the variances of the Gaussian additive noises added on z-value of the high-quality 3D shape, whose normal map is shown on the first column.

4.3   Qualitative Evaluation

We qualitatively evaluate the performance of the proposed STM in removing noise presented in low-quality 3D faces and recovering their geometric shapes. In Fig. 4. we add Gaussian noise with different variance strengths to a high-quality 3D face and show the six strongest feature maps before and after the STM.

As can be seen, the information in the output feature map corrupts severer and severer with the noise intensity increases. What's more, the features before the STM contain more noise, while the features after the STM are less affected by noise, and the feature response is more cleaner, which means that the proposed method does help relieve the effect of noise on feature extraction.

5 Conclusion

In this paper, we propose a trainable soft thresholding module to explicitly recover 3D faces from highly noised inputs. Extensive qualitative and quantitative experiments are conducted to evaluate the effectiveness of our method. Experimental results show that the proposed soft thresholding module is able to remove much noise presented in low-quality 3D face data and is helpful for recovering the geometric shape for 3D FR. Moreover, the proposed method achieves state-of-the-art recognition accuracy on Lock3DFace and Extended-Multi-Dim.

Acknowledgement. This work is supported by the National Natural Science Foundation of China (61773270).

References

1. Cao, Q., Shen, L., Xie, W., Parkhi, O.M., Zisserman, A.: Vggface2: a dataset for recognising faces across pose and age. In: 2018 13th IEEE International Conference on Automatic Face & Gesture Recognition (FG 2018), pp. 67–74. IEEE (2018)
2. Guo, Y., Zhang, L., Hu, Y., He, X., Gao, J.: Ms-celeb-1m: a dataset and benchmark for large-scale face recognition. In: European Conference on Computer Vision, pp. 87–102. Springer, Cham (2016)
3. Deng, J., Guo, J., Xue, N., Zafeiriou, S.: Arcface: additive angular margin loss for deep face recognition. In: Proceedings of the IEEE/CVF Conference on Computer Vision and Pattern Recognition, pp. 4690–4699 (2019)
4. Li, P., Wang, B., Zhang, L.: Adversarial pose regression network for pose-invariant face recognitions. In: Proceedings of the AAAI Conference on Artificial Intelligence, vol. 35, pp. 1940–1948 (2021)
5. Gilani, S.Z., Mian, A.: Learning from millions of 3d scans for large-scale 3d face recognition. In: Proceedings of the IEEE Conference on Computer Vision and Pattern Recognition, pp. 1896–1905 (2018)
6. Kim, D., Hernandez, M., Choi, J., Medioni, G.: Deep 3d face identification. In: 2017 IEEE International Joint Conference on Biometrics (IJCB), pp. 133–142. IEEE (2017)
7. Min, R., Kose, N., Dugelay, J.L.: Kinectfacedb: a kinect database for face recognition. IEEE Trans. Syst, Man Cybern. Syst. **44**(11), 1534–1548 (2014)
8. Phillips, P.J., et al.: Overview of the face recognition grand challenge. In: 2005 IEEE Computer Society Conference on Computer Vision and Pattern Recognition (CVPR 2005), vol. 1, pp. 947–954. IEEE (2005)
9. Savran, A., et al.: Bosphorus database for 3d face analysis. In: Schouten, B., Juul, N.C., Drygajlo, A., Tistarelli, M. (eds.) BioID 2008. LNCS, vol. 5372, pp. 47–56. Springer, Heidelberg (2008). https://doi.org/10.1007/978-3-540-89991-4_6

10. Zhang, J., Huang, D., Wang, Y., Sun, J.: Lock3dface: A large-scale database of low-cost kinect 3D faces. In: 2016 International Conference on Biometrics (ICB), pp. 1–8. IEEE (2016)
11. Mu, G., Huang, D., Hu, G., Sun, J., Wang, Y.: Led3d: a lightweight and efficient deep approach to recognizing low-quality 3d faces. In: Proceedings of the IEEE/CVF Conference on Computer Vision and Pattern Recognition, pp. 5773–5782 (2019)
12. Zhang, Z., Yu, C., Xu, S., Li, H.: Learning flexibly distributional representation for low-quality 3d face recognition. In: Proceedings of the AAAI Conference on Artificial Intelligence, vol. 35, pp. 3465–3473 (2021)
13. Zhao, M., Zhong, S., Fu, X., Tang, B., Pecht, M.: Deep residual shrinkage networks for fault diagnosis. IEEE Trans. Ind. Inform. **16**(7), 4681–4690 (2019)
14. Simonyan, K., Zisserman, A.: Very deep convolutional networks for large-scale image recognition. arXiv preprint arXiv:1409.1556 (2014)
15. He, K., Zhang, X., Ren, S., Sun, J.: Deep residual learning for image recognition. In: Proceedings of the IEEE Conference on Computer Vision and Pattern Recognition, pp. 770–778 (2016)
16. Ioffe, S., Szegedy, C.: Batch normalization: accelerating deep network training by reducing internal covariate shift. In: International Conference on Machine Learning, pp. 448–456. PMLR (2015)
17. Howard, A., Zhmoginov, A., Chen, L.C., Sandler, M., Zhu, M.: Inverted residuals and linear bottlenecks: Mobile networks for classification, detection and segmentation (2018)
18. Hu, Z., et al.: Boosting depth-based face recognition from a quality perspective. Sensors **19**(19), 4124 (2019)
19. Donoho, D.L.: De-noising by soft-thresholding. IEEE Trans. Inf. Theor. **41**(3), 613–627 (1995)
20. Isogawa, K., Ida, T., Shiodera, T., Takeguchi, T.: Deep shrinkage convolutional neural network for adaptive noise reduction. IEEE Sig. Process. Lett. **25**(2), 224–228 (2017)
21. Yang, X., Huang, D., Wang, Y., Chen, L.: Automatic 3d facial expression recognition using geometric scattering representation. In: 2015 11th IEEE International Conference and Workshops on Automatic Face and Gesture Recognition (FG), vol. 1, pp. 1–6. IEEE (2015)

Research on Face Degraded Image Generation Algorithm for Practical Application Scenes

Li Yu[1,2(✉)], Wenhao Xian[1], and Mengyao Jiang[1]

[1] School of Automation, University of Electronic Science and Technology of China, Chengdu 611731, China
lyu@uestc.edu.cn
[2] Intelligent Terminal Key Laboratory of Sichuan Province, Yibin, China

Abstract. In general face super-resolution (FSR) networks, the degraded model usually adopts a simple bicubic down-sampling, without considering more complex degradation conditions and actual scenes. Although this can verify the basic effectiveness of the model, it makes the model lack of generalization. Therefore, in order to solve the problem of poor generalization ability, this paper constructs a Degraded Generative Adversarial Network (DGAN), which replaces the method of bicubic down-sampling to realize implicit modeling of degradation process, and generates degraded images in real scene. Combining DGAN and face super-resolution networks DIC/DICGAN, a new FSR network is trained to recognize the low- resolution (LR) face of real scene. The face recognition test under FSR reconstruction is carried out using SCFace dataset constructed by actual monitoring camera. It is proved that DGAN can effectively simulate the degradation conditions of actual scenes, and improve the generalization of face reconstruction model, so that the SR algorithm can better adapt to face recognition in actual scenes.

Keywords: Bicubic · Face super-resolution · GAN · Face recognition

1 Introduction

Face super-resolution (FSR) plays an important role in solving the problem of low-resolution (LR) face recognition. Many studies have shown that improving the resolution of LR face can improve the accuracy of face recognition. However, many FSR networks simply use bicubic down-sampling method to simulate degraded images in training. So far, only a few scholars pay attention to the mismatch between training images and actual degraded test images. This problem affects the generalization ability of FSR reconstruction model, and has a great influence on face recognition, face detection and other advanced visual tasks. At present, the literatures on FSR reconstruction usually focus on generalization of facial features (such as generalization about the changes of posture, facial expression, occlusion or misalignment), but rarely involve the problem of degenerative mismatch. The key point of this problem is to simulate the complex degradation model in the real scene, and build a training set closer to the real scene, so

© Springer Nature Switzerland AG 2021
J. Feng et al. (Eds.): CCBR 2021, LNCS 12878, pp. 428–436, 2021.
https://doi.org/10.1007/978-3-030-86608-2_47

that the network can learn the correct mapping relationship. The existing solutions are as follows:

The first scheme attempts to estimate the blur kernel and noise from the actual degraded image, so as to simulate the image degradation model: Gu et al. [1] trained the kernel estimator and corrector of CNN on the premise that the dimension reduction kernel belongs to a Gaussian filter family, and took the estimated kernel as the input of the SR model. In order to restore high-resolution (HR) from LR images with arbitrary fuzzy kernel, Zhang et al. [2] proposed a depth plug and play framework, which uses the existing blind deblurring method to estimate the fuzzy kernel. However, the reconstruction effect of this method varies with the degradation degree, and it is unable to capture the complex degradation and compression degradation.

The second solution is to create image data sets based on real scenes, which are captured by multiple cameras with different focal lengths, so that LR/HR image pairs in real scenes can be obtained [3, 4]. However, the construction cost of this method is large, and the steps are cumbersome. There may be an inherent problem of misalignment between LR and HR image pairs. And up to now, researchers have not produced such data sets based on face images.

The third solution tries to apply unsupervised domain adaptation (UDA) in the SR process. The method of UDA has achieved some success. This method trains the model by using unpaired real LR and HR data and the cycle consistency loss formula. However, the two tasks (maintaining the consistency of visual features and image super-resolution) are carried out simultaneously, which makes the training process of the model become tense and difficult to converge to the optimal parameters. At the same time, it shows that the end-to-end model training is invalid, and it is difficult to carry out gradient back propagation between two convolutional neural networks in parallel.

In order to solve the problem that the degenerative model is too simple in previous methods, this paper designs a DGAN which can implicitly model the degenerative process, and then trains a new SR network by combining DGAN with DIC/DICGAN network proposed by Ma [5]. Finally, the face data set from the monitoring scene is used to evaluate the model. The experimental results show that DGAN successfully realizes the implicit modeling of complex degenerate model, improves the generalization of the original model, restores the SR from LR face in the actual scene, and improves the recognition rate of LR face.

2   Structure of DGAN

DGAN can be understood as a down-sampling network with specific multiple. The reason why the network can implicitly simulate degradation model is that: during the training, two kinds of "mismatched" data sets are used: the first type of data set is high-definition face data set, which includes pre-aligned HR face images, such as CelebA, VGGFace and other data sets. The second kind of data set is the wide-angle and street view face data set in the real-world scene, which includes the fuzzy low-quality LR facial images from outdoor scenes. For example, the Widerface [6] data set, which is often used for outdoor face detection tasks, performs face detection and clipping operations. After the data set processing is completed, the method of confrontation training is adopted: the generator change the input HR image to LR image, and the discriminator judge the LR image by "true or false", so that the generator can simulate the data distribution of the actual degraded image as much as possible, and then an implicit degradation model is obtained. The overall network structure of DGAN is shown in Fig. 1.

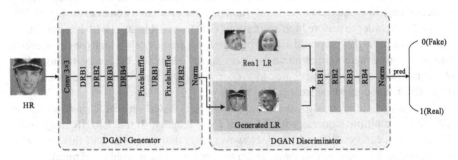

Fig. 1. Network structure of DGAN

2.1 Generator of DGAN

The generator uses the HR data set as the input image, and the structure is similar to that used in SRGAN. In the first layer of the network, HR image is concatenated with a random noise vector as the input of the network. The random noise vector has the same size as an HR image after mapping and reconstruction of the full connection layer. By paralleling the above noise vectors with HR images to build the model, our method can simulate a variety of different degradation situations. The generator of DGAN is essentially similar to conditional GAN, where the label is HR image.

The generator network uses encoder decoder structure. The whole system consists of six residual blocks, including four down sampling and two up-sampling. Firstly, the network uses four down-sampling residual blocks (DRB) to reduce the resolution. DRB has pooling layer, which can gradually reduce the resolution by 16 times, that is, from 128×128 down to 8×8 pixels. Then, two up-sample residual blocks (URB) are used to improve the resolution step by step. There is no pooling layer in the URB, and finally the pixel value can be increased to 32×32. The structure of DRB and URB of DGAN generator is shown in Fig. 2.

2.2 Discriminator of DGAN

The structure of the discriminator is shown in Fig. 1, and the structure of the residual block used in discriminator is shown in Fig. 3. The whole discriminator follows the Resnet based architecture, which is composed of four residual blocks without batch norm, and then a fully connected layer, which maps the output to 0 and 1, so as to judge whether the image belongs to the real image or the generated image. The input resolution of DGAN discriminator is 32×32. Therefore, the max pooling layer of the first two residual blocks is omitted, and only the last two residual blocks are down sampled and integrated.

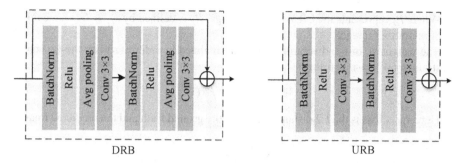

Fig. 2. Structure of DRB and URB of DGAN generator

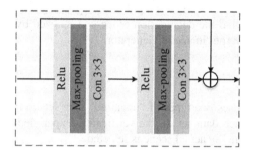

Fig. 3. Structure of the residual block of discriminator

2.3 Loss Function

The generator and discriminator networks of DGAN network are trained with the combination of GAN loss and L2 pixel loss. DGAN network is a simulated degradation network, which uses an unpaired training setting. The LR image in the Widerface dataset is used as the reference value to constrain the output of the generator. Because the main task is to simulate the degradation model, the main role and status of GAN loss and pixel loss are different at this time. The loss function of DGAN is centered on GAN loss, which drives the main image degradation process, contaminates the HR image input with noise and artifacts in Widerface dataset, and L2 pixel loss plays an auxiliary role in preserving the basic features of the face image, constraining the approximate contour of the face image, and preventing the generation of face image with excessively damaged structure.

The loss function l is defined as follows: where α and β are the corresponding weight. The GAN loss mentioned above plays a major role, while L2 pixels assist in the generation of constraint network.

$$l = \alpha l_{pixel} + \beta l_{GAN} \tag{1}$$

We used the hinge loss defined as:

$$l_{GAN} = E_{x \sim P_r}[\min(0, -1 + D(x))] + E_{x' \sim P_g}[\min(0, -1 - D(x'_G))] \tag{2}$$

Where P_r represents the LR Widerface image. P_g is defined by $x'_G = G(x)$, meaning generator output image.

The weight W of the discriminator are normalized in order to satisfy the Lipschitz constraint $\sigma(W) = 1$ as follows:

$$W_{SN}(W) = W/\sigma(W) \tag{3}$$

Here, l_{pixel} loss is the L2 distance between the ground truth and the predicted image.

$$l_{pixel} = \frac{1}{WH} \sum_{i=1}^{W} \sum_{j=1}^{H} \left(F\left(I^{hr}\right)_{i,j} - G_{\theta_G}\left(I^{hr}\right)_{i,j} \right)^2 \tag{4}$$

Among them, W and H represent the width and height of the generated output image, F is a simple degradation function to map the corresponding original HR image I^{hr} to the output resolution, and the degradation process is realized by the average pooling layer. $G_{\theta_G}\left(I^{hr}\right)$ is the output image of Generator.

3 Experiments

In this paper, DGAN uses two types of "unpaired" data sets: one is HR face data set, and the other is LR face data set. In the verification experiment of DGAN, the face recognition test set from the actual scene is selected.

1) HR data set: We combine two datasets to create a HR face training set containing about 150000 images. Firstly, 60000 faces are randomly selected from CelebA, which mainly include the front photos with good illumination and no occlusion. Secondly, about 9000 characters were randomly selected from VGGFace, and each character had 10 photos with big changes in posture: mainly including side face photos and big changes in expression, etc.

2) LR data set: LR data sets from real scenes are created from Widerface data set. Widerface contains large scale and diverse face data, covering faces affected by various degradation and noise types. About 50000 images are selected from Widerface data set. This paper uses the face detector in Openface. For HR dataset and LR data set, the resolution of the face image is adjusted to 128×128 and 32×32, respectively.

3) Face test set in real scene: This section uses the surveillance cameras face database SCFace [7]. The subjects were in an unconstrained indoor environment. Five video surveillance cameras of different quality were used for shooting. All cameras were installed and fixed in the same position, and did not move during the whole shooting process. The dataset contains 4160 images of 130 subjects. The images obtained by different quality surveillance cameras can represent a variety of degradation conditions in the real world. The images of subjects can be divided into the following categories: one high-resolution frontal photo of each subject, multiple photos of five different surveillance cameras (one surveillance camera contains three photos with different focal lengths, but not fully aligned), and photos taken by two surveillance cameras using night vision mode.

The SCFace dataset has a person's identity tag (No. 001–130), so it can be used for face recognition test, and can serve for different law enforcement scenarios and security monitoring scenarios. Some samples are shown in the Fig. 4.

In the subsequent reconstruction experiments, the resolution of all images is normalized to 32 × 32, and reconstruct image is 4 times magnification.

Firstly, in order to detect and cut all facial images, face detector in Openface [8] is used when preprocessing the Widerface data set. Secondly, the data set is simply expanded, and the diversity of the data set is increased. The random image flipping, zooming and rotation are used. Then, for the random noise input in DGAN, the noise vector is s randomly set to simulate a large number of image degradation types. The DGAN network trained 100 epochs, and the update ratio between discriminator and generator was 5:1. The learning rate is maintained throughout the training process. In the setting of loss function, the sum is used in formula (1) with $\alpha = 1$, $\beta = 0.05$, and the optimizer selects Adam.

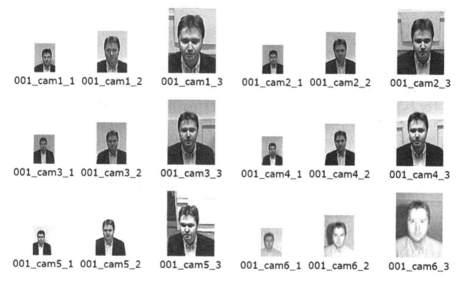

Fig. 4. Samples of SCFace

3.1 Output Image of DGAN

The following figure shows some degradation examples of DGAN generator output. We can see that the examples contain a variety of degradation types with different degrees, such as illumination change, noise, different blur kernel, color change and artifacts similar to JPEG compression. The diversity of scenes in Widerface can give DGAN with the ability to judge the specific noise types that may be contained in specific scenes (such as indoor, night, outdoor scenes, etc.) according to different scenes, so as to achieve accurate degradation (Fig. 5).

3.2 Reconstruction Results of DG-DIC/DG-DICGAN

DGAN will be used to instead of bicubic down-sampling to train a new DIC/DICGAN model (named DG-DIC/DG-DICGAN), and verify the reconstruction performance of

HR input   Output of LR

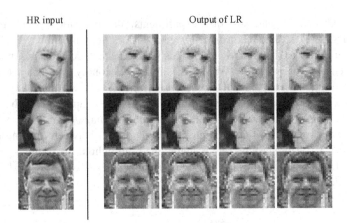

Fig. 5. Degradation examples of DGAN

DG-DIC/DG-DICGAN in real scenes. Specifically, we will test the face recognition rate with SCFace dataset.

The SCface dataset contains a total of 2860 face images. We selected 1200 face pairs for testing. There are 600 pairs from same characters and 600 pairs from different characters. The Arcface face recognition model [9] is used to test.

Figure 6 shows the reconstruction effect comparison of different methods, which are bicubic interpolation, DICGAN using bicubic down-sampling, DG-DIC and DG-DICGAN using DGAN down-sampling training. The selected sample contains images taken at two distances (the distance means the degree of degradation).

It can be seen from the Fig. 6 that: firstly, serious artifacts appear in the original DICGAN reconstruction, especially in the face edge region of the first group of images and the eye region of the fifth group of images, which have a great impact on the face recognition performance. These artifacts are caused by the deviation of the degradation of the training set and the test set discussed above. Secondly, bicubic interpolation method reconstructed image is more natural, there is no large area of artifacts, the face structure is normal, but the whole image is still in a fuzzy state. Finally, the proposed DGAN replaces the bicubic down-sampling methods used in DG-DIC and DG- DICGAN, and achieves the best visual effect. In the case of closer shooting (group 1, 4 and 5), it restores very good face details, and there is no artifacts in DG-DIC/DG- DICGAN. In the case of medium distance shooting (group 2 and group 3), our methods can restore the clearer local details, complete the face structure, and remove the stripe artifacts of surveillance cameras.

The following Table 1 shows the quantitative experimental results of these models. The recognition rates of DIC and DICGAN are the worst two results of all models. Bicubic method ranks third, and its recognition rate is slightly higher than the former two, which proves that interpolation method may be a better method in complex degradation environment. The DG-DIC and DG- DICGAN proposed in this paper have achieved the top two recognition rates, and the latter has achieved 75.3%, which is 5% higher than bicubic method.

| Bicubic | DICGAN | DG-DIC | DG-DICGAN |

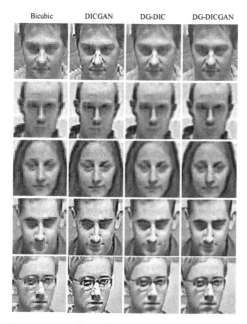

Fig. 6. The reconstruction effect comparison of different methods

Table 1. The quantitative experimental results of these models

SR model	Bicubic	DIC	DICGAN	DG-DIC	DG-DICGAN
Recognition rates (%)	0.700	0.668	0.681	0.724	0.753

4   Conclusion

This paper analyzes the serious influence of complex degradation model and degradation condition deviation on the reconstruction model, proposed a specific DGAN network, and uses mismatched HR/LR image pairs to train the DGAN, so that the DGAN has the ability to simulate the actual scene degradation model, and uses this network as the down sampling model to train DG-DIC/DG-DICGAN. Subsequently, the face recognition rate is tested in the surveillance camera face data set SCFace, and the results show that DG-DICGAN method achieves good reconstruction and recognition results.

Acknowledgments. This work was supported in part by University of Electronic Science and Technology of China Excellent course construction project for graduate students under Grant JPKC20192-29 and open project fund of Intelligent Terminal Key Laboratory of Sichuan Province (2019–2020)SCITLAB-0015.

References

1. Gu, J., Lu, H., Zuo, W., et al.: Blind super-resolution with iterative kernel correction. In: Proceedings of the IEEE/CVF Conference on Computer Vision and Pattern Recognition, pp. 1604–1613 (2019)
2. Zhang, K., Zuo, W., Zhang, L.: Deep plug-and-play super-resolution for arbitrary blur kernels. In: Proceedings of the IEEE/CVF Conference on Computer Vision and Pattern Recognition, pp. 1671–1681 (2019)
3. Cai, J., Zeng, H., Yong, H., et al.: Toward real-world single image super-resolution: a new benchmark and a new model. In: Proceedings of the IEEE/CVF International Conference on Computer Vision, pp. 3086–3095 (2019)
4. Joze, H.R.V., Zharkov, I., Powell, K., et al.: ImagePairs: realistic super resolution dataset via beam splitter camera rig. In: Proceedings of the IEEE/CVF Conference on Computer Vision and Pattern Recognition Workshops, pp. 518–519 (2020)
5. Ma, C., Jiang, Z., Rao, Y., et al.: Deep face super-resolution with iterative collaboration between attentive recovery and landmark estimation. In: Proceedings of the IEEE Conference on Computer Vision and Pattern Recognition, pp. 5568–5578 (2020)
6. Yang, S., Luo, P., Loy, C.C., et al.: Wider face: a face detection benchmark. In: Proceedings of the IEEE Conference on Computer Vision and Pattern Recognition, pp. 5525–5533 (2016)
7. Grgic, M., Delac, K., Grgic, S.: SCface–surveillance cameras face database. Multimedia Tools Appl. **51**(3), 863–879 (2011)
8. Baltrusaitis, T., Zadeh, A., Lim, Y.C., et al.: Openface 2.0: facial behavior analysis toolkit. In: The 13th IEEE International Conference on Automatic Face and Gesture Recognition (FG 2018), pp. 59–66. IEEE (2018)
9. Deng, J., Guo, J., Xue, N., Zafeiriou, S.: Additive angular margin loss for deep face recognition. In: Proceedings of IEEE/CVF Conference on Computer Vision and Pattern Recognition, pp. 4685–4694 (2019)

Embedding Fast Temporal Information Model to Improve Face Anti-spoofing

Yaowen Xu, Lifang Wu[✉], Yongluo Liu, and Zhuming Wang

Beijing University of Technology, Beijing 100124, China
lfwu@bjut.edu.cn, liuyongluo@emails.bjut.edu.cn

Abstract. Face anti-spoofing technology is a vital part of the face recognition system. For a quick response, many single-frame-based methods have been studied and made remarkable progress. However, some researchers improve performance by learning temporal features from video sequences without considering efficiency. Although the additional temporal features can improve face anti-spoofing, its computational efficiency is low. In this paper, we propose a fast temporal information model (Fast TIM) to learn temporal features. Fast TIM contains an efficient data dimensionality reduction method to retain temporal information and a lightweight network with 617 KB parameters to extract features. Fast TIM runs with 72 FPS real-time response and effectively improves the performance of the single-frame-based method. Experiments demonstrate that the proposed framework outperforms the state-of-the-art methods.

Keywords: Face anti-spoofing · Quick response · Temporal features · Dimensionality reduction · Lightweight

1 Introduction

Face-based biometric technology is widely used in our daily lives, such as smartphone unlocking, checking-in, and financial services. However, face images are easily obtained by hackers and used to attack face recognition systems. To address the problem, the face anti-spoofing (FAS) algorithm has been extensively studied, especially in dealing with photo and video attacks. However, FAS is a challenging task because face recognition systems are usually deployed in uncontrolled scenes, which requires high robustness of the FAS.

Early methods are usually based on hand-crafted features [1,2]. With the development of deep learning, the FAS algorithm based on deep learning [3] shows better performance. Recently, the method based on auxiliary supervision [4,5] has achieved excellent results in cross-database FAS. In the state-of-the-art methods, the methods [6] of introducing temporal information have better performance than the methods [7] based on single frame image. But the cost is the slower detection speed, which leads to a non-real-time response.

© Springer Nature Switzerland AG 2021
J. Feng et al. (Eds.): CCBR 2021, LNCS 12878, pp. 437–445, 2021.
https://doi.org/10.1007/978-3-030-86608-2_48

In fact, face anti-spoofing is a quick response task. Many works deprecate temporal information and classify faces from a single frame for quick response, such as [4,7]. However, the dynamic information on the video sequence is a robust clue in the FAS task [6]. In order to improve the performance of the algorithm, the temporal information is introduced in the methods [6,8] without considering the efficiency. These methods roughly employ optical flow [9], RNN [5,10], 3D CNN [11], etc. to extract temporal dynamic information, which increases the amount of calculation and reduces the efficiency. Based on this, an effective and fast algorithm for extracting temporal information is worth further study.

Motivated by the discussions above, we propose a fast temporal information model (Fast TIM) for extracting temporal information from a video clip to improve the performance of the single-frame-based FAS method. The commonly used temporal information extraction network, e.g., optical flow, RNN, 3D CNN, is not efficient for two reasons: (1) Many parameters of deep learning networks lead to a large amount of calculation. (2) Multiple images in the video clips input to the network will cause the network to process a large amount of information. And there is a lot of redundant information in this information. For example, each image contains the same or similar texture detail information. Our proposed Fast TIM solves these two problems from data and network. We use the non-parametric regional difference method to remove the redundant texture information. The data can be reduced from a 3D video clip to a 2D single image, and the temporal information is effectively preserved. In terms of network, we design a super lightweight network with a parameter of only 617 KB, a fully convolutional network with four convolutional layers. For the FAS task, the proposed framework is a two-stream network, including a single-frame-based FAS network and the Fast TIM, as shown in Fig. 1.

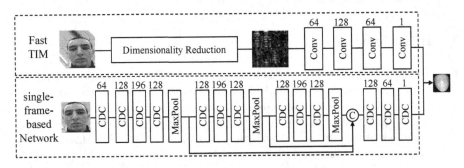

Fig. 1. The framework of the proposed method. "Conv" and "CDC" represent vanilla and central difference convolution. "C" suggests concatenation operation. The number above each layer represents the amount of output channels.

The main contributions of this work are summarized as follows:

(1) The non-parametric regional difference method is proposed to reduce dimensions from the video clip to a single image effectively and quickly.

(2) A fully convolutional network with only 617 KB parameters is designed, which effectively extracts the temporal information.

(3) We propose a fast temporal information model (Fast TIM) to improve the performance of the single-frame-based method and solve the problem of the low efficiency of the video-clip-based method. The experimental results demonstrate that the proposed Fast TIM reduces the error rate by 2.6% and achieves a real-time processing speed of 72 FPS.

2   Proposed Framework

As illustrated in Fig. 1, the proposed framework is a two-stream network that consists of two main models: Fast TIM and a single-frame-based model. Fast TIM is divided into two parts. One is data dimensionality reduction, and the other is network. In this section, the details of these two parts and the overall framework would be described.

2.1   Dimensionality Reduction for Fast TIM

The data dimensionality reduction module only retains the temporal information of the video sequence and removes the spatial details of the face image. The spatial details can be learned in a single-frame-based network from a single image, so the time complexity of the overall framework can be reduced. We leverage the non-parametric regional difference method to achieve data dimensionality reduction. This method is a simple calculation without a parametric model, and computation speed meets real-time response.

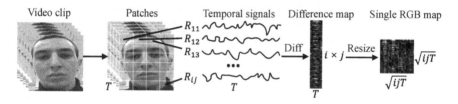

Fig. 2. Dimensionality reduction with the non-parametric regional difference method.

The dimensionality reduction process is shown in Fig. 2. For the detected face region, we cut the same region from the next consecutive T frames to get a video clip. Each frame of the video clip is gridded and divided into $i \times j$ patches. The average value of each patch in RGB channels is calculated, and the temporal signals $\{R_{11}, R_{12}, R_{13}, \ldots, R_{ij}\}$ can be obtained by connecting these average values in the time direction. In order to highlight the temporal pixel change and weaken the spatial pixel relationship, we perform difference calculations on the adjacent values of the temporal signals one by one. After splicing all the difference values of the temporal signals, a difference map with height $i \times j$ and width T can be obtained. To input into the convolution network, the difference map is finally resized into a square.

2.2   Network for Fast TIM

In the FAS task, the model should be able to distinguish the temporal information between real face and spoof face. Previous work design or employ deep neural networks, such as ResNet [12] and 3D CNN [11], to dig out temporal features from video information. In this paper, the temporal information has been exposed from the video information through dimensionality reduction, and then we no longer need to mine deep semantic features with deep networks. Therefore, we design a fully convolutional network with only four convolutional layers.

The structure of the proposed lightweight network for learning temporal features is shown in the Fast TIM of Fig. 1. The network consists of four convolutional layers with a kernel size of 3, stride of 2, and padding of 1. Each convolutional layer is followed by a batch normalization (BN) layer and a rectified linear unit (ReLU) layer. In particular, the stride of the last convolutional layer is 1, and there is no BN after the layer. The overall parameter of the network is 617 KB. The output of the network is a single-channel small-size feature map. Under the supervision of all labels with values of 1 or 0 in a map, the classification of real face or spoofing is learned with the mean square error (MSE) loss function, which is formulated:

$$\frac{1}{m}\sum_{i=1}^{m}(x_i - y_i)^2, \tag{1}$$

where x and y are the predicted map and the target map respectively, and m is the number of samples.

Fast TIM is used to learn temporal features from video clips, which can compensate for the inability to temporal of the single-frame-based method with a small amount of calculation. In this paper, the single-frame-based network CDCN [7] is used as the baseline, which utilizes central difference convolution to extract the fine-grained spatial features. The input of CDCN is a batch of single face images. The output is a face depth map of no more than 1 for a real face or a map with a value of 0 for spoofing. We combine the two output maps of the network in the two-stream framework, and the product of the two maps is used as the final output. If the average value of the final map is close to 1, it can be judged as a real face, and when it is close to 0, it is judged as spoofing.

3   Experiments

3.1   Database and Evaluation Metrics

Database. The most popular public database Oulu-NPU [13] is used in the experiments. The database with high resolutions of 1920 × 1080 contains spoofing (photo attack and replay attack) videos in four different mediums and real face videos. These videos are collected by the camera of six different smartphones in complex scenarios. There are 5,940 videos of both real faces and spoofing of 55 subjects in total. In the database, four intra-database testing protocols are used to validate the performance of the method from three aspects: illumination

Table 1. Comparison to temporal feature extraction methods. Lower values of the evaluation metrics indicate more advantages of the method.

Method	Mean ± std ACER (%)	Parameters	Time spent per data processing	Time spent per forward	Total time
Flownet2.0 [9] +Alexnet [15]	8.7 ± 1.2	650.1 MB +282.6 MB	641.28 ms	1.58 ms	642.86 ms
Flownet2.0 [9] +Resnet101 [12]	5.8 ± 2.3	650.1 MB +170.7 MB	641.28 ms	12.55 ms	653.83 ms
MPLN [16]	2.5 ± 2.8	1.8 MB	96.96 ms	1.46 ms	98.42 ms
Fast TIM (ours)	**0.4 ± 0.9**	**617 KB**	**13.24 ms**	**0.6 ms**	**13.84 ms**

variations, different spoof mediums, different camera devices. Among them, Protocol 4 combines all the above-mentioned variations to comprehensively evaluate the generalization ability of the model.

Metrics. For fair comparisons, we report the performance with Attack Presentation Classification Error Rate (APCER), Bona Fide Presentation Classification Error Rate (BPCER), and Average Classification Error Rate (ACER) [14].

3.2 Implementation Details

The proposed framework is a two-stream network that consists of Fast TIM and the single-frame-based network CDCN. The two networks can be trained separately. In Fast TIM, the sequence length T is 8, and the number i of patch grids in the height direction is 16, and the number j in the width direction is 8. Under this setting, the map size after dimensionality reduction is 32×32, and the output size of Fast TIM is 4×4. In CDCN, the inputs are the face images after resize to 256×256, and the output size is 32×32. The final result is obtained by multiplying the mean values of the outputs of the Fast TIM and CDCN.

3.3 Experimental Comparison on Efficiency

The Fast TIM is compared with the temporal feature extraction methods based on optical flow or 3D CNN. Optical flow Flownet2.0 extracts the movement changes between two frames and forms an optical flow map. Eight optical flow maps are input into CNN (Alexnet [15], Resnet [12]) and voted to get the final result. The MPLN [16] is a lightweight 3D CNN for learning temporal features. Faces in the 8-frame image need to be aligned by a preprocessing algorithm and then input to the network as a 3D video sequence. Because the detection results of photo attacks can better reflect the temporal feature extraction ability of the algorithm [16], all schemes are tested on Protocol 4 of Oulu-NPU without video attacks. All experiments are conducted on a single NVIDIA TITAN X GPU.

Table 2. Comparison to the baseline. The ACER (%) is reported, in which the average ± standard deviation of ACER is reported in Protocols 3 and 4 because of six tests in these protocols. The lower, the better.

Method	Prot. 1	Prot. 2	Prot. 3	Prot. 4
CDCN [7] (baseline)	1.0	1.5	2.3 ± 1.4	6.9 ± 2.9
Fast TIM + CDCN (ours)	0.4	1.3	1.9 ± 1.5	4.3 ± 2.3

The results can be summarised in Table 1. FAS test results ACER, model parameters, and run-time are reported. The Flownet2.0 based methods have more parameters and cost more time than our method because optical flow estimation is a high time-consuming preprocessing algorithm. The error rate ACER of The Flownet2.0 based methods is higher than ours due to the difference between movement changes of optical flow estimation and temporal features. The performance of the lightweight MPLN is worse than that of ours because there is redundant information irrelevant to temporal information in its input. And its face alignment preprocessing takes longer than our data dimensionality reduction preprocessing. In general, our method is superior to other methods in all aspects. In particular, the time consumption of single discrimination is 13.84 ms, i.e., the calculation speed reaches 72 FPS.

3.4   Experimental Comparison on Performance

In order to verify the effect of our proposed Fast TIM on the single-frame-based method, the method of embedding the Fast TIM is compared with the baseline. From the results in Table 2, we can see that the Fast TIM can improve the performance of the single-frame-based method on all four protocols of Oulu-NPU. Especially in the most challenging Protocol 4, the error rate ACER was reduced by 2.6%.

The proposed framework is compared with the state-of-the-art methods in Table 3. The methods Auxiliary [5] and RSGB+STPM [8] are video-based methods, and the methods BCN [18] and Zhang et al. [17] are single-frame-based methods. The single-frame-based methods can improve performance by voting on the results of multiple frames, but the amount of calculation multiplies. We embed the Fast TIM network with a speed of 72 FPS on the single-frame-based method, and its performance exceeds other state-of-the-art methods on the four protocols of Oulu-NPU. The results demonstrate that Fast TIM is not only fast but also effective, and the proposed framework is an efficient and high-performance scheme.

Table 3. Comparison to the state-of-the-art methods on Oulu-NPU database.

Prot.	Method	APCER (%)	BPCER (%)	ACER (%)
1	Auxiliary [5]	1.6	1.6	1.6
	Zhang et al. [17]	1.7	0.8	1.3
	RSGB+STPM [8]	2.0	0.0	1.0
	BCN [18]	0.0	1.6	0.8
	Ours	0.0	0.8	**0.4**
2	Auxiliary [5]	2.7	2.7	2.7
	Zhang et al. [17]	1.1	3.6	2.4
	RSGB+STPM [8]	2.5	1.3	1.9
	BCN [18]	2.6	0.8	1.7
	Ours	2.5	0.2	**1.3**
3	Auxiliary [5]	2.7 ± 1.3	3.1 ± 1.7	2.9 ± 1.5
	RSGB+STPM [8]	3.2 ± 2.0	2.2 ± 1.4	2.7 ± 0.6
	BCN [18]	2.8 ± 2.4	2.3 ± 2.8	2.5 ± 1.1
	Zhang et al. [17]	2.8 ± 2.2	1.7 ± 2.6	2.2 ± 2.2
	Ours	2.2 ± 1.9	1.6 ± 1.1	**1.9 ± 1.5**
4	Auxiliary [5]	9.3 ± 5.6	10.4 ± 6.0	9.5 ± 6.0
	BCN [18]	2.9 ± 4.0	7.5 ± 6.9	5.2 ± 3.7
	RSGB+STPM [8]	6.7 ± 7.5	3.3 ± 4.1	5.0 ± 2.2
	Zhang et al. [17]	5.4 ± 2.9	3.3 ± 6.0	4.4 ± 3.0
	Ours	2.0 ± 1.7	6.6 ± 3.7	**4.3 ± 2.3**

4   Conclusion

This paper identifies that additional temporal features can improve face anti-spoofing, but the calculation should be reduced during model design to achieve a real-time response. We propose a fast temporal information model (Fast TIM), which consists of a dimensionality reduction method and a lightweight network. The proposed non-parametric regional difference method can reduce dimensions from the video clip to a single image. A light fully-convolutional network with only 617 KB parameters can extracts the temporal information from the single image after dimensionality reduction. Fast TIM with 72 FPS real-time response can effectively improve the performance of the single-frame-based method. Experiments demonstrate that the proposed framework outperforms the state-of-the-art methods.

Acknowledgments. This work was supported in part by the Beijing Municipal Education Committee Science Foundation under Grant KM201910005024 and in part by the Beijing Postdoctoral Research Foundation under Grant ZZ2019-63.

References

1. Peixoto, B., Michelassi, C., Rocha, A.: Face liveness detection under bad illumination conditions. In: 18th IEEE International Conference on Image Processing (ICIP), pp. 3557–3560 (2011)
2. Boulkenafet, Z., Komulainen, J., Hadid, A.: Face spoofing detection using colour texture analysis. IEEE Trans. Inf. Forensics Secur. 11(8), 1818–1830 (2016)
3. Yang, J., Lei, Z., Li, S.Z.: Learn convolutional neural network for face anti-spoofing. arXiv preprint arXiv:1408.5601 (2014)
4. Atoum, Y., Liu, Y., Jourabloo, A., Liu, X.: Face anti-spoofing using patch and depth-based CNNs. In: IEEE International Joint Conference on Biometrics (IJCB), pp. 319–328 (2017)
5. Liu, Y., Jourabloo, A., Liu, X.: Learning deep models for face anti-spoofing: binary or auxiliary supervision. In: IEEE Conference on Computer Vision and Pattern Recognition (CVPR), pp. 389–398 (2018)
6. Yu, Z., Wan, J., Qin, Y., Li, X., Li, S.Z., Zhao, G.: NAS-FAS: static-dynamic central difference network search for face anti-spoofing. IEEE Trans. Pattern Anal. Mach. Intell. 1 (2020)
7. Yu, Z., et al.: Searching central difference convolutional networks for face anti-spoofing. In: IEEE/CVF Conference on Computer Vision and Pattern Recognition (CVPR), pp. 5295–5305 (2020)
8. Wang, Z., et al.: Deep spatial gradient and temporal depth learning for face anti-spoofing. In: IEEE/CVF Conference on Computer Vision and Pattern Recognition (CVPR), pp. 5042–5051 (2020)
9. Ilg, E., Mayer, N., Saikia, T., Keuper, M., Dosovitskiy, A., Brox, T.: FlowNet 2.0: evolution of optical flow estimation with deep networks. In: Proceedings of the IEEE Conference on Computer Vision and Pattern Recognition (CVPR), pp. 2462–2470 (2017)
10. Xu, Z., Li, S., Deng, W.: Learning temporal features using LSTM-CNN architecture for face anti-spoofing. In: 2015 3rd IAPR Asian Conference on Pattern Recognition (ACPR), pp. 141–145. IEEE (2015)
11. Tran, D., Bourdev, L., Fergus, R., Torresani, L., Paluri, M.: Learning spatiotemporal features with 3D convolutional networks. In: Proceedings of the IEEE International Conference on Computer Vision (ICCV), pp. 4489–4497. (2015)
12. He, K., Zhang, X., Ren, S., Sun, J.: Deep residual learning for image recognition. In: Proceedings of the IEEE Conference on Computer Vision and Pattern Recognition, pp. 770–778 (2016)
13. Boulkenafet, Z., Komulainen, J., Li, L., Feng, X., Hadid, A.: OULU-NPU: a mobile face presentation attack database with real-world variations. In: 12th IEEE International Conference on Automatic Face & Gesture Recognition (FG), pp. 612–618 (2017)
14. ISO/IEC JTC 1/SC 37 Biometrics: Information technology - biometric presentation attack detection - Part 1: Framework., International organization for standardization (2016)
15. Krizhevsky, A., Sutskever, I., Hinton, G.E.: ImageNet classification with deep convolutional neural networks. Adv. Neural Inf. Process. Syst. 25, 1097–1105 (2012)
16. Xu, Y., Wang, Z., Han, H., Wu, L., Liu, Y.: Exploiting non-uniform inherent cues to improve presentation attack detection. In: IEEE International Joint Conference on Biometrics (IJCB) (2021)

17. Zhang, K.-Y., et al.: Face anti-spoofing via disentangled representation learning. In: Vedaldi, A., Bischof, H., Brox, T., Frahm, J.-M. (eds.) ECCV 2020. LNCS, vol. 12364, pp. 641–657. Springer, Cham (2020). https://doi.org/10.1007/978-3-030-58529-7_38

18. Yu, Z., Li, X., Niu, X., Shi, J., Zhao, G.: Face anti-spoofing with human material perception. In: Vedaldi, A., Bischof, H., Brox, T., Frahm, J.-M. (eds.) ECCV 2020. LNCS, vol. 12352, pp. 557–575. Springer, Cham (2020). https://doi.org/10.1007/978-3-030-58571-6_33

Speech Biometrics

Jointing Multi-task Learning and Gradient Reversal Layer for Far-Field Speaker Verification

Wei Xu[1], Xinghao Wang[1], Hao Wan[1,2], Xin Guo[3], Junhong Zhao[1(✉)],
Feiqi Deng[1], and Wenxiong Kang[1]

[1] School of Automation Science and Engineering, South China University
of Technology, Guangzhou 510641, China
{jhzhao,auwxkang}@scut.edu.cn
[2] Guangdong Baiyun Airport Information Technology Co., Ltd. Postdoctoral
Innovation Base, Guangzhou, China
[3] Guangdong Communication Polytechnic, Guangzhou, China

Abstract. Far-field speaker verification is challenging, because of interferences caused by different distances between the speaker and the recorder. In this paper, a distance discriminator, which determines whether two utterances are recorded at the same distance, is used as an auxiliary task to learn distance discrepancy information. There are two identical auxiliary tasks, one is added before the speaker embedding layer to learn distance discrepancy information via multi-task learning, and then the other is added after that layer to suppress the learned discrepancy via a gradient reversal layer. In addition, to avoid conflicts among the optimization directions of all tasks, the loss weight of every task is updated dynamically during training. Experiments on AISHELL Wake-up show a relatively 7% and 10.3% reduction of equal error rate (EER) on far-far speaker verification and near-far speaker verification respectively, compared with the single-task model, demonstrating the effectiveness of the proposed method.

Keywords: Far-field speaker verification · Multi-task learning · Gradient reversal layer · Dynamic loss weights strategy

1 Introduction

Speaker verification [1] is used to determine whether two given utterances are from the same person. In the smart home scenarios, speaker verification wakes up the smart devices with fixed words from a range of distances between the user and the device. Various distances cause different signal-to-noise ratio (SNR) in the utterances captured by the device, which deteriorates speaker verification system. Usually, registered utterances have a higher SNR than that of verification utterances, because users register in the device from a near distance while waking up the device from random distances and directions. This mismatch makes it

© Springer Nature Switzerland AG 2021
J. Feng et al. (Eds.): CCBR 2021, LNCS 12878, pp. 449–457, 2021.
https://doi.org/10.1007/978-3-030-86608-2_49

harder to determine whether two utterances with different SNR belong to the same person. There are two types of methods to address this problem in previous studies.

One is speech enhancement, which eliminates the mismatch by signal processing technologies. There are two main interferences, lower SNR and reverberation, in far-field utterances compared with near-field clean utterances. To remove these interferences, Tong et al. [2] enhance the quality of far-field utterance with weighted prediction error (WPE) [3] and Beamforming [4]. In contrast, [5,6] add noise or reverberation to clean near-field utterances to make them have the similar SNRs with far-field utterances.

The other is domain adaptation (DA) [7], which aims to find a common feature space for data from different domains. Utterances from different distances can be split into different domains, so DA is also applied in far-field speaker verification. Probabilistic Linear Discriminant Analysis (PLDA) [8] decomposes speaker embedding into the inter subspace to compensate the gap between near-field utterances and far-field utterances [9]. Zhang et al. [10] use a domain classifier to discriminate near-field utterances and far-field utterances, and train it with speaker classifier. Chen et al. [11] minimize the discrepancy between different distances by a distance discriminator. To avoid negative adaptation, Liu et al. [12] extract distance-invariant speaker embedding through adversarial domain separation network (DSN) [13].

The methods mentioned above alleviate mismatches by suppressing the discrepancy between near-field utterances and far-field utterances, but there is no mechanism to encourage the model to learn discrepancy information. Inspired by [14] that multi-task learning (MTL) can encourage the representation of some certain information and gradient reversal layer (GRL) [15] can suppress that information, we use MTL to learn discrepancy information first and then suppress it by a GRL in this paper. Specifically, we add one distance discriminator before the speaker embedding layer first, and then the other is added after the speaker embedding layer via a GRL. In addition, to balance the weights of the loss value of different tasks in the total loss value during training, we apply dynamic loss weights strategy instead of fixing the loss weight of every task.

2   The Proposed Method

As mentioned above, MTL can encourage the model to learn some information and GRL can remove that information from the model. In this paper, MTL and GRL are jointed to eliminate the adverse effects of distance discrepancy on far-field speaker verification. The proposed structure is shown in Fig. 1. In the following, main parts of the model will be described in detail.

2.1   Multi Tasks in the Model

Different tasks can motivate the model to learn different information. In this paper, the speaker classification and the distance discrimination are applied to

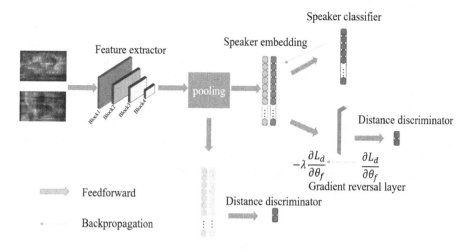

Fig. 1. Jointing multi-task learning and gradient reversal layer

learn speaker embedding and distance discrepancy respectively. The distance discrepancy helps to extract distance-invariant speaker embedding, which improves far-field speaker verification. Totally, there are three tasks in the model, one speaker classifier and two identical distance discriminators as shown in Fig. 1.

The speaker classifier is used as main task to discriminate different speakers. During the training process, we optimize the model to minimize a metric learning objective for speaker classification. The objective is calculated from prototypical loss [16], which makes the distinction between utterances of the same speaker smaller and the distinction between utterances of different speakers larger.

The distance discriminator is used as an auxiliary task, the aim of which is to determine whether two utterances have the same distance label. The auxiliary task is proposed to learn information representing distance discrepancy. Contrast loss [17] is used for this task. Assuming that the Euclidean distance between two speaker embedding vectors is d, the loss of distance discriminator is:

$$l_{dis} = \frac{1}{2N} \sum_{n=1}^{N} \left(y_n d_n^2 + (1 - y_n) \, max \, (margin - d_n, 0)^2 \right) \tag{1}$$

where N denotes the total number of samples. y_n equals 1 when two utterances have the same distance label, otherwise y_n equals 0. The margin serves to prevent two utterances with a large gap from causing damage to the training process. When the Euclidean distance between two utterances is greater than the value of margin, the loss is set to 0, such that it does not participate in updating the parameters.

Notably, the auxiliary task only works in the training, it is not involved in the generation of speaker embedding in the testing.

2.2 Gradient Reversal Layer

The gradient reversal layer is a special fully connected layer that maps the input identically to the output in the forward propagation, but multiplies the gradient by a negative value before passing it to the previous layer in the back propagation.

In this paper, the GRL is inserted between the speaker embedding layer and the distance discriminator, which removes distance discrepancy learned by MTL from speaker embedding. The auxiliary task is proposed to learn information representing distance discrepancy, and GRL is used to suppress that discrepancy. During training, learning distance discrepancy via MTL and suppressing the discrepancy by GRL motivates the model to generate speaker embedding that is resistant to distance variation.

2.3 Dynamic Loss Weights Strategy

Due to the quantitative differences in the loss values of different tasks, fixing the loss weight of every task leads to conflicts of gradient descent directions among tasks. Specifically, if the loss of a certain task is so large that it dominates the optimization of the model, other tasks are prevented from being optimized. Therefore, the loss weight of every task needs to be dynamically updated according to the loss value during training. In [18], the uncertainty is used to balance the loss weight for every task. Similar strategy is applied in this paper.

There are three tasks in the model. The losses of the three tasks are assumed to be l_{spk} (the loss of speaker classifier),l_{mtl} (the loss of distance discriminator before speaker embedding layer), and l_{grl} (the loss of distance discriminator with GRL) respectively, and an uncertainty parameter σ is estimated for the loss weight of every task, denoted as σ_{spk},σ_{mtl} and σ_{grl}. The total loss is:

$$l_{total} = \frac{1}{2\sigma_{spk}^2} l_{spk}\left(W\right) + \frac{1}{2\sigma_{mtl}^2} l_{mtl}\left(W\right) + \frac{1}{2\sigma_{grl}^2} l_{grl}\left(W\right) + \log(\sigma_{spk}\sigma_{mtl}\sigma_{grl}) \quad (2)$$

When the uncertainty of a task increases, its corresponding weight becomes smaller to reduce the interference with other tasks. By minimizing the total loss value, the model weights and the uncertainty parameters are optimized simultaneously to achieve the purpose of dynamically updating the loss weight of every task according to its loss value during training.

3 Experimental Results

3.1 Dataset and Data Preparation

Experiments are conducted on AISHELL wake-up dataset [19], which contains utterances of fixed words, "ni hao, mi ya" in Chinese, with distance labels of 0.25 m, 1 m, 3 m or 5 m. Utterances from 0.25 m are regarded as near-field ones and the others far-field. The speakers in development set and evaluation set, totally

296, are used for training and the other 44 speakers from test set is used for testing. Test pairs are provided by two files, which correspond to two far-field speaker verification tasks, one (near-far) is for near-field registration (0.25 m) with far-field verification (1 m, 3 m, 5 m) and the other (far-far) is for far-field registration (1 m) with far-field verification (1 m, 3 m, 5 m).

All utterances are converted from time domain to frequency domain to get richer feature. The feature used in this paper is 40-dimensional (39-dimensional filter bank feature and energy) with a frame shift of 10 ms and a window width of 25 ms.

3.2 Experiments on Different Part of the Proposed Model

The feature extractor in Fig. 1 is a thin ResNet34 [21] with four residual blocks. Experiments are conducted to find out which part of the model is the best node to apply auxiliary task. The architecture, with one distance discriminator before a certain part and the other is added after that part via GRL, is applied on block2, block3, block4 and speaker embedding layer respectively. The experimental results are shown in Table 1. The baseline is a single-task model, and only the speaker classification task is optimized during training

Table 1. Jointing MTL and GRL at different parts (EER %)

Block	Far-far	Near-far
Baseline	7.47	7.90
Block2	7.77	8.13
Block3	7.17	7.42
Block4	7.47	7.71
Speaker embedding layer	**6.95**	**7.09**

The experimental results show that adding auxiliary task to the shallow part degrades far-field speaker verification, which is caused by the fact that the shallow layer only learns simple local features and does not fuse the global features. In contrast, the results are improved when applying the auxiliary tasks to relatively deeper parts, block3, block4 and speaker embedding layer. The best results can be obtained by adding the auxiliary task before and after the speaker embedding layer. Compared with the baseline model, the EERs of two far-field speaker verification tasks are reduced to 6.95% and 7.09%, with a relative reduction of 7.0% and 10.3%.

In Table 2. Ablation experiments are conducted at speaker embedding layer. We apply MTL before this layer and apply GRL after this layer respectively. Experimental results show that jointing MTL and GRL performs better than using them separately.

Table 2. Ablation experiments at speaker embedding layer (EER %)

	Far-far	Near-far
Baseline	7.47	7.90
MTL before speaker embedding layer	7.26	7.68
GRL after speaker embedding layer	7.17	7.46
Joint	**6.95**	**7.09**

Table 3. Dynamic loss weights strategy (EER %)

$\frac{1}{2\sigma_{spk}^2}$	$\frac{1}{2\sigma_{mtl}^2}, \frac{1}{2\sigma_{grl}^2}$	Far-far	Near-far	Diff. (%)
1	0	7.47	7.90	0.43
0.33	0.33	7.36	7.80	0.44
1	10	8.31	8.80	0.49
1	1	7.30	7.43	0.13
1	0.1	**6.89**	7.48	**0.59**
1	0.01	**6.80**	7.23	**0.43**
1	0.001	7.51	7.91	0.40
Learned	Learned	**6.95**	7.09	**0.14**

3.3 Experiments on Dynamic Loss Weights Strategy

In this section, to verify the effectiveness of the dynamic loss weights strategy, we evaluate its performance by comparing it with different fixed loss weights. Experimental results are shown in Table 3.

In Table 3, the Diff. is the difference of EERs between the two far-field speaker verification tasks, which can also measure the ability of the proposed structure in eliminating the distance discrepancy. A smaller Diff. indicates that the structure is more capable of eliminating the distance discrepancy. 'Learned' means that the corresponding parameters in Eq. 2 are learnable during the training process. Compared with setting the weights of the tasks to 1, 0.01 and 0.01 respectively, the dynamic loss weights strategy gets an EER of 6.95% in far-far task, which is slightly higher than the EER of 6.80% of the fixed loss weight. However, the dynamic loss weights strategy substantially improves the performance of near-far task, reducing the EER from 7.23% to 7.09%. In addition, the Diff. decreases from 0.43% to 0.14%, with a relatively reduction of 67%. In the near-far task, the difference between the registration and verification utterance is larger, so the experimental results further indicate that the dynamic loss weights strategy can fully exploit the distance discrepancy information in the utterances. In addition, the strategy helps quickly determine the loss weights of different tasks and avoids the tedious process of manually tuning parameters.

3.4   Comparison with the Prevailing Single-Task Models

In Table 4, experiments of three remarkable models are conducted on AISHELL Wake-up dataset. These models are the most important works in the field of speaker verification in recent years and have achieved the best verification results on many datasets. Experimental results show that the proposed method performs better than the existing single-task models on far-field speaker verification.

Table 4. Comparison with the prevailing single-task models (EER %)

Model	Year	Far-far	Near-far
Snyder et al. [6]	2018	11.23	12.2
Xie et al. [20]	2019	8.09	8.27
Chung et al. [21]	2020	7.47	7.90
The proposed	2021	**6.95**	**7.09**

4   Conclusion

To remove distance discrepancy between near-field utterances and far-field utterances, the proposed structure first encourages the model to learn distance discrepancy information via MTL, and then suppresses that discrepancy via GRL. The distance discriminator is used as an auxiliary task to apply supervisory information of distance label during training. This paper provides a simple and effective method to extract distance-invariant speaker embedding, because the auxiliary task helps to remove distance discrepancy in the training but not involves in the generation of speaker embedding in the testing. In addition, a dynamic loss weights strategy is used to adjust the loss weight of each task in the total loss value during training. The loss weights are dynamically adjusted according to the learning of every task, so that every task can reach the optimization simultaneously. The strategy helps to fully exploit the distance discrepancy information between near-field utterances and far-field utterances. Experiments show that the proposed method achieves EER of 6.95% and 7.09% on far-far task and near-far task respectively, which performs better than the prevailing single-task models.

Acknowledgments. This work was supported by the National Natural Science Foundation of China under Grant 61573151 and Grant 61976095 and the Science and Technology Planning Project of Guangdong Province under Grant 2018B030323026.

References

1. Bai, Z., Zhang, X.L.: Speaker recognition based on deep learning: an overview. Neural Netw. (2021)
2. Tong, Y., et al.: The JD AI speaker verification system for the FFSVC 2020 challenge. In: Proceedings of Interspeech 2020, pp. 3476–3480 (2020)
3. Nakatani, T., Yoshioka, T., Kinoshita, K., Miyoshi, M., Juang, B.H.: Speech dereverberation based on variance-normalized delayed linear prediction. IEEE Trans. Audio Speech Lang. Process. 18(7), 1717–1731 (2010)
4. Mošner, L., Matějka, P., Novotný, O., Černocký, J.H.: Dereverberation and beamforming in far-field speaker recognition. In: 2018 IEEE International Conference on Acoustics, Speech and Signal Processing (ICASSP), pp. 5254–5258. IEEE (2018)
5. Qin, X., Cai, D., Li, M.: Far-field End-to-end text-dependent speaker verification based on mixed training data with transfer learning and enrollment data augmentation. In: Interspeech, pp. 4045–4049 (2019)
6. Snyder, D., Garcia-Romero, D., Sell, G., Povey, D., Khudanpur, S.: X-vectors: robust DNN embeddings for speaker recognition. In: 2018 IEEE International Conference on Acoustics, Speech and Signal Processing (ICASSP), pp. 5329–5333. IEEE (2018)
7. Pan, S.J., Tsang, I.W., Kwok, J.T., Yang, Q.: Domain Adaptation via transfer component analysis. IEEE Trans. Neural Netw. 22(2), 199–210 (2010)
8. Prince, S.J., Elder, J.H.: Probabilistic linear discriminant analysis for inferences about identity. In: 2007 IEEE 11th International Conference on Computer Vision, pp. 1–8. IEEE (2007)
9. Burget, L., Novotny, O., Glembek, O.: Analysis of BUT submission in far-field scenarios of voices 2019 challenge. In: Proceedings of Interspeech (2019)
10. Zhang, L., Wu, J., Xie, L.: NPU speaker verification system for Interspeech 2020 far-field speaker verification challenge. arXiv preprint arXiv:2008.03521 (2020)
11. Chen, Z., Miao, X., Xiao, R., Wang, W.: Cross-domain speaker recognition using domain adversarial Siamese network with a domain discriminator. Electron. Lett. 56(14), 737–739 (2020)
12. Yi, L., Mak, M.W.: Adversarial separation and adaptation network for far-field speaker verification. In: INTERSPEECH, pp. 4298–4302 (2020)
13. Bousmalis, K., Trigeorgis, G., Silberman, N., Krishnan, D., Erhan, D.: Domain separation networks. arXiv preprint arXiv:1608.06019 (2016)
14. Chen, Z., Wang, S., Qian, Y., Yu, K.: Channel invariant speaker embedding learning with joint multi-task and adversarial training. In: ICASSP 2020–2020 IEEE International Conference on Acoustics, Speech and Signal Processing (ICASSP), pp. 6574–6578. IEEE (2020)
15. Ganin, Y., Lempitsky, V.: Unsupervised domain adaptation by backpropagation. In: International Conference on Machine Learning, PMLR, pp. 1180–1189 (2015)
16. Snell, J., Swersky, K., Zemel, R.S.: Prototypical networks for few-shot learning. arXiv preprint arXiv:1703.05175 (2017)
17. Hadsell, R., Chopra, S., LeCun, Y.: Dimensionality reduction by learning an invariant mapping. In: 2006 IEEE Computer Society Conference on Computer Vision and Pattern Recognition (CVPR 2006), IEEE, vol. 2, pp. 1735–1742 (2006)
18. Kendall, A., Gal, Y., Cipolla, R.: Multi-task learning using uncertainty to weigh losses for scene geometry and semantics. In: Proceedings of the IEEE Conference on Computer Vision and Pattern Recognition, pp. 7482–7491 (2018)

19. Qin, X., Bu, H., Li, M.: HI-MIA: a far-field text-dependent speaker verification database and the baselines. In: ICASSP 2020–2020 IEEE International Conference on Acoustics, Speech and Signal Processing (ICASSP), pp. 7609–7613. IEEE (2020)
20. Xie, W., Nagrani, A., Chung, J.S., Zisserman, A.: Utterance-level aggregation for speaker recognition in the wild. In: ICASSP 2019–2019 IEEE International Conference on Acoustics, Speech and Signal Processing (ICASSP), pp. 5791–5795. IEEE (2019)
21. Chung, J.S., et al.: In defence of metric learning for speaker recognition. arXiv preprint arXiv:2003.11982 (2020)

Attention Network with GMM Based Feature for ASV Spoofing Detection

Zhenchun Lei[✉], Hui Yu, Yingen Yang, and Minglei Ma

School of Computer and Information Engineering, Jiangxi Normal University, Nanchang, China
zhenchun.lei@hotmail.com, huiyu@jxnu.edu.cn, yyg1999@sina.com,
sljsmml@163.com

Abstract. Automatic Speaker Verification (ASV) is widely used for its convenience, but is vulnerable to spoofing attack. The 2-class Gaussian Mixture Model classifier for genuine and spoofed speech is usually used as the baseline in ASVspoof challenge. The GMM accumulates the scores on all frames in a speech independently, and does not consider its context. We propose the self-attention network spoofing detection model whose input is the log-probabilities of the speech frames on the GMM components. The model relies on the self-attention mechanism which directly draws the global dependencies of the inputs. The model considers not only the score distribution on GMM components, but also the relationship of frames. And the pooling layer is used to capture long-term characteristics for detection. We also proposed the two-path attention network, which is based on two GMMs trained on genuine and spoofed speech respectively. Experiments on the ASVspoof 2019 challenge logical and physical access scenarios show that the proposed models can improve performance greatly compared with the baseline systems. LFCC feature is more suitable for our models than CQCC in experiments.

Keywords: ASV spoofing detection · Self-attention network · Gaussian probability feature · Gaussian Mixture Model

1 Introduction

Over the past few years, Automatic Speaker Verification (ASV) [1] systems have improved performance due to the advancements in deep learning technology. However, the ASV technologies are vulnerable, which make ASV systems exposed to various spoofing attacks [2, 3]. There are four well-known attacks that perform logical access (LA) or physical access (PA) spoofing attacks in ASV systems, namely, mimicry [4], text-to-speech (TTS) [5], voice conversion (VC) [6], and replay [7].

A lot of different spoofing technologies have been put forward to improve detection performance. Most of them focus on designing discriminative features [8]. For example, Constant Q Cepstral Coefficients (CQCCs) [9], which use the constant Q transform (CQT) instead of the short-time Fourier transform (STFT) to process speech signals, perform better than common Mel-Frequency Cepstral Coefficients (MFCCs) [10]. Linear

© Springer Nature Switzerland AG 2021
J. Feng et al. (Eds.): CCBR 2021, LNCS 12878, pp. 458–465, 2021.
https://doi.org/10.1007/978-3-030-86608-2_50

Frequency Cepstral Coefficients (LFCCs) [11] is integrated using triangular filter bank and the filters spaced in linear scale, which have been shown to be effective front-ends for spoofing detection.

In the aspect of classifiers, the classical Gaussian Mixture Model (GMM) is general used as the baseline system. With the development of deep learning technology, more and more neural network models are applied to spoofing speech detection. Galina [12] employed Light Convolutional Neural Networks (LCNN) with max filter map activation function, which get the best performance in ASVspoof 2017 challenge. Alejandro [13] proposed a hybrid LCNN plus RNN architecture which combines the ability of the LCNNs for extracting discriminative features at frame level with the capacity of gated recurrent unit (GRU) based RNNs for learning long-term dependencies of the subsequent deep features. Moustafa [14] proposed deep residual neural networks for audio spoofing detection, which process MFCC, CQCC and spectrogram input features, respectively. Cheng-I [15] proposed attentive filtering network, which is composed of an attention-based filtering mechanism that enhances feature representation in both the frequency and time domains, and a ResNet-based classifier.

In the classical GMM, the scores are accumulated on all feature frames independently, and the Gaussian component score distribution information is discarded. the relationship between adjacent frames along the time axis is also been ignored. So, the frame context information is not used in GMM. To address these issues, we applied attention mechanism with gaussian probability feature for spoofing speech detection in this paper. Self-attention [16] is an attention mechanism that computes the representation of a single sequence by relating different positions in it. Francis [17] proposed a visual attention mechanism based on class activation mapping for replay attack detection.

The remainder of the paper is organized as follows. In Sect. 2, extracting of Gaussian probability feature is presented. Section 3 describes the self-attention network model and two-path attention network model for spoofing detection. In Sect. 4, the experimental setup, results and discussion are presented. Finally, Sect. 5 provides the conclusions.

2 Gaussian Probability Feature

2.1 Gaussian Mixture Model

The Gaussian Mixture Model is a general model for estimating an unknown probability density function, and the virtues of the model lie mainly in its good approximation properties. The model assumes that the unknown density can be written as a weighted finite sum of Gaussian kernels, with different mixing weights and different parameters, namely, means and covariance matrices. For a D-dimensional feature vector, x, the mixture density used for the likelihood function has the following form:

$$p(x) = \sum_{i=1}^{M} w_i p_i(x) \tag{1}$$

The density is a weighted linear combination of M unimodal Gaussian densities, $p_i(x)$, each parameterized by a mean $D \times 1$ vector, μ_i, and a $D \times D$ covariance matrix, Σ_i:

$$p_i(x) = \frac{1}{(2\pi)^{D/2}|\Sigma_i|^{1/2}} \exp\{-\frac{1}{2}(x - \mu_i)'\Sigma_i^{-1}(x - \mu_i)\} \tag{2}$$

The estimation of the parameters of the model is carried out by the Expectation Maximization (EM) algorithm, aiming at maximizing the likelihood of a set of samples drawn independently from the unknown density.

In ASV spoofing detection field, the GMM based system is general used as the baseline system, which includes two GMMs: one for genuine speech and one for spoof speech. For a given test speech utterance $X = \{x_1, x_2, \ldots, x_N\}$, the log-likelihood ratio is used to make the human/spoof decision, and the log-likelihood ratio is defined in the flowing form:

$$\text{score}_{baseline} = \log p(X|\lambda_h) - \log p(X|\lambda_s) \tag{3}$$

where λ_h and λ_s are the GMMs for human and spoof speech respectively.

2.2 Gaussian Probability Feature

For a speech feature sequence, the GMM accumulates the scores on all frames independently, and does not consider the contribution of every Gaussian component to the final score. Moreover, the relationship between adjacent frames is also been ignored. So, we want to model the score distribution on every GMM component, and use the Gaussian probability feature.

For a raw frame feature x_i (LFCC or CQCC in our experiments), the size of new feature f_i is the order of GMM and the component f_{ij} is:

$$f_{ij} = \log(w_j \bullet p_j(x_i)) \tag{4}$$

After that, the mean μ_f and standard deviation σ_f on the whole training data are calculated and used for mean and variance normalization for each utterance:

$$f'_i = \frac{f_i - \mu_f}{\sigma_f} \tag{5}$$

3   Two-Path Attention Network

3.1   Attention Network

The attention mechanism has been widely used in areas such as speech recognition and natural language processing. In these areas, the attention model is used to weigh the importance of specific inputs. The transformer successfully replaced recurrent neural networks such as LSTMs with sinusoidal positional encoding and the self-attention mechanism to be context-aware on input embeddings.

In this paper, we employ the self-attention formulation by Vaswani et al. [16]. Given a matrix of n query vectors $Q \in R^{n \times d}$, keys $K \in R^{n \times d}$ and values $V \in R^{n \times d}$, the scaled dot-product attention computes the attention scores based on the following equation:

$$\text{Attention}(Q, K, V) = \text{softmax}\left(\frac{QK^T}{\sqrt{d}}\right)V \tag{6}$$

where d is the number of hidden units. The multi-head attention mechanism first maps the matrix of input vectors $X \in R^{t \times d}$ to queries, keys and values matrices by using different linear projections. Then h parallel heads are employed to focus on different part of channels of the value vectors. Then the scaled dot-product attention is used to compute the mixed representations:

$$M_i = \text{Attention}(QW_i^Q, KW_i^K, VW_i^V) \tag{7}$$

where W_i^Q, W_i^K, W_i^V are parameter matrices corresponding to queries, keys and values for the i-th head. The vectors produced by h heads are catenated together to form a single vector, and a linear map is used to mix different channels from different heads:

$$M = \text{Concat}(M_1, \ldots, M_h) \tag{8}$$

$$Y = MW^O \tag{9}$$

where $M \in R^{n \times d}$ and $W^O \in R^{d \times d}$.

In order to make use of the order of the feature sequence, the positional encodings are added to the input embeddings. The position encodings have the same dimension as the inputs, so that can be summed. Our systems use the sine and cosine functions of different frequencies proposed by Vaswani et al. [16]. Unlike the position embedding approach, this approach does not introduce additional parameters.

We apply the multi-head attention mechanism to model the Gaussian probability feature. The new model considers not only the frame scores on GMM components, but also the local relationship between frames. Figure 1 shows the overview of attention mechanism based model for spoofing detection.

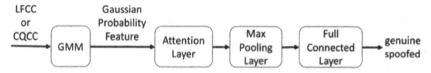

Fig. 1. Flow diagram of attention network model for spoofing detection.

The GMM is trained on the whole training dataset without labels. The attention layer takes the log-probabilities as input features. Then a 1-D max-overtime pooling operation is applied over the feature map and the maximum value is taken as the feature. The idea is to capture the most important feature—one with the highest value—for each feature map. This pooling scheme performs down-sampling and naturally deals with variable speech lengths. Final output of model is the probability distribution over genuine and spoofed speech labels. In our experiments, we employ h = 8 parallel attention heads, and $d/h = 64$.

3.2 Two-Path Attention Network

We also propose the two-path attention network for spoofing speech detection, which is based on two GMMs trained on genuine and spoofed speech respectively. The proposed flow diagram is depicted in Fig. 2.

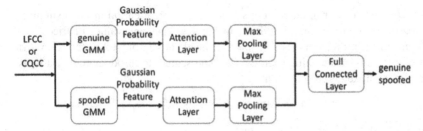

Fig. 2. Flow diagram of two-path attention network model for spoofing detection.

The two-path attention network contains two identical attention networks, each of which has the same architecture in previous section except for the fully connected layer. The input of attention network is log-probabilities calculated separately by two GMMs in the baseline system. The branches of attention networks are trained simultaneously on training dataset and they create two same dimension embedding vectors. Then we concatenate two vectors and input it to the fully connected layer with softmax output.

The unified feature map [18] is also used for the different lengths of evaluation utterances. This method divides the whole utterance into segments with length 400 frames and overlap 200 frames. The score of utterance is computed by averaging the scores of all its segments.

4   Experiments

4.1   Setup

The experiments were run on the ASVspoof 2019 [19] database consisting of bona fide and spoofed speech signals. The database encompasses two partitions for the assessment of logical access (LA) and physical access (PA) scenarios. The LA scenario involves spoofing attacks that are injected directly into the ASV system. Attacks in the LA scenario are generated using the text-to-speech synthesis (TTS) and voice conversion (VC) technologies. For the PA scenario, speech data is assumed to be captured by a microphone in a physical, reverberant space. ASVspoof 2019 corpus is divided into three no speakers overlap subsets: training, development and evaluation. More detailed description of these subsets can be found in [19]. Performance is measured in terms of EER and minimum t-DCF.

In the experiments, we used LFCC and CQCC as the raw acoustic features for anti-spoofing. The feature extractors are matlab implementation of spoofing detection baseline system provided by the organizers. The feature extractors use the default configuration.

The baseline is two separate GMMs system, which are trained using maximum-likelihood criteria from genuine and spoofed speech-data respectively. We train GMMs with 512 mixtures and 30 EM iterations using the MSR Identity Toolbox [20] implementation. The log-likelihood ratio of each tested speech sample from the genuine model and spoofed model is taken as the final score during evaluation.

We implement our neural network models using PyTorch and train models using a machine with a GTX 2080 Ti GPU. Cross-entropy loss is adopted as the loss criterion and Adam optimizer with learning rate of 0.0001 is used during the training process. The batch size is set to 64 in all experiments.

4.2   Results on ASVspoof 2019 LA Scenario

Table 1 shows the results on the ASVspoof 2019 LA scenario obtained by the baseline systems and the attention network systems using LFCC and CQCC respectively.

Table 1. Results on ASVspoof 2019 logical access in terms of EER (%) and min-tDCF.

Feature	Model	Dev		Eval	
		EER (%)	Min-tDCF	EER (%)	Min-tDCF
CQCC	GMM	0.237	0.007	8.97	0.214
	Attention	0.276	0.008	8.67	0.208
	Two-path attention	0.117	0.003	8.48	0.217
LFCC	GMM	3.77	0.103	7.59	0.208
	Attention	0.469	0.014	2.42	0.070
	Two-path attention	0.394	0.009	2.19	0.062

The proposed two-path attention network system outperforms the baseline system on the development and evaluation datasets obviously. Specifically, the LFCC+two-path attention network system improves the baseline system EER and min-tDCF by 71.1% and 70.2% on the evaluation dataset respectively. Both attention network and two-path attention network with CQCC feature can get little performance improvement compared with the GMM system. Maybe our models are more compatible with LFCC feature on LA scenario.

4.3   Results on ASVspoof 2019 PA Scenario

The physical access condition considers spoofing attacks that are performed at the sensor level. Spoofing attacks in this scenario are therefore referred to as replay attacks, whereby a recording of a bona fide access attempt is first captured, presumably surreptitiously, before being replayed to the ASV microphone. Table 2 shows the results on the ASVspoof 2019 PA scenario obtained by the baseline systems and our attention network systems using LFCC and CQCC respectively.

The performance improvement can also be obtained on the PA dataset. The two-path attention network system can get the best performance, but it is more compatible with CQCC feature. The CQCC+two-path attention network system achieves a relative 70.7% and 67.3% better performance than CQCC+GMM on the evaluation set in EER and min-tDCF respectively.

Table 2. Results on ASVspoof 2019 physical access in terms of EER (%) and min-tDCF.

Feature	Model	Dev		Eval	
		EER (%)	Min-tDCF	EER (%)	Min-tDCF
CQCC	GMM	9.72	0.184	11.34	0.254
	Attention	5.00	0.131	5.41	0.145
	Two-path attention	3.37	0.077	3.32	0.083
LFCC	GMM	11.22	0.236	12.90	0.287
	Attention	6.69	0.163	7.74	0.201
	Two-path attention	4.57	0.111	5.41	0.136

5   Conclusions

In this paper, we proposed attention network and two-path attention network models with Gaussian probability feature for spoofing speech detection. The classical GMM accumulates the scores on all frames independently, and does not consider the contribution of every Gaussian component to the final score. And the relationship between adjacent frames is also been ignored. For an utterance, the Gaussian probability feature includes the score distribution on each GMM component. We adopt the multi-head attention to ASV spoofing detection. The model considers not only the frame scores on GMM, but also the relationship between frames. We also propose a two-path attention network for spoofing speech detection, which is based on two GMMs trained on genuine and spoofed speech respectively. The experimental results on the ASVspoof 2019 database show that the proposed two-path attention network can improve performance greatly. For future work, it is essential to explore new neural network architecture to model Gaussian probability feature.

Acknowledgments. This work is supported by National Natural Science Foundation of P.R. China (62067004), and by Educational Commission of Jiangxi Province of P.R. China (GJJ170205).

References

1. Wu, Z., Evans, N., Kinnunen, T., Yamagishi, J., Alegre, F., Li, H.: Spoofing and countermeasures for speaker verification: a survey. Speech Commun. **66**, 130–153 (2015)
2. Kinnunen, T., Wu, Z.Z., Lee, K.A., Sedlak, F., Chng, E.S., Li, H.: Vulnerability of speaker verification systems against voice conversion spoofing attacks: The Case of telephone speech. In: IEEE International Conference on Acoustic, Speech and Signal Processing (ICASSP), pp. 4401–4404 (2012)
3. Lindberg, J., Blomberg, M.: Vulnerability in speaker verification–a study of technical impostor techniques. In: European Conference on Speech Communication and Technology (1999)
4. Hautamäki, R.S., et al.: Automatic versus human speaker verification: the case of voice mimicry. Speech Commun. **72**, 13–31 (2015)

5. Toda, T., Black, A.W., Tokuda, K.: Voice conversion based on maximum-likelihood estimation of spectral parameter trajectory. IEEE Trans. Audio, Speech, Lang. Process. **15**(8), 2222–2235 (2007)

6. Galka, J., Grzywacz, M., Samborski, R.: Playback attack detection for text-dependent speaker verification over telephone channels. Speech Commun. **67**, 143–153 (2015)

7. Sahidullah, M., Kinnunen, T., Hanilci, C.: A comparison of features for synthetic speech detection. In: Proceedings of the INTERSPEECH, pp. 2087–2091 (2015)

8. Todisco, M., Delgado, H., Evans, N.: Constant Q cepstral coefficients: a spoofing countermeasure for automatic speaker verification. Comput. Speech Lang. **45**, 516–535 (2017)

9. Davis, S.B., Mermelstein, P.: Comparison of parametric representation for monosyllabic word recognition in continuously spoken sentences. IEEE Trans. Acoust. Speech Signal Process. **28**(4), 357–366 (1980)

10. Alegre, F., Amehraye, A., Evans, N.: A one-class classification approach to generalised speaker verification spoofing countermeasures using local binary patterns. In: IEEE Sixth International Conference on Biometrics: Theory, Applications and Systems (BTAS). pp. 1–8 (2013)

11. Lavrentyeva, G., Novoselov, S., Malykh, E., Kozlov, A., Kudashev, O., Shchemelinin, V.: Audio replay attack detection with deep learning frameworks. In: INTERSPEECH, pp. 82–86 (2017)

12. Gomez-Alanis, A., Peinado, A.M., Gonzalez, J.A., Gomez, A.M.: A light convolutional GRU-RNN deep feature extractor for ASV spoofing detection. In: INTERSPEECH, pp. 1068–1072 (2019)

13. Alzantot, M., Wang, Z., Srivastava, M.B.: Deep residual neural networks for audio spoofing detection. In: INTERSPEECH, pp. 1078–1082 (2019)

14. Lai, C-I., Abad, A., Richmond, K., Yamagishi, J., Dehak, N., King, S.: Attentive filtering networks for audio replay attack detection. In: ICASSP, pp. 6316–6320 (2019)

15. Vaswani, A., et al.: Attention is all you need. arXiv preprint arXiv:1706.03762 (2017)

16. Tom, F., Jain, M., Dey, P.: End-to-end audio replay attack detection using deep convolutional networks with attention. In: INTERSPEECH, pp. 681–685 (2018)

17. Lai, C., Chen, N., Villalba, J., Dehak, N.: ASSERT: anti-spoofing with squeeze-excitation and residual networks. In: INTERSPEECH (2019)

18. Todisco, M., et al.: ASVspoof 2019: future horizons in spoofed and fake audio detection. In: INTERSPEECH (2019)

19. Sadjadi, S.O., et al.: MSR Identity Toolbox v1.0: A MATLAB toolbox for speaker recognition research. Speech and Lang. Process. Tech. Committee Newsl. (2013)

Cross-Corpus Speech Emotion Recognition Based on Sparse Subspace Transfer Learning

Keke Zhao[1], Peng Song[1(✉)], Wenjing Zhang[1], Weijian Zhang[1], Shaokai Li[1], Dongliang Chen[1], and Wenming Zheng[2]

[1] School of Computer and Control Engineering, Yantai University,
264005 Yantai, China
pengsong@ytu.edu.cn

[2] Key Laboratory of Child Development and Learning Science of Ministry
of Education, Southeast University, 210096 Nanjing, China

Abstract. Cross-corpus speech emotion recognition (SER) has become a hot-spot research topic in recent years. In actual situations, the problem that how to efficiently find the corpus invariant feature representations is still a big challenge. To solve this problem, in this paper, we propose a novel cross-corpus SER method based on sparse subspace transfer learning (SSTL). First, we introduce the discriminative subspace learning to learn a robust common subspace projection. Second, a sparse reconstruction based on $\ell_{2,1}$-norm is deployed to transfer the knowledge from source corpus to target corpus, in which the target samples will be well represented as a linear combination of the source data. Finally, we conduct experiments on three classical databases, and the experimental results show that the proposed method is superior to the other classical subspace transfer learning methods for cross-corpus SER tasks.

Keywords: Speech emotion recognition · Subspace learning · Transfer learning · Sparse representation

1 Introduction

Speech emotion recognition (SER) has been widely studied in the fields of affective computing and human-computer interaction. The goal of SER is to learn a suitable classifier to effectively recognize human emotions or emotional states from speech, e.g., anger, disgust, fear, happiness, and sadness [1,2]. The application fields of SER are extremely widespread, such as medical assistance, online education, car systems, telephone customer service, and so on [2]. However, with the explosive growth of data, the assumption of traditional SER, i.e., the training and testing data follow the same feature distributions, does not often hold. In actual situations, the training and testing data are often obtained in different scenarios, e.g., different languages, or different recording devices, where the recognition performance will be significantly reduced [3].

© Springer Nature Switzerland AG 2021
J. Feng et al. (Eds.): CCBR 2021, LNCS 12878, pp. 466–473, 2021.
https://doi.org/10.1007/978-3-030-86608-2_51

In order to solve the above problems, with the rapid development of transfer learning [4,5], many transfer learning algorithms have been introduced for cross-corpus SER [6–10]. For example, in [6], Deng et al. present a feature subspace transfer learning method for cross-corpus SER. In [7], Zong et al. carry out cross-corpus SER based on a domain adaptive least squares regression method. In [8], Huang et al. develop a PCANet based feature transfer algorithm for cross-corpus SER. In [9], Gideon et al. propose an adversarial discriminative domain generalization method for cross-corpus SER. In [3], Song et al. propose a transfer linear subspace learning approach for cross-corpus SER. In [10], Zhang et al. propose a transfer sparse discriminant subspace learning method for cross-corpus SER.

Most of the above-mentioned algorithms measure the distance discrepancy between source and target databases by using the maximum mean discrepancy (MMD), which is one of the most popular and efficient distance metrics for transfer learning [4,11]. However, MMD can only narrow the probability distribution, neglecting the linear relationship between the source and target databases. This will make the samples from different databases cannot interweave well.

Different from the above-mentioned methods, in this paper, we propose a novel transfer learning algorithm, called sparse subspace transfer learning (SSTL), for cross-corpus SER. Our method jointly combines sparse subspace learning and transfer feature representation to learn a corpus invariant feature representation. It can effectively transfer knowledge and align the features of different corpora into a new common subspace. In this way, the data of target corpus can be well represented by the data of source corpus, and the recognition performance will be significantly improved.

2 The Proposed SSTL Method

2.1 Objective Function

Sparse Discriminant Subspace Learning. The main idea of linear discriminant subspace (LDA) is to learn a projection matrix, in which the samples in the same class are as close as possible, and the samples of different classes are as far away as possible. Thus, it can be formulated as a trace difference form [12]:

$$\min_{W} \mathrm{Tr}\left(W^T \left(S_w - \mu S_b\right) W\right) \tag{1}$$

where μ is a small positive constant, S_w and S_b are the intra-class and inter-class scatter matrices, respectively, W is the projection matrix, and $\mathrm{Tr}(\cdot)$ denotes the trace of a matrix. Specifically, S_w and S_b can be obtained by the following formulas:

$$S_w = \frac{1}{n} \sum_{i=1}^{k} \sum_{j=1}^{n_i} \left(x_j^i - u_i\right)\left(x_j^i - u_i\right)^T \tag{2}$$

$$S_b = \frac{1}{n} \sum_{i=1}^{k} n_i \left(u_i - u\right)\left(u_i - u\right)^T \tag{3}$$

where k is the number of categories, $u_i = \frac{1}{n_i} \sum_{j=1}^{n_i} x_j^i$ denotes the mean of samples belonging to the $i-$th class, $u = \frac{1}{n} \sum_{i=1}^{k} \sum_{j=1}^{n_i} x_j^i$ denotes the mean of all samples, and x_j^i means the $j-$th sample in the $i-$th class.

Inspired by the idea of feature selection, which can help select the most representative features from the original data for classification [13]. We restrict W by introducing an $\ell_{2,1}$-norm to reduce the unnecessary redundant features, which can be formulated as

$$\|W\|_{2,1} = \sum_{i=1}^{d} \sqrt{\sum_{j=1}^{c} w_{ij}^2} \tag{4}$$

Then, by combining Eq. (1) and Eq. (4), we can obtain

$$\min_{W} \mathrm{Tr}\left(W^T \left(S_w - \mu S_b\right) W\right) + \alpha \|W\|_{2,1} \tag{5}$$

where α is a regularization parameter.

Transfer Feature Representation. To reduce the difference of feature distributions between source and target databases, in this work, we introduce a data reconstruction strategy, in which the target data can be linearly reconstructed by the source data in the learned common subspace. In this way, the distributions of the target and the source data are approximately the same. Thus, this problem can be formulated as

$$W^T X_t = W^T X_s Z \tag{6}$$

where $Z \in R^{n_s \times n_t}$ is a reconstruction coefficient matrix. Equation (6) can be rewritten as

$$\min_{W,Z} \|W^T X_t - W^T X_s Z\|_F^2 \tag{7}$$

Then, we also impose an $\ell_{2,1}$-norm constraint on Z, which can select the best reconstruction coefficient. Thus, we can get the following formula:

$$\min_{W,Z} \|W^T X_t - W^T X_s Z\|_F^2 + \gamma \|Z\|_{2,1} \tag{8}$$

where $\|\cdot\|_F$ denotes the Frobenius norm, and γ is a regularization factor. Similar as Eq. (4), the $\ell_{2,1}$-norm on Z can be expressed as $\|Z\|_{2,1} = \sum_{i=1}^{n_s} \sqrt{\sum_{j=1}^{n_t} z_{ij}^2}$.

Objective Function. By combining Eq. (5) with Eq. (8), we can obtain the objective function of SSTL as

$$\min_{W,Z} \mathrm{Tr}\left(W^T \left(S_w - \mu S_b\right) W\right) + \alpha \|W\|_{2,1} + \beta \left\|W^T X_t - W^T X_s Z\right\|_F^2 + \gamma \|Z\|_{2,1}$$

$$\text{s.t. } W^T W = I$$

$$\tag{9}$$

where β is a regularization parameter for the transfer learning item. To avoid getting a trivial solution, we add an orthogonal constraint $W^T W = I$ on W, so that the obtained projection matrix is more in line with our requirements.

2.2   Optimization

To solve the objective function of SSTL, we propose an iterative optimization algorithm. First, according to [14], $\|W\|_{2,1}$ can be expressed as

$$\|W\|_{2,1} = 2 \operatorname{Tr}(W^T D W) \tag{10}$$

Similarly, $\|Z\|_{2,1}$ can be expressed as

$$\|Z\|_{2,1} = 2 \operatorname{Tr}(Z^T G Z) \tag{11}$$

where $D \in R^{m \times m}$ and $G \in R^{n_s \times n_s}$ are diagonal matrices, $D = \frac{1}{2\|W_i\|^2}$, and W_i means the i-th row of W. In the same way, $G = \frac{1}{2\|Z_i\|^2}$, in which Z_i means the i-th row of Z.

In our iterative optimization algorithm, when one variable is solved, the other variables remain unchanged. It mainly includes two processes as follows:

Update W: Fixing the reconstruction coefficient Z and solve the projection matrix W. Then the objective function in Eq. (9) can be transformed into the form of the Lagrangian function as follows:

$$\begin{aligned} L(W) = \operatorname{Tr}\left(W^T \left(S_w - \mu S_b\right) W\right) &+ 2\alpha \operatorname{Tr}(W^T D W) \\ &+ \beta \left\|W^T X_t - W^T X_s Z\right\|_F^2 + \Phi(I - W^T W) \end{aligned} \tag{12}$$

where Φ is a Lagrange parameter. For convenience, we make $V = X_t - X_s Z$, and can get the partial derivative of $L(W)$ w.r.t. W as

$$\frac{\partial L(W)}{\partial W} = (S_w - \mu S_b)W + \alpha DW + \beta V V^T W - \phi W \tag{13}$$

Setting $\frac{\partial L(W)}{\partial W} = 0$, we can get the following generalized eigen-decomposition problem:

$$(S_w - \mu S_b)W + \alpha DW + \beta V V^T W = \phi W \tag{14}$$

Thus, the problem of solving W can be simplified as a eigen-decomposition problem.

Update Z: Fixing the projection matrix W and solve the reconstruction coefficient Z. The objective function in Eq. (9) is transformed into a form of Lagrangian function as follows:

$$L(Z) = \beta\|W^T X_t - W^T X_s Z\|_F^2 + 2\gamma \operatorname{Tr}(Z^T G Z) \tag{15}$$

Taking the partial derivative of $L(Z)$ w.r.t. Z as

$$\frac{\partial L(Z)}{\partial Z} = \gamma G Z + \beta(X_s^T W W^T X_s Z - X_s^T W W^T X_t) \tag{16}$$

Setting $\frac{\partial L(Z)}{\partial Z} = 0$, we can obtain

$$Z = \beta(\gamma G + \beta X_s^T W W^T X_s)^{-1} X_s^T W W^T X_t \tag{17}$$

The above two processes are conducted iteratively until convergence or the maximum number of iterations is reached.

3   Experiments and Results

3.1   Experimental Environment

To prove the effectiveness of the proposed method, we select three widely used emotional databases, including Berlin database [15], eNTERFACE database [16] and RML database [17]. And we compare the proposed method with several related classical subspace learning and transfer learning algorithms, including principal component analysis (PCA) [18], linear discriminant analysis (LDA) [19], semi-supervised discriminant analysis (SDA) [20], transfer component analysis (TCA) [4], joint distribution adaptation (JDA) [21], transfer linear discriminant analysis (TLDA) [11], transfer joint matching (TJM) [22] and transfer sparse discriminant subspace learning (TSDSL) [10].

For these three databases, we choose any two of them for cross-corpus SER, in which one is used as the source corpus and the other is used as the target corpus. There are total six experimental settings, including Be-e, Be-R, e-Be, e-R, R-Be, and R-e, where Be, e and R represent Berlin, eNTERFACE and RML, respectively.

Among these emotional categories, we select the common five emotional categories for evaluation, including anger, disgust, fear, happiness and sadness. And we select all the source data and 4/5 of the target data as the training data, and the remaining 1/5 of the target data are used as the testing data.

For parameter settings, we optimally set $\mu = 0.1$, the regularization parameters α and γ, and the transfer feature representation parameter β are selected in $\{0.001, 0.01, 0.1, 1, 10, 100, 1000\}$. The dimension is set to 5, and the algorithm are repeated 50 times. In our experiments, we report the results with the best optimal values for all methods.

3.2   Results and Analysis

Table 1 gives the recognition results of different methods in six different cases. As can be seen from the table, we can find that, first, the average performance of the proposed SSTL method is much higher than that of the traditional methods. The reason is that the traditional methods ignore the difference of data distribution between different databases. In cross-corpus SER, the data of source and target databases are often collected from different scenes, and directly using the traditional method may lead to poor recognition performance. Second, compared with the other transfer subspace learning algorithms, the proposed SSTL method also achieves better average recognition performance, with an average classification accuracy of 47.11%, which has an 8.95% higher than the second best baseline method TSDSL. These results show that the proposed SSTL method can obtain more transferable feature representation for cross-corpus SER task.

We further discuss the influence of the regularization parameters by the ablation study. There are two main parameters in the objective function, i.e., the feature selection parameter α and transfer feature representation parameter β. Specifically, we consider the following two situations:

Table 1. The recognition accuracy (%) of different methods in different situations.

Cases	Traditional methods			Transfer learning methods					SSTL
	PCA	LDA	SDA	TCA	JDA	TLDA	TJM	TSDSL	
Be-e	36.02	39.58	30.23	38.60	38.14	37.21	39.53	**43.25**	41.40
Be-R	22.22	30.54	22.69	26.39	25.93	32.87	29.63	30.09	**44.17**
e-Be	32.35	29.41	25.00	39.71	45.59	32.35	41.18	50.00	**60.29**
e-R	31.48	30.28	31.94	28.24	28.24	28.24	31.02	31.01	**46.67**
R-Be	17.65	17.65	17.65	22.06	38.24	19.12	29.41	41.17	**52.94**
R-e	27.95	**38.14**	14.42	31.16	31.63	26.05	29.77	33.48	37.21
Average	27.94	30.93	23.65	31.02	34.62	29.30	33.42	38.16	**47.11**

- SSTL$_1$: Let the feature selection item in Eq. (9) be zero, that is, $\alpha = 0$.
- SSTL$_2$: Let the transfer feature representation items in Eq. (9) be zero, that is $\beta = 0$ and $\gamma = 0$.

In Fig. 1(a), we give the recognition results of SSTL and its two special cases, i.e., SSTL$_1$ and SSTL$_2$. From the figure, it can be seen that the recognition performance of SSTL$_1$ and SSTL$_2$ are worse than SSTL, which demonstrates that the feature selection item and the transfer feature representation term have a positive influence on the performance of the model.

In addition, we give the objective values with varying number of iterations in Fig. 1(b). From the figure, we observe that the objective values decrease steadily with the increase of number of iterations, and converges within 50 iterations, which proves the convergence of the proposed method.

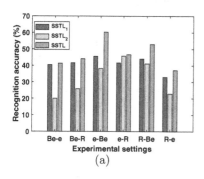
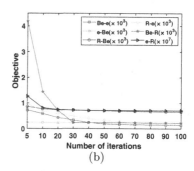

(a)   (b)

Fig. 1. Effectiveness analysis under six experimental settings: (a) the recognition accuracy of our method and two special cases; (b) the convergence curves.

4 Conclusion

To resolve the problem of cross-corpus SER, we propose a novel transfer subspace learning approach called SSTL. In SSTL, we first learn a common feature subspace. Then we introduce the idea of sparse reconstruction, in which the data in target corpus can be linearly represented by the data in source corpus. In addition, we use the $\ell_{2,1}-$norm to constrain the projection matrix and reconstruction coefficients, which can obtain more effective features and avoid trivial solutions. We conduct experiments on three classic emotional databases. The results demonstrate the superiority of the proposed method.

Acknowledgments. This work was supported in part by the Fundamental Research Funds for the Central Universities (2242021k30014 and 2242021k30059), in part by the National Natural Science Foundation of China (61703360 and 61801415), and in part by the Graduate Innovation Foundation of Yantai University (GIFYTU).

References

1. El Ayadi, M., Kamel, M.S., Karray, F.: Survey on speech emotion recognition: features, classification schemes, and databases. Pattern Recogn. **44**(3), 572–587 (2011)
2. Akçay, M.B., Oğuz, K.: Speech emotion recognition: emotional models, databases, features, preprocessing methods, supporting modalities, and classifiers. Speech Commun. **116**, 56–76 (2020)
3. Song, P.: Transfer linear subspace learning for cross-corpus speech emotion recognition. IEEE Trans. Affect. Comput. **10**(2), 265–275 (2019)
4. Pan, S.J., Tsang, I.W., Kwok, J.T., Yang, Q.: Domain adaptation via transfer component analysis. IEEE Trans. Neural Netw. **22**(2), 199–210 (2010)
5. Zhang, J., Li, W., Ogunbona, P., Xu, D.: Recent advances in transfer learning for cross-dataset visual recognition: a problem-oriented perspective. ACM Comput. Surv. (CSUR) **52**(1), 1–38 (2019)
6. Deng, J., Zhang, Z., Schuller, B.: Linked source and target domain subspace feature transfer learning-exemplified by speech emotion recognition. In: 2014 22nd International Conference on Pattern Recognition, pp. 761–766. IEEE (2014)
7. Zong, Y., Zheng, W., Zhang, T., Huang, X.: Cross-corpus speech emotion recognition based on domain-adaptive least-squares regression. IEEE Signal Process. Lett. **23**(5), 585–589 (2016)
8. Huang, Z., Xue, W., Mao, Q., Zhan, Y.: Unsupervised domain adaptation for speech emotion recognition using PCANet. Multimed. Tools Appl. **76**(5), 6785–6799 (2017)
9. Gideon, J., McInnis, M., Provost, E.M.: Improving cross-corpus speech emotion recognition with adversarial discriminative domain generalization (ADDoG). IEEE Trans. Affect. Comput. (2019)
10. Zhang, W., Song, P.: Transfer sparse discriminant subspace learning for cross-corpus speech emotion recognition. IEEE/ACM Trans. Audio Speech Lang. Process. **28**, 307–318 (2020)
11. Song, P., Zheng, W.: Feature selection based transfer subspace learning for speech emotion recognition. IEEE Trans. Affect. Comput. **11**(3), 373–382 (2018)

12. Guo, Y.F., Li, S.J., Yang, J.Y., Shu, T.T., Wu, L.D.: A generalized Foley-Sammon transform based on generalized fisher discriminant criterion and its application to face recognition. Pattern Recogn. Lett. **24**(1–3), 147–158 (2003)
13. Gui, J., Sun, Z., Ji, S., Tao, D., Tan, T.: Feature selection based on structured sparsity: a comprehensive study. IEEE Trans. Neural Netw. Learn. Syst. **28**(7), 1490–1507 (2016)
14. Nie, F., Huang, H., Cai, X., Ding, C.: Efficient and robust feature selection via joint l2, 1-norms minimization. Adv. Neural Inf. Process. Syst. **23**, 1813–1821 (2010)
15. Burkhardt, F., Paeschke, A., Rolfes, M., Sendlmeier, W.F., Weiss, B.: A database of German emotional speech. In: Ninth European Conference on Speech Communication and Technology (2005)
16. Martin, O., Kotsia, I., Macq, B., Pitas, I.: The eNTERFACE'05 audio-visual emotion database. In: 22nd International Conference on Data Engineering Workshops (ICDEW 2006), p. 8. IEEE (2006)
17. Wang, Y., Guan, L.: Recognizing human emotional state from audiovisual signals. IEEE Trans. Multimed. **10**(5), 936–946 (2008)
18. Wold, S., Esbensen, K., Geladi, P.: Principal component analysis. Chemometr. Intell. Lab. Syst. **2**(1–3), 37–52 (1987)
19. Belhumeur, P.N., Hespanha, J.P., Kriegman, D.J.: Eigenfaces vs. fisherfaces: recognition using class specific linear projection. IEEE Trans. Pattern Anal. Mach. Intell. **19**(7), 711–720 (1997)
20. Zhang, Y., Yeung, D.Y.: Semi-supervised discriminant analysis using robust path-based similarity. In: 2008 IEEE Conference on Computer Vision and Pattern Recognition, pp. 1–8. IEEE (2008)
21. Long, M., Wang, J., Ding, G., Sun, J., Yu, P.S.: Transfer feature learning with joint distribution adaptation. In: Proceedings of the IEEE International Conference on Computer Vision, pp. 2200–2207 (2013)
22. Long, M., Wang, J., Ding, G., Sun, J., Yu, P.S.: Transfer joint matching for unsupervised domain adaptation. In: Proceedings of the IEEE International Conference on Computer Vision, pp. 1410–1417 (2014)

Channel Enhanced Temporal-Shift Module for Efficient Lipreading

Hao Li[1], Mutallip Mamut[2], Nurbiya Yadikar[1], Yali Zhu[1], and Kurban Ubul[1(✉)]

[1] School of Information Science and Engineering, Xinjiang University, Urumqi, China
kurbanu@xju.edu.cn
[2] Library of Xinjiang University, Urumqi, China

Abstract. Lipreading, also known as visual speech recognition (VSR), refers to recognizing people's speech content only through the sequence of lip movements. Benefit from the development of deep learning, research on lipreading has made great progress in recent years. At present, 3D CNN and 2D CNN are mixed to extract spatio-temporal features in the front-end network of most lipreading models. In this paper, to make 2D convolution have the ability of 3D convolution in the feature extraction stage without increasing model calculation, we combined TSM with several channel attention modules and conduct ablation studies to validate their effectiveness. Then, we inserted the TSM-SE module that proposed into the front-end network so that 2D convolution has the ability to extract fine-grained spatio-temporal features. On the other hand, we solved the potential impact of the time shift module on the dependence between channels. We verified the effectiveness of the proposed method on LRW and LRW-1000 which are challenging large-scale word-level lipreading datasets and reached a new state-of-the-art.

Keywords: Lipreading · Deep learning · Attention module · Temporal-Shift module

1 Introduction

Speech recognition has been the focus of many researchers. Although great progress has been made over the years, it still easy to be affected by noise and reduce the recognition effect because the input signal is audio information. In contrast, visual signals are not affected by the intensity of noise and speech signals, so lipreading can achieve better performance in speech recognition in noisy environment [1].

Benefit from the development of deep learning and the publication of some large data sets, the effect of lipreading has been significantly improved in recent years. Most lipreading models consist of front-end and back-end modules. The front-end network pays more attention to the local feature extraction of the image, while the back-end network is focused more on the temporal dynamics of the whole sequence. In the whole process of lipreading, in addition to the common challenges in image processing, such as angle, imaging conditions, low resolution and high noise, we also need to face the impact of homonyms and near syllables because these words are very similar in pronunciation

© Springer Nature Switzerland AG 2021
J. Feng et al. (Eds.): CCBR 2021, LNCS 12878, pp. 474–482, 2021.
https://doi.org/10.1007/978-3-030-86608-2_52

and mouth shape but the meaning is very different. For example, "back" and "pack" in English, and "dumpling" and "sleep" in Chinese are very similar in tone and phoneme. If they are not combined with context information, it is difficult for the model to distinguish them.

To address these issues, researchers have focused on how data can be more effectively utilized. [13] focused on processing the input image sequence, first performing face alignment to reduce jitter in lip position between frames, and subsequently using the cutout technique with the model focusing on muscle movements beyond the lip. [15] focused more on the contextual information of the target words to make the classification results of the model more accurate by passing the boundary variables of the words. [10] introduced Mixup as an additional way of data augmentation, by first selecting two samples and then generating a new sample by weighted linear interpolation.

Back to the model itself, today, all lipreading models basically combine 3D CNN and 2D CNN as front-end, because this model can not only obtain the performance of the 3D network but also maintain the speed of the 2D network. In this paper, in order to further enable the 2D CNN to have the ability of 3D CNN in the feature extraction stage without increasing the computational load of the model, we introduce the Temporal-Shift module in each residual block, which enables 2D convolution to extract fine-grained spatial features between adjacent frames by moving forward and backward channels in the temporal dimension. However, we realize that this may ignore the correlation between adjacent frames. To solve this problem, we combine the Temporal-Shift module with the channel attention module. Specifically, in each residual block, we first use the Temporal-Shift module to move some channels along the temporal dimension to learn the information of adjacent frames, and then use the channel attention module to fit the complex correlation between the channels at the end of the residual block. We verified the effectiveness of our method on the large-scale word-level benchmark LRW [6] and LRW-1000 [7], and the performance has increased to 88.61% and 57.78%, respectively, which achieved the new state-of-the-art.

2 Related Work

Visual speech recognition, as its name suggests, is an intersection of computer vision and language recognition, often combining the advantages of both fields.

The traditional lipreading system consists of two steps. The first step is to use manual algorithm to extract and classify the lip region of interest [2]. Among them, the common feature extraction methods include Local Binary Pattern extracted from three orthogonal planes (LBP-TOP) [3], Histogram of Oriented Gradients (HOG) [4] and Discrete Cosine Transform (DCT) [5]. The second step is to use neural classifiers such as TDNN and HMM to model the temporal evolution of features and then obtain the reasoning results.

With the rise of deep learning, the recognition effect of lipreading task has been greatly improved by using deep neural network to extract features. As the publisher of English word level dataset LRW, Chung and Zisserman [6] were the first to use CNN as the feature extraction network. Since lipreading task involves temporal sequence, they compared 2D CNN network with 3D CNN network, and finally found that the feature extraction ability of the former is better than the latter. After that, more and more studies have shown that the spatio-temporal feature extraction ability of 3D convolution cannot be ignored. For instance, Themos and Georgios [8] combined residual network with 3D convolution. First, the input lip image is passed to the 3D convolution head and then deep features are extracted utilizing 2D convolutions with strong spatial feature extraction capabilities. Finally, the obtained one-dimensional vector is transferred to bidirectional LSTM network for temporal feature extraction. It is worth mentioning that such a network structure has gradually become the consensus among lipreading researchers. B. Martinez, et al. [12] used multi-scale TCN as back-end network and variable length amplification, and achieved good results. Usually, in the data processing stage of lipreading task, we prefer to let the model focus on the lip region, because it is considered to be the main location of muscle movement during pronunciation while the rest of the facial region could be a burden for lipreading learning. However, Zhang et al. [13] found that it is more conducive to improve the performance of lipreading by combining the face region other than the lip after face alignment.

As mentioned above, either changing the backbone of the front-end and back-end networks or directly processing the data with additional processing, are designed to extract features more effectively to enhance the network's recognition ability. Based on these methods, this paper optimized the existing lipreading models. Compared with them, we focus more on how to easily improve the performance of classical lipreading models, while the structure of the entire network remains unchanged, and the interme-diate structure we proposed which has a strong generalization can easily be placed in other backbones.

3   Proposed Approach

In this section, we propose a complete framework for lipreading. The front-end network of the framework is ResNet-18, which combines the TSM with the channel attention module, while the back-end network uses GRU. Figure 1 shows the overall structure of our lipreading network.

3.1   Temporal-Shift Module (TSM)

For the video processing task, the traditional 2D CNN cannot capture the long-term temporal relationship, although the computing cost is very low; 3D CNN can achieve better performance, but it needs higher cost of computation and deployment. Based on the above problems, J. Lin et al. proposed TSM [11] which can be applied in 2D CNN.

Its core idea is to move some channels along the temporal dimension, so as to promote the information exchange between adjacent frames. As shown in Fig. 2, we only describe a tensor with T frames and C channels, without showing other irrelevant parameters. Among them, the color of each row is different, which means that they are not in the same temporal dimension. We move part of the channel in both directions along the temporal dimension so that the model can learn not only the information of the current frame but also the information of adjacent frames. After temporal shifting, there will be empty channels at the boundary, and we pad the empty space with zeros.

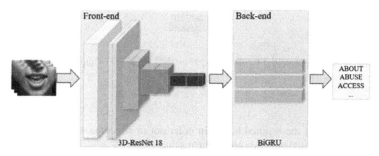

Fig. 1. The overall architecture of the model. The preprocessed image first goes through the front-end network based on 3D-ResNet-18, and then the feature vector is transferred to three-layers BiGRUs for sequence modeling.

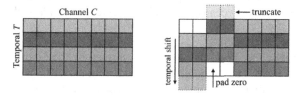

Fig. 2. Temporal-shift module. We move part of the channel along temporal dimension and pad the empty space with zeros.

3.2 Squeeze-Excitation Network (SE)

Hu et al. [14] proposed the Squeeze-Excitation network, which can enhance the network's sensitivity to channel information, thereby enhancing the useful features of current tasks according to different weights, and suppressing the useless features.

The SE module can be divided into two steps: squeeze and excitation. Squeeze is to compress the global spatial information into channel descriptors by global average pooling, so that each unit can use the context information of other units. Then, in the excitation operation, a simple Sigmoid activation is used to obtain the correlation between channels from the compressed information. It is worth noting that the weight of the excitation output can be regarded as the description of the importance of each channel after feature selection, and it is weighted to the main feature channel by channel through multiplication, so as to complete the re-calibration of the original feature.

3.3 Network Structure

Front-End Network: We use 3D-ResNet-18 as the front-end backbone. In this way, we can not only extract the temporal dynamics between frames, but also the spatial features within frames. To preserve the ability of extracting 2D convolution spatial features and the network to extract adjacent frame temporal information, we put the TSM into the residual block. Along the temporal dimension, we shift 1/4 channels by −1, another quarter by+1, and leaving the rest half un-shifted. In this way, we mix the information of frame T − 1, frame T, and frame T + 1 so that the current frame gets the information of

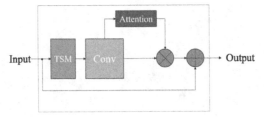

Fig. 3. The structure of the residual block. In order not to affect the ability of spatial feature extraction, TSM and spatial attention are on the residual branch.

adjacent frames. Besides, we shift one channel at a time and pad the empty space with "0". To compensate for the potential disruption of channel dependencies by Temporal-Shift modules, we added a channel attention module at the end of each residual block to fit complex correlations between channels. The structure of residual block is shown in Fig. 3.

Back-End Network: Our back-end network is formed by three-layers BiGRUs with 1024 hidden units. BiGRU is composed of two unidirectional GRUs with opposite directions, and the final output is determined by both of them. Perform sequence modeling on the 512-dimensional feature vector output by the front-end network and extract the temporal dynamics. Finally, the output is classified through a full connection layer.

4   Experiment

4.1 Dataset

We trained and evaluated two large-scale word-level lipreading datasets, LRW and LRW-1000.

Among them, LRW is a video clip extracted from the BBC TV broadcast. Each clip has 29 frames of images. It contains more than 1000 speakers and 500 English words. The LRW-1000 includes 1,000 Chinese word classes, as well as clips from TV programs that include more than 2,000 speakers. Both datasets have been preassigned for training, validation, and testing, and in LRW-1000 the publisher has even cropped the faces. In addition, the speakers in both datasets are diverse in posture, age and skin color, which is the largest and most challenging lipreading dataset currently recognized.

4.2 Data Preprocessing

Face alignment is helpful to improve the results of face recognition tasks based on muscle units, such as expression recognition. So, for LRW, we use the method proposed in [13], first align the faces, and use the Dlib toolkit to get the key points of faces, then extract the lip area. Because the speaker's posture is different, there will be multiple viewing angles, so we used the method used in [10] to do the similarity transformation for each picture, and the LRW-1000 has been pre-edited into a picture, so this is not necessary. We normalized all the pictures and used a fixed 88 × 88 rectangle clips its center. For training datasets, we not only randomly clip and flip all pictures, but also use a 44 × 44 window-size cutout to improve the generalization of the model. In addition, we have introduced word boundary [15], which provides as much context and environmental information as possible for categorizing target words by passing in word boundary variables. At last, we use label smooth and Mixup to reduce overfitting.

4.3 Compare the Effectiveness of Attention Modules Combined with TSM

In order to verify the effectiveness of the attention module for feature extraction, we first compare several different attention mechanisms.

Woo and Sang Hyun et al. [16] proposed CBAM, which consists of two modules, which perform feature attention in space and channel respectively. In the channel attention block, in order to reduce the loss of information in the pooling process, CBAM uses the parallel connection mode of average pooling and maximum pooling. In recent work, different from transforms the feature tensor into a single feature vector through global pooling, Hou, Qi et al. [17] proposed coordinate attention, which decomposes the channel attention into two parallel 1D feature encoding processes. In this way, the two feature graphs embedded with specific directional information are then encoded as two attention maps, each of which captures the long-term dependence of the input feature along a spatial direction.

Table 1. Comparison of different attention module on LRW

Module	Accuracy	FLOPs
Baseline	87.15%	10.56G
Only TSM	87.71%	–
TSM-CBAM	87.38%	–
TSM-Coordinate	87.86%	–
TSM-SE	88.61%	10.57G

We insert these attention modules into the residual block of the front-end network respectively and put them behind the Temporal-Shift module to enhance the extraction capacity of the channel features. The results are shown in Table 1 and Fig. 4. Here, the baseline is the network structure of 3D-ResNet-18 and BiGRU. It can be seen that with the addition of the TSM module, the model can learn the spatio-temporal features from the information of adjacent frames, thereby increasing the baseline by 0.6%. However, because the Temporal-Shift module moves part of the channel, the intra-frame correlation may be disrupted, so we assume that the channel attention will allow the model to better fit the correlation between channels. For CBAM and Coordinated Attention, both take into account both spatial and channel features, but CBAM only considers local information by taking the maximum and average values of multiple channels at each location as weighting factors, so coordinated attention perform better. Surprisingly, the

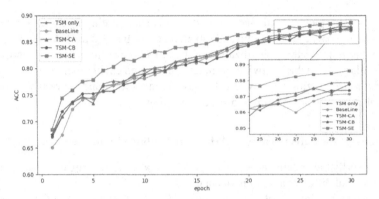

Fig. 4. Classification accuracy on LRW with different attention module

SE module which focuses only on channel attention did the best, and we suspect that the 3D convolution head makes it difficult for spatial attention to perform. Furthermore, we calculated the FLOPs (floating-point operations per second) of baseline and the model fused with TSM-SE. We can see that the model fused with TSM-SE improves the performance by 1.6%, but the computational effort hardly increases.

4.4 Comparison with Some State-of-the-Arts

Finally, we chose the SE module to extract short-term temporal series features in conjunction with TSM and compared them with recent work. The classification accuracy on LRW-1000 was shown in Fig. 5.

As shown in Table 2. Themos and Georgia [8] first fused the residual network with 3D convolution, and achieved 83% recognition rate in LRW; Wang [18] proposed a multi-grained spatio-temporal network which fused the information of different granularity with a learnable spatial attention mechanism; X. Weng and K. Kitani [9] used I3D CNN instead of shallow 3D convolution head, and input the optical flow data and gray sequence into the network respectively; B. Martinez, P. Ma [12] used multi-scale TCN as back-end network, and used variable-length data enhancement method; Zhang and Yang [13] added face alignment and clipping in the preprocessing to further improve the generalization of the model; Feng, Yang et al. [10] added many effective image processing training methods and processing methods to the lipreading task, and the recognition rate of LRW and LRW-1000 reached 88.4% and 55.7% respectively, which was the best result before then. The recognition rate of the proposed method is 88.61% on LRW and 57.79% on LRW-1000, which is a new SOTA for the current lipreading task.

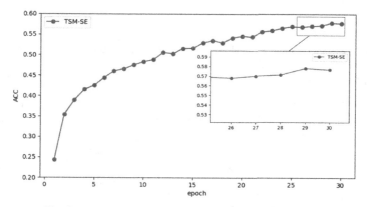

Fig. 5. Classification accuracy on LRW-1000 with TSM-SE

Table 2. Comparison with some existing methods.

Year	Methods	LRW	LRW-1000
2017	ResNet-18 [8]	83.00%	–
2019	Multi-graine ResNet-18 [18]	83.30%	36.90%
2019	Two-stream I3D [9]	84.11%	–
2020	MSTCN [12]	85.30%	41.40%
2020	CBAM (Cutout) [13]	85.02%	45.24%
2021	SE-ResNet-18 (Face Aligned) [10]	88.40%	55.70%
	Ours (TSM-SE (Face Aligned))	**88.61%**	**57.78%**

5 Conclusion

In this paper, we focus on how to make 2D convolutional have the ability to extract temporal information without increasing model calculation. Although the Temporal-Shift Module solves the above problem, it may affect the correlation between channels. Therefore, we combined the channel attention module with TSM to strengthen the weight of some channels to reduce the impact that TSM brings. The experiment shows that TSM combined with SE can effectively help to extract spatio-temporal features of lip movement in two-dimensional convolution. We have carried out experiments on two of the largest word-level lipreading benchmarks and reached a new state-of-the-art. Beyond lipreading, we believe the model also has great potential for other vision tasks.

Acknowledgments. This work was supported by the National Natural Science Foundation of China under Grant (No. 62061045, 61862061, 61563052). The Funds for Creative Groups of Higher Educational Research Plan in Xinjiang Uyghur Autonomous, China under Grant (No. XJEDU2017T002), and 2018th Scientific Research Initiate Program of Doctors of Xinjiang University under Grant No. 24470.

References

1. Zhou, Z., Zhao, G., Hong, X., et al.: A review of recent advances in visual speech decoding. Image Vis. Comput. **32**(9), 590–605 (2014)
2. Zhou, Z., Zhao, G., Pietikäinen, M.: Towards a practical lipreading system. In: CVPR 2011, 137–144. IEEE (2011)
3. Zhou, Z., Hong, X., Zhao, G., et al.: A compact representation of visual speech data using latent variables. IEEE Trans. Pattern Anal. Mach. Intell. **36**(1), 1 (2013)
4. Pei, Y., Kim, T.K., Zha, H.: Unsupervised random forest manifold alignment for lipreading. In: Proceedings of the IEEE International Conference on Computer Vision, 129–136 (2013)
5. Potamianos, G., Neti, C., Iyengar, G., et al.: A cascade visual front end for speaker independent automatic speechreading. Int. J. Speech Technol. **4**(3), 193–208 (2001)
6. Chung, J.S., Zisserman, A.: Lip reading in the wild. In: Lai, S.-H., Lepetit, V., Nishino, K., Sato, Y. (eds.) ACCV 2016. LNCS, vol. 10112, pp. 87–103. Springer, Cham (2017). https://doi.org/10.1007/978-3-319-54184-6_6
7. Yang, S., Zhang, Y., Feng, D., et al.: LRW-1000: a naturally-distributed large-scale benchmark for lip reading in the wild. arXiv e-prints arXiv:1810.06990 (2018)
8. Stafylakis, T., Tzimiropoulos, G.: Combining residual networks with LSTMs for lipreading. arXiv preprint arXiv:1703.04105 (2017)
9. Weng, X., Kitani, K.: Learning spatio-temporal features with two-stream deep 3D CNNS for lipreading. arXiv preprint arXiv:1905.02540 (2019)
10. Feng, D., Yang, S., Shan, S., et al.: Learn an effective lip reading model without pains. arXiv preprint arXiv:2011.07557 (2020)
11. Lin, J., Gan, C., Han, S.: Tsm: Temporal shift module for efficient video understanding. In: Proceedings of the IEEE/CVF International Conference on Computer Vision, pp. 7083–7093 (2019)
12. Martinez, B., Ma, P., Petridis, S., et al.: Lipreading using temporal convolutional networks. In: ICASSP 2020–2020 IEEE International Conference on Acoustics, Speech and Signal Processing (ICASSP), 6319–6323. IEEE (2020)
13. Zhang, Y., Yang, S., Xiao, J., et al.: Can we read speech beyond the lips? rethinking roi selection for deep visual speech recognition. arXiv preprint arXiv:2003.03206 (2020)
14. Hu, J., Shen, L., Sun, G.: Squeeze-and-excitation networks. In: Proceedings of the IEEE Conference on Computer Vision and Pattern Recognition, pp. 7132–7141 (2018)
15. Stafylakis, T., Khan, M.H., Tzimiropoulos, G.: Pushing the boundaries of audiovisual word recognition using residual networks and LSTMs. Comput. Vis. Image Underst. **176**, 22–32 (2018)
16. Woo, S., Park, J., Lee, J.-Y., Kweon, I.S.: Cbam: convolutional block attention module. In: Ferrari, V., Hebert, M., Sminchisescu, C., Weiss, Y. (eds.) ECCV 2018. LNCS, vol. 11211, pp. 3–19. Springer, Cham (2018). https://doi.org/10.1007/978-3-030-01234-2_1
17. Hou, Q., Zhou, D., Feng, J.: Coordinate attention for efficient mobile network design. arXiv preprint arXiv:2103.02907 (2021)
18. Wang, C.: Multi-grained spatio-temporal modeling for lip-reading. arXiv preprint arXiv:1908.1161 (2019)

Explore the Use of Self-supervised Pre-trained Acoustic Features on Disguised Speech Detection

Jie Quan[✉] and Yingchun Yang[✉]

School of Computer Science and Technology, Zhejiang University,
Yugu Road. 34, Hangzhou, China
{21921163,yyc}@zju.edu.cn

Abstract. Nowadays disguised voice presents an increasing tendency towards daily life: it has become more and more important and difficult to identify whether an audio file has been disguised. However, researches on such detection are generally based on traditional acoustic features and traditional machine learning classifiers. Our experiment has shown that these methods have two issues: (1) the accuracy needs to be improved, (2) the generalization performance is poor. We considered two ways to figure them out, one is the feature, and the other is the classifier. Thus, we proposed Kekaimalu, based on CNN. Different from previous blind detection methods, Kekaimalu took speaker-independent phonetic characteristics into account in the training process. To test the proposed approach, we first confirmed that vqwav2vec representation carried clear phonetic information. Next, we observed that LCNN with layer normalization can further improve the differentiation. Finally, we merged statistical moments of traditional acoustic features and phonetic characteristics. The extensive experiment demonstrates that detection rates higher than 97%.

Keywords: Voice disguise · Blind detection · vqwav2vec · Feature fusion

1 Introduction

This paper studies the problem of speaker identification of disguised speech. As we can see, the wide application of digital audio editing software makes the voice disguise easier. Disguised speech has a great negative impact on social security. The principle of disguise consists in modifying the voice in one person to sound differently (mechanic alteration), or sound like another person (conversion) [1]. Generally, disguising methods can be divided into two categories: non-electronic and electronic [2]. Non-electronic methods include using the falsetto, pinching nostrils, speaking with object of mouth, etc.

The existing concrete solutions to detection of disguised voice are usually based on traditional acoustic features. There are two stages on these methods.

© Springer Nature Switzerland AG 2021
J. Feng et al. (Eds.): CCBR 2021, LNCS 12878, pp. 483–490, 2021.
https://doi.org/10.1007/978-3-030-86608-2_53

Firstly, extract features such as MFCC, LFCC, CQCC. Secondly, classify the features using SVM, LR, etc. Wang Y investigated the principle of electronic voice transformation and proposed a blind detection method based on MFCC and VQ-SVM [3]. Wu H did some research on statistical moments and proposed an improved method based on statistical moments of MFCC and SVM [4].

As we all know, traditional features are much more interpretable. However, extracting features manually is cumbersome and traditional features can not reflect the difference between original voice and disguised voice comprehensively. We considered using end-to-end model for automatically extracting the corresponding features of this task. Few studies were conducted on representations. We explored self-supervised training and utilized the pre-trained vqwav2vec encoder to extract acoustic representations. Ma D compared features of two conventional and four pre-trained systems in some simple frame-level phonetic classification tasks, with classifiers trained on features from one version of the TIMIT dataset and tested on features from another [5]. Pre-trained systems, including wav2vec [6], vq-wav2vec [7], mockingjay [8], DeCoAR [9], show that learning vector representations by neural network of acoustic data is possible.

Except for pre-trained encoder, we also used feature fusion to improve performance. The integration of multiple media, with associated features, or the intermediate decisions in order to perform an analysis task is referred to as multi-modal fusion [10]. As it proved, multi-modal fusion provides benefit for various multimedia analysis tasks. In this paper, to combine the two strengths of traditional acoustic features and pre-trained acoustic representations, we refer to the multi-modal fusion method of feature fusion stage.

This paper aims to distinguish normal voice and disguised voice by raised and lowered pitch. Kekaimalu combines traditional acoustic features and pre-trained representations. The experiment proved that this model comparing to traditional methods performs better. It combines the advantages of traditional features and depth features. Hence, we gave the name Kekaimalu, which is the name of the first captive-bred cetacean.

The rest of this paper is organized as follows. In Sect. 2, related work including speech representation and features fusion is introduced. In Sect. 3, we propose the concrete network for detection of disguised voice. In Sect. 4, a series of experiment results are presented. In Sect. 5, we discuss the experiment results. Finally, in Sect. 6, conclusion and future work are given.

2   Related Work

The traditional methods of tamper detection are described above. Here we introduce the work related to representation learning and feature fusion.

Representation learning means to learn transformation of data that makes it easier to extract useful information when building classifiers or other predictors [11]. With the rapid development of deep learning, there has been increasing interest in pre-trained representations. Inspired by the success of pre-trained word representation [12], more studies have considered learning distributed representation of acoustic data.

Except for the four models mentioned above, there is several excellent related works. Wav2vec [6] proposed a fully convolutional neural network optimized via a noise contrastive binary classification and was applied to WSJ ASR tasks. DeCoAR [9] combined the bidirectional of ELMo and the reconstruction objective of APC to give deep contextualized acoustic features. vqwav2vec [7] proposed a gunnel softmax approach as well as online k-means clustering, similar to VQ-VAE, to discretize the speech signal and then applied NLP algorithms to speech data. Mockingjay [8] used multi-layer transformer encoders and multi-head self-attention under the proposed Masked Acoustic Model (MAM) to achieve bidirectional encoding. Problem-agnostic speech encoder (PASE) [13] was an improved self-supervised method, where a single neural encoder is followed by multiple workers that jointly solve different self-supervised tasks. wav2vec2.0 [14] masked the speech input in the latent space and solved a contrastive task defined over a quantization of the latent representations which are jointly learned.

Feature fusion is an effective way to improve performance. Generally, it can be divided by level of fusion into two methods. One is fusing the information on feature level, the other is at decision level. For feature level, it refers to feature fusion, including early fusion and late fusion. Common methods base on rank, DNN, LSTM or generative models. Here, this paper focuses on network based on rank. TFN [15] is tailored to the volatile nature of spoken language in online videos as well as accompanying gestures and voice. Low-rank Multi-modal Fusion method (LMF) [16] performs multi-modal fusion using low-rank tensors to improve efficiency.

3 Kekaimalu

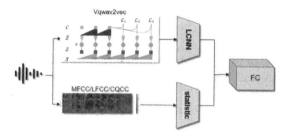

Fig. 1. Overall network architecture of Kekaimalu

As is mentioned above, the overall network architecture contains four parts. The first part is the vq-wav2vec network, learning self-supervised features from audio. The second part is the preprocessing network for traditional acoustic features, it learns statistical characteristics from MFCC, LFCC, CQCC. The third part is the adjusted Light CNN, it reduce dimensions for these two kinds of features. Then we used matrix operations for feature fusion. And the final part is the feed-forward network for classifying post-fusion feature. The whole architecture is shown in Fig. 1.

VQ-wav2vec is a wav2vec-style self-supervised model for learning discrete representations [7]. The CNN-based encoder wav2vec transforms raw waveform inputs into a batch of sequence of 512 dimensional vectors [6]. VQ-wav2vec model was trained in the unlabeled version of librispeech, then the authors discrete the same data with the resulting model to estimate a BERT model. Finally, they train a wav2letter acoustic model on WSJ by inputting either the BERT or vqwav2vec representations instead of log-mel filter banks [7].

To verify that features extracted by vqwav2vec are informative for phonetic characteristics. We used t-SNE, a non-linear dimension reduction technique to verify the effectiveness of the generated features. We randomly selected 100 positive samples and 100 negative samples. The red points present positive samples and the blue present negative samples.As we can see from Fig. 2, comparing with traditional acoustic features, the features generated by pre-trained vqwav2vec encoder have better performance.

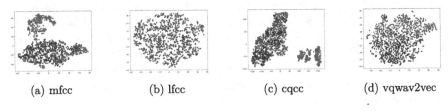

(a) mfcc   (b) lfcc   (c) cqcc   (d) vqwav2vec

Fig. 2. The dimension reduction results of several features

Light convolution neural network was first proposed to face recognition [17]. It was presented to learn compact embedding on large-scale face data. Compared with CNN models, light CNN had better effect, simpler structure, lower computation.

The core module of LCNN is Max-Feature-Map (MFM), designed for obtaining a compact representation and perform feature filter selection.

$$y_{ij}^k = \max\left(x_{ij}^k, x_{ij}^{k+N/2}\right) \tag{1}$$

$$\forall i = \overline{1, H}, j = \overline{1, W}, k = \overline{1, N/2} \tag{2}$$

Wherein, X is the output feature map of a certain layer, and its dimension is $N \times H \times W$, and y is the picture after MSM is used, whose dimension is $N/2 \times H \times W$, where i and j are the coordinates representing the two spatial dimensions, and k is the label of the channel. The intuitive meaning is to divide X into two feature blocks of the same size along the direction of the channel, and then corresponding to the channel feature graph in pairs Maximize between. The purpose of MFM is to describe the relationship between channels, to simplify the input, the output is compressed to half the input, which keeps the model compact and robust. MFM suppresses neuron by competitive relationship. That's to say, the MFM plays a role of feature selector [18].

For disguised speech detection, we used the reduced version of the LCNN network architectures [17]. Specifically, it contains four convolutions neural network block, four Max-pooling layers, ten Max-Feature-Map layers and two linear layers. Each convolution layer is a combination of two independent convolution parts calculated of layer's input. Max-FeatureMap activation function is used to calculate element-wise maximum of these parts.

Lavrentyeva G [18] investigated single CNN and combined with RNN approaches. They explored the applicability of the deep learning approach for solution the problem of replay attack spoofing detection. On the basis of their research, we used Layer Normalization [19]. Wu X removed batch normalization from the original residual block [17]. They thought that batch normalization [20] is domain specific which may be failed when test samples come from different domains compared with training data. We explored other normalization methods and chose layer normalization [19] to improve our network.

4   Experiments

In this section, we evaluated our model on disguised detection task. We first introduced our dataset, and then presented traditional state-of-the-art methods, as well as algorithms analysis.

4.1   Dataset

The TIMIT corpus of read speech, which is designed to provide speech data for acoustic-phonetic studies, contains broadband recordings of 630 speakers of eight major dialects of American English [21].

There are several leading disguise softwares or algorithms, including Cool Edit, Audacity, PRAAT. In my work, we use Audacity to disguise. I consider 12 kinds of disguised voice with disguising factors in $\pm 2, \pm 4, \pm 6, \pm 8, \pm 10$. For each factor, we randomly selected 500 samples for training dataset and 200 samples for test dataset. That's to say, in training dataset, there are 2000 real samples and 4000 disguised samples. Meanwhile, in test dataset, there are 1600 real samples and 800 disguised samples.

4.2   Statistical Moments for Traditional Features

Since MFCCs/CQCCs/LFCCs can be used to well describe frequency spectral properties. we used the statistical moments including mean values and correlations coefficients. We concatenated statistical moments of these three kinds of traditional acoustic features. Then an algorithm based on the extracted features and support vector machine classifiers is proposed to be regarded as our baseline.

For $x(n)$ with N, assuming $v_{i,j}$ to be the jth component of the MFCC/LFCC/CQCC vector of the ith frame, and V_j to be the set of all the jth components, V_j can be expressed as:

$$V_j = \{v_{1j}, v_{2j}, \ldots, v_{Nj}\}, \quad j = 1, 2, \ldots, L \tag{3}$$

Mean values and correlations coefficients can be calculated by the following formula.

$$E_j = E(V_j), \quad j = 1, 2, \ldots, L \tag{4}$$

$$CR_{jj'} = \frac{\text{cov}(V_j, V_{j'})}{\sqrt{VAR(V_j)}\sqrt{VAR(V_{j'})}}, \quad 1 \le j < j' \le L \tag{5}$$

We took MFCC as example, the results E_j and $CR_{jj'}$ are combined to form the statistical moments W_{MFCC} of the L-dimensional MFCC vectors. In our experiment, we set L to 24.

$$W_{MFCC} = [E_1, E_2, \ldots, E_L, CR_{12}, CR_{13}, \ldots, CR_{L-1\,L}] \tag{6}$$

Similarly, the statistical moments $W_{\delta MFCC}$ and $W_{\delta\delta MFCC}$. And we concatenated W_{MFCC}, $W_{\delta MFCC}$ and $W_{\delta\delta MFCC}$ as W. Since the dimension of MFCC is 24, the dimension of CR is 288, and the dimension of W is 867. In addition, we do the same thing for CQCC and LFCC. We get W_{LFCC} and W_{CQCC}.

4.3   Feature Fusion

We modified the number of output nodes of the last full connection layer of LCNN from 2 to 128. And then we got 2 hidden weights, we regarded them as H_t and H_{vq}. Based on matrix operation, we fuse the two features.

$$\mathbf{H}^m = \begin{bmatrix} \mathbf{H_t}^l \\ 1 \end{bmatrix} \otimes \begin{bmatrix} \mathbf{H_{vq}}^v \\ 1 \end{bmatrix} \tag{7}$$

Here $\otimes$ indicates the outer product between vectors. Since Tensor Fusion is mathematically formed by an outer product, it has no learnable parameters and we empirically observed that although the output tensor is high dimensional, chances of over-fitting are low.

5   Discussion

Firstly, we compared the effects of several traditional features. We used SVM, NB, and LR as classifiers respectively. As we can see from Table 1, for these classifiers, CQCC performs better than MFCC and LFCC. And for these traditional features, SVM performs better than NB and LR. Most importantly, it's obvious that the statistics are much better than the original feature for these three features.

Next, we introduced LCNN as classifier and vqwav2vec for extracting feature. Helped by LCNN, we can improve accuracy significantly. Finally, by future fusion, the accuracy of Kekaimalu is 97.2%. As we can see from Table 2

Table 1. The results of traditional methods

Model	MFCC + SVM	MFCC + NB	MFCC + LR
Precision	0.752	0.668	0.721
Model	LFCC + SVM	LFCC + NB	LFCC + LR
Precision	0.712	0.617	0.668
Model	CQCC + SVM	CQCC + NB	CQCC + LR
Precision	0.765	0.731	0.775
Model	W_{MFCC} + SVM	W_{MFCC} + NB	W_{MFCC} + LR
Precision	0.871	0.735	0.876
Model	W_{LFCC} + SVM	W_{LFCC} + NB	W_{LFCC} + LR
Precision	0.735	0.661	0.737
Model	W_{CQCC} + SVM	W_{CQCC} + NB	W_{CQCC} + LR
Precision	0.884	0.821	0.869

Table 2. The results of deep learning methods

Model	W_{MFCC} + LCNN	W_{LFCC} + LCNN	W_{CQCC} + LCNN
Precision	0.916	0.932	0.912
Model	vqwav2vec + LCNN	vqwav2vec + LCNN	vqwav2vec + LCNN
Precision	0.951	0.957	0.969
Model	Kekaimalu		
Precision	0.972		

6   Conclusions

In this paper we explored the use of the pre-trained vqwav2vec encoder in disguised detection. We compared the prediction results with pre-trained features (vqwav2vec for audio) and traditional features (MFCC/CQCC/LFCC). We proved that self-supervised representation perform better in tamper detection. And we add LayerNorm in original Light CNN, which is valid for sequential data. Finally, we used mathematically method for feature fusion. In conclusion, we improved the accuracy from 0.752 to 0.972. However, many researches indicated transformer is more useful for feature extraction of sequence data than vqwav2vec, which is based on CNN. Thus, we are doing research on other pre-trained model.

References

1. Perrot, P., Aversano, G., Chollet, G.: Voice disguise and automatic detection: review and perspectives. Prog. Nonlinear Speech Process. 101–117 (2007)
2. Kaur, H., Singh, A.G.: Speaker identification of disguised voices using MFCC statistical moment and SVM classifier (2017)

3. Wang, Y., Deng, Y., Wu, H., Huang, J.: Blind detection of electronic voice transformation with natural disguise. In: Shi, Y.Q., Kim, H.-J., Pérez-González, F. (eds.) IWDW 2012. LNCS, vol. 7809, pp. 336–343. Springer, Heidelberg (2013). https://doi.org/10.1007/978-3-642-40099-5_28

4. Wu, H., Wang, Y., Huang, J.: Blind detection of electronic disguised voice. In: 2013 IEEE International Conference on Acoustics, Speech and Signal Processing, IEEE, pp. 3013–3017 (2013)

5. Ma, D., Ryant, N., Liberman, M.: Probing acoustic representations for phonetic properties. In: ICASSP 2021–2021 IEEE International Conference on Acoustics, Speech and Signal Processing (ICASSP), pp. 311–315. IEEE (2021)

6. Schneider, S., Baevski, A., Collobert, R., et al.: wav2vec: unsupervised pre-training for speech recognition. arXiv preprint arXiv:1904.05862 (2019)

7. Baevski, A,. Schneider, S., Auli, M.: vq-wav2vec: self-supervised learning of discrete speech representations. arXiv preprint arXiv:1910.05453 (2019)

8. Liu, A.T., Yang, S., Chi, P.H., et al.: Mockingjay: unsupervised speech representation learning with deep bidirectional transformer encoders. In: ICASSP 2020–2020 IEEE International Conference on Acoustics, Speech and Signal Processing (ICASSP), pp. 6419–6423. IEEE (2020)

9. Ling, S., Liu, Y., Salazar, J., et al.: Deep contextualized acoustic representations for semi-supervised speech recognition. In: ICASSP 2020–2020 IEEE International Conference on Acoustics, Speech and Signal Processing (ICASSP), pp. 6429–6433. IEEE (2020)

10. Atrey, P.K., Hossain, M.A., El Saddik, A., et al.: Multimodal fusion for multimedia analysis: a survey. Multimed. Syst. 16(6), 345–379 (2010)

11. Bengio, Y., Courville, A., Vincent, P.: Representation learning: a review and new perspectives. IEEE Trans. Pattern Anal. Mach. Intell. 35(8), 1798–1828 (2013)

12. Mikolov, T., Sutskever, I., Chen, K., et al.: Distributed representations of words and phrases and their compositionality. arXiv preprint arXiv:1310.4546 (2013)

13. Pascual, S., Ravanelli, M., Serra, J., et al.: Learning problem-agnostic speech representations from multiple self-supervised tasks. arXiv preprint arXiv:1904.03416 (2019)

14. Baevski, A., Zhou, H., Mohamed, A., et al.: wav2vec 2.0: a framework for self-supervised learning of speech representations. arXiv preprint arXiv:2006.11477 (2020)

15. Zadeh, A., Chen, M., Poria, S., et al.: Tensor fusion network for multimodal sentiment analysis. arXiv preprint arXiv:1707.07250 (2017)

16. Liu, Z., Shen, Y., Lakshminarasimhan, V.B., et al.: Efficient low-rank multimodal fusion with modality-specific factors. arXiv preprint arXiv:1806.00064 (2018)

17. Wu, X., He, R., Sun, Z., et al.: A light CNN for deep face representation with noisy labels. IEEE Trans. Inf. Forensics Secur. 13(11), 2884–2896 (2018)

18. Lavrentyeva, G., Novoselov, S., Malykh, E., et al.: Audio replay attack detection with deep learning frameworks. In: Interspeech, pp. 82–86 (2017)

19. Ba, J.L., Kiros, J.R., Hinton, G.E.: Layer normalization. arXiv preprint arXiv:1607.06450 (2016)

20. Ioffe, S., Szegedy, C.: Batch normalization: accelerating deep network training by reducing internal covariate shift. In: International Conference on Machine Learning. PMLR, pp. 448–456 (2015)

21. Garofolo, J.S.: TIMIT acoustic phonetic continuous speech corpus. Linguistic Data Consortium, 1993 (1993)

Author Index

Printed in the United States
by Baker & Taylor Publisher Services